A PLACE OF RECOURSE

# Ohio University Press Series on
# Law, Society, and Politics in the Midwest

SERIES EDITOR: PAUL FINKELMAN

*The History of Ohio Law*, edited by Michael Les Benedict and John F. Winkler

*Frontiers of Freedom: Cincinnati's Black Community, 1802–1868*, by Nikki M. Taylor

*A Place of Recourse: A History of the U.S. District Court for the Southern District of Ohio, 1803–2003*, by Roberta Sue Alexander

ROBERTA SUE ALEXANDER

# A PLACE OF
# RECOURSE

A History of the U.S. District Court for the
Southern District of Ohio, 1803–2003

Ohio University Press | Athens

Ohio University Press, Athens, Ohio 45701
© 2005 by Ohio University Press
www.ohio.edu/oupress
Printed in the United States of America

Ohio University Press books are printed on acid-free paper ⊗ ™

*Photos on jacket from left, top to bottom.* First column: Sandra Beckwith; Gregory L. Frost; Joseph P. Kinneary; Algenon L. Marbley; John Weld Peck, courtesy Mayhew & Peper, Photographers, Cincinnati; Edmund A. Sargus Jr.; Benjamin Tappan, courtesy Ohio Historical Society. Second column: John Wilson Campbell, courtesy Mayhew & Peper, Photographers, Cincinnati; James L. Graham; David Stewart Porter; George C. Smith; Albert Clifton Thompson, courtesy Mayhew & Peper, Photographers, Cincinnati. Third column: Lester L. Cecil; Smith Hickenlooper; Walter H. Rice; John E. Sater, from *Who Is Who in and from Ohio*, vol. 2 (Cincinnati: Queen City Publishing, 1912). Fourth column: William Creighton, courtesy Ohio Historical Society; Philip B. Swing; Thomas M. Rose; S. Arthur Spiegel; Carl A. Weinman. Fifth column: Susan Dlott; Howard Clark Hollister, from Morris, *The Bench and Bar of Cincinnati* (Cincinnati: New Court House Publishing, 1921); Carl B. Rubin, courtesy Mrs. Carl B. Rubin; William White, from Randall, et al., *History of Ohio* (New York: Century Co., 1912). Sixth column: John H. Druffel; John D. Holschuh; Humphrey H. Leavitt, courtesy Cincinnati Historical Society; Robert R. Nevin; George Read Sage, courtesy Cincinnati Historical Society; Timothy Sylvester Hogan; Herman J. Weber. Central image: the judges of the U.S. District Court, Sourthern District of Ohio, October 2003. *Unless otherwise noted, photos are courtesy Sixth Circuit Archives, Cincinnati.*

13 12 11 10 09 08 07 06 05    5 4 3 2 1

*Library of Congress Cataloging-in-Publication Data*

Alexander, Roberta Sue, 1943–
  A place of recourse : a history of the U.S. District Court for the Southern District of Ohio, 1803–2003 / Roberta Sue Alexander.
     p. cm. — (Ohio University Press series on law, society, and politics in the Midwest)
  Includes bibliographical references and index.
  ISBN 0-8214-1602-2 (cloth : alk. paper)
 1. United States. District Court (Ohio : Southern District)—History. 2. District courts—Ohio—History. I. Title. II. Series.
  KF8755.O363A83  2005

                                                    2005007550

*To the Honorable Walter H. Rice,*

*whose vision inspired this project and*

*whose confidence and support made it all possible*

# CONTENTS

# ILLUSTRATIONS

# TABLES

# FOREWORD

The history of southern Ohio mirrors the history of our nation over the past two hundred years and more. At first, we newly free Americans considered ourselves more as citizens of individual states of residence than as citizens of a federal union, the United States of America. Likewise, the courts of this new political entity began their existence in 1789 as poor stepchildren of the court systems already established in each of the thirteen original states. As the power of the federal government began to grow in importance, in perception and in the acceptance of those who increasingly began to consider themselves Americans, so too did the federal court system grow from what had been basically local tribunals dealing with trifling matters to courts that have literally shaped and reshaped American society. These courts have made our nation one that is blind to color and gender under law, have guaranteed our citizens more individual freedoms and liberties vis-à-vis a strong central government than any nation in the history of the world, and have produced and maintained that delicate balance between the rights of the individual and those of society in areas as disparate as the environment, labor-management relations, consumer protection, freedom of speech, and the free exercise of religion. As such, our federal court system, nationally as well as in southern Ohio, has protected citizens against the potential tyranny of the majority.

That story is here for all to read. Certainly, the judges are present, from the very first of us, Charles Willing Byrd, who gaveled to order the very first session of the then District of Ohio, at Chillicothe, more than two centuries ago; through Humphrey Howe Leavitt, the first judge of the Southern District of Ohio, who presided in Cincinnati after the state was split into a northern and a southern district in 1855; through Joseph P. Kinneary, a legend in his own time, who carried a full civil and a virtually full criminal case load, until retiring a few months short of his ninety-sixth birthday; and through to Gregory Frost, our newest colleague.

Present also are the attorneys who appeared before those judges, attorneys whose imagination, creativity, and vigor brought before the court a myriad of cases, historically and legally significant for their times, cases dealing with slavery, the Industrial Revolution, patent protection, draft resistance, desegregation, civil rights, and the development of intellectual property law in the computer age, cases that would allow our federal court to discharge a significant role in the development of southern Ohio's distinctive legal, social, and economic culture.

The history of any court consists of more than the judges and the attorneys who appear before them. Indeed, without the significant efforts of all those who have supported our court since its inception, bailiffs, courtroom deputies, court reporters, members of the clerk's office, U.S. marshals, probation officers, pretrial services officers, and countless others, the record of this court would be far less exemplary than what is recounted in this volume. We are pleased to take the opportunity to thank each and every one of those members of our court family for their invaluable service to the people of southern Ohio in the cause of justice over the years.

Two others deserve special mention. Dr. Roberta Alexander, the author of this magnum opus, reacted with great enthusiasm when the idea of compiling the history of our court was first broached some years ago and has labored tirelessly and well to bring this project to fruition. She deserves the thanks of each and every member of our court for preserving and telling its story for present generations and all that will follow. Charles Hogan, an attorney and a historian, provided the initial impetus, enthusiasm, and model for this work. If anyone deserves recognition as the "spiritual father of this history," it is he.

WALTER H. RICE, CHIEF JUDGE

*U.S. District Court for the Southern District of Ohio*

*1996–2003*

# ACKNOWLEDGMENTS

One of the great pleasures of writing a book is thanking all of those who made it possible. First and foremost, I wish to thank Judge Walter H. Rice, who as chief judge of the U.S. District Court for the Southern District of Ohio had, as one of his main goals, the writing of a history of this court. At the time, after having long been a Civil War and Reconstruction scholar, I was looking for new research directions. Further, I was fulfilling a lifelong dream of attending law school. These circumstances led to my volunteering for this project. I do not think Judge Rice or I knew what we were getting ourselves into, but we persevered.

I would also like to thank all of the district and magistrate judges, past and present, who agreed to sit with me for hours and to share their insights and their stories during our long interviews. I especially would like to thank Crystal McNamee, Judge Joseph Kinneary's longtime secretary, who helped with the two interviews with the judge who recounted so many stories about the changes in law and lawyering during the past century. John Lyter, former clerk of courts, and Robert Snell, former deputy clerk for Dayton, also provided great tales during their interviews. In addition to their own interviews, Magistrate Judges Mark Abel and Michael Merz helped provide background on several of the judges and some of the major cases. Judge Edmund A. Sargus also offered several helpful suggestions. And Judge Rice was always there with intellectual and moral support when I needed it most. Finally, to all the judges, thank you for agreeing to help support this project financially. Without the funds from the court, publication of this book would not have been possible.

Several people aided in the research of the book. First, the administrative staff of the court in Cincinnati, Columbus, and Dayton opened their doors to me and accompanied me down to their dusty basements to help me plow through the records stored there. I wish to offer a special thanks to Clerk of Courts Jim Murphy and his staff and especially Beth Baird and Jim Murphy's administrative secretary, Judy Allen; Karen Jones, deputy clerk in Cincinnati, and Rebecca Sniveley, deputy clerk in Dayton. Rita Wallace, the historian of the Sixth Circuit Court of Appeals, graciously shared not only all of her files but her vast knowledge of the court. She also provided invaluable assistance in gathering the photographs and illustrations for the book. The staff at the National Archives, Great Lakes Region, offered invaluable help in plodding through the massive collections housed there on the district court. Glenn Longacre and Don Jackanicz were especially helpful. Maggie Yax, at the Cincinnati Historical Society, went far beyond the call of duty when she sat with me for several days in the cold warehouse where the papers of John Weld Peck are stored. The rest of the staff helped search for wonderful photographs that helped enrich this book. Rodney Ross, at the National Archives in Washington, D.C., searched through all the records of the Senate for me. The staff at the National Archives at College Park, Maryland, helped me find relevant records from the mass of material available in the records of the Department of Justice. Michael Hussey was especially helpful in this regard. Susan Elliott, research librarian at the University of Dayton School of Law, provided essential help in tracking down information and locating obscure sources. Dayton attorney Tom Cecil, the son of Judge Lester Cecil, spent hours telling me of life in the 1950s and shared with me his father's scrapbook and other materials. And Shirley Cobb, Judge Rice's administrative assistant, was always there when I needed help hunting down something or someone.

The staff at the Ohio University Press has been supportive throughout. Paul Finkelman read the manuscript with his usual care and saved me from countless embarrassing mistakes. Gillian Berchowitz not only offered several wonderful editing suggestions but was my cheerleader, providing support when I needed it most.

Several people graciously read the manuscript and offered many comments that have made this book a much better work than it otherwise could have been. Magistrate Judge Michael Merz, former reporter on the "court" beat for the *Cincinnati Enquirer*, Ben Kaufman, and the historian of the Sixth Circuit Court of Appeals, Rita Wallace, read all or parts of the book. In addition, Mr. Kaufman graciously offered me all of his clippings from his years covering the court in Cincinnati. All of the judges reviewed portions of the manuscript and many offered important corrections. Of course, any mistakes in fact or interpretation are mine alone.

Finally, I want to thank my husband, Ron Fost, who put up with me through these many years. Not only has he lived through my doubts, my ravings, and my many days away from home doing research but he has always tolerated so many boxes of notes in our shared office that for months he was unable to get near his computer. He is my source of strength and my inspiration.

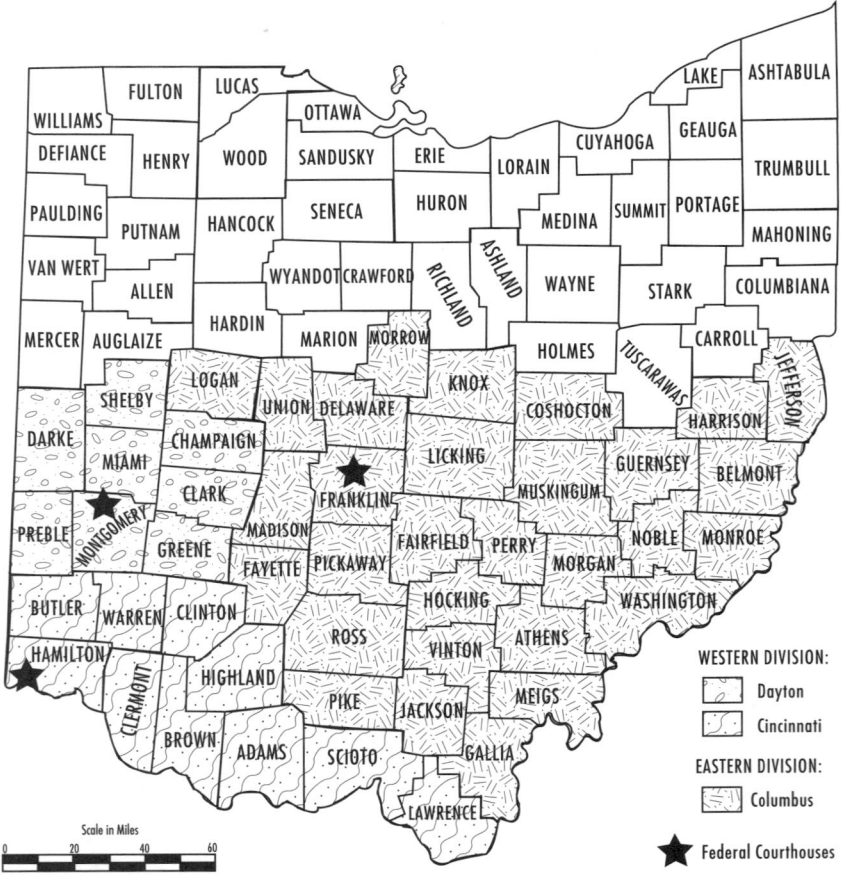

The Southern District of Ohio.

# INTRODUCTION

THOSE WHO SERVE IN the federal district courts as judges or who practice in them as attorneys appreciate the important role these institutions play in American society. To them, a federal district court is "a sacred place," the only "physical place" where an "ordinary citizen," "man or woman, young or old," comes into "contact with the big concept of the federal government." It is the place where the average person can be "restrained in his rights."[1] But it is also the place "where ordinary citizens" can "hold the government account-able."[2] Therefore, it is "a place where the Constitution and all of our history come into being,"[3] a place where "the Constitution continues to live . . . through the vigilance and courage of we the people."[4]

The ninety-one U.S. district courts are, however, more than arenas in which individual citizens come to protect their constitutional rights and free-doms and the federal government enforces its laws against those accused of violations and noncompliance. They also provide forums in which private parties can resolve their disputes peacefully. In hundreds of thousands of cases each year, the federal district courts not only enforce societal norms and protect constitutional liberties but also preserve the peace and promote eco-nomic stability by resolving private disputes. In carrying out these responsi-bilities, the district courts also often influence and make national policy as the first courts to interpret new federal laws and hear constitutional chal-lenges to statutes, administrative proceedings, and executive actions.[5]

Six hundred sixty-three district court judges, "the workhorses of the fed-eral judiciary,"[6] preside over the only courts in the federal system to hear the facts of their cases directly from the litigants and their witnesses. They see this position as "the highest calling of the legal profession."[7] As those who preside over "not only the first but the final court"[8] for most litigants, these judges work to ensure that all "get justice," by providing a forum where the parties "have their day in court" and by refereeing impartially so that all have a level "playing field."[9]

But district courts have not always played such a major role in the nation's life. While the framers of the U.S. Constitution sought to ensure that the new federal government had an independent means of enforcing its own law, they had to balance the desires of those who favored a more centralized government with the concerns of those who feared such a strong entity. Thus, Article III of the Constitution established a federal judiciary to hear cases arising under federal law, federal treaties, and the Constitution, as well as disputes between states, between a state and the federal government, and between individual citizens of different states. But aside from mandating a Supreme Court, Article III left it to Congress to determine whether there were to be any lower courts, and, if there were, to define their scope of authority.

Congress could have chosen to allow state courts to hear all federal cases except those few over which the Constitution gave the Supreme Court original jurisdiction, with appeal then taken from the state courts to the Supreme Court. But the first Congress decided, instead, that there should be a full federal court system, so the federal government could enforce its own laws independent of any state officials. The result was the Judiciary Act of 1789.[10] A compromise between nationalists and localists, the statute created three sets of federal courts. The Supreme Court had original jurisdiction in areas outlined by the U.S. Constitution and appellate jurisdiction in most cases from lower federal courts as well as limited appellate jurisdiction over the highest state courts. Below the Supreme Court, both the district and circuit courts served as trial courts. The circuit courts had appellate jurisdiction over some cases begun at the district level as well as trial responsibilities for major federal civil and criminal cases. In addition, defendants in diversity cases— that is, in litigation between citizens of different states or in which the defendant was an alien—could remove their cases from state to federal court only if the jurisdictional amount exceeded $500.[11]

The Judiciary Act of 1789 restricted the district courts' criminal and civil jurisdiction to minor cases. Immediately, however, the act gave these courts significant power and influence in their communities by granting them exclusive jurisdiction over all admiralty and maritime cases and over suits brought by the United States to collect penalties or to enforce forfeitures imposed on defendants who had been found to have violated federal law. Initially, each state had one district court. By establishing federal courts in every state, the nationalists ensured that there would be federal courts enforcing federal law at the local level. On the other hand, advocates of states' rights hoped that the district court judges would also be influenced by local political and economic forces.[12]

Under the Constitution, the president appointed, with the advice and consent of the Senate, Supreme Court justices and district court judges. Congress, however, authorized no specifically designated circuit court judges. Initially, the state's district court judge sat with two Supreme Court justices to form a circuit court. In 1802, this changed to one district court judge and one Supreme Court justice.[13] But even this alteration did not solve the problems inherent in the two-trial-court system. Supreme Court jurists regularly faced the awkward chore of hearing appeals from their own and their colleagues' lower court decisions. Further, Supreme Court justices grumbled, and some even resigned, over their arduous circuit-riding duties. Supreme Court Justice John McLean, who rode the circuit that included Ohio, as well as Indiana, Illinois, and Michigan, traveled twenty-five hundred miles each year to fulfill his circuit court duties. In May 1837, he complained that "the mud was so deep in Indiana," he had to ride in a common wagon to get to court.[14] But political considerations prevented Congress from beginning to reform the system until the end of the nineteenth century. In 1891, the Evarts Act established independent circuit courts of appeal as intermediary appellate courts between the federal trial courts and the Supreme Court. Each new circuit court of appeal would have a circuit judge. Thus, three judges composed the new courts of appeal—the newly created circuit judge, the circuit justice (that is, the Supreme Court justice appointed to the circuit), and the district judge—and only the presence of two of the three was required for a quorum. But the problems of overlapping jurisdiction remained, for Congress still refused to abolish the old circuit courts as trial courts. Thus, district court judges now heard trial cases in their district courts and in the circuit court as well as sitting as appellate judges on the new courts of appeal.[15] Finally, in 1911, Congress ended this cumbersome system by establishing the district courts as the sole trial court of the federal system, the courts of appeal of the various circuits as the immediate appellate courts, and the Supreme Court as the final court of appeals.[16]

In addition, to help the nation deal with the economic, social, and political issues that arose as the country changed from a small, predominantly rural nation clustered along the Atlantic Ocean to an industrial giant and world leader with millions of citizens who have come from countless countries spread over more than a continent, Congress also transformed the district courts' jurisdiction and thus their role in society. The district courts have evolved from local tribunals dealing with minor infractions and land disputes into courts of tremendous significance dealing with essentially every major issue confronting society: equal rights and equal opportunities in the political and economic arenas; the scope of individual rights under the Constitution, including free speech, the free exercise of religion, and the rights of privacy; the enforcement of federal laws, ranging from environmental regulations to conflicts between labor and management; the enforcement of federal criminal law, especially in the areas of racketeering and the war against drugs; and the relationship between national and state power.

As a result, district court dockets grew more than tenfold during the twentieth century. In 1904, federal courts faced 67 filings per 100,000 adults. In 1985, the 311,915 filings represented an increase to almost 120 per 100,000 adults. This explosion in federal litigation put pressure on district court judges to dispose of cases more quickly. As a result, courts gradually moved from adjudication to negotiation. With pretrial conferences, new settlement techniques, and plea bargaining, judges increasingly see themselves more as case managers than as trial judges.[17] The courts' administrative structure has changed dramatically as well. Now magistrate judges, court administrators, the Administrative Office of the U.S. Courts, the Federal Judicial Center, and other ancillary staff share in the duties of the court or supply the court with the information and resources it needs to do its job more efficiently.[18]

The history of the U.S. District Court for the Southern District of Ohio well illustrates this transformation. In the early nineteenth century, this court, with its one judge, sat three times a year, hearing only a few cases each term, consisting mainly of individual litigants disputing land titles, the federal government trying to collect penalties, or the government and individuals dealing with problems on the Ohio River and other avenues of commerce. Today, the District Court for the Southern District of Ohio serves more than five million people in forty-eight of the state's eighty-eight counties. On average, the eight full-time judges, along with senior and magistrate judges, handle some five hundred criminal cases and three thousand civil cases a year. They have ruled on such economically and socially significant issues as corporate abuse and antitrust violations, the enforcement of the draft and wartime restrictions, and the desegregation of local schools. They have settled major class action suits against drug companies and nuclear power plants. And they have arbitrated heated disputes in their communities over open housing, police practices, and prison conditions. Finally, they regularly hear cases in which litigants seek to expand or to restrict such basic individual rights as free speech, the free exercise of religion, and privacy.[19]

This book describes this transformation. By examining the types of litigation that dominated the court throughout its history, the judges whose decisions affected not only individual litigants but also the state's and the nation's history, and the substantive and procedural transformations that have taken place, it traces the changing role that this federal district court has played in the history of the nation and its locality. Relying primarily on court documents, I detail both the important part the federal District Court for the Southern District of Ohio has played in the development of constitutional law and the role it has had in bringing federal law home to the people of southern Ohio. I show how, in fulfilling its functions, the court has, on numerous occasions, confronted tensions that have arisen between the ideology and values of the majority of the citizens of the southern district and the rights protected by federal law and the U.S. Constitution. But I conclude that throughout its history the court functioned largely as Congress intended—as an enforcer of federal law and the U.S. Constitution. The court's judges, however, have interpreted this role differently in different eras. Initially, judges saw their primary role as enforcers of federal law. Although this role continues today, especially since World War II the judges of the district court see themselves primarily as protectors of individual rights under the federal Constitution—the rights of speech, press, the free exercise of religion, equal protection under the law, and the like.

In addition to tracing the changes in the work of the court and its impact on the development of law and on Ohio's economic, political, and social life during its two-hundred-year history, I provide, especially in the last chapter, brief judicial biographies of all those who have been appointed as district court judges for the Southern District of Ohio. But along with the standard biographical data, I have added the histories of their appointments to the bench. As Judge John Weld Peck explained in a speech before the Toledo Bar Association in 1935, "The selection of judges . . . will ever be . . . political. The elevation to public office . . . cannot in the nature of things be otherwise than political."[20] By describing how the judges in southern Ohio gained appointment, we learn a little more about the role politics has played in judicial appointments.

Such histories of district courts are rare. Although historians have studied the Supreme Court in minute detail, only a few have examined district courts, and most of the more recent detailed histories have focused on southern courts.[21] One of the major reasons few historians have studied federal trial courts is the relative inaccessibility of sources. In the nineteenth century, most decisions went unreported. The courts operated for almost a century before West Publishing produced *Federal Cases,* making reported cases available nationally. Before West, regional reporters printed a limited number of circuit and district court decisions. As one scholar noted, most decisions of the nineteenth-century district court "rest in the obscurity of the pigeon hole, from which there is no present prospect that they will ever emerge."[22] But even today, the bulk of the work of the district courts remains unreported. Most of the "action" occurs during trials or in negotiations for settlements or over other matters. This regular business of the court is almost entirely undocumented. Even when judges issue orders and rulings, many, if not most, remain unpublished by the federal reporter, Westlaw, or Lexis. What court records there are—docket sheets and case records—are either in musty basements in the various federal courthouses of Ohio or in dirty, previously unopened boxes at the Great Lakes Region (Chicago) branch of the National Archives and Records Administration. Finally, few judges have left any personal papers that could help recreate their histories. But by digging into these "pigeon holes" in musty archives, as well as examining newspapers and case files, conducting oral interviews, and tapping other extant records, the history of the U.S. District Court for the Southern District of Ohio emerges.

Understanding the work of lower federal courts is, in the words of Supreme Court Justice Louis Brandeis, "essential" to the nation's "political and social health."[23] Felix Frankfurter and James M. Landis, in their pathbreaking work, *The Business of the Supreme Court,* agreed. "Our national history will not be adequately written until the history of our judicial systems can be adequately told through monograph studies of individual [lower federal] courts."[24] This book is one attempt to fill this gap in our knowledge of the history of the nation's federal courts, focusing on an important midwestern court and its work over its two-hundred-year history.

# THE BEGINNING, 1803–1833

AS THE NINETEENTH CENTURY opened, most of the residents of the territory that would become Ohio "were engaged, literally, in getting out of the woods."[1] As part of the Northwest Territory, these pioneers, averaging one person per square mile, concentrated in two areas—the western community of Cincinnati and the eastern area around Steubenville. Most engaged in farming, primarily exporting wheat and corn as cash crops. But commerce along the Ohio River also played an important role in the frontier economy, especially after the Louisiana Purchase in 1803 guaranteed free commerce down the Mississippi. Ohio's economy boomed as farmers shipped surplus crops down the Ohio and Mississippi rivers to European markets, as settlers poured into the area, and as land prices soared.[2]

On April 30, 1802, Congress specified the process by which the people of this rapidly growing area could transform themselves from residents of a territory into citizens of a new state that would then be admitted into the union "upon the same footing with the original states."[3] Ohioans were to call a constitutional convention, write a constitution, and organize a state government.[4] That done, Congress accepted Ohio as the nation's seventeenth state, declared all federal laws to be operable in the state, and created the U.S. District Court for the District of Ohio to enforce those laws.[5] This new court, presided over by a district judge, who, like all district judges, had to be a resident of his district, was to hold three sessions a year at Chillicothe, the seat of

Ohio's government. Congress set the judge's salary at a substantial $1,000 per year. In addition, Congress authorized the president to appoint "a person learned in the law" as attorney for the United States and a U.S. marshal to execute court orders. Each earned a salary of $200 per year in addition to the fees he collected. Finally, the district judge appointed a clerk as the court's administrative arm.[6]

Until 1807, the District Court for the District of Ohio acted as both district and circuit court for the state. Congress believed it would be too great a burden on a Supreme Court justice to have to travel such a distance to serve on what would be a far-western circuit. By the early 1800s, however, the population of Kentucky, Tennessee, and Ohio had grown so much and the litigation, especially over land disputes, had so increased that Congress realized the need for a new circuit court. Thus, in 1807, Congress created the Seventh Circuit, consisting of these three rapidly growing states, as the first circuit court west of the Appalachian Mountains. Like other circuit courts, the seventh was composed of the district court judge for the state and the Supreme Court justice from the area. Such a composition ensured that those from the locality enforced federal law in their own communities. To provide a Supreme Court justice to sit on this new court, Congress added a seventh justice to the Supreme Court. President Thomas Jefferson appointed Thomas Todd as the

Ohio counties in 1806. *Randolph C. Downes,* Evolution of Ohio County Boundaries *(Columbus: Ohio Historical Society, 1927)*

first western Supreme Court justice. By law, the Seventh Circuit Court held two sessions a year in each district. In Ohio, the Circuit Court for the District of Ohio convened in Chillicothe on the first Monday of January and September, annually. The district court held its sessions on the first Monday of February, June, and October.[7]

## JUDGE CHARLES BYRD, 1803–1828

To preside over the District Court for the District of Ohio, President Jefferson nominated and the Senate confirmed Charles Willing Byrd as the district's first judge.[8] A member of a prominent Virginia planter family, Byrd practiced law in Pennsylvania before moving to Ohio when, in 1799, President John Adams appointed him secretary of the Northwest Territory. Once in Ohio, Byrd became a prominent politician as secretary and then as acting governor of the Northwest Territory before Ohio's statehood, as an active proponent of statehood, and as a delegate to the constitutional convention that drafted Ohio's new constitution. Despite his appointment by the Federalist John Adams, Byrd aligned himself nationally with the Jeffersonian Republicans and locally with the state's moderate Republicans. This faction, headed by Nathaniel Massie, Thomas Worthington, one of Ohio's first U.S. senators, and Edward Tiffin, Ohio's first governor and later a U.S. senator, believed in a democratic government, but one run by a natural aristocracy based on merit. They sought stability, gentility, and order. To help achieve these goals, Byrd and his political cohorts supported an independent judiciary, which Byrd believed to be essential to the protection of property and the maintenance of order.[9]

President Jefferson appointed David Ziegler as U.S. marshal and Michael Baldwin as attorney for the United States as the two other officers of the court.[10] "Many ambitious" young attorneys, viewing these positions as prestigious and lucrative, had "coveted" them, leading to fierce competition before Jefferson made his decisions.[11] Ziegler, from Heidelberg, Germany, had earned distinction as an American Revolutionary War hero and Indian fighter and later as a successful Cincinnati storekeeper. A devoted Jeffersonian, he was part of the group, along with Byrd and Massie, who had vigorously promoted statehood.[12] Michael Baldwin, a successful Chillicothe attorney, had come to Ohio from Connecticut in 1799, after receiving his education at Yale. He, too, was politically "well connected," his brother, Henry Baldwin, serving as U.S. senator from Georgia and then as an associate justice of the Supreme Court. Despite this seemingly conservative background, Baldwin was the most radical of this group of Jeffersonian Republicans. Unlike Byrd, Baldwin rejected notions of deference and rule by a natural aristocracy. Also unlike Byrd, who supported an independent judiciary to protect propertied interests, Baldwin opposed most limits on majority rule and supported an elected judiciary.[13]

On June 6, 1803, the first meeting of the District Court for the District of Ohio convened in Chillicothe, "in a forty by sixty foot stone building" in a courtroom shared with the county court of common pleas and the Ohio Supreme Court.[14] At the opening of court, Byrd, Ziegler, and Baldwin presented their commissions, took their oaths, and posted the required bonds. Byrd quickly admitted five attorneys to practice before the court. The new judge then entered upon his first major task—the creation of a functioning court. To maintain the court's records, he appointed George Hoffman clerk. Next, he proclaimed the procedural rules of the court. In eighteen pages, he outlined ninety rules covering such topics as summoning grand and petit juries, posting bail, serving process, and conducting jury trials. He specified procedures for libel cases, that is, admiralty or equity cases involving the confiscation of ships and other property for violations of federal law. In general, preparation for trial was simple. Instead of the briefs and the lengthy

The first orders of the U.S. District Court for the District of Ohio, proclaimed by Judge Charles W. Byrd on June 6, 1803, the first day of the first session of the court, in Chillicothe, Ohio. *Courtesy of National Archives and Records Administration—Great Lakes Region (Chicago)*

The first building in Ohio to house the federal court (the U.S. District Court for the District of Ohio), Chillicothe, 1803–1820. This stone structure also housed the Ohio Court of Common Pleas and the Ohio Supreme Court. *Courtesy of the Sixth Circuit Archives, Cincinnati*

discovery process common today, Byrd required that, "at least one day" before trial commenced, attorneys for both sides "reduce the . . . facts to writing" and exchange these documents.[15] On the second day of the court's first session, the grand jury convened, the court admitted two more attorneys to its bar, and then the court adjourned, there being no more business.

These events went unnoticed by most Ohioans. The few newspapers published in the frontier state paid essentially no attention to the federal court. While the *Scioto Gazette* announced the president's appointment of Byrd and other federal officers when they were confirmed in March, the paper was silent on the new court's first session. Indeed, although Chillicothe papers printed an occasional legal notice, no extant Chillicothe or Cincinnati newspaper reported the proceedings of the district court for several decades.[16]

For many years, the court saw little activity.[17] From 1803 through 1807, when the court sat as both a district and a circuit court, the grand juries, which convened regularly at each term, returned no criminal indictments. The United States did not file its first civil suit until 1805. After that, it litigated two or three cases a year. These fell into two categories—debt cases and libel cases. Early debt cases generally were pursued by the postal service against postmasters who were not returning their collections to the government. Later cases mainly saw the United States as plaintiff, suing defendants who had not paid taxes, those who owed money to the government for fines or forfeitures, or sureties who had posted bonds for others.[18] The government also instituted libel suits, or cases of confiscation of personal property that violated federal law, which, during this early period, generally meant ships violating federal interstate commerce regulations or people not paying customs or whiskey taxes.[19] These cases, heard by the court sitting in admiralty or equity, began when the government filed a bill of information.

Most of the cases were private civil suits for the collection of money, jurisdiction being based on diversity of citizenship or on the few federal issues litigated in federal district courts, usually land disputes. Indeed, the first case the court heard was a dispute over land begun at its October 1803 term. The two daughters and devisees of Colonel William Crawford, an American Revolutionary War veteran, filed two suits against Thomas Armat and Samuel Finley to recover land in Ohio that their father had received as compensation for his services in the war. In 1804 and 1805, in a suit that became known as *McCormick v. Sullivant,* they initiated proceedings against three more defendants—Lucas Sullivant, John Beasley, and Bernard Thompson. These suits typified some of the complex land disputes early federal courts heard. The parties agreed that the colonel, as payment for his services during the American Revolution, had received a military land warrant for 6,666 and 2/3 acres in the Virginia Military District. They also agreed that the colonel, in his will, had divided the land between his son and his two daughters. Despite the will, the son, John, had surveyed the land and secured a military warrant issued in his name alone. He then had contracted to sell the land to various parties, who then sold it to others. Colonel Crawford's daughters claimed their brother had sold all their father's land without authorization and sought their two-thirds portion. The defendants, of course, claimed to be legal purchasers, who had bought the land for "valuable consideration" from the plaintiffs' brother, whom they believed to be the sole owner of the property.

In February 1805, Judge Byrd held for the defendants. The plaintiffs appealed, and on March 16, 1825, after twenty years of legal maneuvering, the U.S. Supreme Court sustained Byrd. Because Crawford's will had been probated only in Pennsylvania and never in Ohio, the will had no force in Ohio. Ohio law required that wills, to be valid, had to be "duly proved, and admitted to record, in the Court of the county where the testator had his residence at the time of his decease, or . . . in the Court of the county where the land devised lay." Because Ohio did not recognize the will, the court would follow state intestate laws. Applying the intestate law of Virginia, the state in which the land had been located at the time of Crawford's death in 1782, Byrd ruled that John Crawford, as the colonel's only son and thus his "heir at law," had inherited the whole property. Virginia, like Ohio and most other states, did not recognize women as heirs.[20]

Libel cases tended to be more straightforward. These cases involved seizures of goods thought to be in violation of a federal law. In many cases, it was determined that the duties had, indeed, been paid on seized goods. In such cases, however, as long as the government had good cause for the seizure, the claimants were not entitled to costs or damages. They simply got their goods returned.[21] When the seizures were valid, Byrd fined the defendants and ordered them to pay the required duty. Once they did, the government returned their property if the property itself were legal. Illegal property, such as stills, was destroyed. Further, if the property were legal in itself but if the defendant either could not or would not pay his duties, license fees, fines, or other moneys owned, the government sold the goods to cover the debt.[22]

In 1807, after Congress created the Circuit Court for the Districts of Ohio, Kentucky, and Tennessee,[23] Byrd heard major civil and criminal cases as a circuit judge and focused on minor criminal[24] and civil cases, as well as maritime (primarily libel) cases, as a district judge.[25] Until 1820, the court continued to meet in Chillicothe. But after the Ohio legislature moved the state's capital to Columbus, Congress moved the federal district and circuit courts there.[26] Columbus at the time was "a raw village of about eight hundred souls." The federal courthouse fit the town; it was a small building situated on a public square next to the official state buildings.[27]

The business of the district court declined briefly after the creation of the circuit court. Until 1819, a typical term saw anything ranging from an empty docket to approximately twenty cases. The types of cases, however, remained the same—mainly debt cases in which the United States was the plaintiff; libel cases, mainly against those retailing liquor without a license; and litigation between private parties, mainly for debt. At around this time, however, the United States started filing many more debt cases. Indeed, during the September term of 1819, there were 139 such cases. In the vast majority, the defendant did not appear, and the court declared default judgments in favor of the United States. The number of such cases in 1819 was unusually high; during the remainder of Byrd's tenure, the number of debt cases ranged from a handful to between fifty and one hundred per term Most were routine default judgments. One, originally heard by Byrd but not settled until 1831, was of interest only because it involved future president William Henry Harrison. Harrison had acted as surety for a Charles Clarkson, who had posted a bond with the United States when he became assistant paymaster in the U.S. Army. When Clarkson failed to pay out $1,129 of the government's money, the court ordered Harrison to pay that amount, plus interest.[28] Although these cases were routine, sparking no controversy or comment, they did show that the United States was committed to enforcing its own laws, rather than relying on state courts as it had to do before the U.S. Constitution had been ratified.[29]

Byrd was busier than ever with his double duties.[30] To the average citizen, the courts seemed nearly interchangeable, except that those who came to the

The U.S. District Court for the District of Ohio relocated to Columbus in 1820 after the state capital was moved there. The district court met in this building on Broad Street, situated beside the state office building and the State House, from 1820 until 1855, when Congress divided the court into northern and southern districts and moved the seat of the southern district to Cincinnati. *Courtesy of the Sixth Circuit Archives, Cincinnati*

circuit court often got to hear a Supreme Court justice addressing them or charging the jury. Although newspapers failed to report sessions of the district court, the *Scioto Gazette* did report the opening of circuit court and Supreme Court Justice Todd's charge to the grand jury.[31] And in that charge, Todd made explicit the role the federal courts were playing; they were to ensure justice and to enforce federal criminal and civil law, "to punish frauds committed on the bank of the United States," to punish crimes against the government, and especially the post office, and to "regulate trade and intercourse with the Indian tribes, and to preserve peace on the frontiers."[32]

Although the district court saw no major cases of national importance, it did have to arbitrate two disputes that could potentially have pitted the federal fugitive slave law against Ohio's prohibition of slavery. Such disputes were rare in federal court,[33] and these cases have been buried in archival records until now. In September 1817, the court heard its first case of a runaway. Edward and George Jackson, Virginia residents, owned several slaves, including one named Alice. When their mother needed help, they gave Alice as a gift for her use throughout the remainder of her life. Later George moved to Ohio. Four years after his move, his wife died, leaving him to care for his two young daughters. To help, the grandmother agreed to let Alice go to Ohio for a year to tend to the children. Alice readily agreed to the arrangement and arrived in June 1814; six months later, she ran away.[34]

To recover Alice, George Jackson, on behalf of himself and his mother, first applied to an Ohio justice of the peace under provisions of an 1803

Ohio law.[35] After hearing the case, the justice held that Alice was "a free person by the laws of the state of Ohio." Determined to continue litigation, Jackson continued to hold Alice while initiating a suit in federal district court under the Fugitive Slave Act of 1793.[36] But after two Ohio antislavery advocates, Moses and Jacob Ayers, took Alice from Jackson and apparently sent her out of the area, Jackson dropped his original suit and filed another against the Ayers brothers to recover for the loss of the value of his slave.[37]

After the trial, the jury asked Judge Byrd for advice, whether the law was on the side of the plaintiff or the defendant. The answer was by no means clear-cut, and Byrd took two years before he rendered a decision. Extant records provide no clue to the issues Byrd considered or to the basis for his ruling. For whatever reason, on September 16, 1819, Byrd held that the law was on the side of the defendants; Alice and her children were free persons, and therefore the Ayerses were not liable to Jackson for any damages.[38] Thus, Byrd struck a blow for freedom, siding with Ohio's status as a free state over southern pressures for strict comity. Ohio law prohibited slavery. Furthermore, a strict reading of the federal Fugitive Slave Act of 1793 and Article IV of the Constitution reveals that federal law governing the return of runaway slaves covered only those who escaped from a slave state into a free state. This was not, of course, Alice's situation; she was sent to Ohio voluntarily by her master. Nevertheless, northern states at the time struggled with the issue of comity and slave transit. If Alice were "domiciled" in Ohio—that is, living in a free state for a long or unspecified period of time—most courts, including many in the South, would grant her free status. But if she were "sojourning"—that is, living in the state for a brief, specified time—the law was unclear. Historian Don E. Fehrenbacher argues that "sojourning rights were acknowledged" in Ohio by "implicit understanding," and that northern judiciaries "offered no serious challenge to sojourning during the early decades of the Republic."[39] Paul Finkelman, however, cites several cases in which state judges ruled for freedom, although the Ohio Supreme Court "hedg[ed] on the legality of introducing a slave into the state for a short time." Until the 1840s, most Ohio judges adopted U.S. Supreme Court Justice Jessup N. Couch's position, which protected slave owners passing through the state with their slaves, but if the owner "*unlawfully* held [the slave] to labor," courts would declare that slave free. Although few federal courts heard such cases before 1850, one Pennsylvania circuit court case, decided by U.S. Supreme Court Justice Bushrod Washington in 1806, implied that courts would not free sojourner slaves, but would free those domiciled in a free state.[40]

Whether Byrd relied on the reasoning of Ohio's state judges or Justice Washington will never be known. But, based on the slim legal authority at the time, what seems to be at issue was whether Alice was merely "sojourning" in Ohio or whether, by living and working for six months in Ohio with her master's blessings, she was considered to be domiciled in the state. If she were free, the Ayers brothers owed nothing to Jackson, but if she were still his slave, they would owe him damages for his loss. By siding with Alice and the Ayers brothers and the earlier state court decision, Byrd chose to support freedom. Although there is no evidence that Byrd's personal views influenced his decision, no court had ever developed a bright-line rule for determining sojourner versus resident status. Because each situation was fact specific, a judge's personal views on slavery could be decisive. Although Byrd hailed from the slave state of Virginia, his Quaker education led him to oppose slavery.

The other case arose when Ben, traveling from Maryland, through Ohio, to Kentucky with his master, Griffith Davis, escaped. Encouraged by several antislavery Ohioans, Ben refused to return to his owner, insisting that he was free. Davis filed his trespass suit, based on diversity jurisdiction—that is, jurisdiction over controversies between citizens of different states, between citizens of the same state claiming lands under grants from different states, or between citizens of a state and a foreign country, citizens, or subjects—against those who had helped Ben escape. In this case, Ben was clearly a runaway, escaping while merely in transit in Ohio with his master. Although the Fugitive Slave Act, strictly speaking, applied only to slaves who escaped from a slave state into a free state, if Ben were a slave and therefore Davis's property, those who helped him escape could be liable for common-law damages. Most courts before the 1840s upheld the slave owner's claims in such cases.[41] This case settled out of court, the owner probably agreeing to allow antislavery Ohioans to purchase the runaway and then free him.[42]

During Byrd's tenure, the circuit court confronted two cases of great importance to the nation and ones that provoked much controversy in southern Ohio.[43] The first dealt with claims by the Jefferson administration that former vice president Aaron Burr wanted to create his own empire out of Spanish possessions along the Mississippi River south of Ohio. Newspapers reported Burr's activities with interest, especially when Burr passed through southern Ohio. Reports speculated that the former vice president was involved in a "nefarious plot."[44] State senator James Sargent of Washington Township introduced legislation that the Ohio General Assembly quickly enacted, authorizing the arrest of anyone "engaged in unlawful enterprises and the seizure of their goods."[45] Letters to the editor condemned Burr.[46] One wrote, "The western people have been active and successful. They have exhibited an example of their firmness to the general government, and cordially shewn to their eastern brethren in what detestation they hold the man who dares to attempt a separation of the states."[47]

After Burr's acquittal on charges of treason in Virginia in 1807, he and Harman Blennerhassett, a "rich Irish gentleman" who had bought an island in the Ohio River about twelve miles below Marietta, faced charges before the Seventh Circuit Court for launching an expedition to wage war against Spain in Mexico, "a nation with whom the United States was at peace." Justice Todd and Judge Byrd had just convened the first session of the circuit court. At this session in early January 1808, the grand jury, with Return Jonathan Meigs as foreman, after hearing the government's twenty-five witnesses, indicted Burr and Blennerhassett. Both then posted bond and, in anticipation of trial, hired Jacob Burnet and Michael Baldwin to run their defense. Burnet, a Cincinnati attorney, was an old Federalist and longtime acquaintance of Burr. Blennerhassett believed having him represent him and Burr would help their cause "with the decent part of the citizens of Ohio." They selected Baldwin, on the other hand, not only for his brilliance as a trial attorney but also because of his "influence with the rabble." Baldwin had been the first U.S. attorney for the District of Ohio, but after Jefferson replaced him because his alcoholism led him to neglect his duties, he shifted his political allegiance to the Federalists. The court continued the case for several years, but the trial never began, and neither Burr nor Blennerhassett ever appeared. Finally, in the January 1819 term, on a motion by the district attorney, the case was "discontinued."[48]

The second case, *Osborn v. Bank of the United States*,[49] developed out of the heated political debates over the national bank. Ultimately, the controversy centered on the power of the federal government versus the independence of the states. The first issue to be settled was whether the Eleventh Amendment to the U.S. Constitution prohibited the Bank of the United States from suing officials of a state government. Second, did the circuit court have jurisdiction? What did the phrase "arising under" federal law in Article III of the Constitution mean? Finally, what powers did the federal courts have to decide, with finality, the constitutionality of state and federal laws? In their decisions, Byrd and Todd in the circuit court and later the full Supreme Court upheld federal supremacy in the face of widespread opposition by Ohio politicians, newspapers, and the public at large. In fact, the Supreme Court's decision affirming Byrd and Todd is one of the most important cases cited for asserting federal supremacy.[50]

The Bank of the United States, originally created by Congress in February 1791, had always been controversial.[51] After Congress allowed it to expire in 1811, however, there was continued pressure to create another. Thus, in March 1816, President James Madison signed legislation creating the Second Bank of the United States. In 1817, that bank established branches in Cincinnati and Chillicothe. Initially, the bank enjoyed "fairly harmonious" relations with western financiers, but that changed as a depression gripped most of the nation.[52]

Ohio had enjoyed great prosperity from its founding through mid-1818. Especially after the War of 1812, land prices rose rapidly, commercial activity revived, and speculation ran rampant. New settlers poured into the state.[53]

Steamboat construction thrived, new towns sprang up, and new products flooded Ohio's markets. The number of banks mushroomed as entrepreneurs and farmers demanded easy credit so they could try to take advantage of these new opportunities. But prosperity came to an abrupt end in the summer of 1818. By year's end, there was "general bankruptcy, confusion and dismay."[54] Although the greed of speculators using borrowed money was the underlying cause, the policies of the Bank of the United States sparked the immediate crisis. Loans of vast sums of money by the western branches of the bank had drained resources from eastern branches and the parent bank. Inflation plagued the nation. Fearing the stability of its bank notes, the national bank adopted a new policy. State banks had to pay back their loans to the federal bank immediately. Moreover, the national bank's notes could be redeemed only at the branch that issued them.[55] This caused the inflationary bubble to burst. Prices of staple crops dropped dramatically, accelerating the deflationary cycle. In turn, the prices of land and manufactured goods collapsed. Unable to pay their debts, countless Ohioans faced bankruptcy and the loss of their farms and businesses.[56]

Needless to say, the Bank of the United States immediately lost whatever popularity it had had in Ohio. Even before the panic, the legislature had debated a proposal to tax the bank's branches. In December 1817, however, a committee concluded that it "would . . . be impolitic" for Ohio, "one of the youngest and most highly favored [states] in the Union, to be among the first to contravene the acts of the general government."[57] Although the Ohio House of Representatives rejected its committee's report, instead asserting that "the states that compose the American Union are independent sovereign states" and as such have the right to tax the stock of any company, including one created by the U.S. government,[58] the legislators did not enact a tax at that time. In December 1818, when the General Assembly reconvened, the newly elected Democratic governor, Ethan A. Brown, attacked the bank as illegal and unconstitutional and urged the legislature to place a tax on it. Blaming the bank for the state's economic problems, the legislature eagerly complied, imposing a tax of $50,000 a year on each branch of the bank doing business in Ohio after September 1, 1819.[59] The statute further authorized the state auditor to seize funds from the bank to pay the tax if the bank refused to pay.[60]

Before the September deadline, on March 7, 1819, the U.S. Supreme Court unanimously, in *McCulloch v. Maryland,* upheld the constitutionality of the Bank of the United States and proclaimed that no state could tax it or any of its branches.[61] Ignoring the controversial decision, Ohio state auditor Ralph Osborn declared that he still planned to collect Ohio's tax if the bank were still doing business in the state in September. To prevent that from happening, on September 14, 1819, the directors of the national bank received an injunction from the Seventh Circuit Court.[62] Nevertheless, Osborn, on the advice of the Ohio secretary of state and three private attorneys, maintained that the bank agent had improperly informed him of the injunction, never having given him a copy of the writ of injunction. Thus, he concluded, there was no legal injunction.[63] In turn, he authorized Sheriff John L. Harper to enter the Chillicothe branch of the bank to demand payment of the tax and, if payment were refused, to seize $100,000 in bank assets to cover the amount due. This the sheriff did, despite the fact that the bank's officers informed him of the injunction against such a seizure.[64]

The next day, the Seventh Circuit issued another writ of injunction against Osborn and Harper, "restraining them from paying over the money or making report of its collection to the legislature."[65] After the two state officials ignored this injunction, the bank filed suit against them for contempt of court, for trespass, and to recover the funds seized. On January 6, 1820, the court served notice on Osborn and Harper to show cause why "an attachment should not issue against them for contempt" of court for disregarding the injunction.[66]

Most Ohioans supported their state leaders.[67] A legislative committee denounced the idea that the federal courts were the exclusive judge of the U.S. Constitution. Citing the Kentucky and Virginia Resolves,[68] the committee declared that the states had an equal right to decide for themselves whether a federal law was constitutional. The General Assembly approved the committee's report and, to make clear its commitment to exercise its sovereign power, it also enacted a statute withdrawing from the Bank of the United States "the protection and aid of the laws of this state, in certain cases" unless it was willing to pay the Ohio tax. Citizens met and passed resolutions supporting their state leaders. Even those who supported the bank were cautious in their criticism of Ohio's actions. The probank *Cincinnati Inquisitor and Advertiser,* for example, editorialized that a confrontation with the federal government was not the best policy. It argued that, if state officials believed the bank to be unconstitutional, they should challenge it directly rather than indirectly in a way that "subverts the order of our government."[69] But the bank held fast.

Finally, on September 5, 1821, Justice Todd and Judge Byrd issued their opinion. Denouncing Osborn's actions, they delineated the broad powers the federal courts had to control the actions of the states and their officials. The federal courts, they said, determine whether state laws unconstitutionally conflict with federal law; states do not have the right to decide for themselves. And the federal courts had declared the Ohio tax unconstitutional. If state agents ignored federal courts, they would be brought before those courts to answer for their illegal actions. The judges not only ordered Osborn to return the $100,000 seized but also demanded that the defendants pay the bank interest, amounting to $19,380. Moreover, the court "perpetually enjoined" state officials from collecting any state tax from the bank. Finally, the court ordered the defendants to pay the costs the bank had expended in pursuing legal action.[70]

Ohio appealed the circuit court's decision to the U.S. Supreme Court. Nationally renowned politician-lawyers Henry Clay, Daniel Webster, William Wirt, and A. G. Sargent defended the bank; Ohioans Charles Hammond and John C. Wright represented Osborn and the state of Ohio.[71] After listening to arguments on both sides, especially those focusing on the issues of "the constitutionality and effect of the provision in the charter of the Bank, which authorizes it to sue in the Circuit Courts of the Union,"[72] Chief Justice John Marshall, writing for the majority, reaffirmed the Court's decision in *McCulloch v. Maryland*. Further, Marshall held that Congress could authorize the bank to sue in lower federal courts and that the Eleventh Amendment to the U.S. Constitution did not prevent suits against state officials, just against the states themselves.[73] The Court did, however, temper the strong stand taken by Judge Byrd and Justice Todd by holding that, although the $100,000 seized from the bank had to be returned, no interest was due because "the parties were restrained by the authority of the Circuit Court" from using the money.[74]

Besides controversial cases that sometimes pitted federal law against state officials, the federal system of justice experienced some embarrassment because of the problems caused by the unfortunate deterioration of Michael Baldwin, Ohio's first U.S. attorney and then its U.S. marshal. Perhaps one of the most successful attorneys in Chillicothe's early history, Baldwin had, because of his "uncontrollable love of liquor, fun and frolic," begun to neglect most of his duties, especially during the Burr conspiracy. Baldwin's lack of attention to his duties created problems as court papers went undelivered or prosecutions were mishandled or neglected. Dismissed by Jefferson in 1807, Baldwin returned to private practice. Within a few years, his name appeared in court records only for contempt of court or as a defendant in suits for unpaid tavern bills or other debts.[75]

Byrd himself had his own problems, although he kept his dispute with the government from public view. Byrd believed he was not receiving the salary Congress had authorized for him. Therefore, he wrote Justice Todd, requesting that Todd discuss his salary with Congressman William Clay. Byrd insisted that it was Clay's intention, when he introduced the bill creating the Seventh Circuit, to place all judges' pay "on the same footing." Byrd, however, was still receiving only $1,000 a year while the district judges in Kentucky and Tennessee received $1,200.[76]

### BYRD'S SUCCESSORS

Judge Byrd's death on August 11, 1828, ended his twenty-five-year tenure as district court judge. He had accomplished much. Although the court did not yet play a prominent role in the lives of average Ohioans, Byrd had established the federal court as an institution that enforced federal law and federal obligations in what many viewed as a remote outpost. The national government regularly litigated actions to ensure that its taxes would be paid and its custom regulations would be obeyed. Byrd steadfastly upheld federal supremacy in the bank controversy, and, on the slavery issue, he carefully considered comity issues before deciding for freedom. Although many, depending on the issue, might have resented the decisions of the federal courts, its ability to sustain its judgment was clearly established by the mid-1820s.

Byrd's death occasioned a scramble among Ohio's various political factions to influence President John Quincy Adams's choice of a replacement. As a frontier community, Ohio had early aligned itself with the Jeffersonians. At the constitutional convention that created the state, at least two-thirds of the delegates supported Jefferson over the Federalists.[77] But despite the commitment to Jeffersonian Republicanism, most Ohioans were nationalists. They needed the federal government to defend them against Indian attacks, to arbitrate disputes over land titles, and to help pay for roads and the infrastructure needed for commercial development.[78] Such support by the national government spurred Ohio's growth, so by 1820 the state ranked third in the value of produce and fifth in capital invested in factories producing goods for sale at home and abroad. In spite of this growth, Ohio was still predominantly rural: 95 percent of its population lived on farms or in villages of fewer than a hundred people. Only Cincinnati, with a population of almost ten thousand, could be considered a city.[79] Perhaps because of these conflicting economic and social interests, Ohioans of the late 1820s were divided almost evenly between the two emerging political parties, although southern Ohioans tended to favor Andrew Jackson and his more states-rights, laissez-faire approach over John Quincy Adams and Henry Clay, who favored a more activist central government.[80]

In the midst of a reelection campaign, Adams hesitated to nominate a replacement for Byrd, fearing that any choice would alienate some faction he needed to win Ohio.[81] But on November 1, 1828, when it must have been clear to him that the election was lost, he named William Creighton Jr., as a recess appointee.[82] Creighton seemed to be an excellent choice. "A man of the finest legal attainments" and a popular politician, his loyalty to the Jeffersonians had been rewarded when President Jefferson appointed him U.S. attorney for the District of Ohio in 1808. During his four terms as U.S. congressman, however, Creighton eventually aligned himself with the more conservative Adams faction.[83] Politics won out over merit; the Jacksonian-dominated Senate refused to confirm Creighton—or any Adams nominee, determined to keep all the vacant judicial positions open for Jackson, who had won the 1828 election, to fill.[84] Creighton, therefore, served only one term—the December 1828 term—as district court judge. He heard only a handful of cases, all involving litigation with the United States as plaintiff trying to collect money owed it for a variety of reasons.[85]

On March 7, 1829, Jackson's nominee, John W. Campbell, after being confirmed by the Senate, replaced Creighton.[86] A Virginian like Byrd and Creighton, Campbell had also been politically active. He served as a justice of the peace, a county prosecuting attorney, three terms as a member of the Ohio General Assembly, and five terms as a U.S. congressman. But, most important, he had been an early supporter of the new president, Andrew Jackson. Although well educated and a man of integrity, Campbell had not practiced law in many years. Many questioned his qualifications for his new post. Perhaps realizing his deficiencies and taking his new responsibilities seriously, Campbell moved to Columbus, the seat of the court, and rose at 4:00 AM each day to study the law.[87]

### THE CAMPBELL COURT

During the four years Campbell served as judge for the District of Ohio, he had few notable cases. At the district level, he handled fewer than ten cases a term, nearly all of them debt cases, the government seeking to recover money owed it by postmasters, by those who had put up bond, by those who had purchased government-owned property, and the like. The only remotely unusual case extant in the records occurred in the July 1831 term, when a jury rendered judgment in a trespass case against four defendants who had squatted on government land, ordering each to pay $5 in damages plus the cost of prosecution. During his tenure as a district court judge, Campbell probably heard no criminal cases, because there is no record that the grand jury indicted anyone during his term.[88]

Of course, like Byrd before him, Campbell also sat as a circuit court judge. The records generally do not indicate whether, when that court convened, Campbell sat alone or with Justice John McLean, the Supreme Court justice assigned to the Seventh Circuit, or whether McLean sat alone. Any of these possibilities was allowable under the rules of the court.[89] For example, one of the circuit court's most notable cases for this period was *Ewing v. Burnet*.[90] The U.S. Supreme Court's affirmation of the circuit court's holding "is a leading textbook case on adverse possession."[91] But no record exists indicating which judge or judges presided over the case in the Seventh Circuit.[92]

The records do indicate that Judge Campbell presided over the circuit court's most important case for the city of Cincinnati. In *Lessee of White v. Cincinnati*, the plaintiff claimed title by legal conveyances from Mathias Denman to what had become known as the public levee. Denman had bought the land from John Cleves Symmes, who had originally purchased the land from the federal government in 1788. After Symmes sold part of the tract to Denman, Denman sold one-third interests to Israel Ludlow and Robert Patterson. The three then proceeded to lay out the town of Cincinnati. According to their plan, the ground lying between Front Street and the Ohio River was set apart as a common "for the use and benefit of the town for ever." After

Denman sold a small lot that included some of this grant to the plaintiff, the issue became whether Denman's grant to the city for a public common was valid even though there was no writing or deed.[93]

In a conservative decision following the strict letter of the law, Campbell refused to give the jury the instructions the city requested that would have let the jury consider the validity of an unwritten agreement. Instead, his instructions favored private property rights over the claims of the city, insisting that to prevail the plaintiff needed clear proof that the grant was intended to be permanent. Following these instructions, the jury found for the individual claimant against the city. The city then appealed to the Supreme Court, which overruled Campbell's decision. In very Jacksonian language, Justice Smith Thompson, delivering the opinion of the Court, upheld the rights of the community over legal technicalities. He ruled "that no deed or writing was necessary to constitute a valid dedication of the easement." Emphasizing the importance of considering the rights of the public, he asserted that "all public dedications must be considered with reference to the use for which they are made, and streets in a town or city may require a more enlarged right over the use of the land, in order to carry into effect the purposes intended." In this case, the grant "was for the public use, and the convenience and accommodation of the inhabitants of Cincinnati." Further, this grant "doubtless" "greatly enhanced the value of the private property adjoining this common, and thereby compensated" White and other owners of land not included in the public grant.[94]

While the Supreme Court reversed the Circuit Court of Ohio's jury instructions in *Cincinnati v. Lessee of White,* it upheld Campbell on other occasions, which indicates that Campbell was a competent judge, despite some of the criticism that had been raised against him. One case, in particular, demonstrated Campbell's use of textual analysis of statutes as well as common sense to arrive at a decision that Justice McLean praised. In that case, an army paymaster claimed he was due the same pay as a major of cavalry, whereas the government argued that his pay was equivalent to that of a major of infantry. After studying the issues in depth, Campbell concluded that although the current statute did not specify either cavalry or infantry, a comparison of paymaster salaries with those of others employed by the government as well as an analysis of all the statutes Congress had enacted on the subject led to the conclusion that the paymasters' salary was the equivalent of that of a major of infantry. The plaintiff appealed, and the circuit court continued the case until the Supreme Court decided a similar case. Three years after Campbell's death, McLean, sitting as circuit court judge, published Campbell's district court opinion, praising him for arriving, years before the Supreme Court, at the same result the higher court had just reached.[95]

History will never know whether Campbell would have emerged as a prominent jurist, because he died suddenly, on September 24, 1833, at the age of fifty-one, a victim of a cholera epidemic that struck Columbus that year.[96] But he and the judges who preceded him had succeeded in establishing the federal courts in Ohio as institutions to be respected and obeyed, regularly deciding disputes between federal and state jurisdiction, presiding over cases in which the federal government pressed its claims and enforced its law against citizens and state officials who either ignored or challenged its authority, and listening as individuals litigated to uphold their rights under the Constitution and federal law against those who would undermine those rights. And, although all three judges who presided over the court in its early years were Jeffersonians or Jacksonians, they upheld federal authority when called upon to do so. Ohio's next judge, Humphrey H. Leavitt, also a Jacksonian, would go even further in establishing the authority of the federal court and upholding the powers of the federal government as the country faced the crisis of secession and civil war.

# 2

## HUMPHREY H. LEAVITT, 1834–1872

### THE SCRAMBLE FOR A NEW DISTRICT COURT JUDGE

Several prominent politicians and attorneys scrambled to be Andrew Jackson's nominee to fill John W. Campbell's seat as district court judge for Ohio,[1] but it was Benjamin Tappan, of Steubenville, who had the backing of many of Jackson's closest political advisors, including Micajah T. Williams and General Land Office Commissioner Elijah Hayward, "chief dispenser of the administration's Ohio patronage."[2] Tappan had served as an Ohio state senator, a judge of the Fifth Circuit Court of Common Pleas, and a Jackson elector in 1832.[3] Supporters praised him as "among the most learned and able jurists" in the West,[4] but his enemies, led by Ohio's two Whig senators, Thomas Ewing and Benjamin Ruggles, succeeded in convincing the Senate to reject his nomination by an 11 to 28 vote.[5]

To replace Tappan, President Jackson turned to Humphrey H. Leavitt, who had been one of the other candidates he had considered after Campbell's death.[6] In the words of one commentator, Leavitt was, "in appearance, the most venerable official I have ever known."[7] A popular Democratic politician before his appointment to the bench, Leavitt had served as a member of both houses of the Ohio General Assembly and as a three-term representative to Congress, supporting such Jacksonian causes as opposition to the federally chartered Bank of the United States.[8]

In the words of future judge John Weld Peck, Leavitt "bridge[d] the gap between the old times and the new,"[9] serving as judge for thirty-seven years. He presided over the court during the antebellum years, the Civil War, and the Gilded Age as America launched its industrial revolution. In the years before the war, as Ohio and the nation underwent a market revolution with great growth in commerce and banking, Leavitt dealt mainly with cases of debt and cases in admiralty along with land disputes and an occasional criminal case. More and more, however, the government brought suits to collect the increasing number of federal excise and customs taxes. He also presided over bankruptcy cases and the even more important and controversial cases contesting the validity of the federal fugitive slave laws. During the Civil War, a time of great stress and political divisions in Ohio, Leavitt presided over many seizures as the nation tried to prevent the smuggling of goods to the Confederacy as well as cases against those expressing sympathy for the Confederate cause. After the war, bankruptcy cases, as well as diversity cases, dominated Leavitt's judicial life.

## THE DISTRICT COURT DURING THE ANTEBELLUM YEARS: NEW RESPONSIBILITIES AND NEW CHALLENGES

When Leavitt assumed his duties on July 10, 1834, Ohio was still growing rapidly. Between 1826 and 1840, its population increased from 800,000 to more than 1.5 million people, making it the third-most-populous state in the Union. On the eve of the Civil War, its population had increased to more than 2.3 million. Cincinnati emerged as the "Queen City of the West," being one of the most important commercial and manufacturing centers in the country and, by 1860, the sixth-largest city in the nation. Still, farming dominated Ohio's economy, although it was increasingly farming involved in the market economy. To further trade and manufacturing, Ohio expanded its system of transportation with canals and railroads. By 1860, the state had about three thousand miles of railroad track, more than any other state in the Union. After the Civil War, Ohio continued its agricultural and industrial growth, becoming a leading producer of wheat as well as other farm products and coal. It also became heavily involved in iron and steel production.[10] As commerce and industry increased, as America went through boom and bust cycles, and as industry developed, federal courts saw more cases in admiralty and more civil suits based on diversity.

The docket also increased as Congress expanded the role of the federal court. From the district court's inception, Congress had limited its jurisdiction to admiralty and maritime cases, seizures upon land, and suits brought by the United States for penalties and forfeitures and against those in debt to the government. The court also heard cases based on its diversity jurisdiction. Its criminal jurisdiction was limited to minor federal crimes. Judge Leavitt himself explained that when he took up his post as district judge, the whole state of Ohio was one judicial district with "comparatively little business." The two sessions the court held each year "rarely exceeded three weeks in duration."[11]

All this changed in the 1840s and 1850s, as Congress transformed the district court from an institution exercising a narrow role to one of increasing importance in the economic and social issues of the day. In 1842, Congress significantly expanded the district courts' criminal jurisdiction by giving it concurrent jurisdiction with the U.S. circuit courts in all criminal cases except those involving capital crimes.[12] In the civil area, two new pieces of legislation thrust the court into the heated economic and social debates of the antebellum era. Although repealed after only one year of operation, the Bankruptcy Act of 1841 created a uniform bankruptcy system for the nation and designated the district courts to be the system's administrators. The Fugitive Slave Acts of 1793 and 1850 had a more lasting effect, resulting in many dramatic cases along with political and ideological debates that some believe helped lead to secession and civil war.[13]

To relieve Ohio's federal courts, most particularly the circuit court, from their increasingly heavy burden, in 1855 Congress divided the state into the northern and southern districts. The southern, to which Leavitt was assigned, sat in Cincinnati and was composed of thirty-nine counties, including Belmont, Guernsey, Muskingum, Licking, Franklin, Madison, Champaign, Shelby, and Mercer and all the counties south of these.[14] The court, meeting in its new building at the corner of Fourth and Vine streets, held two terms a year both as a circuit and as a district court, convening on the third Tuesdays in April and October.[15] This division of the District Court of Ohio was not without controversy. Columbus was the big loser. The southern district sat in Cincinnati and the northern district met in Cleveland, leaving Columbus without the prestige and patronage of a federal court. For months before Congress approved the change, Columbus's leading newspaper, the *Ohio State Journal,* in numerous editorials, lobbied to defeat the move. It claimed that the docket was not overcrowded, that Judge Leavitt had proven himself quite capable of handling the work load, and that the only reason for the change was to promote "more lucrative jobs" for political patronage and the interests of the legal professions in Cincinnati and Cleveland. Rather than serving any useful purpose, the division of the court, the *Journal* contended, would result only in unnecessary increased costs and greater inconveniences for most Ohioans, who would be better served by one court meeting in Columbus, "which is accessible from all parts of the state."[16]

Judge Leavitt seemed to disagree, claiming that after Congress divided Ohio the new court for the Southern District of Ohio experienced "a very changed state." Now meeting in Cincinnati, "the great commercial center for the State," Leavitt said that the court witnessed "an avalanche" of new business.[17] The records, however, do not bear the judge out. At least initially,

The new U.S. District Court for the Southern District of Ohio held its sessions from 1855 until 1885 in the new federal building, known as the Post Office Building, located at Fourth and Vine in Cincinnati. *Courtesy of the Sixth Circuit Archives, Cincinnati*

despite Congress's expansion of the court's jurisdiction, the court's docket remained much the same as it had from the court's inception. Even after Congress divided the court into two district courts and moved the new southern district to Cincinnati, the pattern changed little. In 1855, for example, there were still only three to ten new cases per term.[18]

Leavitt spent most of his energies on circuit court business, where civil filings averaged two hundred a year.[19] The circuit court dealt with patent and copyright disputes, land title controversies, trespass, assumpsit and chancery cases, personal injury cases, especially against stagecoach companies, and negotiable instrument and other commercial paper disputes. The court also resolved several disputes over the construction of bridges over navigable waters, balancing the interests of river traffic with the needs of commerce over land. In addition, the circuit court heard some dramatic cases involving violations of U.S. neutrality laws, including plots to invade Canada and Cuba and a scheme by Irish émigrés to attack Great Britain. The court was also called upon to define its authority, ruling on whether cases before it were in its jurisdiction. It defined the requirements of diversity and the scope of its subject matter jurisdiction. The circuit court's criminal docket was also crowded, with around forty cases a year, mainly dealing with counterfeiters, forgers, and those who stole from the U.S. post office.[20]

The district court docket included mainly small cases of debt and trespass, as well as admiralty and maritime cases. Debt cases often involved those who had posted bonds for others, either bonds in judicial proceedings or bonds required for office holding. At his first session as judge, in the July term of 1834, for example, Leavitt presided over one quite ironic debt case, as the government sued Benjamin Tappan, whom the Senate had just refused to confirm as district court judge, and who, in this case, had acted as a surety for a Jeremiah Fogg. The jury, however, found that Tappan owed no money because Fogg had not breached his duties in his federal post.[21] The United States also brought actions in trespass against those who illegally settled on or took resources from federal lands. For example, in the December term of 1836 and the July term of 1837, Leavitt dealt with nineteen cases of trespass. All those accused were found liable and assessed damages of between one cent and five dollars. There was another rash of trespass cases in 1845, when the government accused a dozen people of cutting down timber on federal lands, and in 1849, when it sued another eighteen.[22] In these civil cases, the fines and court costs, which were assessed against the losing party, were generally small. Filing a praecipe, administering oaths, or swearing a witness to testify cost ten cents. Copies of pleadings were ten cents a folio. Entering endorsements and decrees, as well as plaintiff's appearances or motions, cost fifteen cents; issuing writs cost a dollar. A notary public charged between $3.00 and $3.50 to take a deposition.[23]

It was in admiralty and maritime cases that the federal government most clearly enforced its laws, and the court arbitrated disputes affecting the area's expanding commercial life. The Judiciary Act of 1789 gave district courts exclusive jurisdiction in admiralty and maritime law. In the 1830s and 1840s, Congress increased the district courts' role by enacting legislation to promote safety on interstate waterways and to make explicit the district courts' jurisdiction over incidents on the nation's lakes and navigable rivers.[24]

Safe and reliable river transportation was essential for the continued growth and prosperity of Cincinnati as well as for the rest of southern Ohio. By the 1830s, Cincinnati had become not only a major commercial port but also an important center for shipbuilding. Moreover, because roads generally were in poor condition, rivers, and especially the Ohio River for southern Ohio, played a key role in the development of the economy, providing farmers with a means to market their crops and a convenient route for those moving west.[25] Indeed, reliable river transportation was so important to the area that river safety became a significant topic of debate. After one steamboat, the *Moselle,* considered "the very paragon of Western steamboats," exploded, a group of citizens at a public meeting held in Cincinnati, at which the mayor presided, passed several resolutions urging Congress to enact stronger regulations to ensure that steam vessels would be driven by qualified pilots and maintained by trained engineers.[26] Leavitt, by arbitrating disputes that arose in this important commercial arena, enforcing federal regulations, and expanding federal authority through creative jurisprudence, helped promote the well-regulated society most Americans—or at least most political and economic leaders—seemed to desire.[27] Leavitt himself described the increased burden these cases placed on him. Noting that before the court's move to Cincinnati, there were "few" admiralty cases, he explained that by the 1850s such cases were "numerous and many of them very important, involving great labor in trying and disposing them." Indeed, cases became so numerous and complex that the judge was "compelled" to undertake a "study of maritime law" so he could dispose of them wisely.[28]

For the Southern District of Ohio, four basic types of admiralty and maritime cases dominated the docket.[29] The first involved the seizure of goods for violations of revenue laws, especially the nonpayment of import duties. In such cases, customs or revenue officials generally seized the ship or the goods, the marshal then published information about the seizure in state newspapers, and finally the court, at its next term, heard the case. If a violation were found, the court ordered the goods sold. On occasion, someone claimed the goods, paid the tax, and the goods were returned.[30]

Second, the government litigated to enforce commercial safety and federal regulations of ships, especially the 1838 act requiring the licensing and use of pilots for all steamboats engaged in interstate commerce.[31] The case of the *United States v. The Steam Boat Warren* typified such proceedings. After government agents seized the *Warren* for operating without a license, its owner, John Moore, posted bond in double the amount of the penalty to get his boat back. Then, at the court's next term, a jury, after a short trial, found Moore guilty of operating an unlicensed ship. Leavitt fined him $500 plus court costs. To collect the fine, the government sold the boat and divided the $500, as required by law, between itself and the informer.[32]

The third category of admiralty cases involved individuals suing ship owners. Seamen sued for unpaid wages. Independent contractors sought money due them.[33] Shippers sued to resolve contract disputes, usually involving the nondelivery or the late delivery of goods shipped or for damages to goods transported.[34]

Collisions, a fourth type of admiralty case, presented the most difficulty because they required that the judge determine which ship had the right of way or failed to obey the rules of the river.[35] Leavitt considered these cases of the greatest importance to the promotion of commerce. Safe shipping and water travel were essential to public confidence in emerging technologies. Therefore, courts had to enforce maritime law vigorously to ensure "unremitting vigilance and care on the part of those intrusted with the navigation of vessels" in order to minimize the chances for collisions.[36] The case of the steamboat *Atlantic* well illustrates the difficulties involved in collision cases. The *Atlantic,* a large passenger steamboat, collided with the *Ogdensburgh,* a freight boat, resulting in the sinking of the *Atlantic* and the loss of two hundred lives. Leavitt had to determine exactly what happened before he could decide which ship was responsible for the collision. The problem, typical in such cases, was that, although there was "a great mass of testimony," there was, " in some material points, great conflict" in that testimony.[37] Leavitt finally found the testimony of "the many experienced and highly intelligent navigators, who testified as experts" for the *Ogdensburgh* most persuasive and therefore held the *Atlantic* liable for the $3,000 in damages it caused to the freighter while allowing nothing to the owners of the *Atlantic,* who lost their ship in the wreck.[38] Justice McLean, hearing the appeal in circuit court, reversed Leavitt's decision, holding that "the weight of the responsibility for this great calamity lies on the Propeller *Ogdensburgh.* The *Atlantic* was at fault, but not in the same degree as the propeller." Therefore, he held, "where the fault is mutual, the damages are divided."[39] The U.S. Supreme Court affirmed McLean's judgment.[40]

Whereas the *Ogdensburgh* case challenged the judges' ability to weigh conflicting evidence, *McGinnis v. The Pontiac* required Leavitt to search for the appropriate law to apply. This provided Leavitt with the opportunity to use creative jurisprudence to ensure river safety, but at a reasonable cost to shipowners, thereby also encouraging greater economic activity. Michael N. McGinnis filed suit, claiming the rights as a salvor for saving the *Pontiac* from "imminent peril" and bringing her and her freight safely to Cincinnati after a gorge of ice threatened the ship on a cold January evening in 1852. McGinnis was a passenger on one of the many other ships stuck in the ice on the Ohio River that night, all of them colliding with each other, unable to steer. The *Pontiac,* however, faced a more severe crisis. Her captain had taken ill, so the passengers and some of the crew had left the ship, fearing it would sink. One of the ship's owners, who was on the steamboat, asked McGinnis, who was himself a master pilot, if he would try to save the ship and then sail it to Cincinnati. This McGinnis did, fighting the ice and the other ships the entire night, finally freeing the *Pontiac* and sailing her safely to Cincinnati, arriving six days later.

After McGinnis's heroic efforts saved the ship, the *Pontiac's* owners claimed they had merely hired McGinnis as a ship's captain and therefore they owed him only a captain's salary and not a salvor's rights. Leavitt disagreed. The judge conceded that the maritime rule that ships' masters have an obligation to save their vessels and cargoes and have no right to assert claims for salvage was an important one, "founded on good sense." Such a rule, he granted, must be "rigidly observed," based as it was on public policy "designed for the protection of the great interests of navigation and commerce." But, Leavitt pointed out, McGinnis, as a passenger on another ship, was "under no obligation to take command" of the *Pontiac.* Further, Leavitt concluded that no one would assume such a responsibility "for the trifling pecuniary remuneration he would be entitled to as master . . . for the few days that he would be employed as such."

Describing his decision-making process in this case of first impression, Leavitt explained that he had reached his conclusions "without the aid of any authorities bearing on the point. In looking into the few books on maritime law, which are accessible to me, I have found no case reported, or principle settled, which directly touches the inquiry here involved." Thus, he declared, he would use common sense, and common sense led him to conclude that McGinnis had earned the right to be treated as a salvor. But Leavitt tempered the economic cost of this decision by limiting McGinnis's compensation to a modest amount. Again employing his commonsense approach to the case at hand, Leavitt rejected precedents established in salvage cases on the high seas, arguing that such cases did not properly fit the lower risks of river navigation because "the peril of life, in cases of disaster on our rivers . . . is not equal to those resulting from disasters on the ocean." This analysis led Leavitt to proclaim an important principle adopted by other courts and still cited in treatises for salvor cases occurring on rivers and lakes: that salvor claims should be set only after a fair assessment of the "peril incurred," the "labor sustained," and the "value of the freight saved."[41]

Not only were admiralty and maritime cases important for the nation's economic growth, promoting safe commerce and arbitrating contractual disputes involving shipping, but they also occasionally afforded the court the opportunity to delineate the scope of federal authority over the states in the area of commerce. In the *McGinnis* salvage case, for example, the owners of the *Pontiac* challenged the district court's jurisdiction, claiming that the ship was not in the tidal waters, which, they claimed, was the limits of federal maritime authority. Judge Leavitt, asserting broad federal power, pointed to the decision of the U.S. Supreme Court in *Genesee Chief v. Fitzhugh*,[42] proclaiming it "authoritative in all the courts of the Union," settling decisively this issue: "the admiralty and maritime jurisdiction granted to the federal government by the constitution [sic] of the United States is not limited to tidewaters, but extends to all public navigable lakes and rivers, where commerce is carried on between different states."[43]

This principle was an extremely important one for those litigating against ship owners, especially seamen and common laborers. Throughout the antebellum period, many opposed the expansion of federal power over commerce, seeking to confine maritime jurisdiction in the United States only to the high seas, that being the limits of English admiralty courts. But even states rights—oriented Jacksonians like Chief Justice Roger B. Taney recognized that the invention of the steamboat required an expansion of federal law. If the federal government's power to regulate interstate commerce was to mean anything, its courts had to be able to arbitrate disputes that arose on any avenue of commerce.

Therefore, rather than blindly following English traditions, both Taney and Leavitt, when dealing with changing technologies, employed an instrumental approach to carry out what they saw as the intent of the Constitution. In the *Genesee Chief* case, Taney argued the Jacksonian principle of equality. He maintained that western states would not have the same protection as did eastern seaboard states if commerce on lakes and rivers were not protected by the federal courts. Leavitt took the same position in *McGinnis v. The Pontiac.* Although an occasional steamboat owner grumbled that this new doctrine granted seamen the status of "wards of admiralty," giving "crews a means to harass" owners "unreasonably," the doctrine slowly gained acceptance as Leavitt and other district judges regularly reinforced the message.[44]

Broadening the scope of federal commerce powers was only one of the ways in which Leavitt strengthened the authority of the federal government in the economic arena. In a case of first impression, he used a purpose approach to statutory interpretation to increase federal powers. Asserting that judges should not rely on a narrow textual jurisprudence when interpreting congressional statutes, Leavitt insisted that they must strive, instead, to carry out Congress's intent. Therefore, in *United States v. Bougher,* when the United States filed an action of debt to collect a penalty imposed by the court on a steamboat owner for operating his boat without a licensed pilot, Leavitt held that the federal government could institute suits in its own name despite the fact that the statute in question specified only that informers could sue.[45] To read the statute narrowly, he stated, would defeat Congress's goals. Having established the government's power to institute its own suits, Leavitt proceeded to expand federal authority further by applying what he claimed to be "settled principles of the common law." He ruled that, not only could the government initiate suits, but when it did so, it was free to choose how it would proceed against alleged violators. It could file a libel in admiralty court or it could proceed with "the milder form of an action of debt." Finally, taking an expansive view of the district courts' jurisdiction, Leavitt added that, if the government chose to proceed with an action of debt, it could institute that suit in district court based on the provisions of the Judiciary Act of 1789, declaring that these courts "have cognizance of all suits at common law, where the United States sue."[46]

The third way Leavitt strengthened federal power over interstate commerce was his insistence on federal supremacy when the authority of federal courts clashed with that of state courts. When an Ohio court and the federal district court ordered the sale of the same boat to pay that boat's debts, Leavitt explained that the state's proceedings must give way; state courts may not "interfere with a rightful exercise of the admiralty law." To do so "would be a violation of the constitution and the laws of the Union." Although each state can regulate its own commerce, federal admiralty law is superior when the two are in conflict or overlap.[47]

Developing the policies and procedures necessary to implement the nation's new uniform bankruptcy system established by Congress on August 19, 1841, gave Leavitt another opportunity to provide Ohioans with the benefits of federal law as well as to bring home to them the broad scope of federal power.[48] His first step was to issue an order on February 2, 1842, establishing the rules and regulations the court would follow in administering the act. All attorneys admitted to practice before the circuit court could, upon taking an oath to support the Constitution and faithfully discharge their duties, practice before the U.S. District Court for the District of Ohio sitting in Bankruptcy. Debtors and creditors would present their petitions to the judge either during a session of the district court or at the judge's "residence." All petitions would be docketed, numbered, and then published in newspapers designated by the court for three successive weeks before any hearing would be held. Leavitt also spelled out the rules and procedures for the new commissioners of bankruptcy that the act mandated the court to appoint in each of the state's counties. The commissioners would hold office during the pleasure of the court. Their varied duties included notifying creditors, verifying claims, and holding hearings if they believed such were necessary. The court would then use their reports in its proceedings. A debtor wishing to challenge his designation as a bankrupt by one of his creditors could file for a jury trial, which would then determine whether, indeed, he should be declared bankrupt. Most bankruptcy proceedings, however, were in the form of a hearing before the district court judge. Leavitt also established rules for taking depositions, applying for continuances or postponements, and selling a bankrupt's property. Further, he described his procedures for appointing assignees and methods he expected them to use in keeping records and reporting to the court. Finally, he established a fee schedule as well as compensation amounts for assignees and commissioners. In addition, Leavitt created twenty-one forms for bankrupts or creditors to complete at various stages of the proceedings. He also created two preprinted forms for the clerk of court to use in recording the various stages of the bankruptcy proceedings.[49]

The passage of the Bankruptcy Act of 1841 increased the court's case load dramatically. During the district court's first term sitting as a bankruptcy court, in 1842, more than five hundred creditors and debtors filed at least one bankruptcy form.[50] Although most cases were routine and were dispatched quickly, Leavitt sometimes had to deal with complicated litigation interpreting the statute, deciding what property would be included in the bankruptcy, and how assets would be distributed among creditors.[51] In sum, the new statute created "an immense amount of labor" for the judge, often involving "questions of great intricacy and importance."[52]

In the area of criminal law, despite the fact that Congress, in 1842, expanded the district court's docket by giving it concurrent jurisdiction with the circuit court over all federal crimes except capital cases, at least the District

Court for the District of Ohio experienced no increase in the number of cases until the mid-1850s. During the October 1854 term, Leavitt presided over two counterfeiting cases for the first time as a district court judge.[53] After that, the district court started handling many of the criminal cases previously heard in circuit court—cases involving theft of the mails, forgery, and counterfeiting.[54]

Although the increasing importance of admiralty and interstate commerce law, the new federal bankruptcy statute, and the expanded criminal jurisdiction enhanced the role the federal district court played in the economic, social, and political life of Ohio, nothing embroiled the court in state and national debates more than litigation arising under federal fugitive slave laws. As historian Paul Finkelman has explained, "Ohio, more than any other state, faced the problems and dilemmas of slave transit." With the Cumberland (National) Road crossing the state and the Ohio River bordering Virginia and Kentucky, Ohio was the major land and water route both for slave owners moving slaves and engaging in trade and for runaways trying to escape to freedom.[55] Thus, for Ohio in general, and southern Ohio and especially Cincinnati in particular, the issues of runaway slaves, abolitionism, and the status of free blacks produced volatile conditions, continual debate, and occasional violence, eventually resulting in changing attitudes and laws.[56]

From its founding, southern Ohio exhibited ambiguity on the topics of slavery, fugitive slave legislation, and the status of African Americans in the body politic. Many Ohioans hailed from Virginia, Maryland, North Carolina, Kentucky, and other southern states.[57] Twenty-five percent of the 1825–26 Ohio legislature, for example, came from the South, and, even as late as 1840, 19 percent of Ohio's legislators had been born in the South.[58] Politically, these southerners, who led the Jeffersonian coalition that controlled Ohio from statehood through the 1820s, sympathized with southern slaveholders, although there were some, including men like Tappan, who had migrated from New England, or others from the South with Quaker beliefs who supported equality.[59]

Besides familial ties, southern Ohio had important economic links with the South. Farmers and manufacturers shipped their products south. Cincinnati's position as a major commercial port depended on river traffic along the Ohio. Although these ties loosened somewhat in the 1840s and 1850s, as canals and then railroads began to shift trade patterns away from the South and toward the East, good relations with Ohio's southern brethren were necessary for economic prosperity. Moreover, common laborers resented competition from African Americans, fearing that blacks would drive down wages.[60]

These demographic and economic factors contributed to Ohio's early opposition to African American migrants, its support of fugitive slave laws, and its opposition to abolitionism. From the beginning, Ohio adopted so-called

Black Laws discriminating against African Americans. The state's first constitution denied blacks suffrage. In 1804, the legislature required African Americans entering the state to prove their freedom and to register with the county clerk. Three years later, a new statute required all African American migrants to obtain the signatures of two sureties for a $500 bond. Another state law prohibited them from testifying against whites in court. Additional antebellum legislation placed other restrictions on Ohio's increasing black population. They could not serve on juries. Until the 1830s, state law excluded them from public schools, and it was not until 1853 that the state required boards of education to establish schools for African Americans when the number of potential black students in the district reached thirty. But the law was not well enforced. On the eve of the Civil War, "of 517 districts containing Negro children . . . , 416 had no schools at all." Nevertheless, although it was not "general practice," some communities did admit blacks to white schools.[61]

In 1849, after Free-Soilers gained enough influence in the legislature to pressure "reluctant Democrats," the Ohio General Assembly repealed most of the Black Laws, though African Americans still could not vote or serve on juries. Moreover, blacks continued to face private discrimination. In the 1850s, a recent emigrant to Ohio, John Stewart, complained of his treatment by whites in this free state. Having purchased his freedom, he moved to Ohio from North Carolina. But instead of opportunity, he found abuse "by all classes of white men" and no employment.[62] Even more damaging was the occasional violence launched against southern Ohio's African American population. Black Ohioans could not readily forget the Cincinnati antiblack riot of 1829, during which whites drove half the city's African American population out of town.[63] Similar mob actions occurred in 1836 and in 1841. Perhaps because of such antagonism, Ohio's African American population remained small. In 1820, 10 percent of Cincinnati's population was black, but, by 1840, that percentage had dropped to a mere 5 percent. By 1859, the percentage had declined further—to one in thirty-seven, a mere 2.7 percent. And in 1860, Ohio's 36,673 blacks represented only 1.6 percent of the state's population.[64]

Initially, the Fugitive Slave Act of 1793, which required both state and federal officials to aid in the return of runaway slaves whenever claimants proved ownership to their satisfaction by oral testimony or affidavit,[65] did not spark much debate nor create new tensions. Until 1839 Ohio laws had accommodated the 1793 act, requiring its enforcement by state judges and justices of the peace. In 1839, however, Ohio imposed tougher standards for rendition by state officials, giving alleged runaways the right to be heard and requiring proof of ownership to the satisfaction of Ohio judges. Nevertheless, the law did provide penalties for harboring or concealing fugitive slaves and for interfering in any way with their recapture, making such activities a state crime as well as a federal offense; however, Ohio also had strict kidnapping laws that barred slave catchers from simply seizing alleged runaways and taking them out of the state. The few state cases recorded before 1840 show a reluctance in some cases to return fugitives, but a general commitment to comply with state and federal law.[66]

In Ohio, as elsewhere in the North, however, abolitionist activity steadily increased during the antebellum years.[67] By the 1840s, many white Ohioans had become abolitionists, determined to take whatever action was necessary to protect fugitive slaves and obstruct the implementation of the federal fugitive slave laws. Lane Seminary students in Cincinnati debated slavery for eighteen nights in 1834. Then, after the trustees voted to suppress further discussion, most of the students, along with some of the teachers, left that institution to establish Oberlin College, "the nation's first self-proclaimed integrationist institution of higher learning and a hotbed of abolitionist activity."[68] In 1835, the Ohio Anti-Slavery Society was founded. By 1837, nearly fifteen thousand Ohioans residing in towns along the Ohio River belonged to antislavery societies. In 1841, the Liberty Party held a state convention, with more than two hundred in attendance. Four years later, more than two thousand delegates attended the party's meeting in Cincinnati. Benjamin Lundy of St. Clairsville, Ohio, and later James G. Birney, of Cincinnati, published antislavery journals. And Salmon Chase, a prominent Ohio politician and attorney who would later become chief justice of the U.S. Supreme Court, volunteered to defend fugitive slaves and those accused of harboring them. Indeed, by the 1850s, he was "the antislavery crusaders' premier legal strategist." His "nation-wide legal strategy," based on his slogan "Freedom National, Slavery Local," strove to make slavery a purely local institution unprotected by federal statute. He argued that the fugitive slave laws were unconstitutional, having no force in the free states.[69] As the number of runaways increased, some Ohioans turned to extralegal means to aid fugitives. Many participated in Underground Railroad activities. One historian estimates that between forty thousand and fifty thousand slaves escaped through Ohio during the antebellum period. And Levi Coffin, a North Carolina Quaker who migrated to Ohio in 1847, was dubbed the president of the "Underground Railways."[70]

Others, however, especially those in Cincinnati and Dayton interested in trading with the South, took a dim view of abolitionists and others who they believed endangered friendly relations with the South. Some, like a New Lisbon citizen, explained that, while nearly all opposed slavery, "'not one in twenty' was an abolitionist." Moreover, he continued, "all 'right thinking men'" agreed that slave owners were entitled to come North to recapture their runaways.[71] Some radical opponents took the law into their own hands to defeat abolitionists. Cincinnati mobs attacked Birney and his abolitionist newspaper offices on several occasions, while a meeting of "respectable" men met to resolve that "no abolition paper should be published or distributed in town." Finally, a large meeting condemned mob action but urged colonization as the best way to end slavery.[72]

It was inevitable that slave owners, increasingly frustrated in their attempts to capture runaways, would turn to the courts for help. And most of these cases arising under the 1793 fugitive slave law originated in southern Ohio.[73] Both Ohio and the federal courts of southern Ohio heard cases, but each jurisdiction approached the law differently. By the 1840s, although the Ohio Supreme Court declared Ohio's antikidnapping statute unconstitutional when applied to those operating under the provisions of the Fugitive Slave Act of 1793, it limited the scope of the federal law by holding that it applied only to those African Americans who had escaped from a slave state into a free state; the fugitive slave clause of the Constitution, it held, did not cover slaves escaping in Ohio or other free states after their masters had voluntarily brought them there.[74] In other cases, several Ohio courts undermined what southerners considered their sacred sojourner rights. Before the 1830s, all northern states, either by law or, as in Ohio, by "implicit understanding," allowed southerners to bring their slaves with them to free states as temporary sojourners.[75] In the 1830s, however, the Supreme Judicial Court of Massachusetts became the first northern court to challenge this understanding.[76] In the 1840s, two Ohio lower courts and an Ohio Supreme Court justice agreed with the Massachusetts court. By the mid-1840s, "it was clear that Ohio had joined Massachusetts on the forefront of antislavery decision making"; slave owners voluntarily bringing their slaves into Ohio risked forfeiture.[77]

Despite the willingness of Ohio court judges to look for legal loopholes that would protect alleged fugitives and those accused of harboring them, slave owners filed most of their pre-1850 cases in state court. The federal court met infrequently, and the cost of a federal suit was often more than the runaway was worth.[78] But the District of Ohio heard two important cases under the 1793 Fugitive Slave Act. And in both, as was generally the case in federal courts, the judges and jurors enforced federal law more strictly than did the Ohio courts.

In *Jones v. Van Zandt*, a slave owner sued abolitionist John Van Zandt for the value of a slave Van Zandt had allegedly helped to escape. On April 22, 1842, nine of Wharton Jones's slaves escaped from Kentucky into Ohio. Van Zandt, driving his wagon back to his farm from Cincinnati, found the slaves and offered them a ride. Several slave catchers, however, caught up with Van Zandt and the slaves, capturing seven of the runaways and taking them back to Kentucky. Jones then sued Van Zandt for the value of the two slaves who escaped. Salmon Chase, representing the defendant in the circuit court trial, argued that his client did not have legal notice that those he helped were slaves, that the 1793 Fugitive Slave Act required such notice, and that the act itself was unconstitutional. In charging the jury, Justice McLean accepted much of Chase's argument. Sounding much like some state judges, McLean told the jurors that in Ohio "every person . . . is presumed to be free." But, McLean added, the defendant need not have "formal notice" to be found guilty of harboring. Following these instructions, the jury rendered two verdicts in favor of the slave owner, awarding him a total of $1,200 in damages for the loss of his slave as well as the $500 statutory penalty imposed by the Fugitive Slave Act. After long delays, the U.S. Supreme Court, in 1847, affirmed McLean's ruling that the only evidence needed was that those aiding fugitives knew that the fugitives were escaping from service.[79]

Despite the fact that Chase, knowing McLean's antislavery views, shaped his arguments to convince the judge to take a more natural law approach to jurisprudence, McLean maintained what one historian has labeled "the judge-as-moral-automaton" positivism.[80] The justice explained that to preserve a well-ordered society, judges had to adhere to positive law. It was up to the people and their representatives to consider issues of morality and natural law; judges must look only to the law. To do otherwise "would undermine and overturn the social compact." Legislatures, not courts, repeal unjust laws.[81]

The facts in *Driskill v. Parrish* were similar to those in the Van Zandt case. Again a slave owner sued an Ohio abolitionist for concealing runaway slaves and hindering their recapture. The abolitionist denied guilt, claiming he was only attempting to ensure that the alleged fugitives had a fair hearing. Although Justice McLean instructed the jury that the slave owner could arrest fugitives and remove them from Ohio "without judicial sanction," the jury could not agree on a verdict. But at a second trial, Judge Leavitt presided. He told the jurors that obstruction did not require "a resort to violence." Further, he reminded them of their duty to uphold federal law despite any personal opposition to slavery. This second jury, like the jury in *Jones,* sided with the slaveholder, awarding him the $500 statutory penalty under the Fugitive Slave Act.[82]

When Congress enacted a stronger fugitive slave law in 1850, the role played by the federal government and the federal courts in recapturing runaway slaves increased dramatically. For the first time, Congress established a federal bureaucracy to aid slaveholders in their efforts to "reclaim fugitives" by creating special federal commissioners to hear fugitive rendition proceedings and to issue certificates of removal. The statute permitted the commissioners or the courts to hear only ex parte testimony by the slaveholders or their agents; it prohibited any testimony by the alleged runaway. Further, a commissioner received ten dollars for each certificate he issued, but only five dollars if he found against a slave owner's claim. The establishment of these new commissioners made federal proceedings more accessible to those seeking to capture runaways. Besides having commissioners available in every county, those seeking to reclaim fugitives no longer had to wait for a federal court to convene one of its semiannual sessions. In addition, the statute required federal marshals and deputy marshals to aid those seeking to find runaways. Moreover, it authorized commissioners to appoint other "suitable persons" to help execute the warrants they issued as well as to form posses to arrest fugitives. Particularly disturbing to an increasing number of northerners, the statute also required "bystanders" to help capture runaways. Finally, the statute provided that those accused of knowingly and willingly obstructing or hindering the arrest of any fugitive slave would be tried in federal district court and, if found guilty, would be subject to fines not exceeding $1,000 and imprisonment of up to six months. In addition, such persons could be subject to civil damage suits by slave owners, again in proceedings to be held in federal district courts.[83]

Many Ohioans saw this new statute as a way to end sectional tensions and preserve the union. "An enthusiastic" Dayton crowd applauded Democratic congressman Clement L. Vallandigham's praise of the act. Ohio governor Reuben Wood also urged all Buckeyes to support the law, and most did comply.[84] Further, although antislavery forces won the statewide Ohio elections in 1855, electing Salmon Chase governor, in Hamilton County, the largest county in the Southern District of Ohio, Chase polled only 4,518 of 23,280 votes cast.[85] Moreover, most southern Ohioans placed no obstructions in the path of those trying to reclaim fugitives, and many even "volunteer[ed] their personal Assistance and extend[ed] the kindest hospitality" to those pursuing runaways.[86]

Nevertheless, opposition to the enforcement of the 1850 Fugitive Slave Act increased throughout the decade. In 1856, for example, Cincinnati's mayor fired two policemen "for aiding in the capture of fugitive slaves." The next year the Ohio General Assembly enacted a personal liberty law to counter some of the effects of the federal statute. That law established penalties for kidnapping free blacks and prohibited Ohio jails from holding fugitives.[87] And tensions mounted as abolitionists, although still a minority in southern Ohio, increased in number and became more determined than ever to help slaves escape, even if it meant defying federal law. When they did, it was up to the federal judges of the Southern District of Ohio to resolve these explosive cases.

The first case heard in Ohio under the new statute began in August of 1853, when a U.S. deputy marshal, acting upon an informer's tip, arrested George "Wash" McQuerry in Troy, Ohio, where McQuerry had lived for four years after running away from his Kentucky master. The marshal first brought the fugitive before U.S. Commissioner S. S. Carpenter in Cincinnati. But because this was Ohio's first case under the 1850 law, Carpenter turned the proceedings over to Justice McLean, sitting as circuit judge. The city was tense. Blacks and whites filled the courtroom as police surrounded the courthouse to maintain order. John Jolliffe, McQuerry's attorney, in addition to making an "impassioned plea" for his client based on simple justice, argued that the Fugitive Slave Act was unconstitutional because it denied

McQuerry his constitutional right to a jury trial. McLean, again refusing to look to natural or common law, maintained his positivist jurisprudence and upheld the statute. He ruled that the Constitution's Seventh Amendment guarantees trial by juries only in "suits at common law." Cases arising under the Fugitive Slave Act could not be suits at common law, because the common law opposed slavery. Rather, he concluded, such suits arose under the Constitution and federal law and thus were not subject to the constitutional requirement of a jury trial.[88]

Judge Leavitt presided over at least twelve cases under the Fugitive Slave Act of 1850. Pitting slave owners against runaway slaves or those harboring them, these trials were often intense, even poignant, but in general the juries found for the slave owner plaintiffs. Leavitt's first major case in district court began in 1854. Lewis Weimer, a Kentucky slaveholder, filed suit against Rush R. Sloane for $12,000 in damages plus the $1,000 penalty imposed by the 1850 act. Weimer accused Sloane of hindering his efforts to recapture George, Matilda, and Ellen, three of his slaves. During the three-day trial, the jury heard conflicting testimony from the many witnesses, who disagreed about whether Sloane had knowledge that the slaves were fugitives being legally detained by James Patton, Weimer's agent, and whether he actually aided in the fugitives' escape. Patton testified that he had arrested the runaways in Sandusky, but then a large crowd of black and white Sandusky residents gathered, so he took the slaves to the mayor's office. The mayor, however, refused to take action, arguing that he had no authority to do so. As the crowd grew restless, Sloane, an attorney, first tried to find some legal loophole by which he could insist that Patton release the slaves. He focused especially on the authority Patton had gotten to arrest them. In his defense, he argued that because Patton had no written warrant, the arrest was not legal. But Sloane, allegedly, was not willing to rely solely on legal maneuvers. The plaintiff's witnesses testified that, after questioning Patton, Sloane "took off his hat, and waved it over his head and said, Colored friends, arise, and take those colored friends of yours out of the room." In response, a crowd of about twenty African Americans, "some of them armed with clubs, rushed towards the slaves, and forced them out of the room, with a rush." Defense witnesses argued that Sloane did not signal or call on the blacks to launch an escape, but that he was acting only in his capacity as counsel for the runaways. Sloane argued that the crowd carried out the escape without any action on his part. After hearing Leavitt's charge to them, which summarized the evidence and spelled out the law, the jury determined that the plaintiff's witnesses were more credible. They found Sloane liable and awarded Weimer $3,000 in damages plus court costs.[89]

In emotional and controversial cases such as these, the judge's charge to the jury is of utmost importance. Leavitt, like McLean, personally opposed slavery.[90] In his *Autobiography*, while claiming that it "was with the greatest reluctance" that he "aided in any way" in enforcing such an "odious" law, he explained that he could not adopt the "extremist" view that because slavery violated God's law "no human authority could give it validity." His job, he said, was to uphold his oath of office by enforcing the Constitution and federal law. "Any other course of action . . . would be subversive of the first principles of our government and lead inevitably to its overthrow."[91] Thus, in *Weimer v. Sloane,* Leavitt told the jury that their personal opinions about slavery and the Fugitive Slave Act should not enter into their deliberations. If they were satisfied that those arrested were, indeed, fugitive slaves legally in Patton's custody and that the defendant knew that this were true and that he aided or assisted in their escape, they must find for the plaintiff. Even with such a clear charge, initially the jury could not agree. They asked Leavitt whether, to find the defendant liable for the escape, "it was necessary to be proved that he *intended,* by his acts . . . to cause an escape." Leavitt replied that the defendant's intentions were not at issue; what the jury needed to determine was whether the fugitives' escape was "the reasonable and natural consequences" of the defendant's actions. After these instructions, the jury returned its findings for the plaintiff.[92]

But while enforcing this controversial federal law, Leavitt did at least insist that plaintiffs follow the letter of the law. Thus, in a companion case, *Gibbons v. Sloane,* the results were different because Gibbons had not complied with the strict requirements of the 1850 statute when executing a power of attorney so his agent, Patton, could act in his behalf. Leavitt used this lapse to encourage the jury to release the defendant, which they did after the judge instructed them that Patton did not have proper authorization to arrest Gibbons's slaves.[93]

After McLean and Leavitt exhibited such a strong determination to enforce federal law, abolitionists sought an alternative forum: the state courts. The result was a series of bitter confrontations between state and federal jurists. These confrontations, begun in the judicial system, spilled over into the political arena. Newspapers praised or condemned the actions of various judges, depending on their political positions, and judicial decisions became the topic of heated political campaigns.[94] Indeed, Chase argued that Leavitt's decisions alienated public opinion and "no doubt contributed much" to the Republican victory in 1860.[95]

The first confrontation arose in 1855 when a master tried to reclaim sixteen-year-old Rosetta Armstead. A probate judge ordered Armstead free after hearing testimony from several Cincinnati free blacks who claimed that her master had voluntarily brought her to Ohio. The master then obtained a warrant from a U.S. commissioner for Armstead's capture. To counter that warrant, Armstead's state-appointed guardian sought and received a writ of habeas corpus from a state court. When the U.S. marshal refused to obey the state writ, the state judge held him in contempt and ordered his arrest. Justice

McLean then issued a federal writ of habeas corpus, ordering the marshal's release. Claiming that the state judge's actions freeing Armstead from the federal marshal was "without precedent," he reminded state officials of the supremacy of federal law: "A sense of duty compels me to say that the proceedings of the honorable judge were not only without the authority of law, but against law . . . and I am bound to treat them as a nullity."[96] Eventually, the commissioner released Armstead, agreeing with state officials that she was not a fugitive, thus ending the confrontation.[97]

The following year, the case of Margaret Garner[98] and her fellow fugitives caused another "state of excitement." Caught by pursuers, Garner murdered one of her children and attempted to kill the others so they would not be returned to slavery. Again, federal and state officials filed competing writs, with U.S. Marshal Robinson resisting service and compliance to state court orders. Meanwhile, officials repeatedly moved the runaways from federal to state authority and back as the two jurisdictions fought for supremacy. But then, in a new twist, Garner's attorney, to prevent his client's return to slavery, obtained a murder indictment against his client, hoping this would place her under state jurisdiction. Judge Leavitt, citing McLean's decision in the Armstead case, refused to honor the state's writ of habeas corpus. He held that once fugitives, under a valid warrant, were in federal custody, state processes could not be honored, even if the state were pressing criminal murder charges. "As to the demands of Ohio justice," Leavitt said, he had no doubt that Kentucky would return the slave to Ohio for trial if Ohio pursued its charges. Moreover, Leavitt concluded, the state could not detain any federal official acting in pursuance of federal law. The atmosphere in Cincinnati was tense, as antislavery men protested Leavitt's decisions. On the other hand, the Cincinnati *Daily Gazette,* sounding much like Leavitt, called for "self-restraint and public order," claiming that resistance to the Fugitive Slave Act would "manufacture pro-slavery sentiments ten thousand times more rapidly than the work can be accomplished by the slavery propagandists of the South."[99]

Federal officials acted quickly once Leavitt issued his decision. Within an hour of Leavitt's order allowing the removal of the slaves from the county jail into federal custody, Robinson, "with a large force of assistants," returned the Garners and the other escaped slaves to Kentucky. Speaking to a group of Kentuckians after he arrived in the slave state, Robinson argued that in upholding Kentucky's sovereignty he was also upholding the sovereignty of Ohio and all the other states, thereby adding "one more link to the glorious chain that bound the Union together." But the drama was not over. Ohio Governor Chase immediately wrote Kentucky Governor Charles S. Morehead, requesting that Morehead return Garner to Ohio so she could stand trial for murder. Although Morehead agreed, Archibald Gains, Garner's owner, sold her along with the rest of his recalcitrant slaves "down the river."[100]

Udney Hyde, abolitionist and partici-
pant in the Underground Railroad.
*Ohio Historical Society, Columbus*

The home of Udney Hyde, Champaign County, site of the arrest of Russell Hyde and three others for aiding and abetting the escape of a fugitive. The incident led to the decision in *Ex parte Sifford*, 22 F. Cas. 105 (S.D. Ohio 1857) (No. 12,848), in which Judge Leavitt proclaimed important principles of federal supremacy over state laws and actions of state officials when the U.S. government acts within its constitutional sphere. *Ohio Historical Society, Columbus*

Yet another crisis developed the following year. It started near Mechanics-burg, in Champaign County, in May 1857. After Udney Hyde, along with his sons and neighbors, thwarted several slave catchers' attempt to seize Addison White, a Kentucky fugitive who had been living and working for Hyde for sev-eral months, the five Kentuckians returned to Hyde's farm with two deputy marshals to arrest Hyde for hindering the capture of a fugitive in violation of the Fugitive Slave Act of 1850. Unable to find Hyde, who had gone into hid-ing, the posse arrested his son Russell along with three others, charging them with aiding and abetting the escape of a fugitive slave. As the posse traveled south on their way to Cincinnati with their prisoners, they encountered continual resistance. Several state officials, ranging from county sheriffs to judges in Champaign, Clark, and Greene counties, tried to undermine the posse's work. One sheriff attempted to seize the prisoners, using a writ of habeas corpus issued by a county probate judge. Then a large armed force seized the federal marshals and the rest of the posse and brought them before a Clark County justice of the peace, who charged them with assaulting the county sheriff and released their prisoners.[101]

The crisis between state and federal officials escalated as the marshal filed charges against the judge and other state officials for obstructing federal law, and Governor Chase directed the Ohio attorney general, Christopher P. Wolcott, to represent them at trial before Judge Leavitt in what became known as *Ex parte Sifford*. As the Democratic *Cincinnati Enquirer* noted, this "designation of the Attorney-General" by the governor to represent these county officials who acted to obstruct federal officials was the "equivalent to a declaration of war on the part of Chase and his abolition crew against the United States courts."[102]

Leavitt's charge to the jury was a clear attempt to stem the mounting tensions. As he saw it, he had two duties. First, he needed to maintain the supremacy of federal law against interference by state authorities. And second, he had to find a way to stop what he saw as the potential threat of "anarchy" if citizens continued to take the law into their own hands. Therefore, Leavitt sternly condemned the actions of all the state officials involved, reminding them that the U.S. Supreme Court "has stated . . . with great force and accuracy" that an official, having arrested a prisoner by authority of a warrant issued by a U.S. court, acting under the authority of the U.S. Constitution or congressional law, is not subject to any legal proceeding by any state. Although Leavitt conceded that federal judges must "tread with cautious steps upon the line dividing the national and state sovereignties," he reminded his listeners that the federal government, acting within its constitutional sphere, "is supreme and its action is paramount."

Appealing for law and order, Leavitt continued: "It cannot be controverted, that there was a settled purpose, in at least a portion of the community in which these occurrences took place, to prevent, either by direct or indirect means, the execution of a law of the United States." Such "extreme views," held by those who believed they were above the law, were dangerous to a civilized society. He asserted that "every right-thinking and right-hearted American citizen" has an "obligation" to the laws of both "the Union as well as of the state in which he resides." While conceding that most in the "free states" hold a "deep seated hostility to the fugitive-slave act of 1850," and that there was an "almost unanimous sentiment in opposition to slavery" among the people of Ohio, he insisted that none of these realities justified "attempts to defeat the national laws." Federal law "must be respected and obeyed." While every citizen has a right to express his opposition to congressional legislation, and even to the Constitution, he must still obey that law until he can get it changed lawfully. "If one man is to be tolerated in [an] evasion or resistance, in regard to one law, others may do the same as to other laws. The result would be, that every man, being a law unto himself, and acting under some vague notion of a higher law, would choose for himself what laws he would obey. This would produce a state of unmitigated anarchy, and effectually undermine the foundations of the social fabric."[103] Indeed, in hindsight Leavitt argued that the stance he and other federal judges took before secession upholding slaveholders' rights prevented the South from having the "vantage ground" during the Civil War. "The fact that the general Government was able to exhibit to the country and the world a fair record on this subject . . . deprived the South of all pretense of justification" for rebelling.[104]

Democratic president James Buchanan and his administration supported Leavitt and Ohio's other federal officials in their attempt to enforce the federal law. Buchanan's attorney general, Jeremiah S. Black, wrote the U.S. marshal and the U.S. attorney for the Southern District of Ohio, emphasizing that neither they nor any other federal official should honor any order by any state court that interfered with their duties nor surrender any federal prisoner to any state official. Further, "in case of an attack upon you by State Officers, you must defend yourself, and maintain the rights of the United States, against all lawless aggressions."[105]

But Leavitt's strong nationalist stance quickly became embroiled in Ohio's political campaigns. During the fall state elections, Republicans subjected his decisions to repeated attacks. The *Ohio State Journal* denounced Leavitt's insistence on the supremacy of federal law as a "monstrous doctrine" that undermined state authority and individual liberties and contributed to "the centralizing tendencies of the United States Government under Democratic and proslavery control."[106] The Republican state platform of 1857 criticized federal prosecutions of state officials and state citizens, insisting that state courts be allowed to proceed "without interference," and the party's press continually editorialized against Leavitt and other federal judges with "life tenure" imposing "pro-slavery Federalism" on the state.[107] On the other hand, the *Cincinnati Enquirer,* the *Mount Vernon Banner,* and other Democratic newspapers praised Leavitt's wisdom. Even the *New York Herald* lauded this Ohio judge.[108]

While Leavitt continued to see that federal law was enforced, that law itself was clearly alienating more and more Ohioans. Another controversial case that occurred in 1858 well illustrates this growing antagonism. Stanley Matthews, the U.S. attorney for the Southern District of Ohio, charged Cincinnati newspaperman William M. Connelly with hiding two slaves in his office. After a two-day trial, the jury found Connelly guilty, and Leavitt denied the defense's motions to set aside the verdict or to grant a new trial. But the jury verdict and Leavitt's sentencing of Connelly to twenty days in the Hamilton County jail and a $10 fine plus court costs only made the newspaper man a public martyr. Every day he spent in jail, "the ladies" of Cincinnati brought him presents and food. Public school teachers "headed processions," and church ministers regularly visited. Then, after he served his time, "a torch-light procession [of leading Cincinnatians] headed by a band of music" escorted him from jail.[109]

The debate over slavery also embroiled Leavitt in a contentious religious controversy. In 1845, the southern Methodists withdrew from the Methodist Episcopal Church, forming the Methodist Episcopal Church, South, because their northern brethren condemned slaveholding and wanted to limit the right of church leaders to own slaves. Once the division took place, the two branches fought over the disposition of the church's property. The southerners filed suit in the Southern District of Ohio, seeking their pro rata share of the assets of the Book Concern of the Methodist Episcopal Church, a charitable fund incorporated in Cincinnati under Ohio law with property in houses, printing presses, books, cash, and other items worth more than $200,000. Perhaps reflecting his regional biases, Leavitt ruled for the northern-based parent organization, holding that the General Conference of the Methodist Episcopal Church had no authority to approve the division of the church into two conferences. Although preachers were free to leave the organization, they were not entitled to take any of the church's property with them, including any share of the Book Concern.[110]

Although the U.S. Supreme Court disagreed, holding that the General Conference of the Methodist Episcopal Church did, indeed, have the authority to allow the southerners to leave and to take certain property with them, Leavitt continued to believe his ruling was the correct one. Arguing that this was one of his "most important cases," he noted that both Justice McLean and Thomas Ewing, one of the lead counsel for the defendants, praised his decision and that even one of plaintiff's attorneys admitted that Leavitt's view "of the law and the legal rights of the parties . . . were . . . unanswerable."[111] Despite his personal views, however, after the Supreme Court ordered him to oversee the division of the funds, he did so.[112]

Besides exercising his responsibility to administer the law fairly, Leavitt had the pleasant duty of granting citizenship to immigrants. Because of its expanding economy, southern Ohio attracted thousands of immigrants from all over Europe. While those from Ireland predominated among those Leavitt naturalized, many hailed from Bavaria, Hanover, Prussia, England, Scotland, and Spain. There were also a handful from elsewhere in the world, mainly from Mexico.[113]

On one occasion at least, however, the government questioned the loyalty of some of these newly naturalized citizens. The highly publicized, emotionally charged case of *United States v. Lumsden* involved twelve naturalized citizens originally from Ireland who settled in Cumminsville, a Cincinnati suburb, whom the government accused of planning an invasion of Ireland to free it from English rule. During the month-long preliminary hearing, huge, predominantly Irish crowds thronged the courtroom and the surrounding streets. After the government presented its evidence, Leavitt held that that evidence was insufficient for presentation to the grand jury and ordered the accused to be released.[114]

Denying that he had given in to public opinion or outside pressure, as the prosecution charged, Leavitt emphasized the technical nature of his ruling, a ruling, he claimed, that had "put a heavy strain on his intellect."[115] He released the defendants only because the government had failed to present any evidence that the defendants had committed an overt act in violation of America's neutrality laws. Rather, the government had shown only that they harbored "feelings of deep-rooted hostility to England, and a too ardent desire for the redress of the alleged wrongs of Ireland." Perhaps giving in to classic stereotyping, Leavitt said that the government merely showed that the defendants, exhibiting "the almost proverbial warmth and excitability of the Irish temperament," had "been imprudent, or indiscreet in words or action." Nevertheless, Leavitt warned the accused that this dismissal was no bar to a future indictment. He then used the occasion of his decision to again spread his message about the obligation of citizens to their nation and its laws. The evidence, he said, had shown that some were beginning to form an organization to launch an invasion of Ireland. He warned them that, if they went further, they would be prosecuted. He also said that, although he sympathized with their desire to restore to Ireland "the rights of its people," he reminded them that they were now U.S. citizens. There could be no such thing as divided loyalty. The government had conferred upon them all the rights of citizenship. They, in turn, owed the government their loyalty and obedience to the laws of their adopted country.[116]

Finally, Leavitt had to deal with the unpleasant task of disciplining those who had not faithfully executed the duties of their offices.[117] Leavitt presided over the government's civil suit against Charles K. Smith, secretary of the territory of Minnesota. The president had removed Smith from office after discovering that he had retained public monies collected on behalf of the United States. At trial, the issue was whether Smith was entitled to his salary for the entire year even though he was removed midyear. The jury found that Smith owed the government almost $2,000 after Leavitt ruled that he was not entitled to any pay after his removal from office.[118] In a criminal case, a jury found U.S. marshal John Patterson guilty of the misdemeanor offense of paying the deputies he appointed to take the Sixth Census (1840) in depreciated currency, pocketing the difference between the money he received from the government and the depreciated dollars, and Leavitt imposed the $500 statutory penalty.[119]

Some federal officials in southern Ohio became involved in political squabbles, exacerbating tensions in the state and drawing the court into more political machinations. In the late 1850s, the Democratic Party divided into factions, one supporting Senator Stephen Douglas and his popular sovereignty position for dealing with the issue of slavery in the territories, and the other James Buchanan, the president, with his more pro-southern stance. In June 1857, Lewis W. Sifford, the U.S. marshal for the Southern District of Ohio, wrote to George E. Pugh, Ohio's U.S. senator from Cincinnati, reporting that John H. O'Neill, the district's U.S. attorney, was neglecting his duties. Sifford claimed that O'Neill was not showing up to prosecute cases. Rather, he was sitting "in the saloons of this city unqualified by intemperance to discharge any of his official duties."[120] Three years later, the shoe was on the other foot. Sifford now complained that there was "a movement afoot" to remove him because he supported Buchanan.[121] Despite such backbiting, the Buchanan administration made no changes in the federal personnel.

## LEAVITT DURING THE CIVIL WAR YEARS

After the Civil War broke out, in 1861, Judge Leavitt and the court of the Southern District of Ohio faced new challenges. The state was deeply divided. Tens of thousands of Ohioans volunteered to fight for the Union, and the Republican Party won most statewide elections, running on a platform promising to prosecute the war vigorously. But southern Ohio was also home to many leading peace Democrats, led by Clement L. Vallandigham, George Pugh, and others, who believed the war to be unwise and constitutionally unjustified. Many merchants with close commercial ties to the South opposed the war for economic reasons. During this grave constitutional crisis, Leavitt took an activist position, viewing the South as engaging in a "wicked rebellion" and seeing his duty as a judge as upholding the Constitution, enforcing federal laws, and helping to preserve the Union.[122]

Leavitt's first task was to enforce the blockade against trade with the South. Therefore, besides the regular docket of admiralty and debt cases, criminal prosecutions, and trespasses,[123] Leavitt presided over hundreds of libel cases in which the government seized such contraband as food, whiskey, sulphate quinine, pistols, ammunition, and military clothing. For most cases, after the government published the information in local newspapers, as required by law, the court found the seized goods properly seized; the goods were then forfeited, condemned, and sold at auction to the highest bidder.[124]

Only two cases appear in the records, both early in the war, in which Leavitt found that the goods were improperly seized. In the first, on May 16, 1861, a month after the war began, the government seized thirteen revolvers being transported from New York to Louisville, Kentucky. After a quick bench trial, Leavitt found that the goods were not contraband, but rather were bound for "loyal citizens" in Owensboro, Kentucky, to be used against "negro insurrections and marauding parties."[125] The second case, however, required Leavitt, very early in the war, to rule on the nature of that war. The government had taken possession of six boxes of arms being shipped from Baltimore to Little Rock, Arkansas, after a group of citizens in Cincinnati had taken the law into their own hands and seized them while they were passing through the city on April 17, only two days after President Abraham Lincoln had proclaimed certain areas to be insurrectionary. At the time, however, Arkansas had not yet seceded from the Union and was not part of Lincoln's proclamation. Leavitt held that, although it was a "well-settled rule of the law of nations, where a war exists between two distinct and independent powers," all commercial activities cease, President Lincoln had "cautiously avoided the recognition of the Southern Confederacy, as an independent sovereignty." Thus, because Arkansas had not seceded at the time the goods were shipped or at the time they stopped at Cincinnati, the arms had been improperly seized and had to be returned to their owner, who promised to sell the goods "to the Union defense committee of New York."[126]

In addition to enforcing proclamations against the shipping of contraband, Leavitt enforced Congress's 1862 Confiscation Act, which authorized government agents to seize and confiscate rebel property.[127] Once having established rules for proceeding under the new law, Leavitt presided over fairly routine matters. After the government seized the property that those allegedly in rebellion held in southern Ohio, the court generally proceeded via bench trials. With the defendant rarely present, Leavitt would hear testimony that the person whose property was at issue had taken up arms against the government and would then order that person's life estate in that real estate condemned as enemy property, appraised, and sold.[128]

After Congress enacted new revenue laws taxing liquor and other such items, Leavitt's docket increased dramatically as the government seized and sold the goods of "those trying to fraudulently evade payment of the taxes imposed."[129] Leavitt insisted, however, that those whose property was seized had their full constitutional rights. The 1864 Revenue Act had authorized forfeiture cases to proceed "in rem," that is, against the property rather than the person. The government argued that, because this was normally a procedure used in admiralty court, the court should proceed under the rules of admiralty, which meant no trial by jury. Leavitt rejected this argument, saying that "it would be an impeachment of the intelligence" of Congress "to suppose they intended a seizure on land" be considered a proper subject for admiralty jurisdiction. Quoting a recent U.S. Supreme Court ruling, Leavitt held that, in cases of seizures of land under revenue laws, the district court would proceed "as a court of common law, according to the course of exchequer informations in rem; and the trial of issues of fact is to be by jury."[130]

Although most of Leavitt's time was spent enforcing the blockade and revenue laws, he is best known for how he dealt with the few cases of treason that appeared on his docket. Initially, Leavitt carefully distinguished between treason, the most "odious" of crimes, and "mere expressions" of sympathy with the rebellion. In his 1861 charge to the grand jury, he cautioned the jurors to keep this distinction in mind. Only treason was a criminal offense that could be tried in federal courts. Further, because treason was "the highest crime against society" and because the "mere suspicion of guilt often brings down upon its object a strong feeling of public indignation," jurors had to insist that the government present evidence in accord with the strict constitutional requirements. Treason consisted of an overt act of levying war against the government or aiding and abetting those who were levying war. Obviously, those in actual armed rebellion or those who gave money, arms, or other supplies to support that armed rebellion were committing treason; however, the overt act had to be confirmed by the testimony of two witnesses to that act. Jurors had to consider the evidence calmly and carefully "exclude from their minds all influences originating in mere popular excitement." Whereas, "on the principle of self-preservation," the government might have to arrest some people under its military authority for "mere expressions of opinion indicative of sympathy with the public enemy," such speech did not constitute treason.[131]

After hearing his charge, the grand jury indicted James M. Chenoweth for treason. Sitting as district court judge, Leavitt granted bail to the accused. The case was then tried in circuit court in its April 1862 term.[132] Although the proceedings and the jury's verdict are unreported,[133] in *Ex parte Vallandigham*, Leavitt stated that the court continued to adhere to the definition of treason as he spelled it out in his charge to the grand jury. One could not be convicted of treason simply by engaging in a conspiracy to aid the rebellion; the accused must have committed an overt act, witnessed by two people.[134]

*Ex parte Vallandigham* was perhaps Leavitt's most famous case. Then and now this is a leading case on the scope of free speech during wartime. At the time, Clement L. Vallandigham's arrest "focused national attention on the meaning of free speech . . . , on the relation of free speech to democratic government, and on civil liberties for critics of the Lincoln administration."[135] Vallandigham was a prominent politician and former Dayton congressman who headed Ohio's peace Democrats. Though opposed to secession, he did not believe that war was necessary. He believed that President Lincoln, if he wished, could successfully negotiate with the southern states to achieve reunion. Defeated in his reelection bid for Congress in 1862 after Ohio Republicans gerrymandered the Third Congressional District to include the heavily Republican Warren County, Vallandigham remained determined to keep himself in the public eye while preparing to run for governor in 1864. General Ambrose Burnside, however, the new commander of the Army of the Ohio stationed at Cincinnati, was equally determined to stifle what he saw as Vallandigham's treasonous dissent. Thus, on April 13, 1863, Burnside issued General Orders No. 38, prohibiting the declaration of "sympathies for the enemy."[136] Seeing the opportunity to become a martyr, thereby enhancing his political clout, Vallandigham deliberately violated the order in a speech at Mt. Vernon, Ohio, on May 1, 1863. In response, Burnside ordered Vallandigham's arrest. Dozens of soldiers dragged the former congressman from his Dayton home and took him to Cincinnati, where he was tried and convicted by a military court. Lincoln, embarrassed by the proceedings, commuted Vallandigham's sentence of close confinement, sending him to the South instead.[137]

Meanwhile in May of 1863, George E. Pugh, Vallandigham's cocounsel at the military commission trial, filed a petition for a writ of habeas corpus in federal court, arguing that a military trial of a civilian violated a citizen's constitutional right to a civil trial by a jury of one's peers. Because the new circuit justice, Noah Swayne,[138] was not present, Leavitt heard arguments alone. While Pugh spoke eloquently for the protection of American liberties, Flamen Ball, the U.S. attorney for the Southern District of Ohio, insisted that the country had rights, too, including the right to wage war effectively. The suspension of the writ of habeas corpus, which Lincoln had ordered, was one such right.[139]

Leavitt issued his decision to a "packed" crowd in the circuit court's "dingy, cheerless, and comfortless" courtroom.[140] Narrowing the issues to one—whether his court had jurisdiction over the case—the judge found a way to avoid the embarrassment of the court issuing an order that the military would ignore. Refusing to issue the writ, Leavitt cited what he claimed to be binding precedent. In the *Case of Rupert,* decided the previous year by Swayne and himself, Swayne had held, "in an opinion of some length," that a federal court could not grant a writ of habeas corpus when one was detained under "military authority." The president, as commander in chief, controlled the military, so recourse must be to him, not to the courts. Leavitt then noted that in Vallandigham's case the government's evidence was even more compelling than it had been against Rupert. Whereas Rupert had presented evidence "tending to disprove the charge of disloyal conduct imputed to him," Vallandigham had not. Moreover, "Rupert was a man in humble position, unknown beyond the narrow circle in which he moved, while the present petitioner has a widespread fame as a prominent politician and statesman. . . . If any distinction were allowable, it would be against him of admitted intelligence and distinguished talents."[141]

But Leavitt was not satisfied with issuing a mere technical holding. In dicta, he took a staunchly progovernment stance, throwing the prestige of the federal courts firmly behind strong Unionist measures against the peace wing of the Ohio Democratic Party. Especially during war, Leavitt declared, the executive branch had wide latitude to defend the nation and preserve the Constitution. Further, at a time when the very existence of the nation is threatened, it is the duty of every patriot "to concede to the constitution such a capacity of adaptation to circumstances as may be necessary to meet a great emergency." Although the Constitution's framers never foresaw "a period when the people of a large geographical section would be guilty of the madness and the crime of arraying themselves in rebellion" against their country, in their wisdom they endowed the president as commander in chief of the armed forces with the power to deal with such situations. To illustrate his point, Leavitt cited the recently issued Emancipation Proclamation as an example of the president's expansive powers as commander in chief to act as he saw fit to preserve the Union.[142] Thus, not only did Leavitt avoid a confrontation with military authorities by holding that the court had "no sufficient ground" for granting a writ of habeas corpus, but he also upheld, albeit in dicta, the constitutionality of the Emancipation Proclamation and the president's position that he had all those powers he deemed necessary to save the Union.[143]

Finally, Leavitt, making no effort to maintain any impartiality, took a decidedly hostile stance toward antiwar speech. Taking this opportunity to lecture his fellow southern Ohioans about the threat they all faced from "disloyalty in [this] community," Leavitt used highly charged rhetoric to attack that "class of men" in Ohio and elsewhere in the North "who seem to have no just appreciation of the deep criminality of those who are in arms." He reminded his listeners that while America has bestowed its blessings on all its citizens, some men were ungratefully determined to destroy that nation and replace its democracy with an "odious and despotic oligarchy " by engaging in a rebellion totally "destitute of excuse or vindication." And those who gave these rebels support by their speech were "morally guilt[y]," although they might not technically be guilty of treason. Their actions were "a gross offence against their country." "Those who live under the protection and enjoy the blessings of our benignant government," Leavitt concluded, "must learn that they cannot stab its vitals with impunity."[144]

Although Leavitt took his duties as a federal judge seriously, even enforcing laws like the fugitive slave acts despite the fact that he found them "odious," during the Civil War he took a distinctly partisan, some might say, unjudgelike stance. He was pleased that most Ohio Republican newspapers and politicians cheered his Vallandigham ruling. And he expressed pride in the fact that some believed that his decision "contributed . . . to the decisive political triumph of the Republican party in Ohio at the succeeding autumn election."[145]

As one might expect, Democratic newspapers condemned Leavitt and his decision. The *Detroit Free Press,* for example, wrote that Leavitt had put "the Republic . . . in the deepest peril" by suppressing free speech. While at the time the leading Democratic newspaper in southern Ohio, the *Cincinnati Enquirer,* muted its criticism after General Burnside visited its editors, threatening to arrest them also,[146] upon Leavitt's death, it condemned the judge's decision as a "great blot" on his "judicial character," accusing him of cowardice for not doing his duty by not standing up to the "rabid partisan majority" supporting the war.[147]

Despite this Democratic criticism, for the remainder of the war Leavitt continued to support vigorous prosecutions of those who he saw as threatening the Union. Dealing with two treason cases, Leavitt rejected defendants' demurrers, allowing the cases to proceed to trial. In so doing, Leavitt again took the opportunity to pronounce the Union as one and indivisible and denounce defense counsel's arguments that secession was legal and that the United States was merely a compact of sovereign states. He held that such assertions were in direct conflict with numerous rulings by the U.S. Supreme Court, the language of the Constitution, and the history of the Constitution's formation and adoption.[148]

In *United States v. Hughes,* however, Leavitt dismissed charges against one treason defendant. Hughes had been indicted for giving aid and comfort to the Confederate raider Captain John Morgan when he invaded Ohio. Subsequently, though, Hughes had been allowed to take the oath of allegiance proscribed by Lincoln's Amnesty Proclamation of December 8, 1863. Although the government argued that northerners could not take advantage of this proclamation, Leavitt disagreed, ruling that the language of the statute offered grace "to all persons who have directly or by implication participated in the existing rebellion." This, he declared, included Hughes. Further, although a clarifying statute that might have excluded Hughes was enacted March 26, 1864, Hughes had taken his oath of allegiance on March 1. Leavitt held that the government, once granting amnesty, could not take it back.[149]

While Leavitt was dealing with civil and criminal cases involving the preservation of the Union, some of those associated with the district court occasionally faced charges of malfeasance in office. The war provided many opportunities for corruption, and the District Court for the Southern District of Ohio was not immune. The Department of Justice launched an investigation of Alexander C. Sands, U.S. marshal for the district, accused of submitting illegal charges of mileage for guards he had not employed. The final report concluded that Judge Leavitt had authorized the charges, but that "*all* the officers connected with this affair were loose—*Judge, Clerk, Attorney and Marshal.*" The government also accused Sands of charging auctioneers' fees for confiscated goods, but it dropped the charges because, although Sands had charged the fees, he stopped as soon as he discovered that he could not legally do so. Finally, Sands was rumored to have extorted money from prisoners. Again, a Department of Justice investigative report concluded that the charges were unfounded.[150]

### THE LEAVITT COURT DURING THE POSTWAR YEARS

After the Civil War, while Leavitt no longer had to deal with treason cases or cases involving blockade violations,[151] his docket increased with the expansion of federal law. The Republican-dominated Congress enacted several new statutes that shifted power from the states to the federal government, including the Civil Rights Acts of 1866 and 1875, the Bankruptcy Act of 1867, the Habeas Corpus Act of 1867, and the Jurisdiction and Removal Act of 1875.[152] Although the initial impetus for much of this legislation was Congress's concern for protecting the rights of newly freed African Americans in the South, by 1875 Congress shifted its sympathies to "entrepreneurial interests." Responding to the demands of business leaders for consistent rules for commerce and industry as well as their desire to avoid hostile state courts "infected with Granger resentment toward eastern capitalists," Congress vastly increased litigants' opportunity to remove cases from state to federal courts. Even if one of the parties lived in the forum state, as long as the dispute was between diverse parties or if the suit involved a federal question, either party could initiate a removal petition.[153]

Recognizing the increased pressure these new statutes had placed on federal courts, and most especially on the U.S. Supreme Court, Congress set the stage for a drastic reorganization of the federal court system. This reorganization would eventually transform the district courts into far more significant institutions. Congress's first change, in 1866, simply altered the composition of the circuits while reducing the number of Supreme Court justices to seven. Congress assigned Ohio, along with Kentucky, Tennessee, and Michigan, to the Sixth Circuit, where they remain today.[154] More significant, in 1869 Congress established separate judgeships for the U.S. circuit courts. Although still unwilling to establish independent courts of appeal and make district courts the sole trial court, this law reduced the circuit court responsibilities of Supreme Court justices; they now only had to attend each of their assigned circuits once every two years. The new judges had the same powers as did Supreme Court justices when they were sitting on the circuit courts. The circuit courts could meet when any one of the following were present: the circuit justice (that is, the Supreme Court justice riding the circuit), the new circuit judge, or the district judge. This change was the first step toward placing sole responsibility for federal trials in the hands of the district courts.[155]

The federal docket also grew after the Civil War because Ohio, along with the rest of the nation, was involved in more industry, commerce, and business. As commercial transactions increased, so did litigation, especially when combined with the new removal rules. Leavitt heard nearly a hundred cases a year, requiring him to work constantly for at least nine months of each year.[156] Reliable statistics are hard to come by. Extant sources do not list all cases, and bankruptcy and admiralty cases were often recorded in different journals, which are now missing. Table 2.1 represents the minimum number of cases Leavitt heard during three postwar years. In addition to those listed, he occasionally presided over trials to determine, in cases of seizures for tax

## Table 2.1 Cases before the District Court for the Southern District of Ohio, 1867–1870

| Type of Case | 1867 (both terms) | January–March 1868 | January–March 1870 |
|---|---|---|---|
| Seizures (violation of revenue laws) | 35 | 88 | 33 |
| Libel | 12 | 9 | 2 |
| Collisions | 4 | 5 | — |
| Admiralty (wages, debts) | 4 | 8 | 6 |
| Violation of steamboat law | — | 1 | — |
| Debt (U.S. as plaintiff) | 23 | — | 6 |
| Bankruptcy | — | — | 1 |
| Chancery | — | — | 2 |
| Assumpsit | — | — | 6 |
| Contract—diversity cases | 2 | 3 | — |
| Criminal | 18 | — | 18 |
| **Total** | **98** | **114** | **74** |

Note: Dashes indicate that no cases were found in those categories.

*Sources:* Journals, W. Div., vols. 1 and 2; Court Docket Books, 1863–1872, W. Div., vol. 2, RG 21.

evasions, who the first informer was, because that person was entitled to part of the proceeds from the sale of the seized goods.[157]

Southern Ohio's federal docket differed significantly from those in the southern states. Whereas southern courts heard many cases brought under federal civil rights legislation, table 2.1 illustrates that such was not the case in Ohio or, for that matter, in other northern courts. Leavitt heard only one civil rights case during the postwar years. In *United States v. Canter,* the government indicted Lewis Canter and his son, Henry, for violating a Reconstruction law enacted in 1870 to ensure the right of all citizens to vote in elections.[158] Jacob Stuart and Jupiter Wilson, African American citizens of Lawrence County, had tried to vote in the October 1870 elections for state and county officials as well as for a representative to Congress. On approaching the polling place, a crowd gathered. Lewis Canter told them that he would not allow any "colored man" to vote, "that he would die first, and would cut the heart out of any one who would protect them." Intimidated by the crowd and Lewis's threats, Stuart and Wilson left without voting.[159]

Leavitt, when charging the jury, was obviously well aware of Ohioans' ambivalent attitude toward African Americans. While the state legislature had ratified the Thirteenth and Fourteenth Amendments, requiring equal protection of the laws for all, Ohioans, in 1867 by referendum, had rejected black suffrage and elected a Democratic majority to the General Assembly.

Race prejudice and support for the Democratic position against black rights was particularly strong in southern Ohio. When the Democrat-controlled legislature convened, it rescinded Ohio's ratification of the Fourteenth Amendment and rejected the proposed Fifteenth Amendment to the U.S. Constitution prohibiting discrimination based on race in voting. It was not until the next election, after the Democrats lost their control of the legislature, that Ohio ratified the Fifteenth Amendment, and then only by the narrowest of margins.[160] And it was not until the 1880s and 1890s that the Republican-dominated General Assembly provided for school desegregation, repealed the state's antimiscegenation law, and enacted a prohibition against discrimination in areas of public accommodation.[161] Thus, Leavitt emphasized that the jurors needed to put aside any individual views they might have "as to the policy and expediency of the extension of the right of suffrage" to African Americans. Under the Fourteenth Amendment, he reminded them, "all native-born male persons" were "guarant[eed] . . . the full rights of citizenship, irrespective of race, color, or previous condition." Because that amendment was now part of the Constitution, "all laws passed in pursuance of it are obligatory upon every citizen."[162]

Then, boldly asserting a broader interpretation of the Fourteenth Amendment than most supposed it to have, Leavitt declared that its guarantee of the full rights of citizenship "implies obviously the right of suffrage and includes clearly the African race." Leavitt then articulated a broad vision of democracy, asking jurors to take a stand for full equality. He told them that the extension of the franchise to all adult male citizens was "in strict accordance with the great principles which underlie our free republican government. And there is good reason to hope that the experiment will work auspiciously to the promotion of the stability and success of our free institutions." He hoped that granting suffrage to blacks would "stimulate them to such efforts in the acquirement of knowledge and intelligence, as will result in their moral and intellectual elevation, and qualify them fully for the right discharge of all their duties and obligations as free and independent members and citizens of our country." On the basis of the evidence and Leavitt's charge, the jury found Lewis Canter guilty and Henry Canter not guilty, and Leavitt sentenced the father to six months in the county jail.[163]

The bulk of Leavitt's docket, as was typical of northern courts, centered on economic issues. As table 2.1 indicates, from one-third to more than one-half of Leavitt's case load dealt with seizures under the new federal revenue laws, especially those dealing with the sale of liquor and tobacco. To handle this increased load, Leavitt adopted several rules to standardize procedures.[164] Basically, revenue agents seized and attached the goods said to have violated the law. They then placed advertisements in local newspapers announcing the seizure and providing the date for the judicial hearing. The goods were then appraised and testimony taken verifying proper notification via newspaper advertisement. In most instances, no claimant appeared at the scheduled hearing. In those cases, Leavitt ordered the goods sold, the stills destroyed, and the proceeds distributed to the United States and the informer, if there were one. If a claimant did appear, Leavitt held a jury or bench trial. If Leavitt or the jury found that there were no violation, which happened in most trials, the government returned the seized goods. If the fact finder held that the goods had been properly seized, Leavitt declared them forfeited.[165] In addition to seizures, Leavitt heard a significant number of debt cases, which mainly consisted of prosecutions by the government for nonpayment of taxes imposed by the Revenue Act of 1864.[166]

When trials occurred, Judge Leavitt was called upon to rule on a variety of issues. First, of course, Leavitt sometimes had to interpret sections of the statutes when defendants challenged the applicability of the law to their particular situations.[167] Leavitt preferred a commonsense approach to the law over the technical application of, from his point of view, the antiquated common law. Justice, to Leavitt, was more important than the technical requirements of out-of-date law. Thus, in a dispute over the validity of a transportation bond, Leavitt instructed the jury that there was no reason to apply "the ancient law" that required the use of seals to validate a written instrument. The jury needed only to decide whether the clerk who signed the instrument had proper authorization to do so.[168] If precedent were clear, however, Leavitt would enforce the law even if the result went against "reason and justice." Articulating a philosophy of judicial restraint, he explained that he was not "at liberty" to decide otherwise. Nevertheless, he urged the legislature "to remedy what I must regard as a defect in the law, as held by the courts."[169]

Most disputes during trial dealt with evidence. In these cases, Leavitt held the government to strict standards of proof. For example, in a five-week trial of four men for fraud of the internal revenue laws dealing with unpaid duties on whiskey they had allegedly manufactured, the government wanted to introduce evidence that those honestly conducting businesses distilling liquor were not making much of a profit, but the defendants were becoming quite wealthy. The government hoped that the jury, hearing this evidence, would conclude that the defendants must be illegally conducting their business if they were making money at it. Leavitt rejected the government's request, holding that the government had to abide by the same rules of evidence as did private parties, so evidence on mere collateral issues was not to be allowed.[170]

The Bankruptcy Act of 1867, the first to cover corporations, established a new federal bankruptcy system generous to bankrupts, hoping to give entrepreneurs fresh starts.[171] On May 27 and June 17, 1867, to put the judicial machinery in place to enforce the new law, Leavitt laid down rules, created forms, and established procedures that included the manner in which registers would be appointed to supervise bankruptcy petitions. All issues would be certified to the judge by the register; the judge would hear no oral or writ-

ten arguments by the parties unless he granted them special leave.[172] Therefore, most of the cases that reached Leavitt dealt with the priority or the validity of claims against the bankrupt.[173] Some decisions resulted in grave
hardship for the petitioner, but Leavitt tended to enforce the law as Congress
intended, generally having sympathy for honest debtors,[174] although showing
little compassion toward those who exercised poor judgment. For example,
Ellen Manley had loaned her brother some of her possessions, taking a chattel mortgage to secure the debt. The court held that this mortgage did not vest
a title to the property in Manley; rather it was the property of her brother, the
bankrupt, and thus subject to sale with the proceeds distributed to his creditors. Leavitt admitted that Manly's counsel had "eloquently" described the
"great hardship" she would endure if her property were taken from her. But,
he concluded, he could find no case that supported Manly's position. Moreover, he said, "if she is a sufferer it is her own fault." She could have taken
full possession of the mortgaged property when her brother failed to make
timely payment. Instead, from either "a desire to aid him, or a misplaced
confidence in the pecuniary ability of her brother she permitted him to retain possession of the property, and carry on business as before." By allowing
her brother to continue in business, she permitted him to induce honest men
to give him credit. Therefore, she had "no just grounds for complaint."[175]

In addition to enforcing federal revenue laws and administering the new
bankruptcy system, Leavitt upheld the supremacy of federal treaties when he
extradited Patrick Ross, fugitive from a charge of murder in his native Ireland. Leavitt held that the evidence presented to him was sufficient and that
the United States' treaty with Great Britain required the extradition. Rather
than returning to Great Britain for trial, Ross cut his own throat.[176]

Leavitt occasionally had to clarify the scope of the district court's jurisdiction. In doing so, he again took the opportunity to assert broad federal authority when applicable precedent or law was available. *The Cheeseman v. Two
Ferryboats* pitted the owners of the *Cheeseman*, who claimed salvage compensation, against two ferryboats the *Cheeseman* rescued from danger on the Ohio
River. The ferryboat owners argued that the case was not within the court's
admiralty jurisdiction because the boats, at the time, were "lying at the shore
on the Ohio side of the river."[177] Rejecting this argument, Leavitt again, as he
had done in antebellum admiralty cases, interpreted the federal government's commerce powers broadly. Citing the U.S. Supreme Court's 1851
*Genesee Chief* decision,[178] Leavitt held that ferryboats operating between two
cities of different states fall within the scope of congressional legislation and
are therefore subject to admiralty jurisdiction.[179] In a revenue case, however,
the court rejected the plaintiff's request for the judge to restrain the collector
of internal revenue from collecting a tax he felt was unconstitutional, finding
that Congress, by statute, had specified a different forum for such appeals.
Leavitt held that, although the Constitution gives federal courts jurisdiction

over cases arising under federal law, that clause was not "self-executing." Thus the plaintiff had to follow the provisions of the relevant law, which in this case required him first to seek redress from the district assessor and, failing satisfaction there, to appeal to the commissioner of internal revenue.[180]

Leavitt, embroiled in controversy during the Civil War, provoked little comment during his postbellum years on the bench. But the actions of others associated with the administration of federal justice in southern Ohio caused brief periods of debate that could have affected the court's reputation for objectivity and integrity. Ohio Republicans were divided over whether to support President Andrew Johnson, Lincoln's successor. Although Johnson had been elected vice president as President Lincoln's running mate, Lincoln chose him only to balance the ticket during what he feared would be a close election in the middle of the Civil War. Johnson remained a Jacksonian Democrat. Further, coming from Tennessee, he was sympathetic to the South and antagonistic to the rights of African Americans. Within a few years after Johnson became president following Lincoln's assassination, most Republicans broke with him. The U.S. marshal for the Southern District, General Andrew Hickenlooper, however, remained loyal. Therefore, when Grant won the presidency in 1868, Hickenlooper tendered his resignation. Despite some controversy about the composition of grand and petit juries during Hickenlooper's tenure and some accusations that he appointed Democrats as deputy marshals, letters of support for the marshal assured Grant that there was no reason for him to leave his position. One wrote that "it is the desire of nearly all Republicans here that he be retained." Another said that he was the "best marshal in anyone's memory." Grant kept him on.[181]

The district's U.S. attorney also came under attack. A detective investigating revenue fraud in Ohio accused him of either incompetence or negligence in not prosecuting cases of "well established fraud." Rather, he continued the cases "from term to term . . . , until the witnesses of the Government cannot be found, or if found vulnerable from lapse of time to recall with certainty the facts of the case." Although the government failed to launch an investigation into these changes, the detective was correct when he asserted that many cases appeared in the docket for years without prosecution.[182]

On April 1, 1871, at the age of seventy-five, Judge Leavitt retired after thirty-seven years on the bench, making him the longest-serving judge in the history of the District Court for the Southern District of Ohio.[183] Two years later, Leavitt died at his home in Springfield, Ohio. The members of the federal bar praised his service to the court. Leavitt, they resolved, had "discharged the duties of his high office with marked ability." He was learned, a man of integrity, patience, industry, and modesty, who was "loved by all." He was a man of the people, who walked daily, greeting local citizens, making himself accessible to them. Although appointed as a Jacksonian Democrat with the expectation that he would maintain states rights over attempts to expand federal authority, Leavitt became a staunch nationalist determined to interpret federal commerce clause powers broadly, to view presidential power in time of war expansively, and to insist on strict compliance with federal law. Moreover, at key points during his long career, he adopted an activist stance, reminding the citizens of southern Ohio of their duty to their nation and the U.S. Constitution.[184]

# 3

## THE DISTRICT COURT AT THE TURN OF THE CENTURY

*The Gilded Age, 1871–1898*

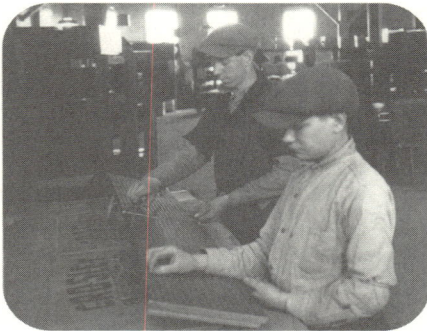

DURING THE GILDED AGE, AS America became an industrial giant, immigrants flocked to its shores in record numbers, and banking, commerce, and industry expanded rapidly. Although, for Ohio, the rate of growth declined compared to the boom years of the antebellum era, the state changed significantly. From a predominantly agricultural state, Ohio emerged, by the end of the nineteenth century, industrialized, urbanized, and pluralistic, with all the social and economic problems those changes entailed. Whereas agriculture remained a vital part of the state's economy, mining and manufacturing soon outstripped farming as the most important aspects of the state's economy. In 1870, Cincinnati was the state's industrial center, but other regions in southern Ohio developed rapidly. Dayton and Springfield became leaders in the manufacture of farm implements. Dayton, too, thrived after John Patterson took over the National Cash Register Company in 1884. In Columbus, the number of manufacturing establishments increased from thirty-eight before the Civil War to more than three hundred by 1908, with printing and binding concerns and wagon and carriage industries leading the way. Industries developed even more quickly in northern Ohio. Cleveland not only became a center for the steel industry but also emerged as the oil capital of the nation with the rise of John D. Rockefeller and Standard Oil Company. Akron, the home of Goodyear and Firestone rubber companies, also became a thriving factory town. To foster this economic growth, railroads and transportation along the Great Lakes took over from rivers and canals as the area's chief source of conveyance, although canals were still important, especially in the life of Dayton, where industry sprung up along the Miami and Lake Erie Canal.[1]

As life became more complex and impersonal, dominated by urbanization and industrialization, Ohioans, along with others throughout the nation, called on their government to ensure fair prices, genuine competition, and efficient city and state services. But political corruption plagued city and state governments, especially in Cincinnati with Boss George B. Cox. Statewide, the government tended to support the industrialists over labor. For example, Republican governor Joseph B. Foraker, elected in 1885, had been a Cincinnati attorney whose clients included railroads, public utilities, and leading corporations, but the Ohio legislature, responding to public pressure, enacted a number of regulatory measures, including regulations for Ohio's coal mining industry.[2]

Still, with such rapid changes, racial, social, and economic tensions sometimes exploded into strikes, riots, and lynchings.[3] Many turned to the federal courts to resolve conflicts that arose in the areas of commerce, disputes between labor and management, and questions of the extent of governmental power over business. The two judges who presided over the U.S. District Court for the Southern District of Ohio during this era represented the conservative-to-balanced orientation of Ohio politics. Phillip B. Swing, serving from 1871 to 1882, was, from boyhood, a close personal friend of President Ulysses S. Grant, who appointed him to replace Judge Leavitt.[4] Raised in rural Ohio, Swing remained a small-town lawyer and then prosecuting attorney in Batavia before his appointment as a federal judge. But his thriving practice included admiralty and patent as well as general civil and criminal law.[5] After Swing's death on October 30, 1882, political wrangling left the judicial seat open until February 1883, when President Chester A. Arthur nominated George R. Sage, of Lebanon, to fill the vacancy.[6] Aligned with Murat Halstead, editor of the *Cincinnati Commercial* and leader of the Independent Republicans in Ohio, Sage was considered a moderate and a reformer. Having grown up the son of a poor Baptist minister, Sage had to work his way through college and law school. Despite his humble beginnings, Sage soon developed a thriving law practice both in Cincinnati and in Lebanon, associating himself with leading Republicans, including his father-in-law, Whig governor and U.S. senator Thomas Corwin, and Republican governor Charles Anderson. His firms represented leading businesses as well as common people. Like Swing, Sage was known especially for his expertise in patent and criminal law. He loved trial work because he saw it as a way of "discharg[ing] his high functions near the people."[7]

The court these new judges presided over was a court that was slowly being transformed by the post–Civil War Congresses. The Reconstruction Congresses, although concerned with an overburdened federal docket, continued to enact legislation expanding the jurisdiction of the federal courts. To deal with the resulting burgeoning case load, Congress made significant structural changes both in the federal court system in general and for the Southern District of Ohio in particular. In 1891, the Circuit Court of Appeals Act, popularly known as the Evarts Act after Senator William Evarts, the bill's author, reduced the role of the old circuit courts, inaugurating the modern appellate system. After establishing independent circuit courts of appeal and creating the new position of circuit judge, the statute gave the Supreme Court some discretion in determining which cases it would hear and stipulated that there would be no appeal to the Supreme Court in diversity suits and in several other categories of cases unless the new circuit courts of appeal certified the case to the higher court. Three judges made up each of the nine newly created courts of appeal—the circuit justice (that is, the Supreme Court justice appointed to the circuit), the circuit judge, and the district judge—and the presence of two of the three was required for a quorum; however, no district judge could hear, on appeal, a case that he had had before him at the district court level.[8]

Although the new law shifted the appellate case load from the Supreme Court to the new courts of appeal, thus dramatically reducing the Supreme Court's docket,[9] it had little immediate impact on the district courts. Because the statute was a compromise with those who still clung to the old system, it left intact the two federal trial courts, a situation which Congress did not repair until 1911. By the Civil War, however, the lower court judges themselves had already, in reality, nearly obliterated the distinction between the district and circuit courts.[10] For example, in the 1870s, single district judges handled about two-thirds of the case load of the circuit courts. By the 1880s, that figure increased to nearly 90 percent. But this merely made matters more embarrassing, because district judges often heard appeals from their own decisions. Now, at least, the new law shifted some of the weight off the shoulders of the district court judges by creating these more independent courts of appeal.[11]

Of greater immediate significance to the judges was the district's reconfiguration. In 1880 Congress shifted seven counties from the Northern District of Ohio to the Southern District and then divided the Southern District into an eastern division and a western division. The Eastern Division, composed of twenty-nine counties, would meet in Columbus, whereas the Western Division, comprising nineteen counties, would sit in Cincinnati. The district, however, still had only one judge, one clerk of courts, and one U.S. marshal

In 1885, the U.S. District Court for the Southern District of Ohio, Western Division, moved to this new federal building. *Courtesy of the Sixth Circuit Archives, Cincinnati*

Interior of the Columbus federal building used between 1887 and 1934. *Ohio Historical Society, Columbus*

This U.S. Courthouse and Post Office Building, opened in 1887, was the first federal building in Columbus since the federal courthouse had closed in 1855. It housed the post office, the federal courts, and other federal governmental agencies, such as the Internal Revenue Service. Located on State House Square, this building, an example of Romanesque Revival architecture, was used until the court moved to the new federal building in 1935. *Ohio Historical Society, Columbus*

to handle the work of both divisions.[12] But at least in Cincinnati, the judge would have new facilities. After eleven years of construction, at a cost of $4.5 million, the government completed a new pillared, sandstone post office building across from Fountain Square. The federal courts moved "into [their] spacious quarters on the third floor" in 1886.[13]

The docket Swing and Sage handled was changing dramatically during these years, as Congress significantly expanded the jurisdiction of the federal courts. During the Reconstruction era, Congress had already expanded the court's role in the life of the average citizen by enacting civil rights laws, a new bankruptcy statute, and other substantive legislation. But its most significant piece of legislation affecting the federal courts was the Jurisdiction and Removal Act of 1875, which would transform the role the federal courts would play in America's changing economy. For the first time, Congress established federal-question jurisdiction, authorizing a plaintiff to file his suit in federal courts if his claim involved a federal question valued at $500 or more. Of course, the courts still retained their diversity jurisdiction. In addition, the new statute made it possible for either litigant to remove a case from state to federal court when a federal question was at issue or when there was diversity of parties.[14]

Pointing out that Congress enacted this statute the same day it passed the Civil Rights Act of 1875, many contend that the Republicans, not trusting southern state courts to enforce civil rights legislation, believed this expanded jurisdiction was an essential protection for those seeking to vindicate rights guaranteed to them by the Constitution and federal law. Others, however, argue that these congressmen, influenced by a powerful business lobby, voted to expand federal jurisdiction in order to achieve the uniform system of law desired by an ever-growing number of national corporations and to protect out-of-state corporations from local bias. Whatever the initial motivation behind the legislation, federal diversity jurisdiction, coupled with the expansive removal provisions of the statute and accompanied by new Supreme Court doctrines, allowed railroads and other large corporations to move their cases from state to federal court, especially when they were defendants in tort litigation or contract disputes. Corporations and the public alike believed that such removals favored corporations over individual litigants. Many believed that federal judges, independent of popular pressures because of their life tenure, favored business.[15]

Even if this belief were not true, corporations "gained powerful legal and extralegal advantages by using the federal courts."[16] After *Swift v. Tyson*,[17] federal courts developed and applied a national, uniform common law.[18] Further, federal juries, drawn from larger pools than juries in state courts, might render decisions freer from local prejudice. Corporate attorneys also believed that their familiarity with federal court procedures gave them an advantage over the more inexperienced attorney representing an individual litigant. Finally, numerous informal legal processes seemed to give an advantage to big business.[19] Farmers and reformers worked to limit these new removal procedures, but succeeded only in having the jurisdictional amount increased slightly.[20] Businesses continued to lobby Congress to retain the new system. Several Cincinnati organizations joined the petition drive; the Cincinnati Board of Trade and Transportation, the Alms and Doepke Company, and the John Shillito Company all petitioned Congress in 1884.[21]

Judges Swing and Sage issued several rulings following the lead of the U.S. Supreme Court, which assured that this expanded jurisdiction would be interpreted broadly. Immediately after Congress enacted the statute, Swing held that, even when a case had been heard in state court, it could by removed to federal court if the state supreme court had reversed and remanded the original lower court decision; the reversal started the case anew.[22] The following year, Swing further held that where there is diverse citizenship and multiple defendants, the case can be removed to federal court by petition of just one of the several defendants.[23] Sage's rulings sometimes favored the individual litigant over the corporation. Although in *Wills v. Baltimore & Ohio Railroad Co.* he broadly held that the moment a petitioner files for removal, state jurisdiction ceases and any error on the part of the state clerk in form does not prevent removal,[24] in other cases he denied requests by a railroad company and a printing company to remove, holding that they failed to meet certain requirements of the removal provisions.[25]

## THE DOCKET OF THE DISTRICT COURT DURING THE GILDED AGE

Although businesses believed retaining the option to remove litigation to federal courts served their interests, and although legal scholars have documented the validity of those beliefs, based on extant records, at least during the Gilded Age neither Swing nor Sage had an unusually heavy docket. Nationally between 1873 and 1890, cases pending before district courts rose 86 percent, from 29,000 to 54,000.[26] But records from the Office of the Attorney General indicate that the case load in the Southern District of Ohio was considerably lighter. The types of cases, however, did change; the judges saw a significant increase in civil suits based on diversity, demonstrating the effect of the new congressional legislation. As table 3.1 indicates, during the Gilded Age, Swing and Sage terminated slightly fewer civil cases in which the United States was a party than the national average, more civil diversity suits (that is, civil suits in which the United States was not a party), and considerably fewer criminal cases.[27] Bankruptcy cases accounted for about 40 percent of the civil dockets. Swing and Sage, like their colleagues across the country, supervised the dissolution and reorganization of numerous businesses, but most especially the railroads; they oversaw their reorganizations when they faced financial crises and in other ways exercised federal power in ways that affected the local and national economy. Many legal scholars view these receivership cases as examples of federal judges playing a leading role in the nation's economic development by supporting the maintenance of national railroad systems rather than their division and sale following bankruptcy.[28] But extant records do not provide sufficient evidence for any conclusions about how the judges of the Southern District of Ohio operated.[29]

Another 40 percent of the judges' case load were admiralty cases, including cases of collisions between river boats and libel actions against shipowners or their cargo. The remainder of the cases involved diversity suits other than bankruptcy, tax litigation, including seizures of untaxed goods, and a handful of cases in which the federal government sued to collect money allegedly owed it.[30]

After the district split into two divisions, business in Cincinnati declined, but not drastically; several years passed before the Eastern Division handled many cases. Swing, on March 1, 1880, convened the first meeting of the Eastern Division of the District Court for the Southern District of Ohio.[31] After he opened court, no case was listed for the rest of the term. Finally, in December, during the second week of its session, the court heard its first case. During that session, plaintiffs filed four cases. There was no significant increase after Sage took over in 1883. Not until the end of the June 1886 term was case number twenty docketed.[32]

For the Southern District of Ohio during the Gilded Age, in the civil arena, a typical day[33] might start with a review of the accounts of the clerk, the commissioners, the U.S. attorney, and any special commissioners or receivers appointed by the court. The judge might then order fees and other compensation to be paid. Next, he might deal with receivership issues and other disputes in equity, determining who held valid title to some property, whether a claim against the railroad or the bank in receivership was valid, or what the appropriate priority of claims in bankruptcy or admiralty were.[34] He would then deal with cases of seizure—the government condemning brandy, liquor, cigars, stills, distilleries, and the like for nonpayment of taxes.[35] The judge might also hear a variety of debt or money cases. In these cases, the United States was generally the plaintiff, trying to enforce a judgment on a bond, to collect money due on taxes or for fines for violations of laws such as navigation statutes and laws regulating steam boats, or to sue government officials who had not made a proper accounting of the money they had collected on behalf of the government. There were also private suits based on diversity jurisdiction. The judge might also handle several procedural matters, issuing subpoenas, hearing motions for joinder or substitution of parties, declaring defendants in default for not answering or appearing, and the like. Often, especially in libel cases and cases of bankruptcy, defendants failed to appear or respond. The court then issued decrees pro confesso and ordered the case to be heard ex parte.[36]

Both Swing and Sage were conservative jurists who tended to promote free enterprise over government or court control. Thus, for example, in *United*

# Table 3.1 Cases Terminated for Fiscal Years Ending June 30, 1876–1895

| Year | Civil Suits, U.S. a Party | | | | Civil Suits, U.S. Not a Party | | | Criminal Prosecutions | | | | | |
|---|---|---|---|---|---|---|---|---|---|---|---|---|---|
| | Internal Revenue | Post Office | Miscellaneous | Total | Admiralty | Other | Total | Internal Revenue | Post Office | Embezzlement | Pension | Misc. | Total |
| 1876 | 1,867/25 | 87/1 | 1,249/16 | 3,203/42 | — | — | — | 4,750/63 | 311/4 | 34/.5 | — | 1,848/24 | 6,943/91 |
| | 23 | 1 | 7 | 31 | — | — | — | 23 | 9 | 0 | — | 29 | 61 |
| 1877 | 1,042/14 | 90/1 | 1,584/21 | 2,716/36 | — | — | — | 5,890/78 | 347/5 | 37/.5 | — | 1,595/21 | 7,869/104 |
| | 21 | 2 | 9 | 32 | — | — | — | 12 | 11 | 0 | — | 59 | 83 |
| 1878 | 1,056/15 | 96/1 | 1,437/19 | 2,589/34 | 2,202/29 | 7,660/101 | 9,862/139 | 5,701/75 | 404/5 | 37/.5 | — | 4,705/62 | 10,847/143 |
| | 11 | 4 | 15 | 30 | 23 | 177 | 200 | 43 | 21 | 0 | — | 51 | 115 |
| 1880 | — | — | — | 2,423/32 | 1,463/19 | 7,140/94 | 8,603/113 | 6,341/83 | 439/6 | 40/.5 | — | 2,379/31 | 9,199/121 |
| | — | — | — | 25 | 17 | 119 | 136 | 75 | 22 | 1 | — | 38 | 136 |
| 1885 | 480/6 | 59/1 | 1,097/14 | 1,636/22 | 1,973/26 | 6,979/92 | 8,952/118 | 4,738/62 | 502/7 | 41/.5 | — | 1,636/22 | 6,917/91 |
| | 10 | 8 | 2 | 20 | 15 | 115 | 130 | 8 | 22 | 1 | — | 42 | 73 |
| 1890 | 158/2 | 67/1 | 1,503/20 | 1,728/23 | — | — | — | 6,720/88 | 883/12 | 55/1 | 246/3 | 8,112/107 | 16,016/211 |
| | 2 | 2 | 5 | 9 | — | — | — | 10 | 26 | 2 | 7 | 10 | 55 |
| 1895 | 564/7 | 179/2 | 1,947/26 | 2,690/35 | 1,805/24 | 8,177/108 | 9,982/131 | 10,394/137 | 1,485/20 | 86/1 | 506/7 | 13,253/174 | 25,724/338 |
| | 1 | 1 | 18 | 20 | 5 | 158 | 163 | 18 | 30 | 0 | 4 | 18 | 70 |

Notes: Dashes indicate that no figures are provided.

In each column, the first row represents the totals for all districts/average per district for all districts (e.g., 1,867/23 means that nationwide, there were a total of 1,867 cases in that category with 23, on average, for each district court). The second row lists the number of cases for the Southern District of Ohio. Thus, using rows 1 and 2, the reader can compare the numbers for the Southern District of Ohio with the national averages per district.

Source: U.S. attorney general, *Annual Reports of the Attorney General of the United States*, 1876–1895.

*States v. Thornburg,* Swing, in charging the jury, promoted more independent decision making by shipping companies and more freedom from government regulations by taking a narrow view of the word "practicable" in a statute regulating the transportation of petroleum, nitroglycerine, and other explosives and dangerous products on passenger vessels. The statute prohibited the transportation of such goods on passenger steamers unless there were no other "practicable" route. The government, arguing that "practicable" meant any route available, contended that because there was an all-rail route from Marietta to Cincinnati, the shipper could have used it to transport his explosives. By not using that route, the government maintained, the shipper had violated the law. Swing, however, took the approach advocated by the defense. He defined "practicable" as "commercially practicable, as distinguished from physically or mechanically practicable." That is, if the all-rail route was so expensive as to leave no profit, it was not "practicable."[37]

In admiralty cases involving seamen, contractors, or salvors trying to collect money owed them by ship owners, however, the judges often upheld the rights of the individual against the defendant steamboat or corporation. In *Longstreet v. Steam-Boat R. R. Springer,* for example, Swing held that, based on "well-established" doctrines of admiralty law, a seaman injured, without his fault, while working on a ship, was entitled to full wages for the trip.[38] In debt disputes, he insisted that seamen's wages had priority over mortgages and construction claims.[39] In a widely cited collision case, Swing adopted the position taken by Chief Justice Salmon Chase on circuit duty, that a widow could initiate a libel in rem in admiralty for the wrongful death of her passenger husband due to the negligence of the ship captain and crew, independent of statutory remedies. This conclusion was contrary to common law and to decisions in admiralty in England.[40]

Sage, however, tended to view negligence suits with suspicion. In collision cases and in cases of accidents in which workers were injured and even killed, he was reluctant to find liability. By viewing accidents as merely the inevitable result of boat traffic, Sage promoted the more rapid growth of commerce. In *Kineon v. The New Mary Houston,* for example, the cables of a river boat moored to a wharf broke loose. The captain of the river boat extinguished his lights to avoid fire breaking out if he struck bridge piers. Doing so, however, meant that the coal barges coming down the river could not see the river boat. The result was a collision that caused a total loss of the barges. Citing the standard treatise on such accidents, *Marsden on Collisions at Sea,* Sage held that in cases of sudden danger not caused by a person's own negligence, the ship captain is required only to exercise ordinary skill. Essentially, Sage concluded, this was just one of the "inevitable" accidents that occur on rivers; no one should be held liable.[41] An even more tragic accident occurred on board a steamer traveling from Memphis to Cincinnati. Its flue collapsed, and the escaping steam scalded twenty-four of the crew, fourteen of them dying from their injuries.

Sage found that the collapse of the flue was not caused by any negligence on the part of the steamboat owner, and thus he was not liable.[42]

As commerce increased from the economic expansion occurring after the Civil War, it was almost inevitable that federal judges would have to decide cases in which state and federal power conflicted. In 1887, Congress passed the Interstate Commerce Act, creating the Interstate Commerce Commission (ICC) to regulate railroads and their rates. Although Congress gave the ICC the power to determine whether railroad rates were unreasonable, it did not specifically authorize it to set rates. Sage's narrow interpretation of the statute, concluding that the only powers the ICC had were administrative, not legislative, followed the pattern of decisions in the Supreme Court and most other federal courts. Most agreed that the ICC had no power to fix rates. Moreover, Sage held that railroads were free to enter into special contracts "to meet the necessities of commerce, and, generally, to manage their interests upon business principles."[43]

In other cases, however, Sage bucked the trend seen in other federal courts and the Supreme Court, clinging to a narrower interpretation of the commerce clause that allowed states to exercise more economic control. In *I.C.C. v. Bellaire, Zanesville & Columbus Railway Co.,* for example, Sage held that a railroad whose line was totally within the state of Ohio, even though it carried freight destined for places beyond the state's borders, because it did not issue or receive bills of lading beyond its own lines, was not engaged in interstate commerce and was thus beyond the reach of the ICC's power.[44] And even when Ohio tried to prohibit the manufacture or sale of oleomargarine unless it was sold in a separate and distinct form, Sage, although he held that this was an invalid regulation of interstate commerce in conflict with Congress's regulation of the product, stopped short of declaring Ohio's statute unconstitutional. Drawing a fine line between interstate commerce and a state's police powers, Sage said that Ohio not only could regulate oleomargarine manufactured in the state but also could regulate the sale of oleomargarine produced in other states once the packages coming from out of state had been broken in Ohio stores.[45]

Although Sage's decisions in admiralty and commerce cases did not consistently reflect conservative, laissez-faire jurisprudence or conform to national doctrine, in the field of labor law his rulings established one of the lynchpins of conservatism. Toward the end of the century, courts across the nation began to confront the inevitable result of rapid industrial development—conflicts between labor and management. As unions began to form in earnest in the 1870s, tensions between workers and owners resulted in strikes and violence.[46] Slowly these problems wound up in federal court. Although acknowledging the right of unions to strike, within certain limits,[47] Sage became "the first Federal judge [to blaze] the way for that class of decisions which have since become so well known as 'Government by Injunction.'"[48] Sage's

Workers setting type at a printing press in Cincinnati. It was a strike by workers like these that led to the decision in *Casey v. Cincinnati Typographical Union No. 3*, 45 F. 135 (C.C.S.D. Ohio 1891), in which Judge Sage became the first federal judge to prevent, by injunction, a strike, holding that the property of one citizen was being destroyed by a conspiracy of others. *Cincinnati Museum Center—Cincinnati Historical Society Library*

decision in *Casey v. Cincinnati Typographical Union No. 3*[49] "emerged as the seminal authority."[50] Holding that union boycotts of companies they were trying to unionize were illegal conspiracies that courts, sitting in equity, could enjoin, Sage won "the honor of being the first Federal Judge to prevent, by injunction, the property of one citizen being destroyed by a conspiracy of others to destroy it."[51]

In *Casey*, the company's owner had, after promising to unionize his business, fired all the members of the typographical union and vowed not to hire any union members. The workers, in response, printed advertisements encouraging a boycott. Sage admitted that in its actions the union had threatened no one, but, he concluded, the very "word 'boycott' is in itself a threat" and thus could be enjoined. Relying simply on the principles of general equity relief, Sage asserted that "equity had jurisdiction to restrain an attempted intimidation" as well as the potential loss of business.[52] Granting that individual union members had the right to try to persuade others not to work for someone who would not pay the wages they demanded or recognize their union, Sage insisted that "persuasion, with the hootings of a *mob,* is not peaceable persuasion." He assured the business community and the public at large that "the courts will be ready for the emergency whenever and wherever the *spirit of anarchy* may manifest itself . . . , and the American people, if need be, will rise in their majesty and their might, and crush it as a trip-hammer would crush an eggshell."[53]

Following Sage's rationale, which became the standard position of judges in the Southern District of Ohio until the 1930s, federal courts abandoned conspiracy prosecutions for strike activities, which had been the method used extensively during the antebellum years to curb strikes, and adopted the labor injunction as a distinctive American device.[54] One scholar conservatively estimated that federal courts issued at least forty-three hundred injunctions between 1880 and 1930. The injunction thus became the leading means by which courts enforced order in industrial regions.[55]

Although such problems involving commerce and industry affected most states at the turn of the century, historians have tended to view the issue of segregation and civil rights as a southern problem. But southern Ohio, too, had to deal with this sensitive issue. The Ohio legislature enacted a strong civil rights statute in 1884 and a "model" antilynching law in the early 1890s.[56] But even before the state legislature acted, Swing took a progressive stance. In 1871, he appointed George W. Hays the first African American to have a position in the District Court for the Southern District of Ohio. A former fugitive slave, having escaped from the Confederate Army during the Civil War, Hays served as crier of the court from 1871 until his death, at the age of eighty-two, in 1929.[57]

Far more significant was Swing's judicial decision in *Gray v. Cincinnati Southern Railway Co.* The case came to trial when an African American woman sued the railroad company for violating her rights under the Civil Rights Act of 1875. Silena Gray had purchased a first-class, round-trip ticket from Lexington, Kentucky, to Cincinnati. The trip to Cincinnati was uneventful. But when this woman of "lady-like . . . appearance and bearing" tried to board the train in Cincinnati for her return to Kentucky, carrying her sick child and accompanied by her Baptist minister husband, the brakeman and the conductor stopped her. They insisted she ride in the second-class car filled with men, most of whom were smoking, rather than in the first-class ladies' car which carried ladies and gentlemen. The brakeman admitted that the only reason they denied her admittance to the ladies' car was because she was "colored." Gray refused to ride in the smoking car, returning home via another mode of transportation.[58]

In 1882, the Civil Rights Act of 1875 was still the law of the land, and it provided that "all persons . . . shall be entitled to the full and equal enjoyment of accommodations" on public conveyances.[59] Immediately after Congress enacted this statute, African Americans went to court to ensure its enforcement.

They also pushed U.S. attorneys to file suits, as the law required. This was even before the U.S. attorneys had received copies of the statute. Indeed, Warner H. Bateman, U.S. attorney for the Southern District of Ohio, telegraphed U.S. attorney general George H. Williams asking for guidance and a copy of the law. Supporters of the statute and of civil rights realized that the fate of the statute and enforcement of civil rights depended on vigorous prosecution by federal officials and favorable rulings in federal courts.[60]

In the first few years after Congress enacted the civil rights law, several district and circuit courts heard cases of discrimination by railroads. Although some argue that the statute mandated desegregation,[61] every reported federal court opinion that applied the statute upheld the common-law decisions that predated the legislation, which required those providing public transportation to accommodate all persons but permitted carriers to provide separate but equal facilities as a "reasonable" regulation of their property.[62] Four courts, however, refused to apply the law, declaring it unconstitutional.[63]

Swing sided with those supporting a strict application of the separate but equal doctrine. Refusing to enter into a discussion "as to the nature and character" of the Civil Rights Act of 1875 and whether Congress had the power to confer on citizens of the United States those rights state citizens had had under the common law, Swing simply applied the common law as Ohio had interpreted it since the antebellum era. Citing an 1858 Michigan Supreme Court case as precedent, Swing, in his charge to the jury, declared that the train company "was bound to provide for her such accommodations as were provided for the white women." If they did not, she was entitled to travel in the only first-class car available. He reminded the jury that "in the eye of the law we all stand now upon the same footing. We stand before the law equal. Whatever the social relations of life may be, before the law we all stand upon the broad plane of equality. And this company was bound to provide for this colored woman precisely such accommodations, in every respect, as were provided upon their train for white women." The company, in refusing her equal accommodations, was liable for damages. The jury, following these instructions, awarded Mrs. Gray the then quite significant sum of $1,000 in damages, covering not only the cost of her ticket but also the loss of her time and the "inconvenience she was put to" as well as money as a "vindication" of her right to equality before the law.[64]

Patricia Hagler Minter argues that Gray's lawyer wisely chose to sue not only under the Civil Rights Act of 1875 but also under the common-law concept of reasonableness. This made it easier for Swing to deliver a charge to the jury that would be most favorable to his client because the issue of access was defined not as a civil or a social right but as a common-law right to reasonable accommodation.[65] Other historians, however, have praised Swing for at least making clear that equality should be enforced. Further, William Singer argues that while the case "purported to adopt the 'separate but equal' doctrine, [it] nonetheless went a long way to promote integration." He contends that judges realized that if courts continued to enforce the "equal" requirement strictly, economic concerns would force integration.[66]

The court also dealt with issues of personal rights. In *Hallam v. Post Publishing Co.*, Judge Sage, in a leading case on defamation, articulated a rationale eventually adopted by the majority of the courts at the time for addressing the tensions between the First Amendment right to a free press and the right of an individual not to be defamed. In his charge to the jury, Sage claimed that public acts of public men could be criticized by the press but that false allegations of fact were not privileged.[67] Judge William Howard Taft, on appeal, agreed, emphasizing that untrue statements, even those made in good faith, were not privileged; the press had to prove all statements of fact.[68]

In the area of criminal violations, as table 3.1 indicates, the southern Ohio district judges generally handled fewer cases than the average district judge, nationwide. Also, after a peak in 1880, when the district terminated 136 criminal cases, the numbers declined dramatically. As one might expect, in view of the newness of the Eastern Division, Columbus handled fewer cases than did Cincinnati. In Columbus, during the 1880s, cases ranged from four to seventeen per term and never more than twenty in any one year. In Cincinnati, from 1888 to 1891, judges heard between fourteen and twenty-eight cases a year.[69] Most crimes fell into one of four categories: violations of revenue laws, especially those regulating the manufacture and sale of cigars and other tobacco products; crimes against the postal service, including breaking into a post office, stealing letters, or mailing obscene material; crimes against the purity of federal money and other federal documents, including counterfeiting and forgery; and presenting false claims to the government, including perjury. After 1880, pension cases added another category of crimes. There were also at least three indictments for illegal voting or procuring an illegal vote. One person was indicted for violating the oleomargarine laws and another for violating the national banking laws.[70]

A sample of Cincinnati cases from 1888 through 1890 indicates that defendants, once indicted by the grand jury, had about a 50 percent chance of conviction. During these years, ten defendants pleaded guilty and eighteen went to trial. Of those who were tried, ten were found guilty and eight were found not guilty. The government, however, chose not to prosecute fifteen of those indicted.[71] Although it was rare for the judge to record any ruling in a criminal case, Sage, especially, was known as a law-and-order judge. Lawyers commented that he "administer[ed] the criminal law with a firm hand and to inflict adequate punishment upon malefactors." Indeed, William Howard Taft claimed that Sage considered himself "the instrument appointed to preserve society from malefactors." Specifically, he believed that it was his job as a judge, first, to control the jury by his rulings, thereby saving them "from errors of prejudice, passion or weak sentimentality," and then, if the defendant were convicted, to impose "deterrent sentences that freed his jurisdiction from further depredations."[72]

While most criminal cases dealt with routine federal crimes, *United States v. Britton* presented an interesting exception. The defendant, indicted for mailing an obscene letter, tried to argue that the federal statute did not include the mailing of objectionable material in a sealed letter. And even if it did, he claimed, what he mailed was not obscene or indecent. The U.S. commissioner hearing the case, quoting an Ohio circuit court ruling, rejected this argument and established a very expansive definition of obscenity. Obscenity, he declared, was anything that had a "tendency . . . to deprave and corrupt the morals of those whose minds are open to such influences." Moreover, the contents of the letter, not the motive of the sender, is what matters. Congress, by using such plain words as "obscene," "lewd," and "indecent," clearly indicated that it intended that "nothing should circulate in the mail which would disseminate immorality in any form to the people."[73]

In addition to its disposition of cases, the court continued naturalizing citizens at a steady pace. Although Cincinnati, Columbus, and Dayton did not experience the vast numbers of immigrants flooding into its cities like major industrial areas such as New York, Chicago, and Cleveland did, significant numbers of immigrants sought naturalization. All, it is interesting to note, were men. In Cincinnati, in the first two years of the 1880s, for example, Swing naturalized more than three hundred.[74]

The federal judges of the Gilded Age in the Southern District of Ohio generally practiced a conservative jurisprudence, supporting business over labor, issuing rulings that contributed not only to economic expansion but also to corporate growth. Further, they did not seem to be as concerned with promoting nationalism as had Leavitt and his predecessors. They sometimes favored state authority over an expanding federal power. Moreover, they tempered their conservatism with decisions that upheld civil rights and liberties and often supported individual litigants against corporations, steamboat companies, and the railroads.

# 4

## THE PROGRESSIVE ERA AND
## WORLD WAR I, 1898–1919

As America entered the twentieth century, it faced numerous problems. Rapid industrialization, led by the so-called robber barons, created vast disparities in wealth. Corporations formed monopolies and trusts to achieve better efficiency and higher profits, but, once they controlled their industries, they imposed predatory pricing on the nation. Unskilled workers struggled to survive: wives and children, along with husbands, worked in factories and mines without effective safety standards, earning wages often below the subsistence level. Workers attempting to unionize faced opposition from their employers and the courts alike. America's population also changed. Floods of immigrants from southern and eastern Europe, including Catholics and Jews, came to the United States in record numbers, seeking opportunities in the expanding economy. They sought work in the rapidly growing cities, in coal mines, and with railroads. In addition, many native-born citizens left rural America for opportunities in the cities. The result was rapid urbanization and the accompanying problems of crime, slums, and health concerns.

Although most Americans entered the new century with great optimism, some had grave concerns about the future. Many middle-class Protestants worried that the new immigrants, holding what they viewed as strange customs and beliefs, would undermine America's traditional Protestant values and Victorian morals. Others feared that they would be squeezed by some large, impersonal organization over which they had no control, be it a large corporation, a labor union, or a political boss system. America had risen to greatness, they believed, because it provided for individual opportunity, that is, a single person who could succeed and rise from rags to riches, by dint of his or her own efforts. Now, they feared, this was no longer possible. Faced with concentrations of power in the economy and in politics, they turned to the government for help. Business, too, saw the need for change. Often industrialists led the calls for reform, seeking to rationalize and systematize economic life. Congress, during the Progressive Era, enacted a raft of new laws regulating the economy and established a bureaucracy to administer these regulations. Statutes regulated railroads, trusts, food and drugs, labor relations, and such morally vested concerns as prostitution, child labor, and the sale of lottery tickets.[1]

Ohio represented a microcosm of the nation, experiencing all of the progress and the problems the nation faced. By 1900, its population of 4.5 million participated in a diverse and increasingly impersonal economy. In 1902, 25,000 men worked in Ohio's coal mines, producing 20 million tons of coal valued at over $23,000,000. Railroads employed 60,000 men and had gross receipts of $101,000,000.[2] By 1905, Dayton, a center for innovation and invention, ranked second in the country in manufacturing automobiles and led in the new field of automobile parts manufacturing.[3] Faced with a burgeoning population, rapid economic growth, an inadequate tax system, labor strife, political corruption, and the stresses of rapid urbanization and immigration, many of Ohio's business and labor leaders, middle-class reformers, lawyers, and clergy supported progressive reform.[4] Judge Howard Hollister, who presided over the court in Cincinnati from 1910 to 1919, summarized the attitude of many Ohio progressives. He maintained that, although "the people of to-day are living in the most glorious period in the country's history," they face serious problems, including "the tendency toward monopoly, the development of the cities at the expense of the country, . . . the frequent apparent lack of high ideals, the apparent importance given to the possession of wealth and the dangers of great wealth recently acquired in the hands of selfish and irresponsible persons." The "welfare of the people and of institutions," he contended, depended on finding "proper solutions" to these problems. For Hollister, lawyers would play the leading role in finding these solutions.[5]

Whether attorneys or not, Ohio reformers sought legal solutions to the myriad problems the state faced. Led by the state's progressive governors, the Ohio legislature enacted compulsory worker's compensation, a variety of labor laws, including a prohibition against child labor, an eight-hour day for many workers, and laws prescribing safety regulations. Civil service, municipal reform, and other political innovations aimed to end corruption by political bosses and bribery by lobbyists. "Crusading" attorney general Timothy S. Hogan prosecuted bossism and corruption while defending the rights of labor.[6]

As the state courts and the state attorney general pursued progressive goals, many progressives viewed the federal courts with suspicion, believing federal judges and federal common law to be probusiness and antireform.[7] But Congress, through its myriad of progressive statutes as well as its transformation of the judicial structure, significantly expanded the role of the district courts, which would now have to determine whether the new regulations were constitutionally valid and, if they were, how they should be enforced. At least in the Southern District of Ohio, contrary to stereotypes about the antiprogressive views of federal judges, the district judges often showed a progressive bent. In some areas, however, conservative jurisprudence still prevailed.

### CONGRESS CHANGES THE FUNCTION AND THE STRUCTURE OF THE DISTRICT COURT

Until 1907, a single judge still presided over the Southern District of Ohio's two divisions during this time of increasing responsibilities. In that year, Congress authorized a second, but temporary, judgeship, and President Theodore Roosevelt nominated Columbus attorney John E. Sater to the post.[8] In 1910, Congress made this second judgeship permanent.[9] Congress also reorganized the district. From 1907 on, the circuit and district courts would sit in Dayton twice a year in addition to their sessions in Cincinnati and Columbus.[10] Then, in 1915 Congress rearranged the divisions again, establishing court sessions in Steubenville as well as in Cincinnati, Dayton, and Columbus, provided suitable accommodations, "free of expense to the Government," could be found for holding federal court there.[11]

But the most significant legislation of the era was the Judicial Code of 1911, which finally ended the old circuit court system, with its two trial courts and Supreme Court justices riding the circuit. In its place, Congress established the current system with a three-tier court structure. The district courts became the only trial court. The nine U.S. circuit courts of appeal heard appeals from the district courts. Finally, based on the system established in the Evarts Act of 1891, the Supreme Court heard appeals from the courts of appeal.[12]

Albert C. Thompson, appointed in 1898 by his personal friend, President William McKinley, served under the old two-court trial system. A Portsmouth attorney and prominent Republican politician, he had served in Congress for three terms before his appointment to the bench, supporting such probusiness legislation as a high protective tariff.[13] Contemporaries described the new judge as "a magistrate of the highest order" with a "clear, solid, logical mind," a wide-ranging knowledge of the law, and a "high sense of right and justice."[14] Thompson served on the federal bench until his death, in Cincinnati, on January 26, 1910.[15]

In 1907, John E. Sater joined Thompson as the newly authorized second judge for the Southern District of Ohio. Born on a farm near New Haven, Ohio, and orphaned at the age of ten, Sater grew up under humble circumstances, working his way through college and teaching for many years before becoming a lawyer.[16] As an attorney, Sater had a successful civil practice, representing, in the words of one supporter, clients "in all walks of life." Although his firm, Sater, Seymour & Sater, was "closely identified with the business interests" of Columbus, it also represented labor unions.[17] Seen as a public-spirited community leader, Sater had the near-unanimous support of the Columbus bar for the new judgeship, that bar being anxious to have one of its own appointed as the judge who would be sitting in their city. But the bar also emphasized that Sater supported Roosevelt's progressive agenda; he, too, supported trust-busting and compromises between organized labor and business.[18]

Serving with Sater after Thompson's death in 1910 was Howard Clark Hollister. Respected and popular, Hollister was a close personal friend and Yale classmate of the president, William Howard Taft. He also had the endorsement of the Cincinnati Bar Association, the support of U.S. Supreme Court Justice Horace Lurton, who had sat on the Sixth Circuit Court of Appeals, and the backing of leading businessmen, bankers, and railroad presidents.[19] Unlike Sater, Hollister, from "old stock," grew up in the affluent Cincinnati community of Mt. Auburn, the son of a prominent Cincinnati attorney. But like Sater, he supported many progressive principles. An independent Republican and Roosevelt-Taft supporter, he fought against Cincinnati's Boss Cox and Cox's Hamilton County Republican organization. On the bench, he vigorously enforced antitrust legislation, condemning the ruthless practices employed by National Cash Register's corporate officers. But he also praised Taft as circuit court judge for the way he handled the prosecution of the Pullman workers under the same antitrust statute, believing all combinations, whether in labor or business, illegal.[20] Still, many immigrants loved him. Under the auspices of the American House, they bought "a handsome floral piece" with money raised from many "small voluntary contributions," which they sent to Hollister's home after his death. The card they enclosed thanked the judge for serving as their "inspiration and example."[21] But like many middle-class Protestant progressives, Hollister believed society would be best served by the preservation of Victorian values, a stance that some might see as anti-immigrant. Thus, for example, as "a bitter foe of the liquor traffic," he often refused citizenship to saloonkeepers.[22]

## THE DOCKET OF THE DISTRICT COURT DURING THE PROGRESSIVE ERA

Although the menu of cases changed significantly during the Progressive Era, the first decade of the new century saw little change. Judge Thompson, sitting as the sole judge of the Southern District of Ohio, handled the usual array of civil cases—cases in which the United States sued to enforce internal revenue and postal regulations, cases of seizures for violations of various revenue and regulatory statutes, suits alleging patent and copyright infringement, and a handful of diversity cases. Criminal prosecutions remained few. Until 1908, Columbus never heard more than ten criminal cases a year, while Cincinnati handled, on average, about twenty-five annually. The pattern for criminal cases was similar to that seen during the Gilded Age—robbing the mails, misusing the mails to defraud, forgery, counterfeiting, filing false pension claims, and carrying on certain businesses without a license.[23] But as the only judge, having to travel between two cities, Thompson faced a monumental task. As the *Ohio Law Reporter* noted, his "docket [was] so heavy as to be beyond the power of any one man to handle." Thompson pushed for trials so speedy that they "sometimes took away the breath of counsel," and he instructed juries that it was their duty to "agree upon a verdict without unnecessary delay." Despite the rapidity with which Thompson dispensed justice, the appellate courts rarely overturned either his decisions or those rendered by juries in cases over which he presided. On the one hand, only attorneys with good cases brought them to him. On the other hand, his work load increased as those seeking a well-run court filed in his jurisdiction.[24]

In addition to handling the routine cases filed in federal court, Thompson had to undertake the major tasks of establishing the rules for the Bankruptcy Act of 1898, appointing the referees who were to supervise bankruptcies, and creating new forms and procedures to administer the act.[25] In addition, the new flood of bankruptcy cases required Thompson to interpret various provisions of this new statute, rule on jurisdictional issues, and determine the validity and priority of claims.[26]

Thompson's second major challenge was to interpret the many statutes Congress was enacting as part of its progressive program, especially those regulating the economy through its constitutionally granted power to regulate interstate commerce. In carrying out this duty, Thompson adopted a cautious, yet generally progressive, approach, tending to read congressional authority broadly. For example, in 1903, in *United States v. Geddes,* the United States sued to enforce provisions of the Safety Appliance Act passed in 1893. Taking a narrow view of the scope of Congress's interstate commerce power, Thompson held that when a carrier merely transports a product to a railroad company's platform, even though those goods are destined to be transported to another state, that intrastate railroad is not engaged in interstate commerce. The law, he proclaimed, is "limited strictly to interstate commerce and was not intended to affect railroads operated wholly within a state."[27] On the other hand, in *I.C.C. v. Cincinnati, Hamilton, & Dayton Railway Co.,* Thompson, anticipating new congressional legislation and later Supreme Court decisions, granted the ICC broad powers, declaring that the ICC's findings of fact are conclusive and will not be reviewed by the district court de novo. Moreover, he agreed that the ICC was acting within its power when it ordered a railroad company to desist from reclassifying less than carloads of common soap so it could charge more.[28]

In a widely cited and discussed case of bank fraud, Thompson again took a broad view, this time when interpreting a criminal statute. In 1872, under U.S. Revised Statutes section 5480, Congress, for the first time, made mail fraud a federal crime. There was no legislative history or congressional debates on this provision other than a comment by one congressman that laws should stop "thieves" and others from "deceiving . . . innocent people." Whereas the Supreme Court upheld the constitutionality of the statute, lower courts split on its scope. Strict constructionists emphasized that proper indictments had to focus solely on the fraudulent use of the mail. Thompson sided with the broad constructionists, who "did not let the mail-emphasizing language limit their definition of a scheme to defraud." Rather, he held that anyone who intentionally used the mail in any fraudulent scheme fell under the scope of the act and that the statute applied to a wide variety of schemes not recognized as illegal by either common law or state law. In *United States v. Horman*, Thompson took one of the broadest views of the time, declaring that the statute applied to a blackmail scheme whereby the defendant simply used the mail as a vehicle to send letters to three people for the purpose of blackmailing them.[29] Thompson admitted that he was initially inclined to side with the defendant, but, after reflecting on "the broad purpose" the statute "was intended to serve," he changed his mind. Congress, he declared, meant to prevent "the prostitution of the mails of the United States in furtherance of dishonest schemes . . . of any kind."[30]

Thompson was also called upon to adjudicate a labor dispute between printing companies and the International Printing Pressmen and Assistants' Union in *Barnes v. Berry*. In this case, he exhibited the most prounion leaning of any of the judges of the Southern District of Ohio during the late nineteenth and early twentieth centuries. The union had negotiated a contract that the officers of the union had signed establishing wages and abolishing strikes, lockouts, and boycotts for the period of the contract. Therefore, Thompson granted the injunction sought by the printing companies against the officers of the union to prevent them from inciting their members to strike for an eight-hour day and a closed shop, points they failed to achieve while negotiating the contract. Thompson, though, held narrowly that the injunction applied only to the officers, requiring them to live up to the contract they had signed; it did not apply to the workers, who were free to strike if they wished. To force people to stay on the job, Thompson held, would be tantamount to slavery. Further, continuing this prounion stance, Thompson lifted the injunction against the union officers and dismissed the companies' complaint against them after the union officers demonstrated that the contract, to be binding, needed to be ratified by the union at its national convention, something the convention had refused to do.[31]

In *Kelly v. Herrman,* Thompson "rendered a decision of great interest to the 'fans'" of professional baseball.[32] In 1903, the two "major" leagues—the National League and the American League—along with the "minor" National Association signed a national agreement for the governance of professional baseball. That agreement not only established the rules for playing professional baseball but also stipulated the clubs' rights to reserve or sell players to other clubs. Michael Kelly, president, general manager, and occasional first baseman for the minor league St. Paul Baseball Club, had signed a contract with the club's owner, a Mr. Lennon, in 1901, and had worked successfully for the club until he and the owner had a falling-out, at which point the owner traded (that is, "sold") him to the St. Louis American League club. Kelly objected, arguing that Lennon had no right to sell him because he had never signed a player's contract as required under the national agreement. Thompson agreed. Though never challenging the national agreement, Thompson held that Kelly had a contract independent of the national agreement, signed two years before that agreement was formed. Because Kelly was not subject to its stipulations, Thompson issued an injunction to prevent Lennon or anyone associated with professional baseball from blackballing Kelly, which would have prevented him from negotiating successfully with any other club.[33]

During the next decade, the district court became much more involved in enforcing new federal laws enacted by the progressive Congresses to regulate health and safety as well as to ensure competition in the marketplace. Tables 4.1, 4.2, 4.3, and 4.4 show that the court, although it continued to handle cases involving federal tax laws, the postal service, admiralty, bankruptcy, and routine federal crimes like counterfeiting, spent more time enforcing new laws. These laws were wide ranging, regulating industries as diverse as railroads, banking, interstate commerce, and the transportation of food and drugs. In this area, the court disposed of several significant cases involving the constitutionality of these federal statutes in addition to deciding some major cases questioning the constitutionality of progressive measures enacted by the Ohio legislature. The court also presided over significant antitrust cases and heard numerous cases involving violations of statutes promoting morality, such as the Mann Act, known at the time as the White Slavery Act, which made transportation of women and girls across state lines for immoral purposes a federal crime. Moreover, for the first time the court handled immigration cases, deporting those considered undesirable or who had entered the country illegally. The result, of course, was a significant increase in the docket, especially from 1912 on.[34]

Although the numbers of cases increased, the judges dispatched most of them quickly. For example, for most seizures under the Food and Drug Act, the defendant did not appear and the goods were sold.[35] Even in patent cases, which continued to make up a significant portion of the court's docket, the judges were able to decide quickly whether a product could properly be patented and, if it could, whether the defendant had violated that patent.[36]

Table 4.1 Criminal Cases Commenced in the Western Division, District Court for the Southern District of Ohio, 1906–1912

| Year | Number of Cases | Comments |
|---|---|---|
| April–December | | |
| 1906 | 6 | |
| 1907 | 27 | |
| 1908 | 36[a] | Included 2 cases of contempt; 9 violations of the Food and Drug Act |
| 1909 | 37 | Included 11 violations of Food and Drug Act; 2 violations of the Quarantine Act (transporting agricultural products subject to quarantine); 1 case of false testimony in naturalization proceedings; 1 embezzlement |
| 1910 | 49 | 25 violations of Food and Drug Act (19 pleaded guilty—fined from \$5 to \$200; 5 pleaded nolo contendere—fined \$25 each; 1 dismissed); 4 violations of Quarantine Act; 2 violations of Oleomargarine Act; 1 violation of Bankruptcy Act; 17 violations of criminal code, including 2 cases of blackmailing, 2 of counterfeiting, several postal service violations, and 4 cases of sending obscene matter through the mails |
| 1911 | 53 | Bulk were violations of Food and Drug Act; 1 violation of Copyright Act; 1 violation of Interstate Commerce Act; 5 violations of Mann Act; 5 charged with blackmail |
| 1912 | 104 | 53 violations of Food and Drug Act (vast majority handled quickly with guilty pleas and small fines); 9 violations of Mann Act; 6 violations of Quarantine Act; 8 violations of Interstate Commerce Act; 27 violations of various provisions of penal code and revised statutes; antitrust proceedings against officers of National Cash Register Corp. |

[a]In 1908 there were 33 cases in the Eastern Division, including mailing obscene material, counterfeiting, misusing the mail to defraud, and violations of the oleomargarine law. Surprisingly, there were no prosecutions for violations of the Food and Drug Act. No other statistics are available for the Eastern Division.

Source: Compiled from records at the National Archives (RG 21) and at the Cincinnati and Columbus courthouses.

## Table 4.2 Civil Cases Commenced in the Western Division, District Court for the Southern District of Ohio, 1906–1912

| Year | Number of Cases | Comments |
|---|---|---|
| 1906 | 10 | Included seizures; patent infringements; admiralty; equity; habeas corpus; cancellation of citizenship; U.S. as plaintiff for money due it |
| 1907 | 68 | Most were U.S. as plaintiff for money due it; some railroad receiverships; application for search warrant; cancellation of citizenship; habeas corpus; admiralty (petition to limit liability) |
| 1908 | 25 | Actions for money; 3 cancellations of citizenship; admiralty; forfeitures (whiskey, coffee, butter); bankruptcies; corporations suing to collect monies due |
| 1909 | 30 | Several cancellations of citizenship; several seizures; many bankruptcy cases, mainly in equity |
| 1910 | 27 | Actions for money (including to recover penalties for violations of regulatory laws like Safety Appliance Act); seizures (including under Food and Drug Act); habeas corpus; 1 cancellation of citizenship; several bankruptcy cases, most in equity |
| 1911 | 23 | 8 cases, U.S. as plaintiff against railroads for violation of Twenty-Eight-Hour Law; 7 cases for violation of Safety Appliance Act; cancellations of citizenship; habeas corpus |
| 1912 | 117 | U.S. as plaintiff to collect money for violations of various regulatory laws or for taxes; 7 diversity suits (personal injury, contract, etc.); bankruptcy cases; patent disputes; petitions for removal; seizures under Food and Drug Act |

Source: Compiled from records at the National Archives (RG 21) and at the Cincinnati courthouse.

Similarly, in the criminal area, not only did the southern Ohio district court generally hear fewer criminal cases than the nation's district courts, on average, but, except for the National Cash Register case to be discussed below, most were routine prosecutions of violations of internal revenue and post office laws, counterfeiting, forgery, and the like.[37] Hollister, however, vigorously enforcing the progressive morality laws, was known to punish severely those found guilty of violating the Mann Act. For example, after a chauffeur pleaded guilty to bringing women from Kentucky to Cincinnati for immoral purposes, Hollister not only sentenced him to four years in the federal penitentiary but also took the opportunity "to express his contempt for a man who

# Table 4.3 Civil Cases Commenced for Fiscal Years Ending June 30, 1913–1919

| Year | Civil Suits, U.S. a Party | | | | | | | | | | | | Civil Suits, U.S. Not a Party | | |
|---|---|---|---|---|---|---|---|---|---|---|---|---|---|---|---|
| | Internal Revenue | Post Office | Safety Appliance Act | Land Laws/ Trespass | Twenty-Eight-Hour Law | Hours of Service Act | Forfeit FDA | Antitrust | Immigration | Customs | Miscellaneous | Total | Admiralty Bankruptcy | Others Except | Total |
| 1913 | 803/10<br>15 | 15/–<br>– | 226/3<br>5 | 283/3<br>– | 293/4<br>11 | 290/3<br>17 | 363/4<br>8 | 21/–<br>– | 108/1<br>1 | 165/2<br>6 | 1,185/14<br>3 | 3,752/45<br>66 | 2,008/24<br>– | 9,175/109<br>142 | 12,146/144<br>142 |
| 1914 | 492/6<br>12 | 13/–<br>– | 264/3<br>7 | 223/3<br>– | 910/11<br>42 | 218/6<br>5 | 350/4<br>19 | 9/–<br>– | 180/2<br>1 | 465/6<br>8 | 1,018/12<br>– | 4,142/49<br>95 | 1,879/22<br>1 | 10,267/122<br>146 | 11,183/133<br>147 |
| 1915 | 321/4<br>3 | 11/–<br>– | 155/2<br>5 | 295/4<br>– | 468/6<br>5 | 126/2<br>2 | 668/8<br>17 | 3/–<br>– | 194/2<br>5 | 373/4<br>11 | 964/11<br>4 | 3,578/43<br>52 | 2,065/25<br>1 | 9,625/115<br>116 | 11,690/139<br>117 |
| 1916 | 302/4<br>5 | 17/–<br>– | 264/3<br>9 | 323/4<br>– | 389/5<br>2 | 157/2<br>2 | 6,057/72<br>16 | 1/–<br>– | 79/1<br>1 | 342/4<br>– | 1,021/12<br>1 | 3,500/42<br>36 | 2,313/28<br>2 | 11,539/137<br>139 | 13,852/165<br>141 |
| 1917 | 307/4<br>18 | 25/–<br>– | 221/3<br>11 | 264/3<br>– | 891/11<br>12 | 129/2<br>6 | 428/5<br>4 | 4/–<br>– | 38/–<br>– | 210/2<br>1 | 1,017/12<br>5 | 3,532/42<br>57 | 2,527/30<br>14 | 11,490/137<br>309 | 14,017/167<br>323 |
| 1918 | 472/6<br>3 | 29/–<br>– | 165/2<br>3 | 5,498/65<br>– | 1,246/14<br>10 | 124/1<br>1 | 125/1<br>11 | 13/–<br>– | 63/–<br>– | 271/3<br>– | 1,092/13<br>3 | 9,098/108<br>31 | 2,677/31<br>1 | 11,202/133<br>114 | 13,879/165<br>115 |
| 1919 | 441/5<br>1 | 25/–<br>1 | 14/–<br>– | 199/2<br>– | 816/10<br>25 | 8/–<br>– | 1,128/13<br>35 | 3/–<br>1 | 84/1<br>– | 139/2<br>– | 2,118/25<br>14 | 4,975/59<br>80 | 2,605/31<br>1 | 11,220/134<br>128 | 13,825/165<br>129 |

Note: In each column, the first line represents the totals for all districts, based on eighty-four district courts and the second line is the case load for the southern district of Ohio.

Source: U.S. attorney general, Annual Reports of the Attorney General of the United States, 1913–1919.

## Table 4.4 Criminal Cases Commenced for Fiscal Years Ending June 30, 1913–1919

| Year | Customs | Internal Revenue | Post Office | Banking | Land Laws/ Trespass | Mann Act | FDA | Antitrust | ICC Laws | Counter-feiting | Miscellaneous | Selective Draft Act | Espionage Act | Total |
|---|---|---|---|---|---|---|---|---|---|---|---|---|---|---|
| 1913 | 308/4 | 4,104/49 | 1,923/23 | 62/1 | 65/1 | — | 809/19 | 10/— | 344/4 | 237/3 | 8,891/106 | — | — | 16,753/199 |
|  | — | 11 | 41 | 4 | — | — | 31 | — | 3 | 1 | 22 | — | — | 113 |
| 1914 | 405/5 | 3,452/41 | 1,940/23 | 62/1 | 67/1 | — | 450/5 | 6/— | 760/9 | 219/3 | 11,038/131 | — | — | 18,399/219 |
|  | — | 29 | 23 | — | — | — | 8 | — | 4 | 2 | 29 | — | — | 95 |
| 1915 | 435/5 | 4,410/53 | 2,253/27 | 119/1 | 37/— | — | 384/5 | 21/— | 446/5 | 303/4 | 11,446/136 | — | — | 19,868/237 |
|  | — | 13 | 33 | 1 | — | 2 | — | — | — | 2 | 13 | — | — | 64 |
| 1916 | 523/6 | 5,676/68 | 2,169/26 | 109/1 | 48/— | — | 466/6 | 4/— | 421/5 | 285/3 | 10,542/126 | — | — | 20,243/241 |
|  | — | 44 | 43 | 7 | — | — | 14 | — | 2 | 7 | 36 | — | — | 153 |
| 1917 | 421/5 | 4,598/55 | 2,066/25 | 81/1 | 44/— | — | 486/6 | 11/— | 625/7 | 150/2 | 11,146/136 | — | — | 19,628/234 |
|  | — | 8 | 37 | — | — | — | 10 | — | — | — | 26 | — | — | 81 |
| 1918 | 420/5 | 3,900/46 | 1,968/23 | 66/1 | 72/1 | 435/5 | 384/5 | 10/— | 1,597/19 | 165/2 | 13,282/158 | 11,809/141 | 968/12 | 35,096/418 |
|  | — | 19 | 30 | 2 | — | 11 | 16 | — | 18 | 4 | 43 | 206 | 9 | 358 |
| 1919 | 408/5 | 5,807/69 | 2,092/25 | 83/1 | 117/1 | 438/5 | 393/5 | 3/— | 2,597/31 | 149/2 | 19,126/228 | 15,262/182 | 968/12 | 47,443/565 |
|  | — | 27 | 36 | 2 | — | 3 | 5 | — | 45 | — | 137 | 198 | 6 | 459 |

Note: In each column, the first line represents the totals for all districts/average per district for all districts based on eighty-four districts, and the second line is the case load for the Southern District of Ohio.

Source: U.S. attorney general, Annual Reports of the Attorney General of the United States, 1913–1919.

would live upon the earnings of a woman. "The Court," Hollister declared, "will have no mercy on any man who is proved to have been guilty of such an offense."[38]

It is difficult to categorize Sater's and Hollister's jurisprudential approaches. Neither falls easily into the conservative or progressive camp. Toward the end of the nineteenth century, conservative judges in state and federal courts had developed the doctrine of substantive due process to protect businesses from arbitrary and unreasonable regulations. Courts were called on to decide whether state laws violated a company's due process and equal protection rights under the Fourteenth Amendment and whether, if a state regulation were contested, that regulation unconstitutionally infringed on Congress's power to regulate interstate commerce. Progressives called for judicial restraint, arguing that legislatures should be free to determine the wisdom of laws regulating various businesses. This latter view became more prevalent during the Progressive Era, as more citizens, legislators, and judges saw a need for regulation. Moreover, recognizing the increasingly national nature of the economy, federal courts developed the notion of a national police power, allowing Congress, through the exercise of its power to tax and to regulate interstate commerce, to regulate certain products and industries for the general welfare.[39]

Sater and Hollister, both Republicans, generally ruled as moderate progressives, sometimes upholding the state's power to regulate, especially when regulations did not directly clash with a congressional statute, while, at other times striking down a state law as infringing upon federal commerce power. Their progressive leanings more clearly show in their willingness to uphold both state and federal regulatory statutes, rejecting arguments by the industries involved that such laws violated their Fourteenth Amendment equal protection rights or their right not to be deprived of their property without due process of law.

On several occasions, for example, the district court had to decide whether state laws conflicted with federal statutes or the Constitution. Perhaps the court's most widely cited decision, and one that established significant legal precedent, came in *Ohio River & Western Railway Co. v. Dittey*, popularly referred to as the *Ohio Tax Cases*. Ruling on challenges based on both Fourteenth Amendment and interstate commerce clause claims, a three-judge panel composed of Sater, along with Judge William L. Day of the Northern District of Ohio and Circuit Judge John W. Warrington, upheld Ohio's excise tax on the gross intrastate earnings of railroads and other public utilities. First, the jurists declared that the tax did not violate the Fourteenth Amendment's equal protection clause; that provision, the panel declared, "was not intended to prevent a state from adjusting its system of taxation in all proper and reasonable ways," including classifying different property differently and allowing reasonable exemptions. Second, the panel held that the tax did not burden interstate commerce "because gross intrastate earnings can be readily separated from all other earnings."[40] By upholding the tax, the court helped preserve the state's tax base against corporate challenge.

Another three-judge panel, composed of district judges Sater and Hollister along with Circuit Judge Warrington, again ruled in favor of state police powers in *Hebe Co. v. Calvert,* holding that the Ohio statute prohibiting the manufacture or sale of condensed milk made from skimmed milk did not conflict with the Pure Food and Drug Act. Writing for the court, Sater held that just because the producer of "Hebe," the adulterated condensed milk, shipped the skimmed milk and coconut oil into Ohio via interstate commerce and just because that shipment was properly labeled according to the provisions of the Pure Food and Drug Act does not prevent the state of Ohio from exercising its police powers. Congressional power to regulate goods under its interstate commerce power is not exclusive; a state still has the power to protect its citizens from deception. Declaring that, for state statutes, the construction given to it by the state's highest court is determinative, the judges accepted the Ohio Supreme Court's decision that the purpose of the statute was to prevent the deception of consumers. Moreover, exercising judicial restraint, as progressives urged courts to do, the panel declared that whether "Hebe" was as nutritious as its producer claimed was debatable and the state legislature's judgment would not be overruled by the court. Then, emphasizing the fraudulent and deceptive practices of the Hebe Company, Sater concluded that a state has the "undoubted power to protect the health of its people and to impose restrictions having reasonable relation to that end." Articulating progressive dogma, the panel held that the regulation, being neither unreasonable nor arbitrary, did not conflict with federal law nor did it violate the Fourteenth Amendment's prohibition against a deprivation of property without due process of law.[41]

Although upholding state statutes in both the *Ohio Tax Cases* and in *Hebe* might be viewed as undermining federal supremacy, the judges did further progressive goals by making corporations pay their fair share of taxes and produce healthy products, labeled properly. But the district court struck down the Ohio legislature's attempt to regulate stocks and securities by holding Ohio's "blue sky" law, requiring a license to sell stocks and securities in the state, to be unconstitutional. The court held that these regulations, unlike those in *Hebe,* did directly affect interstate commerce.[42] It also found that Ohio's law requiring inspection of train boilers on railroads operating within the state was an unconstitutional infringement on Congress's plenary power to regulate interstate commerce. The court held that Congress had preempted legislation on this issue, at least as it was applied to railroads operating in interstate commerce, with the federal Boiler Inspection Act.[43]

Hollister further enhanced federal power as well as progressive goals when he took an expansive view of the powers of the secretary of agriculture under the Pure Food and Drug Act. In *United States v. Frank,* he declared that the secretary was free to set standards for all products covered by that act, which, incidentally, Hollister concluded, was "one of the most beneficent legislative enactments of recent times." He held that anyone shipping an adulterated or misbranded product in violation of the secretary's standards could be prosecuted.[44] In *United States v. Ferger,* however, Hollister took a narrower view of Congress's power, dismissing an indictment against August Ferger, Thomas Dugan, and Robert Rasch for forging interstate bills of lading and depositing them in a bank as collateral. Hollister ruled that, because no interstate transportation was contemplated, Congress could not punish such forgeries; it would be up to the state to prosecute. The Supreme Court disagreed, broadly declaring that Congress has the power not only to regulate articles that affect commerce directly and indirectly but also to protect the "credit and confidence" people have in interstate commerce.[45]

Another area often disputed was the jurisdiction of the district court and whether a party could remove a case from state to federal court.[46] In all these cases, the Progressive Era judges read the relevant statutes strictly, thus tending to support individual plaintiffs against corporations seeking removal to the supposedly more friendly federal court. For example, in *J. N. Green v. Chesapeake & Ohio Railway Co.,* Hollister granted the plaintiff the right to have his case heard in state court after the defendant had petitioned for removal to federal court. Hollister held that the statute under which the plaintiff was suing, the Employers' Liability Act of 1908, clearly declared that cases such as the one at issue were nonremovable. "The effect of the statute," Hollister concluded, "is that the plaintiff may chose [*sic*] whether he will proceed in the district court of the United States or in the state court." Because Congress has the power to prescribe the scope of the jurisdiction for federal courts, such power includes the "authority to take away, as well as to bestow, the right to remove causes."[47]

As labor and management continued the battle that had begun in the Gilded Age over open versus closed shops and the recognition of unions, however, the Progressive Era judges, citing Sage's opinion in *Casey v. Cincinnati Typographical Union,* continued a conservative approach, issuing injunctions to prevent union members from congregating around plants, from approaching or intimidating anyone choosing to work for the company they were striking, from "congregating" around any sidewalks or approaches to the picketed plant or on the streets in the neighborhood, from going "singly or collectively" to any employee's residence "for the purpose of intimidating or threatening them" or their families, from "calling them scabs or other opprobrious names and epithets; from threatening, intimidating, coercing by menacing attitudes, expressions, gestures, or otherwise any of said . . . person," or from combining or working with others "for the purpose of doing or causing to be done" any of the prohibited acts.[48]

In an article detailing the history of America's labor movement and the federal courts' use of injunctions to curtail labor organization activities, Michael H. Leroy and John H. Johnson IV argue that, until Congress enacted the National Labor Relations Act in 1935 to curtail the courts' intervention in labor strikes, corporations "contrived ways to meet citizenship diversity so as to invoke federal jurisdiction" because they recognized that federal courts were more willing than state courts "to issue overbroad injunctions" against labor.[49] In Ohio, business was particularly interested in filing in federal court as state judges often displayed sympathy for unions and their strikes.[50]

*Niles-Bement-Pond Co. v. Iron Moulders' Union Local No. 68* well illustrates the antiunion bias of at least one judge of the district court for the Southern District of Ohio by showing both Sater's stern opposition to strikes as well as his determination to stretch the court's jurisdictional limits to allow companies to get a hearing in federal court rather than having to seek recourse in the state court system. At the start of World War I, the Iron Moulders struck the Niles Tool Company of Hamilton, Ohio, to achieve a closed shop. The strike turned violent, the company hiring replacements and guards to protect them from the strikers who, in at least two instances, physically attacked the strikebreakers. Sater issued what was becoming the standard injunction in the district, decreeing that union members could not congregate, approach in any intimidating manner, or otherwise intimidate or try to coerce those who had replaced them. Although conceding labor's right to strike, Sater also insisted that "the company has the right to run an open shop" and all Americans in this "free country" have the right to work for whomever they please under whatever terms they choose. Declaring "a mob or an unlawful assemblage" "a cowardly thing" and those who encourage violence or mob rule "vicious and evil-disposed leaders" "subverting the law," he criticized labor leaders for not controlling their members. "Lawful picketing," he declared, "is permissible, but the number of pickets should not be large. There is power in numbers, and when the number is large and unfriendly, it intimidates and terrorizes." All have a right to go to work "without fear or molestation." Union members can invite people to listen to them, but if those people choose not to listen, the union members must let them go. "The streets and highways are for the use of all law-abiding people. To such they should be free as the air." Because nonstriking workers had to be escorted to and from work by guards, he concluded, it was clear that "there was something radically wrong with the conduct of the strike."[51]

The chief problem with Sater's opinion was that he should not have heard the case in the first place. For the case to be heard in federal court, there had to be diverse parties. Therefore, the parent company, Niles-Bement-Pond, incorporated in New Jersey, filed suit against its subsidiary in Hamilton, Ohio, the Niles Tool Company, as well as against the union. The Sixth Circuit Court of Appeals reversed Sater's decision, dismissing the injunction because the district court lacked jurisdiction. It held that Niles, the subsidiary corporation, had the same interest as the parent company and thus could not be a defendant. There was therefore no basis for diversity jurisdiction; the suit should have been between Niles, as an Ohio corporation, and an Ohio union, heard in state court.[52]

The judges of the District Court for the Southern District of Ohio also took a strict approach to deportation proceedings. The immigration department challenged the right of several Chinese to be in the United States, claiming that they had entered the country illegally in violation of the Chinese Exclusion Act of 1888. Long Chong, who spoke no English and testified via a translator, claimed that he was a native American born in San Francisco and that his certificate of residence was illegible because it fell in water. Sater was skeptical. After comparing the photograph on the blurred certificate with the defendant, listening to witnesses he found not to be credible, and reasoning that anyone born in the United States should at least be able to speak some English, Sater concluded that the defendant was not who he claimed to be. Although Chong now owned a business in Dayton and was a law-abiding property owner, Sater held that he had, indeed, entered the country illegally and ordered him deported.[53] In the case of Lee Shew, Hollister explained in detail his decisions to deport Chinese defendants. Hollister wrote that he had "run the gamut of nearly all the Chinese cases in the Federal Reports, and their number," he noted, "is legion" because each case is based on its own peculiar facts. But after his study, Hollister concluded that "the spirit of the Exclusion Laws" was to prevent "the unlawful coming of Chinamen into this country." Therefore, "no Chinaman, who is smuggled in by sea or land, or who, in any other way should slip by the Immigration Officials, should *ever* be considered anything else than an interloper, who should be *always undesirable* and therefore liable to have to go back whence he came. This is harsh law, but is the inevitable conclusion one reaches after studying the History of this Legislation, and following the language of the learned Judges of the United States Courts who have passed upon these questions."[54]

The court also cancelled the citizenship of other immigrants not of Chinese descent when it was adjudged that they entered the country fraudulently.[55] From the records, it is impossible to know whether the judges rendered their decisions purely on clear statutory language and precedent or whether their rulings were tinged by some biases they held against Chinese or other immigrants. Although Hollister showed a determination to enforce morality legislation, which many believe was aimed, at least in part, against immigrants and although he railed against saloonkeepers, many of whom were immigrants or children of immigrants, he did reappoint George Hays, the court's one African American employee, as court crier.[56]

Hollister had two occasions to express his very procompetition, free-market views. The first was an unusual case involving Ford Motor Company's suit against the Union Motor Sales Company of Dayton, seeking to enjoin it from selling Fords below the price fixed by Ford Motor Company. Union Motors was the Costco or Sam's Club of the 1910s. People paid $10 to join the organization. In return, Union Motors sold to its members, through Ford's licensee-dealers, cars at below the normal price. Ford, on the other hand, had contracts with all who sold its cars to sell those cars at a fixed price. Ford claimed that, because it manufactured its cars under its patent, it had the right to sell only through licensees who agreed to its terms.

In rendering his decision, Hollister conceded that the Supreme Court had approved contracts whereby a patentee gives to another a license to manufacture and sell at a fixed price, retaining a small royalty. But, asserting the importance of preserving competition in the marketplace, he argued that there was "a marked difference" between what the Supreme Court had approved and what Ford was doing. Although the rights of a patentee should be liberally construed, it should not be extended, through judicial construction, in such a way as to extinguish competition. Rejecting Ford's position that the legal title of the car remained with it until its dealers sold the car at full price, Hollister held that, once the dealers paid Ford the price it asked, they controlled the car. Citing recent Supreme Court decisions as authority, Hollister refused to enforce contracts whose sole purpose was "to prevent competition." Patent law, he concluded, does not "confer power on the patentee to prevent competition among those who have purchased the patented article from him."[57]

The most important case heard in the Southern District of Ohio during the Progressive Era was the government's civil and criminal prosecutions of the National Cash Register Corporation (NCR), the major employer in Dayton, Ohio.[58] "Perhaps the greatest" antitrust case ever heard in Cincinnati, according to the *Cincinnati Enquirer,* it was the government's only major successful criminal prosecution under the Sherman Act during these pre–World War I years.[59] John H. Patterson had purchased the patent for a new product, a cash register, from its inventor James Ritty and had created a company that came to control 95 percent of its market. The government charged, however, that NCR's success was achieved by "savagery" employed to squash all potential competitors.

In February 1912, the government filed two suits. One sought to enjoin NCR from further illegal practices in violation of the Sherman Act. The other was a criminal prosecution of Patterson, NCR's president, Edward A. Deeds, NCR's vice president and general manager, Thomas Watson, another company officer who later founded IBM, and twenty-five other officers and agents for "knowingly [engaging in a] corrupt conspiracy [to restrain] interstate trade and commerce." The government pursued the criminal indictment first, charging Patterson and his fellow officers with bribing the employees and others associated with its competitors to obtain trade secrets and information about orders, intimidating retailers to sell only NCR products, engaging in

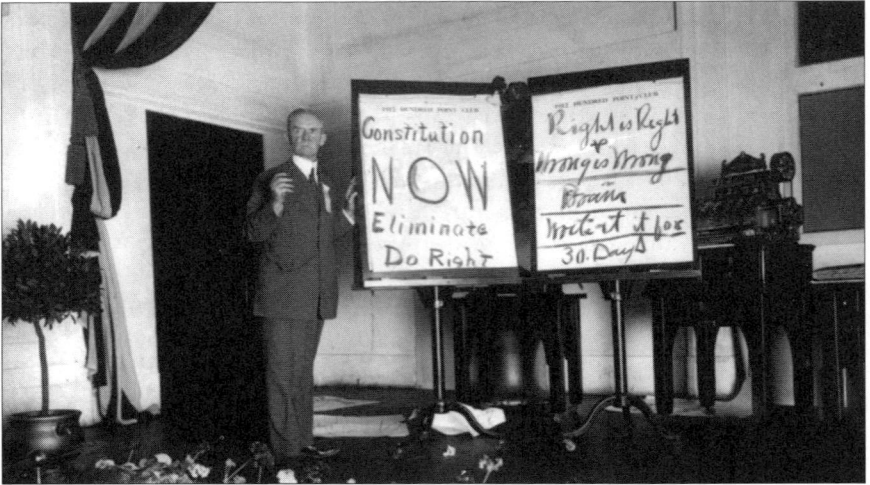

The president of NCR, John H. Patterson, addresses his sales force. It was NCR's sales and marketing practices that led the federal government to pursue both criminal and civil antitrust action against Patterson, other NCR officers, and NCR. These cases were major tests of the effectiveness of federal antitrust legislation. *The NCR Archive at the Montgomery County Historical Society*

predatory pricing practices to drive out competition, threatening competitors and purchasers of competitors' products with suits for patent infringements when they knew such suits were not warranted, and by, in a variety of ways, depicting competitors' products as unreliable "junk." One ingenious technique NCR used was to produce "knock-out" machines, that is, machines that were "in such close similitude of the competitive cash register" as to make purchasers believe they were buying the competitive machine; but these machines were of such "cheap and poor construction" as to convince buyers that purchasing one would be "a waste of money."[60]

U.S. district attorney for the Southern District of Ohio, Sherman T. McPherson, a committed trustbuster, served as lead attorney for the government. Lawrence Maxwell of Cincinnati, former solicitor general of the United States in the Cleveland administration, John F. Miller of Chicago, who had represented Standard Oil Company and the meat packers in their antitrust trials, John A. McMahon, a fifty-eight-year trial court veteran known as "the dean of the Ohio Bar," Columbus attorney John F. Wilson, and Dayton attorneys Charles Craighead and D. B. VanPelt represented NCR.[61]

Hollister, whose antitrust, procompetition views were already apparent in the Ford case, presided, giving him an even better opportunity to express his strong free-enterprise position. The defense's first strategy was to try to get the case heard in Dayton rather than Cincinnati, arguing that Patterson and the other defendants were needed in Dayton to supervise the daily operations of a corporation that employed more than six hundred people. In denying the motion, Hollister probably gave the defense attorneys their first indication of his view of their clients. Although noting that every accused was presumed innocent, he pointed out that those called on to defend themselves were often inconvenienced. Indeed, many have had to "abandon their businesses" to prepare their defense. "The defendants cannot be treated any differently," he ruled, "than other persons charged with a crime." Moreover, he maintained, "the inconvenience to the defendants and the loss to the NCR Company" in this case were not as great as the defense made out. Indeed, he argued, the true reason the defendants wanted the trial moved to Dayton was because of the company's monetary value to that city and because of the loyalty the people of Dayton had shown toward the company. Thus, Hollister concluded, besides the fact that Dayton did not have the necessary facilities for such a trial, the city would not be "the proper place for a fair trial" because the "local atmosphere" might be such as to bias the jury. And it was "the duty of the court . . . to take such steps as to insure, so far as possible, an absolutely fair trial."[62]

Hollister also refused to allow defense attorneys to present "evidence" attempting to prove that those whom NCR drove out of business were patent infringers. Obviously annoyed that the attorneys would think that even legitimate ends justified NCR's means, Hollister took the opportunity to lecture NCR's leadership about the proper procedure one should use to deal with patent infringers. Granting that patents needed to be protected, Hollister pointed out that, if a person believed his patent had been infringed, he should take the alleged violator to court. One did not, Hollister went on, engage in acts of unfair competition to protect oneself from patent infringements. Nor should so-called leaders of a corporation engage in such "shocking" activities as "burn[ing] their competitor's factory, or destroy[ing] the competing . . . machines, by violence." If patent laws protected such practices, he declared, "it is high time that the patent laws be amended." But, of course patent law did not protect such outrageous actions.[63]

On February 13, 1913, the jurors, after the forty-six-day trial, took only twelve hours to cast eighty-seven ballots (twenty-nine defendants times three counts per defendant), convicting all but one defendant. Indeed, the jury foreman told the press that the jurors had their minds made up before they entered the jury room: "on the first ballot they were unanimous for a verdict of guilty."[64] Attorney General George Wickersham, congratulating Hollister on the impartial and efficient way he conducted the trial, expressed his satisfaction with the verdict, which he saw as "a great vindication of justice." Believing the case to be of the utmost importance and one that was difficult to conduct because of its complexity, Wickersham explained why he saw this case as an essential test for the future of antitrust litigation. If the jury had "failed to convict on the evidence the government" presented, he maintained, "the Sherman Law as a criminal statute might just as well be torn up."[65]

A week after the jury had rendered its verdict, Hollister sentenced Patterson, Deeds, Watson, and most of the others to one year in jail and a $5,000 fine each plus court costs. For the three minor defendants, he imposed only a nine-month prison sentence in addition to their fines.[66] The defendants were shocked, having expected fines but not incarceration.[67]

In sentencing them, Hollister reminded the defendants that they "belong to the walk of life which should set the example." But they lost that opportunity. In words that sound familiar in the twenty-first century, plagued by a myriad of unethical activities committed by leading businessmen and accountants, Hollister chastised the convicted officers: "In your desire for gain you forgot everything else. The government is strong enough to protect its people whether the protection extends to the transportation of dynamite across the land for the purpose of blowing up bridges or to the laying of hands upon men who seek to stifle competition by illegal business methods."[68]

Attorney General Wickersham wrote Hollister immediately after reading his remarks, praising the judge for "the clear and forceful way" he had explained to the defendants "the real nature of their offense and the character of the law they violated."[69] Individuals from across the nation also sent letters to the judge thanking him for "the courage and manhood" he demonstrated in imposing jail sentences on NCR's corporate officers.[70] Most newspapers joined the bandwagon of praise. The *Philadelphia Record* concluded that the defendants were convicted because they pushed "their business by methods 'so despicable that they ought not to be even contemplated by a businessman in good standing.'" Joseph Pulitzer's *New York World* praised Hollister for enforcing "the idea of personal guilt" when imposing his sentence and arguing that the sentence was "the first official response" carrying out "the will of the people that was expressed in the election of [progressive president] Woodrow Wilson."[71]

On the other hand, Dayton newspapers defended the company and its officers. Dayton citizens, they maintained, stood by their corporation and were "shocked beyond measure at the severity of the sentence imposed."[72] Herbert E. Orton, a native Daytonian who had moved to Chicago, summed up the attitude of Daytonians well when, in a letter to Hollister, he condemned the "unjust" sentences imposed on "the best citizens of Dayton." NCR, he explained, was a "model factory" where these corporate officers who Hollister had just sent to jail treated their employees as well as any company in America.[73]

The defendants, of course, appealed. And on March 13, 1915, the Sixth Circuit Court of Appeals overturned the conviction, holding that two of the three counts in the indictment were duplicative, and remanded the case back to the district court for a new trial. The U.S. attorney decided not to reprosecute the case, so Hollister ordered the indictments dismissed on February 1, 1916. Perhaps the government's success in its civil suit against NCR influenced the U.S. attorney's decision; NCR had agreed to a decree enjoining it from ever engaging in any of the activities with which it had been charged in the criminal case. Perhaps more important, the chance of success in a second criminal proceeding looked bleak. First, the Sixth Circuit had narrowly construed the original indictment, making conviction unlikely. Further, Patterson had become a national hero after he took the lead in organizing relief following the devastating Dayton flood of 1913. Hundreds of people from across the nation had telegraphed President Wilson requesting a presidential pardon for Patterson.[74]

Two years after the NCR trial, Hollister presided over another criminal prosecution that also received national attention. The case against Roy Van Tress and his cohorts was closely watched by hundreds of "humble" people who had been defrauded in a scheme by which Van Tress sold supposedly Indian-owned land that the government was, he claimed, about to sell at public auction. The trial took ten weeks, with five thousand pages of testimony and more than a hundred witnesses. The jury convicted Van Tress of conspiracy to commit mail fraud and trying to improperly influence potential witnesses; Hollister sentenced all the defendants to three to six months each. But, although Hollister held that the evidence was sufficient to connect Van Tress with the scheme to prove conspiracy, the court of appeals disagreed, reversing and remanding the case back for a new trial.[75]

The most notorious trial in Hollister's court, however, was the prosecution of Edward Bathgate and dozens of others for election fraud. All were charged with buying votes or voting multiple times for the Republican ticket in the presidential and congressional elections of 1916. Hollister dismissed the indictments reluctantly, concluding that the federal court had no jurisdiction, that it could hear cases of crimes only within some provision of some federal statute; there were no federal common-law crimes. But, in dismissing the case, he did not miss the opportunity to lecture the defendants and to encourage Hamilton County prosecutors, in whose hands Congress placed the power to punish "bribery at elections," to file charges against them. He decried the evident fact that "in the last general election" there was "wholesale bribery by saloon keepers, members of the City council and by many deputy officials." The rights of all Americans to a fair election had been undermined.[76]

### THE DISTRICT COURT'S ROLE IN WORLD WAR I

The docket confronting Sater and Hollister changed dramatically after the United States entered World War I, in 1917. When the war broke out, the U.S. attorney general, in his 1918 annual report, noted the increase in litigation because of "war conditions." While "mindful of the fact that this department not only is responsible for law enforcement, but, in a larger sense, is responsible for the protection of civil liberties," he pledged that he would confine the activities of his office "strictly to the legal powers conferred upon it." He also thanked Congress for enacting the new laws the nation needed to wage war effectively—the Espionage Act, the Sabotage Act, the Sedition Act, the Trading with the Enemies Act, and the Selective Service Act.[77]

Ohioans held widely divergent views about America's entry into the war on the side of the Allies. Many German Americans opposed the war against their homeland, even though they had no love for the Kaiser. Many Irish Americans objected to American support for Great Britain. Draft dodging was "rampant."[78] Socialists, who saw the war as a capitalist conspiracy, attracted wide support. Quakers, Amish, Mennonites, and other pacifists refused military service. In local elections in 1917, 44 percent of Dayton's electorate and 11.9 percent of Cincinnati's voted for the Socialist ticket.[79] To counter such sentiments, the state government, supporting mobilization, created departments and boards to stimulate production, promote conservation, and boost civilian morale. Government-produced propaganda, coordinated by the new Americanization Committee, whipped up sentiment for the war and against those who opposed America's policies. They were so successful that anti-German sentiment persisted even after the war. A 1919 statute prohibited teaching German in any Ohio grammar school while also requiring all classes to be conducted only in English. Violence occasionally erupted as tempers flared. A mob kidnapped and beat up pacifist-socialist Herbert S. Bigelow for his alleged pro-German opinions. U.S. attorney for the Southern District of Ohio, Stuart R. Bolin, refused to pursue Bigelow's attackers, bluntly stating, "Our courts are not permitting persons who have taken a stand against the Government in this war to seek shelter behind the Constitution. . . . The Constitution is being virtually suspended during the time when America is facing this tremendous crisis."[80]

The judges of the Southern District seemed to agree with Bolin. Both Sater and Hollister vigorously enforced federal laws and policies designed to curtail antiwar activities. And Hollister, even before America entered the war, sided with the Allies. Never even attempting to appear impartial, he "aroused the wrath of many pro-Germans by signing a protest against Belgian outrages."[81]

Even without new laws, the Department of Justice arrested and jailed more than a hundred German and Austrian immigrants living in the Ohio valley, especially in Cincinnati and Dayton, as "detained enemy aliens." Acting under the orders of the president, the attorney general ordered U.S. attorneys to detain those who might pose "a danger to the public peace and safety . . . until further order of the President." Those jailed were generally charged with being in a restricted zone, usually in or near a military base or a factory engaged in producing war materials and equipment, without a permit, or with uttering seditious statements. Most of those jailed had expressed some sympathy with the German cause or had expressed their opposition to the war.[82]

Once Congress enacted new laws, Bolin vigorously prosecuted alleged violators. Although the normal variety of cases continued, albeit in declining numbers, the court was inundated with criminal and civil cases enforcing the

Selective Service Act, the Espionage Act, and acts regulating prices and rents. Table 4.4 shows that the Southern District of Ohio was slightly above the national average in criminal prosecutions under the draft law. And, as table 4.5 shows, Cincinnati was the focal point for these prosecutions. Not only did it hear more than the average number of cases for violations of the various provisions of the Selective Service Act but it also handled one of the three prosecutions in the nation under the Sabotage Act and one of the three cases charging threats against the president.[83]

Although the number of cases Hollister handled was astonishing, as table 4.5 demonstrates, he disposed of most of them rapidly. In general, the defendants pleaded guilty and received short sentences in a local jail. The judge released many accused of trying to evade the draft so they could have "the opportunity to report as directed by the Local Exemption Board." Those selling liquor to soldiers or running houses of prostitution near military bases generally received small fines or a few days in jail.[84]

Nevertheless, both Sater and Hollister heard several more challenging cases. In *United States v. Casey,* Sater refused to dismiss an indictment against the defendants who were accused of conspiracy to violate section 13 of the Selective Service Act by operating a house of prostitution near the Columbus barracks. The defendants' attorney argued that section 13 unconstitutionally delegated to the secretary of war legislative power to designate which areas fell under the statute. He also maintained that the law unconstitutionally attempted to interfere with the police powers reserved to the state to regulate the morals of its citizens. In a sweeping decision, Sater declared that Congress and the executive branch of government had virtually unlimited powers to prosecute the war. Those branches of government, he maintained, had "unrestricted" "plenary and exclusive" powers to preserve the nation. Congress's power to wage war "is as great, at least, as its power under the commerce clause," giving it complete choice as to the means by which it will carry out its delegated war powers. Therefore, to carry out its policies, it can delegate to the secretary of war virtually any power it wished. Moreover, although states have the power to regulate morality, Congress enacted section 13 under its war power. Even if the state chose to indict Casey for engaging in prostitution, the federal government could also prosecute him for engaging in an activity it had prohibited in certain places.[85]

A grand jury indicted Pemberton W. Stickrath under the new federal law making it a crime to threaten to kill the president, after he declared that "President Wilson ought to be killed. It is a wonder some one has not done it already. If I had an opportunity I would do it myself." Stickrath, in challenging the indictment, argued that his language did not amount to a true threat and that, with the president hundreds of miles away, his words failed to pose any danger to Wilson. Sater denied the defendant's motion, holding that Stickrath's words were sufficient for an indictment under the law and the case

## Table 4.5 Criminal Indictments in the Southern District of Ohio during World War I

| Year | Violation | Number Charged in Cincinnati | Disposition | Number Charged in Columbus | Disposition |
|---|---|---|---|---|---|
| 1917 | "Slacker" Act of May 18, 1917 | 9 | 1 nolle prosequi; 8 pleaded guilty (15 days to 6 months in jail, most sentenced to 3 months) | 0 | — |
| | Espionage Act of June 15, 1917 | 1 | Pleaded guilty (30 days in jail, plus $100 fine) | 0 | — |
| 1918 | Selective Service Act | | | | |
| | Section 5 (failure to report, etc.) | 13 | 12 pleaded guilty (1 hour to 1 year in jail); 1 nolle prosequi | 0 | — |
| | Section 6 (false questionnaire) | 16 | 11 pleaded guilty (1 hour to one year in jail); 1 jury trial (found not guilty); 4 nolle prosequis | 2 | 1 pleaded guilty (sixty days in jail); 1 nolle prosequi |
| | Section 12 (selling liquor to members of the armed services within dry zones declared by the secretary of war) | 79 | 68 pleaded guilty (1 hour to 10 months in jail); 4 jury trials (3 found guilty, 1 not guilty: those found guilty had sentences similar to those who pleaded guilty); 7 nolle prosequis | 26 | 11 pleaded guilty (30 days to 10 months in jail, plus $100 fine); 13 jury trials (10 found guilty, 3 found not guilty: those found guilty had sentences from 60 days to 11 months in jail, plus $200 fine); 2 nolle prosequis |
| | Section 13 (operating houses of prostitution in areas near military camps) | 52 | 45 pleaded guilty (same sentences as under Section 12); 2 jury trials (1 found guilty; 1 hung jury, later nolle prosequi); 5 nolle prosequis | 6 | 5 pleaded guilty (75 days to 9 months in jail or $20 to $25 fine); 1 nolle prosequi |
| | No section listed | 11 | 9 pleaded guilty (same range of sentence as under sections 12 and 13); 2 nolle prosequis | 0 | — |
| | "Slacker" (Act of May 18, 1917) | 20 | 15 pleaded guilty; 2 jury trials (1 found guilty, the other not guilty); 3 nolle prosequis | 0 | — |
| | Proclamation of President of U.S., May 18, 1917 | 1 | Pleaded guilty (6 months in jail) | 3 | 2 pleaded guilty (5 to 20 days in jail); 1 nolle prosequi |
| | Espionage Act of June 15, 1917 | 4 | 1 pleaded guilty (5 years in penitentiary); 2 jury trials (both found guilty; 1 sentenced to 15 years in penitentiary, the other to 20 years in penitentiary); 1 nolle prosequi | 3 | All pleaded guilty (1 received $25 fine; 1 received 3 years in penitentiary; 1 received 5 years in penitentiary) |

Source: Columbus Courthouse Criminal Docket, vol. 3; Criminal Dockets, W. Div., vol. 3.

could proceed to trial. Sater then took the opportunity to praise Congress for enacting the law and to lecture Stickrath on the severity of his alleged crime. Sater contended that in a country like the United States, where the people are sovereign and the president merely their representative, a threat to kill the president "is an affront to all loyal and right-thinking persons, inflam[ing] their minds [and] provok[ing] disorder" and is therefore "akin to treason."[86]

Hollister heard three Espionage Act cases. None involved espionage as it is defined today. Rather, all were prosecutions of defendants who had simply made statements opposing the war. William Bago, charged with wilfully obstructing enlistment, was convicted for saying, "I won't give a nickel to the Red Cross. . . . They are nothing but a lot of ***** grafters. . . . The war is carried on by a lot of grafters . . . for the benefit of the moneyed men." Witnesses at Bago's trial also testified that the defendant had expressed sympathy for Germany and the Kaiser. On the basis of these statements, the jury convicted him of violating the Espionage Act, and Hollister sentenced him to fifteen years in the penitentiary.[87] Fred Bisdorf received twenty years in the Atlanta penitentiary after a jury convicted him of criticizing the war as being prosecuted for "money men" and saying that he hoped "the wooden soldiers over at Camp Sherman are taken to Germany and blown to *****."[88] Jacob Benner, after saying to Raymond Kuhn, a man subject to the draft, that "the thing to do is to go home, and shoot the first man that comes after you," pleaded guilty to violating the Espionage Act. He received only a thirty-day jail sentence and a $100 fine.[89]

Far more serious was the sabotage case against Homer DeBolt and Fred Kelso. The Sabotage Act made it a crime to destroy war materiel or "willfully attempt" to do so. The government charged DeBolt and Kelso with attempting to influence others to defectively make the railroad cars being produced at the Ralston Steel Car Company's plant in Columbus. These cars were to be used by the army in France. Although the defendants may have been guilty of what they were accused of doing, their motives had nothing to do with the war effort. They had been involved in efforts to unionize the plant and had been discharged for these activities. At a union meeting, the indictment alleged, the disgruntled former employees agreed that one of their fellow union members who had not been discharged, a Mr. Fox, would remain employed for the purpose of destroying the company's equipment. Fox was caught before anything could be done. Thus, the defendants argued, they could not be indicted; mere solicitation to commit a crime, they claimed, is not a step taken or an act done toward the commission of that crime. Refusing to grant a directed verdict for the defense, Sater held that mere words could constitute the offense of attempt. "The indictment," he held, "charges an aggravated offense much more prejudicial to the community than an incitement to steal,—an incitement or solicitation to commit an offense which, if committed, would inevitably cripple the nation in the prosecution of the present war, prolong

# DOWN WITH CONSCRIPTION

### The 1st Amendment to the Federal Constitution.

Congress shall make no law respecting an establishment of religion, or prohibiting the free exercise thereof; or abridging the freedom of SPEECH, or of the press; or the right of the people peaceably to assemble, and to petition the Government for a redress of grievances.

### The 13th Amendment to the Constitution of the United States reads:

"Neither slavery nor involuntary servitude, except as a punishment for crime, whereof the party shall have been duly convicted, shall exist within the United States or any places subject to their jurisdiction."

## CONSCRIPTION IS THE WORST FORM OF INVOLUNTARY SERVITUDE

The conscription law which the Wilson adminstration intends to put into effect proposes that the young men of this nation shall be taken from their homes against their will, and sent to the trenches of France to murder and be murdered in a war over the commercial interests of the capitalist class.

Daniel Webster, one of the greatest American statesman, said this of conscription in Congress of this country, Dec. 9, 1814:

"Is this consistent with the character of a free government? Is this civil liberty? Is this the real character of our constitution? No sir, it is not. The constitution is libeled, foully libeled. The people of this country have not established for themselves such a fabric of despotism. They have not purchased at a vast expense of their treasures and their own blood a Magna Charta to be slaves. Where is it written in the constitution, in what article or section is it contained, that you may take 'children from their parents . . . . . compel them to fight the battles of any war in which the follies or the wickedness of the government may engage? Under what concealment has this power lain hidden which now for the first time comes forth, with a tremendous and baleful aspect, to trample down and destroy the dearest right of personal liberty.

Every man who is determined to uphold the "dearest right of personal liberty," every man who refuses to become a victim of the war declared by the government to protect the millions loaned the Allies by the capitalist of this country, should

## REFUSE TO REGISTER FOR CONSCRIPTION

The Socialist party of Ohio has shown the way in the fight against conscription by adoption of this resolution:

Resolved, by the Socialist Party in joint meeting assembled, that we denounce the law proposing "involuntary servitude," in violation of the 13th amendment of the constitution of the United States, in the form of conscription to murder our fellow human beings in other lands, and recommend to and urge all members of the party, and the workers generally, that they refuse to register, [illegible] ... [illegible] pledge to them our financial and moral support in their refusal to become the victims of the ruling class.

One of the millions of leaflets issued by the Socialist Party
SOCIALIST PARTY OF OHIO—1291 Cook Ave., Lakewood, O.

A flyer distributed by Thomas Hammerschmidt and others in the Socialist Party of Ohio. For printing and distributing this flyer, in a trial presided over by Judge Hollister, a jury convicted Hammerschmidt and twelve others of conspiracy to defraud the United States by impairing, obstructing, and defeating the lawful functioning of the Selective Service Act of May 18, 1917. Although the Sixth Circuit Court of Appeals upheld Hollister's many rulings and the conviction in *Hammerschmidt v. U.S.*, 287 F. 817 (6th Cir. 1923), the U.S. Supreme Court overturned the conviction in *Hammerschmidt v. U.S.*, 262 U.S. 736 (1923). *Courtesy of National Archives and Records Administration—Great Lakes Region (Chicago)* its duration, increase its cost, and multiply the number of killed and wounded Americans." Such incitement is "provocative of disorder."[90] Despite Sater's instructions, the jury acquitted the defendants. Nevertheless, the U.S. attorney general praised the judge for settling an "important question of law"— that an attempt to influence someone was a sufficient step taken to constitute attempted sabotage under the requirements of the statute.[91]

The case of socialist Thomas Hammerschmidt and twelve others for conspiracy to obstruct registration for military service presented the most direct challenge to the First Amendment's right to free speech. The defendants had printed a flyer entitled "Down with Conscription," charging that the draft violated the Thirteenth Amendment's prohibition against slavery and urging men to refuse to register. "The Socialist Party of Ohio," the flyer declared, "has shown the way in the fight against conscription" by denouncing the law and recommending that all workers refuse to register. During the court proceedings, the defendants unsuccessfully challenged the sufficiency of the indictment, the composition of the grand jury, and several of Hollister's rulings. Hollister held that "to print or cause to be printed a circular . . . and to deliver [it] to the persons named, may never result in bringing the circular to the attention of anyone sought to be influenced," but the "intent to do so is alleged, and it is for the jury to say whether the conspiracy was entered into and the overt act . . . done with the intent to bring about the results charged." He therefore submitted the case to the jury, which convicted the defendants. After Hollister's death, Judge John Weld Peck, who replaced him on the bench, denied the defendants' motion for a new trial. The Sixth Circuit Court of Appeals upheld the conviction, but, in 1923, the Supreme Court overturned it, remanding the case back to the district court. The U.S. attorney then dropped the case.[92]

Despite this reversal, the judges of the Southern District of Ohio during the Progressive Era and World War I had accomplished what they saw as their primary tasks: they had upheld federal authority, maintained law and order, and fostered free competition. They also furthered progressive goals by rejecting arguments by corporate defendants that state and federal regulatory statutes violated businesses' Fourteenth Amendment rights to equal protection and due process of law.

# 5

## FROM PROSPERITY, TO THE GREAT DEPRESSION AND WAR, AND BACK AGAIN, 1920–1960

### THE 1920s: THE TENSIONS OF MODERNITY

After World War I, Americans went back to the business of business. They returned to their lives as farmers, mechanics, laborers, professionals, small businessmen, and corporate leaders. It was a time of general prosperity, but also an era of tension between the past, with its personal relations in small towns and in rural America, and the future, with advances in science and technology, urbanization, and the impersonal corporation. Radio, movies, advertising, and mass-circulation magazines promoted a national, secular culture that emphasized consumption, pleasure, and even sex. Frightened, many clung to their Victorian morality, denouncing flappers, drinking, and the new immigrants from southern and eastern Europe who had come to America over the preceding decades with "alien" religions and "strange" values. In response to these fears, Congress enacted immigration restriction, while the states ratified the Eighteenth Amendment, inaugurating prohibition. The District Court for the Southern District of Ohio forthrightly faced the task of enforcing these new statutes as well as dealing with the social and economic conflicts that resulted in a docket dominated by prohibition and labor-management litigation.[1]

Four judges presided over the Southern District of Ohio during this decade. To serve with Sater as a replacement for Hollister, who died suddenly in the fall of 1919, President Wilson selected John Weld Peck.[2] Part of a distinguished family of lawyers and judges, Peck, at the time of his appointment, was one of Cincinnati's most prominent attorneys, with a clientele that included the Cincinnati Southern Railroad, Cincinnati Gas and Electric Company, Cincinnati Street Railway Company, Western Bank & Trust Company, and many other industrial and financial institutions. Politically active in the Democratic Party, having held office himself as well as campaigning for others, Peck considered himself an "Independent," or, in the words of the *Cincinnati Times–Star,* a "Jeffersonian" Democrat, viewing with suspicion expansive federal powers or any regulatory statute that might call into question the constitutional right of businesses not to be deprived of property without due process of law.[3]

Peck remained on the bench for only four years before returning to private practice.[4] President Warren G. Harding replaced him with Smith Hickenlooper,[5] a native Cincinnatian and "scion of one of the oldest families in the United States."[6] Although Hickenlooper, like Peck, started his career in private practice, after twelve years he switched to the public sector, joining the Hamilton County prosecutor's office as an assistant in charge of the civil division. He then served as superior court judge in Cincinnati until assuming his duties as a federal judge. An expert on patent law, Hickenlooper was considered a brilliant jurist.[7]

When Sater retired at the end of 1924, Harding chose Benson Hough as his replacement. A brigadier general in the Ohio National Guard and a World War I veteran and decorated war hero, Hough had held numerous public law–related positions before his appointment to the federal bench, including serving as a member of the Ohio Supreme Court for three years and as the U.S. attorney for the Southern District of Ohio for two years.[8] A "kind," "considerate," and understanding person,[9] Hough saw his job as doing "what [was] exactly right and just."[10]

### THE DOCKET OF THE DISTRICT COURT IN THE 1920s

The calendar of every federal court changed dramatically in the 1920s. As tables 5.1, 5.2, 5.3, 5.4, and 5.5 demonstrate, many of the same types of cases the court had been hearing remained on its dockets. In addition, some litigation involved matters left over from World War I, with average citizens using the court to press their claims for war benefits they believed due them. But even when cases fell into the same categories as seen in earlier decades, as these tables indicate, the variety of cases increased as the Ohio legislature and the U.S. Congress enacted more and more regulatory laws. Now there were prosecutions for violations of acts regulating banking, food and drugs, hours and wages, and prostitution, as well as litigation over patents and tax disputes that had been pressed from the court's inception.[11] The district judges had to interpret numerous state and federal statutes as corporations initiated suits challenging the new regulations.

## Table 5.1 Civil Cases Commenced for Fiscal Year Ending June 30, 1920

| Year | Civil Suits, U.S. a Party | | | | | | | | | | Civil Suits, U.S. Not a Party | | |
| --- | --- | --- | --- | --- | --- | --- | --- | --- | --- | --- | --- | --- | --- |
| | Internal Revenue | Post Office | Safety Appliance Act | Twenty-Eight-Hour and Hours of Service Act | Forfeit FDA | Antitrust | Immigration | National Prohibition Act | Miscellaneous[a] | Total | Admiralty | Others Except Bankruptcy | Total |
| 1920 | 487/6 1 | 12/1 — | 68/1 2 | 363/4 2 | 1,401/17 43 | 7/1 — | 70/1 — | 611/7 — | 2,708/32 7 | 5,726/68 55 | 3,221/38 2 | 13,162/157 290 | 16,383/195 292 |

Note: In each column, the first line represents the totals for all districts/average per district for all districts based on eighty-four district courts; the second line is the Southern District of Ohio.

[a]Miscellaneous for the national figures includes customs cases and cases involving land laws and timber trespass, which are never brought before the courts of the Southern District of Ohio.

*Source:* Attorney general of the United States, *Annual Reports of the Attorney General of the United States,* 1920.

## Table 5.2 Civil Cases Commenced for Fiscal Years Ending June 30, 1925 and 1930

| Year | Civil Suits, U.S. a Party | | | | | | | | | | Civil Suits, U.S. Not a Party | | |
| --- | --- | --- | --- | --- | --- | --- | --- | --- | --- | --- | --- | --- | --- |
| | Internal Revenue | Post Office | Regulation of Commerce[a] | Public Health and Safety[b] | Banking and Finance[c] | Liability and Insurance[d] | Foreign Relations[e] | Public Lands[f] | Miscellaneous[g] | Total | Admiralty | Others Except Bankruptcy | Total |
| 1925 | 1,329/16 10 | 75/1 — | 1,557/19 37 | 8,039/96 13 | 22/1 — | 219/3 — | 1,673/20 24 | 394/5 — | 3,011/36 11 | 16,319/194 95 | 2,918/35 — | 18,798/224 265 | 21,716/259 265 |
| 1930 | 2,657/32 27 | 27/1 — | 1,494/18 27 | 13,269/158 115 | 6/1 — | 2,231/27 33 | 781/9 2 | 772/9 — | 3,697/44 6 | 24,934/297 210 | 2,505/30 — | 20,886/249 207 | 23,391/278 207 |

Note: In each column, the first line represents the totals for all districts/average per district for all districts based on eighty-four district courts; the second line is the Southern District of Ohio.

[a]Includes antitrust, regulation of public utilities (ICC, Hours of Service, Twenty-Eight-Hour Law, Safety Appliance, thefts, and other such cases), regulation of food and fuel (FDA, Meat Inspection, and other such cases); and miscellaneous regulations (quarantine acts, game-bird acts, insecticide and fungicide acts, virus acts, shipping acts, and other such acts)

[b]Includes National Prohibition Act and other liquor violations, white slavery (Mann Act), Harrison Antinarcotic and other antinarcotic acts, and miscellaneous cases

[c]Includes national banking laws, Federal Reserve Act, Federal Farm Loan Act, War Finance Corporation Act, and others

[d]Includes war risk insurance, federal employees compensation acts, Pension Act, Federal Retirement Act, and other such cases

[e]Includes immigration and naturalization cases, violations of the Trading with the Enemy Act, alien property, war trade and industries, admiralty, and other such cases

[f]Includes public lands, reservations, Indian lands; condemnation proceedings; reclamation and water rights, and other such cases

[g]Includes customs cases, selective service, and other cases

*Source:* Attorney general of the United States, *Annual Reports of the Attorney General of the United States,* 1925 and 1930.

## Table 5.3 Criminal Cases Commenced for Fiscal Year ending June 30, 1920

| Year | Internal Revenue | Post Office | Banking and Finance | Mann Act | FDA | Antitrust | ICC Laws | Counterfeiting | Selective Service Act[a] | National Prohibition Act | Miscellaneous[b] | Total |
|---|---|---|---|---|---|---|---|---|---|---|---|---|
| 1920 | 8,401/100 | 1,984/24 | 93/1 | 477/6 | 613/7 | 5/— | 1,024/12 | 321/4 | 19,830/236 | 7,291/87 | 15,550/185 | 55,587/662 |
| | 78 | 19 | — | 1 | 4 | — | 11 | 4 | — | 56 | 105 | 278 |

Note: In each column, the first line represents the totals for all districts, based on eighty-four district courts; the second line is the Southern District of Ohio.

[a]Includes the few espionage cases remaining from World War I.

[b]Miscellaneous for the national figures includes customs cases and cases involving land laws and timber trespass, which are never brought before the courts of the Southern District of Ohio.

*Source:* Attorney general of the United States, *Annual Reports of the Attorney General of the United States,* 1920.

## Table 5.4 Criminal Cases Commenced for Fiscal Years ending June 30, 1925 and 1930

| Year | Internal Revenue | Post Office | Regulation of Commerce[a] | Public Health and Safety[b] | Banking and Finance[c] | Liability and Insurance[d] | Foreign Relations[e] | Public Lands[f] | Miscellaneous[g] | Total |
|---|---|---|---|---|---|---|---|---|---|---|
| 1925 | 430/5 | 2,600/31 | 3,007/36 | 58,128/692 | 219/3 | 68/1 | 1,532/18 | 151/2 | 9,173/109 | 75,038/893 |
| | 1 | 37 | 32 | 359 | 4 | — | — | — | 5 | 438 |
| 1930 | 584/7 | 2,117/25 | 2,573/31 | 62,960/750 | 676/8 | 119/1 | 7,080/84 | 106/1 | 11,090/132 | 87,305/1,039 |
| | 2 | 21 | 46 | 352 | 5 | — | 2 | — | 77 | 505 |

Note: In each column, the first line represents the totals for all districts, based on eighty-four district courts; the second line is the Southern District of Ohio.

[a]Includes antitrust, regulation of public utilities (ICC, Hours of Service, Twenty-Eight-Hour Law, Safety Appliance, thefts, and other such cases), regulation of food and fuel (FDA, Meat Inspection, and other such cases); and miscellaneous regulations (quarantine acts, game-bird acts, insecticide and fungicide acts, virus acts, shipping acts, and other such acts)

[b]Includes National Prohibition Act and other liquor violations, white slavery (Mann Act), Harrison Antinarcotic and other antinarcotic acts, peonage, and miscellaneous cases

[c]Includes national banking laws, Federal Reserve Act, Federal Farm Loan Act, War Finance Corporation Act, and others

[d]Includes war risk insurance, federal employees compensation acts, Pension Act, Federal Retirement Act, and other such cases

[e]Includes immigration and naturalization cases, violations of the Trading with the Enemy Act, alien property, war trade and industries, admiralty, and other such cases

[f]Includes public lands, reservations, Indian lands; condemnation proceedings; reclamation and water rights, and other such cases

[g]Includes customs cases, selective service, and other cases

*Source:* Attorney general of the United States, *Annual Reports of the Attorney General of the United States,* 1925 and 1930.

### Table 5.5 Criminal and Civil Dockets, July 1, 1927–June 30, 1930

| | Southern District of Ohio | | All Districts | |
| --- | --- | --- | --- | --- |
| | Total Number | Percentage of Total | Total Number | Percentage of Total |
| Criminal docket | | | | |
| Liquor | 1,813 | 69.8 | 58,235 | 80.1 |
| Nonliquor | | | | |
| Drugs | 185 | 7.1 | 5,213 | 7.2 |
| Motor vehicle theft | 162 | 6.3 | 1,730 | 2.4 |
| White slavery | 29 | 1.1 | 242 | 0.3 |
| Postal offenses | 109 | 4.2 | 2,499 | 3.4 |
| Offenses against currency and coinage | 27 | 1.0 | 458 | 0.6 |
| Offenses against national banking system | 15 | 0.6 | 257 | 0.4 |
| Violations of bankruptcy laws | 6 | 0.2 | 538 | 0.7 |
| Offenses against interstate commerce | 41 | 1.6 | 833 | 1.1 |
| Violations of immigration and naturalization laws | 2 | 0.1 | 683 | 1.0 |
| Offenses against government property | 55 | 2.1 | 602 | 0.8 |
| Violations of income tax laws | 7 | 0.3 | 145 | 0.2 |
| Miscellaneous | 145 | 5.6 | 1,301 | 1.8 |
| Total nonliquor violations | 783 | 30.2 | 14,501 | 19.9 |
| Civil docket | | | | |
| Total civil docket | 428 | | 9,852 | |
| Government cases | 180 | 42.0 | 5,664 | 57.5 |
| Quasi-criminal cases[a] | 159 | 37.1 | 4,342 | 44.1 |
| Liquor cases | 134 | | 3,845 | |

[a]Includes violation of liquor laws (U.S. action for tax, penalty, forfeiture, padlock, etc.) and actions of penalty of forfeiture in cases of violations of immigration laws, interstate commerce, and food and drug laws.

Source: American Law Institute, *A Study of the Business of the Federal Court*, part I, Criminal Cases (Philadelphia: American Law Institute, 1934).

Although there were no truly dramatic cases challenging these regulations, individuals and corporations regularly turned to the federal courts when they believed that local or state officials had acted unconstitutionally. In turn, the judges of the District Court for the Southern District of Ohio tended to hold conservative jurisprudential views, generally ruling in favor of these plaintiffs over the regulators. The judges decided more than a dozen cases challenging a variety of taxes imposed by the state, orders issued by the Ohio Public Utilities Commission, rates set by cities for utilities, and the state requirement that goods traveling in interstate commerce be inspected. In general, they held rates established by a city or state agency to be confiscatory or in violation of a valid contract, but occasionally the judges would support a city ordinance or state regulation. For example, in a decision that made him extremely popular with his fellow Columbus residents, Hough declared the Columbus ordinance regulating gas rates to be constitutional and not confiscatory, thereby preserving the low gas rates mandated by the city.[12]

When a state regulation was challenged for interfering with federal power, the judges of the 1920s tended to support state powers. For example, the court declared that the state of Ohio could regulate, tax, and inspect transit companies and goods traveling in Ohio as long as doing so did not burden interstate commerce or conflict with federal laws.[13] But in *Ex parte Willman,* Peck upheld federal power against a state law mandating a certain type of headlight on motor vehicles. In that case the state law conflicted directly with the U.S. postmaster general's specifications for headlights on trucks carrying the U.S. mail. If Peck had held that the state law applied to the mail trucks, the federal government would have had to spend significant sums to refit its delivery vehicles. But Peck sided with the federal government, affirming the supremacy of the federal government in its sphere. He held that, because the Constitution grants Congress the power to establish post offices and post roads, to extend state authority over vehicles delivering the mail along designated post roads would subordinate the federal government to the laws of the states. That would mean that the federal government was not supreme in the selection of instrumentalities for carrying of the mail. "Such a conclusion," Peck ruled, was "inadmissible."[14] On another occasion, however, Peck showed his generally probusiness, antiregulatory views by refusing to extend the federal government's regulatory arm when it tried to operate under what he concluded to be vaguely worded statutory authority. Thus, he held that a section of the Pure Food and Drug Act did not cover false or misleading statements in separate circulars enclosed with the product at issue, forcing Congress to amend its law to clarify its purpose.[15]

The 1920s also witnessed the continued conflict between labor and management. In this area, the judges continued the antiunion policies of the past. Although Peck refused a coal company's request that he send marshals to protect the company, pointing out that this was not a power the court possessed,[16] the judges of the Southern District continued to issue broad injunctions against striking union workers. In 1922, after hearing both sides in a labor dispute during one of his sessions in Steubenville, Sater permanently enjoined the officers and members of the Amalgamated Association of Iron, Steel and Tin Workers of North America and others sympathetic to them from interfering with the Wheeling Steel and Iron Company, against which they were striking. According to the company's petition seeking a temporary restraining order, the entire town was united behind the union. The company claimed that the mayor and other town officials were jailing potential strikebreakers while the union was working to prevent strikebreakers from entering the plant. Sater enjoined them all. He allowed only two picketers at the plant's entrance and ordered that all approaches to the plant be kept clear, that no one congregate in or around the plant, and that no one stop or annoy anyone or use any "profanity . . . or indecent language" or epithets such as "scab." While acknowledging, as he had done in earlier cases,[17] that union members had the right to try to peacefully persuade others not to work for the company, he emphasized that they had no right to intimidate, threaten, or annoy anyone who did not want to talk with them. To control the picketers further, he also ordered the union to submit the names of all picketers to the company prior to the time the picketers began their picket duties. After issuing the injunction, Sater enforced it by jailing several union members from one-and-a-half to four months after finding them guilty of criminal contempt for violating some portions of his injunctions.[18]

The United Mine Workers struck all the coal companies in Jefferson, Harrison, and Belmont counties in eastern Ohio in 1927. The mine owners immediately sought federal court protection. Judge Hough quickly complied, granting a temporary restraining order and later an injunction similar to the ones Sater had issued. He enjoined the strikers from "gathering or loitering in groups, crowds, assemblages and picket file formation or any other formation" in or around the mines or in the residential neighborhoods, from blocking any public highway, or from intimidating those who wanted to work. Moreover, based on his belief that "persuasion in the presence of three or more persons congregated with the persuader is not peaceful persuasion," Hough limited the number of picketers to three persons per picket post with picket posts required to be at least one hundred feet apart. Moreover, Hough required union leaders to submit lists with the names of the picketers to the U.S. marshal "along with rough plats showing picket posts." Even more restrictive of free speech, Hough also prohibited strikers from displaying, within a ten-mile radius of any of the mines, "any signs or banners containing any words or language designed to intimidate or insult employes [sic] or prospective employes [sic]." Specifically, Hough forbade the use of any derogatory words such as "scab," "rat," or "yellow dog."[19] Determined that his injunction be enforced, Hough allegedly warned, "[I]f the marshals can't enforce my decrees, the Thirty-Seventh division [of the Ohio National Guard]," the unit he had previously commanded, will.[20]

The strike in the coalfields presented an additional complication. Workers lived in company housing, with the rent money coming out of their paychecks. Acting upon a bill of complaint from the mine companies, Hough decided that he could appropriately use his equity power to order the striking workers to leave their homes to make room for new employees willing to work. Because it was midwinter, "near the holiday time, and a most inconvenient and hazardous time for families to break up homes and acquire and take up new abodes," however, he did allow the strikers to stay in their company houses until the first of April.[21]

Although regulatory disputes and labor confrontations held important places on the court's docket, the most important story of the 1920s revolved around the enforcement of prohibition. In 1919 the country ratified the Eighteenth Amendment, authorizing Congress to regulate the sale of alcohol. In enforcing prohibition vigorously, federal judges not only brought home to Ohio citizens the force of federal law and federal authority but also reflected the sentiments of most Ohioans. If Ohio legislators and state judicial officers reflected public sentiment, then most Ohioans supported prohibition. The Ohio General Assembly, after the Eighteenth Amendment was ratified, established an office of the prohibition commissioner to enforce the law, and state officials arrested and convicted thousands.[22]

But although state officials, like their federal counterparts, supported vigorous enforcement of prohibition, many citizens continued to drink. This kept the courts very busy. Nationally, in 1920, the number of liquor cases was still small, accounting for fewer than 2 percent of the civil cases terminated. By 1925, though, they represented 43 percent of the docket. In 1927, they constituted almost 53 percent of all cases terminated. The percentage stayed in that range until prohibition's repeal in 1933.[23]

The pattern in the Southern District followed that of the nation, although there were some variations between the Western and Eastern Divisions. In the Western Division for 1928, 51 of the 142 civil cases involved violations of liquor laws.[24] But most prohibition violations were prosecuted criminally in the Southern District of Ohio. As early as 1920, in the Western Division, 105 of the 172 criminal cases involved liquor violations. They were disposed of rapidly. In 73 of the cases, the defendants pleaded guilty.[25] The prosecutor chose not to prosecute 17. Therefore, only 15 cases went to trial. Juries convicted in 10 and found 4 not guilty; the result of the fifteenth trial is not known. The judges fined those guilty of illicit distilling between $100 and $1,000, with most fines being either $100 or $500. About half also received jail terms of thirty days to six months. They fined those guilty of violating the National Prohibition Act $50 to $300, with most in the $100 range. Some of those also received jail terms, but rarely more than thirty days.[26] The Eastern Division had a more even distribution of cases between liquor violators and others. In 1925, forty-three of the ninety-seven criminal cases were violations of the National Prohibition Act. As in Cincinnati, most pleaded guilty or were otherwise quickly dispatched in one-day trials.[27]

Although most cases were routine and handled quickly, in 1923 Judge Peck presided over one of the largest, if not the largest, criminal conspiracy trials brought under the National Prohibition Act. Indeed, circuit court judge Maurice H. Donahue, upholding the convictions, said the conspiracy was "extraordinary . . . both as to the time of its continuance and the number of offenses."[28] The indictment against George Remus and his thirteen co-defendants included three hundred offenses for the unlawful transportation of intoxicating liquor and three thousand offenses for the unlawful sale of liquor.[29]

A German-born American, Remus was a lifelong teetotaler who became the richest bootlegger in America. Indeed, the *St. Louis Dispatch* claimed that "Remus was to bootlegging what Rockefeller was to oil."[30] A self-made man, Remus began his entrepreneurial rise to riches in Chicago, first working in his uncle's drug store. He then became a licensed pharmacologist, and later a certified optometrist, and finally, at age twenty-four, an attorney. Specializing in criminal law, divorce law, and labor law for the unions, Remus built a lucrative practice. But when America went dry, Remus moved to Cincinnati to seize the opportunity he saw to make a vast fortune. Using his life savings of $100,000, Remus started acquiring distilleries. With his legal training, he knew how to manipulate the law, so he sought and got permission to remove the whiskey from the distilleries and sell it to drug companies licensed to sell medicinal whiskey. He then moved beyond the law, selling directly to bootleggers and private customers. By 1924, he owned fourteen distilleries, employed three thousand people, including shippers, drivers, salesmen, bodyguards, and accountants, and controlled almost one-seventh of all the medicinal liquor distilled in the United States. Grossing more than $25 million a year, Remus used his vast wealth to try to buy his way into Cincinnati society, building a huge estate in the Price Hill area of Cincinnati and throwing lavish parties where he "slipped $100 bills under his guests' plates." Indeed, some have speculated that F. Scott Fitzgerald modeled Jay Gatsby, in his novel *The Great Gatsby,* after Remus, the self-made man who threw lavish parties but was never quite accepted by refined society.[31]

With such a large operation and with only a small amount of the liquor going to pharmacies, Remus needed a place to store his whiskey before he repackaged and bottled it. Eventually, he found an "isolated farmhouse" in the rural Cincinnati suburb of Westwood, renamed it Death Valley Farm, and remodeled it for his purposes. A fortified enclave accessible by only one small dirt road, with floodlights and armed guards, it seemed safe and secure. Further, Remus employed "almost the entire police force" of Cincinnati "either as convoy guards or as salesmen on commission" and bribed federal law enforcement officers to keep clear of the farm. But on April 15, 1922, a quiet Sunday afternoon, Franklin L. Dodge Jr., a special federal agent, drove into Death Valley Farm with a squad of raiders. The men at the gate assumed they were customers, and they were admitted without the use of force. Once inside, they showed their search warrant and uncovered the storage cellars, the bottling plant, and hundreds of gallons of whiskey.[32]

A grand jury indicted Remus and twelve coconspirators for conspiracy to violate prohibition laws and for maintaining a nuisance by selling and keeping liquor. The government charged that Remus and his staff received, almost daily, truck-size deliveries of whiskey at their farm, and then took the whiskey from the farm, by car, to retailers who would sell it to customers. Often, the government alleged, Remus delivered five or six truckloads of whiskey a week.

After a jury convicted all the defendants on both counts, Peck sentenced Remus to two years in the Atlanta penitentiary and fined him $10,000 on the conspiracy charge. He sentenced his codefendants to lesser terms and fines.

Death Valley Farm, the site where George Remus, one of the biggest bootleggers in the nation, stored his illegal whiskey. It was the site of the raid that led to Remus's arrest in 1922. *Courtesy of Jack Doll, Cincinnati*

On the nuisance charge, Peck sentenced all the defendants to one year in the Montgomery County jail.[33]

The defendants appealed their convictions on several grounds. First, they argued that neither the indictment in the conspiracy case nor the information in the nuisance case was sufficient. The appellate court disagreed. Next, the defendants contended that the jury was prejudiced, several being members of the Law and Order League or the Anti-Saloon League. The appellate court overruled that argument too, citing "a long line of authorities to the effect that membership" in such organizations "does not per se render the juror incompetent." Finally, the defendants took exception to the prosecutor's closing argument, contending that it was inflammatory and prejudicial. After citing World War I as proof that law and order could easily be threatened, the prosecutor had told the jurors that the evidence he presented established "a wholesale reckless attempt" on the part of the defendants "to contravene the law and Constitution of the United States." Such an attempt, he said, by so many individuals contemplating the "continuous flagrant violations of the law and defiance of the provisions of the federal Constitution imperil the efficiency of a government in the maintenance of law and order, and that a failure to maintain law and order would place the United States in a class" with countries that have failed as democracies. Peck held, and the Sixth Circuit Court of Appeals affirmed, that, although he did not favorably regard attempts by any attorney to inflame jurors, the U.S. attorney did have a right and a duty to present the government's case forcibly. Finally, the

George Remus in the federal penitentiary in Atlanta, 1923.
*Courtesy of Jack Doll, Cincinnati*

defendants argued that they did not have to serve their jail sentences after serving their time in the penitentiary, because the two sentences were to be concurrent. Judge Hickenlooper, who took over the case after Peck's resignation from the court, agreed, applying the general rule that when the sentences do not state whether they are to be served concurrently or consecutively, they "will run concurrently." The appellate court overruled him, holding that the fact that the same judge pronounced the two sentences and did not stipulate that they should run concurrently but instead designated two separate places for serving the sentences led to the conclusion that they should be served consecutively.[34] In January 1924, after the Sixth Circuit rejected all of the defendants' appeals and the Supreme Court refused to grant certiorari, Remus boarded a train bound for Atlanta to serve his time, his bootlegging career at an end.[35]

The judges of the district court along with those on the Sixth Circuit Court of Appeals decided several more legally significant—although less spectacular—cases involving defendants' constitutional rights against illegal searches and seizures. In *United States v. Borkowski* (1920), Sater helped establish, in a case of first impression, the minimum requirements for a constitutional search warrant. Aware of the significance of the issue, Sater declared that he was issuing his ruling as "a guide in the future on the subject of search warrants." Officers of the law would have to follow all formalities strictly to assure that their searches complied with the requirements of the Fourth Amendment to the U.S. Constitution. And, based on a textual analysis of that amendment and legal treatises on the subject, Sater concluded that the Fourth Amendment required that search warrants be issued only upon probable cause, the affidavit describing with specificity the place to be searched, the thing to be seized, and the basis for probable cause. The name of the accused, if at all possible, should be stated, although John Doe warrants could be issued if absolutely necessary. Moreover, searches should be conducted in the daytime; if a search was to be done at night, that fact should be stated clearly on the warrant along with the authority upon which a night search was authorized. Finally, court officers issuing search warrants must not do so pro forma. Rather, they had to be convinced, using their sound judgment, that the testimony underlying the affidavits was sufficient.[36] Courts across the country cited Sater's decision, establishing a national standard for issuing proper search warrants.[37]

Four months later, Sater reinforced *Borkowski* in three companion cases involving the searches of private homes and businesses and the seizure of stills in Dayton, Ohio. In all three cases, Sater ruled the searches and seizures unconstitutional because the search warrants did not comply with the requirements he had spelled out in *Borkowski*. Sater went on at great length, describing to those responsible for issuing warrants and for those seeking warrants the minimum constitutional requirements for a valid search, citing legal sources for their reference and the textual language they should follow so they could meet constitutional standards. If law enforcement officials would only follow his guidelines, he fumed, he would not have to release those who had clearly violated the law and should have been punished. But, he emphasized, the Fourth and Fifth Amendments to the Constitution are "as sacred" as the prohibition amendment. Moreover, the Volstead Act, which Congress passed to enforce prohibition, should be enforced only "along legal lines, lest the law be made odious and the ultimate result be the defeat of justice."[38]

The following year, Peck, in a decision as significant as *Borkowski*, defined the requirements for a valid consent to a search. Looking for liquor, two probation officers and two Cincinnati city policemen went to a Mr. Slusser's home without a warrant. After Slusser answered their knock, the agents displayed their badges and said they were going to search for liquor. Slusser responded, "All right; go ahead." Thinking they had a valid consent, they entered his home, searched, and found nothing. They then searched his garage, where they found the liquor. Peck held the whole process to be unconstitutional. First, establishing what was to become a national standard for consent, Peck ruled that Slusser had not consented to the search. Under the circumstances, Slusser had not waived his constitutional rights, but had merely peacefully submitted to officers of the law. Citing no precedent, Peck simply declared that one needs to agree freely to a search, not merely acquiesce to a police demand. Further, Peck held, the right to be secure in one's home includes one's garage as well as one's business. "An unlawful search cannot be justified by what is found"; officers were not free to search wherever they pleased. Their discretion was no "substitute in law for a search warrant issued by a proper magistrate." Finally, Peck ruled, no evidence obtained from an illegal search could be used to secure a person's conviction or subject his or her goods to forfeiture. Therefore, Peck ordered the case dismissed and Slusser's seized automobile returned to him.[39]

Although the judges vigorously enforced the liquor laws unless law enforcement officers violated the accused person's constitutional rights, apparently some federal and local officials did not. In June 1929, the U.S. attorney general wrote Hough, informing him of a complaint by the prohibition department against some of the U.S. commissioners in Cincinnati, whose job it was to hear many of the smaller cases of prohibition violations. Hough agreed to allow the Bureau of Investigation to launch an investigation of the alleged "irregularities."[40] Perhaps he agreed, because four years earlier Hickenlooper had presided over a case in which seventy-one Cincinnati policemen and village prohibition enforcement agents were convicted of "accepting bribes for 'protecting' violators of federal liquor and narcotic laws."[41]

Except for the criminal prosecutions of prohibition violators, criminal cases in the Southern District of Ohio tended to be routine, with the judges having a reputation for sternness, tempered by compassion when warranted, although Hough was particularly hard on narcotics "peddlers."[42] Although most criminal prosecutions were routine, the court did hear two notorious cases allegedly involving dishonesty and scandal. One was of minor importance except to baseball fans. In *Magee v. Chicago National League Ball Club,* the plaintiff sued the ball club for breach of contract. Despite his contract to play with the club, the club had refused to let him play or to pay his salary because, they alleged, he was betting against his team and then playing poorly to win his bets. A jury agreed, and Magee was out of baseball.[43]

A case of far more political significance involved Mally S. Daugherty, the brother of Harry M. Daugherty, President Harding's attorney general, who had been forced to resign after accusations surfaced that he had been involved in the Teapot Dome Scandal, that he had failed to prosecute corporations violating the Sherman and Clayton antitrust acts, and that he had failed to enforce many other federal statutes. The Senate subpoenaed Mally Daugherty, president of Midland National Bank of Washington Court House, Ohio, to testify before a committee investigating his brother. It also subpoenaed certain bank documents, obviously to determine whether Harry Daugherty had used the bank as a vehicle to hide the proceeds from his alleged bribery and corruption. Mally refused to appear, so the Senate issued a warrant for his arrest. Justice Andrew M. J. Cochran of the District Court for the Eastern District of Kentucky, sitting by designation in the Southern District of Ohio, granted Mally a writ of habeas corpus, releasing him from custody. Although the Senate had the power to subpoena private citizens as witnesses in order to carry out its legislative functions, it could not force a private citizen to appear for investigations having nonlegislative purposes. And, Cochran concluded, the Senate, in its own resolution, admitted that its goal in investigating Daugherty was nonlegislative. Moreover, Cochran added, the Senate's words were reinforced by action—"the extreme personal cast of the original resolutions; the spirit of hostility towards the then Attorney General . . . are calculated to create the impression that the idea of legislative action being in contemplation was an afterthought."[44] The Supreme Court disagreed, concluding that the Senate investigation did have a legislative purpose.[45]

Historians cite *Scripps v. Scripps* as another case of note, not because of the law at issue, but because of the parties and their attorneys. The case pitted the estate of Edward W. Scripps, the founder of Scripps newspapers, against the estate of James G. Scripps, Edward's eldest son and, after his father's retirement, comanager, along with his brother John, of the newspaper conglomerate. At issue was half the profits of this vast fortune. Josephine S. Scripps, the executrix of James's will, and her attorneys, Charles Evan Hughes, later to be chief justice of the Supreme Court, John Weld Peck, former district court judge for the Southern District of Ohio, and Nathan R. Margold, who became solicitor of the United States under President Franklin Roosevelt, along with others, claimed that Edward had promised his sons this money. Newton D. Baker, former secretary of war and potential Democratic presidential candidate, represented Edward Scripps's estate. Hickenlooper, ruling for Edward Scripps's estate, held that the father never created any "binding or legal obligation"; in paying his sons half the profits while he was alive, he was merely "acting within the sphere of parental bounty." The Sixth Circuit Court of Appeals affirmed Hickenlooper's decision. Edward Scripps's heirs would continue to collect all the profits from the newspaper conglomerate.[46]

Although cases involving the rich and famous like Daughtery and Scripps fascinated the public, the federal courts' significant work involved determining the fate of reform legislation. But what characterized the legal history of the 1920s was not the resolution of disputes between the government and those businesses being regulated, but the implementation of prohibition. Inundated with cases charging violation of liquor laws, the district court struggled to enforce federal law while still preserving individual rights guaranteed by the U.S. Constitution to be secure in one's home against illegal searches and seizures.

## THE CONSTITUTION IN THE ERA OF THE
## GREAT DEPRESSION AND THE NEW DEAL

The concerns of most Americans changed dramatically on October 23, 1929, Black Thursday, when the prosperity of the 1920s ended with the collapse of the stock market. Republican president Herbert Hoover took some initial steps to stimulate the economy, but he lacked the vision needed to deal with such a crisis. By 1933, one-third of the nation was unemployed. Each year, the number of bankruptcies mounted, exacerbating economic woes. Because state and local governments could not handle such a severe economic downturn, Ohioans, like others around the nation, turned to the federal government for help. In the face of the economic crisis, the new president, Franklin D. Roosevelt, elected in the 1932 Democratic landslide, inaugurated the New Deal. By the end of the decade, Congress had enacted legislation regulating every facet of the economy—agriculture, banking, the stock market, and labor relations, to name a few.[47] These programs made the federal government a "powerful force in the lives of Ohioans."[48] Farmers and urban workers alike benefited from the Agricultural Adjustment Act, the Soil Conservation and Domestic Allotment Act, the Civilian Conservation Corps, the Public Works Administration, and rural electrification. By 1936, for example, 126,700 Ohio farmers placed 63 percent of Ohio's cropland in the federal government's agriculture soil-conservation program, reaping almost $10 million in conservation payments.[49]

But some farmers and business leaders, seeing these programs more as burdens than as benefits, challenged them in federal district court. Initially, many district court judges agreed with the plaintiffs, striking down much of the early New Deal legislation. These judges held that some of the challenged statutes deprived the complainants of their liberty or property without due process of law, in violation of the Fifth Amendment. They held that others unconstitutionally delegated legislative powers to federal administrative boards and agencies or that they exceeded the interstate commerce and taxing powers of Congress, thereby infringing upon the police powers of the states in violation of the Tenth Amendment.

The four judges of the Southern District of Ohio during this decade, however, whether appointed by Republican presidents in the 1920s or by Roosevelt in the 1930s, regularly upheld challenged statutes, deferring to the legislature, be it city, state, or federal. Hough continued to preside over the court in Columbus until his death on November 19, 1935. Despite his stern treatment of strikers in the 1920s, Hough had exhibited progressive tendencies by upholding municipal taxation and a number of regulatory statutes. In 1935, President Roosevelt filled the Columbus vacancy left by Hough's death with Mell Underwood, who had risen through the political rather than legal or judicial ranks.[50] Born on a farm in Morgan County, he had to work his way through college and law school. After serving as Perry County prosecuting attorney for four years, Underwood was elected to Congress in 1922, where he remained until Roosevelt appointed him to the federal bench. Despite his Democratic Party affiliation, in the 1920s Underwood had actively protected the interests of Ohio's coal industry and had authored the Underwood Bill restricting immigration. But Roosevelt expected that Underwood, after so many years in Congress, would have a high regard for that body and would thus uphold its legislation and insist that the law be applied as written.[51]

Serving first with Hough and then with Underwood was Robert R. (Jake) Nevin, who had been nominated by President Calvin Coolidge on January 4, 1929, to replace Hickenlooper, whom Coolidge had elevated to the Sixth Circuit Court of Appeals.[52] Nevin was a native Daytonian and the son of a prominent Dayton lawyer and longtime Republican congressman from the Third Congressional District. A superb trial lawyer specializing in corporate law, he had represented several major railroad companies and had served as chief trial counsel for NCR in the antitrust litigation of the 1910s. Although his background was stereotypically conservative Republican, Nevin also had done legal work for the International Brotherhood of Carpenters and had served for many years as a member of an impartial board for arbitration matters between newspaper publishers and the typographers' unions. Once appointed to the federal bench, he earned a reputation for fairness and impartiality, dispensing justice with "a human touch." He explained that his "sole ambition [was] to keep the administration of the Federal courts on a high plane."[53]

In 1937, John H. Druffel joined Nevin and Underwood after Congress approved an additional judgeship for the Southern District of Ohio.[54] A native Cincinnatian, Druffel was educated not only in Cincinnati's public and parochial schools but also in the city's Eighth Ward, bucking Mike Muller, the boss of this Republican stronghold, to organize a successful Democratic club. He then worked for various Democratic politicians before becoming an active reformer himself, serving from 1929 to 1932 as vice mayor and as a member of Cincinnati city council as a Charterite, or member of Cincinnati's reform party, and authoring several important pieces of legislation, including the first effective building code for Cincinnati and antifraud legislation that remains on the books today, regulating scales, weights and measures, deception in the sale of petroleum products, and the like. Roosevelt, therefore, could assume that he would support the federal regulatory statutes of the New Deal. Both as a Hamilton County Common Pleas Court judge during the early 1930s and then as a district court judge, Druffel tended to exercise judicial restraint when reviewing regulatory statutes.[55]

As a general rule, each of these judges presided independently over his own court. When the president nominates and the Senate approves judicial

In Cincinnati, the judges of the U.S. District Court for the Southern District of Ohio now hold their sessions in the Potter Stewart U.S. Courthouse. They moved to this building in 1939. This federal building also serves as the headquarters of the Sixth Circuit Court of Appeals and the supporting staff and library of the Sixth Circuit. *Courtesy of the Sixth Circuit Archives, Cincinnati*

appointments, they do not designate where the judges will sit. Ever since 1880, when Congress divided the Southern District of Ohio into two divisions, by tradition there has always been one judge from the western part of the state, generally the Cincinnati area, and one from the east, generally Columbus. Indeed, on several occasions when vacancies developed, attorneys and politicians from the area having the vacancy actively sought to preserve this tradition. When Congress created the third judgeship for the Southern District of Ohio, a new tradition developed. Nevin moved to Dayton, and, from that point on, one judge regularly has sat in Dayton along with those regularly presiding in Cincinnati and Columbus. Congress also authorized the judges of the Eastern Division to hold court in Steubenville, which they have done with some regularity, but there has never been a permanent sitting judge there.[56]

The judges in Cincinnati and Columbus presided over courts in new federal facilities. In 1939, Druffel moved into Cincinnati's new federal building, authorized by Congress to accommodate the increased federal activities

The Joseph P. Kinneary United States Courthouse, Columbus. *Courtesy of the U.S. District Court, Southern District of Ohio*

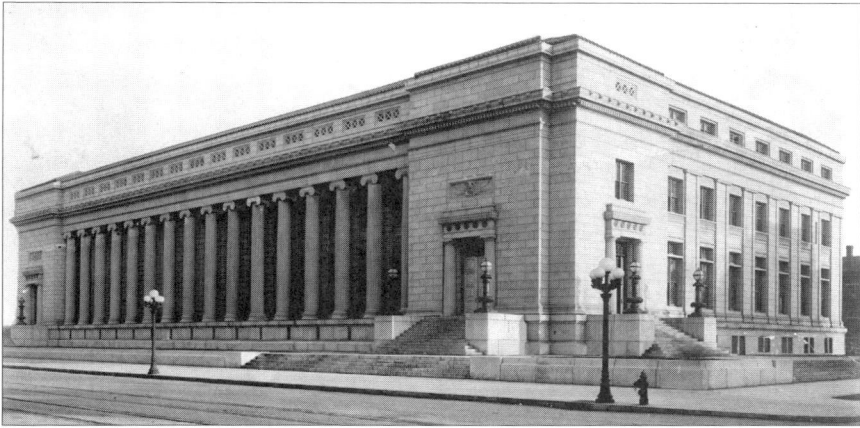

The first federal building in Dayton housed the district court and other federal agencies. *Courtesy of the Sixth Circuit Archives, Cincinnati*

The current federal building in Dayton, home of the district court judges sitting in Dayton as well as other federal agencies. *Courtesy of the Sixth Circuit Archives, Cincinnati*

centered in that city largely because of the administration of New Deal programs. Whereas the new Cincinnati courthouse was considered a beautiful
building, the new Columbus courthouse looked "dumpy." Ironically, it was
Congressman Underwood who had insisted on using Ohio limestone rather
than white marble for the building's exterior, wanting to put people in southern Ohio to work and to use Ohio materials. But when he became judge, he
hated the building's drab appearance.[57]

## THE DOCKET OF THE DISTRICT COURT DURING THE DEPRESSION YEARS

In light of the expansiveness of the New Deal, one might expect that the District Court for the Southern District of Ohio, as well as other district courts,
would be inundated with suits contesting the new laws. Surprisingly, this was
not the case. Most cases commenced nationwide and in the Southern District
of Ohio were criminal cases (see table 6.2, *infra*). Nationwide, in 1935, nearly
80 percent of the cases commenced were criminal. This declined to 59 percent in 1939. Only 20 percent and 19 percent, respectively, were civil cases in
which the United States was a party. Most of the criminal cases were routine
crimes against property—theft, larceny, embezzlement, and the like. The
judges generally handled them quickly, and guilty pleas were the basis for
about 90 percent of all convictions.[58] The so-called *Cemetery Case* was a notable
exception, the government prosecuting forty defendants for using the mails
to defraud the public in a scheme for selling cemetery lots. The Columbus
trial lasted from September 1939 until April 1940, before the jury convicted
all the defendants.[59] Another case that started in 1946 was not tried until
1957. But, at the time, it made headlines as the government prosecuted the
mobster George C. "Bugs" Moran and his cohorts for committing larceny of
a federal bank.[60]

Because of the Depression, bankruptcy cases flooded in, and the Southern
District of Ohio heard many more than the national average—2,331, for example, filed in 1935 in the Southern District of Ohio compared to an average of only 823 per district overall. But the U.S. commissioners disposed of
most of these cases, with the district court judges hearing appeals only when
constitutional issues or questions of statutory interpretation arose.[61]

*In re Cole* exemplifies the controversial cases. It also points up the battle between the Democratic Congress and the conservative Supreme Court over the
constitutionality of New Deal legislation and illustrates the judicial restraint
philosophy embraced by the judges in southern Ohio. Congress had enacted
the Frazier Lemke Act to provide debt relief to farmers. Section 75(s) placed
a moratorium on foreclosures, authorizing district court judges to restrain
secured creditors from seeking to foreclose, in proceedings in state courts,
farm property for nonpayment of mortgages and other debts.[62] After the
Supreme Court declared section 75(s) unconstitutional,[63] Congress, on August 28, 1935, enacted an amended version to overcome the Court's objec-

tions. At issue in *In re Cole* was the constitutionality of the amended section 75(s). Already, one circuit court and two district judges elsewhere in the nation had declared the amended section unconstitutional, but two other district court judges had upheld the provision.[64]

*In re Cole* involved fifteen bankruptcy cases filed by groups of secured creditors against debtor farmers. Before his death, Hough had enjoined the creditors from continuing foreclosure proceedings in state courts against their debtors. After Congress enacted the amended section 75(s), the debtors again filed petitions seeking bankruptcy protection. The secured creditors protested, filing motions challenging the amended legislation's constitutionality. They argued, as they had argued against the original act, that the law exceeded Congress's authority because its purpose was not to legislate for bankrupts but to provide "a moratorium to farmer debtors—a relief not within the bankruptcy jurisdiction of Congress."[65] Second, the creditors insisted that the statute deprived them of their property without due process of law in violation of the Fifth Amendment because it deprived them from taking action against those in default of their loans. Finally, they contended that the law violates Section I of Article IV of the U.S. Constitution by denying full faith and credit to the judgments of state courts.

Judge Nevin sided with the debtors, summarizing the classic argument for judicial restraint. He maintained that there were two "cardinal principles" judges must follow when considering the constitutionality of congressional legislation. First, the exercise of judicial review "is one of grave responsibility and a matter of much delicacy. Courts should approach constitutional questions with great deliberation, exercising their power in this respect with the greatest possible caution and even reluctance. They should *never* declare a statute void, unless its invalidity, in their judgment, *is beyond reasonable doubt.*"[66] Second, Nevin stated, "the legal presumption is that every law enacted by Congress is constitutional" and that plaintiffs have the burden of proving otherwise. Thus, Nevin concluded, he would presume the law constitutional "until and unless it has been declared otherwise either by the United States Circuit Court of Appeals of this (Sixth) Circuit, or the Supreme Court of the United States."[67]

In the civil arena, the judges continued to hear many of the same kinds of routine cases traditional in federal courts, with private parties litigating contract or patent disputes and the like. The number of patent cases, however, increased for the Southern District of Ohio, perhaps due to the national reputations of Nevin and Druffel as experts in this highly specialized area. Both regularly assessed whether patents were valid, whether new products were patentable, and whether others had infringed on valid patents.[68] The one unusual civil case dealt with freedom of speech and the press. In *Zimmerman v. Village of London,* Judge Underwood granted the Jehovah's Witnesses a permanent injunction, enjoining village officials from enforcing the village's ordinance against door-to-door solicitation against them. He held that restricting this religious group from distributing their pamphlets denied their rights to free speech and a free press "protected against state infringement by the Fourteenth Amendment."[69]

The court also heard several cases dealing with the new Federal Rules of Civil Procedure that had been adopted in 1938. The judges needed to define the requirements for summary judgment and delineate the scope of discovery.[70] In addition, the judges began experimenting with a new technique that would alter their role as adjudicators. The pretrial conference emerged as a natural outgrowth of the new rules of civil procedure. By 1941, 111 of the 178 district court judges reported using pretrial conferences not only to promote settlements but also to clarify issues, handle evidentiary disputes before trial, and establish a calendar for trial preparation. Underwood was reported to hold pretrial conferences in 40 to 50 percent of his cases, an unusually large number for the times.[71] Eventually this innovation would contribute to the emergence of federal judges as administrators as well as adjudicators, with much of their time being spent outside the courtroom.[72]

Although criminal prosecutions, bankruptcy cases, and procedural issues took up much of the court's time, challenges to New Deal legislation, to regulations by the state of Ohio and various municipalities, and to governmental authority were most significant. In many districts, judges struck down much of this legislation, finding that the challenged laws deprived complainants of their liberty and property without due process of law in violation of the Fifth and Fourteenth Amendments, or that federal laws infringed upon the powers of the state in violation of the Tenth Amendment or unconstitutionally delegated legislative powers to administrative boards. The judges of the Southern District of Ohio, however, regularly upheld challenged statutes, deferring to the legislature, be it city, state, or federal.

The judges first confronted litigation challenging New Deal–style regulations by the state of Ohio and various municipalities. In 1936, in *Walker v. Chapman,* Nevin and Underwood along with circuit judge Florence Allen, sitting as a three-judge panel, upheld Ohio's minimum wage law a year before the Supreme Court upheld a Washington state minimum wage statute in *West Coast Hotel v. Parrish.*[73] Distinguishing Ohio's statute from a Washington, D.C., minimum wage law the Supreme Court had struck down in 1923 in *Adkins v. Children's Hospital,*[74] the panel found that Ohio's law did not deprive complainants of their liberty or property without due process of law or deny them the equal protection of the laws because it fixed the minimum wage as a "fair wage" "commensurate with the value of the service or class of service rendered."[75] In *Feldman v. City of Cincinnati,* city barbers challenged a Cincinnati ordinance regulating the hours barber shops could be open as a violation of their Fourteenth Amendment due process and equal protection rights. Citing *West Coast Hotel,* which had just been decided, Nevin, again exercising judicial restraint, upheld the regulation, broadly proclaiming that governmental bodies have wide discretion in exercising their police powers and that courts will not examine the justice, wisdom, or expedience of their laws. Though admitting that he had grave doubts about the wisdom and constitutionality of the statute, he said that doubt is resolved in favor of a statute's validity; only clearly unreasonable laws would be struck down as violating the Fourteenth Amendment.[76]

The judges also adjudicated disputes between state and federal authority. For example, in *United Fuel Gas Co. v. PUCO,* a three-judge panel composed of Allen, Nevin, and Underwood declared that once Congress regulated the sale of natural gas in interstate commerce in the Natural Gas Act it had preempted the field, thus invalidating the Ohio Public Utilities Commission's attempt to regulate rates within the state.[77]

On the federal level, the judges were often called upon to rule in the relatively new area of administrative law. Here, too, they tended to uphold the authority of administrative agencies to make rules and regulations to carry out the legislation they were administering and declaring that such rules and regulations had the force of law. For example, in 1934 in *Ohio v. United States* and *Wheeling & Lake Erie Railway Co. v. United States,* a three-judge panel composed of now circuit judge Hickenlooper along with district judges Hough and Nevin upheld the delegation of broad powers to the new administrative agencies created by the myriad of New Deal laws. Specifically, in this case, the panel first held that, in reviewing orders by the ICC, the court would inquire only whether the agency made its decision on sufficient evidence but would not examine its wisdom or its reasoning. Second, the panel affirmed the commission's power to adjust intrastate rates when it found that necessary to prevent discrimination between intrastate and interstate rates.[78] Similarly, in *Ohio v. United States Civil Service Commission,* Underwood held that all administrative agencies have rule-making power and those rules and regulations have the force of law as if passed by Congress.[79]

Finally, the judges of the Southern District of Ohio regularly upheld New Deal legislation, construing statutes liberally to carry out what they viewed as Congress's purpose. Nevin explicitly declared that all acts of Congress were to be presumed constitutional and the burden of proving otherwise was on the party challenging them. Of course many judges made similar avowals, but Nevin meant it.[80] However, no matter what their personal views were of the law, the judges had to follow the Supreme Court's decisions. In *Lohrey v. Conner, P. Lorillard Co. v. Conner,* and almost twenty other suits,[81] several grocers, tobacco producers, and others challenged the Agricultural Adjustment Act's processing tax. In 1936, Nevin reluctantly issued an injunction to prevent the tax from being collected based on the Supreme Court's ruling in *United States v. Butler*[82] that the statute was unconstitutional.[83] This was the only time the court did not enforce a New Deal statute.

When there was no clear mandate from the Supreme Court to do otherwise, the judges of the Southern District of Ohio followed their own proregulatory instincts. In doing so, they brought to Ohioans another clear message about the supremacy of federal law, often in opposition to the views of the majority of Ohio's citizens. Although the New Deal had helped countless Ohio farmers, business people, and average citizens, by 1938 the majority of Ohio's voters turned against the Democratic program, electing John W. Bricker governor and Robert Taft U.S. senator. According to one historian, the Republican victory in Ohio in 1938 "reflected a populist uprising . . . in small towns, rural areas, and cities such as Columbus against the growing assertiveness of labor and the celebration of government as the solution to Ohio's woes."[84] Ignoring such sentiment, Nevin refused to restrain the National Labor Relations Board from proceeding with a hearing against the Ohio Custom Garment Company.[85] In *Dayton Power & Light Co. v. Mathewson*[86] and *Ohio Custom Garment Co. v. Locket*,[87] the court upheld the National Labor Relations Act, even applying it to a Dayton utility company that did business only in the Dayton area.[88]

The court most clearly showed its willingness to recognize the federal government's broad power to deal with the economy in *United States v. Krechting*. The government filed suit against twenty-four independent Cincinnati milk producers that failed to comply with the Agricultural Marketing Agreement Act of 1937, having disagreed with the Department of Agriculture's conclusion that the statute applied to them. They argued that this could not be the case because they produced milk only for a local market and that none of their products ever entered "the current of commerce." Further, they contended that, even if the law could be applied to them, the statute was invalid because it unconstitutionally delegated legislative power to the secretary of agriculture. Finally, they maintained that the act deprived them of their property without due process of law in violation of the Fifth Amendment. After Judge Druffel listened to four days of "heated" arguments from both sides, he rejected each of defendants' contentions. Citing a recent Supreme Court decision, he first simply declared that the act did not unconstitutionally delegate power to the secretary of agriculture nor take property in violation of the Fifth Amendment. The government had provided the dairies sufficient due process by holding hearings at which they had testified and by allowing all the dairies to vote on appropriate allotments.[89]

But most important, in answering the dairies' challenge to the scope of Congress's interstate commerce power, Druffel anticipated the Supreme Court's decision in *Wickard v. Filburn*.[90] He explained, "Whether or not the defendants are engaged in the business of handling milk in the current of interstate commerce . . . must depend upon whether their business is to be treated as local and individual, or whether the milk industry in the marketing area is to be treated as an entirety." Taking an expansive view, Druffel found that to accomplish Congress's purpose to regulate the industry as a whole, the local dairies must come within the scope of the law. Congressional efforts "would be futile if individual handlers and producers were permitted to pursue their own individual and separate courses." And whereas America protects the sanctity of private property and contract rights, neither is "absolute; for government cannot exist if the citizen may at will use his property to the detriment of his fellows, or exercise his freedom of contract to work them harm. Equally fundamental with the private right is that of the public to regulate it in the common interest."[91]

*Wickard v. Filburn,* known as *Filburn v. Helke* when a three-judge district court heard it, is probably the most significant case ever decided in the District Court for the Southern District of Ohio. The Supreme Court's ruling on appeal represented the culmination of the New Deal's constitutional revolution, whereby that Court expanded the commerce clause to enable Congress to regulate anything that had a "substantial economic effect" on commerce, using the "aggregation" principle. That is, the courts did not look at the economic effect of a single person but how that person's contribution to the economy, taken with all others similarly situated, affected commerce. Culminating with *Filburn,* federalism was transformed. As the Supreme Court later said in *United States v. Lopez, Filburn* was "perhaps the most far reaching example of Commerce Clause authority over intrastate activity."[92]

Ironically, when Druffel, Nevin, and Allen heard the case, they did not see it in such a light. The case started when Roscoe Filburn, a small farmer in Montgomery County who raised poultry and dairy cattle and some wheat, sought an injunction enjoining Secretary of Agriculture Claude R. Wickard from collecting a penalty tax Wickard had imposed on Filburn for growing twice his allotment of wheat. Filburn claimed that he was not subject to the wheat allotment because all of his wheat was consumed on his farm and thus never entered interstate commerce. He claimed that the attempt to regulate wheat production not bound for interstate commerce violated the Tenth Amendment by infringing on powers reserved to the state. By a two-to-one decision, Circuit Judge Allen dissenting, the panel granted Filburn his injunction. Druffel, writing for himself and Nevin, focused solely on the penalty imposed. When Filburn planted the wheat, the penalty had been fifteen cents a bushel. But before harvesting, wheat farmers in a national referendum approved a new marketing quota with a new penalty of forty-nine cents per bushel. Filburn claimed the referendum was invalid because the farmers had been misled by Wickard's statements. That claim was not as important to the panel as was the retroactive nature of the penalty, which, Druffel held, amounted "to a taking of plaintiff's property without due process." But this decision never invalidated the statute itself; it simply enjoined the secretary of agriculture "from collecting the penalty for the farm marketing excess over and above fifteen cents per bushel." Indeed, the court never reviewed the validity of the Agricultural Adjustment Act or the constitutionality of regulating the amount of wheat locally. Implicitly, however, the court upheld the statute by enjoining only any penalty over the original fifteen cents.[93]

It was only on appeal that the Supreme Court transformed the case into a major decision on federalism, upholding both the penalty and the statute, even when it applied to homegrown wheat. First, it declared that just because a penalty might lead to an inequitable result does not mean it deprives one of his property without due process of law in violation of the Fifth Amendment. But more important, the Court, sounding much like Druffel in *Krechting*, held that regulating the production of homegrown wheat fell within Congress's commerce power and therefore did not violate the Tenth Amendment. "A factor of such volume and variability as home-consumed wheat would have a substantial influence on price and market conditions. . . . Home-grown wheat in this sense competes with wheat in commerce." Thus, Congress could properly regulate the amount of wheat grown for home consumption because of its "substantial effect" on the total supply and demand of the crop.[94]

## THE IMPACT OF WORLD WAR II ON THE SOUTHERN DISTRICT OF OHIO

With America's entry into World War II in December 1941, the United States geared up for an all-out effort. In anticipation of war, Congress passed the Selective Service Act and the Second War Powers Act, created the Office of Price Administration (OPA) to control the prices of all sorts of war-related materials, consumer goods, and rents, and enacted other statutes related to the war effort like those requiring the registration of aliens or making it illegal to falsely wear a uniform. These new laws and other war-related activities dramatically increased the number of civil cases brought in the district courts. The percentage of civil cases in which the United States was a party rose steeply. In 1934, private civil cases had exceeded those in which the government was involved three to one. But by the end of 1941, the situation was reversed; civil cases in which the government was a party slightly exceeded the number of private cases. And by the end of 1944, the number of U.S. civil cases was twice the number of private civil cases. Patent and copyright litigation as well as private civil litigation based on diversity dropped, because most people became more preoccupied with war activities and litigants, witnesses, and lawyers went off to war.[95]

In 1941, government land condemnations were responsible for the initial increase, representing more than half the civil docket in that year, when the government took land for defense programs and other war-related activities. The government condemned land throughout the Southern District of Ohio, in rural areas like Pickaway, Perry, Guernsey, Coshocton, Washington, and Monroe counties as well as in Columbus and Dayton.[96] These land condemnations often created hardships for those who lost their facilities. Nevin told the story of the government's condemnation of four of the fourteen stories of the Third National Bank Building in Dayton in April 1942. Forty-six tenants, including well-established law firms, real estate companies, financial enterprises, and large insurance companies, many of which had occupied their offices for years and held long-term leases, lost their office space and were then unable to find other accommodations because of the "demands of war." Still, Nevin approved the condemnation, which Congress had authorized in the Second War Powers Act, explaining that Congress had full power to pursue the war vigorously, including the power to condemn property needed for "military, naval, or other war purposes."[97]

Violations of price and rent controls imposed by the OPA soon overtook land condemnations as the major type of case heard by the court. For the Southern District of Ohio, specifically, of the 594 civil cases commenced by the United States in the fiscal year ending June 1945, 354 were actions by the OPA. Of the 527 criminal cases commenced during the same year, 132 were violations of OPA regulations.[98] But, although the government was determined to enforce OPA regulations vigorously, on most occasions it merely sought to enjoin the wrongdoer. Most were routine cases, the defendant generally failing to appear and the court granting a default judgment.[99] On occasion, however, more serious legal issues arose. Druffel willingly gave the government extensive powers. In *United States v. Lichter,* for example, he broadly upheld the government's ability, based on its war powers, to determine whether a government contractor received excessive profits from his war contracts, even if the contractor had negotiated his war contract before the statute's passage as long as the contractor received the money after the statute went into effect. Moreover, Druffel held that Congress's decision to grant the federal tax court exclusive jurisdiction to determine all questions of law and fact was not an unconstitutional delegation of power nor did it deprive defendants of their property without due process.[100]

The few extant cases do not indicate much enthusiasm on the part of Underwood for giving the federal government free reign. For example, in an OPA suit to recover damages from a defendant charged with selling merchandise above the ceiling price, the government, during discovery, sought answers to interrogatories that would have required the company to do a complete audit of all its records. Underwood denied the request, holding it to be too "burdensome, vexatious and onerous."[101]

Violations of the Selective Service Act, while another significant component of the court's docket, never reached the numbers seen during World War I. Violations included failure to register, failure to have a registration card, failure to return the required questionnaire, giving false information on the registration form or the questionnaire, failure to report for one's physical examination, failure to report for induction, or interference with government officials in the administration of the draft. Nationwide, between October 1940 and June 30, 1941, there were 31,640 reported violations, but, according to the Administrative Office of the United States Courts, most were "unintentional."[102] Thus, the government prosecuted only a small portion. During the three and a half years of World War II, the government prosecuted only 22,000 violations of the Selective Service Act, compared to the 47,000 violations prosecuted for violations in less than two years during World War I.[103]

In the Southern District of Ohio, violations of the Selective Service Act represented only about 10 to 15 percent of the court's criminal docket. For example, of the 527 criminal cases commenced in fiscal 1945, only 55 were for violations of the Selective Service Act. And even at the height of the war, in 1942 and 1943, the Southern District of Ohio tried only 60 to 100 violations each year.[104] Moreover, for southern Ohio, there were no spectacular cases as there had been during World War I.[105] Routine cases of those who refused to be drafted and could not get any exemption generally resulted in five years imprisonment. And there was not much hope for those who believed they should have been granted an exemption. Juries convicted the defendants in all twenty-one cases that went to trial in Dayton in 1943.[106]

In *In re Berue* the court willingly extended the military's jurisdiction over a civilian under special circumstances. Jacob Berue was a merchant seaman on a ship that was part of a large convoy carrying military supplies to Africa through "waters infested by submarines and other naval craft of the Axis Nations." During the trip, "an incident occurred" between Berue and "certain officers and members of the crew." Once the convoy reached Casablanca, the army convened a general court-martial, which convicted Berue of violating military regulations. After sentencing, Berue was sent to the federal reformatory in Chillicothe, Ohio. Berue then filed a writ of habeas corpus, challenging the army's jurisdiction over him as a civilian. Underwood held that Berue was subject to court martial for violations of military regulations, citing the Second Article of War in the U.S. Code, which provided that "all persons accompanying . . . the Armies of the United States" during time of war were subject to military jurisdiction. Although Underwood carefully documented in what ways he concluded the Berue was, indeed, a person "accompanying" the army in time of war, he never questioned the constitutionality of the war article.[107]

After the war, the court had to deal with many cases involving veterans' rights. In the Selective Service Act, Congress had protected the jobs and seniority rights of those who served in the armed forces. This privilege sometimes clashed with union collective bargaining contracts. At other times, the employer claimed there were no positions open with which to recognize the returning soldier's seniority privileges. Although the court held that the veterans' rights were independent of any union contract,[108] it allowed employers some time and flexibility to make adjustments based on the needs of their businesses.[109] And the court was not going to allow veterans more benefits than the statute provided. Underwood, for example, dismissed Roy Brown's suit to have his time spent in the army in World War II counted for the purpose of determining how much vacation he was due.[110]

## THE 1950s

Although in most ways life returned to normal after World War II, the federal government continued to play a significant role in Ohio's economic life, subsidizing highway construction, industrial and commercial growth, and the development of new technologies, especially those related to military needs and the aircraft industry. With continued federal regulations and an increasingly nationalized economy, the federal district court dockets continued to grow. The Southern District of Ohio experienced dramatic increases. In the first four years of the 1950s, its docket nearly doubled. At the start of the decade, litigants filed slightly fewer than a thousand cases a year. Of them, 37 percent were criminal cases, 46 percent civil cases in which the United States was a party, and only 17 percent civil cases between private parties. Four years later, parties filed 1,813 cases, although the distribution of cases remained about the same. This meant that the Southern District of Ohio's civil case load was larger than the national average (292 cases per Southern District of Ohio judge compared to 222 nationwide), whereas its criminal docket averaged slightly less that the national average (162 cases per judge in the Southern District of Ohio compared to 169 nationally).[111]

Although every Southern District of Ohio judge experienced this increasing case load, each heard different types of cases based on differences in the local communities. In the criminal area, the highest percentage of crimes in Cincinnati at the start of the decade were crimes against property, such as theft, embezzlement, and the like, representing 25 percent of all criminal cases. Second, at 17 percent, were postal-related violations, such as theft of mails or sending obscene matter through the mails. Drug-related violations and making false statements on some government form tied for third at 14 percent. In Columbus, the leading category of crime was drug-related violations, at 32 percent. Seventeen percent were crimes against property, with violations of interstate commerce regulations and income tax evasion tied for third at 10 percent each. In Dayton, as in Columbus, drug-related violations dominated the criminal docket, representing 46 percent of all indictments; almost 30 percent of the docket were thefts and the like. Dayton maintained this pattern throughout the decade. Columbus, however, during the next two years, experienced a rash of men refusing induction into the armed services, with some even refusing civilian alternative service. There was also an increase in those charged with income tax evasion. Such cases continued throughout the rest of the decade.[112]

In the civil area, approximately half the government's cases in the Southern District of Ohio were against those violating rent maximums that had been imposed during World War II and continued after the war. The other half involved government efforts to collect money owed it, generally for defaults of Federal Housing Administration or Veterans Administration loans or to collect for overpayments it had made for various allowances due servicemen and their families. There were also several cases in the Dayton area to collect fines against farmers who had exceeded their wheat or other farm allotments. Diversity cases exhibited the same pattern as they had for years—mostly personal injury cases, breach of contract cases, and patent, trademark, and copyright litigation. Occasionally the court was also called upon to decide labor-management disputes over collective bargaining agreements.[113]

Initially, the three judges presiding over these dockets were Nevin in Dayton, Underwood in Columbus, and Druffel in Cincinnati. In early 1953, however, President Dwight D. Eisenhower nominated Lester L. Cecil to replace Nevin, who had died suddenly at the end of 1952.[114] Cecil was Eisenhower's first judicial appointment. He won the nomination largely because of his impressive credentials and his personal popularity. Born on a farm near Piqua, in Miami County, Ohio, Cecil grew up in West Milton, where his father worked for $17.50 a week, twelve hours a day, seven days a week, fueling a boiler to run a traction line. Always wanting to be a lawyer, the future judge worked from the time he was thirteen to make that dream come true. After serving in World War I, Cecil finally began his legal career, serving as prosecuting attorney for the city of Dayton, a judge in Dayton's municipal court, and then judge of the Montgomery County Court of Common Pleas. A moderate, Cecil believed the court's main function was to "secure justice" and protect individual rights.[115]

The judges, in approaching their cases, generally continued to support broad powers for the federal government, enforcing federal law vigorously and interpreting federal statutes broadly. Although most litigation was ordinary and routine, the judges demonstrated this jurisprudential approach in a few landmark cases. In a criminal case brought under the Sherman Act, the grand jury indicted several milk distributors for conspiracy to fix prices in violation of the antitrust laws. The defendants moved to dismiss, arguing that their conspiracy did not involve interstate commerce. Nevin denied their motion, taking a broad view of interstate commerce and the Sherman Act. First, he declared, that, based on the Sherman Act, "price fixing is illegal per se." Moreover, he held that the conspiracy here charged operated as a direct restraint on such commerce by causing a decrease in the volume of milk sold. Nevin noted that, even if the quantity involved is small, "it is not the substantial quantity" that matters. "It is the substantial effect on interstate commerce."[116]

In addition to vigilantly prosecuting conspiracies restraining trade in the United States, in the 1950s, the Department of Justice attacked a number of private international cartels. In *United States v. Holophane Co.,* after a two-day bench trial, Underwood found that Holophane had violated the Sherman Act by agreeing with several foreign corporations to divide the marketing area to suppress competition. Underwood held that the evidence showed that these agreements were not necessary to protect the defendants' businesses. Rather, they were designed to restrain trade. But more important, Underwood asserted broad federal court jurisdiction, placing the case in the mainstream of federal court decisions maintaining the government's power to exercise control over not only transnational business transactions, but also foreign corporations, voiding agreements made outside the United States as long as it involved American corporations and trade within the United States.[117]

The Southern District of Ohio also heard the first case in the nation charging a union official with filing a false affidavit in violation of the Taft-Hartley Act of 1947, which required union officials to swear that they were not members of the Communist Party. The government filed its indictment in Dayton, and Cecil initially denied defendant E. Melvin Hupman's motion to dismiss, but also refused the government's request to increase the bail. On the motion of the U.S. attorney, the case then moved to Druffel's courtroom in Cincinnati. The trial, a lengthy and hard-fought battle, began on August 19, 1953. After four days of voir dire, challenges, and objections, the jury was finally empanelled. After two weeks of testimony, the jurors deliberated for two days before advising Druffel that they could not agree. He discharged them, but overruled defense's motions to dismiss or to return the trial to Dayton. The second trial began in Cincinnati on January 6, 1954. After two days spent empanelling the jury, both sides presented their evidence in a week's time. On January 15, the jury found Hupman guilty, and Druffel sentenced him to five years imprisonment and a $5,000 fine.[118]

On appeal, Hupman claimed that Druffel had improperly charged the jury on the standard needed to prove perjury. The defense asked Druffel to include in his jury instructions the rule, followed by the Supreme Court, "that a statement made under oath can be proved false only by two oaths directly asserting the contrary, or one such oath supported by corroborative evidence." If that instruction had been given, Hupman probably would have been acquitted, because the evidence against him was circumstantial. Druffel refused, employing the common-law exception to the rule that provides that where "the nature of the defendant's statement was such that its falsity could not be proved by direct evidence, circumstantial evidence is sufficient." The Sixth Circuit Court of Appeals sided with Druffel, upholding Hupman's conviction. It found Druffel's instructions to the jury to be "fair, substantially cover[ing] the crucial questions of the law," and the evidence to be sufficient for conviction. Moreover, the appellate court praised Druffel for his patience in assuring that the defendant had "a fair trial." The court noted that Druffel had "remained commendably calm and impartial," despite "the continual interruptions, exceptions, and complaints of appellant's counsel."

And after the Department of Justice circulated Druffel's charge to the jury, these instructions became the model judges used across the nation.[119]

The Southern District of Ohio also heard one of the first challenges to school desegregation in a northern state after the landmark 1954 Supreme Court decision, *Brown v. Board of Education*.[120] The case pitting the Hillsboro Board of Education against several African American families drew "nation-wide attention"[121] and national legal talent. Thurgood Marshall, who would later be appointed to the Supreme Court, and NAACP attorney Constance Baker Motley of New York, along with Dayton attorney James H. McGee, who later became mayor of that city, and Russell L. Carter represented the African American plaintiffs. The Hillsboro city solicitor, James D. Hapner, aided by Timothy S. Hogan, soon to be appointed a judge for the Southern District of Ohio, represented the Hillsboro Board of Education.[122]

All parties agreed to the basic facts leading to the suit. Hillsboro, Ohio, although it had an integrated high school and had integrated students in the seventh and eighth grades, had, for at least fifteen years, segregated its elementary schoolchildren. Whites attended Washington and Webster schools, where each classroom had its own white teacher who taught separate grades in separate rooms. African American children went to Lincoln School, where African American teachers taught all six grades in two classrooms. Immediately after the *Brown* decision, seven black school children registered at the white schools. Initially, each was assigned a seat, but the school board then closed the schools. A week later, it reassigned the black children to Lincoln School after it developed, for the first time, school attendance zones. The zone for Lincoln comprised two completely separate parts of the city in order to include African American children who lived in the northeastern section of the city as well as those who lived in the southeast. The African American families then filed suit in Druffel's court, seeking a preliminary and then a permanent injunction enjoining the Hillsboro Board of Education from enforcing its policy of racial segregation. The board argued that it planned to integrate the schools once it rebuilt the two white schools but that construction would not be completed until 1956 or 1957. Until then, overcrowding dictated the organization of school zones as the board had mandated them.[123]

Initially, in a decision that some speculated "may set something of a national precedent,"[124] Druffel sought a strategy of delay, ordering that all proceedings be continued until two weeks after the Supreme Court formulated a final enforcement decree in the *Brown* case.[125] The plaintiffs appealed to the Sixth Circuit Court of Appeals, which ordered Druffel to proceed with a trial.[126] Druffel obeyed, but, after the trial, although Ohio and federal law prohibited segregation and Druffel found that the development of the school zones was a mere "subterfuge to permit the continuance of Lincoln School for Negro children exclusively," he denied the injunction on the grounds that it would disrupt the white schools. Pointing out that the school board was "officially on record as favoring complete integration," he held that, under Ohio law, school boards had broad discretionary power and he was not going to interfere.[127]

The Sixth Circuit Court of Appeals, in strong terms, reversed him. It found that not only had "the Board abused its discretion and violated state and constitutional law" but also that "the District Court [had] abused its discretion in refusing to enjoin this continued violation of law." The court remanded the case back to Druffel, ordering him to rewrite his conclusions of law and to issue the injunction.[128] In an "action described by Cincinnati newsmen as 'unprecedented for his court,'" Druffel said he would refuse the appellate court's order unless the Hillsboro board assured him that the injunction would not cause "chaos and confusion" in the schools. The judge then met privately with the superintendent of schools and not only urged the school board to appeal but also said he would seek an appeal in his own name. He also informed the press that he was going to ask the Cincinnati Bar Association "to appoint someone to represent him before the Supreme Court on the question of whether his court had 'abused its discretion'" in refusing to issue the original injunction.[129] After the Sixth Circuit Court of Appeals denied the board's request for a rehearing and after the Supreme Court denied certiorari, however, Druffel did obey the circuit court mandate, issuing an order requiring the school board to admit the litigants to the white schools immediately and to integrate all elementary schools by the start of the new school year.[130]

Although in the end Druffel upheld the federal law and the orders from the higher court, his protests did nothing to enhance the court's dignity and might have encouraged some to resist federal authority. As the *Hillsboro News-Herald* editorialized, this "small Southern Ohio agricultural community" of "admitted 'gradualists'" resented becoming "the Northern whipping boy of the United States Supreme Court." Citizens believed that they had made a commitment to integration while many other northern communities had not, but that they had real problems that the higher courts refused to acknowledge. As a result, the *News-Herald* claimed, "the faith of some of our residents in law abidance, citizenship and morality . . . has suffered a deep, unhealing wound." The community will have to struggle "to find a way to restore their faith in democracy."[131]

By the middle of the twentieth century, the District Court for the Southern District of Ohio had become a "modern" court. Every day, it faced issues that affected the political, economic, and social order of Ohio and the nation. It had issued important decisions enlarging the scope of federal and regulatory authority, determining the extent of citizens' rights and responsibilities, and confronting the new issue of racial equality in education. Generally, the judges of southern Ohio exercised judicial restraint, deferring to legislatures and viewing the scope of federal power expansively. Their position on individual rights differed with the cases and the times. But, with the exception of the Hillsboro case, they accepted their place within the federal court system, upholding the decisions of the appellate courts even when they might disagree with those decisions.

From the 1960s on, the court would confront an even more litigious world. The judges would face the challenges of ever-increasing dockets of cases whose decisions would continue to affect their communities in a myriad of ways. The judges of southern Ohio developed a variety of innovative techniques to deal with their new challenges.

# 6

# THE COURT TRANSFORMED

*Adjudication, Arbitration, and Administration, 1960–2003*

THE 1960S BEGAN THE FINAL transformation of district courts. New issues and a tremendous increase in litigation confronted the judges. With new federal statutes and new constitutional interpretations developed by the Supreme Court, district court judges became arbiters in disputes over the meaning and extent of constitutional rights.[1] This role became extremely important as Ohioans experienced the frustrations of life at the end of the twentieth century. Economically, Ohio stagnated. Both agriculture and industry experienced hard times. Although agribusiness still made Ohio a leading agricultural state, those who owned family farms found it increasingly difficult to compete. By 1985, the number of Ohio farms had decreased by more than 50 percent, while the average size of a farm had nearly doubled. Obsolete factories, unimaginative corporate leadership, and high labor costs threatened Ohio's industrial base. And as Ohio's industries struggled to compete with other regions and nations, unions lost influence. In the 1970s alone, for example, Ohio suffered over an 18 percent decline in jobs. Attempted corporate takeovers, labor conflicts, and other economic disputes wound up in litigation in district court. Noneconomic issues also plagued the state. Pollution from uranium plants such as Fernald, near

Cincinnati, protests over the war in Vietnam, and demands from various groups for protection of their civil rights raised fears among many "that traditional values were disintegrating."[2]

Ohioans increasingly looked to the judges of the federal district court to help them solve such problems. Some saw the court as an institution that could right the wrongs they believed governments had inflicted on them, wrongs that violated their civil rights and civil liberties. The government asked judges and juries to enforce its laws so it could protect citizens against drugs, fraud, and other problems plaguing modern society. Corporations and average citizens filed suits, hoping the judicial system could resolve their economic, political, or rights-based disputes. Thus, the impact of the decisions rendered by the judges and juries on their communities and the nation become increasingly significant. As a reporter for the *Dayton Daily News* noted, as Americans embark on the twenty-first century federal judges carry the burden of deciding "the limits of our most basic freedoms, including those of privacy, reproduction, dying and speech."[3]

With these new responsibilities, the work load of the district court increased steadily, and the cases became more complex. There were desegregation cases, litigation over the state's reapportionment, and massive class action disputes involving billions of dollars. By 1985, the District Court for the Southern District of Ohio was the busiest in the nation. More civil cases were filed and closed by that court than in any other. Even so, the court had more civil cases pending per judge than in any other federal district court.[4]

Congress finally saw the need for additional judges to help ease the work load. At the start of the 1960s, the Southern District of Ohio had three authorized judges. Since then, Congress has increased that number almost threefold. In 1961, Congress authorized one additional judgeship; it then added two more in the 1970s, one more in 1984, and the last in 1990, bringing the total to eight authorized judges.[5]

At the beginning of the 1960s, Judge Carl A. Weinman sat in Dayton, Underwood in Columbus, and Druffel in Cincinnati. President Eisenhower had nominated Weinman in 1959 to replace Cecil, whom he had appointed to the Sixth Circuit Court of Appeals. From Steubenville, Weinman had been active in local politics, a member of the state Republican committee, a two-term city solicitor, and a Jefferson County Court of Common Pleas judge for twelve years before returning to private practice, where he remained until his appointment to the federal bench.[6]

In 1961, Weinman, Druffel, and Underwood were joined by John Weld Peck, nominated by Democratic president John F. Kennedy to replace Druffel, who took senior status although he maintained an active docket until his death in 1967. The nephew of the district judge John W. Peck of the 1920s, the new appointee was known as Cincinnati's "resident judge" because of the family's longtime roots in that city. Born in the Cincinnati suburban town of

Wyoming and educated locally, Peck joined his father's law firm after he was admitted to the bar in 1938. After serving in World War II, he returned to private practice and political involvement, being one of the cofounders of the Hamilton County Democratic Veterans' Club. He served on Ohio's Tax Commission, the Hamilton County Court of Common Pleas, and the Ohio Supreme Court. An "incurable idealist," he opposed the death penalty. When sentencing defendants in criminal cases, he strove to find a "balance between justice and mercy." Peck was also innovative, using pretrial conferences, jury questionnaires, and judge-run voir dire to help dispose of cases more quickly and keep the ever-expanding docket under control.[7]

When President Lyndon B. Johnson elevated Peck to the Sixth Circuit Court of Appeals in 1966, he replaced him on the district court with Timothy S. Hogan, originally from Wellston, Ohio. Hogan's father had been Ohio's attorney general from 1910 to 1914, and all of his siblings were lawyers. His nephew is currently a U.S. magistrate judge for the Southern District of Ohio. Upon his return from Europe after World War II, Hogan became a partner in Cohen, Baron, Todd & Hogan, earning the reputation as one of the finest attorneys in southern Ohio. He was also politically active. He joined Peck in founding the Democratic veterans' group, actively campaigned for many Democratic candidates, and ran unsuccessfully for several positions himself. "Probably the most brilliant man who ever sat" on the court of the Southern District of Ohio, he was a casual and unpretentious person.[8]

Hogan was joined in Cincinnati by another judge, the Southern District of Ohio's fourth, after Congress approved the new judgeship in 1966.[9] Johnson nominated David S. Porter for that post. Before his appointment to the federal bench, Porter spent most of his legal career as a judge of the Court of Common Pleas of Miami County. To him, the goal of the courts was to maintain individual rights. "In the area of civil rights," he explained, "the courts are simply doing for the individual what it has done all along for corporations."[10]

In 1966, Columbus too had a new judge, Joseph P. Kinneary, appointed by Johnson to replace Underwood, who took senior status that year. Active in Democratic politics, Kinneary was appointed assistant attorney general of Ohio before he became U.S. attorney for the Southern District of Ohio in 1961. Retiring in 2001, Kinneary served as judge for the Southern District for thirty-five years, making him second in longevity to Judge Leavitt.[11]

The 1970s saw two new judges, one taking a new position authorized by Congress in 1970,[12] and the other a replacement for Weinman, who took senior status in 1973. In 1971, President Richard M. Nixon nominated Carl B. Rubin to the new judgeship. An active Republican, Rubin directed the congressional campaigns of Robert Taft Jr. in 1966 and 1968 and served as field director during Taft's 1970 Senate race. He was a successful trial lawyer before becoming a federal judge. An economic conservative who preached strict constructionism and "eschewed judicial activism," he was a liberal when he came to protecting individual rights. He was also an innovative judge; he was known as "the father of courtroom imaging," being one of the first judges in the country to install imaging and presentation technology in his courtroom so jurors could better understand cases.[13]

Nixon's other nominee was Robert M. Duncan, appointed in June of 1974. The first African American to serve as a federal judge in Ohio, Duncan had served as an attorney in the Worker's Compensation Division of the Ohio attorney general's office, as a Columbus city prosecutor, chief counsel to Ohio Attorney General William Saxbe, a municipal court judge, an Ohio Supreme Court judge, and a judge on the U.S. Court of Military Appeals.[14]

Since 1980, Congress has added two more judges to the U.S. District Court for the Southern District of Ohio, bringing the total authorized judges to eight.[15] These eight, plus the judges who have taken senior status, comprised the court at its two hundredth anniversary. In 1980, Democratic president Jimmy Carter appointed John D. Holschuh, S. Arthur Spiegel, and Walter H. Rice.[16] Holschuh, from Ironton, Ohio, received his B.A. from Miami University and his J.D. from the University of Cincinnati College of Law. One of the top litigators in Columbus, Holschuh spent his legal career in private practice before taking his seat on the federal bench in Columbus.[17] Spiegel, from Cincinnati, was the son of a municipal court judge and the grandson of a judge and the mayor of Cincinnati. After receiving his B.A. from the University of Cincinnati, Spiegel received his J.D. from Harvard Law School. Like Holschuh, Spiegel spent his legal career in private practice before becoming a federal judge sitting in Cincinnati.[18] Rice is one of the few late-twentieth-century judges not born in Ohio. From Pittsburgh, Rice received his B.A. from Northwestern University and his J.D. and M.B.A. from Columbia University. Also unlike Holschuh and Spiegel, Rice, after moving to Dayton, spent most of his prejudicial career in the public arena, first as a prosecutor and then as a municipal court and common pleas court judge. Rice sits in the district court in Dayton.[19]

In the mid-1980s, Republican Ronald Reagan appointed Herman J. Weber, James L. Graham, and George C. Smith to the district court bench.[20] Weber, born in Lima, Ohio, received his B.A. from Otterbein College and his J.D. from the Ohio State University College of Law. He then moved to Fairborn, Ohio, and briefly engaged in private practice before embarking on his judicial career. Before becoming a federal district court judge sitting in Cincinnati, Weber served as a municipal, a common pleas, and an Ohio court of appeals judge.[21] Judge Graham, born in Columbus, received both his B.A. and J.D. from Ohio State. Before joining the district court sitting in Columbus, Graham was in private practice, being one of that city's top litigators.[22] Like Graham, Smith was born in Columbus and received his B.A. and J.D. from Ohio State. But unlike Graham, Smith chose a career in public service, serving as a prosecuting attorney, a municipal court judge, and then a common pleas court judge before assuming his position as a federal district court judge in Columbus.[23]

In 1991, Republican president George Bush nominated Sandra Beckwith to the district court bench in southern Ohio.[24] A member of a prominent Cincinnati family of attorneys and physicians, Beckwith, the first woman to serve as a district judge in the Southern District of Ohio, received her B.S. and J.D. from the University of Cincinnati. From 1969, when she was admitted to the bar, until her assuming her duties as district judge, sitting primarily in Cincinnati, she moved between private practice and public service, holding positions as municipal judge, common pleas court judge, and Hamilton County commissioner.[25]

In the mid-1990s, Democratic president Bill Clinton appointed Susan Dlott, Edmund A. Sargus, and Algenon L. Marbley as district court judges in southern Ohio.[26] Like most judges appointed in the late twentieth century, Dlott is a native Ohioan, born in Dayton. But unlike her fellow judges, she attended college and law school outside Ohio, receiving her B.A. from the University of Pennsylvania and her J.D. from Boston University School of Law. She then returned to Ohio, joining the U.S. Department of Justice as the first woman assistant U.S. attorney for the Southern District of Ohio. Four years later, she went into private practice as one of the chief litigators for the Cincinnati law firm of Graydon, Head & Ritchey, where she remained until her appointment to the federal bench, sitting in Cincinnati.[27] Sargus, from St. Clairsville, received his A.B. from Brown University, in Rhode Island, before returning to Ohio to receive his J.D. from Case Western Reserve University School of Law. While spending several years in private practice in his home town, Sargus became politically active and, in 1993, won appointment as U.S. attorney for the Southern District of Ohio, a position he retained until Clinton appointed him to the federal bench. He sits primarily in Columbus, although he also occasionally holds court in St. Clairsville.[28] Marbley came to Ohio from North Carolina, after receiving his B.A. from the University of North Carolina at Chapel Hill and his J.D. from Northwestern University School of Law. He spent most of his career in private practice in Columbus before becoming a federal judge sitting in Columbus.[29]

Republican president George W. Bush appointed Thomas M. Rose in 2002 and Gregory L. Frost in 2003. Rose, born in Circleville, Ohio, received his B.S. from Ohio University and his J.D. from the University of Cincinnati College of Law. Most of his career was spent in public service as a prosecutor in Greene County before he joined Rice as Dayton's second full-time district court judge. Frost is a lifelong resident of Licking County, Ohio. He received his B.A. from Wittenberg University and his J.D. from Ohio Northern University. After nine years in private practice, he became a municipal court judge. In 1990, he was elected a Licking County Common Pleas Court judge, where he remained until his appointment to the federal bench to sit with the other district court judges in Columbus.[30]

In many ways, the eighteen judges appointed to the bench since 1960 have backgrounds similar to those of most district court judges nationwide. The typical district court judge is a white male who has been politically active in the same party as his appointing president's before assuming his position on the bench. In his early fifties at the time of his appointment, he generally came from a middle to upper-middle class family that had lived and been active in the community for several generations. A graduate of a private college and law school, often a prestigious Ivy League institution, the typical appointee had either judicial or prosecutorial experience before becoming a district court judge.[31]

As the appendix illustrates, all of the judges appointed since 1960 to the District Court for the Southern District of Ohio were members of the same political party as the president who nominated them, all but two are male, and all but two are white. Their average age at the time of their appointments was 51.5 years. Most have deep roots in the community. All but two were born in Ohio, and at least six come from families of attorneys, judges, or successful politicians with years of service in their localities. But at least four came from working-class rather than middle- or upper-middle-class backgrounds. Further, the educational backgrounds of the judges of southern Ohio reinforce their ties to their local communities. Unlike the typical judge, who attended private or Ivy League schools, ten of the judges serving southern Ohio attended Ohio public colleges as undergraduates, and three others attended private Ohio colleges; fourteen of the eighteen graduated from Ohio law schools. Their career paths, however, generally follow the typical pattern, although more of the judges serving southern Ohio had previous judicial or prosecutorial experience than the national average. Among southern Ohio judges, 50 percent had prosecutorial experience, and 50 percent had judicial experience; only 28 percent had neither. This compares to 37 percent, 36 percent, and 27 percent respectively nationwide. This would indicate a better-prepared judge for southern Ohio, one with firm roots in the local community and one from a less elite background than the average judge nationally. However, political connections as well as sound qualifications still were important for appointments. All but four of the modern judges had been politically active before their appointments to the bench, and several had close ties with at least one of Ohio's U.S. senators serving at the time of his or her appointment.[32]

## STRUCTURAL AND JURISDICTIONAL CHANGES

In addition to authorizing new judgeships to handle the ever-increasing district court dockets, Congress has created new types of judges, developed new administrative positions, and established new agencies. In 1939, it established the Administrative Office of the United States Courts, shifting the administrative responsibility of the courts from the executive to the judicial branch. The Administrative Office works under the supervision of the Judicial Conference of the United States, studying the courts and their case loads and making recommendations to Congress to increase judicial efficiency. In 1948, to help coordinate the work of the expanding district courts, Congress authorized the position of chief judge. The chief judge is the most senior active judge in his or her district who has not yet reached the age of seventy. He or she handles the administrative chores of the court as well as coordinating the efforts of the judges who often sit in several different cities. In the Southern District of Ohio, for example, the chief judge handles the administrative chores for the court sitting in Cincinnati, Columbus, Dayton, and occasionally St. Clairsville. In 1967, Congress created the Federal Judicial Center to conduct research and initiate education programs for the federal courts.[33]

But, most significant, in 1968 Congress created an entirely new Article I judgeship—the magistrate judge. This innovation has had increased significance as the decades have progressed. Initially, magistrate judges replaced the U.S. commissioners to help district judges with some of the routine and ministerial duties—issuing warrants, conducting hearings, taking depositions, and performing other duties assigned to them by the district judges, such as conducting pretrial and discovery proceedings or considering applications for posttrial relief. Unlike the earlier commissioners, however, magistrate judges are attorneys who have been admitted to the highest court of their respective states for at least five years. And whereas the commissioners were compensated under the old fee system, magistrate judges receive a fixed salary, making the position attractive to highly qualified lawyers and jurists.[34] As of 2003, the Southern District of Ohio had seven authorized magistrate judges.

District court judges appoint magistrate judges to eight-year, renewable terms. The appointment process for magistrate judges tends to be more apolitical than that for district court judges, magistrate judges often being affiliated with a political party different from that of the majority of judges in their area.[35] As Judge Rice noted, district judges are more concerned with having magistrate judges who share their judicial philosophy on such issues as setting bond or the requirements for a search warrant, because this reduces the number of appeals they might receive.[36] At first, the judges selected magistrate judges from among their former law clerks. For example, two Columbus magistrate judges, Mark Abel and current chief magistrate judge Norah McCann King, are both former law clerks to Kinneary. But within the last ten years the pattern has shifted; the pay structure and the challenges of many federal court cases have attracted former state court judges. By 2003, half the magistrate judges in the Southern District of Ohio were former state court judges, a fact that tends to make attorneys more willing to consent to having them preside over their cases.[37]

U.S. Magistrate Judges, U.S. District Court, Southern District of Ohio, late 1970s or early 1980s. Left to right: Jack Sherman Jr. (Columbus), Norah McCann King (Columbus), Mark R. Abel (Columbus), Michael R. Merz (Dayton), Robert A. Steinberg (Cincinnati), and Terence P. Kemp (Cincinnati). *Courtesy of Magistrate Judge Michael R. Merz*

Magistrate judges' responsibilities continue to grow, having expanded well beyond those of the former commissioners. This is due to several factors. First, Congress recognized the clear need created by the pressures of an expanding federal docket. In 1979, therefore, it gave magistrate judges trial authority, with consent of the parties.[38] In 1990, it changed their title to that of U.S. magistrate judge, to more accurately describe their role as full judicial officers. Second, because of the magistrate judges' stature as well-respected attorneys and judges, parties are increasingly willing to consent to their presiding over cases. Finally, the increasing importance of magistrate judges is a reflection of the expanding role of judges as active agents in effecting settlement.[39]

Table 6.1 illustrates the ever-increasing importance of magistrate judges to the court. In 2000, for example, magistrate judges conducted 213 consent trials, heard 278 Social Security cases, and reviewed 518 prisoner petitions.

In Dayton, magistrate judges also preside over numerous misdemeanor trials, which constitute some 10 to 15 percent of their work load because of the presence of a large federal installation, Wright-Patterson Air Force Base, in the north Dayton suburb of Fairborn, where federal rather than state law applies.[40] In addition, magistrate judges conduct numerous pretrial conferences and handle hundreds of other procedural issues.

Although all the district judges agree that their court would not be able to function effectively without the magistrate judges, each judge uses magistrate judges in very different ways. In Dayton, Magistrate Judge Michael Merz has his own docket of civil cases in addition to pro se and other prisoner cases, Social Security cases, and misdemeanor cases. In general, either Rice or Merz handles a case from its beginning to its final settlement. But to promote consent, Rice developed a system unique in the country—contingent consent. When Rice pretries a case, he asks the parties to consider whether, if he were unavailable when the trial date came up, the parties would consent to a magistrate judge presiding. In general, Merz will hear two or three trials a year this way. On the other hand, in Columbus, the situation is just the opposite. There, magistrate judges do all the pretrial work, handle the preliminary trial conference, deal with all discovery disputes, and preside over most settlement conferences. When it is time to render judgments on dispositive motions, the Article III judge takes over. In Cincinnati, some judges use the Columbus method, whereas others handle their own cases, turning over cases to magistrate judges when the parties consent.[41]

The second significant change in the structure of the district courts was the establishment of separate bankruptcy judges and separate bankruptcy courts. This system replaced the old referee system. Although a bankruptcy court is technically a unit of the district court, judges of the courts of appeal appoint the bankruptcy judges, who hold fourteen-year, renewable terms. These judges now dispose of most bankruptcy cases, with district judges only occasionally being called on to hear appeals.[42]

Another change that has helped district courts handle the increased work load is the creation of "senior status." Judges who retire after reaching the retirement age of sixty-five draw their annual salaries for the rest of their lives. Many judges, however, prefer to continue working past retirement age. Congress has permitted part-time work with the creation of senior status. With this innovation, federal judges have the option of not retiring in the conventional sense. By taking senior status, they are considered retired for the purpose of replacement, and a vacancy is created for which the sitting president can nominate a new judge. Judges on senior status, may, however, still accept as many cases as they like. This allows younger, presumably more energetic judges to assume the bench while also providing a cadre of senior judges to hear cases.[43]

In addition to making these structural and personnel changes, Congress and the courts, by legislation or new procedural rules, have changed the role

## Table 6.1 Magistrate Judges' Case Load, 1972–2000

| Year and Jurisdiction | Defendants Disposed of by Magistrates | | | Matters Disposed of by Magistrates per 28 U.S.C. § 636(a) | | | | Additional Duties under 28 U.S.C. § 636(b), Criminal | | | | | | Additional Duties under 28 U.S.C. § 636(b), Civil | | | |
|---|---|---|---|---|---|---|---|---|---|---|---|---|---|---|---|---|---|
| | Minor Offenses, Except Petty[a] | Petty Offenses[b] | Search and Arrest Warrants[c] | Bail Proceedings and Reviews | Preliminary Exams | Removal Hearings | Probation Revocations | Pretrial Conferences | Motions | Post-indictment Arraignments | Pretrial Conferences[d] | Motions | Prisoner Petitions | Narcotics Addicts Recovery Act | Social Security | All Other[e] | Consent Trials/Terminations |
| **1972** | | | | | | | | | | | | | | | | | |
| Total | 9,167 | 62,915 | 44,171 | 64,518 | 9,554 | 2,480 | — | 5,279 | 5,870 | 10,799 | 7,168 | 6,077 | 6,786 | 705 | 334 | 1311 | — |
| Sixth Circuit | 170 | 2,067 | 4,636 | 5,501 | 898 | 228 | — | 159 | 20 | 1,307 | 526 | 61 | 608 | 96 | 160 | 75 | — |
| S. D. Ohio | 93 | 47 | 730 | 493 | 160 | 69 | — | 60 | 18 | 0 | 314 | 36 | 232 | 0 | 77 | 46 | — |
| **1975** | | | | | | | | | | | | | | | | | |
| Total | 11,403 | 73,102 | 33,456 | 58,121 | 8,144 | 2,198 | 1,407 | — | — | — | — | — | — | — | — | — | — |
| Sixth Circuit | 666 | 4,978 | 4,610 | 6,297 | 813 | 176 | 141 | — | — | — | — | — | — | — | — | — | — |
| S. D. Ohio | 57 | 38 | 599 | 501 | 91 | 14 | 8 | — | — | — | — | — | — | — | — | — | — |
| **1980** | | | | | | | | | | | | | | | | | |
| Total | 12,622 | 77,780 | 16,029 | 43,964 | 3,966 | 1,638 | 874 | 3,433 | 12,778 | 17,512 | 22,531 | 41,700 | 11,578 | — | 4,213 | 4,230 | 597 |
| Sixth Circuit | 421 | 4,168 | 1,748 | 2,925 | 327 | 123 | 45 | 494 | 340 | 1,692 | 1,105 | 2,930 | 1,562 | — | 1,334 | 373 | 112 |
| S. D. Ohio | 15 | 85 | 200 | 227 | 36 | 5 | 10 | 0 | 22 | 213 | 313 | 297 | 322 | — | 236 | 81 | 15 |
| **1985** | | | | | | | | | | | | | | | | | |
| Total | 13,779 | 76,978 | 22,954 | 8,051 | 4,922 | 58,939 | 152 | 2,837 | 24,766 | 42,826 | 36,695 | 91,497 | 20,235 | — | 14,101 | 10,261 | 3,717 |
| Sixth Circuit | 6,842 | 6,424 | 1,726 | 367 | 357 | 3,567 | 5 | 521 | 897 | 1,817 | 2,664 | 9,781 | 3,877 | — | 93 | 745 | 655 |
| S. D. Ohio | 131 | 95 | — | 26 | 65 | 483 | 0 | 0 | 32 | 193 | 774 | 2,073 | 1,149 | — | 23 | 539 | 33 |
| **1990** | | | | | | | | | | | | | | | | | |
| Total | 13,248 | 87,682 | 39,644 | 7,858 | 7,145 | 78,424 | 529 | 3,488 | 26,509 | 34,311 | 45,201 | 61,594 | 21,867 | — | 5,112 | 5,501 | 4,758 |
| Sixth Circuit | 470 | 4,526 | — | 58 | 111 | — | 1 | — | 81 | 114 | 677 | 1,760 | 319 | — | 219 | 306 | 184 |
| S. D. Ohio | 31 | 161 | 373 | — | — | 700 | — | 0 | — | — | — | — | — | — | — | — | — |
| **1996** | | | | | | | | | | | | | | | | | |
| Total | 10,356 | 64,450 | 48,930 | 9,456 | 10,303 | 115,243 | 2,295 | 5,837 | 28,444 | 40,715 | 62,130 | 66,230 | 31,617 | — | 4,603 | 22,265 | 9,948 |
| S. D. Ohio | 60 | 187 | 381 | 34 | 97 | 767 | 33 | 98 | 130 | 70 | 970 | 1,566 | 647 | — | 111 | 244 | 154 |
| **2000** | | | | | | | | | | | | | | | | | |
| Total[f] | 8,990 | 79,459 | 56,704 | 10,741 | 16,589 | 131,223 | 3,109 | 10,965 | 68,656 | 49,740 | 73,979 | 187,397 | 25,013 | — | 5,516 | 3,483 | 11,481 |
| S. D. Ohio | 47 | 158 | 596 | 50 | 133 | 659 | 14 | 0 | 57 | 103 | 1,295 | 3,738 | 518 | — | 278 | 25 | 213 |

Note: The Southern District of Ohio had five magistrates in 1972

[a] Minor offenses other than petty offenses include theft, food and drug, traffic, weapons, assault, fraud, and miscellaneous; from 1990 on, these are referred to as misdemeanor cases

[b] Petty offenses include traffic, immigration, hunting/fishing/camping, drunk/disorderly, trespass, theft, and miscellaneous

[c] From 1980 on, this also includes summonses

[d] In 2000, this also includes settlement conferences

[e] Includes special master reports

[f] In 2000, there was another entry, "Misc Matters," which included seizure/inspection warrants and orders; IRS enforcement; judgment debtor exams, extradition hearings, contempt proceedings, grand and petit juries, and so forth. The overall total for these was 36,813. For the Southern District of Ohio, the total was 396. In 2000, other criminal matters included guilty plea proceedings, mental competency, and writs. The overall total for these was 18,325. For the Southern District of Ohio, the total was nine.

of the district court judges and the way they handle their dockets. In the criminal area, Congress, by promulgating federal sentencing guidelines in 1987, shifted much of the decision making on sentencing away from the district court judges and onto the federal prosecutors by establishing fairly strict rules for judges to follow in sentencing. The result has been an increase in sentencing appeals. As Judge Beckwith has noted, the guidelines have "inspired a whole new area of litigation." After sentencing, those convicted "now . . . file § 2255 attacks on their sentences and the litigation goes on." Judge Smith added that the guidelines have also created a "nightmare for the court of appeals because of all the debates over interpreting them."[44]

In the civil area, largely because of changing procedures and judicial interpretation, the role of the district court judge has also changed. Although it was as true before World War II as after that most cases settled before they came to trial, it has only been since the 1960s that many, if not most, district court judges began to see their role more as arbiters of disputes rather than as triers of cases. For example, Spiegel claims to be in "the dispute resolution business," with the courtroom as "the bottom line, to be avoided, if at all possible."[45] To further that new role, the judges have developed a variety of new techniques and procedures.

Each of the judges of the Southern District of Ohio has his or her own philosophy about settlements and his or her own methodology. Whereas Peck emphasized pretrial conferences, he refused to coerce lawyers into settlements, because he always hated such tactics when he was in private practice. Peck's pretrial conferences simply clarified or eliminated issues, fostered agreement on all possible stipulations of fact, and handled in advance rulings on major questions of admissibility of evidence. Settlement invariably was discussed, but not pushed.[46] Holschuh tends to agree, influenced by his experience as a clerk for Underwood, who he felt pushed the litigating parties too hard to achieve settlement.[47] But most judges of the late twentieth and early twenty-first centuries actively promote settlements.[48]

The judges of the Southern District of Ohio have had many notable successes with settlements. Beckwith negotiated a settlement in the Cincinnati radiation mass tort litigation that allowed the victims some closure and financial compensation.[49] Rice achieved a settlement in the Cincinnati school desegregation case, thereby avoiding a trial that would have further divided the Cincinnati community.[50] Similarly, Dlott, who sees her role as "a referee to level the playing field so that people . . . get justice," got a settlement in the explosive Cincinnati racial profiling case after appointing a conflict resolution firm and then Magistrate Judge Merz to serve as mediators in the lengthy negotiations.[51] Sometimes certifying a case as a class action suit encourages settlement. Weber used this technique effectively in a contract dispute case between physicians and a health maintenance organization.[52] Other judges have used alternative dispute resolution successfully. For example, in a dispute over a more than $32 million contract involving some eighteen hundred gas contracts between producers in seven states, Smith used nonbinding mediation and then managed to negotiate a settlement.[53]

But it is probably Spiegel who has used the greatest variety of techniques to gain settlements. In most cases, he uses the Lloyd's of London method, popularized by a prominent Chicago judge after World War II to get each party to assess realistically his or her chances of winning the case, the amount the winner might expect to receive if he or she did win, and the costs of going to trial. The judge then tries to foster a settlement by finding a middle number that balances these factors.[54]

Spiegel also has been the most active proponent of the summary jury trial. A summary jury trial is an innovative device perfected by its inventor, Judge Thomas Lambros, of the Northern District of Ohio, and Spiegel.[55] In such a trial, the parties "present abbreviated versions of their cases to an advisory jury of six actual jurors, chosen from the court's regular jury pool." After hearing the attorneys' combined opening and closing arguments and a summary of the testimony they would introduce and the exhibits they would show at a full trial, the jurors render a nonbinding verdict. The purpose is to encourage settlement by giving both sides an indication of "how a real jury would decide issues of liability and damages."[56]

Spiegel's record for achieving settlement after summary jury trials, even in very complex cases, is impressive. In the three-year period from 1982 to 1985, for example, Spiegel used summary trial trials in eight cases. In five, the parties settled, one went to a full trial with the result mirroring that of the summary jury, and two others were pending at the time of the report.[57] Perhaps even more significant were the several complex cases that settled after summary jury trials, including the mass tort litigation over radiation exposure at the Fernald plant in southwestern Ohio and a case in which three electric companies charged General Electric with fraud in the construction of the failed Zimmer nuclear processing plant. To make sure that those who have the ultimate power to settle the litigation have this more accurate view of their case and a better understanding of the other side's position, Spiegel has often demanded that the heads of the corporations involved in the litigation sit through this summary trial. Thus, John F. "Jack" Welch, General Electric's chairman of the board, sat through the nonbinding jury trial when the owners of the aborted Zimmer nuclear power station sued General Electric for more than $1 billion. After the parties reached an undisclosed settlement, Welch, in a private note to Spiegel, congratulated the judge for bringing "two factious groups together in an approach that served the country, its legal system and the taxpayers very well." He praised Spiegel's "evenhanded, professional and, at the same time, warm and caring manner." While admitting that "authorizing a multimillion-dollar settlement" was not one of his "favorite tasks," Welch concluded, "We are all fortunate to have you on the bench."[58]

In 1994, Spiegel tried another new device. After hearing on National Public Radio of a collaborative solution used in other cities to resolve disputes between public housing authorities and young mothers who had been denied housing because they were younger than eighteen and unmarried, he appointed a facilitator, and, eventually, a consortium of nine organizations was created to develop standards and screening procedures for public housing applicants. This consortium continues to help teenagers find housing as well as to cope with the myriad of other problems they face.[59]

The judges of the district court have sometimes worked together to implement new devices to foster settlement. In 1984, when the Cincinnati court had "a substantial backlog of cases" because it had "the highest caseload per judge of any federal court in the country," the judges developed a system of "referred, non-binding arbitration."[60] At the time, only three other federal courts nationwide had adopted similar vehicles. Since 1991, Cincinnati has formalized the process by holding settlement weeks. A magistrate judge assigns, schedules, and monitors settlement conferences. In the first year, 43 percent of the fifty-six cases settled. The next year, the success rate climbed to 60 percent.[61] The Columbus court uses experienced litigators to speak with the parties and their attorneys during their settlement week. In 1999, the judges of the Southern District approved another new concept known as the Collaborative Law Project, which is an "alternative dispute resolution mechanism" developed by the Cincinnati-based Collaborative Law Center. The technique allows the parties to stop their litigation and try collaborative negotiations, in which they "commit to a structured, good faith effort to evaluate the merits of a claim or dispute."[62]

This shifting role from trier of cases to resolver of disputes, while keeping many cases out of the courtroom, has created new responsibilities for the judges, increasing the administrative work even more. Now, in addition to trying cases and resolving disputes by alternative methods, they must supervise the settlements they help negotiate. Judges have supervised settlements and consent decrees in cases ranging from school desegregation to the overcrowding of jails; they have overseen the dissemination of notices to thousands of potential members of a class in class action suits; and they administer the distribution of funds in mass tort cases.[63]

In addition to new administrative responsibilities, most judges find another relatively new role, that of "motions clerk," quite bothersome for a variety of reasons. In nearly every civil case, today's federal judge will need to rule on numerous pretrial motions. Sometimes these motions involve sensitive issues of venue,[64] personal jurisdiction,[65] and subject matter jurisdiction.[66] In one case in particular, Porter articulated a "novel proposition," adopted by several other federal courts, that in federal cases involving violations of federal law, the constitutional test for personal jurisdiction is "whether the defendant has certain minimal contacts with the United States" rather than with a particular forum state. He used notions of fair play and due process rather than any federal statutes or federal rules to establish that concept.[67]

Such substantive motions as those challenging venue and jurisdiction are not the type that annoy the federal judges, because they are integral to questions of the court's constitutional authority. Motions that are most troublesome are those involving discovery disputes and for summary judgment. Discovery disputes can take up an enormous amount of time. Dlott, for example, complained that *Iams v. KalKan* was the "case from hell," with lawyers literally filing a motion a day during a one-month period. To resolve this intolerable condition, she finally appointed a special master and got the lawyers to agree to abide by his rulings. But, in general, magistrate judges are able to dispose of most discovery problems.[68]

Motions for summary judgment, which are now filed routinely in almost every civil case, raise a different sort of question. The Federal Rules of Civil Procedure of 1938 first allowed judges to grant motions for summary judgment, that is, to render a judgment without a trial. Because granting such motions denies plaintiffs their day in court, many scholars maintain that judges can make judgments based on hidden biases. For this reason, for many decades the attitude of trial judges was that summary judgment should not be granted except in rare cases. Even today, Rice tends to agree with this view, arguing that the current Supreme Court standards, by encouraging judges to determine whether there is a genuine issue of material fact, "comes . . . perilously close to weighing evidence."[69]

Regardless of their personal feelings, the judges of the Southern District of Ohio must follow the standards established by the Supreme Court[70] and the Sixth Circuit, which in the 1980s ushered in a "new era" of summary judgments, emphasizing that the nonmoving party must present convincing affirmative evidence of the existence of a genuine issue of material fact[71] and insisting that even "complex cases and cases involving state of mind issues are not necessarily inappropriate for summary judgment."[72] Although all the district court judges follow the standards established by the higher courts, some, still working within the current rules, are much stricter in granting summary judgment than are others, often inviting plaintiffs to do more discovery and then resubmit their complaints.[73]

## THE DOCKET: A FORTY-YEAR PERSPECTIVE

Since the 1960s, the Southern District of Ohio has been a very busy court. Table 6.2 charts the changing docket for federal district courts nationwide, the Sixth Circuit Court of Appeals, and the Southern District of Ohio. As that table shows, in 1960 1,359 cases were filed in the Southern District of Ohio. Of them, only 39 percent were criminal cases. Of the 833 civil cases, 565 involved the U.S. government as a party, whereas only 268 were between private litigants. For the judges, the increase in civil cases placed additional

# Table 6.2 Cases Commenced, 1935–2000

| Year | Criminal Cases | U.S. Civil Cases | Private Civil Cases | Total Civil Cases | Total Cases | Bankruptcies Filed |
|---|---|---|---|---|---|---|
| 1935 | | | | | | |
| Total[a] | 19,393/231 (77) | 5,900/70 (23) | Unknown | — | — | 69,153/823 |
| S. D. Ohio | 136 (80) | 35 (20) | — | — | — | 2,331 |
| 1938 | | | | | | |
| Total | 31,322/373 (53) | 11,043/131 (19) | 16,583/197 (28) | 27,626/329 | 58,948 | — |
| S. D. Ohio | 450 (59) | 147 (19) | 167 (22) | 314 | 764 | — |
| 1940 | | | | | | |
| Total | 31,088/370 (54) | 12,586/150 (22) | 14,170/169 (24) | 26,756/319 | 57,844 | 52,171/621 |
| Sixth Circuit[b] | 3,889/432 (59) | 1,039/115 (16) | 1,690/188 (25) | 2,729/303 | 6,618 | — |
| S. D. Ohio | 343 (53) | 126 (20) | 174 (27) | 300 | 643 | 1,568 |
| 1945 | | | | | | |
| Total | 39,429/469 (39) | 43,110/513 (43) | 17,855/213 (18) | 60,965/726 | 100,394 | 12,822/153 |
| Sixth Circuit | 3,709/412 (46) | 3462/385 (43) | 909/101 (11) | 4,371/486 | 8,080 | 2,070/230 |
| S. D. Ohio | 484 (40) | 594 (50) | 114 (10) | 708 | 1,192 | 333 |
| 1950 | | | | | | |
| Total[c] | 37,720/439 (41) | 22,429/261 (24) | 32,193/374 (35) | 54,622/635 | 92,342 | 33,284/387 |
| Sixth Circuit | 3,542/394 (40) | 3,063/341 (35) | 2,172/241 (25) | 5,235/582 | 8,777 | 5,714/635 |
| S. D. Ohio | 510 (37) | 634 (46) | 241 (17) | 875 | 1,385 | 994 |
| 1954 | | | | | | |
| Total | 40,744/474 (46) | 19,167/223 (22) | 29,015/337 (32) | 48,182/560 | 88,926 | 53,033/617 |
| Sixth Circuit | 3,424/381 (33) | 4,409/490 (42) | 2,574/286 (25) | 6,983/776 | 10,407 | 9,304/1,034 |
| S. D. Ohio | 416 (33) | 595 (46) | 268 (21) | 863 | 1,279 | 1,813 |
| 1960 | | | | | | |
| Total | 29,828/347 (37) | 19,804/230 (25) | 30,048/350 (38) | 49,852/580 | 79,680 | 110,034/1,279 |
| Sixth Circuit | 3,537/393 (33) | 4,803/534 (44) | 2,467/274 (23) | 7,270/808 | 10,807 | 22,747/2,527 |
| S. D. Ohio | 526 (39) | 565 (41) | 268 (20) | 833 | 1,359 | 4,641 |
| 1964 | | | | | | |
| Total | 30,268/352 (31) | 22,268/259 (23) | 44,662/519 (46) | 66,930/778 | 97,198 | 171,719/1,997 |
| Sixth Circuit | 3,574/397 (36) | 2,652/295 (26) | 3,824/425 (38) | 6,476/720 | 10,050 | 34,350/3,817 |
| S. D. Ohio | 525 (37) | 410 (29) | 499 (34) | 909 | 1,434 | 7,155 |
| 1970 | | | | | | |
| Total[d] | 39,959/439 (31) | 24,965/274 (20) | 62,356/685 (49) | 87,321/959 | 127,280 | 194,399/2,136 |
| Sixth Circuit | 3,852/428 (32) | 3,016/335 (25) | 5,064/563 (43) | 8,080/898 | 11,932 | 38,061/4,229 |
| S. D. Ohio | 401 (29) | 365 (26) | 632 (45) | 997 | 1,398 | 8,831 |
| 1975 | | | | | | |
| Total | 43,282/476 (27) | 31,779/349 (20) | 85,541/940 (53) | 117,320/1,289 | 160,602 | 254,484/2,797 |
| Sixth Circuit | 4,759/529 (30) | 4,042/449 (25) | 7,308/812 (45) | 11,350/1,261 | 16,109 | 41,856/4,651 |
| S. D. Ohio | 385 (19) | 662 (33) | 938 (48) | 1,600 | 1,985 | 8,753 |
| 1980 | | | | | | |
| Total | 28,921/318 (15) | 63,628/699 (32) | 105,161/1,156 (53) | 168,789/1,855 | 197,710 | 210,364/2,312 |
| Sixth Circuit | 2,378/264 (12) | 7,263/807 (37) | 9,829/1,092 (51) | 17,092/1,899 | 19,470 | 39,511/4,390 |
| S. D. Ohio | 214 (8) | 1,083 (41) | 1,367 (51) | 2,450 | 2,664 | 7,795 |
| 1985 | | | | | | |
| Total | 38,245/420 (12) | 117,488/1,291 (38) | 156,182/1,716 (50) | 273,670/3,007 | 311,915 | 364,536/4,006 |
| Sixth Circuit | 2,565/285 (8) | 15,374/1,708 (45) | 16,053/1,784 (47) | 31,427/3,492 | 33,992 | 49,865/5,540 |
| S. D. Ohio | 332 (6) | 2,589 (46) | 2,736 (48) | 5,325 | 5,657 | 10,149 |
| 1990 | | | | | | |
| Total | 48,904/537 (18) | 56,300/619 (21) | 161,579/1,776 (61) | 217,879/2,395 | 266,783 | 725,484/7,972 |
| Sixth Circuit | 3,444/383 (12) | 5,466/607 (20) | 19,077/2,120 (68) | 24,543/2,727 | 27,987 | 103,357/11,484 |
| S. D. Ohio | 526 (18) | 835 (28) | 1,615 (54) | 2,450 | 2,976 | 19,749 |
| 1996 | | | | | | |
| Total | 47,889/526 (15) | 48,755/536 (15) | 220,377/2,422 (70) | 269,132/2,958 | 317,021 | 1,111,964/12,219 |
| Sixth Circuit | 3,294/366 (10) | 5,344/594 (16) | 23,833/2,648 (74) | 29,177/3,242 | 32,471 | 106,602/11,845 |
| S. D. Ohio | 358 (10) | 621 (18) | 2,455 (72) | 3,076 | 3,434 | 17,024 |
| 2000 | | | | | | |
| Total | 83,963/923 (24) | 71,109/781 (21) | 188,408/2,070 (75) | 259,517/2,851 | 343,480 | 1,262,102/13,869 |
| Sixth Circuit | 5,568/619 (17) | 8,627/959 (26) | 18,801/2,089 (57) | 27,428/3,048 | 32,996 | 159,200/17,689 |
| S. D. Ohio | 508 (13) | 1,223 (32) | 2,150 (55) | 3,373 | 3,881 | 25,858 |

Note: Numbers in parentheses are percentages. Numbers to the left of the slash are totals for all districts; numbers to the right of the slash are the averages per district.

[a] 1935, 84 districts

[b] The Sixth Circuit contains 9 districts

[c] 1950, increase to 86 districts

[d] 1970, increase to 91 districts

Source: AO annual reports for respective years.

burdens on their time. Nationwide, 90 percent of the defendants in criminal cases either plead guilty or nolo contendere, eliminating the need for time-consuming trials. Although the judges in the Southern District of Ohio did spend slightly more of their time presiding over criminal trials, 33 percent compared to 30 percent nationwide, they still faced a tremendous number of the more time-consuming civil cases.[74] Between 1960 and 1964 alone, for example, Peck presided over at least one jury trial a month. In the fiscal year ending June 30, 1965, he completed an astounding 105 civil trials. To keep his docket current, Peck took no vacations. Instead, he worked from 8 AM until early evening, "with trials, pretrial conferences, preparations of jury charges, dictating of correspondence, and a hundred miscellaneous chores incident to the administration of justice."[75]

By 1980, the number of cases filed in the Southern District of Ohio had almost doubled, to 2,664. Only 8 percent were criminal cases. This followed the national trend of declining criminal cases, largely because of a drop in liquor law violation prosecutions.[76] But there were 2,450 new civil cases, with 49 percent involving the United States as a party and 51 percent being between private litigants. From 1980 on, however, the number of civil suits filed by the United States continued to decline as the government initiated fewer cases to recover overpayments of veterans benefits and defaulted student loans.[77] By 2000, in the Southern District of Ohio 55 percent of the civil suits commenced were between private parties.

The Administrative Office of the United States Courts studies case loads of judges. As table 6.3 shows, their figures indicate that in the 1960s the judges of the Southern District handled fewer civil but more criminal cases. By 1970, they were carrying essentially the average load. But in 1980, the average judge in the Southern District of Ohio handled 442 cases compared to a 381 per judge case load nationally. In 1985 the difference was even more dramatic—809 cases per judge for the Southern District of Ohio compared to 545 per judge nationally. In 2000, judges of the Southern District of Ohio were back to carrying about the average national load, but, unlike the 1960s, they handled, on average, more civil and fewer criminal cases.[78]

The types of cases have also changed. In the 1960s, civil rights was not even a category listed in the statistics kept by the courts. The largest category of civil cases for the Southern District of Ohio was the federal government collecting money. State prisoner habeas corpus cases also represented a significant part of the case load. By 1980, state and federal prisoner petitions accounted for the largest category of civil cases, at 19 percent. Indeed, the Southern District of Ohio had, in Porter's words, "the dubious distinction of being seventh in the country in the number of prisoner § 1983 cases filed," with an increase of 188 percent between 1978 and 1979 alone.[79] Social Security cases closely followed behind prisoner petitions as the second-highest category of civil cases, representing 17.5 percent of the total cases filed. Civil

## Table 6.3 Case Load per Judgeship, 1941–2000

| Year and Jurisdiction | Total Civil | Private Civil | Criminal | Overall |
|---|---|---|---|---|
| 1941 | | | | |
| Total (86 districts, 179 judges) | 171 | 81 | 164 | — |
| Sixth Circuit (20 judges) | 158 | 90 | 203 | — |
| S. D. Ohio (3 judges) | 109 | 54 | 148 | — |
| 1950 | | | | |
| Total (86 districts, 200 judges) | 222 | 113 | 169 | — |
| Sixth Circuit (20 judges) | 262 | 109 | 170 | — |
| S. D. Ohio (3 judges) | 292 | 80 | 162 | — |
| 1960 | | | | |
| Total (86 districts, 226 judges) | 221 | 133 | 107 | — |
| Sixth Circuit (24 judges) | 200 | 103 | 139 | — |
| S. D. Ohio (3 judges) | 188 | 89 | 163 | — |

### Weighted Case Load

| Year and Jurisdiction | Total Civil | Private Civil | Criminal | Overall |
|---|---|---|---|---|
| 1964 | | | | |
| Total (86 districts, 289 judges) | 207 | Not available | 57 | — |
| Sixth Circuit (31 judges) | 208 | — | 62 | — |
| S. D. Ohio (3 judges) | 267 | — | 84 | — |
| 1970 | | | | |
| Total (89 districts, 382 judges) | 214 | — | 63 | 277 |
| Sixth Circuit (39 judges) | 217 | — | 64 | 281 |
| S. D. Ohio (5 judges) | 213 | — | 51 | 264 |
| 1975 | | | | |
| Total (91 districts, 396 judges) | 293 | — | 107 | 400 |
| S. D. Ohio (5 judges) | 355 | — | 85 | 420 |

### Weighted and Unweighted Case Load

| Year and Jurisdiction | Total Civil | Private Civil | Criminal | Overall |
|---|---|---|---|---|
| 1980 | | | | |
| Total (91 districts, 511 judges) | 311/328 | — | 47/53 | 358/381 |
| S. D. Ohio (6 judges) | 347/408 | — | 43/34 | 390/442 |
| 1985 | | | | |
| Total (91 districts, 571 judges) | 401/478 | — | 59/67 | 460/545 |
| S. D. Ohio (7 judges) | 574/761 | — | 55/48 | 629/809 |
| 1990 | | | | |
| Total (91 districts, 571 judges) | 390/380 | — | 58/56 | 448/436 |
| S. D. Ohio (7 judges) | 376/350 | — | 64/65 | 440/415 |
| 1996 | | | | |
| Total (91 districts, 643 judges) | 338/388 | — | 134/85 | 472/472 |
| S. D. Ohio (8 judges) | 342/350 | — | 95/59 | 436/409 |
| 2000 | | | | |
| Total (91 districts, 651 judges) | 311/378 | — | 167/110 | 479/488 |
| S. D. Ohio (8 judges) | 337/408 | — | 88/59 | 425/467 |

Note: Case load per judgeship excludes immigration (or so-called wetback prosecutions). The case load per judgeship is obtained by dividing the number of cases commenced by the number of judge-ships existing at the end of the fiscal year. But the numbers can be misleading because they do not reflect times when judges are sick or when there is a vacancy unfilled, the length of trials, the number of corporate reorganizations and bankruptcy reviews, or the number of separate tracts in land con-demnation cases. Nevertheless, the numbers do give a rough comparison among districts.

*Source:* AO annual reports for respective years.

rights cases constituted only 9 percent of the docket. By the 1990s, judges faced additional burdens as the civil cases became more complex with multi-district and mass tort class action suits like the Bendectin drug and the Fernald litigation clogging the docket.[80] But even more dramatic, civil rights cases increased by more than 100 percent in the 1990s. Student loan cases increased by an astonishing 1,333 percent. Thus, in 2000, of the civil cases filed in the Southern District of Ohio, 21 percent involved civil rights litigation, 19 percent student loans, and 14 percent prisoner petitions.

There have also been significant differences among the three cities in which the court sits. In 2000, for example, Cincinnati's civil case load matched the distribution for the district as a whole, although its fourth-largest group of cases, those involving property, represented more than 11 percent of the total, far more than in the other cities. In Columbus, civil rights cases far outnumbered other categories, with student loans second and prisoner cases third, but closely following these categories were labor cases, representing 13 percent of its civil case load. Indeed, Columbus heard 68 percent of all the labor cases in the district. In Dayton, civil rights and student loans ranked first and second, but third were Social Security cases, representing 18 percent of its docket. Prisoner cases represented only 8 percent.

In the criminal area, one sees the same dramatic shifts. First, Congress has federalized many crimes, increasing the variety of criminal cases confronting the courts. Second, the war on drugs has had a significant impact on the types of cases prosecuted. For the four years 1964 through 1967, only one drug-related case was filed in the entire district. Forgery and counterfeiting was the largest category of crime, representing between 25 and 30 percent of the docket. In 1980, only twelve drug-related cases (5 percent of the docket) were filed. But by 1988, drug-related crimes represented 27 percent of the docket, with fraud second at 18 percent. Columbus, especially, witnessed a large increase in cocaine and crack-related cases in the period from 1988 through 1989. In 2000, drug-related cases had increased to 32 percent of the docket, with fraud cases a distant second at 15 percent.

Here, again, there are significant regional differences. First, Columbus has far more criminal cases than the other seats of the court. In 1992, for example, more than half of the district's criminal case filings were in Columbus. And in Columbus, drug cases dominated. By 2000, drug case filings represented 22 percent of the case load, with weapons and firearms cases second at 14 percent, and fraud third at 11 percent. In that same year in Cincinnati, fraud cases ranked first, representing almost 32 percent of all criminal cases, with drug cases representing only 14 percent. In Dayton, like Columbus, drug cases ranked first, representing 25 percent of the case load, followed closely by burglary and larceny at 20 percent.

Though not numerically significant within the total number of cases filed, from 1940 to 1975 the Southern District of Ohio, along with district courts throughout the nation, faced numerous cases involving violations of the Selective Service Act. There was a steady diet of these cases continuing from World War II through Korea. Most disputes involved disagreements over the defendant's classification. Following clear statutory language and established case law, judges imposed jail terms of up to five years in these cases if the defendant refused or failed to report either for active duty or, if classified as a conscientious objector, for alternative "work of national importance."[81] In the 1960s and 1970s, the number of conflicts between draftees and their local draft boards increased as the Vietnam War escalated.[82] Most disputes concerned the draftees' applications for conscientious objector status. According to Magistrate Judge Merz, who represented many of these men, the U.S. attorneys for the Southern District of Ohio settled most cases before the court got involved. If a settlement could not be reached, most men, after their convictions, received probation from the judge as long as they agreed to do the same type of service required of conscientious objectors. Kinneary and Weinman were especially understanding.[83] For example, a grand jury indicted David Green in Columbus in 1968 for burning his draft card. Following a four-day trial, the jury found him guilty. Although Kinneary fined him $1,500, he suspended Green's three-year sentence.[84]

Nevertheless, some who opposed the draft served time. Peck sentenced Peter Irons, now a prominent legal historian,[85] to three years in prison for refusing induction after his appeal for conscientious objector status was denied. At his trial in 1965, Irons tried to argue that the draft law, as written, was an unconstitutional violation of the First Amendment's guarantee of freedom of religion because it required those exempted as conscientious objectors to affirm a belief in a Supreme Being. Peck responded: "What law school did you attend, young man?" In 1974 and then again in 1985, Irons criticized Peck's handling of his case. He condemned Peck's cruelty in imposing a stern sentence and refusing to examine the presentencing report favorably. Peck responded to Irons that he regretted that Irons believed Peck displayed "hostility" to him. Peck tried to assure him that there was nothing personal involved in his decision. "As in hundreds (or thousands) of other cases which have been before me since I first went on the bench in 1949, I was simply applying the law as I understood it."[86]

Another area in which the docket increased for a short period in the late twentieth century involved Social Security benefit appeals from miners suffering from black lung disease based on provisions of the Federal Coal Mine Health and Safety Act of 1969. Appeals from the decisions of the required administrative hearing and review were concentrated in the coal-mining areas of the country. Although four district courts in Kentucky, Pennsylvania, Virginia, and West Virginia heard nearly 70 percent of the cases, the Southern District of Ohio also felt the impact of this litigation. For the southern district, such filings went from none in 1974 to 126 in 1975.[87]

The new statute, while providing benefits for miners who had contracted black lung disease after years of working in the coal mines, limited the district courts' authority when hearing appeals following denial of benefits by the U.S. Department of Health, Education, and Welfare (HEW). District courts could review the HEW secretary's legal conclusions and findings only to determine whether the record of the administrative hearing contained the "substantial evidence" needed to support the contested findings. They had to accept the factual findings of the administrative hearings as conclusive, if based on substantial evidence.[88] Therefore, the judges dismissed most of these denial appeals on motions for summary judgment, and the Sixth Circuit Court of Appeals generally affirmed them in the rare appeal. When cases were not dismissed, the judges generally remanded them to the agency for further proceedings.[89] Duncan, however, did render an important decision, affirmed by the Sixth Circuit Court of Appeals. After a careful analysis of the statute's text, employing all the standard judicial rules for textual analysis, Duncan concluded that HEW had misread the deadline requirements.[90] His ruling permitted many more miners to claim disability benefits.[91] Other early decisions by the district courts continue to have jurisprudential significance and are still referenced in decisions by other courts. Further, because district courts continue to hear appeals in Social Security disability cases, many of the rules and standards adopted in earlier black lung appeals have been incorporated into this area of the law.[92]

The draft cases and the black lung cases illustrate how historical events like the Vietnam War or one piece of legislation like a coal mine safety statute can affect the court's work load. Although federal judges develop new tools to handle their diverse cases, shifting much of their work from the courtroom to their chambers, their case loads are still products of events beyond their control.

# 7

## INTO THE TWENTY-FIRST CENTURY

*The District Court as a Place of Recourse, 1960–2003*

SINCE THE 1960S, FEDERAL COURTS have become increasingly important in the political, economic, and social lives of average citizens. During the years of President Lyndon Johnson's Great Society program, Congress enacted numerous statutes designed to ensure constitutionally protected individual rights, regulate economic activities, and protect society from crime. In several landmark cases in the 1950s and 1960s, the Supreme Court helped transform the federal courts into institutions to which citizens can turn for protection of their constitutionally guaranteed rights. District court judges, as the first judges in the federal court system to interpret new congressional statutes and implement Supreme Court mandates, continually render judgments that affect their communities and help shape the development of national law. Indeed, Spiegel asserted that being a district judge is the "pinnacle" of the legal profession "because a federal judge often sets the tone for a community regarding both civil and individual rights."[1]

The District Court for the Southern District of Ohio has had its most significant impact on the development of law, nationally, and on the community it serves in six major categories of cases: (1) civil rights and equal protection under the laws (including school desegregation; integration, based on race and gender, of police and fire departments; equal employment and housing opportunities; cases of police discrimination and abuse of power;

and litigation involving the regulation of elections, the right to unfettered political associations, and apportionment equal protection issues); (2) Bill of Rights cases, especially litigation involving First Amendment rights of the free exercise of religion and freedom of speech, including obscenity, and the Ninth Amendment right of privacy, especially in the area of abortion; (3) cases enforcing federal and state statutes and arbitrating disputes over federalism, especially those involving Eleventh Amendment questions of state immunity from lawsuits; (4) mass tort and major class action cases, some involving grave abuses by governmental agencies; (5) cases involving major economic issues, including patents, trademarks, and copyrights; antitrust violations and corporate takeovers; disputes between labor and management; bankruptcy litigation; securities and other cases of fraud; disagreements between the Interstate Commerce Commission and the carriers it regulates; and product liability disputes; and (6) major criminal cases, ranging from the famous, like those of Dr. Sam Sheppard and Pete Rose, and large drug conspiracies, like the Short North Posse case, to cases raising criminal justice issues of fairness, the enforcement of sentencing guidelines, and the mandating of prison reform to ensure prisoners' rights against cruel and unusual punishment and to equal protection of the laws.

This chapter analyzes the major cases in the first two categories, emphasizing their importance to legal developments and to the local communities. The next chapter examines how the court has dealt with disagreements over the power of the federal government, especially in its relationship to the states and its officials, mass tort litigation, economic issues, and crime.

### EQUAL PROTECTION OF THE LAW

In the 1960s, black Ohioans still faced segregation, especially in urban schools and in residential housing, and economic discrimination by employers and unions. Although the Ohio General Assembly enacted a new civil rights law outlawing employment discrimination and establishing a civil rights commission to enforce equal rights, until African Americans turned to the courts little changed.[2] Following the success of African Americans, women and other minorities also turned to the federal courts for relief. Their cases have resulted in a society that, though still facing numerous problems of equal access based on race, gender, wealth, and other factors, provides more opportunities than were available before litigation began.

*The Desegregation of the Public Schools: Cincinnati, Columbus, and Dayton*

When federal judges arbitrated disputes over segregation in the public schools, they dealt with one of the most sensitive issues facing communities. Emotions ran high as all parties strove to do what they thought was best for the children. The first desegregation case occurred in Hillsboro in the 1950s, and there Druffel sided with the school board. Whether he opposed integration is not clear, but he certainly believed integration should wait so as not to cause what he saw as a disruption of the educational process.[3]

Within the next two decades, Cincinnati, Columbus, and Dayton each experienced very different suits to integrate their city schools, with very different results. Despite these differences, there were important similarities. All the suits were class action suits. All the parties confronted the same law. First, on the basis of Supreme Court decisions, the plaintiffs had to prove that the school boards had intentionally segregated the schools; the mere presence of de facto segregation was not sufficient. Further, segregation resulting from residential housing patterns would not justify court-ordered remedies. Second, if the court found that the school board had engaged in purposeful segregation, the remedy would be based on the "linkage principle," that is, it would be determined by the nature and the extent of the constitutional violation.[4]

Cincinnati's litigation began in 1963 when Tina Deal and forty-five other African American children filed suit against the Cincinnati Board of Education.[5] The immediate cause was the Cincinnati school board's transfer of pupils from an overcrowded, predominantly black school in the Evanston neighborhood to a predominantly white school in the nearby neighborhood of Oakley. During the first year, the board kept the black students together before they were to be "absorbed fully into their new school's mix the second year." According to the NAACP, this was sufficient evidence that the board had deprived African Americans of their constitutional right to an integrated education.[6] The plaintiffs further claimed that the board had long assigned students to racially segregated schools, intentionally exacerbating patterns of segregation in housing. Pretrial, interrogatories, and discovery went on for two years, and the plaintiffs benefited from full access to the records of the Cincinnati Board of Education.[7] Judge Peck, however, limited the plaintiffs' case theory; following standards established by the Supreme Court, he denied their request to present evidence of intentional segregation in housing. He insisted that, unless they could show a link between intentional residential segregation and the school board, evidence of illegal actions by people and institutions not a party to the lawsuit (that is, realtors, lenders, or others involving in selling and renting housing) would not be permitted.[8]

After the June 1965 bench trial, Peck found that the plaintiffs had failed, even after extensive discovery, to provide any "clear evidence" that the board had denied them their constitutional rights by intentionally segregating the schools or gerrymandering attendance zones.[9] He therefore dismissed the suit, concluding, "It is not for the judicial system to be the initiating factor in sociological reform."[10]

The African American community tried again in 1974 in *Bronson v. Board of Education.* By then, the Dayton and Columbus suits were also being litigated, but the Cincinnati case was unique. The *Deal* decision had a significant limiting impact on the way this second suit against the Cincinnati Board of Education developed. In *Bronson,* the plaintiffs tried a new strategy. They named as defendants not only the Cincinnati school board but also the state board of education, the Hamilton County board of education, and eighteen Hamilton County suburban school boards.[11] The NAACP argued that Hamilton County should be viewed "as one education unit," with city and suburban school and other officials acting together to restrict African Americans to schools in the city.[12] In doing so, however, they faced the impossible task of proving intentional discrimination on the part of the suburban boards, especially after Porter, the first judge assigned to this new case, held that, under the doctrine of issue preclusion, the plaintiffs could not reargue the issues raised but held not to be proven in *Deal.* That meant that the plaintiffs in *Bronson* could present only evidence of school board actions that occurred after July 26, 1965, the date Peck issued his ruling in *Deal* that no segregative intent could be found.[13]

In 1980, Judge Rice, who had been assigned the case after Porter took senior status, heard the plaintiff's request for a modification of Porter's estoppel decision, arguing that they should be entitled to show, without time constraints, that one or more of the suburban districts committed segregative acts within their districts that increased segregation in Cincinnati or that there was collusion between the city and one or more of the suburban districts to maintain segregation. Rice agreed to this modification. After the courts had ruled on the Dayton and Columbus cases, Rice allowed the plaintiffs to present evidence of pre-1954 conditions because those conditions, thought to be irrelevant before the Dayton and Columbus decisions, could now be important. He also held that the plaintiffs were not precluded from examining conditions after 1954 but before 1965 as long as the evidence was used solely to show that the board had not corrected the pre-1954 problems. The Sixth Circuit Court of Appeals, however, reversed Rice, leaving Porter's original estoppel decision in place.[14] Thus, the plaintiffs could not, for example, show any evidence that before 1965 African Americans living in the suburbs were transported to black schools in Cincinnati or that de facto segregation had been part of the state's history before 1954. Without such evidence, plaintiffs could not prove any nexus between the suburban, state, and Cincinnati boards. Rice had no choice but to dismiss the suburbanites as defendants.[15]

Hoping to work out an effective settlement in which the children would ultimately be the winners, Rice next set up regular meetings to monitor the progress of discovery and other issues leading to trial, and, on the morning the trial was scheduled to start, he ordered mediation efforts to begin instead. He explained to the plaintiffs that, although settlement would not give them all they wanted, there were considerable risks in going to trial. With the limitations placed upon them because of the previous *Deal* decision, they would have difficulty proving their case. Moreover, he argued, settlement was

Pulitzer Prize–winning political cartoonist Jim Borgman's depiction of Judge Walter Rice's work in the Cincinnati school desegregation case, *Bronson v. Board of Education*. © *Reprinted with permission of King Features Syndicate*

better than litigating for all concerned.[16] Rice succinctly explained his philosophy of the benefits of negotiation over litigation: "In a case of this magnitude, in a case with this community-wide significance, *neither* party can *afford* to lose, because when one side of the case loses, regardless of which party that is, the entire community is a loser."[17]

Because of the excellent reputation of the superintendent of the Cincinnati schools and Rice's skills as a mediator, the parties succeeded in avoiding a trial. They hammered out a settlement that called for the school district to reduce racial isolation by the use of new and expanded alternative schools, supported by a commitment of $35 million in state funds and the allocation of congressionally authorized federal funds.[18] Rice believed this settlement was reached because of the Cincinnati school superintendent's sincere desire to achieve an integrated school system, which had led to his earning the respect of the African American community. The NAACP and the black parents trusted the superintendent, allowing negotiations to proceed in good faith.[19] On the other hand, David Greer, the Dayton attorney who represented the Dayton school board in its desegregation case, credits Rice's "empathy, patience, and persistence." The judge, Greer maintained, "managed to touch both sides with calm and reason and bring the matter to a peaceful resolution."[20]

In 1991, Rice concluded that Cincinnati was in compliance with respect to certain aspects of the consent decree but not others, so he retained limited jurisdiction. In doing so, he explained how the district court played a vital role protecting those seeking justice: "It is often said that 'no one cares about poor children' or that 'the poor have no constituency among a community's elected and appointed leadership.'" Noting that, at times of financial crisis like the Cincinnati school board was facing in the 1990s, the special needs of the poor are "often disproportionately sacrificed and compromised on the altar of financial necessity and expediency," Rice proclaimed that the district court would not let that happen; it would be the protector of the poor.[21] No case could better illustrate the district court's conception of its role as resolving disputes rather than merely adjudicating them. But it also illustrates the new burdens placed on the court as it must continually monitor the settlements it approves.

The Columbus school case, *Penick v. Columbus Board of Education,* began in June 1973, when Gary Penick and thirteen coplaintiffs filed suit to enjoin the Columbus Board of Education from spending the $89.5 million it had raised in a school bond levy for new school construction until it could demonstrate that the money would be spent to promote integrated educational experiences. The following year, the plaintiffs, now certified as a class, filed an amended complaint alleging that the Columbus school board had intentionally maintained a segregated public school system. Further, they argued that the new construction would only add to that segregation. Finally, they asserted that the Ohio state board of education and the state superintendent of public instruction, among others, were also liable, because, although they knew that the Columbus school system was segregated, they failed to investigate or take any action to desegregate the schools. To remedy this situation, the plaintiffs sought the implementation of a systemwide plan of desegregation, which would include busing. The city was tense, the white community countering that racial isolation in the schools was due solely to housing patterns and not to school board policies and thus a desegregation plan was not warranted.[22]

In 1975, Duncan took over the case originally assigned to Rubin, who had moved to the Dayton court. It is perhaps a twist of fate that Duncan presided over this case: upon graduation from college, he had experienced firsthand the effects of the Columbus school board's discriminatory policies. Because there were no openings for African American teachers due to the board's segregation practices, Duncan, having graduated from Ohio State University as an education major, decided to become an attorney. Although one might expect a natural bias in favor of the plaintiffs in this case, Duncan earned the respect of all the parties and the Columbus community for the way he handled the litigation.

To ensure an efficient handling of the case and to try to reach a settlement without litigation, Duncan began conducting regular pretrial meetings as discovery continued and the issues to be proven clarified. Despite his efforts, the case went to trial on April 19, 1976. It lasted until September 3, with thirty-six trial days, more than seventy witnesses, six hundred exhibits, and a trial transcript numbering more than sixty-six hundred pages. On March 8,

1977, Duncan delivered his findings. He held that, based on the history of the Columbus public schools as well as current practices, the school board had intentionally and purposefully maintained a segregated system, with both students and teachers assigned to different schools on the basis of race. Although he praised the recent efforts by the Columbus board to provide alternative schooling such as magnet schools to decrease the racial isolation, he noted that such efforts had "fallen far short of providing a remedy." Further, he added, clinging to the neighborhood school concept could not be condoned. "A neighborhood school policy . . . cannot be a contributor to unconstitutional deprivation." Duncan bemoaned the fact that the courts ever had to become involved, because "[t]he litigation model is not the most efficient way to solve problems of far-reaching social impact." But, he explained, courts had to get into "the school desegregation business" because other governmental entities failed "to confront and produce answers." The role of the court was to "protect the constitutional rights of all our citizens." He thus ordered the board to develop a districtwide plan that "balances the constitutional right to integrated education" with the desire to have a plan that is not "so burdensome . . . as to impair" the school system's "ability to provide the best possible educational opportunities."[23]

At the remedy stage, Duncan continued to insist on a districtwide solution. The Sixth Circuit Court of Appeals and the Supreme Court affirmed not only his conclusions that the Columbus school board had administered a segregated school system but also his insistence that the solution apply to the entire school district. Duncan continued to reject school board plans until the board came up with one that included busing, all the while patiently trying to educate Columbus citizens. He admitted that many citizens believed that school desegregation was "not worth the trouble of doing it" and that busing abrogated their constitutional rights. But, he reminded them, the Supreme Court and the Sixth Circuit Court of Appeals had proclaimed that all children had a constitutional right to an integrated education and those principles had to be maintained despite the fact "that many . . . in the Columbus community . . . strongly object" to them and the remedy required to achieve them.[24]

Duncan's firm stand, coupled with his continuing effort to educate the Columbus community about the law and principles underlying it, helped alleviate tensions and bring about a smooth implementation of the integration plan. Civil and business leaders, pointing to Columbus's peaceful implementation of integration, even turned "the business of desegregating schools into a way of boosting the city as a great place to live and invest."[25]

In 1985, Duncan ordered the Columbus school system released from court supervision. Noting that he was one of the first judges to remove a desegregation order, he explained, "They did everything I said, and they did it very well. They didn't like it, but they did it well."[26]

Dayton's experience with school desegregation proved the most divisive of the three cities. In 1969, the U.S. Department of Health, Education, and Welfare found that the Dayton school board had been assigning its teachers in a racially discriminatory manner. It also found that other board policies had promoted segregation in the schools. The Ohio Department of Education urged the city to correct its segregated conditions quickly. In response, the Dayton school board created a biracial citizens committee to study school segregation. After the citizens' committee completed its study, the school board passed resolutions admitting that its actions had created a system of "racial isolation of school children" and "unequal educational opportunities for the poor and black students" in Dayton. The board called for new policies to end these racial and economic imbalances. Wayne Carle, the superintendent of Dayton's schools, worked with the board to develop a plan to achieve integration, which included the busing of some school children. Angered by the school board's plans, many in the white community organized to reverse the board's decisions. The "Save Our Schools" forces successfully rallied the city's antibusing forces and won a majority on the school board in the November 1971 elections. When the new board convened in January 1972, it rescinded the previous board's resolutions and fired Carle.[27]

In response, on April 7, 1972, several Daytonians, supported by the NAACP, filed suit against the Dayton Board of Education, as well as state officials, the Ohio Board of Education, and the superintendent of public instruction for the Ohio Department of Education, seeking an injunction to stop their allegedly unconstitutional policy of operating the public schools in Dayton in a manner that perpetuated racial segregation. The plaintiffs filed the original complaint in the Eastern Division of the Southern District of Ohio because that was the location of the state government, rather than in the Western Division, where the local schools are. Judge Rubin held an expedited hearing in November and December 1972 to determine whether the school system in Dayton was intentionally segregated. Through former superintendent Carle's efforts, the plaintiffs had substantial statistical and other evidence of intentionally segregative policies on the part of the Dayton school board, along with documents showing that the board was continuing to maintain the segregation of both students and teachers. After hearing the evidence, Rubin concluded that the Dayton school board had intentionally segregated Dayton schools by using optional attendance zones and implementing other policies that promoted segregation. On February 7, 1973, he ordered the board to come up with a plan to end the segregation of students, teachers, and staff.[28]

The plaintiffs were frankly surprised that they had won so much from Rubin. The NAACP's lead attorney, Nathaniel R. Jones, soon to be appointed to the Sixth Circuit Court of Appeals, was leery of the judge. Because of Rubin's various pretrial comments and decisions, Jones feared the judge was more "preoccupied with form rather than substance." The plaintiffs continually wrangled with the judge over what evidence would be admissible. They also fought Rubin's attempts to limit the issues. To them it seemed that Rubin was inclined to see board actions as merely promoting neighborhood schools rather than maintaining segregation. Moreover, during the trial, Rubin suggested "that the judicial mind should be governed by the technical application of the narrowest possible legal rules." Plaintiffs' attorneys disagreed, arguing that the "process of judging was a considerably more complex task" that required judgments based on "a broad understanding of constitutional history and the human striving for equal justice under the law." Rubin countered by claiming such methods were based on emotions rather than logic and the law. Moreover, throughout the proceedings, Rubin often displayed what one plaintiffs' attorney described as "visible wrath."[29]

Although Rubin went with the evidence and found segregative policies on the part of the Dayton school board, the Nixon-appointed Republican's conservatism and desire to maintain neighborhood schools became clear in the remedy stage. Rubin had concluded that the Dayton board's school construction program was "racially neutral," while the plaintiffs had insisted that the board's practices in school construction "had a segregative effect and contributed substantially to the alleged present duality in pupil assignment." Moreover, the plaintiffs had argued that the board's placement of schools contributed to Dayton's segregated housing patterns. The significance of this dispute became clear when the board presented its first plan to Rubin on March 19, 1973. Both the plaintiffs and a minority of the members of the Dayton board objected to the plan, claiming that it merely froze in place the city's present unconstitutional system. It would, they claimed, "fail to eliminate racially identifiable schools when other alternative remedies, such as busing of children to other schools, were available." Rubin, without holding a hearing, sided with the board's majority and approved their plan with only one minor modification. The Sixth Circuit Court of Appeals reversed Rubin's decision, finding the plan "inadequate to remedy the cumulative violation found by the District Court."[30] Then, after the court of appeals finally approved a revamped plan,[31] the Supreme Court vacated that judgment, holding that the evidence was insufficient to justify the remedy and remanded the case back yet again, ordering Rubin to hold additional hearings and make more specific findings.[32]

In a case that came to be known as "Dayton II," Rubin reversed himself, finding that the board's intentional segregation had ended over twenty years before this litigation, that there was nothing unconstitutional about establishing and maintaining neighborhood schools and thus that the plaintiffs had failed to prove that recent policies had a "segregative intent." The problem with Dayton was its almost completely segregated residential patterns. The east side of the Miami River was almost entirely white, whereas the west side was almost entirely black. That, Rubin concluded, caused the racial isolation one saw in the schools, not any deliberate plan by the Dayton school board. And because there was, in Rubin's mind, no evidence that the board had violated the plaintiffs' equal protection rights, he dismissed the complaint.[33] The Sixth Circuit Court of Appeals disagreed, finding that the Dayton board had "intentionally operated a dual school system" at the time of the *Brown* decision and subsequently "never fulfilled their affirmative duty to eliminate the systemwide effects of their prior acts of segregation," thus violating the plaintiffs' equal protection rights. It called for the reinstatement of the systemwide desegregation plan it had approved in July 1976.[34] The Supreme Court affirmed the appellate court's conclusions.[35] In 1976, Rubin finally approved a remedial plan, and the Dayton public school system began operating under it, developing alternative schools as well as carrying out court-ordered busing. Not until 2002 did Judge Rice declare the Dayton school system "unitary" and release it from court supervision.[36]

Throughout the proceedings, Dayton remained tense. Hundreds, perhaps thousands, of "angry callers . . . lit up the telephone lines on radio call-in shows" to protest any change in neighborhood schools.[37] Local newspapers criticized the Sixth Circuit Court of Appeals and the busing solution. And, tragically, in 1974, "an enraged parent of a soon-to-be-bused student" shot and killed Rubin's court-appointed desegregation expert, Dr. Charles Glatt, just a few feet from Rubin's chambers in Dayton's federal courthouse after looking for Rubin and not finding him. But contrary to the fears of many, Dayton did not explode when busing began. After Glatt's murder, Rubin took firm steps to diffuse the issue, establishing a "communitywide panel of citizens from all walks of life" to keep the peace by talking with their neighbors, explaining the purpose of busing and the need to obey the rule of law.[38]

In all three cases, one sees the important role the court played in protecting constitutional rights, often against the wishes of the majority of the community. One also sees the way an individual judge can make a difference and how different approaches, perspectives, and jurisprudential views affect outcomes. Rubin might have exacerbated tensions until he finally determined to implement full integration as ordered by the higher courts. Rice, on the other hand, seeking a just outcome while avoiding litigation and having other favorable factors going for him, was able to achieve a settlement without increasing tensions in the community. All the judges involved, however, recognized the limitations of litigation and the limits of their power. Sensitive to community concerns, they sought to work with elected officials and community groups during the remedial stage. As Michael W. Combs put it, the remedial process involved both persuasion and negotiation. "Contrary to popular opinion," he concluded, the judges demonstrated their sensitivity "to the impact of desegregation policies on the operation of schools, both educationally and administratively" and tried to work with the community to achieve just and effective plans. But, he observed, working with the community could be "a two-edged sword. It can enable the community to work out an effective plan or it can allow school officials to undermine a desegregation plan."[39] The experience in southern Ohio well demonstrates this two-edged sword as well as the benefits and limitations of the courts and their ability to negotiate and help implement social change.

*Employment: The Case of Equal Opportunities to Serve as Police Officers and Firefighters and Beyond*

Perhaps second only to schools, communities focus on the quality of their police and firefighters. But for African Americans and women in the 1970s, the police and fire departments were seen as the bastions of white men. Many African Americans, especially, felt that their communities were threatened rather than protected by these "public servants." Therefore, blacks and women in Columbus, Cincinnati, and Dayton sought equal opportunities to serve in these capacities. Title VII of the Civil Rights Act of 1964 prohibits discrimination in employment based on race or gender and gives the federal courts jurisdiction over such claims.[40]

Both racial minorities and women, in a series of suits, complained about the testing procedures, the interviewing techniques, and other requirements imposed on applicants for fire-fighting or police positions, claiming that they were discriminatory rather than job related. Once hired, they also filed complaints against promotion procedures. In Columbus and Cincinnati, in response to court orders, the defendants signed consent decrees establishing hiring goals, promotion goals in some cases, and new recruiting techniques and testing procedures to assure more access while maintaining qualified forces. In Columbus, in 1973, for example, a group of African American applicants to the Columbus Fire Department filed suit, challenging the department's employment practices. After lengthy hearings, Kinneary concluded that the department's testing and hiring procedures involved several practices that were not related to a candidate's ability to perform as a firefighter, but had a discriminatory effect against African American applicants. Therefore, he ordered the department to devise new tests and procedures and to adopt a goal "to be reached over a period of time" that would lead to having African American firefighters "in the approximate percentage" to their percentage in the general Columbus population. He retained jurisdiction until these goals were achieved.[41] Similar hearings on similar evidence resulted in Duncan and Kinneary issuing similar orders regarding the hiring and promotion of women and African Americans by the city's fire and police departments.[42] In 1992, however, Graham, after hearing a challenge by male firefighter applicants to the consent decree approved by Kinneary in 1989, ordered the decree set aside and enjoined the city from selecting firefighters in the manner provided for in that decree. He based his order on a recent Supreme Court decision, *City of Richmond v. Croson*,[43] holding that "mere statistical imbalance" was insufficient proof of past discrimination.[44] He did, however, uphold the new tests the department had developed and ordered the city to develop hiring procedures that did not discriminate against either men or women. Job-related tests, even if they exclude most women, are constitutional, but the department must be cautious not to use tests that discriminate unnecessarily.[45]

In Cincinnati, Judge Porter helped minority firefighters and the city negotiate an acceptable consent decree whereby the city, though denying that it had discriminated, adopted new recruitment, testing, and promotion policies and procedures with the goal of "significantly" increasing the number of minority firefighters.[46] In 1989, Rubin, after hearing claims by white applicants that their rights were being violated by these new procedures, ordered the decree dissolved.[47] Rubin claimed that, although racial balance had not been achieved, "the violations that provoked [the original suit] no longer existed."[48] In his order, however, he highlighted his general opposition to continued court supervision. Expressing his jurisprudence of judicial restraint, he insisted that "courts should not be the arbiters of every social question." For him, "the basic question to be answered is that if fifteen years of supervision is not enough, what is?" He emphasized that the district court should not "permanently engraft itself upon the appointment procedures of the City of Cincinnati while there exist well established and adequate statutes providing for a nondiscriminatory framework for such appointments." The Sixth Circuit Court of Appeals disagreed, holding that Rubin had not resolved all the objections against dissolution.[49]

In the 1980s, newly hired minorities sued to maintain their gains in the face of layoffs. Rubin initially decided that Cincinnati had to use affirmative action guidelines in laying off police. But after the Supreme Court ruled in *Firefighters Local Union No. 1784 v. Stotts* that courts cannot overrule seniority systems to protect gains in minority hiring,[50] Rubin reversed himself in the Cincinnati police litigation and Porter dismissed a similar suit filed by African American firefighters. This clearly illustrates the limitations imposed upon district court judges. Rubin criticized both the Department of Justice and the Supreme Court for changing positions. First, he noted, the Justice Department challenged the city's hiring practices. But in the 1980s, the department supported seniority. The Supreme Court, likewise, first supported and then limited affirmative action.[51]

Employment discrimination against minorities and women obviously goes well beyond fire and police departments. In almost every occupation, litigation by individuals suing their employers or prospective employers (be they private or public) for alleged discrimination based on race, gender, or sexual orientation continues to keep federal courts busy.[52] One of the earliest such cases had a major impact on the Dayton community. An African American employee of General Motors's Inland Division, an employer of almost six thousand people at two Dayton plants, sued, alleging racial discrimination in the selection of supervisory personnel. After a bench trial, Rubin found that the plaintiff represented a definable class of persons who had been denied opportunities for promotion based on race, in violation of Title VII of the Civil Rights Act of 1964. He awarded the plaintiff, as well as others in the class, back pay equivalent to "the difference between the pay received by supervisory employees and that actually received by the employee in question during the dates" covered by the decision.[53]

Even more significant in the history of the court and the economy of the local community were the suits, initiated beginning in the 1970s, to end discrimination in craft unions. African Americans successfully sued the plumbers and the electricians unions to gain entry and, once members, to prohibit them from awarding jobs based on seniority.[54] They also sought and won an injunction against the state of Ohio, preventing it from entering into any contracts with those who used contractors or unions that discriminated.[55] Although these decisions opened up new opportunities for minorities who had been barred from skilled craft jobs for decades, the victory has been somewhat limited by the Supreme Court's *Croson* decision. After *Croson* held that local governments could establish so-called set-aside programs that favored minority-owned businesses only if they could prove that such programs were enacted to correct specific past discriminatory practices, Judge Graham, using the strict scrutiny standards established by the Supreme Court, overturned Columbus's set-aside programs, holding that these programs unconstitutionally denied majority-owned businesses equal protection of the law in violation of the Fourteenth Amendment because Columbus could not provide any evidence of specific past discriminatory practices. By following the Supreme Court's analysis, Graham upheld new federal interpretations, reversing earlier decisions by the Ohio Supreme Court, thereby maintaining federal supremacy and uniformity.[56]

### Housing and Race

Although discrimination in education and employment were the chief concerns of the African American community, beginning in the 1960s, African Americans also sought help from the district court to end discrimination in housing, to stop redlining (that is, discriminatory lending policies to maintain segregated residential patterns), and to halt urban renewal projects they believed were designed to perpetuate segregated housing patterns. Judges in the Southern District of Ohio agreed that depriving African Americans of their right to buy or rent anywhere they chose violated the Thirteenth Amendment, the Civil Rights Act of 1866, the Civil Rights Act of 1968, and the Fair Housing Act. But to win, plaintiffs had to prove they were denied these rights on the basis of race.[57]

The practice of redlining presented a clear barrier to equal rights in housing. In 1976, Porter presided over one of the first cases in the country challenging this practice. In his widely cited *Laufman v. Oakley Building and Loan Co.*, he established the standard for interpreting recently enacted civil rights legislation. Rejecting the defendant's *"expressio unius est exclusio alterius"* argument for interpreting the Civil Rights Acts of 1964 and 1968, Porter held that that rule of statutory construction must be subordinated to the more modern doctrine that courts will construe legislative provisions in a manner that conforms to the statute's "general purpose," reading "the text in light of its context" so as to carry out Congress's legislative purposes. Relying on interpretations of the statutes by the Department of Housing and Urban Development and the Federal Home Loan Bank Board, as well as the legislative history of the statutes, Porter concluded that Congress had, indeed, intended to outlaw discriminatory loans in a broad number of areas.[58]

More difficult to sustain were suits filed by African Americans to halt urban renewal projects to preserve their neighborhoods. Although the plaintiffs had no difficulty proving that these projects had an adverse effect on their neighborhoods, they generally failed to meet the heavy burden of proving that the government's purpose was discriminatory, and absent that proof, no law prevented government entities from undertaking those projects they believed to be best for the communities.[59]

Despite their failure to halt urban renewal projects, African Americans won important victories in the District Court for the Southern District of Ohio from the 1960s on. Spiegel, praising Porter and the work of other pioneers in civil rights statutory interpretation, explained that the decisions in school desegregation, in employment by the fire department, in discriminatory housing practices, and in "many other less well known cases concerning equal rights in housing and employment" let "it be known to the community that discrimination would not be tolerated."[60]

*Racial Profiling, Police, and the Community*

Racial profiling and the entire issue of the relationship between the police and the citizens they serve has resulted, in Cincinnati, in "the biggest case" that city has seen in years, making national headlines for more than a year. The outcome of this racial-profiling lawsuit dramatically illustrates the increasingly important role district courts play in their communities. It also illustrates the new techniques district courts use, promoting mediation rather than trials to resolve community problems. District court judges are now resolvers of disputes, and this case well represents this proactive role.

In April 2001, after a Cincinnati police officer shot and killed an unarmed African American youth, Timothy Thomas, the city experienced its worse race riots in thirty-three years. In response, Mayor Tom Luken invited the Department of Justice to Cincinnati to investigate Cincinnati police practices. A month before the shooting, the American Civil Liberties Union (ACLU) and local African American activists sought to join in a suit filed in 1999, *Tyehimba v. Cincinnati,* and turn it into a class action suit against the Cincinnati police for discriminatory practices against African Americans. Thus, "the city was confronted with two major legal problems." The first was the investigation by the justice department into Cincinnati police procedures to determine whether those practices contributed to Thomas's shooting and the April riots. The second was the pending racial profiling lawsuit, accusing the police of singling out African Americans for traffic stops because of the color of their skin. The subject of racial profiling made front-page news "amid allegations that it was a widespread social and legal problem." Racial tensions remained high.[61]

As the Department of Justice investigation moved along, the city, the ACLU, and black citizen groups asked Judge Dlott to "take unprecedented action to mediate the . . . case." Dlott took control, putting the plaintiff's request to amend the *Tyehimba* suit to certify a class on hold and establishing an innovative, special collaborative procedure "to address the social conflicts alleged" in the racial profiling lawsuit. Dlott appointed Jay Rothman and his conflict-resolution firm to "manage the collaborative procedure." During the process, Dlott continually monitored the negotiations, holding periodic status conferences to ensure that everything was kept on track and that all sides were committed to the negotiation process. Eventually all groups involved in both disputes were linked together in marathon negotiation sessions that included representatives of the Department of Justice, the ACLU, the Fraternal Order of Police, the city of Cincinnati, and the Cincinnati Black United Front, a local civil rights group. After Rothman and his firm had worked for a year, Magistrate Judge Merz took over the final stages of negotiations.[62]

Once a settlement was reached, Dlott held a fairness hearing before approving the "historic," "groundbreaking" agreement that many thought could become a model for other communities throughout the country facing similar problems. According to ACLU attorney Scott Greenwood, this was the first time anywhere in the country that a "binding agreement" was put in place "so the community and the rank-and-file officers can work together to fundamentally change policing" in a community. The agreement called for the creation of a Citizen Complaint Authority and other procedures to track citizen complaints and the development of new police policies on the use of force, foot pursuits, and the interaction between the police and the community. The court appointed a monitor to oversee adherence by the police and the citizens of Cincinnati, while Merz serves as conciliator—that is, a liaison between the monitor and Dlott—reviewing the monitor's quarterly reports. Dlott and the district court retain jurisdiction.[63]

In the mid-1980s, allegations of police misconduct in Dayton aroused "constant media attention and community concern." The three-year controversy began after Dayton police shot an apparently innocent man in a raid undertaken under a search warrant based on false affidavits. An investigation revealed not only lax standards for securing search warrants but also unconstitutional tactics used by the police and "sweetheart relationships" between the police and some state and local judges.[64] As a result, Rice presided over two lengthy, media-charged trials. In the first, a jury awarded the widow of the innocent man shot by police the "staggering sum" of $3.5 million in her wrongful death suit against the city, encouraging the city to tighten up procedures.[65] The second case began after a grand jury indicted Robert H. Clemmer and Charles E. Gentry, two Dayton police detectives with a reputation for successful drug busting, for conspiring with drug lords to undermine criminal investigations and for filing false income tax returns. After a long trial, the jury acquitted the two on the more serious conspiracy charges but convicted them on one minor tax count. Although Rice believed Clemmer was entitled to a judgment of acquittal because the jury verdict was based on improper information, the Sixth Circuit Court of Appeals disagreed and ordered the guilty verdict reinstated.[66]

In both Cincinnati and Dayton, one sees the new role the federal district court plays after two hundred years of ever-expanding jurisdiction. By the end of the twentieth century, citizens increasingly turn to the court to help them fight those government officials they believe are depriving them of their constitutional rights.

### Other Areas Involving the Equal Protection of the Law

The right to be free from discrimination based on one's sexual orientation emerged as a new concept toward the end of the twentieth century, and in this area, too, the judges of the Southern District of Ohio have consistently upheld the nondiscriminatory principle.[67] And in one case, Spiegel broke new ground, becoming the first federal district court judge to declare that gays, lesbians, and bisexuals were entitled to constitutional protection from discrimination based on sexual orientation. Declaring that gays and lesbians were a "quasi-suspect class," he ruled that any law limiting their rights, to be constitutional, must further an important governmental interest. This, he concluded, the Cincinnati charter amendment at issue in *Equality Foundation of Greater Cincinnati, Inc. v. City of Cincinnati* did not do.[68]

The case arose after Cincinnati voters, on November 2, 1993, passed an initiative, generally labeled Issue 3, preventing the city from enacting any ordinance that provides that those with a homosexual or bisexual orientation are entitled to "any claim to minority or protected status." The effect was to repeal a Cincinnati city council ordinance that had banned, among other things, private discrimination based on sexual orientation in employment, housing, or public accommodation. Holding that Issue 3 violated plaintiffs' rights to equal protection of the law in violation of the Fourteenth Amendment, Spiegel explained that the Charter amendment imposed burdens on "an identifiable group of citizens" "without being rationally related to any legitimate governmental purpose." Specifically, it "fences out" gays, lesbians, and bisexuals "from the political process by imposing upon them an added and significant burden on their quest for favorable legislation." As such, in addition to denying the plaintiffs their equal protection rights, it deprived them of their First Amendment right to free speech and free political association.[69] Spiegel explained that, unlike statutes that regulate conduct, the Charter amendment was directed toward a person's "orientation," which the plaintiffs clearly demonstrated was determined by the time one was one or two years of age. Therefore, one had almost as little control over sexual orientation as over race or gender.[70]

Realizing that this was an explosive issue, Spiegel emphasized that his decision "in no way [gave] any group any rights above and beyond those enjoyed by all citizens." Rather, he said, his decision "simply" prevented a "group of citizens from being deprived of the very rights we all share." Conceding that it might "*seem* unfair" to overturn the majority will of a community on such a "deeply emotional" issue, he tried to educate the citizens of Cincinnati on the underlying principles and "deeply rooted" traditions of America—that "rights protected by the Constitution can never be subordinated to the vote of the majority."[71]

Judge Robert B. Krupansky, writing for a three-judge Sixth Circuit Court of Appeals panel, rejected Spiegel's "novel" approach, ruling instead that homosexuals were not an "identifiable class" entitled to any special constitutional protections, that Issue 3 did not exclude homosexuals from the political process, that city governments have no obligation to outlaw private discrimination by individuals against gays and lesbians, and that Issue 3 was rationally related to permissible governmental goals.[72] But the following year, the Supreme Court, in *Romer v. Evans,* overturned a nearly identical Colorado antigay statute.[73] It then vacated the appellate court's decision in *Equality Foundation* and remanded the case "for further consideration in light of *Romer.*"[74] A deeply divided Sixth Circuit Court of Appeals refused en banc review, holding that *Romer* had no precedential value in the Cincinnati case because *Romer* dealt with a state law whereas Issue 3 was a mere city ordinance. Judge Danny Boggs, concurring in the appellate court's denial of rehearing en banc, explained: "Cincinnati's Issue 3 merely reflects the kind of social and political experimentation that is such a common characteristic of city government."[75] On appeal, the Supreme Court refused to review the appellate court's decision. Justice David H. Souter told Spiegel that the high court decided to deny certiorari largely because the issue involved only one "small community."[76]

*Voting Rights: Equal Protection and Citizen Rights under the First Amendment*

As Spiegel argued in *Equality Foundation,* some of the most basic rights in a democratic government are the right to vote and the right to unfettered political association. Indeed, a three-judge district court panel declared that "no right is more precious in a free country than that of having a voice in the election of those who make the laws under which . . . we must live."[77] But the state of Ohio, by its election laws, has denied at least some of its citizens these fundamental rights. Beginning in the 1960s, various groups began to challenge the state's discriminatory practices.

First, a variety of citizens' groups challenged the way the Ohio state legislature was apportioned and the way candidates were elected. Initially, in 1963, citizens from Cuyahoga (Cleveland) and Hamilton (Cincinnati) counties challenged the apportionment of the state House of Representatives whereby each county was guaranteed one representative regardless of population. The plaintiffs argued that this apportionment violated the Civil Rights Act by denying them equal protection and the principle of one person, one vote. Although a three-judge district court panel disagreed, the Supreme Court reversed that decision, forcing the Ohio legislature to develop a new method of apportionment.[78] Challenges by African American citizens to at-large elections for municipal and state judges and for Cincinnati city council, however, failed. In all cases, the judges rejected the plaintiffs' contentions that at-large elections violated the Voting Rights Act of 1965 by impermissibly diluting minority votes.[79]

More successful were challenges to those Ohio election laws that curtailed not only citizens' rights to equal protection of the laws but also their First Amendment rights to free political association. Since the 1950s, Ohio required new parties seeking to place candidates on a ballot to file petitions that had been signed by qualified voters totaling 15 percent of the vote in the last gubernatorial election, whereas established parties needed signatures totaling only 10 percent. In addition, these new parties had to file their petitions ninety days before the primary.[80] In 1968, the Socialist Labor Party launched the first challenge to these laws, focusing on the requirement for the large number of signatures needed to be placed on the ballot. Three weeks later, George Wallace's American Independent Party filed a more general attack on all of Ohio's election law statutes.[81] In *Socialist Labor Party v. Rhodes* and *Williams v. Rhodes,* a three-judge panel composed of Cecil, Kinneary, and Weinman declared much of Ohio's election code unconstitutional, holding that the code made it virtually impossible for new political parties, even those with wide support, to gain a place on the state ballot. But although the three agreed that Ohio's presidential ballot had to provide space for write-in votes, Cecil and Weinman refused to order the state to print the names of the minority parties' candidates on that ballot. The Supreme Court settled the issue by requiring the state to place the names of the Wallace electors on the ballot but not the names of the candidates for the Socialist Labor Party. It held that, not only were the socialists a small organization, but they had also filed their protest too close to the election.[82]

In response, Ohio enacted new election laws. Two years later, the Socialist Labor Party challenged these new laws, and again a three-judge panel declared most provisions unconstitutional. Ohio, the court held, could not require a political party to hold a nominating convention or require so many signatures on a petition that the requirement became unreasonable. But the state could require candidates to take a loyalty oath, swearing that their party was not engaged in an attempt to overthrow the government by force or violence.[83]

The state legislature then changed Ohio's election laws for a third time. It was still clear, however, that the General Assembly sought to limit the efforts of independent candidates and various socialist parties. A decade later, in 1982, an independent candidate challenged the Ohio requirement that independents file nominating papers two and a half months before a primary election. Duncan held that provision to be an unconstitutional deprivation of citizens' First Amendment right to political association without any compelling state need.[84] Finally, that same year the Socialist Workers' Party challenged Ohio's requirement that the party had to disclose campaign income and expenses. After heated discovery fights in which the government claimed that its investigation of the party was privileged and, in response, the court demanded in camera inspection, a district court panel concluded that the reporting provision, at least as applied to the Socialist Workers' Party, was unconstitutional since compelling disclosure by minor political parties could subject their members to threats and harassment.[85] The Supreme Court affirmed the panel.[86] For three decades thereafter, the District Court for the Southern District of Ohio has repeatedly confirmed that only when there is a compelling state interest can the state of Ohio restrict ballot choices. The state cannot, through its election laws, curtail fundamental rights in its effort to "eliminat[e] . . . third party and independent candidates from Ohio elections."[87]

Other candidates have challenged Ohio's election laws prohibiting false statements by political candidates as another abridgement of the First Amendment, this time that amendment's guarantee to the right to free speech. Here, although the court held the regulation to be an unconstitutional restriction of free speech because it was too vague and because it was not subject to judicial review, it ruled that the state can forbid false speech if it is proven false and if it is proven, by clear and convincing evidence, that the speaker knew it was false.[88]

## THE BILL OF RIGHTS IN THE SOUTHERN DISTRICT OF OHIO

### The First Amendment

In the last four decades, the U.S. District Court for the Southern District of Ohio has handled several high-profile civil liberties cases in which it has defined the scope of First Amendment rights to free speech and the free exercise of one's religion. As Judge Graham noted, most of the time district court judges deal with individual litigants, helping people settle their disputes, but occasionally they get a case of significant public interest or cases in which the decision will affect the public significantly. These First Amendment cases fall into the latter category.[89]

In 1989, after hearing the first of these cases, Graham held that the Delaware County nativity scene on the courthouse lawn violated the establishment clause of the First Amendment. In this case, the district court clarified for Ohioans the restrictions on government entanglement with religious symbols.[90] The case also offers an excellent illustration of how a district court judge decides a case. District court judges in this region are bound to follow precedents established by the U.S. Supreme Court and the Sixth Circuit Court of Appeals. Many scholars claim that much judicial activism occurs at the district court level.[91] This may be true in some cases, but at least the district judges for the Southern District of Ohio take seriously the constraints of precedent. Thus, in the Delaware County case, Graham postponed his decision until the Supreme Court decided an analogous case in Allegheny County, Pennsylvania. Then, with the guidance of the Supreme Court, Graham helped the parties work out a settlement agreement.[92]

Although the Supreme Court established a clear standard against government-sponsored nativity scenes, the right of religious groups to use public forums is less clear-cut. Rubin first addressed the issue in two cases involving the use of Fountain Square in Cincinnati. Holding that the square was a traditional public forum, he ruled that the city could not prohibit a group of ultraorthodox Jews from putting up a menorah during Chanukah or the Ku Klux Klan from erecting a cross at Christmas; both were protected speech. Further, the Klan's cross could not be prohibited as "fighting words," as Cincinnati city council claimed.[93] Rubin told city officials that they "should worry more about protecting free speech" and less about "restricting it." Even anti-Semites and racists have a right to use Fountain Square, he explained. "The Constitution of the United States does not protect only good people. It protects bad people as well."[94]

Judge Graham faced the same issue in Columbus, when the Klan wanted to erect a cross on Capitol Square. As Rubin did in Cincinnati, Graham held Capitol Square to be a traditional public forum. By contrast, perhaps because of his views on the separation of church and state, Graham analyzed the case in terms of not only the First Amendment's free speech clause but also its establishment clause. First, he held that the Klan was entitled to erect a Latin cross in such a public arena based on its First Amendment right to free speech. In a ringing endorsement for the importance of free speech in a free society Graham wrote, "The constitutional right of freedom of speech would be meaningless if it did not apply equally to all groups, popular and unpopular alike." But further, he held that the display of an unattended cross on a public square, even in front of the state capitol, was not an impermissible endorsement of religion. Distinguishing this case from the Delaware County case, he maintained that, in the case of the Klan, a private party was displaying a religious symbol on a public square that was a focal point for the exchange of ideas. There was no government entanglement or endorsement, as there had been in Delaware County.[95] The Supreme Court's decision affirming Graham's ruling is considered a landmark case. Commentators have labeled the decision "far reaching," "signaling a shift in First Amendment jurisprudence" by weakening the state-endorsement prong of the traditional *Lemon* test[96] and focusing instead on the issue of equal access to public forums. Others, who prefer more scope for the free exercise of religion, lament that the Supreme Court did not set down a bright-line rule protecting all speech in public arenas.[97]

More recently, Graham, in "Capitol Square II," upheld Ohio's state motto, "With God All Things Are Possible," which is engraved on the plaza at the entrance to the Statehouse. Although the motto comes from the New Testament, Graham held that the words had been completely removed from their religious context and served a legitimate secular purpose of inculcating hope and acknowledging "the humility that government leaders frequently feel in grappling with difficult public policy issues."[98] Relying on the Supreme Court's decision in *Marsh v. Chambers*,[99] which upheld the practice of a prayer before the opening of a legislative session, Graham concluded that "viewed in the context of a long tradition of government acknowledgment of religion in mottoes, oaths, and anthems, the Ohio motto does not have the primary or principal purpose of advancing religion, and it does not foster excessive government entanglement with religion."[100] In a similar vein, Dlott upheld the constitutionality of Christmas as a legal public holiday, finding that such a designation merely acknowledges the secular cultural aspects of the occasion and does not impermissibly endorse religion or excessively entangle government with religion.[101]

The court has confronted several other important First Amendment issues since the 1960s. One of the most publicized, addressing questions of what is obscenity and what is protected speech, began in 1989 when Cincinnati's Contemporary Arts Center (CAC) exhibited Robert Mapplethorpe's allegedly sadomasochistic and homoerotic photographs. City and county officials with "a long history of zealously prosecuting anyone who violated what they considered to be community standards of decency," won an indictment against the CAC and its director, Dennis Barrie, for two misdemeanor offenses—pandering obscenity and the illegal use of minors in nudity-oriented material. The ensuing trial in municipal court, "the first . . . in the United States" in which "an arts institution and its director [went] on trial for pandering obscenity," "reinforced Cincinnati's reputation as a bastion of conservatism." Although the national media criticized Cincinnati's "prudery," many local citizens supported their elected officials' efforts to protect what they believed to be traditional community values.[102]

Rubin issued a preliminary injunction preventing the county prosecutor, the county sheriff, and the city police from interfering with the exhibit. Until a court determined whether the photographs were obscene, the CAC was free to continue the exhibit. Local officials had no authority to determine legal issues. After the exhibit was shown, a municipal court jury acquitted the CAC and Barrie of the misdemeanor charges.[103]

Other judges have had to resolve disputes over the limits, if any, that may be placed on political speech. Dlott, for example, rejected attempts by the Southwest Ohio Regional Transit Authority (SORTA) to restrict advertising by a labor union that the company maintained was unsightly and controversial. The Sixth Circuit Court of Appeals, in affirming Dlott, went even further, proclaiming that, based on its practices rather than its written policies, SORTA had demonstrated its intent to designate advertising space on its buses as a public forum. Therefore, any restrictions were subject to strict scrutiny.[104] Before the appellate court rendered its decision, however, Beckwith, holding that SORTA had not made its buses public forums, refused to issue an order requiring the bus company to accept advertising signs from a Hamilton County commission candidate.[105] After the Sixth Circuit Court of Appeals rendered its decision in the Dlott case, however, Beckwith reversed herself *sua sponte* to comply with the higher court's decision.[106] These decisions by Dlott, Beckwith, and the panel of the Sixth Circuit Court of Appeals well illustrate not only the opportunities judges have to determine the extent of individual rights in different situations based on their personal views of the law and the facts of a given case but also the limited opportunities district court judges have for policy making. Once the appellate court has spoken clearly on an issue, the district court judges, no matter what their own views, follow the higher court's doctrine.

*The Protection of Other Fundamental Rights*

In addition to protecting citizens' First Amendment rights, district court judges are regularly called upon to interpret the scope of other rights protected by the Bill of Rights and federal statutes. They have, for example, handled challenges to gun regulations on Second Amendment grounds[107] and numerous Fourth Amendment search and seizure cases.[108] One case that received a great deal of publicity illustrates the importance of federal courts in protecting the rights of the powerless. Carolyn Wade sued seven defendants for violating her civil rights by ordering and then performing a forced sterilization on her when she was seventeen years old, because government officials had determined that she was "feeble minded." In resolving the issue of immunity, which was a necessary prerequisite for the suit to proceed, Kinneary held that the probate judge who ordered the girl to submit to sterilization had no judicial immunity because he acted beyond his scope of authority; the doctor who performed the operation and the hospital in which the surgery was performed were not public officials or institutions and therefore not immune from liability; and the officials of the Muskingum County Children's Services Board are individually responsible for their actions. Only the Children's Services Board itself, as an agency of the state, was immune from litigation.[109]

By making individual officials responsible for their actions, Kinneary ensured that judges and government officials could not hide behind the argument that they were just following orders. After Kinneary's decision on the immunity issue, the case went to trial. By then Wade was a married adult. Although she had an IQ lower than "normal," she was able to work and support herself. And at trial, she understood the attorney's questions and gave effective testimony, telling the jurors that she very much wanted to have children and was greatly distressed because, after the sterilization operation, she could not. After Wade's testimony, the parties settled for an undisclosed amount.[110]

### The Right to Privacy and Abortion Protest

Cases dealing with the privacy rights of women to have abortions and the rights of those who oppose abortion to protest that right continue to receive widespread publicity as county officials and state legislators continue to try to place restrictions on women's access to abortions. By upholding constitutional rights as regularly reasserted by the Supreme Court, the judges of the District Court for the Southern District of Ohio have reaffirmed, on numerous occasions, the privacy rights of women to have abortions.[111] Dlott has twice held that Hamilton County officials may not prohibit female prisoners' access to abortion services. She declared, first, that inmates still have basic constitutional rights, and, second, that one of those rights, as repeatedly affirmed by the Supreme Court, is not to place undue burdens on a woman's decision about whether to terminate her pregnancy. She reminded the Hamilton County sheriff, Simon Leis, that no matter what his view was toward abortion, "ours is a government of laws, not of men."[112]

More controversial were two decisions by Rice declaring unconstitutional two attempts by the Ohio legislature to outlaw certain procedures often referred to as partial-birth abortions. Relying on the Supreme Court's ruling in *Planned Parenthood v. Casey*,[113] Rice held that Ohio may not enact regulations that place substantial obstacles against a woman's decision to seek an abortion before the fetus is viable. Further, he held that, even after viability, although the state may regulate, it may not do so in a manner that could have an adverse impact on the life or health of the pregnant woman.[114] He explained that the evidence in the cases before him showed that the procedure at issue was not used as a means of late pregnancy birth control. Rather, doctors used it only in those very rare cases when they believed it was the best option open to protect the physical or psychological health of the woman.[115]

The judges of the Southern District of Ohio have also affirmed the right of doctors who perform abortions and clinics that provide abortion services to be protected against undue harassment. Smith, for example, upheld the city of Upper Arlington's ordinance prohibiting residential picketing and ruled that it could be applied to prevent continuous picketing in front of a physician's home. The abortion protestors had claimed that the ordinance deprived them of their First and Fourteenth Amendment rights to free speech; the city and its citizens argued that they were entitled to the rights of privacy and the sanctity of their homes. Relying heavily on the Supreme Court's decision in *Frisby v. Schultz*,[116] Smith ruled that the ordinance could not be enforced to prevent picketing, but picketing could be limited. Describing the picketing as rising to the level of a "siege" as defined in *Frisby* so as to constitute an "invasion of residential privacy," Smith established a "bright-line standard" to "best serve the competing interests" and the police who had to enforce the ordinance while also trying to protect the free speech rights of the picketers. He ruled that no picketing would be allowed in front of the physician's home or in front of the two homes on either side of the physician's home.[117] The Sixth Circuit Court of Appeals, however, reversed Smith, holding that an overbroad ordinance could not be saved by a judge narrowing its enforcement; an ordinance that broadly prohibited residential picketing was an unconstitutional deprivation of free speech, not being narrowly tailored to balance the right of free speech against the city's interest in residential privacy.[118]

After Congress enacted the Freedom of Access to Clinic Entrances Act in 1994,[119] Rice upheld it against abortion protestors' claims that it violated their First and Tenth Amendment rights. Rice held that Congress, exercising its commerce clause powers, could prevent obstruction of access to facilities providing abortion services. The defendants, therefore, if found guilty, would be liable for blockading entrances to such clinics or directing others to do so.[120]

Although the district judges in southern Ohio often enforced federal laws and Supreme Court rulings against demonstrations by citizens opposed to abortions, actions by state officials, and legislation by elected representatives, at least one case demonstrates that some citizens agree that violence is no way to resolve social issues. Cincinnati jurors showed no sympathy for Clayton Lee Waager's campaign to stop abortions by threatening abortion clinics. Waager had sent the clinics fake anthrax letters and vowed to kill any doctor who performed an abortion. At trial, Waager represented himself. His defense was that he was simply doing God's work. Further, God proved that He was on Waager's side by helping Waager elude police during his ten-month run after escaping from Illinois authorities. After a four-day trial in which Dlott presided, a jury convicted Waager of firearms and stolen weapons charges.[121]

As Ohioans enter the twenty-first century, they continue to turn to the federal courts to protect their constitutional rights from governmental actions they view as restrictive. The judges of the District Court for the Southern District of Ohio have had a tremendous impact on life in their communities, as they preside over, adjudicate, and mediate these disputes. In resolving these cases, the judges have generally insisted that governmental officials treat all equally and that minorities and women have equal access to schools, jobs, and the ballot box. They have also protected individual rights to free speech, free religious expression, and privacy. Although they sometimes have discretion in rendering decisions, given the facts of a case and the broad doctrines of the higher courts, the district court judges work within the confines of the law as enacted by Congress and interpreted by the Sixth Circuit Court of Appeals and the U.S. Supreme Court. When the opportunity presents itself and the situation seems to call for a unique decision, they may exercise judicial activism to help resolve community tensions, but when a higher court speaks clearly, they obey its mandate. The judges use this same approach in interpreting regulatory statutes, in resolving disputes affecting the economic life of southern Ohio, and in adjudicating civil and criminal cases that affect not only the individuals involved but also the economic and social well-being of Ohio and the nation.

# 8

## THE DISTRICT COURT AS ARBITER, INTERPRETER, AND INNOVATOR, 1960–2003

IN 1803, OHIOANS WELCOMED their status as citizens of a new state. They were proud of their full-fledged affiliation with the nation. Nevertheless, although they embraced the nation and the opportunities it offered, many also resented some occasions when the national government imposed its power on them. And when resentments flared, citizens viewed the federal district court with suspicion; it was the place where the government went to collect its taxes, enforce its regulations, and impose on unwilling citizens such "undemocratic" institutions and laws as the national bank or the fugitive slave acts. Two hundred years later, although average citizens now turn to the court as a place of recourse where they can go to seek protection of their rights and liberties, the court continues to play its original role. Indeed, the court's role as enforcer of federal law has increased in importance as the federal government has come to regulate more aspects of the national economy and is involved in more areas of American life. Besides enforcing such legislation as the Selective Service Act, provisions of the Social Security Act, and numerous civil rights and voting rights mandates, as well as protecting liberties guaranteed by the Bill of Rights and the Fourteenth Amendment to the Constitution, the judges of the federal district court adjudicate hundreds of criminal and civil cases that affect not only the individual litigants or the criminally accused but also the economic and social well-being of Ohio and the entire nation. As interpreters of federal law, arbitrators of power between the states and the federal government, and adjudicators of civil disputes and criminal prosecutions, the judges of the U.S. District Court for the Southern District of Ohio have a continuing impact on the political, social, and economic lives of their community.

## INTERPRETING REGULATORY STATUTES

As the federal government continues to enact legislation regulating economic and social issues, the courts are increasingly called upon to interpret the statutes and arbitrate disputes concerning their scope and their meaning.

In 1982, Duncan heard an environmental case that illustrates important points both about how citizens use the law and about the clear lines between legislative and administrative authority on the one hand and judicial authority on the other. In March 1979, the secretary of the U.S. Air Force announced the sharp curtailment of activities at Rickenbacker Air National Guard Base near Groveport, a suburban area south of Columbus, Ohio. Before 1979, Rickenbacker was a fully operational Strategic Air Command (SAC) base employing approximately 1,800 military personnel and 1,200 civilians. By July 1979, however, SAC activities at Rickenbacker ceased and the base was turned over to the Ohio Air National Guard. Eventually, after the air force completed its planned phaseout, only 148 military personnel and 768 civilians would remain.

Hoping to prevent further cutbacks, in October 1980 a group of retired air force personnel who wanted to ensure that they would continue to obtain goods and medical services at the substantial discounts given retired military, filed a civil suit under the provisions of the National Environmental Policy Act (NEPA), hoping to prevent the abandonment of facilities they believed to be vital to national defense just to save money and to prevent the loss of a facility that provided important economic benefits to the region. They claimed the air force's environmental impact study did not sufficiently consider the economic ramifications of the decision.

In the meantime, the city of Columbus and several of the surrounding suburbs formed the Rickenbacker Port Authority (RPA) to negotiate a joint use agreement with the air force for the development of the abandoned area into an air cargo facility. But citizens in the area around the old base worried about the noise the new plan would generate. Therefore, after Duncan refused to grant the original plaintiffs the injunctive relief they sought, an expanded group of plaintiffs amended the complaint to challenge the sufficiency of the air force's environmental impact study on noise pollution. After hearing four days of testimony, Duncan, though emphasizing the narrow scope of the court's reviewing power, concluded that further study was, indeed, needed on the noise issue to comply with federal law and regulations. He was, however, quick to underscore the fact that, although "NEPA establishes 'significant substantive goals for the Nation,' it does not wrest from administrative agencies their traditional decisionmaking power." Ultimately, Duncan pointed out, "the final decision on how best to use the facilities at Rickenbacker rests exclusively with the Secretary of the Air Force, not this Court."[1]

Although Duncan emphasized the limits of judicial power when Congress delegated authority to an administrative agency or a department in the executive branch of government, Rubin, as the first judge in the nation to interpret the "Superfund" statute (CERCLA—the Comprehensive Environmental Response, Compensation, and Liability Act) on the issue of liability, enhanced the ability of plaintiffs to recover for harms done in major environmental cases and, in the words of two legal scholars, provided for "a more equitable distribution of liability."[2] The issue in *United States v. Chem-Dyne Corp.* was whether CERCLA allowed joint and several liability. The statute itself was silent on the subject, so Rubin turned to legislative history. After detailed analysis, he concluded that Congress's omission of any mention of joint and several liability did not mean that such liability could never be imposed. Rather, Rubin held that by remaining silent on the subject, Congress intended the courts to rely on common law. Applying the *Restatement (Second) of Torts,* Rubin held that joint and several liability applied when two or more persons caused a single, indivisible harm, but each party was liable for his or her share of the harm when each caused a separate harm for which "there is a reasonable basis for division." Further, defendants seeking to limit or share liability had the burden of proof.[3] *Chem-Dyne,* being the first case to deal with this issue, became "the seminal" one "on the issue of joint and several liability" in CERCLA litigation."[4]

The *Chem-Dyne* litigation illustrates the influential role judges can play in implementing federal statutes. Another major case, *Gravitt v. General Electric,* shows the important role federal courts have in America's constitutional system of checks and balances. By using its power to hold other branches of government accountable and force them to do their jobs as federal statutes require, the courts prevent sweetheart deals between government agencies and their major contractors, thereby protecting the public's interest. In the *Gravitt* case, Rubin ensured that the Department of Justice did not allow a major defense contractor to defraud taxpayers. John Michael Gravitt, a machinist foreman at General Electric's Aircraft Engineer Division in the Cincinnati suburb of Evendale, filed his "whistleblower" suit in 1984 under the federal False Claims Act, an antiprofiteering statute enacted more than a hundred years earlier during the Civil War to prevent government contractors from overcharging the government. The statute allows an individual citizen to sue on behalf of the government; if the government then wins the suit, the person initiating the suit will share in the recovered damages. Gravitt had reported the violations he saw to GE's executive vice president Brian Rowe in 1983. Although an internal audit verified Gravitt's complaints, GE laid Gravitt off. Claiming that his "layoff" was due in large part to his refusal to go along with GE's ongoing fraudulent activities, Gravitt filed his qui tam suit accusing GE of billing the Department of Defense for idle time and for jet engine work done for others. A Vietnam Marine Corps veteran and recipient of a Purple Heart, Gravitt wanted to protect the taxpayers from "shenanigans and fraud" that "ran up costs" in government contracts.[5]

The Department of Justice took over the investigation and negotiated a settlement with GE whereby the company agreed to pay $234,000 in civil penalties. Gravitt and his attorney, James B. Helmer Jr. fought the settlement, arguing that it was "a 'sweetheart deal' that denied the public millions in recovered payments and penalties." Overturning the report and recommendation by Magistrate Judge Robert A. Steinberg, Rubin agreed with Gravitt and his lawyer. In his order rejecting the settlement proposal as "inadequate," Rubin said he was "puzzled" by the government's handling of the case. "The Justice Department's civil attorneys took no depositions, interviewed no witnesses and confined its efforts to opposing Helmer's attempts to do the same." Indeed, all Rubin saw was a "remarkable lack of cooperation" by the Department of Justice. He then allowed the suit to continue under the more liberal 1986 amendment to the False Claims Act, which no longer required the whistleblower to prove "an intent" to defraud the government and established lower levels of proof needed to win the amended, higher civil penalties "from profiteering companies."[6] Eventually, five years after Gravitt filed his suit, GE settled with the government for $3.5 million. Gravitt and the three other plaintiffs who filed suits subsequent to Gravitt's divided 22 percent of the settlement—$770,000. The balance went to the U.S. Treasury. The payment was the largest made "in a suit brought by individuals under the False Claims Act."[7] Gravitt believed he had accomplished something important: "We slowed them down a bit. . . . I don't know if we stopped them. But there's an army of bounty-hunters out there now."[8] Although Gravitt's persistence was responsible for the victory, so was Rubin's insistence that the government pursue the case vigorously. When Department of Justice attorneys tried to tell Rubin that his only role in the case was to approve its proposed $234,000 settlement, the "blast from the bench" was like "trying to take a bone from a hungry Doberman who then growled and showed his teeth."[9]

## FEDERALISM AND THE ELEVENTH AMENDMENT

Although the enforcement of federal statutes and the adjudication of disputes can be controversial because both require interpretation of often ambiguously worded statutes and regulations, one of the major issues that has most divided the judges of the district court for southern Ohio in the last several decades is the scope of federal authority over the state and its officials. The Eleventh Amendment to the Constitution protects states from being sued without their consent by citizens of other states or by foreign countries. Until the Sixth Circuit Court of Appeals and the Supreme Court developed sufficiently clear doctrine, the issue the district judges grappled with was the scope of Ohio's Eleventh Amendment immunity.

In the 1980s and early 1990s, Duncan, Rubin, and Smith, following the Supreme Court's 1908 decision in *Ex parte Young*,[10] held that state officials, within a narrow set of rules, could be sued for violating federal law. Duncan explained that *Ex parte Young* held that plaintiffs could "obtain prospective injunctive relief," including reinstatement, although not retroactive relief or damages, from state officials who had violated federal law. Federal courts, however, had no jurisdiction to hear suits accusing state officials of violating state law. Thus, he held that a disabled plaintiff could, under the authority of the equal protection clause of the Fourteenth Amendment, enjoin the Ohio Department of Youth Services from terminating him because of his epilepsy, in violation of the federal Rehabilitation Act of 1973.[11] Smith agreed, enjoining Governor George Voinovich, the Ohio Department of Mental Retardation and Developmental Disabilities and its director, and the Ohio Department of Human Services and its director, from depriving mentally retarded and developmentally disabled Ohioans of their equal protection and due process rights and from violating the Rehabilitation Act, the Americans with Disabilities Act (ADA), Medicaid statutes, and regulations enforceable under 42 U.S.C.A. § 1983. Further, Smith upheld the federal statute requiring the state to provide "sufficient resources," ruling that although this constituted prospective relief, Congress had made its intention to abrogate the states' Eleventh Amendment immunity "unmistakably clear" in the language of the ADA and the Rehabilitation Act.[12]

But in 1996, the Supreme Court, in *Seminole Tribe of Florida v. Florida*,[13] held that Congress could not abrogate Eleventh Amendment immunity in any statute passed pursuant to its Article I enumerated powers, including its spending, commerce, bankruptcy, or intellectual property powers. The states' immunity could be abrogated only when the substantive statute was enacted pursuant to Congress's powers under Section 5 of the Fourteenth Amendment. The following year, in *City of Boerne v. Flores,* the Court went further, holding that Congress's ability to abrogate states' immunity under Section 5 was limited to statutes enforcing substantive Fourteenth Amendment guarantees.[14] District court judges now had to decide under what authority Congress enacted various regulatory and remedial statutes.

*Wilson-Jones v. Caviness* clearly illustrates the impact these Supreme Court decisions have had. Graham initially upheld what had been, before 1996, the Supreme Court's view that Congress could broadly abrogate states' Eleventh Amendment immunity, allowing a suit against the Ohio Civil Rights

Commission under the Fair Labor Standards Act to proceed. Hearing the commission's appeal after the Supreme Court's *Seminole Tribe* decision, however, the Sixth Circuit vacated Graham's decision, holding that Congress could not waive Ohio's Eleventh Amendment immunity in statutes such as the Fair Labor Standards Act, passed pursuant to Congress's Article I interstate commerce powers.[15]

After this, the district court judges came to very different conclusions on how to apply Supreme Court doctrine. Judges appointed by Democratic presidents tended to find authority under Section 5 of the Fourteenth Amendment, while those appointed by Republican presidents did not. For example, when analyzing the ADA, the Rehabilitation Act, and the Age Discrimination in Employment Act (ADEA), Dlott, Marbley, Sargus, and Spiegel held that Congress enacted these statutes pursuant to its powers under Section 5 of the Fourteenth Amendment, that Congress's clear language abrogating the states' Eleventh Amendment immunity was in force, and that plaintiffs could sue state officials to enforce these statutes. Believing that the Fourteenth Amendment fundamentally changed the structure of government, granting additional powers to the federal government, these judges emphasized that courts should defer to Congress's judgment as much as possible as to what legislation is "necessary to secure the guarantees of the Fourteenth Amendment." Examining the statutes' text, stated purposes, and legislative history, they found the legislation appropriate under the Fourteenth Amendment's equal protection clause. As Marbley succinctly concluded, "The state can't hide behind the Eleventh Amendment."[16]

Sargus's 1997 decision in *Value Behavioral v. Ohio Department of Mental Health* illustrates the stance of these judges. Clearly resisting any further restrictions on Congress's power to abrogate the states' Eleventh Amendment immunity, Sargus carefully analyzed several conflicting Supreme Court decisions.[17] Because the Supreme Court had not yet reconciled its *Seminole Tribe* ruling with its previous decision in *Maine v. Thiboutot*,[18] he held that the high court's decisions still permitted Congress to abrogate the states' Eleventh Amendment immunity under section 1983 of the U.S. Code.[19] Thus, because Ohio had accepted federal Medicaid money and because its bidding process violated certain provisions of the Social Security Act, Sargus granted an unsuccessful bidder's request for a permanent injunction prohibiting the state from implementing the contract it had improperly awarded for a managed care system in its Medicaid program.[20] Although the Sixth Circuit Court of Appeals vacated his ruling, Sargus, admitting that his decision in the case was probably his "most assertive," still believes his reading of the law was correct.[21]

Graham, on the other hand, became the first judge in the Southern District of Ohio to rule that Congress violated the Eleventh Amendment when it applied the ADA to the states. Examining the substance of the ADA and the Rehabilitation Act, Graham concluded that certain provisions went beyond equal protection to mandate preferential treatment. Requirements in the ADA and the Rehabilitation Act mandating "accommodations" for disabled persons created new entitlements, he concluded, thus exceeding Congress's Fourteenth Amendment powers.[22] In a similar vein, both Graham and Weber held that Congress could not abrogate the states' immunity under the Family and Medical Leave Act (FMLA). First, Graham held that the Fourteenth Amendment "contains rather specific constitutional goals, such as the elimination of race discrimination by state actors" as well as "general goals, such as the guarantee to every citizen of equal protection of the laws."[23] Arguing that if the courts were to apply these general goals broadly Congress would have carte blanche to abrogate state immunity, Graham analyzed FMLA by applying the three tests set out by the Supreme Court in *Katzenbach v. Morgan*[24] in light of the Court's rulings in *Seminole Tribe* and *City of Boerne*. He concluded that, although Congress claimed to have enacted the statute pursuant to its Fourteenth Amendment powers and although the statute was designed, at least in part, to stop gender discrimination by creating an "affirmative entitlement to leave," Congress attempted "to dictate that the Equal Protection Clause . . . requires that employees be furnished twelve weeks of leave. . . . This is patently the sort of substantive legislation that exceeds the proper scope of Congress' authority under § 5 [of the Fourteenth Amendment]."[25]

By the beginning of the twenty-first century, the Supreme Court and the Sixth Circuit Court of Appeals had settled Eleventh Amendment doctrine. The current view dictates that, with only two exceptions, the Eleventh Amendment prohibits individuals from suing states or state agencies in federal court, although individuals can still sue state officials, but only for "prospective injunctive relief."[26] Once the higher courts ruled clearly on this issue, the district judges ended their "activism" and their differing judgments. Whatever their personal views on sovereign immunity, they take seriously their responsibility to uphold binding precedent. Thus Marbley, for example, in 2000, dismissed a claim against the Ohio State University under the ADA, holding that the Supreme Court and the Sixth Circuit have "unambiguously" held that Congress cannot abrogate the states' sovereign immunity except pursuant to the Fourteenth Amendment and that, in the ADA, Congress exceeded its Fourteenth Amendment authority.[27] On the other side, when the Sixth Circuit Court of Appeals held that there was a private right of action under Title IX for gender discrimination against employees of state institutions, Graham applied that law even though he disagreed with it and invited future appeals court panels to rethink the current binding precedent.[28]

Under current Eleventh Amendment jurisprudence, federal courts continue to fulfill their role as enforcer of federal law against reluctant states, although, at least when it is done through suits filed by individuals, relief is most often through injunction rather than via monetary damages. As Smith explained when he allowed a suit by mentally retarded and developmentally disabled people to go forward against the state of Ohio for injunctive relief under the ADA and the Rehabilitation Act, "This federal court cannot shrink from its duty to apply the law and reach conclusions on these profound issues."[29]

## MASS TORT LITIGATION

The U.S. District Court for the Southern District of Ohio has adjudicated several major mass tort cases that have contributed significantly to the development of the law in that field. Indeed, the first mass tort claim in the country originated with Rubin in 1977 in *In re Beverly Hills Fire Litigation*.[30] Since then, mass tort litigation has "become the most critical aspect of federal civil litigation." By 1990, mass tort claims comprised 75 percent of all new product liability filings. It is now the "single largest category of personal injury litigation."[31] Mass tort claims fall into three broad categories—mass accident claims, such as the Beverly Hills Supper Club fire or the Markland Dam disaster; mass exposure claims involving accidental or intentional exposure to toxic substances, such as atomic radiation at the Fernald plant in southwestern Ohio or experiments on humans as in *In re Cincinnati Radiation;* and product liability litigation over such products as nausea medication and pacemakers. In each category, the District Court for the Southern District of Ohio has taken the lead in developing new approaches to handle complex litigation.

### *Mass Accident Claims*

On May 28, 1977, a fire at the Beverly Hills Supper Club in the greater Cincinnati area killed 165 people and injured another 116.[32] The result was the "first class action ever in the field of torts." Rubin, who presided over the first trial, told the lead counsel for the plaintiffs, attorney Stanley Chesley of Cincinnati, that he was "not going to permit one or two lawyers to come in here and raid whatever is left" of the small amount of money the supper club owners had. "There will be parity," Rubin declared. Chesley initially opposed proceeding with the case as a class action. It was Rubin's insistence on equality for all who had been killed or injured that launched this revolutionary approach to tort litigation.[33]

Dealing with the new form of litigation, Rubin presided "with enthusiasm and an open mind to resolving problems unique" to the case. To organize the litigation, Rubin pioneered new practices and procedures others now imitate. Proceeding under Rule 23 of the Federal Rules of Civil Procedure,[34] he bifurcated the trial to present the juries with simplified issues. The first trial would focus solely on causation. The Sixth Circuit Court of Appeals affirmed Rubin's innovation.[35] Suspecting that an electrical problem had started the fire and that toxic smoke from the furnishings had killed many of the victims, Chesley sued not only the owners of the supper club but also the electric and aluminum wiring companies that had manufactured and installed the wiring at the nightclub as well as whole industries making aluminum

Devastation from the fire at the Beverly Hills Supper Club in the Cincinnati sub-urban community of Southgate, Kentucky. The tragedy led to the first class action suit ever filed in the field of torts, a case presided over by Judge Rubin. *Cincinnati Museum Center—Cincinnati Historical Society Library*

wiring or supplying PVC wire covering, carpets, paneling, upholstery, and similar products. This innovative strategy initiated the concept of "enter-prise liability," in which attorneys sue a whole industry. After a twenty-two-day trial that lasted more than eleven weeks, the jury found none but the supper club owners liable. The owners of the supper club then decided to settle for $2.9 million. The plaintiffs, however, won a more meaningful victory on ap-peal. The Sixth Circuit Court of Appeals reversed the jury's judgment and ordered a new trial after it became known that one of the jurors had per-formed an unauthorized experiment in his home that influenced the jurors, thereby denying the plaintiffs a fair trial. Eventually, after failing to achieve favorable rulings on several motions, Union Light, Heat and Power, which had provided the aluminum wiring for the supper club, and those who pro-vided the PVC settled with the plaintiffs for more than $14.5 million.[36]

In the late 1970s and 1980s, Spiegel faced perhaps an even more compli-cated case. The Ohio River Disaster Litigation added to the massive tort liti-gation the complication of the issue of sovereign immunity.[37] January 1978 was one of the most severe winter months in southwestern Ohio history. The Ohio River rose rapidly, from 29.6 feet at Cincinnati on January 25 to its crest of 53.9 feet five days later. Ice accumulation became such a significant problem that river traffic in the Cincinnati area upstream of the Markland Dam was at a standstill. On January 27, because of actions and decisions by the Army Corps of Engineers, which had built the dam between Cincinnati and Louisville and was now in charge of its operations, the massive ice jam broke, sending "a wall of ice and water" downstream and causing "probably the greatest single disaster to hit the Ohio river in modern times. Barges, towboats, and docks were swept onto or through Markland Dam; barges and towboats were sunk; Big Bone Island was simply shaved off, and does not now exist." Owners of barges damaged as a result of this disaster brought action against the United States under the Suits in Admiralty Act, charging negligence on the part of the Army Corps of Engineers in monitoring the crisis and operating the dam.[38] Years of discovery and bench trials followed. The parties took more than a week just to present testimony about what happened.

The major obstacle the plaintiffs had to overcome was the United States' sovereign immunity. Congress had waived the government's immunity in a limited number of situations spelled out in the Federal Tort Claims Act. The court first had to decide whether that statute applied to suits in admiralty. Both Spiegel and the Sixth Circuit Court of Appeals agreed that it did; the United States had generally waived its immunity in admiralty as well as in tort litigation. Thus, Spiegel, after presiding over a long bench trial, awarded two barge companies more than $2.7 million in damages, having found that the Army Corps of Engineers acted negligently in handling the crisis. On hearing the government's appeal, however, the Sixth Circuit Court of Appeals reversed Spiegel's decision and the award, holding that the Army Corps of Engineers did, indeed, have sovereign immunity. In the Federal Tort Claims Act, Congress had not waived sovereign immunity in cases in which its employees, "exercising due care," were undertaking discretionary acts authorized by federal statutes or regulations. Unlike Spiegel, the Sixth Circuit concluded that the Corps, in handling the crisis, fell under this exception. Although the higher court conceded that Spiegel handled this "long and difficult case" well, having "struggled valiantly with many complex issues," its decision to overturn his ruling meant that the barge companies would receive no compensation. They would be forced to rely on whatever resources they could muster to put themselves back in business.[39]

*Mass Exposure Cases*

Mass exposure claims are perhaps even more dramatic, involving tragic personal injuries and deaths. But the main issue involved, like that in the Beverly Hills fire and, to a lesser extent, the Markland Dam disaster, is the issue of causation. And the disadvantage to the plaintiffs of a divided trial is seen even more clearly in these cases than in the Beverly Hills fire case. The first of this type of mass tort litigation in the Southern District of Ohio was the Bendectin product liability lawsuit. Plaintiffs filed numerous lawsuits against the suburban Cincinnati corporation Merrell Dow Pharmaceuticals on behalf of children born with birth defects after their mothers had taken an antinausea drug, Bendectin, during their pregnancies. They sued Merrell Dow for negligence, breach of warranty, strict liability, fraud, and gross negligence. The case represented a fairly new legal device—multidistrict litigation. In 1968, Congress authorized the temporary transfer of cases filed in several different district courts but which involve one or more common questions of fact to a single district for coordinated or consolidated pretrial proceedings.[40] Here the Judicial Panel on Multidistrict Litigation transferred the forty-five cases pending in twenty-two districts to the Southern District of Ohio, where Merrell Dow had its headquarters, and to Rubin, who volunteered to "preside over the complex, demanding case."[41]

Eventually, out of the hundreds of cases filed in state and federal courts, Rubin heard 818 of them in a consolidated trial held in 1985, making it one of the ten largest cases in the country to that point.[42] As lead plaintiff attorney Stanley Chesley explained, "We're involved in the type of trial that, to the best of my knowledge, has never occurred before. It's the first consolidation . . . involving a drug. It's one of the most innovative means from the standpoint of what it would mean to the plaintiffs. Imagine if everybody had to go to 381 courts—there aren't enough courts."[43] From Rubin's point of view, certifying the case as a class action was essential for efficiency and to preserve judicial resources. He explained that the Bendectin litigation was but "one example of massive product liability lawsuits involving large numbers of plaintiffs, protracted trials, and substantial litigation costs. The traditional court system is simply unequipped to handle such litigation in a conventional manner."[44] But the case was the most significant of all the Bendectin trials not only because both sides invested significant resources and because so many cases had been consolidated but also because Rubin trifurcated the trial, ordering separate trials on general causation, liability, and specific causation and damages. The plaintiffs had to prevail at each stage to proceed to the next.

The first trial, lasting twenty-two days, focused solely on the issue of causation. The six-person jury was only to decide whether the plaintiffs established, by a preponderance of the evidence, that the taking of Bendectin by women during pregnancy was "a proximate cause of human birth defects." All the jury heard was seventy-three hours of testimony from nineteen experts dealing solely with scientific evidence. Because Rubin would not allow any commingling of the elements, he forbade plaintiffs from introducing any evidence on issues of fault or damages. In fact, Rubin even "barred from the courtroom all plaintiffs with obvious physical disabilities and all plaintiffs under ten years of age so that the jury would not be influenced by damages issues." He even refused the plaintiffs' "modest efforts to introduce evidence that went to the breach of duty element, excluding from evidence a letter from Dr. Smithells to Merrell that would have co-mingled the issues of causation and breach of duty." This trial was the only one out of the thirty trials to exclude that letter. Rubin also restricted the number of expert witnesses each side could call.

The plaintiffs argued that Rubin's major procedural rulings created "a sterile or laboratory atmosphere" that made it impossible for them to win. "By isolating jurors from the deformed children and not allowing attorneys for the families to introduce certain evidence critical of Merrell Dow's testing methods, Rubin made it impossible for the jury to get a feel for the 'humanistic aspect of this investigation.'"[45] Further, by refusing to allow the commingling of issues, plaintiffs could not "balance a weak case on causation against a stronger case on breach and damages." But most important, it prevented plaintiffs from telling their story, a story about how Merrell was allegedly negligent in testing its new drug. When trials allowed commingling, plaintiffs won. But in this case, as in most others, the defense prevailed. Because the jury found that plaintiffs had not proven that taking Bendectin was the proximate cause of birth defects, the case ended without ever moving on to the second stage concerning liability.[46]

Judges Beckwith and Spiegel handled two other significant mass tort suits in very different ways. *In re Cincinnati Radiation Litigation,* a case dealing with abuse and deception by the federal government and other public institutions, concerned the right of people to be able to control what is done to them. Beckwith presided over this class action lawsuit against physicians employed by the Department of Defense and two Cincinnati hospitals (the University of Cincinnati Hospital, called Cincinnati General Hospital at the time, and Children's Hospital), the city of Cincinnati, the University of Cincinnati, and the U.S. government by the families of almost ninety cancer patients who were, without their knowledge or permission, used as human guinea pigs for experiments sponsored by the Department of Defense between 1960 and 1972 to study how radiation might affect soldiers during a nuclear war. Most of the patients were indigent, poorly educated, and of lower than average intelligence. The majority of them were African American. Although they were all diagnosed as terminally ill, they were still healthy, some having at least two years to live. But rather than being informed of the risks involved in the radiation "treatments," patients were told they were being given treatments to prolong their lives. Instead, the treatments shortened their lives by months, if not years.

Frankly proclaiming that "the allegations . . . make out an outrageous tale of government perfidy in dealing with some of its most vulnerable citizens," Beckwith creatively ruled that one of the basic constitutional rights held by American citizens was the right to be free from unwarranted bodily intrusions.[47] Thus, the defendants were found to have deprived the patients of their

Fourteenth Amendment substantive and procedural due process rights, their right to equal protection under the law, their right to privacy, and their right to access to the courts. Beckwith ruled further that the defendants had violated the federal government's directive that this nation would comply with the so-called Nuremberg Code developed after the trials of Nazi war criminals at the end of World War II, which mandated that "voluntary consent of the human subject" to medical tests "is absolutely essential."[48]

Throughout the five-year case, Beckwith insisted on full disclosure and a fair settlement. She initially refused to certify any plaintiffs as a class, because their attorneys had not made effective efforts to identify all the victims and because she believed that the defendants' claims of limited resources were not proven.[49] But she worked hard to achieve a settlement rather than see the case litigated. She worried that there were so many procedural bars to the plaintiffs' ultimate success that they needed to settle to achieve any sort of victory.[50] Finally, she helped craft a $3.5 million settlement for the one surviving patient and the families of sixty-four others who had died before the litigation was concluded. Each received approximately $40,000. The money came from the federal government, the city of Cincinnati, the hospitals, and insurance companies. In addition to the financial settlement, the federal government apologized and installed a large plaque in University Hospital's pavilion courtyard, inscribed: "In Memoriam, Cancer Patients Radiation Effects Study, 1960–1972."[51] After she approved the settlement, Beckwith said that she hoped this will help those "who have carried this as a wound" close the matter and allow the wound to heal.[52]

As the first case "in which the federal government was held accountable for experimenting on people,"[53] Beckwith's opinion has become a landmark of civil rights law, "the subject of law review commentary, and . . . standard reading in civil rights classes in law schools."[54] At a ceremony remembering the victims, Beckwith said, "This lawsuit was a call on conscience for the entire country and the government." John H. Metz, one of the attorneys representing the families of the victims, said, "The United States is the only nation in the world where ordinary citizens can hold the government accountable, and the radiation case shows 'the Constitution continues to live, but only through the vigilance and courage of we the people.'"[55]

Spiegel handled his several mass tort cases in still other ways. Here, too, were cases of government failure to protect its citizens from toxic substances. Like *In re Cincinnati Radiation*, the key issue was the accountability of the federal government and its agencies. Also like *In re Cincinnati Radiation*, none of Spiegel's cases went to a full jury. But Spiegel used innovative summary jury trials to gain some of his settlements.[56] The first two cases, *In re Fernald Litigation* and *Day v. NLO*, arose in the mid-1980s out of the operation of a facility about thirty miles northwest of Cincinnati, owned and operated by the U.S. Department of Energy (DOE) and managed for DOE by the National Lead Company

(NL) and its wholly owned subsidiary, National Lead of Ohio (NLO). The plant, which produced unenriched uranium billets, was shut down because it was exposing workers and residents of the area to unacceptable levels of radiation. The first set of litigants included property owners, residents, and employees living and working within a five-mile radius of the plant. They sought damages for the diminution of their property values, for compensation for the emotional distress caused by the negligent operation of the facility, and for a fund to pay the costs of medical monitoring and epidemiology to determine the adverse health effects caused by the negligent operation of the plant. The second set of litigants included former employees and their spouses and independent contractors who had worked at the facility as well as any others who had done business at Fernald for at least six weeks and thus had been exposed to radioactive material for a significant period. They sued, claiming harm from an increased risk of disease, the emotional distress caused by that increased risk, and the disease itself.[57]

One of the first issues was whether plaintiffs could sue—that is, were they suing the U.S. government, and, if so, had the government abrogated its sovereign immunity in such cases? In its efforts to assert sovereign immunity, the DOE argued that NLO was merely a "government contractor" and therefore immune from suit. To prove that the DOE and not a private firm was in charge, the energy department admitted that it had polluted the environment, exposed area residents to radiation, and ignored warnings by NLO that problems needed to be solved. Shocked by such admissions, Thomas A. Luken, a congressman from Fernald's district, "decried [the government's] 'the king can do no wrong' defense." He ordered subcommittee hearings to investigate the DOE's admission of "conducting a form of chemical warfare against the people in the Fernald area."[58] After hearing arguments by both sides, Spiegel held that the suit was between private parties—the plaintiffs and the contractor, NL. He admitted that he knew that the federal government would reimburse NL, but, he declared, "that's something you [National Lead] can take up with the Federal Government. As far as I'm concerned, you're the defendant in this case."[59]

Having rejected the defense's various attempts to get the suit dismissed, Spiegel used a summary jury trial to help promote settlement.[60] In the first case, In re Fernald, Spiegel held a ten-day summary jury trial; at the end, the jurors awarded the plaintiffs $136 million. A week later—and four and a half years after the plaintiffs had filed their complaint—the parties reached a tentative $73 million settlement, which, after a fairness hearing, became the final settlement. The settlement provided compensation not only for the decrease in property values and emotional distress but also for funding for the medical monitoring of the residents and workers. Moreover, the settlement still allowed individual plaintiffs to file injury claims for specific diseases they personally might develop as a result of the exposure to radiation.[61]

Spiegel wanted a summary jury trial for the second case, *Day v. NLO*, but the defendants resisted and the Sixth Circuit Court of Appeals concluded that he could not compel them to participate. Thus, a trial on the merits of the case commenced on July 5, 1994. After a nine-day trial, the parties reached a settlement. This settlement, too, was a "first," because it included the cost of medical monitoring for all plaintiffs, funded by $5 million from the DOE, to be supplemented by the department as needed by the plaintiffs. In addition, the settlement provided $15 million to compensate class members for emotional distress. Family members of deceased workers shared in this fund even though statutes of limitation had expired in most of the cases. Finally, the settlement allowed individual workers to file claims for specific physical injuries either under workers' compensation or via a suit against the defendants.[62] Spiegel still administers this fund.[63]

In addition to their significance to the litigants, these cases, the first in the country to declare the DOE liable for its actions, reinforced the notion that this is a government of laws and even the federal government must be accountable to its citizens for its actions. As attorney Stanley Chesley noted, the settlements "proved the virtue of using the U.S. District Court to bring out evidence of mismanagement . . . and win a settlement."[64]

## THE RELATIONSHIP BETWEEN THE COURT AND THE ECONOMIC PROSPERITY OF SOUTHERN OHIO

District courts are often called upon to decide cases that have enormous economic implications for their communities. By hearing antitrust suits by both the government and private parties, disputes between labor and management,[65] claims of patent, trademark, and copyright infringement,[66] disputes in bankruptcy cases,[67] securities and other cases of fraud,[68] and disputes between the ICC and the carriers it regulates[69] district courts ensure that the marketplace is free for all to compete on as fair a basis as possible based on existing statutory law. In examining the decisions of the district court judges for the Southern District of Ohio in such litigation, no pattern that seems to favor one group over the other can be discerned. And most attorneys representing all classes of litigants say that most times the judges take neutral stances. If they have any bias, it is that most prefer settlement to litigation and will pursue a variety of techniques, including summary jury trials and mediation, to achieve that result.

Several antitrust and corporate takeover cases well illustrate the kind of impact the outcome of such litigation can have on the economic and psychological health of the community. The government's success in forcing Scripps Newspapers, in the early 1970s, to divest itself of certain newspaper holdings affected the independence of one of two Cincinnati newspapers as well as the financial health of one of Cincinnati's major corporations, American Financial, which eventually bought the *Cincinnati Enquirer* from the E. W. Scripps Company.[70] At the same time, the government reached a settlement with Mead Corporation, one of Dayton's major companies, whereby Mead agreed to divest itself of several fine paper merchant houses. To ensure compliance, the court retained supervision over the agreement for sixteen years.[71] The federal government's effort to prosecute General Electric Company, one of Cincinnati's two largest employers, for conspiracy to raise the price of industrial diamonds in violation of the Sherman Act, failed completely. In this complicated case, "one of the largest antitrust actions" brought in the Southern District of Ohio "in many years," Smith used "progressive pretrial and trial management procedures" to finally bring the case to trial. But he then granted General Electric's motion for a judgment of acquittal, holding that the government failed to prove its case.[72]

Of far greater importance to the area's economy was the private antitrust suit Dayton-based Elder-Beerman department stores filed against Federated department stores with headquarters in Cincinnati. Here is an example of how the court had to allow the legal system to run its course, to the economic detriment of the private companies involved as well as the entire Dayton community. The case pitted the two major department stores in downtown Dayton against each other in a bitter dispute. Elder-Beerman charged Federated's Rike's department store with forcing suppliers of quality merchandise to deal exclusively with Rike's, thus making certain products unavailable at Elder-Beerman stores and destroying its ability to compete fairly. Rike's claimed that its relationship with its suppliers violated no law. Unable to settle their differences, the parties exhausted themselves in a six-month trial. A jury finally awarded Elder-Beerman more than $1 million, which was trebled under the provisions of the Sherman Antitrust Act to almost $4 million, "a staggering sum by the standards of the day." The Sixth Circuit Court of Appeals, however, reversed that judgment, agreeing with the defense theory that Elder-Beerman had market alternatives. Both sides, "too exhausted" to go on, finally settled out of court. Moreover, the issue was moot, since by the time the trial was half over, most suppliers had agreed to sell to the plaintiff.[73] The story ended tragically for downtown Dayton and Elder-Beerman. Neither department store remains downtown, and Elder-Beerman filed for bankruptcy in 1997.[74]

Even more was at stake in several hostile takeover attempts in the last three decades. The most dramatic began in August 1978 when Armand Hammer and his corporation, Occidental Petroleum, attempted a takeover of Dayton's Mead Corporation.[75] This was at a critical time for the city of Dayton. Dayton's population had declined by more than 50,000 during the 1970s. Its largest employers, NCR and Frigidaire, a major General Motors division, were in decline, laying off thousands of workers. By 1978, Mead was Dayton's "leading corporate citizen," with its high-rise office tower the center of the newly renovated Courthouse Square in the heart of downtown Dayton. If Mead went, Daytonians feared, Dayton would never recover. Mead convinced the Department of Justice to file suit in the U.S. District Court for the Southern District of Ohio, giving Mead the hometown advantage of Judge Rubin and the Dayton courtroom. The Department of Justice asked Rubin to issue a restraining order to block Occidental from asking its shareholders to vote for a merger with Mead, arguing that the takeover would violate federal antitrust laws.[76] After a lengthy trial that attracted national media attention, on December 10, 1978, Rubin granted the government its request and issued a preliminary injunction prohibiting Occidental from proceeding with its tender offer. Three weeks later, Occidental abandoned its takeover bid.[77]

Although Mead and its lawyers managed to prevent a takeover by Occidental, other local companies have not been as successful. In 1981, Mobil Oil attempted to take over Marathon Oil Company, the nation's seventeenth-largest oil company at the time and a major corporation in southern Ohio. Less successful than Mead, Marathon was able to prevent the hostile takeover only by merging with U.S. Steel. Although Judge Kinneary issued a temporary restraining order blocking the use of an Ohio statute that would have prevented the takeover, he refused to stop the merger between Marathon and U.S. Steel.[78] The $6.2 billion deal was at the time the second-largest corporate takeover in American history.[79] Attorney James L. Graham, later a district judge himself, was one of the attorneys representing the board of directors of Marathon Oil fighting the takeover. Noting the significance of the case, he pointed out that it made the front page of the *New York Times*.[80] Once the Marathon–U.S. Steel deal was completed, saving Marathon's identity and jobs in southern Ohio, minority shareholders sued Marathon's board of directors, charging that board members violated the Securities and Exchange Act, committed common-law fraud, and breached their fiduciary duties by ignoring the better offer from Mobil Oil. After a month-long trial in Rubin's court, that included testimony in favor of the Marathon–U.S. Steel merger by former astronaut Neil Armstrong, a nonemployee member of Marathon's board, the six-person jury took five hours to decide against the minority Marathon litigants.[81]

As judge, Graham faced a similar case in 1995, when Luxottica took over U.S. Shoe, a Cincinnati corporation. The Cincinnati company tried to use a recently enacted Ohio statute, the Control Share Acquisition Act, to thwart the hostile bid, but Graham enjoined them from doing so, pointing out that the federal Williams Act regulating hostile takeovers had preempted the field in this limited area. His decision was an important assertion of the supremacy of federal law over state attempts to curtail hostile takeovers, but it cost Cincinnati the corporate headquarters of a major company. Although Luxottica still maintains a presence in Cincinnati, U.S. Shoe disappeared as a corporation along with its headquarters and the economic benefits that a locally based corporation brings to a city.[82]

In other cases, the court, in interpreting and enforcing federal law, has directly affected the region's economic base. In *Wheeling–Pittsburgh Steel Corp. v. Mitsui & Co.*, for example, an American steel producer sued to stop Russian and Japanese manufacturers from selling hot-rolled steel in Ohio and elsewhere in the United States at prices substantially less than their market value. This litigation was especially important to eastern Ohio, Pittsburgh Steel being the main employer in that area. In a case of first impression, Sargus, interpreting an old statute in a new context, held that although the federal Antidumping Act of 1916 authorized suits for treble damages, attorney's fees, and costs, Congress had not given federal courts the power to grant injunctive relief. Thus, Wheeling-Pittsburgh could sue for damages, but could not get injunctive relief from the district court. If they wanted to prevent foreign manufactures from "dumping" their products on U.S. markets, the American companies would have to appeal to the president, who had the power to negotiate trade agreements as part of his power over foreign affairs and to the U.S. Court of International Trade, which Congress had created to deal with such controversies.[83]

Private litigation of economic disputes has also resulted in the development of new legal doctrines. Three, in particular, stand out. The first, a products liability case involving the Ford Pinto, was the first "second-collision tort" case in the Sixth Circuit and one of the early cases in the United States. In 1972, Pandora Anton was riding in a 1972 Ford Pinto driven by her brother-in-law, Jack Dodrill. Dodrill's wife and daughter were also in the car. Another Ford, a 1969 LTD station wagon speeding down the street in excess of 75 miles per hour, struck the Pinto in the rear, causing the rear window frame and glass to pop out of the vehicle and rupturing the vehicle's gasoline tank. Anton was thrown out of the Pinto through the rear window opening and sustained burns from the fuel, which had spewed from the Pinto and ignited. No one else was burned. The station wagon hitting the Pinto was the first collision; the second was the gas tank explosion. Although the law clearly places liability on the driver of the LTD, the issue before the court was whether the Ford Motor Company was also liable.[84]

In considering Ford's motion for summary judgment, Duncan focused on whether products liability law "imposes a duty of safe design upon the manufacturers of automobiles, and, if so, whether the complaint sufficiently alleges a breach of such a duty." That issue was, at the time, a "hotly debated" one. Did auto makers have a duty "to make the car 'crashworthy,' or in other words, to prevent injury from what has been called the 'second collision,' when the plaintiff comes in contact with some part of the automobile after the crash?" Although most early court decisions denied any duty to protect against second collisions, holding that the second collision was not an intended use of the car, Duncan followed the reasoning of a few more recent decisions that had held that the danger was foreseeable, arising out of the car's intended use. But Duncan's decision was moderate and balanced in its exercise, to use his own words, of "the hazards of prophecy." Because the accident occurred in Ohio, it was Duncan's duty to follow Ohio law on products liability, but no Ohio appellate court had confronted this issue. Thus, Duncan examined the history, over the past century, of Ohio products liability law, concluding that Ohio "has been at the forefront of those states which have shaped the format of modern products liability law." In one case, for example, the Ohio Supreme Court acknowledged it was overturning years of precedent, but explained that "occasions may arise when it is fitting and wholesome to discard legal concepts of the past to meet new conditions and practices of our changing and progressing civilization." On the basis of this analysis, Duncan concluded that, although no Ohio case specifically defined the duties of the manufacturer relative to product design, if the Ohio Supreme Court were to decide the issue, it would "impose upon the automobile manufacturer only the duty not to design an unreasonably dangerous product." Though this might sound like a victory for the car manufacturer, Duncan temporized. He concluded that each case must be judged on its particular facts and that in this case, because the parties had stipulated that some other design involving the gas tank would have prevented the rupture of the gas tank, there were enough issues of fact to turn the case over to a jury to decide if the design was unreasonably dangerous. Finally, he listed those factors a jury would need to consider to determine whether the design was, indeed, unreasonably dangerous. Duncan's reasoning and analysis then became a standard, widely cited throughout the country in products liability litigation.[85]

The second case involved the battle over the construction of the Zimmer Nuclear Power Plant in Moscow, Ohio. Three electric companies, Cincinnati Gas and Electric, Dayton Power and Light, and Columbus & Southern Ohio Electric, initially sued Sargent & Lundy Engineers, the architectural and engineering designers of the plant, and General Electric Company, the firm that had contracted with them to supply nuclear energy. The plaintiffs alleged that they had expended hundreds of millions of dollars for a plant that was useless as a nuclear plant because it was "unable to withstand the violent forces generated" by the nuclear steam supply system GE had designed.

The plaintiffs sued on a variety of legal theories in both tort and contract as well as under the Racketeer Influenced and Corrupt Organizations Act (RICO). They claimed that Zimmer's design was faulty and that the defendants had hidden these flaws. The defendants maintained that they had done nothing wrong, but that the problems were created by construction mismanagement and ineffective quality control. Spiegel dismissed the complaints in torts, but allowed the suit to proceed for rescission and restitution and damages for breach of contract and for fraud under RICO. To help facilitate a settlement, Spiegel decided on a closed summary jury trial in which six jurors would hear evidence on the fraud and racketeering as well as the contract charges. Area newspapers filed a motion to intervene, however, challenging the closure of the summary jury trial. Spiegel held that the district court had the power to conduct such trials and that the newspapers had no First Amendment right of access to such proceedings. Although agreeing with the newspapers that the trial would highlight issues "central to the merits of this case," matters that were "of paramount public concern," Spiegel concluded that a summary jury trial was not a trial for First Amendment purposes. Rather, it was a "settlement technique," held "with the cooperation of the parties." Eventually, after the closed summary trial, the parties did settle. The incident had an enormous impact not only on these major companies in southwestern Ohio, whose economic health is vital to the community, but also on all taxpayers, because the enormous costs involved with construction, repair, and litigation drove up energy prices for years. The press and the public seized upon the story of fraud, mismanagement, and incredible bungling of a major undertaking.[86] Ultimately, however, when GE settled with the utilities companies, the consumers also won. General Electric would bear at least some of the cost of the failed nuclear plant and its conversion to coal.[87]

The third and perhaps the most interesting case dealing with developments in private litigation was the case of *CompuServe Inc. v. Cyber Promotions, Inc.* Graham adapted the ancient common-law doctrine of trespass to chattel to a modern technological problem—the flooding of Compuserve's server with unsolicited e-mail advertisements. Graham held that "the public interest," as well as the private interests of CompuServe and its subscribers, is best "advanced by the Court's protection of the common-law rights of individuals and entities to their personal property." Rejecting the defendant's claim that preventing him from sending mass unsolicited e-mails violated his First Amendment rights to free speech, Graham wrote that the "high volumes of junk e-mail devour computer processing and storage capacity, slow down data transfer between computers over the Internet . . . , and cause recipients to spend time and money wading through messages that they do not want. It is ironic that if defendants were to prevail on their First Amendment arguments, the viability of electronic mail as an effective means of communication for the rest of society would be put at risk." Thus, he found such arguments were "without merit." His decision has been widely discussed and quoted in many other cases and law review articles dealing with adapting law to the new technology of cyberspace.[88]

### CRIMINAL PROSECUTIONS IN THE DISTRICT COURT FOR THE SOUTHERN DISTRICT OF OHIO

Although criminal cases are often dramatic and are obviously important to both the defendant, whose freedom and sometimes whose life is at risk, and the community that seeks law and order, most do not advance the development of law. Judges routinely hear cases involving violations of federal laws.

As such, they, like trial judges in state courts, regularly decide whether to suppress certain evidence or statements because law enforcement officials might have violated constitutional guarantees against unreasonable searches and seizures.[89] Judges also routinely review cases to prevent prosecutorial misconduct or ineffective assistance of counsel.[90] In addition, in decisions aimed at protecting the rights of the innocent, they review the constitutionality of state criminal laws. Both Beckwith and Dlott, for example, have held that the application of Ohio's automobile seizure statute to owners of automobiles seized when their spouses committed a driving violation while driving their cars without their knowledge deprived innocent people of their property without procedural due process rights, in violation of the Fourteenth Amendment.[91]

Some cases, however, gain notoriety simply because of the persons involved. One such case, which is still a topic of conversation among sports fans everywhere, involved litigation against the Cincinnati Red's All Star Pete Rose. Judge Holschuh heard the civil suit Rose brought against Major League Baseball Commissioner A. Bartlett Giamatti, to enjoin the commissioner from conducting a disciplinary hearing concerning allegations that Rose had bet on baseball games. Never, Holschuh said, had he had a case with such intense media attention. After the judge refused to return the case to state court where Rose had originally filed it, the parties agreed to a settlement that included Rose's suspension from professional baseball.[92] In a related case, Spiegel accepted Rose's guilty plea on two counts of tax fraud and sentenced him to five months in prison, then three months in a halfway house, followed by 1,000 hours of community service.[93]

Other criminal cases are important because of their sheer magnitude and their impact on the community. Perhaps the biggest criminal case in Columbus history was the drug conspiracy case known as the Short North Posse case. The grand jury indicted forty-one defendants on 186 counts of federal drug and firearms violations, making it the largest number of defendants indicted in a criminal case in the history of the Southern District of Ohio. Judge Smith said it was his most "major case," because he felt "that of all the things I've done in my entire career, that these people were the most dangerous." Not only were they dealing drugs but they also had automatic weapons. They intimidated an entire neighborhood, making it almost unlivable. "They were beating people up. There were a lot of bullets flying at cars." It took a major effort to coordinate the case and the trial. Smith issued extensive trial orders, prepared a jury questionnaire so a jury could be empaneled quickly, and held several pretrial meetings with attorneys to handle motions in limine and the like. For two months the jury heard five to six hours a day of uninterrupted testimony. Smith refused to recess the trial to hear evidentiary or other motions unless the attorney could show that the matter could not have been raised sooner. Although all but eight of the defendants plea bargained before trial and then testified against the leaders, the trial lasted two months.[94]

This case was important on two levels. First, major drug prosecutions can have a significant impact on the community. With the Short North Posse behind bars, the neighborhood is now undergoing revitalization.[95] Second, the case illustrates the difference between prosecution in state versus federal court and the dramatic effect that can result when prosecutors have the choice. Many of the defendants were shocked when they discovered the stiff penalties they faced under federal law compared to state law. Also in federal court there is "a presumption against bail" in major drug cases, so the defendants stayed in jail awaiting trial or sentencing rather than being able to return to the community they had been terrorizing before the trial began.[96]

A few of the criminal cases heard by the District Court for the Southern District of Ohio since the 1960s have advanced important legal principles. In the Sixth Circuit's first RICO trial under the Organized Crime Control Act of 1970, the appellate court generally affirmed Rubin's rulings in *U.S. v. Sutton,* broadly defining the scope of the federal enterprise racketeering statute by relying on a textual, plain-meaning interpretation and upholding the convictions and sentences of the nine defendants for drug offenses, fraud, and racketeering. The decision opened the way for the widespread use of RICO to prosecute organized crime and drug conspiracies.[97]

*United States ex rel. Shott v. Tehan* made legal history by establishing the basic rule regarding retroactivity. Edgar I. Shott Jr., a Cincinnati attorney, was tried in state court for his participation in a Ponzi scheme. When Shott chose not to testify in his own behalf, the prosecutor, in closing arguments, commented extensively on that fact. Although federal courts prohibited such statements, at the time they were routine in Ohio courts, sanctioned by a provision of the Ohio constitution.[98] States considered such statements constitutionally proper, the U.S. Supreme Court having held that states were not required to apply federal standards to their criminal prosecutions. It was on that basis that Peck dismissed Shott's appeal. But after Peck's decision, the Supreme Court reversed itself and began to apply federal constitutional protections to state court defendants. The Sixth Circuit Court of Appeals then held that Shott's constitutional rights were violated. The appeal to the Supreme Court focused on whether the Supreme Court's new application of federal standards to the states was retroactive. In declaring that it was not, the Supreme Court articulated a basic philosophy on criminal procedure as it considered the purpose of retroactivity, the nature of the rule against self-incrimination, and the effect retroactive application of its new decision would have on the administration of justice. First, it concluded that the Fifth's Amendment's privilege against self-incrimination is not essential to ascertaining the truth, which is the main purpose of a trial. Rather, the privilege against self-incrimination reflects society's concern that each individual has a right to be left alone. Thus, the application of its new decision to old cases would not further ascertain "truth." Moreover, states had relied on the earlier Supreme Court rulings in good faith. Finally, the Court concluded that to require the states involved to void the conviction of every person who did not testify at his trial "would have an impact upon the administration of their criminal law so devastating as to need no elaboration."[99]

Judge Weinman's decision in the habeas corpus case of Sam Sheppard, the Cleveland physician who had been tried and convicted amid tremendous publicity in state court for the murder of his wife, became a landmark on the need to control publicity to ensure a defendant a fair trial.[100] Weinman courageously granted Sheppard his writ of habeas corpus,[101] basing his decision on five grounds, all of which, he held, violated Sheppard's constitutional rights to a fair trial: the court's failure to grant a change of venue given the massive amount of newspaper publicity before the trial; the inability to maintain impartial jurors in light of the publicity during the trial; the failure of the trial judge to disqualify himself although many found him partial; the improper admission of lie detector test testimony; and the unauthorized communications between jurors and third persons during jury deliberations, when the bailiffs allowed them to make unmonitored outside calls.[102]

Many praised Weinman for his decision. The Steubenville newspaper, for example, in its eulogy to the judge, wrote that Weinman's decision "called the attention of the nation to Judge Weinman's competence, fairness and his courage in making difficult decisions." Weinman, himself, said that of all the decisions he had rendered during his long judicial career, this was the one he was most proud of. When Weinman received word that the Sixth Circuit Court of Appeals had reversed him, he was so outraged he adjourned court for the day. By contrast, when he found out that the Supreme Court reversed the appellate court, he was ecstatic.[103] The Supreme Court, in affirming Weinman, broadly proclaimed that a trial judge had a duty to maintain proper courtroom decorum and an atmosphere in which a defendant is able to get a fair hearing. This decision has forced trial courts to develop a variety of ways to limit undue pretrial and trial publicity, but it has also opened them up to criticism that they are "gagging" the press and preventing the public from being informed.[104]

Two areas in criminal law that create problems for judges and consume inordinate amounts of time are sentencing, with many appeals now being taken over disputes with the U.S. Sentencing Guidelines, and with petitions for writs of habeas corpus by state and federal prisoners. Most judges currently serving in southern Ohio have some concerns about the sentencing guidelines. Although most say that the guidelines reflect what most of them do, they find them, at times, "restrictive and confining, sometimes excessively punitive," especially in the sentencing of those convicted of possession of crack cocaine as compared with powdered cocaine.[105] Moreover, they are disturbed about the issue of separation of powers. What judges see is Congress interfering with the judiciary in an area outside its constitutional purview, taking discretionary power away from the courts and giving it to the U.S. attorneys and probation officers.[106]

Thus judges often feel justified in departing from the guidelines, within the rules established by Congress. In the Southern District of Ohio, the judges depart downward in approximately 35 percent of their criminal cases, mostly in cooperation with prosecutors or probation officers.[107] But it is the upward departures that reach the appellate court. In 1989, two years after the sentencing commission promulgated the sentencing guidelines, the Sixth Circuit Court of Appeals heard its first challenge to an upward departure. In that case, the appellate court upheld Graham's sentencing of Felino Rodriguez, who had been convicted by a jury of the possession of cocaine with intent to distribute. Ignoring the recommended thirty to thirty-seven months imprisonment, Graham sentenced Rodriguez to seventy-two months without parole. In affirming this departure, the Sixth Circuit, "adopting a three-step analysis developed by colleagues in New England for examining factors used to justify longer sentences," declared that the upward departure was warranted because of the defendant's criminal conviction in Cuba, his exhibition of a propensity to commit future crimes, and his maintenance of a "criminal livelihood."[108] Ten days later, the circuit court upheld Smith's upward departure in the case of Franklin Joan, who had pleaded guilty to possession of marijuana with intent to distribute and being a felon in possession of a firearm. Smith sentenced Joan to 120 months imprisonment rather than the 57- to 71-month range found in the sentencing guidelines. The Sixth Circuit agreed with Smith's assessment that such a dramatic upward departure was justified because of the defendant's "dangerous criminal history" and the "lenient treatment" he had previously received from the criminal justice system.[109] Beckwith, on the other hand, refused to depart from the guidelines, turning down a white-collar criminal's petition for postconviction relief after he had pleaded guilty to mail fraud and tax evasion. She held that all relevant factors had been considered and no error had been made; her order requiring restitution stood regardless of the defendant's resources or his dependents' needs.[110] When Beckwith held, in *United States v. Moored,* that the district court was not precluded by a plea bargain agreement from making different calculations than the prosecutor had of the offense level, however, the court of appeals disagreed.[111]

Death penalty cases are perhaps the most difficult cases judges confront. Although Ohio had enacted its current death penalty statute in 1981, no person was executed in the state until 1999. Then, during the next three years, Ohio executed five men.[112] In two cases, the District Court for the Southern District of Ohio heard appeals. Wilford Lee Berry, the first to be executed, requested that no more appeals be made in his behalf and that he be allowed to die. His mother and sister filed a motion to gain a new hearing, arguing that Berry was mentally incompetent. Marbley, determined to make a *judicial* decision despite the politically charged atmosphere surrounding the case, granted a temporary stay of execution so an evidentiary hearing could be held, but the court of appeals vacated his order, holding that the state court's finding of competence was binding on the federal court.[113] On remand, Marbley then wrote: "Simply put, this court has never had authority to consider any evidence—new or old—of Berry's actual competence."[114]

John W. Byrd's attempts to avoid the death penalty began after his 1983 conviction for the stabbing death of a convenience store clerk. After Byrd exhausted his state court appeals and his state postconviction relief attempts, he filed for a stay of execution and sought a writ of habeas corpus in Rubin's court. On March 14, 1994, Rubin denied Byrd's request to stay his execution on the ground of delay, pointing out that Byrd had filed his request only eight days before his scheduled execution, six years after the U.S. Supreme Court had denied certiorari in his first direct appeal, and eleven years after the murder. The Sixth Circuit Court of Appeals reversed, and, in an unusual move, removed Rubin from the case, remanding it to another district judge,[115] Graham then issued rulings on Byrd's various legal arguments in his many petitions. Finally, the appeals court ordered additional hearings. To comply with this order, Magistrate Judge Merz held extensive hearings on Byrd's claims of innocence of the death penalty and of actual innocence. He concluded that Byrd could not prove any of his claims by the standards demanded by the rules of the court. The court of appeals affirmed Merz's recommendations and rescinded the earlier stay of execution. The state executed Byrd by lethal injection on February 19, 2002.[116]

Judges also have to address prisoners' petitions for writs of habeas corpus to vacate sentences imposed by state courts. Such petitions have increased greatly in numbers and are terribly time consuming. Judges, however, understand their necessity. Every person, as Rubin explained, has the right to appeal the fact or duration of his or her physical imprisonment. And many see such petitions as a necessity in protecting the constitutionally granted procedural rights of the accused and convicted against violations in the state judicial system. Because of recent congressional legislation and Supreme Court rulings, influenced by those who believe such federal review of state court proceedings intrude on state sovereignty, however, the federal district courts are limited in the decisions they can render. Such appeals, when from state court, must first exhaust state court remedies. Then the state court findings of fact are presumed correct and binding on the federal court unless that presumption is rebutted by clear and convincing evidence. Further, state court legal rulings are controlling unless the state court decision was contrary to clearly established federal law as determined by the Supreme Court.[117]

Prisoner "civil rights complaints," filed pursuant to 42 U.S.C. § 1983, question not the fact or duration of one's imprisonment, but the conditions in prison. Such complaints have increased even more than petitions asserting procedural violations by state courts. Normally filed pro se, prisoners in these civil rights suits claim that some certain practice in the prison violates their First, Eighth, or Fourteenth Amendment due process rights. From 1970 to 1982, civil rights claims rose from 2,793 to 15,575 nationwide. The District Court for the Southern District of Ohio experienced one of the sharpest increases. In 1978, for example, in Chief Judge David Porter's words, the Southern District of Ohio had "the dubious distinction of being seventh in the country" in § 1983 cases, having experienced an increase of 188 percent over the previous year. That year, the district had 35 petitions to vacate sentences, 229 habeas corpus petitions, and 318 civil rights petitions. Columbus handled the bulk of this latter group, receiving 200 filings in 1978 versus 114 for Cincinnati and only 4 for Dayton. To handle the ever-increasing numbers, courts, including those in the Southern District of Ohio, have appointed pro se law clerks and developed screening procedures. More recently, most have been assigned to magistrate judges.[118]

Although some judges see these petitions as providing an important safety valve to prisoners so they can gain the attention of the federal court when their constitutional rights are being violated,[119] others claim that "probably ninety-nine percent [are] meritless."[120] Rubin argued that for prisoners these filings are really a "no-lose" situation. Prisoners can file interrogatories, request the production of documents, gain the right to a day away from prison as a petitioner in court, and even gain points with their fellow inmates by getting them a day away from prison when they call them as witnesses. Eventually, however, prisoners lose most of their petitions.[121]

Whether it is because of their lack of merit or because Congress and the Supreme Court have limited the cases in which relief will be granted, most prisoners fail to obtain the relief they seek.[122] For example, the judges of the Southern District of Ohio, citing Supreme Court and Sixth Circuit Court of Appeals precedent, have taken a narrow view of the First Amendment's free exercise clause when it comes to rights of prisoners, and even the rights of prison officials, versus the state's need for discipline and uniformity. Rubin, for example, denied an inmate's request for an injunction to prevent prison officials from cutting his hair, which he maintained violated the religious beliefs of his tribe, the Lakota Indians.[123] Smith denied a Muslim prisoner's request to wear his tarboosh in the prison dining room and denied a correctional officer's challenge to the Ohio Department of Rehabilitation and Correction's requirement for "collar length or shorter" hair. In both cases, he held that plaintiffs' First Amendment claim to wear a head covering or an eight-inch ponytail as part of their religious belief system had to give way to the state's compelling need for security and uniformity in its correctional institutions.[124]

But several cases have resulted in the court supervising prisons to ensure that inmates are not denied their Eighth Amendment rights against cruel or unusual punishment. In the 1970s, Hogan, after a week-long bench trial held, in response to a class-action suit initiated by several inmates, that the practice of "double celling" at the maximum-security Southern Ohio Correctional Facility (SOCF) at Lucasville, when done on a long-term basis, constituted unconstitutional cruel and unusual punishment and had to be stopped immediately. Further, in setting a fifty-square-foot standard as the minimum acceptable space for a prisoner, Hogan became the first federal judge to establish "a space standard for long-term prisoners." Quoting the 1910 Supreme Court decision *Weems v. United States,* Hogan explained that "the 'cruel and unusual punishment' clause of the Eighth Amendment is 'progressive and is not fastened to the obsolete but may acquire meaning as public opinion becomes enlightened by humane justice.'" The Sixth Circuit Court of Appeals affirmed Hogan's judgment, but the Supreme Court, in a landmark case, reversed the lower courts.[125]

The district court judges also dealt with overcrowding and other problems plaguing city and county jails. In Hamilton County, Porter presided over a class-action lawsuit filed by the Legal Aid Society in 1977 to halt overcrowding, "unbearable" conditions such as poor food, filth, no beds, and violence resulting from an "underworld" running the Hamilton County jail. Jose M. Arcaya, a criminal justice professor at the University of Cincinnati, testified that the Hamilton County jail lacked "some of the most basic amenities of life," producing "an atmosphere of brutality and rage." After nine years of negotiations, Porter finally approved a consent decree, which he then continued to monitor. After two more years of confrontation with county officials, Porter finally threatened the Hamilton County commissioners with fines and jail sentences unless they corrected conditions and provided the facilities they had agreed to in the consent decree. After Porter's death, Weber continued to hear complaints well into the 1990s.[126]

In the 1980s, Rice spearheaded negotiations to end overcrowding in the Montgomery County jail and facilities in other southwestern Ohio counties. Eventually, as a result of Rice's efforts, Montgomery, Greene, Shelby, Preble, Miami, and Champaign counties all built new jails to relieve overcrowded conditions. Then, in the late 1990s, Rice dealt with complaints about the overcrowded conditions at the Dayton Human Rehabilitation Center, the city's seventy-three-year-old jail. After Rice repeatedly ruled that conditions violated inmates' Eighth Amendment constitutional guarantees, the Dayton city commission finally decided to build a new wing. In a 2000 settlement, city officials also pledged to improve medical care, clothing, meals, cleanliness, and health care, develop procedures to ensure better responses to inmate complaints, and improve the work-release education and training programs.[127]

The court also faced the issue of the segregation of prisoners. In 1979, Duncan enjoined officials at the Columbus correctional facility from segregating inmates by race and in using physical restraints without sufficient reason and without providing immediate medical attention after restraints were used. This decision was carried out without incident.[128] In 1993, however, after some inmates at the SOCF in Lucasville challenged the racial segregation there, prison officials negotiated a consent decree, agreeing to prohibit cell assignments based on race unless the warden found that a segregated cell was necessary to prevent violence.[129] The result was an eleven-day uprising, partly brought on by racial tensions that were exacerbated when cell assignments were no longer made on the basis of race. The violence resulted in the murder of one prison guard and nine inmates. Thus, Spiegel modified the consent decree, but pushed for single-celling, which was agreed to.[130] Then inmates who had not participated in the riot brought a civil rights action against prison officials, claiming that officials knew about the volatile conditions but let them continue and that during the uprising innocent inmates were deprived of water, toilets, and medical care, were subjected to excessive force, and had their personal property destroyed. Spiegel ordered a summary jury trial to help foster a settlement and a new consent decree. After the trial in the summer of 1996, negotiations continued with the aid of the court. Finally, in early 1997, the parties reached a settlement, creating a $4.1 million fund to cover inmate damage claims as well as attorneys' fees and expenses. More important, the agreement reached consensus on eleven "quality of inmate life" issues, including single-celling, transfers of lower security inmates to other prisons, addressing parole problems, piloting a program for hearing alleged rule violations, improving racial and cultural relations, providing more out-of-cell time, and allowing greater freedom for inmates to practice their religious beliefs. Spiegel still oversees this settlement.[131]

This story of the transformation of the District Court for the Southern District of Ohio is one of great change as the nation—and Ohio—moved from a small frontier community to a complex society composed of people from varying ethnic, economic, and social backgrounds pursuing countless different occupations, practicing different religions, and holding different values. The court's changes paralleled those of the nation. It has been transformed from one judge, holding court two or three times a year to hear a handful of minor civil and criminal cases to a court with eight authorized judges, seven magistrate judges, judges on senior status, and clerks, secretaries, and other staff members working in three courthouses to administer a docket of more than three thousand new cases a year. The court's business touches the lives of most citizens of Ohio in one way or another, be it in supervising the schools, in delineating the limits of free speech or the free exercise of one's religion, or in prosecuting drug abusers so communities are safer places in which to live. It is, in the words of Judge Sandra Beckwith, "the place of recourse for citizens" who feel that a federal law, a state law, or some other action has been applied to them in some "unfair or discriminatory way."[132]

# 9

## WHO'S WHO

*The Judges of the Southern District of Ohio*

IN 1966, ERWIN SURRENCY BEMOANED THE FACT THAT "MANY OF THE judges on the District Courts who molded the Federal law are . . . virtually unknown."[1] Thirty-seven years later, another *Federal Rules Decision* article again lamented the fact that so few records are available and so few histories detail "the contributions of the district court judges, who played as a group, a significant role" in shaping federal justice.[2]

Jurists and legal scholars alike agree that understanding a judge's background helps one understand his or her judicial views. As Justice Antonin Scalia wrote in a recent Supreme Court decision, "It is virtually impossible to find a judge who does not have preconceptions about the law." Quoting Chief Justice William Rehnquist, Scalia pointed out that it would be highly unusual if judicial appointees came to the bench without "at least some tentative notions that would influence them in their interpretation of the sweeping clauses of the Constitution." Indeed, Scalia continued, "even if it were possible to select judges who did not have preconceived views on legal issues, it would hardly be desirable to do so." Such a judge, Scalia and Rehnquist believe, would lack the qualifications for the job.[3]

Although legal scholars have written histories of a few district courts,[4] detailed information on hundreds of district court judges still remains buried in obscure sources. Political scientists have begun filling these gaps by analyzing their backgrounds, their rulings, and their appointment experiences using statistical models as an analytical tool. These studies have demonstrated two things: first, that partisanship and patronage have always played important roles in the process of appointing federal judges, and second, that judges' backgrounds, ideologies, and political affiliations might influence at least some of their opinions.

Over the past fifty years, the public has learned a great deal about the historical evolution of the recruitment and appointment process which, as historian Kermit Hall has pointed out, is linked to the perception of the legitimacy of the lower federal judiciary. Citizens believe judges should represent the popular will. Yet, at the same time, they—and especially members of the legal profession—seek professionally competent judges, that is, appointees who have displayed a "dedication to the standards, values, and technical attributes of the legal profession." They seek judges with "integrity, persistence, commitment, diligence, and a 'judicial temperament.'"[5] The process by which federal judges are appointed has evolved to accommodate both views. Senatorial courtesy, involvement by local political leaders, and participation by the executive branch all promote popular input. At the same time, local leaders and later the American Bar Association, bipartisan committees, and other interest groups have pushed for well-qualified candidates.

In the nineteenth century, the president took an active role in appointments, but by the end of that century, the president's direct involvement declined as the attorney general and the staff of the Department of Justice took charge of compiling information and making recommendations to the president.[6] Of course, this process varied from president to president. Several modern presidents, especially Lyndon Johnson and Ronald Reagan, have taken very active roles, whereas others have used a committee system, relying on input from local leaders.[7] But no matter how actively involved the president has been in selecting his district court judges, other groups have influenced his choices. Initially, as Hall has demonstrated, kinship and friendship acted to limit appointees to those from the highest ranks of the society. But in the nineteenth century, although "merit and ability" were never ignored, local political connections became more important, thus opening up opportunities for "the children of the cabins," that is, those from more modest social origins, to rise to become federal judges.[8] During this era, for both the president and the local politicians, party loyalty was the chief criterion for judicial appointments.[9] By the twentieth century, presidents, some claim, placed greater emphasis on the nominees' qualifications. And after World War II, many presidents relied increasingly on the ratings of the American Bar Association to help them make their selections.[10]

In addition to the president and the local political leaders, from the beginning the U.S. Senate, with its explicit constitutional role, has played an important part in the appointment process. The idea of senatorial courtesy— that is, that the senators of the president's party either select or have a deciding say in judicial selections—began in the Washington administration, and all presidents since "have relied rather heavily on senatorial input for district court appointments." Indeed, on occasion, even when the senators from the state where the vacancy has occurred are from a party different from the president, the president has listened to their choices, using judicial appointments to curry favor from that senator in other legislative matters.[11] Although senatorial courtesy declined somewhat during the last quarter of the nineteenth century, it reemerged in the twentieth century and has played an important role in judicial selections ever since. Only two presidents in the twentieth century have tried to modify senatorial courtesy—Herbert Hoover and Jimmy Carter—neither with notable success. In recent years, though, presidents have limited the influence of senators. Until Carter, senators generally submitted only one name for each vacancy. During the Carter administration, however, the standard became three to five names for each available judgeship.[12] In addition to having a strong say in the president's choice for district court judge, senators have used their power in very partisan ways to block nominations. Indeed, from the early nineteenth century, the Senate has often either slowed down or stalled a president's nomination during lame duck periods or when the sitting president is being seriously challenged for reelection.[13]

In addition to senators and local political leaders, interest groups have played roles of varying importance. In addition to bipartisan nominating committees widely used during the Carter administration and by several senators in recent years, the Committee on the Federal Judiciary of the American Bar Association, local bar groups, and political action committees have made recommendations and sought to influence presidential choices.[14]

While the appointment process has always been a partisan one, this does not mean that judges have not been qualified. Nor does it mean that judges have blindly followed their appointing president's political agenda. Many scholars have demonstrated, and this study confirms, that on the bench district court judges render decisions that reflect many influences. Some even change their views as they continue to serve. Hall, for example, has shown that those judges appointed by the states-rights-oriented presidents Thomas Jefferson and Andrew Jackson enforced federal law against state challenges on numerous occasions.[15] Studies of judicial behavior of appointees since World War II demonstrate only "weak and inconsistent" correlations between a judge's decisions and the agenda of his or her appointing president. Although in recent years Democratic judges have tended to be more liberal than Republican judges, the deviations are not "terribly large."[16]

Nevertheless, scholars continue to analyze factors that might influence a judge's decisions. Ronald Stidham and Robert A. Carp argue that "United States trial judges have historically had strong ties with the state and region in which their courts are located," generally having been born and educated in the region where they serve. The result, they argue, is that federal district judges "tend to be products of their respective regional and local cultures" and that their decisions reflect this regionalism.[17] Beyond regionalism, Carp and Rowland argue, there is a "causal relationship between judges' background characteristics and their subsequent judicial behavior." In another study, however, Stidham and Carp concede that the correlation between background and beliefs on the one hand and judicial behavior on the other is less for district than for appellate court judges. Indeed, trial court judges, they admit, have less opportunity to shape the law, because they are limited by controlling law from the circuit and Supreme courts. They conclude, therefore, that because of the judges' integrity, training, and values, most decisions show little bias. Indeed, they admit that "the best way to predict the outcome of any given case is to determine which litigant has the weightiest evidence and the best controlling precedents." But for a "small but substantively important group of cases" where the area of law is new or the "precedents and evidence are ambiguous or contradictory," "factors such as the judges' basic philosophy, the mores and traditions of their particular circuit or state, and the attitudes and values reflected in their own political backgrounds do indeed measurably affect their judicial decision making."[18]

This study has sought to identify not only the leading cases judges have decided in the Southern District of Ohio but also the changing patterns of their cases over time. Throughout, this study shows that judges, following precedent and enforcing the law as written, have made decisions that they philosophically or morally opposed. On occasion, a judge's decision reflected his or her background or values or the values and interests of his or her community. This chapter will more specifically summarize the backgrounds of the judges and examine what factors might have influenced their jurisprudential views. It also examines the appointment process, delineating those factors that have gone into the selection of the judges of the U.S. District Court for the Southern District of Ohio. It is hoped that this information will provide further insights into the nature of the court and provide others with additional information for further study.

### CHARLES WILLING BYRD, 1803–1828

Nominated by President Thomas Jefferson, Charles Willing Byrd served as the first district judge for the District of Ohio.[19] Although many others competed for the post, attracted by the prestige and what was considered at the time the decent salary of $1,000 a year, Byrd had the strong support of two of Ohio's most influential men, Thomas Worthington, one of Ohio's first U.S. senators, and Edward Tiffin, Ohio's first governor and later a U.S. senator. In addition, Byrd was himself a prominent and popular Ohio politician. Moreover, he used his Virginia connections to lobby Secretary of State James Madison and President Jefferson.[20]

Typical of late-eighteenth- and early-nineteenth-century jurists, Byrd was one of early America's elite.[21] The son of Colonel William Byrd, a wealthy

Mrs. Elmer Fulton, a descendent, unveils a memorial marker to Judge Charles Willing Byrd, October 19, 1941, in Sinking Spring, Ohio. Judge Byrd, the first judge of the District of Ohio, served from 1803 to 1828. *From the collections of the Ohio Historical Society, Columbus*

planter and American Revolutionary War officer who served under General George Washington, and prominent Philadelphian Mary Willing Byrd, Byrd was born on a Virginia plantation along the James River in 1770. After his father's death in 1777, Byrd moved with his mother to Philadelphia and continued to associate with elite society. His early education under the tutelage of William Powell, a wealthy Quaker, probably shaped his strong views against slavery and for temperance. After receiving his classical education, Byrd read law with Gouveneur Morris, an influential politician of the time and a member of the convention that drafted the U.S. Constitution, and was admitted to the state bar in 1794. Then, as an agent of Robert Morris, a prominent financier of the American Revolution, Byrd traveled to Kentucky to sell land. There he met and married Sarah Waters Meade in 1797. He then returned to Philadelphia and engaged in the private practice of law for two years until 1799, when President John Adams appointed him secretary of the Northwest Territory. Through marriage Byrd had established strong ties to Ohio. His wife's sister married General Nathaniel Massie, one of the largest landowners in the territory and the founder of Chillicothe, Ohio's first seat of government.[22]

Despite his appointment by the Federalist John Adams, Bryd aligned himself with the dominant Jeffersonian Republicans and clashed with the Federalist territorial governor Arthur St. Clair. The feud between St. Clair and Byrd became public in December 1802. St. Clair accused Byrd of neglecting his duties and trying to have him removed from his territorial office. In response, Byrd accused St. Clair of trying to defeat his candidacy as a delegate to the state's constitutional convention. After that election, Byrd considered himself vindicated. Not only was he elected to the convention, but Jefferson removed St. Clair and appointed Byrd to serve as acting governor as well as still serving as secretary of the territory.[23]

After Ohio became a state and Jefferson appointed Byrd to the District Court of Ohio, Byrd initially maintained his residence in Cincinnati, on what was then known as Byrd Street (now Fifth Street), although he was required to attend court in Chillicothe three times a year. In June 1807, he purchased a six-hundred-acre tract in Adams County, known as Buckeye Station and Hurricane Hill, overlooking the Ohio River. He lived there with his wife and four children until his wife's death in 1814, after which he sold the land and moved to Chillicothe for about a year. In 1816, he returned to Adams County, moving to West Union, where he lived for seven years. There, in 1818, he met and married Hannah Miles, a widow with two children. Byrd had another two children with her. After his second wife's death, in 1823, Charles bought a large tract of land in Sinking Springs, in Highland County, and built a brick home for himself and his children. There he remained until his death, at the age of fifty-eight, on August 11, 1828. He is buried in Sinking Springs.[24]

Notwithstanding his elite upbringing, Byrd, in his personal life, "had a strong taste for the quiet and spiritual life."[25] He indicated in his diary that he moved to "Sinking Springs because he believed the waters there promoted health." He was near fanatical about a proper diet, limiting his intake of sugar, fat, and the like. Devout, his moral ideals were shaped, at least in part, by Quakers and Shakers. He strictly observed the Sabbath, even refusing to ride horses on Sundays. He opposed slavery and supported temperance, choosing to abstain from the consumption of liquor himself.[26]

Politically, Byrd was a moderate Republican. This faction of the party believed in a democratic government, but one run by a natural aristocracy based on merit. They sought stability, gentility, and order. To help achieve these goals, Byrd and his moderate colleagues supported an independent judiciary, which Byrd believed to be essential to the protection of property and the maintenance of order.[27]

## WILLIAM CREIGHTON, RECESS APPOINTMENT, 1828–1829

When Byrd died, John Quincy Adams was president. At the time the nation was in the throes of one of the most contentious presidential races it would ever see. Since 1824, when the House of Representatives had selected Adams over Andrew Jackson, after no candidate received a majority of the electoral votes, Jackson vowed to gain the position he considered had been stolen from him by a "corrupt bargain." Jackson believed Adams and Henry Clay had conspired to throw the 1824 election to Adams. In return, Adams had appointed Clay secretary of state, which was then considered the position of heir apparent to the presidency. As a result, political tensions mounted, the so-called Era of Good

William Creighton, a recess appointment, 1828–1829. *From the collections of the Ohio Historical Society, Columbus*

Feelings ended, and the seeds were sown for what historians have labeled the "second American party system."[28]

Byrd's death created a political dilemma for Adams. Nominating a replacement would help perpetuate his philosophy of government and provide patronage for his political supporters. Many supporters, such as Thomas C. Flournoy of Columbus, however, urged the president to wait, fearing that any appointment would alienate some faction Adams needed to win reelection. Although Adams followed this advice, it did not help; he lost the election to Jackson anyway.[29] On November 1, 1828, when it must have been clear to him that the election was lost, he appointed William Creighton Jr. to be the new district court judge for the District of Ohio on an interim basis.[30] Creighton seemed to be an excellent choice. Born October 29, 1778, in Berkeley County, Virginia (now West Virginia), the son of Colonel William and Elizabeth Creighton, young William attended Dickinson College in Pennsylvania, where he was a classmate of Roger Taney, whom President Jackson would appoint chief justice of the U.S. Supreme Court. After graduating with distinction, Creighton studied law in western Virginia before moving to Chillicothe in 1799, where he was admitted to the Ohio bar. He became a member of what was known as the "Chillicothe Junto," a group of Virginians that included Byrd who were instrumental in gaining statehood for Ohio. His wife, Elizabeth Meade, whom he married in 1805, was the daughter of Colonel David Meade, another prominent and popular Ohioan.

In 1803, in recognition of his abilities, Ohioans elected Creighton to be their first secretary of state. While serving in that office, he designed the Great Seal of Ohio. He held that office until Thomas Jefferson appointed him U.S. attorney for the District of Ohio in 1808. In 1813, his constituents elected him to the U.S. Congress, where he served two terms before returning to private practice. As a lawyer, he gained prominence when he defended two Ohio judges whom the Ohio House of Representatives had impeached for declaring an act of the state legislature unconstitutional. Their acquittal established the principle of judicial review in Ohio. In the 1820s, Creighton associated himself with the conservative wing of the Jeffersonian Republican Party, and voters in his district again elected him to Congress in 1826 and 1828 despite the Jackson landslide.[31] Flournoy, who had recommended Creighton for the federal judgeship, asserted that he was "a man of the finest legal attainments, and undoubtedly the most popular man in Ohio."[32]

When Congress reconvened in December 1828, Adams informed the Senate of the temporary commission and officially nominated Creighton.[33] The Jacksonian-dominated Senate, however, refused to act, and the Judiciary Committee reported that it believed it was "not expedient to act" on the nomination "during the present session."[34] Obviously determined to keep all the vacant judicial positions open for Jackson appointees, the Senate refused to consider any of Adams's nominations. The "correspondent" to the *Cincinnati*

*Advertiser,* reporting on the Senate proceedings, strongly criticized this action, calling the Senate "irresponsible" and "factious" for failing to do its constitutional duty. Arguing that "it was not supposed that they would ever refuse to consider the President's nominations," the correspondent asserted that the "Senate was bound by usage, by courtesy, by the Constitution, to give the nominations an immediate and respectful consideration and either to confirm them, or in case they had objections to the qualifications, to reject them, and thereby enable the President to nominate other persons." The judgeships they refused to vote on, he maintained, were "necessary to the public welfare," and those nominated "were known to be honest, capable, and faithful to the Constitution." But, he continued, "arrogant . . . Jackson Senators" refused to fill these vacancies until "they could fill them with their own adherents."[35]

Although the *Advertiser* was correct that the Jacksonians were determined to keep patronage positions open for their supporters and although Jackson wanted only those loyal to him and his views to serve in government posts, there was no evidence that judicial philosophy played a role in Creighton's rejection. Jacksonians were more interested in patronage. In nominating their own people or in rejecting Adams's nominees, Jacksonians in the Senate never discussed the candidates' jurisprudence.[36] As a supporter of the national bank and president of its Chillicothe branch, however, Creighton's political views certainly did not coincide with those of Jackson.[37] Creighton did serve as district court judge for one term, the December 1828 term, handling only a few cases with the United States as plaintiff trying to collect money owed it for a variety of reasons.[38]

### JOHN W. CAMPBELL, 1829–1833

To fill the position created by Byrd's death and Creighton's nonconfirmation, Jackson nominated John W. Campbell on March 6, 1829. The Senate confirmed him the next day.[39] Campbell, too, was a Virginian, born February 23, 1782, in Augusta County, Virginia. He received his Latin and classical education under the tutelage of the Reverend John Dunlevy and the Reverend Robert Finley after he moved with his parents, William and Elizabeth Campbell, to Brown County, Ohio, in 1798. Growing up poor, he paid for his education "by clearing ground and teaching school." He then read law with his uncle, Thomas Wilson, in Morgantown, Virginia, and was admitted to the Ohio bar in 1808. Setting up practice in West Union, he was elected justice of the peace for Tiffin Township in 1807 and appointed prosecuting attorney for Adams County. In 1810, his constituents elected him to the Ohio legislature, where he served three terms until, in 1816, voters elected him to the U.S. Congress, where he served five consecutive terms. After leaving Congress, Campbell moved to Brown County, where he purchased a small farm in what is now Jefferson Township and ran for governor as a Jacksonian Democrat in 1828.[40]

John Wilson Campbell, 1829–1833. *Courtesy of Mayhew & Peper, Photographers, Cincinnati*

Jackson appreciated the importance of federal judicial positions. He relied on loyal supporters to recommend only those with "sound and well-fixed" constitutional principles.[41] Jackson saw the judicial position in Ohio as particularly important because of the fierce competition in the state between the conservative National Republicans and the Jacksonian Democrats. Although Jackson narrowly won Ohio in 1828, the National Republicans won the governorship, Allen Trimble defeating Campbell by a slim two-thousand-vote margin.[42] Without Democratic senators or a well-developed state party organization, individual party leaders vigorously vied for Jackson's ear.

Many prominent Jacksonians urged Jackson to reward Campbell for his loyalty. Thomas Gillespie pointed out that Campbell, unlike others who had jumped on Jackson's bandwagon when he looked like a winner, had been a long and loyal supporter. Further, Gillespie claimed, Campbell's appointment "would please the majority of the people" of Ohio more than any other.[43] Elijah Hayward, the Cincinnati editor of one of Ohio's leading Democratic newspapers, an early organizer of Ohio's Jacksonian Democrats, and "chief dispenser of the Jackson administration's Ohio patronage," went to Washington to lobby for Campbell. Hayward emphasized how Campbell had faithfully served both Jackson and the party. As a congressman, Campbell had cast one of Ohio's two votes for Jackson in the disputed 1824 election. Then, in 1828, Campbell sacrificed his congressional career to be the party's candidate for governor. He then lost not only the race for governor but also the race for the Senate to Jacob Burnett.[44] Ohio representative William Russell also argued that fairness dictated Campbell's appointment, because Campbell had "suffered two defeats on party grounds." Moreover, Russell added, Campbell's "appointment would do more to strengthen the hands of the new administration in Ohio, than that of any other individual."[45]

Campbell's supporters were quick to point out that their candidate was not only a good political choice but also well qualified. Campbell, they argued, was a man of "unimpeached integrity, and a character without a single blemish."[46] He was a devout Presbyterian who, in the words of one biographer, "carried with him on the bench the same unbending integrity, and good sense, which had marked his public course."[47] Others praised him for his "common sense" along with his "industry," "integrity," and "good judgment."[48] But Campbell had not practiced law in many years and had no judicial experience. His appointment was clearly based on political considerations more than on considerations of merit. Campbell, however, was conscientious. Perhaps realizing his deficiencies and taking his new responsibilities seriously, he moved to Columbus, the seat of the court, and rose early each morning to study the law. Still, no one ever praised Campbell for his knowledge of the law; they spoke only of his common sense and his integrity.[49]

History will never know whether Campbell would have emerged as a prominent jurist, because he died suddenly on September 24, 1833, at the age of fifty-one. In 1811, Campbell had married Eleanor Doak, also from Augusta County, Virginia. Although they had had no children of their own, they did adopt a daughter. During the cholera epidemic of 1833, Campbell remained in Columbus to tend to his stricken daughter and others. Exhausted after their daughter's death, Campbell and his wife traveled to Delaware Springs to rest, but "overwork" and exposure to the cholera during his relief work was too much for the judge. He "took a chill, followed by high fever," and died soon thereafter.[50]

### BENJAMIN TAPPAN, RECESS APPOINTMENT, 1833–1834

After Campbell's death, several prominent politicians and attorneys vied to gain the nomination from President Jackson. After Jackson's veto of the bill to reauthorize the national bank, the president was more determined than ever that his district court nominees share his constitutional and political views on the bank and the Fugitive Slave Act, which he wished to be strictly enforced. Although eight men seriously contended for the nomination, Benjamin Tappan and Humphrey H. Leavitt, both of Steubenville, emerged as the leading candidates.[51] But Leavitt had just been reelected to a third term in Congress. If Jackson appointed him judge, the Whigs and conservative Democrats who controlled the Ohio legislative and executive branches would be able to appoint his replacement. Thus, Jackson decided against Leavitt, rejecting the recommendation of Ohio's Democratic congressional delegation. Instead, Jackson chose Tappan, who was being pushed by many of Jackson's close political advisors, including Vice

Benjamin Tappan, a recess appointment, 1833–1834. *Ohio Historical Society, Columbus*

President Martin Van Buren, Ohioan Micajah T. Williams, and Elijah Hayward, the Cincinnati newspaperman who had earlier advocated Campbell's appointment.[52]

On paper, Tappan was highly qualified. Born May 25, 1773, in Northampton, Massachusetts, Tappan was the eldest son of Benjamin Tappan, Sr., a Congregational minister, goldsmith, and dry-goods merchant. Sarah Homes Tappan, young Benjamin's mother, was the grandniece of Benjamin Franklin. Growing up in comfortable surroundings, Tappan attended common schools, apprenticed as an engraver, and then read law with Gideon Granger of Connecticut. In 1799, rebelling against his family's Federalism and Calvinism, Tappan moved to northern Ohio, where he set up his legal practice and entered into politics as a Jeffersonian. After serving in the state senate from Trumbull County, Tappan and his wife, Nancy Wright, moved to Steubenville. From 1816 to 1828, Tappan served as presiding judge of the Fifth Circuit of the Court of Common Pleas. He then returned to a lucrative private practice, while also remaining politically active, serving as a Jackson elector in 1832.[53] Supporters praised Tappan as "among the most learned and able jurists" in the West, as a sound Democrat "dedicated to the Jacksonian cause" who had supported the president from the beginning, and as "a man of integrity."[54]

Jackson appointed Tappan on an interim basis on October 12, 1833, hoping that, having begun his duties as district court judge, Tappan would be more easily confirmed. And, indeed, Tappan held court for the three-day December 1833 term. But on January 20, 1834, after the Senate reconvened and Jackson officially named Tappan, the Senate pigeonholed the nomination. This session proved to be "one of the most rancorous in Senate history." And Tappan had made many enemies. First, many believed his "uncompromising" partisanship inappropriate for a future judge. Indeed, Tappan fanned the fires when he continued his legislative lobbying and "signed a call for a Jefferson County Jackson–Van Buren meeting" after accepting Jackson's recess appointment as district judge. In addition to being labeled too political, Tappan alienated others who saw him as irreligious. But "the most . . . devastating critique" came from Tappan's former business partner Bezaleel Wells. Wells wrote to Ohio's Whig senator Thomas Ewing that Tappan was "a complete political demagogue," "unfit" for a judgeship. Despite his legal knowledge and skill as a lawyer, Tappan, Wells argued, would be unable "to divest himself" of the belief that the ends justify the means. The anti-Tappan campaign, led by Ewing and fellow Whig Benjamin Ruggles, who had not won reelection to the Senate in 1834, succeeded. The Senate, on May 29, rejected the nominee by a vote of 11 to 28.[55]

## HUMPHREY H. LEAVITT, 1834–1871

To replace Tappan, President Jackson turned to Humphrey H. Leavitt, whom Jackson had considered before he finally chose Tappan. Although Jackson

Humphrey Howe Leavitt, 1834–1871.
*Cincinnati Museum Center—Cincinnati Historical Society Library*

had rejected him previously, largely due to political considerations, Leavitt was still eager for the position of district court judge and quickly renewed his lobbying efforts, turning to his many influential supporters. In addition to Ohio's Democratic congressional delegation, which had supported Leavitt over Tappan from the beginning, John Patterson, the U.S. marshal for the District of Ohio, James Polk, then a congressman from Tennessee and later president of the United States, and Vice President Van Buren, after his first choice (Tappan) was rejected, wrote in favor of Leavitt's nomination.[56] On June 28, 1834, Jackson finally nominated Leavitt and the Senate confirmed his appointment the same day.[57]

With a reputation as an "able lawyer free from controversy," many considered Leavitt to be "the best that could be nominated from the Jacksonian ranks."[58] Born in Connecticut on June 18, 1796, Leavitt grew up in a family that always had struggled financially. Leavitt's father, John, whose ancestry went back to the early Pilgrims, worked as a farmer and a merchant, never experiencing much success in either. His mother, Fitch, struggled continually to make ends meet. In 1800, the family moved to the Ohio frontier, hoping for new opportunities. A few years later, they moved on to the small town of Warren in Trumbull County, where Leavitt finally gained the rudiments of an education. But at age sixteen, his formal education ended; he had to work to help his family. His first jobs were as a store clerk and teacher. At eighteen, he began to read law in the office of future Whig senator Ruggles, of St. Clairsville, and later with John C. Wirth, of Steubenville. In 1816, he gained admittance to the Ohio bar. He began practicing law in St. Clairsville with Ruggles, his mentor, and then moved nearby to Cadiz. Thus, Leavitt, more than any other antebellum judge from the District of Ohio, embodied the type Kermit Hall described as "children of the cabins," the men able to rise from "modest social origins . . . not through kinship and friendship connections," but through "partisan commitment and political activism."[59] But Leavitt never did rise financially above his modest beginnings. Because he held a series of government positions rather than establish a potentially more lucrative private practice, he never acquired much wealth and was always concerned about being able to support his wife, his daughter, and his three sons. He struggled even after his appointment to the federal bench, receiving only $1,500 a year until 1855. Then, after Congress divided the district in two, it raised Leavitt's salary to $2,500, relieving much of Leavitt's financial anxieties. Even so, he continued to worry about money throughout his life.[60]

Three years after Leavitt had become a lawyer, he moved to Steubenville to enter practice with John M. Goodenow, another prominent politician and, like Ruggles, a political opponent of Tappan and his faction. In 1823, Leavitt became Jefferson County's prosecuting attorney. Two years after that, he was elected to the Ohio House of Representatives. In the next election, his constituents sent him to the Ohio Senate. After briefly returning to private practice in 1828, Leavitt was elected as a Jacksonian Democrat to a seat in Congress.[61] Leavitt supported Jackson because of the president's "energy," "patriotism," and "liberal political principles."[62]

Leavitt held views Jackson considered essential for a judicial appointee, being one of only three of Ohio's congressional representatives who voted against the recharter of the national bank. Leavitt doubted its constitutionality as well as its merits. He said he feared an institution like the bank, which was "capable of wielding so potent an influence over the business and monetary interests of the country to say nothing of its temptation and its ability to interfere with and control the political affairs of the nation."[63] Leavitt's views on Jackson's other key political issue, the vigorous enforcement of the federal Fugitive Slave Act, were unknown at the time. Later, Leavitt made it clear that personally he opposed slavery and found the fugitive slave laws "harsh and repulsive." But as district court judge, he enforced the law, albeit "with the greatest reluctance," believing that he "had no power to nullify and set aside an act of Congress passed according to the forms of the Constitution, and held to be constitutional by the highest Court of the nation."[64] It was only after his retirement in 1871 that Leavitt was finally able to express his views publicly, and, in 1872, he attended a world convention on racial problems.[65]

Leavitt assumed his new duties as district judge with a mixture of joy and dread. He and his wife looked forward to enjoying the "peaceful" life of a judge, a life free from the turmoil and stress of politics, from which they both had an "intense desire to escape."[66] But, like Campbell, Leavitt had not practiced law for many years, so he feared that he lacked the qualifications necessary to do his new job well. Circuit Judge and Supreme Court Justice John McLean served as an important mentor to the young Leavitt. Moreover, when sitting on circuit court, Leavitt generally deferred to McLean and for years rarely prepared an opinion. Leavitt was particularly fearful after the court's division and his move to Cincinnati as judge for the U.S. District Court for the new Southern District of Ohio. He knew that the move to this "great center of commerce" would cause his docket to increase dramatically.

Again McLean quieted Leavitt's fears, and Leavitt went on to distinguish himself as an outstanding jurist.[67]

Nevertheless, although the president of the Cincinnati Bar Association, upon Leavitt's retirement in 1871, lauded the judge for his "strict impartiality," his "courteous demeanor," and his desire to provide "equal and exact justice to all,"[68] during his tenure as judge Leavitt expressed his disappointment that he had no "indication from any quarter" that he was doing well. Though some criticized or praised individual decisions, such comments were "few and far between." Finally, in 1869, members of the bar of southern Ohio raised money for a full-length portrait to be placed in the court room as an "indication" of the high regard with which they held Leavitt.[69] Leavitt, however, insisted that he never sought popularity. Rather, he explained, it was his "honest purpose . . . to do my duty in my official capacity."[70]

Leavitt served as district judge longer than any other person in the court's history. Indeed, at the time of his retirement, at the age of seventy-five, he was among the most elderly of the federal judges and with one exception was then the longest serving judge in the nation.[71] After his retirement, Leavitt remained politically active. In 1872, as a delegate appointed by the Ohio legislature, he attended an international conference on prison reform held in London. At the age of seventy-seven, on March 15, 1873, Leavitt died at his home in Springfield, Ohio, the town he had chosen over Cincinnati for his retirement years.[72]

### PHILIP B. SWING, 1871–1882

President Ulysses S. Grant chose his boyhood friend Phillip Swing to replace the retiring Leavitt. Many prominent attorneys, well aware that Leavitt was planning to resign, scrambled to gain the appointment as the next district court judge. The life tenure, the intellectual challenges, and the newly increased $4,000 annual salary were attractive features to many southern Ohio attorneys.[73] At least thirteen actively sought the post. Leavitt supported R. M. Corwine, the U.S. attorney serving while Leavitt was judge. It was a not well-guarded secret, however, that Grant intended to appoint his lifelong friend. And, indeed, many prominent politicians and lawyers, including members of the bar of Warren

Philip Bergan Swing, 1871–1882.
*Courtesy of the Sixth Circuit Archives, Cincinnati*

and Clermont counties as well as the Speaker of the U.S. House of Representatives, supported Swing's appointment, praising his abilities. They claimed his qualifications were "second to none," calling him a lawyer who occupied "a distinguished place in the front of his profession" and was "eminently fitted in all aspects." He not only had "a legal mind of the highest order" but was "honest," of "high character," and had "christian integrity."[74]

But others vigorously opposed Swing's appointment. Joseph H. Barret and B. Eggleston, of Cincinnati, wrote Grant, claiming that it was the near "unanimous opinion" of Grant's "true political friends" that Swing's appointment would be "unpopular and distasteful" both to the bar and to "influential Republicans, to whom you must look for support."[75] Others, too, were working to undermine Swing's nomination, because several people wrote Grant to dispel the rumors that they had heard were circulating in Washington that Swing was not qualified and that most lawyers opposed his nomination. These rumors, they told Grant, were simply untrue. Those who knew Swing professionally, they wrote, knew him to be "industrious and laborious," to have a fine mind, and to be engaged in a practice that included admiralty and patent cases as well as general civil and criminal law.[76] But Grant was unconcerned about any rumors or comments. Ever loyal to his friends, he nominated Swing on March 30, 1871. The Senate unanimously confirmed him that day.[77] On April 6, five days after Leavitt's retirement went into effect, Swing presented his commission to the court and took the oath of office.[78] He served for eleven years, until his death at his home in Batavia on October 30, 1882.[79]

Born in Milford, Ohio, in Miami Township, Clermont County, on October 22, 1820, Swing was the first native Ohioan to serve as district court judge of the Southern District of Ohio. The sixth child of Michael and Ruth Gatch Swing, he grew up in a rural community. As a boy, he often visited Bethel, Ohio, where he became the friend of future president Grant, whose father owned a tannery there. At the age of twenty, Swing went to study law with Judge Owen T. Fishback, of Batavia; he was admitted to the bar two years later. Two years after that, he married Mary Hafer, and the couple had four children. After five years in private practice in Batavia, he became prosecuting attorney of Clermont County. Active in his community, he was a member of the Batavia town council, the treasurer of the county agricultural society, and a leader of the Whig and, subsequently, the Republican Party in Clermont County.[80]

## WILLIAM WHITE, 1883

Swing had been ill for more than a year before his death, unable to perform most of his judicial duties. As a result, the docket piled up. The clerk of court reported that "much work" needed to be done, old bankruptcy cases needed to be closed, and "quite a number of admiralty cases" needed attention.[81] But the clerk of court's pleas for a rapid nomination to replace Swing went un-

William White, 1883. *From E. O. Randall et al.,* History of Ohio *(New York: Century Co., 1912)*

heeded. It was not until February 10, 1883, that Republican president Chester A. Arthur nominated William White, of Springfield.[82]

Factionalism within the Ohio Republican Party contributed to the delay. According to the Democratic *Cincinnati Enquirer,* whereas the business community wanted someone above politics, someone who was not "a politician nor appointed by a politician,"[83] potential candidates lined up political support, knowing that it was the key to an appointment. At least sixteen men vied for the post, but the three top contenders were White, George R. Sage, of Lebanon, and Warren M. Bateman, of Cincinnati. Republican senator John Sherman led the forces pushing for Bateman. Republican Speaker of the House J. Warren Keifer headed the White forces. B. R. Cowen, editor of the influential Republican newspaper the *Ohio State Journal,* of Columbus, spearheaded the movement for Sage, the son-in-law of the late Ohio governor Thomas Corwin. All the candidates solicited hundreds of testimonials, letters, and petitions on their behalf. White had letters from most state officials, including the governor, the attorney general, the secretary of state, the auditor, the commissioner of schools, and the commissioner of railroads. In addition, members of the Ohio Supreme Court, as well as members from the bars of most counties in the Southern District of Ohio, wrote praising White's abilities. Even U.S. Supreme Court Chief Justice Morrison Waite wrote to Attorney General Benjamin Harris Brewster praising White's judicial qualities. Waite maintained that White, as judge of the Ohio Supreme Court since 1863, has earned "the confidence and respect of everybody. He is careful, thoughtful and painstaking in the highest degree." It would be difficult, Waite concluded, to find someone better qualified. Keifer wrote several letters to Arthur, Brewster, and others, praising White's "purity of life and character, his experience and extraordinary attainments as a jurist, [and] his relations to the republican [sic] party." Some, Keifer noted, argued that White was too old—rumors put his age at sixty-five—but, Keifer pointed out, he was only sixty and "in good vigorous health."[84]

Sage, too, had hundreds of letters of support from attorneys and business leaders. Members of the bar from at least four counties petitioned for his appointment. Cowen described him as "one of the leading lawyers" of the state, a man of "very high character," "an active Republican and a hard worker for the party although he has never held an office."[85]

For Arthur, the dilemma was which faction of the party he would support. Cowen described the problem clearly, although in a way most favorable to his candidate, Sage. Writing to Benjamin Butterworth, an influential Ohio congressman and later commissioner of the U.S. Patent Office, on January 2, 1883, Cowen argued that the selection of the new judge would be important to the prospects of the Republican Party in the upcoming state elections. It is of utmost importance, he argued, to "harmonize all the elements." He explained: "We have factions here . . . and they have done us much injury. If we can steer clear of them it will be well. If we do not, Ohio is lost in 1883." He then argued that Bateman's appointment would anger the Sherman faction and that White's nomination would alienate the Keifer group; only Sage, who was "always a Republican of the straightest sect," would not alienate either.[86]

Cowen, however, was not being completely forthright in his assessment. Sage had made powerful enemies, too. He had aligned himself with Murat Halstead, the editor of the influential *Cincinnati Commercial.* Halstead, however, was an independent Republican who opposed a protective tariff and supported the anti-Grant Liberal Republicans in 1871. Because of this relationship, Grant and his friends actively worked to prevent Sage's nomination. Washington McLean, for example, wrote that Sage, "like Halsted [sic] is utterly unfit to fill any position where justice has to be administered." He claimed that "Sage like his master Halsted [sic] has been [a] bitter enemy" of Grant and many other leading Republicans.[87] Cowen tried to counter this opposition. He claimed that he, too, was a friend of Halstead's, but that did not mean that he followed Halstead's politics. Sage, he argued, was "a wholesome influence over Halstead." Besides, Cowen reminded Arthur, it would not hurt the party to placate Halstead, "especially as he is about to enter on a new era of journalism." And finally, Cowen argued, Sage was the best lawyer of the three, and far younger than White, who Cowen said was sixty-five and too old.[88] Andrew S. Hickenlooper, the district's U.S. marshal, reinforced Cowen's arguments. He pointed out that "Sage has not been identified with either of the [major] Republican factions" in the state and was a friend and confidant of the respected Judge William Howard Taft.[89]

After Arthur decided on White, the Senate quickly confirmed him.[90] White, indeed, was well qualified for the post. Born in England on January 28, 1822, he moved to Springfield, Ohio, with an uncle in 1831 after his parents died. At twelve, he was apprenticed to a cabinetmaker, but after serving for six years he bought his remaining time so he could attend high school, while still, during vacations, working as a cabinetmaker. After completing this education, he studied law with William A. Rodgers, of Clark County, teaching school to help support himself. In 1836, he was admitted to the Ohio bar and became Rodgers's partner until Rodgers was appointed to the common pleas bench in 1852. In the meantime, White had been elected prosecuting attorney for Clark County in 1847. Voters reelected him three times to that post, and in 1856 elected him common pleas court judge for the county. In 1864, Governor John Bough appointed White to a vacancy on the Ohio Supreme Court. Ohioans then reelected White every five years. White was serving as chief justice when Arthur appointed him to the District Court for the Southern District of Ohio, in 1883.[91] Unfortunately, Cowen had been right when he claimed White was not in good health. Once confirmed, White declined the position because of illness. He died a month later, on March 12, 1883.[92]

GEORGE R. SAGE, 1883–1898

Acting quickly, on March 20, only eight days after White's death, President Arthur named George Sage to the district court bench as a recess appointment and then officially nominated him when the Senate reconvened in December; the Senate approved his appointment on January 7, 1884.[93]

Born in Erie, Pennsylvania, on August 24, 1828, Sage was the eldest son of O. N.— a Baptist minister—and Elizabeth Sage. After the family moved to Ohio in 1835, Sage learned printing while being educated at home. He graduated from Granville College (now Denison) in 1849, having worked as a typesetter to pay for his education. After graduation, he taught mathematics at an academy in Lebanon, Ohio, while reading law with Alphonso Taft. The first of the district judges in southern Ohio to attend law school, Sage completed his legal training at the Cincinnati Law School, where he later taught, and was admitted to the Ohio and Kentucky bars in 1852. He then entered private practice, first forming the law firm of King, Anderson & Sage. His partners, both influential Republicans, were Rufus King and a future Ohio governor, Charles Anderson. In 1855, Sage married Eva A. Corwin and two years later moved to Lebanon to form a partnership with his father-in-law, former Whig governor and U.S. senator Thomas

George Read Sage, 1883–1898. *Cincinnati Museum Center—Cincinnati Historical Society Library*

Corwin. When Corwin died in 1865, Sage moved back to Cincinnati and, in 1867, established the firm of Sage & Hinkle with his brother-in-law, Thornton M. Hinkle. With a large practice representing several leading area businesses, Sage had a reputation as a fine lawyer. Indeed, the future district court judge John Weld Peck read law with him. Although active in politics before being appointed to the federal bench, the only public position Sage previously held was early in his career when he served as prosecuting attorney of Warren County. In 1861, he had sought the position of U.S. attorney, but failed to win appointment.[94]

Sage served as district court judge from 1883 until August 1898, when he resigned on the occasion of his seventieth birthday, to take advantage of the retirement benefits in the 1869 judiciary act. His resignation was to take effect upon appointment of a successor, but on November 19, he died of a heart attack. For all practical purposes, Sage had retired seven months earlier when, after having suffered several severe attacks, he was confined to bed.[95] Sage was eulogized as a man with "a character beyond reproach and a record as a citizen, as a lawyer, as a Judge, and as a christian, without a stain." He had a "gentle disposition." He considered himself a simple man of the people. Every day, he rode the baggage car of a train from his home in Lebanon to the courthouse in Cincinnati. He told attorneys that if they ever needed to consult him, they could always join him there. A deeply religious man who loved literature and played the flute to relax, Sage's greatest asset as a judge was his self control. He was a "patient" listener and a cautious jurist who applied law to facts. Lawyers especially praised his handling of patent cases. He was "fond of investigating new mechanical inventions" and "no one who tried a patent case before him failed to discover that he was at home in mechanical complications." He also excelled in criminal law, having extensive experience in that area from his six years as prosecuting attorney early in his career and then having defended numerous clients in private practice. Lawyers commented that Sage, a law-and-order judge, "administer[ed] the criminal law with a firm hand and to inflict adequate punishment upon malefactors." Indeed, he considered himself "the instrument appointed to preserve society from malefactors." Specifically, he believed that it was his job as a judge to control the jury by his rulings, thereby saving them "from errors of prejudice, passion or weak sentimentality."[96]

### ALBERT C. THOMPSON, 1898–1910

Immediately upon Sage's resignation, Republican president William McKinley chose his personal friend and former congressional colleague Albert C. Thompson as a recess appointee. Thompson took his oath of office and assumed his duties on September 22, 1898. McKinley then officially nominated him when the Senate reconvened in December, and the Senate quickly confirmed the appointment.[97]

Albert Clifton Thompson, 1898–1910.
*Courtesy of Mayhew & Peper, Photographers, Cincinnati*

Born January 23, 1842, in Brookville, Pennsylvania, the son of the Honorable John Jamison Yipsilanti and Agnes Susan Kennedy Thompson, Thompson entered the preparatory department of Jefferson College in Pennsylvania in 1854. Family financial problems, however, cut his education short. At seventeen, after returning home, he began to read law with a local attorney until the Civil War halted these studies. Enlisting in the Union Army in 1861 as a private, Thompson advanced to the rank of captain before two wounds he received at the second battle of Bull Run forced him to resign. One bullet could not be removed and remained, throughout his life, a painful reminder of his wartime experience. Returning home in 1863, he again studied law and was admitted to the Pennsylvania bar the next year. After moving to Portsmouth, Ohio, in 1865, he opened a private practice and became involved in local politics as a Republican. He also met Ella A. Turley, the daughter of Colonel and Mrs. John A. Turley. Turley was a wealthy Scioto County farmer and prominent Republican who had served as mayor of Portsmouth. They were married on Christmas Day 1867 and eventually had six children.

Thompson then embarked on a career as a jurist and successful Republican politician. In 1868, he was elected probate judge of Scioto County. In 1881, his constituency elected him judge of Ohio's Seventh Judicial District Common Pleas Court. Then, in 1884, the people elected him to Congress where he served for three terms. As congressman, he initially sat on the Private Land Claims Committee and the Invalid Pension Committee. Later, he became an influential member of the Judiciary Committee and the Committee on Foreign Affairs. After a Democrat took his seat in the 1890 election, Thompson returned to a lucrative private practice in Portsmouth, though he also remained active in his community. In 1893, he served as chairman of the Ohio Tax Commission. In 1896, he served as a delegate to the national Republican convention, supporting the soon-to-be president McKinley, whose famous tariff bill, which established one of the highest tariffs the United States ever experienced, Thompson helped to draft. In turn, McKinley, in recognition of Thompson's prominence as a jurist and attorney, appointed him in 1897 to chair the commission created to revise and codify the federal criminal code.[98]

Described as "a magistrate of the highest order," with a wide-ranging knowledge of the law,[99] Thompson controlled his crowded docket by moving trials along rapidly. Despite the speed with which he dispatched the court's business, the appellate court rarely overturned a verdict rendered in his court or a decision or order he issued during his twelve years on the bench. Thompson died in office on January 26, 1910.[100]

## JOHN E. SATER, 1907–1924

In 1907, Columbus attorney John E. Sater joined Thompson as the newly authorized second judge for the Southern District of Ohio. Born on a farm near New Haven, Ohio, on January 16, 1854, the son of John J. and Nancy Larson Sater, Sater's roots went back to Ohio's prestatehood days. Both his parents were native-born Ohioans, and his paternal grandfather had been one of the first settlers of Hamilton County. Orphaned at the age of ten, Sater went to live with his uncle, Joseph Sater, in Hamilton, Ohio. After attending public and select schools, he became a schoolteacher as well as a farm worker until he saved enough money to attend college. Sater then became the first district judge in southern Ohio to receive a college degree. After attending Miami University for two years, he transferred to Marietta College, where he received his A.B. in 1875 and his M.A. in 1878. Upon graduation, he served as superintendent of schools in Wauseon, in Fulton County, until 1881, when he became chief clerk in the office of the state commissioner of common schools in Columbus. It was at that time that he began to read law with J. H. Collins, one of the most prominent attorneys in Columbus and chief counsel for the Baltimore and Ohio Railroad. Admitted to the Ohio bar in 1884, Sater entered private practice but continued to stay active in the field of education. In 1885, he was elected to the Columbus board of education. He was also instrumental in establishing North End High School, which was the first branch high school in Columbus. He also served as trustee and president of the Columbus Public Library.[101]

As an attorney, Sater had a successful civil practice, representing, in the words of one supporter, clients "in all walks of life." His firm, Sater, Seymour & Sater, was not only retained

John Elbert Sater, 1907–1924. *From Who Is Who in and from Ohio, vol. 2 (Cincinnati: Queen City Publishing, 1912)*

by several banks, savings and loan companies, corporations in and around Columbus, and the Masonic Order and the Odd Fellows, but also represented many labor unions.[102] In addition, Sater had a lively real estate law practice. "For the ten years prior to 1907, the firm was counsel in almost every important case before the courts of Franklin County, Ohio."[103]

Sater's major support for the new judgeship came from the Columbus bar and Representative E. L. Taylor, who had authored the bill that had created the new judgeship. Taylor and the Columbus bar were insistent that the new appointee be from Columbus. As Taylor explained in a letter to President Theodore Roosevelt, if the appointee were not a Columbus resident, "the purpose of this Bill will fail."[104] In addition to the near-unanimous endorsement from the Columbus bar, Sater submitted more than a hundred letters of support from people from all over Ohio, including nearly all the state judges, numerous attorneys, and many leaders of labor groups. The letters described him as "a consistent Republican—never a factionalist" as well as a talented and knowledgeable lawyer and "a hard worker."[105]

On March, 18, 1907, after Congress authorized the district's temporary additional judgeship, Republican president Roosevelt appointed Sater as a recess appointment. On December 3, after Congress reconvened, the president officially submitted Sater's name, and the Senate routinely referred the nomination to the Judiciary Committee. But the nomination sat there for a year.[106] Senator Joseph B. Foraker, a Republican from Cincinnati, stalled the hearings, apparently piqued that Roosevelt had ignored senatorial courtesy in making the recess appointment.[107]

There had been a great deal of competition for this position. The chief contenders were Judge John J. Adams of Zanesville, Oscar M. Gottschall of Dayton, George M. Martin of Lancaster, and C. M. Rogers, Edmund B. Dillon, and George S. Marshall, of Columbus, in addition to Sater. All had several letters of support from area attorneys, leading businessmen, and prominent Republicans. From the letters sent to the president, it was clear that all viewed this position as important for reasons of party and policy. Many insisted that their candidate was a true Republican and that only good Republicans should be appointed. But more important to these letter writers was the type of person the candidate was. As mentioned before, Sater's supporters emphasized that his clientele came from all walks of life. Roosevelt, as a progressive Republican, had taken on the corporations as a trustbuster and had negotiated settlements between the unions and the corporations. He was also known to be seeking judges with similar progressive views. Sater supporters stressed that their candidate held such beliefs.[108]

Others identified their candidates as people who would further the interests of the Republican Party.[109] But the unions actively opposed at least two of the candidates—Oscar Gottschall and Judge John Adams. Nine unions wrote to oppose Gottschall, and four condemned Adams.[110] The editor of the *Locomotive Firemen and Engineer's Magazine,* for example, said that Adams opposed organized labor and was a friend of "the Coal Barons, the Packers' Combine, the Railroad Mergers, the Oil syndicates and other interests antagonistic to the public welfare." Believing Roosevelt to be labor's friend, the editor continued, "I think you will agree with me when I say that we already have too many corporate lawyers masquerading as judges."[111]

At the next session of Congress, Roosevelt renominated Sater. Finally, on March 1, 1909, the Senate confirmed the appointment.[112] In general, Sater lived up to the praises of those who had supported him. As a judge he was recognized for his "high ability." The *Ohio State Journal* praised him as "a rapid worker . . . liberal in his tendencies, . . . [and open to] innovations designed to promote the public welfare."[113] Attorneys who practiced before him called him "one of the ablest United States judges" of his time, a man who "took pride in his opinions, many of which became valuable precedents."[114] Not only did he sit in Columbus, Dayton, and Steubenville as a district judge for the Southern District of Ohio but he also served as special judge on many federal benches including courts in Toledo, Grand Rapids, Nashville, Philadelphia, Cleveland, Memphis, and the Sixth Circuit Court of Appeals. He also chaired the commission to review federal judicial procedure. Chief Justice William Howard Taft commended the work of the commission and Congress enacted the proposals submitted by Sater's committee.[115]

After serving seventeen years on the bench, Sater retired in 1924. Retirement opened up new challenges. He returned to private practice, served on the Columbus Chamber of Commerce, was a member of the Ohio convention that urged the repeal of the Eighteenth (Prohibition) Amendment, and authored an article on land titles in Columbus. He died at his home in Columbus on July 18, 1937.[116]

### HOWARD CLARK HOLLISTER, 1910–1919

After Thompson's death in 1910, the Southern District of Ohio would have returned to a one-judge district with Sater being the only judge if Congress had not made the second judgeship, which it had authorized on a temporary basis in 1907, permanent. Indeed, the *Cincinnati Enquirer* speculated that Thompson's death would help speed congressional authorization for a permanent second judgeship, the work load of Thompson and Sater demonstrating the necessity.[117] But the creation of a permanent second judgeship was not accomplished without dissent. Representative James Mann, of Illinois, criticized the bill as political, providing the Republicans with yet another judgeship and more patronage. To counter this charge, Province M. Pogue, a leader in the Cincinnati Bar Association and a member of the delegation that went to Washington to lobby Congress for the passage of the bill, wrote to President Taft, presenting documentation that the push for a new judge was not political. Rather, he contended, the desire for a second judge had wide bipartisan

Howard Clark Hollister, 1910–1919. *From William W. Morris,* The Bench and Bar of Cincinnati *(Cincinnati: New Court House Publishing, 1921)*

support because of the need to "relieve the congested condition of litigation" in the Southern District of Ohio.[118]

Once Congress made the second judgeship permanent, Republican president Taft nominated Howard Clark Hollister to fill the office.[119] "A man of small, spare stature," "extremely nervous," but respected and popular,[120] Hollister was nearly everyone's choice. First, he was a close personal friend and Yale classmate of Taft. Taft, a Cincinnatian and former circuit judge for Ohio's Sixth Circuit Court of Appeals, took an active role in his judicial selections. In the case of Hollister, Taft went even further than he generally did, ignoring senatorial courtesy because he felt that his close connection with Hollister as well as with Ohio's lawyers and judges made him the best qualified to identify the most appropriate candidate. For Taft, that meant "judges who would enforce property rights" and ensure businesses that they would not be "deprived of their property without due process of law."[121] In addition to ignoring Ohio's Republican senators, Taft bypassed Cincinnati's powerful Republican political machine headed by Boss Cox, whom both Taft and Thompson had long opposed. Thus, Taft personally wrote the chairman of the Senate Judiciary Committee, C. D. Clark, urging him to confirm Hollister quickly. In fact, Taft claimed that the opportunity to appoint Hollister to the federal bench was "one of the three or four personal considerations" that made him seek the presidency.[122]

In addition to Taft's support, Hollister had virtually the unanimous support of southern Ohio's bench and bar and prominent local community leaders. He received endorsements from Supreme Court Justice Horace Lurton, several judges of area common pleas courts, the Cincinnati Bar Association, and leading businessmen, bankers, and railroad presidents.[123] Lawyers praised him as a "distinguished," "hard working," "patient," "painstaking judge" with "unusual courage" to make the tough decisions. He was impartial, a man of integrity, skill, and learning. "None of our local judges," said one Cincinnati lawyer, "stands higher, few as high."[124] Indeed, the chairman of the Senate Judiciary Committee claimed that since he had been on that committee he had not seen any other candidate with "such a wealth of expressions of approval from those best qualified to judge of capacity and fitness for judicial position."[125]

Taft nominated Hollister on February 24, 1910, and the Senate confirmed him on March 7.[126] Hollister was a popular choice. "A thorough Cincinnatian," "a gracious and cultured gentleman," and "an extremely conscientious and high-minded judge and an excellent lawyer,"[127] Hollister was the best educated person to be nominated to a district court judgeship for the Southern District of Ohio to that point. Born in Cincinnati on September 11, 1856, Hollister was the eldest son of George Hollister, a prominent member of the Hamilton County bar and a Republican state senator, and Laura B. Strait Hollister, the daughter of a successful Cincinnati lawyer. Coming from "old stock," Hollister's ancestors came to America during the colonial era, three of his great-grandfathers having served as soldiers in the American Revolution. After Hollister graduated from Yale in 1878, he studied law with his father and attended the Cincinnati Law School, which awarded him an LL.B. in 1880, the same year he was admitted to the Ohio bar. After serving as Cincinnati's assistant prosecuting attorney for two years, he became a partner in his father's law firm along with his two brothers. He remained in private practice until he was elected, as a Republican, to the Court of Common Pleas of Hamilton County in 1893. Reelected in 1898, he remained in that position until 1903, when he returned to private practice. In the meantime, he had married Alice Keys, with whom he had four children.

When Hollister died suddenly of a heart attack in the library of his home in the East Walnut Hills area of Cincinnati on September 24, 1919, the Cincinnati bar eulogized him as a sincere man with a kind heart. The *Cincinnati Enquirer* praised his intense patriotism. "His Americanism," it noted, "was manifested often in the examination of candidates for admission to citizenship." But, clearly, he was deeply loved by many of those immigrants, who, under the auspices of the American House, raised money to send "a handsome floral piece" to Hollister's home after his death.[128]

### JOHN WELD PECK, 1919–1924

On October 30, 1919, Democratic president Woodrow Wilson nominated John Weld Peck to replace Hollister. Within a week, the Senate had confirmed him and he immediately assumed his position on the bench.[129] There seemed to be little competition for the position, perhaps because Hollister had died so suddenly. In the Department of Justice files, only one other person, a Dayton circuit court of appeals judge, H. L. Ferneding, had more than a handful of letters of support. Peck, however, was the clear choice, having been endorsed by Ohio's Democratic senator Atlee Pomerene, Governor James M. Cox, former governor Judson Harmon, and former congressman Alfred G. Allen. Moreover, Ohio's Republican senator, Warren G. Harding, had no objections to the nominee. In addition, the members of the bar of southwestern Ohio enthusiastically supported Peck. Unsolicited, the president of the Ohio State Bar Association, Smith W. Bennett, wrote to Attorney

John Weld Peck, 1919–1924. *Courtesy of Mayhew & Peper, Photographers, Cincinnati, Ohio*

General A. Mitchell Palmer, endorsing Peck's candidacy: "In learning, judicial temperament, and upright character, his selection could not be excelled." Both Alfred B. Allen, a Cincinnati attorney, and Senator Pomerene believed Peck to be one of the best trial lawyers in the state.[130]

Born February 5, 1874, in Wyoming, Ohio, the oldest son of Judge Hiram David Peck and Emily Weld Peck, Peck was part of a distinguished, well-established Cincinnati family. After attending public schools in Cincinnati and graduating from Woodward High School, he entered Miami University. After his freshmen year, however, he transferred to Harvard College, where he received his A.B. in 1896. Admitted to the Ohio bar in 1897, he continued his studies at the Cincinnati Law School, earning a bachelor of laws in 1898. The next year, he married Nell Wright, with whom he had two children. He also entered private practice as a member of his father's firm, which was eventually renamed Peck, Shaffer and Peck, and, after his father's death, Peck, Shaffer, and Williams. By the time he was appointed to the bench, he was one of the most prominent attorneys in Cincinnati, with a clientele that included the Cincinnati Southern Railroad, Cincinnati Gas and Electric Company, Cincinnati Street Railway Company, Western Bank and Trust Company, and many other industrial and financial institutions. He also served his community as president of the board of trustees of Miami University, a trustee of the Cincinnati Law Library Association, trustee of the Cincinnati Zoological Society, president of the Cincinnati Bar Association, a member of the county board of the Red Cross, the head of the Salvation Army in his district, and a professor of law at the University of Cincinnati School of Law.

In addition to his professional and community activities, Peck had been quite active in Democratic politics before his appointment to the federal bench. He ran unsuccessfully for mayor of Cincinnati in 1902, helped lead many local Democratic campaigns, and served as a delegate to the Democratic National Convention in 1912 and as a member of the Cincinnati City Council in 1912–1913.[131] Ideologically an "Independent" or "Jeffersonian" Democrat,[132] Peck was much more conservative than the progressive president who appointed him, believing in the economic law of supply and demand, insisting on "the inviolability" of due process, and "deplor[ing] the tendencies" of the time to ignore encroachments on the Bill of Rights by congressional legislation or executive action.[133] In the 1930s, he criticized the New Deal's centralizing tendencies and its involvement in labor-management affairs, in the production and sale of electricity, and in banking and finance. He feared that these "innovations" would lead the country to "Marxian socialism, if not actual communism" and praised the U.S. Supreme Court for the courage it displayed in striking down New Deal legislation.[134]

Peck remained on the bench for only four years before he decided to return to private practice. Perhaps it was the constant stream of mundane prohibition cases that failed to challenge him, but, for whatever reason, on January 16, 1923, Peck wrote to Attorney General Harry M. Daugherty that he desired to escape "the irksomeness of the confinement of this office, which bears upon me very heavily."[135]

### SMITH HICKENLOOPER, 1923–1929

Republican president Warren G. Harding initially nominated Harry Hoffheimmer to replace Peck. Before Harding announced his choice, there seemed to be great concern among Cincinnati attorneys that Harding would appoint someone connected with Cincinnati's corrupt Republican machine. A group calling itself the Cincinnati Lawyers' Committee lobbied the president for "a first-class" appointment.[136] Hoffheimmer seemed to be a satisfactory choice. Although he was nominated on February 28, 1923, and confirmed by the Senate three days later with the blessing of Ohio's two senators, Hoffheimmer, for unknown reasons, declined the appointment. Harding immediately turned to Smith Hickenlooper, whom he nominated on March 3, the day after the Senate had confirmed Hoffheimmer, simply noting that "this appointment [is] in lieu of the appointment of Harry M. Hoffheimmer, whose nomination was confirmed." The Senate confirmed Hickenlooper the same day.[137]

A native Cincinnatian, Hickenlooper was born on February 13, 1880, to Mary L. Smith and General Andrew Hickenlooper. Hickenlooper's father served in the Civil War, reaching the rank of general. After the war, he served as lieutenant governor of Ohio and president of Cincinnati Gas and Electric Company. Smith Hickenlooper graduated from Woodward High School

Smith Hickenlooper, 1923–1929. *Courtesy of the Sixth Circuit Archives, Cincinnati* and then the University of Cincinnati, where he graduated Phi Beta Kappa with a B.A. in 1901. He then went on to Harvard Law School, graduating cum laude in 1904. Admitted to the Ohio bar that year, he joined the firm of Outcalt and Forakes. Meanwhile, he married Anna Bailey Wright, and the couple had three children. Until 1916, Hickenlooper pursued a career in private practice, at which time he was appointed assistant Hamilton County prosecutor in charge of the civil division. He soon left that post to serve in World War I. After the war, he was elected to the superior court in Cincinnati, where he remained until Harding appointed him to the district court judgeship. He served on that court until 1929 when President Herbert Hoover elevated him to the Sixth Circuit Court of Appeals. He stayed on that bench until his death on December 22, 1933.[138] An expert in patent law, Hickenlooper was brilliant, with an "incisive mind" that went, in the words of Peck, "like lightning to the pivotal point of the case."[139] E. W. Edwards, president of the Fifth-Third Union Trust Company, praised him as "one of the most learned and efficient Federal Judges we had on the bench" in Cincinnati. But while he was courteous, capable, and conscientious, he was also a "somewhat severe gentleman."[140]

## BENSON HOUGH, 1925–1935

On Sater's retirement, Harding chose, as his second appointment to the district court for the Southern District of Ohio, Benson Hough. Hough was born on March 5, 1875, in Berkshire, Delaware County, Ohio, the son of Leonard and Mary Linn Hough and the grandson of Crasmus Daniel Hough, an early member of the Ohio General Assembly and a justice of the peace. He was raised on his family's farm and attended area schools. He then went to Ohio Wesleyan University, where he played football and baseball. After graduating with an M.A., he attended Ohio State University College of Law, receiving his bachelor of laws in 1899. He then entered private practice. From 1902 to 1906 he also served as city solicitor of Delaware, Ohio. During that time he married Edith Markel, with whom he had one child. In addition to his law practice, from 1892 to 1897, and then again from 1902 until he resigned in 1916 to join the regular army, Hough served in the Ohio National Guard, reaching the rank of brigadier general. After serving on the Mexican border, Hough fought in World War I as colonel of the Rainbow Division. He returned a decorated hero, having received the French Croix de Guerre along with a citation from General Pershing. Returning to private practice after

Benson Hough, 1925–1935. *Courtesy of the U.S. District Court, Southern District of Ohio*

the war, he was elected, in 1919, at the age of forty-four, to fill an unexpired term as a justice of the Ohio Supreme Court, making him one of the youngest men ever to have served on the state's highest court. Defeated for reelection in 1922, he gained appointment as U.S. attorney for the Southern District of Ohio. Serving in that capacity until Harding appointed him to the federal bench, Hough handled several high-profile cases, including *McGrain v. Daugherty*, involving the scandals in the Harding administration.[141]

Although nominated on January 31, 1925, and confirmed by the Senate on February 9, Hough endured a tough battle before winning appointment over five other leading contenders.[142] Ohio's two Republican senators, F. B. Willis and Simeon D. Fess, each backed a different candidate. Some feared that this split, along with political factionalism in Columbus, would result in the appointment of a judge without the requisite skills for the job. C. E. Thompson, president of the Steel Products Company, urged Harding to keep politics out of the appointment. As someone who litigated patent cases frequently before the federal court, Thompson wanted a person fit for the job.[143]

Hough had the support of Willis, who praised him as "a man of the highest character," "thoroughly qualified in every way."[144] Hough also received endorsements from other prominent Ohioans, including James E. Campbell, the former governor of the state, the Republican executive committees of several counties, and members of the bar of twenty-one counties.[145]

Representative Israel M. Foster, of Athens, the other major contender, had not only the support of Fess, the other Ohio senator, but also letters of endorsement from judges and bar associations from most of the rural counties of the Eastern Division, former Ohio attorney general Timothy S. Hogan, the general secretary of the National Child Labor Commission of New York, the president and vice president of the United Mine Workers of America, the chief of the Children's Bureau of the Department of Labor, the president of Ohio University, and many leading congressmen in and out of Ohio. A graduate of Harvard, Foster received praise as an able lawyer with an excellent record,[146] but Foster also had serious opposition. Mrs. Lyle Evans of Chillicothe wrote Attorney General Harlan F. Stone that Foster was too much of a politician and "a lawyer of small ability." She, along with most others she had spoken with, she claimed, preferred Hough.[147] G. C. Weitzel, the managing officer of three coal companies, wrote that Foster, as a congressman, had tried to solicit a bribe from him to gain his (Foster's) support for the coal companies.[148]

Others supported Roscoe J. Mauch of Gallipolis as a good compromise candidate who could break the deadlock between Ohio's two senators. Indeed, Mauch was Judge Sater's first choice. In a confidential letter to Attorney General Stone, Sater criticized Foster as an "ambulance chasing type of lawyer, fairly capable but not altogether well balanced and lacking the stability of character which a Judge . . . should possess." He did not think much better of Hough. Admitting that Hough had the character he believed Foster lacked, Sater did not think Hough had been a very effective U.S. attorney, "not [being] prepossessed to hard work."[149]

Despite all the controversy, Hough turned out to be "a splendid Federal Judge," who earned the confidence and admiration of all the attorneys who practiced before him.[150] More than six feet tall, Hough was an "impressive figure" on the bench with a "commanding presence."[151] Ralph H. Beaton, a Columbus attorney who worked with Hough on some complicated litigation, eulogized the judge as "a big man, physically, mentally, and morally." Quiet and retiring, with "unfailing modesty," Hough always tried "to do what is exactly right and just."[152] The Columbus *Evening Dispatch* called him a "distinguished jurist" presiding over a court that was a "bulwark of human rights of which he was a virile exponent."[153]

A "devoted admirer of the Federal Judiciary," believing it symbolized justice and all that made America great, Hough regretted the Prohibition era which he believed made his court almost a police court, bringing this great federal court "into a kind of disrepute." So he tried to temper "justice with mercy" when "the poor and simple were caught" while the "higher-ups escaped detection." If he found that the guilty brought before him still had "some worth, he never failed to give them hope and some chance for a new future." But while "kind," "considerate," and especially helpful "to the young and timid" new attorney, Hough was master of his court. Believing that "Justice too long delayed is often Justice denied," he dispatched the court's business swiftly. When he could do so "with justice," he forced "the dismissal of cases that ought never to have been brought." At other times, he would push parties to compromise when such "compromises were wise and just." In the courtroom, he moved his cases along quickly.[154]

Presiding over his court with "great dignity,"[155] Hough never wavered to do "his sworn duty." He believed that "his oath of office bound him in perfect subordination to those whom the Constitution and Congress made his superior." Therefore, "if his own Circuit Court of Appeals or the Supreme Court of the United States had fairly settled the law applicable to a particular case, it never entered his mind to ignore its express decision or the reasonable implications of that decision," even if he would have decided the case otherwise if the higher courts had not settled the question.[156] Hough also insisted that everyone in his courtroom show the court respect. Thus, he never hesitated "to rebuke an attorney, regardless of his standing or reputation, for conduct or language" he deemed inappropriate.[157] After serving "with distinction" for ten years, Hough died on November 19, 1935.[158]

### ROBERT R. (JAKE) NEVIN, 1929–1952

On January 5, 1929, President Calvin Coolidge nominated Robert R. (Jake) Nevin to replace Hickenlooper, whom he had elevated to the Sixth Circuit Court of Appeals. The Senate quickly confirmed Nevin.[159] Nevin was born in

Robert R. (Jake) Nevin, 1929–1952.
*Courtesy of the Sixth Circuit Archives, Cincinnati*

Dayton in 1876, the son of Colonel Robert M. and Emma Frances Reasoner Nevin. Colonel Nevin was a prominent Dayton lawyer and Republican congressman from the Third Congressional District. Indeed, it was Colonel Nevin who secured the passage of the so-called Dayton court bill, the act that provided for court sessions in Dayton. After graduating from Steele High School in Dayton, the future judge Nevin went to Ohio State University for two years before studying law at the University of Cincinnati College of Law. After earning his degree and being admitted to the Ohio bar in 1898, he joined his father in private practice, forming the firm of Nevin and Nevin. Two months later when the Spanish-American War broke out, Nevin enlisted as a private in the First Ohio Volunteer Cavalry. Eventually commissioned a second lieutenant in the U.S. Army, he served until the war ended, when he returned to private practice with his father. He was thought to be one of the best trial attorneys of his time. Specializing in corporate matters, his clients included several major railroad companies. He was also chief trial counsel for NCR in the antitrust litigation of the 1910s. In addition, he did legal work for the International Brotherhood of Carpenters and served for many years as a member of an impartial board for the arbitration of matters between newspaper publishers and the typographers unions. In 1906, he married May Steely, with whom he had two children. An active Republican, he served as prosecuting attorney for Montgomery County from 1906 through 1909, a delegate to the Republican National Convention in 1924 that nominated Coolidge, and the chairman of the Republican Executive Committee in Montgomery County from 1925 through 1926.[160]

"Recognized as one of the nation's top authorities on patent law," Nevin loved being a judge. For example, after the voters elected Republican Dwight D. Eisenhower president in 1952, Nevin could have retired and been replaced by a fellow Republican, but he continued on the bench, explaining: "I like the work and I like my court."[161] How Nevin became a top patent judge tells one a lot about his character. Admitting that he was frightened and worried about becoming a district judge, especially because he "knew nothing" about patent law, he set himself on a plan of study to overcome this shortcoming, knowing he would need such expertise as a judge sitting in Dayton, with the community's numerous research and development facilities, including those at NCR and General Motors. Through self-education, he became so knowledgeable that even federal judges in New York "held up patent cases with the words 'save it for Nevin.'"[162]

People eulogized Nevin as one who brought to the court "a well-trained mind, a broad culture, unusual learning in the law, the practical experience which comes from a varied practice, and above all his insatiable love of justice." "Patient and openminded," "he presided with a grace and dignity which commanded universal respect for his court." He was said to have "a human touch." Even when he handed out a tough sentence to a convicted criminal, he explained the reason for the sentence to him. As one court official said, "He is so kindly about it that even the prisoner likes it." People also admired his wit, and he was often able to use it to good advantage to keep his cases on point. For example, assigned to a patent case involving a device that controlled the curtain at Radio City Music Hall, he held court at the hall in New York so the attorneys could explain the issues. After listening to them drone on for hours, Nevin finally "halted the proceedings and asked: 'Please, gentlemen, can't we have the Rockettes?'"[163]

A 1948 poem demonstrates the admiration in which the bar held Nevin:

> One half a century ago,
> He started briefs and speeches.
> Now he presides o'er us below.
> He practiced; now he preaches.
> Against no man he bears a grudge,
> On earth, in sea or heaven.
> Behold at last a human judge,
> Your friend and mine, Jake Nevin.[164]

Following the passage of the Judiciary Act of 1948, he became the first chief judge of the Southern District of Ohio. Nevin served on the court until his death at his home in Dayton on December 31, 1952.[165]

### MELL UNDERWOOD, 1936–1967

On January 27, 1936, Franklin D. Roosevelt made his first judicial appointment for the Southern District of Ohio, nominating Mell Underwood to replace Hough. The appointment was not without controversy. The Franklin County League of Women Voters protested the nomination as "not in accord with the current campaign of the National League of Women Voters to establish the merit principle of appointment" in governmental positions. Specifically, Mrs. Ralph W. Hoffman, president of the Franklin County League, noted that Underwood was not even "registered to practice in federal court not having taken the required examination."[166] Although Underwood had only minimal experience practicing in federal courts and had not even practiced law for twelve years, he gained the nomination and quick Senate confirmation. He took the oath of office in Columbus on April 11, 1936.[167]

There are no extant records indicating why he chose Underwood, but Roosevelt was known for taking an active role in the selection of lower court judges, insisting that they share his views on the Constitution and the need for New Deal legislation. The president also generally consulted with the state's senators, but, again, there are no records of the views of Ohio's two Democratic senators on Underwood's nomination.[168] According to John Lyter, who clerked for Underwood in 1953 and later became clerk of courts for the Southern District of Ohio, Underwood developed a strategy to win the appointment that proved to be successful. He managed to position himself as everyone's second choice and convinced Jim Farley, Roosevelt's postmaster general and head of the administration's patronage, that he would make a good judge. In view of his record in the 1920s, Underwood seemed to hold more conservative views than did the president. He actively protected the interests of Ohio's coal industry and also authored the Underwood Bill to restrict immigration. And, according to Lyter, on the bench Underwood was a strict constructionist and a very conservative jurist.[169] But after fourteen years in Congress, Underwood had a high regard for Congress, which led him to a jurisprudence of judicial restraint whereby he strove to apply the law as written. This might have been exactly what Roosevelt wanted.

Born on a farm in Morgan County, Ohio, January 30, 1892, Underwood was the son of James G. and Sarah Newlon Underwood, both the children of pioneer Ohioans. Underwood attended public schools, graduating from New Lexington High School in 1911. He attended Ohio University and then taught school in New Lexington, Perry County, before studying law at Ohio State University. After being admitted to the Ohio bar in 1915, he returned to New Lexington, married Flora E. Lewis of Cadiz, Ohio, with whom he had four children, and set up his law practice. From 1917 to 1921, he was the county prosecuting attorney. He soon turned his attention to politics. After running unsuccessfully as the Democratic candidate for Congress in 1920, he won election in 1922, the youngest congressman then in the nation. He served in Congress as the representative from his district until Roosevelt appointed him to the federal bench.[170]

Although he had not practiced law for some time, he immediately took control of

Mell Underwood, 1936–1967. *Courtesy of the U.S. District Court, Southern District of Ohio*

his courtroom. After he was sworn in, he issued procedural orders for attorneys practicing before him. No case, he declared, would be assigned for trial until both sides filed trial briefs with "a concise statement of the case," the law the attorneys would rely on, and citations to authority, with reference only to federal courts, and most especially to the Supreme Court and the Sixth Circuit Court of Appeals. Attorneys were not to exchange these trial briefs, however, as they had done in the nineteenth century in Byrd's court. The briefs submitted in Underwood's court were "for the confidential information of the court only."[171]

Despite his ostensible courtroom authority, Underwood was always, to use his words, "a farm boy from the southern Ohio hills."[172] He was known more for his joviality than for his hard work. He was, in the words of Judge John D. Holschuh, a later district court judge who had clerked for Underwood, a "colorful judge." He kept two pints of Old Grand-Dad secreted behind the volumes of *The Life of Washington* on his bookshelves in his office. Moreover, he was quite casual about judicial procedures, often meeting with attorneys to discuss the substance or the merits of a case without a court reporter present. He also tended to push hard for settlements—in the opinion of some, too hard—putting great pressure on some attorneys. Although he had the reputation as "a no nonsense, common sense" judge and although he prided himself on "calling them as he saw them,"[173] he was neither a hard worker nor a very competent judge. Indeed, in 1965, the judges of the Sixth Circuit Court of Appeals "adopted a secret resolution demanding that . . . Underwood retire," believing that "he was not doing his share of the work." Underwood ignored the appellate jurists, saying they could "go to hell, and you may quote me on that."[174] Underwood stayed on the court until 1967, serving as chief judge from 1953 to 1962. He did take senior status at the end of 1965, however, and retired two years later. He died at the age of eighty, on March 8, 1972, on his farm near New Lexington.

### JOHN H. DRUFFEL, 1937–1967

On November 16, 1937, after Congress approved an additional judge for the Southern District of Ohio, Roosevelt nominated John H. Druffel to fill the new position. Within three weeks, the Senate unanimously confirmed him.[175] Born on February 6, 1886, the son of Henry B. and Mary McGinley Druffel, Druffel attended

John Henry Druffel, 1937–1967. *Courtesy of the Sixth Circuit Archives, Cincinnati*

public and parochial schools before graduating from Xavier University in Cincinnati. As a youth, Druffel became active in politics. Raised in Cincinnati's Eighth Ward, Druffel bucked Mike Muller, the boss of this Republican stronghold, organizing a Democratic club. He then worked as secretary to the city engineer under Mayor John Dempsey and as a jury reporter for the Hamilton County prosecuting attorney, Henry T. Hunt, who became Cincinnati's famous reform mayor. When Hunt was elected mayor, Druffel became secretary to the safety director, Dennis Cash. At this time, Druffel also attended the YMCA night law school, which later became Salmon P. Chase College of Law. After receiving his LL.B. in 1911, he was admitted to the Ohio bar in 1912 and in 1913 joined the firm of Moulinier, Bettman & Hunt. In 1929 he was elected to Cincinnati City Council on the reformist Charter ticket. He served until 1932, two of those years as vice mayor. During this time he married Loretta Barrett, with whom he had three children. In 1932, he ran as an independent against the two endorsed candidates for judge of the Hamilton County Court of Common Pleas. He won and remained there, winning reelection every two years, until Roosevelt appointed him to the federal bench. He took senior status in 1961, keeping an active calendar until his death on May 16, 1967.[176]

Druffel had a reputation as an extremely hardworking but stern judge. Peck said that statistics showed that his was "one of the busiest, single-judge federal courts in the nation." And, in 1958, the Department of Justice recognized his efficiency, citing him as one of the nation's eight top district judges with the least crowded docket. He never took a vacation, and he used pretrial meetings to clarify issues and try to get settlements.

But besides being efficient, he was, in the words of his fellow judges Weinman, Kinneary, Hogan, and Porter, "known, correctly, as a severe judge— more so than average," although he was also known, at least at times, to show patience and "charitable" attributes. Druffel believed the federal court was "a solemn place" that demanded respect. He never banged his gavel to keep order, the *Cincinnati Post & Times-Star* reported. "'Like this,' said Judge John, and tapped two fingers on his desk. That was all he ever needed to keep order. No man ever dared exceed it without penalty." When one famous lawyer ignored Druffel's warning and made faces at the jury to distract a prosecutor, Druffel made the attorney "turn his face to the wall, like a small child being punished," as well as fining him for contempt. On another occasion, he forced two accused bank robbers to wear leg irons during their trial. He said he could see in their eyes that they were going to try to escape. The Sixth Circuit Court of Appeals upheld his order and later Druffel's intuition seemed to be affirmed, as the two escaped from federal prison to rob another bank!

Often controversial, Druffel was still respected. As one attorney said, "It would be wrong to say that every decision that emanated from Judge Druffel's Court won the immediate concurrence from those inside and outside the legal profession. But we will hazard the estimate that every decision was respected as the handiwork of a competent jurist motivated by a deep reverence for the law." Like Nevin, Druffel, too, was an expert in patent law. While working his way through school, he had worked in industrial plants where he acquired knowledge of mechanics. He also was a secretary in a patent law office. Because of his expertise, the government often sent him the tough cases.[177]

## LESTER L. CECIL, 1953–1959

On April 1, 1953, Republican president Dwight D. Eisenhower made his first judicial appointment, nominating Lester L. Cecil to replace Nevin after Nevin's sudden death.[178] Under the Constitution the Democratic incumbent, President Harry S. Truman, had the authority to nominate Nevin's successor, but either in deference to Eisenhower's victory over Adlai Stevenson, the Democratic nominee, or because he believed any nomination he made would not be confirmed anyway, he chose to let Eisenhower make the appointment.[179]

Rumors circulated in Dayton for months as it became clear that no nominee would be named until Eisenhower's inauguration on January 20. Most assumed the nomination would come from one of the eight counties that composed the Dayton docket. The biggest issue was whether it would be someone from Dayton. Six men were considered top contenders: Harry N. Routzohn, a former congressman from Dayton's Third Congressional District, former county probate judge, and prominent railroad attorney; Cecil, then the chief justice of the Montgomery County Common Pleas Court; Herbert D. Mills, from New Lebanon, a powerful Republican central committeeman; and three other judges and leaders of the Republican Party.[180] Members of the Republican Party competed to win the nomination for their favorite. Routzohn, who had the backing of a powerful area Republican national committeewoman, Katharine Kennedy Brown, was assumed to have the inside track, but he was seventy-one years old. Although Cecil was also prominently mentioned, some thought his problem was that he had just been reelected to the court of common pleas; if he were confirmed for the federal bench, Ohio's Democratic governor Frank J. Lausche would appoint Cecil's replacement to the county judgeship.[181]

Both the executive committee of the Montgomery County Republican Party

Lester LeFebre Cecil, 1953–1959. *Courtesy of the Sixth Circuit Archives, Cincinnati*

and the Dayton Bar Association clashed over whether to endorse anyone officially. Eventually the Dayton bar polled its membership, which ranked Cecil first and Routzohn second. After weeks, the Montgomery County Republican Committee endorsed Cecil, but the party remained fractured. The county committee chairman went to Washington to lobby Ohio's two Republican senators, Robert A. Taft and John W. Bricker, for Cecil. Brown, however, continued her battle for Routzohn. This infighting led many to speculate that, because of the political deadlock in Dayton, the president might select someone from another area. Eventually, Cecil supporters convinced Brown to endorse their candidate. This, combined with Taft and Bricker's endorsement, led to Cecil's appointment to the post.[182] Although Cecil struggled to win the nomination, he received unanimous Senate confirmation on April 23, largely because of his impressive credentials and his personal popularity. Dayton congressman Paul F. Schenck noted, "Judge's Cecil's ability, experience and unquestioned integrity is known to thousands of people all over Ohio."[183]

Born on a farm near Piqua, in Miami County, Ohio, November 21, 1893, Cecil was the second son of Harry Everett and Edna Veretta Furrow Cecil. His ancestry goes back to the colonial period, with two descendants fighting in the American Revolution before the family settled in Miami County. Cecil grew up in West Milton, where his father worked for $17.50 a week, twelve hours a day, seven days a week, fueling a boiler to run a traction line. The young Cecil worked from age thirteen to make his dream of becoming a lawyer come true. After graduating from West Milton High School in 1912, he attended the University of Michigan, where he worked his way through school waiting tables, shoveling coal, mopping floors at the boarding house where he lived, and working in a movie theater at night. While at school, he wrote his mother about his struggles: "I like law real well . . . but it is awful hard. They assigned lessons on the bulletin board before school started and we had to start right in reciting. My books cost me twenty-one dollars and a half and over half of them were second hand. Some of them I had to get new." After five years struggling to make ends meet, he earned his LL.B. in 1917.[184]

Admitted to the Ohio bar that year, Cecil began practicing law with Earl H. and Wellmore B. Turner. He had hardly begun practicing, however, before the United States entered World War I. Cecil joined the army and served until November 1918. He returned to the Turner firm, until, on February 1, 1922, he was appointed the prosecuting attorney for the city of Dayton. During that time he also married his childhood sweetheart, Celia Carroll, with whom he had four children. He held the position of prosecuting attorney until January 1926, when he became a judge in Dayton's municipal court. Then, in 1929, the citizens of Montgomery County elected him to the court of common pleas, a post to which he was reelected four times.[185]

Believing that "to be a federal judge is the height of judicial achievement,"[186] Cecil worked to fulfill the trust that had been bestowed on him. Those who practiced before him praised him as a man of "uncompromising honesty and integrity." Developing "a reputation for dignity and fair dealing," Cecil, according to "the consensus of the Bar," provided each person who appeared before him with "exactly what he deserved, no more, no less." The president of the Dayton Bar Association concluded that Cecil "exemplified what a jurist should be."[187] Cecil himself explained best how he viewed the role of the law in society. Law, he said, is "an instrument to secure justice to all men, preserve freedom and protect the sacred rights of the individual under our form of government." The practice of law, he continued, "is a high calling and it should be the aim of every lawyer and judge to so demean himself . . . that it will always merit the confidence and respect of the public."[188] Personally, Cecil was a serious person, said to have little humor. Early in his career on the federal bench, however, a defendant, charged with criminal tax fraud, appeared carrying a Bible. Cecil asked whether he had counsel to represent him. He responded, "Jesus Christ is my counselor and defender." To this Cecil, with a smile, asked, "Do you have local counsel?"[189]

On July 18, 1959, Eisenhower elevated Cecil to the Sixth Circuit Court of Appeals. Cecil remained an active judge on that bench until August 1965, when he took senior status. He died at age eighty-nine, on November 26, 1982.[190]

## CARL A. WEINMAN, 1959–1979

On July 28, 1959, Eisenhower nominated Carl A. Weinman to replace Cecil. After the Senate confirmed him on September 2, Weinman took up the seat in Dayton.[191] Born in Steubenville, Ohio, January 27, 1903, the son of Andrew G. and Dorothea Becker Weinman, Weinman was the first judge in the Southern District of Ohio to be born in the twentieth century. He attended public schools in Steubenville, mastering the trumpet during that time and becoming a member of the musician's union. After high school, Weinman earned his B.A. and LL.B. from the University of Michigan, working to pay for his education by taking the job of director of the University of Michigan's marching band. Admitted to the Ohio bar in 1925, Weinman returned to Steubenville, joined the law firm of Cohen & Gardner, and married Elaine Scherer, with whom he had two children. While maintaining his private practice, he entered politics,

Carl Andrew Weinman, 1959–1979.
*Courtesy of the Sixth Circuit Archives, Cincinnati*

serving two terms as Steubenville's city solicitor from 1932 to 1936. In 1936 his constituents elected him to the Jefferson County Court of Common Pleas. After serving two six-year terms, he returned to private practice as a partner and principal trial attorney in the firm of Beckman, Weinman and Anglin. During this time, he actively worked for the Republican Party as a member of the state Republican committee.[192]

Weinman served as district court judge from his appointment in 1959 until his death after a long illness, on February 5, 1979. From 1962 to 1973, he served as chief judge, after which he took senior status, although he maintained an active case load until his death. While on the bench, Weinman was a leader among jurists. F. Lee Bailey, a renowned trial attorney[193] who became Weinman's friend after the Sam Sheppard case, said, "Of all the judges I've ever appeared before, none was finer than Carl Weinman."[194] Judge John Sirica, chief judge of the District Court for Washington, D.C., believed Weinman to be "one of the outstanding trial judges in the country."[195] His renown led to his appointment to prestigious committees, including the national Multi-District Litigation Panel. He also served for almost twenty years on the Judicial Conference Committee on the Budget, chairing it for nine of those years. In this capacity, his gregarious personality helped win votes for needed appropriations for the courts. Weinman also had the common touch, eating breakfast every morning with truck drivers, swapping tales with reporters, and participating enthusiastically at naturalization ceremonies.[196]

One of the most influential figures in the federal court system during the 1960s and 1970s, Weinman vigorously defended the dignity of the court. His stern appearance and manner prompted one attorney to remark, "You just look at him and you know he's a federal judge."[197] But Weinman was not impassive. Rather, he was a man of strong opinions, which he often expressed in court. He would publicly chastise lawyers for having beards or long hair. When one attorney made the mistake of putting a witness on the stand who was wearing neither a coat nor tie, Weinman gave him a sound "tongue-lashing" in front of the jury about showing disrespect for the court, the country, and all the country's citizens. Weinman treated unprepared lawyers just as harshly. For example, after dismissing a case against a bank official for embezzlement because the prosecution had not proven its case, Weinman told the U.S. attorney, "Never bring me another case like this." Even more eventful was the time during the six-month jury trial of the Beerman-Federated antitrust case, when Weinman "impulsively interrupted the president of Rike's testimony and exclaimed: 'That's a lie!'"[198]

Although he was politically conservative, Weinman was not predictable. When Secret Service agents, U.S. Customs agents, and agents of the Bureau of Alcohol, Tobacco, and Firearms sued the government for the overtime pay they were promised, for example, Weinman very vocally criticized the government for not keeping its word and ordered them to pay the overtime.[199] During the Vietnam War, he worked to avoid sending draft resisters to jail. At the end of the war, he advocated amnesty for the resisters. He judged those who opposed the war by different standards than robbers or those who committed fraud. "Sentencing people who violated public trusts" never bothered him, but he respected the draft resisters' willingness to go to jail for what they believed in. So he tried to persuade them to accept alternative government service. If they refused, he did sentence them to prison, but he never gave them the maximum sentence. He always told them, if they ever changed their mind, to contact him and he would make arrangements to have their sentences reviewed.[200]

### JOHN WELD PECK, 1961–1966

On September 23, 1961, Democratic president John F. Kennedy nominated John Weld Peck as a recess appointment to replace Druffel, who had taken senior status. Peck began presiding over his court in Cincinnati in October. Kennedy officially nominated him on January 15, 1962, and the Senate confirmed him in April. Democratic senators Stephen Young and Frank Lausche, two men with whom Peck had had long personal and professional relationships, enthusiastically supported the appointment.[201]

Born in the Cincinnati suburb of Wyoming, Ohio, on June 23, 1913, the son of Arthur M. and Marguerite Comstock Peck, John W. Peck came from a long line of judges. His grandfather, Hiram D. Peck, served as a judge of the old superior court of Cincinnati and as a member of the Ohio constitutional convention of 1912. His uncle, John Weld Peck, was a district judge for the Southern District of Ohio in the 1920s. The second Judge John W. Peck attended public schools in Wyoming, graduating from Wyoming High School before going to Miami University for his B.A. and the University of Cincinnati College of Law for his J.D., which he received in 1938. After being admitted to the Ohio bar that year, he joined the family's prestigious law firm, Peck, Shaffer & Williams. On March 25, 1942, a month before he was drafted into the U.S. Army, he married Barbara Moeser, with whom he would eventually have three sons. After serving on active duty in the European theater and then in the Judge Advocate General's office in France, he returned to private practice.[202]

John Weld Peck, 1961–1966. *Courtesy of Mayhew & Peper, Photographers, Cincinnati*

In addition to law, Peck loved politics. Thus, upon his return from Europe, he formed, with future district court judges Timothy Hogan and John Druffel, along with Vincent Aug and others who later became distinguished lawyers and jurists, the Hamilton County Democratic Veterans' Club. They actively supported Democratic candidates, including Frank Lausche in his bid for Ohio's gubernatorial nomination. After their initial success, the group branched out, establishing chapters in more than half of Ohio's counties. In return, in 1949, the new Ohio governor Lausche appointed Peck his executive secretary. Lausche then appointed Peck to the Hamilton County Court of Common Pleas to fill a vacancy. After that term expired, Peck served as Ohio's tax commissioner from 1951 to 1953, until he was again appointed to the common pleas bench. During that time, he demonstrated his commitment to racial justice by appointing as his bailiff Arthur C. Elliott, the first African American to hold such a post. When Peck's judicial term expired, he returned to private practice until Governor Michael DiSalle appointed him, in 1959, to fill a vacancy on the Ohio Supreme Court. After serving a year in that position, however, he lost his election bid for a full term.[203] The Democratic Party of Franklin County opposed him because, some speculated, Peck refused to support Mayor M. E. Sensenbrenner's desire to make, in Peck's determination, an illegal appointment. Peck, one newspaper article said, "chose the courageous course in deciding the issue on the basis of precedent and principle rather than of narrow partisanship."[204]

After he returned to private practice, Peck remained active politically until his appointment to the federal bench. Indeed, in his letter to John A. Wiethe, chairman of the Ohio Democratic Central Committee, resigning from the Hamilton County Democratic Policy Committee, Peck said he would always cherish his "quarter of a century of participation in Democratic affairs." Indeed, he said that the only regret he had about his federal appointment was that he would have to give up "active party politics." After Kennedy appointed him to the federal bench, he stayed on the district court until 1966, when President Lyndon B. Johnson elevated him to the Sixth Circuit Court of Appeals.[205]

Known as "the resident judge" because of his lifelong ties to Cincinnati, Peck was a man of integrity and compassion with a natural "judicial temperament." He was also, to use his own words, "an unashamed, unreconstructed, incurable idealist." That idealism focused especially on "the American system of jurisprudence."[206] And, for Peck, despite his years of service on appellate courts, the heart of that system was the trial court. He loved being a trial court judge, because, as he said, "I like people better than books." A trial judge has to make decisions in "the heat of battle." And, unlike appeals court judges, the trial judge has "personal independence."[207]

Peck's goal as a trial judge was to see that "justice was done."[208] For example, he was always careful, when sentencing in criminal cases, "to strike that balance between justice and mercy."[209] He opposed the death penalty, because he "deplore[d] . . . the barbarity of taking human life as punishment."[210] He also fought for racial justice and equality of all. He said that America was a "blending of Protestant, Catholic, Jew; of white, black, yellow; of Irishman, Englishman, German, Italian, Russian." The races, he urged, must associate together to achieve justice. The "quest for civil rights, the open doors of equal opportunity to all people and the fight for freedom are very much in order" in our time.[211]

## TIMOTHY S. HOGAN, 1966–1989

## DAVID S. PORTER, 1966–1989

Known as "twins" because Lyndon Johnson nominated them both on September 30, 1966, the Senate unanimously confirmed them both on October 20, they received their commissions on November 3, and they took their oaths of office on November 10, Hogan and Porter were intertwined as soon as a position on the bench developed after Congress created an additional judgeship for the Southern District of Ohio.[212] Peck had vigorously lobbied for this new position because of the court's rapidly increasing docket. Matters worsened when Johnson elevated Peck to the Sixth Circuit, leaving no judge sitting in Cincinnati. Without a Cincinnati judge, "the wheels of justice" almost ground to a halt. The director of the FBI wrote to the U.S. attorney general complaining that the lack of a judge was delaying federal prosecutions. While the Department of Justice designated Peck back to the district court to handle "routine business," Clerk of Courts John D. Lyter, in September 1966, vacated all settings of civil matters, hearings of motions, pretrial conferences, civil trials, and calendar calls because no judge was available to handle the cases.[213]

Timothy Sylvester Hogan, 1966–1989.
*Courtesy of the Sixth Circuit Archives, Cincinnati*

David Stewart Porter, 1966–1989.
*Courtesy of the Sixth Circuit Archives, Cincinnati*

With the newly authorized position and Peck's appointment to the Sixth Circuit Court of Appeals, in 1966 the district court in Cincinnati had two vacancies that Johnson would fill. The great scramble for these two positions probably contributed to the almost six-month delay between the time the vacancies occurred and the date when Johnson selected Hogan and Porter. The Cincinnati Bar Association appointed a committee to make recommendations to Ohio's two Democratic senators. This committee sent out a questionnaire to fifty judges and lawyers, including Peck and future judge Carl B. Rubin, asking for their evaluation of potential candidates. The committee then made their recommendations based on "potential judicial temperament, practical experience and academic ability." After their investigation, they recommended five men out of the seventeen candidates—two Republicans and three Democrats.[214]

Eventually, Ohio's two senators, Young and Lausche, agreed to submit Hogan's and Porter's names to Johnson. It was Johnson's policy that the state's senators choose the nominees. Indeed, when White House assistant Bill Moyers passed on a suggestion from a powerful Ohio politician, Johnson wrote back: "Senators make the choice." For unknown reasons, however, it took Johnson almost a month to submit the nominations to the Senate after Ohio's senators had agreed on Hogan and Porter.[215]

Hogan was born on September 23, 1909, in Wellston, Ohio, one of seven children of Timothy S. and Mary Adele Deasey Hogan. His father had been Ohio attorney general from 1910 to 1914, and all his siblings became lawyers. He attended Catholic schools, graduating from the Jesuit Campion Academy in Wisconsin in 1926. He then received his B.A. from Xavier University in Cincinnati in 1926, and his J.D. in 1931 from the University of Cincinnati College of Law, graduating first in both classes as well as being awarded the Order of the Coif, all the while paying his own way, working several jobs, including that of a tennis instructor.[216] Indeed, Judge Carl Rubin, eulogizing Hogan, noted, "Tim Hogan was probably the most brilliant man who ever sat on this court."[217]

After passing the Ohio bar in 1931, Hogan joined the firm of Nichols, Wood, Marx & Ginter in Cincinnati. In 1934, he married Evalon Roberts, with whom he had three children. During the Depression years, he was sent to Detroit as part of a team of young attorneys who worked to salvage the banks during President Roosevelt's so-called bank holiday, acting as trial counsel for the receivers of the banks. In 1938, he was appointed assistant attorney general for Ohio, a position he held until the start of World War II. In 1941, Hogan, exempt from the draft because of his age, volunteered for the Army Air Corps, rising to the rank of lieutenant colonel by 1946, serving primarily with the military government in the European theater. During that time one sees an indication of Hogan's integrity. After the war ended, Hogan opposed America's policy of following the Morgenthau plan "that called for the virtual destruction of anything German" while allowing the Soviets to have a free hand.[218] He therefore refused to rewrite a speech for General Lucius Clay endorsing the policy. To discipline Hogan, Clay consigned him to an empty desk for the remainder of his time in the service. After his discharge, Hogan returned to private practice, becoming a partner in the firm of Cohen, Baron, Todd & Hogan. He was considered to be one of the finest trial lawyers in southern Ohio.[219]

While practicing law, Hogan was also a leader of the Democratic Party in Hamilton County. In the 1930s, he and his close friend, Judge Peck, were the "young Turks" of the Democratic Party. Although Hogan ran unsuccessfully for the Ohio House of Representatives, the Ohio Senate, and state attorney general, in 1952, as a supporter of Estes Kefauver, he did serve as a delegate-at-large at the Democratic National Convention. Also, from 1958 to 1962, he was a member of the Hamilton County Democratic Policy Committee.[220]

Hogan earned a reputation as an outstanding jurist. The judges of the Southern District of Ohio described him as "a person whose intelligence, wit, and high moral standards set him apart."[221] He was "known for his creative approaches to sentencing and his ability to simplify complicated legal arguments."[222] For example, after sentencing a man who had pleaded guilty to bank robbery to twenty-five years in prison, he placed the man on five years' probation after learning that he had returned the $1,600 he had stolen. Though admitting that this was highly unusual for such a serious crime as robbing a bank, he said, "I'm interested in what is just for the individual and not in a 10- or 15- or 25-year sentence just because the crime is bank robbery." His compassion and his sensitivity to the problems of the "downtrodden" is seen in his order requiring the reduction of the number of prisoners in the state prison in Lucasville.[223] He also took an active role in assisting those with substance abuse problems. Indeed, "no person who ever left his courtroom would assert a denial of justice."[224]

Hogan also was probably the least pretentious man ever to sit on the court. He kept a sign on the bench that he could see as he faced the jury or the witness; it said: "Hogan, keep your big trap shut." He dressed casually, sometimes not even bothering to match his socks. His speech, too, was casual, even when writing court decisions. But the meaning was always clear. "He avoided legalese." And he was seldom reversed.[225] Hogan also loved simple things like boating and fishing. Indeed, he found out that Johnson had appointed him district court judge while on a houseboat vacation on the Ohio River with Peck. Pulling into the dock at Portsmouth, the dockman told them that the sheriff wanted to speak with them. As they were dressed in old T-shirts, jeans, and tennis shoes, the dockman looked at them as if they had just robbed a bank. All the sheriff wanted to do was to tell Hogan he had been appointed the next federal district court judge for the Southern District of Ohio. His humility and love of fishing is best exemplified by his actions when he was told he had to sit for an official portrait. He resisted for years, hanging a mounted dolphin in the courthouse where his formal portrait would have been hung among the portraits of the other jurists.[226]

A "lean, smiling jurist with glasses pushed up on his bony, balding head,"[227] the future judge David S. Porter was born in Cincinnati on September 29, 1909, the same day as Hogan.[228] The youngest of the twelve children of Charles H. and Caroline Pemberton Porter, Porter attended public schools, graduating from Clifton Elementary School and then Hughes High School, where he was a member of the basketball team. His father was a pioneer in the area of technical education in the Cincinnati public schools. Upon graduation from Hughes, Porter went on to the University of Cincinnati, where he received his B.A. and J.D. in 1932 and 1934, respectively. Admitted to the Ohio bar in 1934 at the depth of the Depression, he could not find employment as a lawyer, so he went to work for the City Ice and Fuel Company, laboring seven days a week, until, in 1935, he finally found a job with the New Deal as an attorney in Knoxville, Tennessee, for the Tennessee Valley Authority. In 1936, he moved to Troy, Ohio, where one of his sisters lived, and established a private practice. During that time he married Marjorie Bluet Ellis, with whom he had three daughters. In 1949, Governor Lausche appointed him to fill a vacancy on the common pleas court of Miami County. He was then elected in his own right in 1954 and reelected in 1960, serving in that position until Johnson appointed him to the federal bench.[229]

Rubin described Porter as the epitome of "courtesy, kindness, [and] patience." Although he could be stern and maintained strict discipline in his courtroom, his friends described him as "the ideal judge, one who projects an image of fairness [and] integrity." Even a defendant Porter had sentenced to prison sent the judge a Christmas card, in which he wrote, "Judge, you have a good reputation up here." Judge Spiegel, who liked to tell others that he tried to emulate Porter, ranked him "among the top jurists of our time." To Porter, the goal of the courts was to maintain the individual's rights preserved in the Constitution. Even though he believed that some litigants "jump the gun and bring cases to federal court before exhausting other procedures," and even though he was assigned many cases he did not want, he believed that "in the area of civil rights, the courts are simply doing for the individual what it has done all along for corporations."[230] But Porter also had his "wacky" side. He loved toys and gadgets, which filled his chambers. One of his most treasured was Ozzie the Clown, which rode a wire from a wall to the top of the flagpole behind the judge's desk. Porter died of a blood disease on January 5, 1989.[231]

### JOSEPH P. KINNEARY, 1966–2001

Lyndon Johnson appointed a third judge, Joseph P. Kinneary, months before Hogan and Porter joined the District Court for the Southern District of Ohio.

Joseph P. Kinneary, 1966–2001.
*Courtesy of the Sixth Circuit Archives, Cincinnati*

Johnson nominated Kinneary to replace Judge Underwood in Columbus,
who took senior status on June 28,
1966. The Senate confirmed Kinneary
July 22, and he assumed his duties on
August 5, 1966.[232]

Born in Cincinnati on September
19, 1905, the son of Joseph and Anne
Mulvihill Kinneary, Kinneary attended
Cincinnati Catholic schools, graduating from St. Xavier High School. Because his father, a salesman, died when
Kinneary was eight, young Joseph was
forced to spend most of his free time
working, caddying at the Cincinnati Country Club while in parochial school
and then selling shoes to help pay for college. After receiving his B.A. in 1928
from the University of Notre Dame, Kinneary returned to Cincinnati and
earned his LL.B. from the University of Cincinnati College of Law in 1935.
He was admitted to the Ohio bar that same year. Although he had chosen a
career in law because "lawyers were respected," when he graduated from law
school at the depths of the Depression few law positions were available. In
response, he rented a small room in the small office of an insurance agent in
the Traction Building on the corner of Fifth and Walnut Streets in Cincinnati, and sought out clients. Having been active in Third Ward politics paid
off. Ward leader Peter McCarthy "shepherded" him around and sent him
people in need of legal services. He eked out a living until, in 1936, he became a speaker on the campaign trail for Franklin Roosevelt, who was seeking
reelection as president. In 1937 Kinneary was appointed assistant attorney
general of Ohio, where he remained until 1939. During World War II, he
served as chief counsel in the food procurement division of the army's Quar-
termaster Corps. After being discharged in 1946 at the rank of captain, Kinneary again went back to being a solo practitioner. In 1950, he married Byrnece
Camille Rogers. Kinneary regularly went in and out of public and private practice during the 1950s, serving from 1949 to 1951 as first assistant attorney general of Ohio and special counsel to the attorney general from 1959 to 1961. He
was also a delegate to the 1952 Democratic National Convention. Because of
his extensive political activities, Kinneary became friends with Ohio's Democratic senators, Frank Lausche and Stephen Young.[233] These connections
probably won him his appointment, in June 1961, as U.S. attorney for the

Southern District of Ohio.[234] Kinneary served in that position until Johnson appointed him to the federal bench. Peck praised Kinneary's appointment, writing to Young that his appointment "will afford the Columbus community a form of judicial service unknown during the past quarter century."[235]

To Kinneary, being a district court judge was the pinnacle of the career ladder for an attorney—and he loved the job. Indeed, on one occasion he told a fellow judge, "If I had the money, I would do [the job] for free."[236] To him, a federal trial judge held a "unique" position because of life tenure. A district court judge, being "completely and absolutely removed from all normal human competition," does not have "to spend one second in consideration of what is the political thing to do." Therefore, the judge can exercise "human compassion" and protect rights without worrying about political consequences.[237] And the job kept him busy. In the 1980s, Kinneary handled more than six hundred cases a year, "two and a half times the number recommended as manageable by the Judicial Conference of the United States." To deal with such a tremendous work load, Kinneary instituted the pretrial system in Columbus.[238]

Attorneys both praised and cursed Kinneary. Almost all agree that he was an affable, decent, and fair person. Kinneary himself said he tried to rule by using compassion, common sense, and fairness. But once he decided, he never looked back. "Decision-making," he said, "has no formula or precise explanations." Therefore while he was guided and restricted by precedent, he decided as best he could using instinct as well as experience, and if he were wrong, "the court of appeals will tell me." Kinneary also was "well known within the local circles for upholding the utmost dignity in the courtroom." That translated, to use the words of Judge Graham, to Kinneary's being quite "gruff" on occasion. Graham was quick to point out, however, that "his gruffness is evenhanded." Like Weinman, Kinneary believed the courtroom was a sacred place and that its sanctity is upheld by proper conduct on the part of all parties. Thus he, too, insisted on proper decorum on the part of attorneys, litigants, defendants, jurors, and witnesses. If people did not conduct themselves properly, Kinneary publicly reprimanded them. For example, Kinneary ordered a lawyer wearing a brightly colored sports jacket to go home to change. He jailed one juror who was late twice and another who was not paying attention and told Kinneary he did not care about the case.[239] If attorneys were unprepared, they might witness Kinneary's drill sergeant–like tactics. Kinneary also interrupted counsel and lectured witnesses. For example, in the 1974 trial of Anthony LaFatch for extortion, Kinneary sternly admonished jurors, imposed a gag rule on reporters, lectured the government's key witness for not answering questions directly and for speaking too softly, took over the examination of witnesses, sometimes for prolonged periods, and once even suggested that the defense attorney object to one of the prosecutor's questions and then, when he did, sustained the objection.[240]

Kinneary served as chief judge from 1973 until 1975. Even after he took senior status at the end of 1986, he kept a nearly full docket. Kinneary served on the bench until his retirement in September 2001, making his thirty-five years as a judge the second-longest tenure for judges in the Southern District of Ohio. Only Leavitt served longer, by two years. He retired only because a stroke made it impossible for him to continue in his work. He died two years later, on February 14, 2003. On September 18, 1998, the U.S. Courthouse in Columbus was officially renamed the "Joseph P. Kinneary United States Courthouse" in honor of his service.[241]

## CARL B. RUBIN, 1971–1995

On April 29, 1971, Republican president Richard M. Nixon nominated Carl B. Rubin to a new judgeship authorized by Congress a year earlier. The Senate confirmed him on May 19, and he assumed his duties on June 25.[242] He remained on the bench until his death on August 2, 1995, serving as chief judge from September 1979 to March 1990. Rubin was also the only judge in the Southern District of Ohio to serve at all three of the district's major locations—first in Columbus, then in Dayton, and finally in Cincinnati.[243]

Born in Cincinnati, March 27, 1920, to Russian immigrants, John I. and Ethel Friedman Rubin, Rubin attended grade school in the Cincinnati neighborhood of North Avondale with the future Judge Arthur Spiegel. He graduated from Walnut Hills High School before going on to receive his B.A. and LL.B. from the University of Cincinnati in 1942 and 1944, respectively. After passing the bar, he married Gloria Weiland, with whom he had four children, and entered private practice, eventually becoming a partner in the firm he cofounded in the 1960s, Tyler, Kane and Rubin. While remaining in private practice until Nixon appointed him to the federal bench, he also served briefly as assistant prosecuting attorney for Hamilton County in the early 1950s, mostly in the civil division, dealing with such issues as public finances, especially the issuance and sale of county bonds. From 1960 to 1966, he served on the Cincinnati Civil Service Commission, chairing that organization during his last year of service. In 1971, he was elected president of the Southwest Ohio Regional Transit Authority. He had also been active in Republican politics, directing the 1966 and 1968 congressional campaigns of Robert Taft Jr. and being the field director for Taft's 1970 senatorial race.[244]

Carl Bernard Rubin, 1971–1995. *Courtesy of Mrs. Carl B. Rubin*

Rubin had a distinguished judicial career. Many called him "brilliant," one of the brightest judges in the country.[245] Rubin, himself, said being a federal judge was "the highest honor a man can achieve," and he worked night and day at it. Peck, himself a workaholic, wrote Rubin that he was "the only real full-time judge I've ever known. The rest of us may work pretty hard . . . , but we also have our workshops, golf courses, paintbrushes, sailboats, whatever, but except for time devoted to your family, only you eat, sleep and live law."[246] To Rubin, the law was "the last hope of civilization." He said: "We used to send people with spears, now we send them with lawyers, and the judges are there to make everybody behave."[247]

Economically conservative, he was "liberal in terms of protecting the rights of individuals." He cared about "the little guy." For him, the court was where people came to get justice—and that justice must come in a "meaningful" time frame. He was insistent, for example, that the victims of the Beverly Hills fire be compensated as quickly as possible.[248] In several cases he also upheld the free exercise of religion and free speech against attempted government encroachments.[249]

Overall, however, Rubin was a jurisprudential conservative who believed strongly in the rule of law and the importance of precedent. He "eschewed judicial activism."[250] He drew "a conceptual difference between the role of legislatures and executives and the role of judges."[251] Thus, there was a limit to the extent to which he would protect rights. Courts, he insisted, cannot be "the arbiters of every social question."[252]

Although in his rulings he often exhibited his conservative leanings, Rubin was "innovative" in many ways. He was the first judge in the country to preside over a class action, mass tort case. He divided the issues in complex tort litigation, insisting the plaintiff prove each element separately. In suits against manufacturers of asbestos, he established expert panels to screen suing workers and render nonbinding decisions on who had untreatable lung diseases.[253] He was also known as "the father of courtroom imaging" being, in 1991, one of the first judges to install imaging and presentation technology permanently in his courtroom. He believed jurors could better understand and remember information that they could see. Using ten monitors that displayed text or videotape on twenty-one-inch screens placed around the courtroom in a complicated securities fraud case, the plaintiffs' estimated that they cut trial time nearly in half.[254] Rubin was also committed to legal education. He founded the Cincinnati chapter of the American Inns of Courts and the judge-in-residence program at the University of Cincinnati College of Law.[255]

Rubin could also be stern and domineering. Attorneys who tried to argue with him were told to go down the hall to the Sixth Circuit Court of Appeals and file an appeal. Learning from Kinneary, he, too demanded strict courtroom decorum. He would require attorneys to stand behind the lectern, not allowing them to move about the courtroom. Believing as he did that the jury was all important, to assure that they could concentrate fully, he would order the federal marshals to lock the doors to the courtroom and let no one in or out during the attorneys' closing arguments. He was also a man of strong opinions. When Congress rejected a 51 percent pay raise for federal judges, he started a slowdown. Previously known as one of the fastest judges in the country, Rubin vowed to hear no more than two trials a month. When Congress would not move, he finally relented.[256]

## ROBERT M. DUNCAN, 1974–1985

When Carl Weinman took senior status at the end of 1973, President Nixon had the opportunity to make a second appointment to the bench in the Southern District of Ohio. Anticipating Weinman's change of status and knowing that Nixon respected senatorial courtesy, especially for lower-court judgeships,[257] in the fall of 1973 Ohio's two Republican senators, William Saxbe and Robert Taft, selected Robert M. Duncan as their choice to fill the vacancy. The nomination stalled when the Nixon administration, preoccupied with the Watergate scandal, ignored judicial appointments. After the Saturday Night Massacre, Saxbe, a close friend and mentor of Duncan's for years, became Nixon's attorney general. He then continually prodded Nixon, until finally, in May 1974, Nixon sent Duncan's name to the Senate. A month later, the Senate confirmed him. A month after that, Duncan began presiding over his court in Columbus.[258]

Duncan, the first African American judge on the southern Ohio court, was born August 24, 1927, in Urbana, Ohio, in Champaign County. His community was settled originally by free persons of color who came to Ohio from the late 1820s to the Civil War to gain more opportunities than they had as free blacks in the South. While Duncan was growing up, Urbana was a community of African Americans with a strong work ethic who valued education highly. After his parents divorced when he was two, Duncan was raised primarily by his grandparents, although his father, a factory worker, lived with them. His grandfather was waiter, bellman, janitor, and generally the man-of-all-trades for the Douglas Inn, while his grandmother worked as a maid and babysitter. It was she who got Duncan interested early on in politics as an "Abraham Lincoln Republican." During high school and college, Duncan was involved with the Young Republicans. In addition, in college and law school, he worked for Roger Tracy, treasurer of the state of Ohio.

Robert M. Duncan, 1974–1985.
*Courtesy of Judge Robert M. Duncan*

After graduating from high school in Urbana with a solid liberal arts education, Duncan enrolled at Ohio State University. Starting out as a journalism major, he soon became interested in education. After graduating in 1948 with a B.S. in education with a social sciences major and a biological sciences minor, Duncan found that there were no teaching jobs in Ohio for African Americans at the secondary level except in all–African American high schools, and these had long waiting lists. His mother, who had moved to Chicago, encouraged him to attend law school. He had liked Ohio State so much he decided to continue there, earning his J.D. in 1952. After serving in the army for two and a half years, stationed in Alaska, Duncan returned to Ohio and eventually went to work in the workers' compensation section of the attorney general's office where he met William Saxbe, who was at the time the attorney general of Ohio and who would become his mentor and friend. During this time, he also married Shirley A. Duncan, with whom he had three children. When the Republicans were defeated in 1960, Duncan became the Columbus city prosecutor, trying criminal misdemeanor cases. Following Saxbe's re-election, Duncan went back to state government service, first as chief of the workers' compensation section and then as chief counsel to Saxbe, doing advocacy work in the Ohio Supreme Court and the Sixth Circuit Court of Appeals as well as working closely with Governor James Rhodes and his cabinet on legal matters. When a position opened up on municipal court in Columbus in 1966, Rhodes, having gotten to know Duncan, appointed him to that position. In 1968, Rhodes appointed Duncan to the Ohio Supreme Court. He served there until 1971, when the opportunity to join the U.S. Court of Military Appeals presented itself. That court was rather new, created after World War II to alleviate some of the rigidity of military justice. This three-judge (now five-judge) court works to balance the needs of the military to have enough authority to perform its mission with the constitutional rights of individuals in the military. As part of that experience, Duncan heard the My Lai massacre trial of Lieutenant William Calley. Duncan served on that court for three years until Nixon appointed him district court judge for the Southern District of Ohio.

Philosophically, Duncan could be described as an economic conservative, believing strongly in the free market model. But he also has a strong commitment to individual rights and racial justice. To him, the court is there to ensure that all persons are given all the rights due them under the Constitution.[259] Duncan served on the district court for eleven years, presiding over several high-profile cases, including the Columbus school desegregation case. Then, effective April 15, 1985, he resigned to enter private practice, becoming a partner in Jones, Day, Reavis and Pogue. He saw this as an opportunity not only to return to litigation but also to train and recruit others, especially young minority lawyers.[260]

The judges of the U.S. District Court, Southern District of Ohio, October 2003. *Front row, left to right:* James L. Graham, Walter H. Rice, Sandra Beckwith, George C. Smith. *Back row, left to right:* Algenon L. Marbley, Gregory L. Frost, Thomas M. Rose, John D. Holschuh, Edmund A. Sargus Jr., Herman J. Weber, S. Arthur Spiegel, and Susan Dlott. *Courtesy of the Sixth Circuit Archives, Cincinnati*

### JOHN D. HOLSCHUH, 1980 TO THE PRESENT

### S. ARTHUR SPIEGEL, 1980 TO THE PRESENT

### WALTER H. RICE, 1980 TO THE PRESENT

When Congress authorized a new judgeship for the Southern District of Ohio in 1980, President Jimmy Carter chose John D. Holschuh. At the same time, two vacancies developed when judges Porter and Hogan took senior status. To replace them, Carter nominated S. Arthur Spiegel and Walter H. Rice. The Senate confirmed all three on May 20, 1980, but Holschuh gained seniority by assuming his duties in May. Spiegel and Rice did not begin until June.[261] All were nominated after selection by a bipartisan screening committee established by John Glenn and Howard Metzenbaum, Ohio's two Democratic senators. Carter had urged senators to establish such committees, seeking to make fundamental changes in the selection process by shifting from a highly political system to a process emphasizing professional competence.[262] In Ohio, the committee members came from all walks of life. They worked closely with the Ohio Bar Association, soliciting applications from leading attorneys and jurists. The committee and then the senators, after evaluating individual merit as well as who the candidates were and what they stood for, chose Holschuh, who had never been involved in politics, and Spiegel, who merely contributed to some Democratic causes, over politically active attorneys who had been endorsed by the Democratic Party. For example, although Metzenbaum had never before met Spiegel, he was impressed with his work in integrating a Cincinnati swim and tennis club. Indeed, several people actively opposed Spiegel's nomination because of his civil rights activities. They especially feared what he might do if he inherited the Cincinnati school desegregation case from Porter. Rice, also a product of this committee selection process, had been more politically active before his appointment to the federal bench, having run for election for his state judicial position as a Democrat and actively campaigned for other Democratic office seekers.[263]

Born October 12, 1926, in Ironton, Ohio, the son of Edward A. and Helen Ebert Holschuh, Holschuh grew up during the Depression. He watched his father, a successful businessman, be wiped out by economic forces over which he had no control. Refusing to declare bankruptcy, Edward Holschuh finally found work as a foreman on a Works Progress Administration project and then as a millwright doing physical work at a coke plant in Ashland, Kentucky. It took more than ten years of hard work, but he finally paid back all his debts from his failed business. The future Judge Holschuh, upon graduating from Ironton High School in 1944, was able to attend Miami University on a scholarship. Graduating Phi Beta Kappa and cum laude, Holschuh won another scholarship to the University of Cincinnati College of Law. He graduated first in his class, served as editor-in-chief of the *Cincinnati Law Review,* and became a member of the Order of the Coif. He then clerked for Judge Underwood in Columbus before entering private practice. At around the same time, he married Carol Stouder, with whom he had one child. One of the top litigators in Columbus as a partner in the firm of Alexander, Ebinger, Holschuh, Fisher & McAlister, he was a general practitioner whose work included personal injury and wrongful death cases, representing both plaintiffs and defendants, as well as antitrust, acquisition and mergers, and other corporate cases.[264]

The Depression taught Holschuh the importance of compassion and the understanding that a person could be poor through no fault of his or her own. Also, growing up in a socially segregated community, he saw the unfairness of discrimination. He later served as president of the board of Neighborhood House, a settlement house in a Columbus black neighborhood, as well as on the board of the United Way. Attorneys praise him as "an outstanding judge" with a "superb demeanor." He is "fair-minded," with "no biases or prejudices that would affect his judgment."[265]

Spiegel was born on October 24, 1920, in Cincinnati, the son of Arthur M. Spiegel, a Cincinnati municipal court judge, and the grandson of Frederick S. Spiegel, a German immigrant who served as mayor of Cincinnati from 1914 to 1916 and a judge of the superior court of Hamilton County. After receiving his B.A. from the University of Cincinnati in 1942, Spiegel enlisted in the Marines, serving for four years during and after World War II before studying law at Harvard Law School. After receiving his LL.B. in 1948, Spiegel entered private practice. For many years, he was a solo practitioner, the major law firms either not needing new attorneys or refusing to hire Jews. Eventually, after a brief stint with another attorney, Spiegel joined the firm of Cohen, Baron, Druffel and Hogan, later to become Cohen, Todd, Kite & Spiegel. Spiegel's father and grandfather had been active Republicans. While in the state legislature, his father roomed with the future president Warren G. Harding, was close friends with Senator Robert Taft, and supported Taft's isolationist positions before World War I. After his wartime experience and his legal education at Harvard, the younger Spiegel aligned himself with the Democratic Party, convinced of the need for an activist foreign policy and the social legislation of the New Deal.

Two themes run through Spiegel's legal and judicial career. The first is his dedication to the least powerful in this society. Before his elevation to the bench, Spiegel was active in the civil rights movement. He spearheaded the drive to integrate his private swim club, chaired the Cincinnati mayor's Friendly Relations Commission, and served as the first chairman, from 1965 to 1967, of the Cincinnati Human Relations Commission. In recognition of his work in this area, that commission presented him with the Elthelrie Hooper Humanitarian Reward. Noting that the position of district court judge is "the 'pinnacle' of the legal profession because a federal judge often sets the tone for a community regarding both civil and individual rights," Spiegel explained that it is "his duty" as judge "to protect the minority from the 'tyranny of the majority.'"[266]

The second theme is his creativity in fashioning good results from litigation, "moving beyond the 'winner take all' syndrome of the standard trial." He has used summary jury trials and other techniques to promote creative settlements in some of the most difficult cases of recent years, including the Zimmer Power Station litigation, the Fernald litigation, and the Merrill Lynch Boxcar Securities Fraud litigation.[267]

Rice was born May 27, 1937, in Pittsburgh, Pennsylvania, the son of a drug and wholesale tobacco jobber. After receiving his B.A. from Northwestern University and his J.D. and M.B.A. from Columbia, he came to Dayton in 1963 and became an assistant prosecutor for Montgomery County. After two years in that post, he went into private practice with the law firm of Gallon & Miller. In 1970, he began his judicial career after winning election as a municipal court judge. He then served on the court of common pleas for Montgomery County for nine years, until President Carter appointed him to the federal bench. Patient and courteous to all, Rice, like Spiegel, sees one of the major roles of the federal court to be dispute resolution. "A skilled mediator as well as a skilled judge," he has the ability to persuade opposing parties to find common ground so that both can serve their own interests. Thus, to Rice, his most noteworthy case was the Cincinnati school desegregation case in which, "on the eve of trial," he achieved a comprehensive settlement, thereby avoiding the tensions a trial would have exacerbated. Rice's achievement in school desegregation also represents the second of his significant contributions to the court; he is seen as "an activist judge who has been a major force for racial justice both on and off the bench." Although Rice says that the court's primary function is "to make certain that the Constitution works in such a way as to protect the rights of the minority," he also argues that district court judges should *not* make policy. Rather, it is their job to apply the law as interpreted by the Supreme Court and the Sixth Circuit Court of Appeals.[268]

### HERMAN J. WEBER, 1985 TO THE PRESENT

Herman J. Weber became the first of three judges appointed to the District Court for the Southern District of Ohio in the mid-1980s by Republican president Ronald Reagan. Weber was selected to fill a judgeship Congress had just created. The son and grandson of lawyers, Weber was born in Lima, Ohio, on May 20, 1927. His parents died in an automobile accident when he was five, so he was raised by his maternal uncle, a United Brethren minister, in central and northern Ohio. After graduating from the public high school in Fremont, Ohio, Weber enlisted in the navy and served for more than a year at the end of World War II. After the navy, Weber went to Otterbein College, where he received his B.A., and then went on to Ohio State University College of Law, receiving his J.D. summa cum laude in 1951. During this time, he also met and married his wife Barbara Rice, to whom he has been married for more than fifty years. Upon passing the bar in 1951, Weber moved to Fairborn, Ohio, and formed his own law firm—Weber & Hogue. He also became active politically, serving as a member of city council from 1955 to 1959 and vice mayor from 1955 to 1957. At that time, he also began his judicial career as judge of Fairborn's mayor's court. In 1961, his constituents elected him to the court of common pleas for Greene County. He served in that post until elected to the Ohio court of appeals for the second district in 1982. From there, Reagan elevated him to the federal bench.[269]

Although Reagan was determined that the judges he appointed held views that would further his conservative political goals,[270] Weber's appointment came largely from recommendations of area congressmen and other influential Republicans. Because at the time both of Ohio's senators were Democrats, Ohio's Republican congressmen played a more influential role in the judicial selection process. Having held elected judgeships for almost twenty-five years, Weber had met most of the area's political leaders. This was especially true in his court of appeals campaigns, which covered six southwestern Ohio counties. During this time, Weber also developed a close professional relationship with Michael DeWine, who had been county prosecutor from Weber's home, Greene County. (DeWine would later become a U.S. senator from Ohio.) At the time Congress created the new judgeship, DeWine, then a second-term congressman, actively supported Weber's nomination. With this support as well as the support of other area leaders, Weber won the nomination. Reagan sent his name to the Senate on February 28, 1985. After being quickly confirmed, Weber joined the court in Cincinnati on April 4.[271]

Advocating a jurisprudence of judicial restraint, Weber sees the role of a district court judge as applying the law and the Constitution as written and as interpreted by the Supreme Court and the Sixth Circuit Court of Appeals; judges should not make law. Thus, he describes his role as one that ensures that the individual receives all those rights due him or her. But, perhaps more important, his job is to resolve disputes justly. He sees any settlement as a great triumph. Lawyers seem to agree that Weber has achieved his goals. They find him demanding but fair. They also say that because he strongly believes in the jury system, he is less likely than some to grant summary judgment.[272]

### JAMES L. GRAHAM, 1986 TO THE PRESENT

For nineteen months Duncan's seat remained vacant, the longest delay in the court's history, due largely to "politically squabbling in Washington."[273] After Duncan resigned his judgeship, the Franklin County Republican organization developed a selection process whereby a committee solicited nominations among the area lawyers and judges. After some thirty-plus candidates submitted their names, a screening committee interviewed all of them. The candidates included several prominent Republican politicians and judges, including the person many speculated was the leading contender, Greg Lashutka, who later became mayor of Columbus. The committee recommended five names to a group of Ohio congressmen. Graham, along with Lashutka and a "very popular state judge," were among these five finalists, despite the fact that Graham had not been very active politically, having served only as campaign chairman or treasurer for some judicial candidates and, for a short time, as counsel for the local Republican Party. Reagan then insisted that Ohio's congressional delegation submit two names to him. They chose Graham and the judge. Both then underwent extensive interviews with members of the Department of Justice. The interviewers grilled them not only on substantive law but also on their jurisprudential views, especially their views on judicial activism versus judicial restraint. "They wanted judges who would interpret and apply the law, not make it up."[274] In the meantime, it is also possible that Reagan was using the vacancy as leverage to gain votes for his domestic policies. Rubin told of a "a second-hand rumor" he had heard that an Ohio Republican congressman had finally won a promise from the White

House "to appoint Duncan's successor in exchange for supporting Reagan's tax reforms."[275] Another possible reason for the delay in naming Graham was that the American Bar Association's Standing Committee on the Federal Judiciary had given him only a rating of "qualified," with a minority rating him "not qualified." In the words of Paul D. Kamenar, senior executive counsel for the conservative Washington Legal Foundation, in his testimony before the Senate Judiciary Committee in 1988 attacking the ABA's methodology, this rating was "astounding" given Graham's impeccable credentials and his recognition at the time among his fellow attorneys as one of the area's top litigators. Kamenar speculates that the reason for the ABA's low rating lies with the committee's consideration of Graham's conservative religious beliefs, which some committee members might have feared could interfere with his ability to render unbiased opinions and uphold higher court precedents.[276]

No matter what caused the delay, Reagan finally selected Graham for the post, sending his name to the Senate on August 5, 1986. The Senate quickly confirmed him, and Graham entered upon his duties on November 17, 1986.[277]

Born in Columbus, April 20, 1939, the son of Lowell and Violet Watts Graham, Judge Graham attended Columbus public schools before going on to Ohio State University, where he received his B.A. and J.D., summa cum laude. During this time he married Phyllis Jean Bryant, with whom he had four children. Until becoming a federal judge, his legal career was spent in private practice, where he specialized in business litigation, products liability, and malpractice suits. He represented both plaintiffs and defendants, although the main portion of his practice was defense work, representing insurance companies and corporate clients. He participated in many high-profile cases, including representing the board of directors of Marathon Oil in the Mobile-Marathon takeover litigation. To Graham, being a federal judge is "one of the highest callings in our society" and "the highest calling of the legal profession." He demands a lot from himself and from the lawyers who practice before him. Lawyers describe Graham "as an extremely smart and conscientious judge who enjoys analyzing legal issues and will listen to your arguments." Although seen as strict in criminal cases and one who follows the sentencing guidelines fairly closely, he is also praised for being fair.[278]

### GEORGE C. SMITH, 1987 TO THE PRESENT

On July 1, 1987, Reagan nominated George C. Smith to replace Kinneary, who decided to take senior status after witnessing the nineteen-month delay between Duncan's departure and Graham's appointment. Wanting to be sure a qualified judge would be named quickly, before announcing his decision Kinneary received assurances from Michael Colley, the chair of the Ohio Republican Party, that Colley would immediately call a meeting of the party's eighteen-member Committee on Nominations and Appointments to consider applications and interview candidates. Thus, Smith went through essentially the same process as did Graham.[279] The committee eventually selected three candidates to recommend to Ohio's congressional delegation. That group, in turn, made two recommendations to Reagan's Department of Justice, which then recommended Smith to the president.[280] Smith took up his post on December 4.

Born in Columbus, August 8, 1935, the son of George B. Smith, a small businessman, and Dorothy Smith, the future judge received his B.A. and J.D. from Ohio State University. Upon graduation, Smith chose to enter public service, preferring that to private practice. Therefore, after passing the Ohio bar in 1959, he took the position of assistant city attorney for the city of Columbus. Three years later, at the age of twenty-six, he became executive assistant to the Columbus mayor, a cabinet position. Two years after that, he was appointed an assistant attorney general of Ohio. Soon thereafter, he was appointed chief counsel to the prosecuting attorney of Franklin County. He then became the Franklin County prosecuting attorney before being appointed judge of the Franklin County Municipal Court in 1980. In 1985, he won a seat on the common pleas court of Franklin County, where he remained until Reagan appointed him to the federal bench. Until that time, Smith was very active in politics. As a boy, he collected political buttons. In college, he served as president of the Young Republican Club. Later, he was active in national and state campaigns for many Republican candidates and served on the executive committee of the Franklin County Republican Club. Unlike many state judges, Smith enjoyed his many campaigns for judicial positions. Indeed, his only regret on becoming a federal judge was that he would have to give up campaigning. As judge, Smith prides himself on his ability to move cases to settlement, using his persuasive techniques, summary jury trials, and, as he has said, "when all else fails, his sense of humor."[281]

## SANDRA BECKWITH, 1992 TO THE PRESENT

Nominated by Republican president George Bush on July 26, 1991, Sandra Beckwith became the first woman to serve as district court judge for the Southern District of Ohio when she took her oath of office on February 21, 1992. In doing so, she also became the district's eighth judge.[282] Beckwith's appointment process was quite similar to that experienced by Graham and Smith. When Congress established the new judgeship on December 1, 1990, Ohio still had no Republican senators, so the state Republicans appointed another screening committee that included heads of the county Republican organizations as well as Republican congressmen. Beckwith emerged as the leading contender after that committee interviewed seventy-five applicants. Three names went to the White House because "that's the tradition," but Beckwith was clearly the committee's choice, and Hamilton County Republican chairman Ralph Kohnen Jr. admitted that the White House sent only

Beckwith's name to the FBI for a background check.[283] Beckwith had been active in Republican politics throughout her career, so she was well known and respected. After Beckwith interviewed with area congressmen and the Department of Justice in Washington, President Bush chose her as his nominee.[284]

Although born December 4, 1943, in Norfolk, Virginia, where her father was posted during World War II, Beckwith is in fact a native Cincinnatian. Her parents and her grandparents all are from Cincinnati. Her father, Charles Shank, was an attorney, and her paternal grandfather, Dr. Reed A. Shank, was a prominent surgeon and team physician for the Cincinnati Reds, the Cincinnati Bengals, and the University of Cincinnati. Educated at the University of Cincinnati as an undergraduate and in law school, Beckwith joined her father in his private practice once she had gained admittance to the bar in 1969. From that date until her appointment to the federal bench, she moved in and out of public service. In 1976, Governor James A. Rhodes appointed her to the Hamilton County municipal bench. She later won election to that post as well as election as judge of the Hamilton County Court of Common Pleas, Division of Domestic Relations, and to the Hamilton County Board of Commissioners. In between, she practiced law as a solo practitioner and then joined the firm of Graydon, Head & Ritchey. Even in private practice, she remained active politically and in her community. From 1984 to 1990, she served on the Ohio governor's commission on prison overcrowding and from 1990 to 1992 she chaired the Hamilton County domestic violence task force. She is married to Thomas R. Ammann, a former assistant chief of the Cincinnati police department.

As a judge, Beckwith has worked especially hard at developing a variety of alternatives to incarceration. She supports mandatory counseling for drug and alcohol offenders. Earning a reputation as a fair and efficient judge, she operates under two principles. First, saying justice delayed is justice denied, she establishes and enforces timetables to keep cases moving. And second, she is committed to ensuring fair trials, which means that attorneys must strictly adhere to all courtroom rules. She also stresses the virtue of consistency. Lawyers, she explains, should be able to rely on a judge to follow the same procedures, the same rules, and the same precedents no matter what the case or which side is challenging a point. She hopes that no one will ever be able to look at a case assigned to her and know how it will come out because he or she knows what her personal philosophy is in that area. But, overall, Beckwith seeks to do the right thing in the long run, searching for enlightened decisions that respect individual rights and other points of view. Having a conservative bent, she cautiously operates under a jurisprudence of judicial restraint. If confronted with legislation she thinks unwise, she may drop a footnote in her decision urging the legislature to reexamine the issue, but she respects the separation of powers and believes that judges who overstep those bounds "are rightly criticized." Similarly, if she believes a higher court's precedent is incorrect, she will, in her decision, follow that precedent but invite the circuit or Supreme Court to revisit its decision. Finally, she is inclined "to think that judicial resolution of a problem should be tailored to the specific problem"; it is not for the court "to address every injustice in society."[285]

## SUSAN DLOTT, 1995 TO THE PRESENT

When Judge Spiegel took senior status in 1995, Democrat Bill Clinton had become president. Senator John Glenn, Ohio's Democratic senator, again established a bipartisan committee to make recommendations to him. That committee recommended Susan Dlott over more than twenty-five other lawyers and attorneys. Glenn concurred and sent the recommendation on to Clinton in April 1995. Clinton, in turn, sent her name to the Senate on August 10, which confirmed her on December 22. After taking her oath of office, she assumed her duties on December 29.[286] Dlott's selection was not without controversy. She was to sit in Columbus, where Beckwith had originally been assigned, with Beckwith, having more seniority, moving to Cincinnati to fill the slot left by Spiegel's taking senior status. The Columbus legal community grumbled over Glenn's selection of a Cincinnati resident for what they saw as a "Columbus" judgeship. Others complained that Dlott's selection was simply a political payoff, Dlott's lawyer–husband, Stanley Chesley, having been a major contributor to President Clinton's campaign as well as to the campaigns of many Ohio Democrats.[287] Politics may have influenced Glenn and Clinton's choices, but Dlott was well qualified for her new post. Indeed, she had broader experience than many of the other current judges had before their appointments.

Born September 11, 1949, in Dayton, Ohio, Dlott is the granddaughter of Russian immigrants and the daughter of native Daytonians, her father becoming a successful businessman. After receiving her B.A. from the University of Pennsylvania and her J.D. from Boston University School of Law, she clerked for two Ohio appellate court judges before becoming, in 1975, the first woman assistant U.S. attorney in the Southern District of Ohio. In 1979, she joined the law firm of Graydon, Head & Ritchey, where she practiced until her appointment to the federal bench. The first female partner at Graydon, Head & Ritchey, Dlott litigated many major cases including the highly publicized case involving the collapse of Home State Savings and Loan and Marvin Warner. In 1981 she won an acquittal for a doctor accused of improperly billing the state Medicaid program. At the time, it was the longest criminal trial ever in Hamilton County. Moreover, before becoming a federal judge, she was active politically, being a founding member of the Women's Council of the Democratic Senatorial Campaign Committee and a member of the Cincinnati Women's Political Caucus.[288]

As a federal judge, some see her as "sometimes eccentric [and] often unconventional." Her two Cavalier King Charles spaniels, Dickens and Crumpet, are always in her chambers. Stuffed animals fill her windowsills, and dog clocks, dog prints and papier-mâché dogs, dog bones and water dishes, and a dog bed and a doggie cart fill her office. But Dlott is "tough" and highly effective. Attorneys especially praise her mediation skills. Her style is "Listen, intuit, nudge."[289] And she will keep parties at it. She has been known to keep litigants in her chambers working for hours toward a settlement, with only M&Ms or Jenny Craig diet bars to snack on. She also admits to being a judicial activist. By that, she means that she does not "blindly follow precedent." If she feels something is wrong, and if she can, "intellectually and honestly," distinguish the situation from existing precedent, she will do that to achieve the "right result."[290]

### EDMUND A. SARGUS JR., 1996 TO THE PRESENT

When Rubin died in August 1995, Columbus and Cincinnati vied to get "their" person in as his replacement. Regionalism seemed the primary concern. The Columbus legal community, still upset that a Cincinnatian occupied what they saw as a "Columbus" judgeship, pushed hard for the appointment of someone from their area to replace Rubin. They urged Chief Judge Holschuh to assign Dlott to Cincinnati in place of Rubin, opening the way for a new Columbus-area judge to replace Dlott in their city. On the other hand, Cincinnatians expected a Cincinnati lawyer or judge to replace Rubin, the *Cincinnati Enquirer*, for example, speculating about several area Democrats it said were being "screened." By this time, although Clinton was president, Ohio had one Democratic and one Republican senator (Senators Glenn and DeWine). Senator Glenn, as he had done routinely with all judicial nominations, appointed a five-person bipartisan committee to screen applicants. After interviewing ten or eleven candidates, the committee selected Edmund Sargus, at that time the U.S. attorney for the Southern District of Ohio and a close friend of both Howard Metzenbaum, Ohio's recently retired, long-serving Democratic senator, and Glenn. Clinton nominated Sargus on December 22, 1995, but it was not until May 9, 1996, that the Senate Committee on the Judiciary finally reported him favorably to the full Senate. Then the Senate delayed his confirmation until July 22, almost three months later. Ironically, it was Republican senator DeWine who helped push through his appointment, the Republicans generally refusing to vote on judicial nominations until after the 1996 presidential elections.[291]

Born July 2, 1953, Sargus was raised in St. Clairsville, Belmont County, Ohio, where he still lives. His paternal grandparents immigrated from Lebanon, opening a store in Bellaire, Ohio, then a bustling steel mill town. Although they never learned to read or write English, they did well enough to send their son, Sargus's father, to college and law school. At the age of forty, Sargus's father graduated from the University of Notre Dame Law School. He practiced law in St. Clairsville from 1951 through 1966. From 1961 through

1967, he served as a state senator and in 1966 was elected to the Belmont County Court of Common Pleas, Probate and Juvenile Division. He died after serving in the position for only four weeks. Following his death, his friends began a campaign to fulfill one of the elder Sargus's wishes, the creation of a facility separate from the county jail that could be used to house juvenile offenders. In 1972, the facility, known as the Sargus Juvenile Center, the first such multicounty facility, was opened in St. Clairsville, where it continues to operate. Sargus's mother, of Irish descent, was a schoolteacher.

After receiving his A.B. from Brown University in 1975 and his J.D. from Case Western Reserve University School of Law in 1978, Sargus joined the firm of Cinque, Banker, Linch, Groman & White in Bellaire. In 1979, he began a fourteen-year stint as special counsel to the Ohio attorney general while maintaining a private law practice. In 1982, he and Stanley G. Burech formed the firm of Burech & Sargus in St. Clairsville. During this time he met and married his wife, Jennifer, who now is a judge in the Belmont County Court of Common Pleas. He also served on St. Clairsville's city council and as law director for the city of Bellaire.

In 1993, Clinton appointed Sargus U.S. attorney for the Southern District of Ohio. During his three and a half years as U.S. attorney, Sargus handled a number of important cases, including the biggest drug case brought in that time period—the Short North Posse prosecution. This case required Sargus to coordinate the work of several law enforcement agencies, including the Bureau of Alcohol, Tobacco, and Firearms and the narcotics bureau of the Columbus Division of Police. To ensure that all agencies' operating procedures were consistent required coordination, negotiation, and a great deal of tact. Sargus also tried a highly publicized three-week murder-for-hire trial involving "a fairly notorious" Columbus accountant, Barry Kessler, which resulted in a conviction by a jury in a case presided over by Judge Graham. He also tried the first interstate domestic violence case brought in Ohio under a 1994 congressional statute. Moreover, his office brought a number of high-profile health care fraud cases, including one against a major health care provider, Caremark, Inc., which resulted in a fine of $161 million, a sum the company paid in full.

Before becoming U.S. attorney, Sargus had been active in Democratic politics, campaigning for Howard Metzenbaum, serving as a delegate to the 1984 Democratic National Convention, and being a member of the Belmont County Democratic Central Committee. On occasion, he served as legal counsel for both Metzenbaum and Glenn. For example, in Metzenbaum's 1988 reelection campaign, Sargus was designated as chief legal counsel, a volunteer position, but one that dealt with a number of legal issues related to the campaign and campaign issues.

As a judge, he is known as "conscientious and accommodating" with "excellent legal abilities." He uses hands-on mediation techniques to ensure either a fair settlement or an efficient trial. Jurisprudentially, he argues that for most cases, the judge's primary role is to ensure fair and swift justice. For the rare constitutional case, if precedent is not settled, he believes that in the economic sphere, deference should be paid to Congress. It is not the court's job to determine whether a statute is wise or fair. In the realm of individual rights, the judge should look carefully for possible infringements.[292]

### ALGENON L. MARBLEY, 1997 TO THE PRESENT

On July 3, 1997, Clinton nominated Algenon L. Marbley to replace Holschuh when he took senior status. After Senate confirmation, Marbley took his oath of office and assumed his new duties on November 11. Marbley underwent the same selection process as did Dlott and Sargus. Glenn again established a five-person bipartisan committee. Each candidate completed a detailed questionnaire, submitted letters of recommendation, and then interviewed with the committee. The committee's work was basically apolitical. Marbley confirmed what Sargus and Dlott also described; no one asked him about his jurisprudential approach or his political views. They did not even ask him about his party affiliation. Then, again like Sargus, once Clinton nominated Marbley, DeWine helped him through the confirmation process, again enforcing Marbley's "nonpartisan" experience.[293]

The second African American to serve on the court, Marbley was born in Nashville, North Carolina, in 1954. Both his parents were schoolteachers. After his parents divorced, however, he lived with his maternal grandparents, attending North Carolina's segregated public schools until high school, when the state integrated its schools. He then received his B.A. from the University of North Carolina at Chapel Hill, in 1976, and his J.D. from Northwestern University School of Law, in 1979. Except for five years as assistant regional attorney for the U.S. Department of Health and Human Services, he spent his entire legal career in private practice, becoming a partner at Vorys, Sater, Seymour and Pease in Columbus before his appointment to the federal bench. For Marbley, being a federal district court judge is one's "highest calling." He especially values the freedom to make decisions "insulated absolutely from political pressure." He gave up his lucrative position in a private law firm because he believes that as a federal judge he could make "a positive impact on my community and on the law," bringing an important perspective to the bench, having experienced racism and discrimination firsthand.[294]

### THOMAS M. ROSE, 2002 TO THE PRESENT

Thomas M. Rose was nominated by George W. Bush on January 23, 2002, to replace Weber, who had taken senior status. Unanimously confirmed by the Senate on May 9, 2002, Rose took his oath of office June 21. Born October 20, 1948, in Circleville, Ohio, he received his B.S. from Ohio University in 1970 and his J.D. at the University of Cincinnati College of Law in 1973.

After passing the bar, he entered private practice, but much of his career has been in public service. He has served as assistant prosecutor for Greene County, chief juvenile court referee for the Greene County Court of Common Pleas, and chief assistant in charge of the civil division in the Greene County prosecutor's office before becoming a judge for the Greene County Court of Common Pleas. Rose sits in Dayton with Rice. This is the first time Dayton has had two full-time judges.[295]

### GREGORY L. FROST, 2003 TO THE PRESENT

George W. Bush nominated Gregory L. Frost on August 1, 2002, to replace Smith, who took senior status, and the Senate confirmed him on March 10, 2003. Frost was sworn in in Columbus on March 19. Born April 19, 1949, in Newark, Ohio, Frost is a lifelong resident of Licking County. After attending public schools in Newark, Frost received his B.A. from Wittenberg University and his J.D. from Ohio Northern University Law School. After being admitted to the Ohio bar in 1974, he served as assistant Licking County prosecutor for four and a half years. While assistant prosecutor, he also maintained a private practice, becoming a partner in the law firm of Schaller, Frost, Hostetter & Campbell. In 1983, Frost was appointed and then elected to the Licking County municipal bench, where he served until 1990, when he was elected judge of the common pleas court of Licking County. Reelected twice, he served in that position until he assumed his new position as a district court judge. Frost and his wife Kristina Dix Frost have three sons.[296]

THE JUDGES OF THE U.S. District Court for the Southern District of Ohio are a distinguished group of men and women who have come from a variety of backgrounds and experiences. Of the nine judges who were appointed in the nineteenth century, four came from prominent, wealthy families with important political connections, while two grew up in middle-class families, and two came from poor families (one judge's background is not known). All were politically active, and their activities tended to be much more extensive than those of most judges appointed in the twentieth and twenty-first centuries. Of the nine, eight held elective office before their appointment to the bench. Four had been congressmen, five had prosecutorial experience, and three had judicial experience. In the nineteenth century, political activism and family connections to influential politicians characterized the judicial appointees. Two knew the appointing president personally; four were probably appointed largely because of family and political connections; and the appointment of three was most likely a reward for party loyalty.

Of the twenty-eight judges appointed in the twentieth and twenty-first centuries, nine had parents who were attorneys or judges, and four had fathers who held important elective offices. At least eight came from families who had long been politically and socially active in their communities and had probably imbued their children with the importance of service. Most grew up in comfortable or upper-class families, but several came from lower- or lower-middle-class backgrounds. The fathers of two of the judges were hourly workers, one was a tailor, two were teachers, and three were farmers. Only twenty-three of the judges had been politically active, and only one had been a congressman. Fourteen had prosecutorial experience, and fifteen had judicial experience, but many had neither. Their appointments came for a variety of reasons. At least ten were personal friends of an Ohio senator, the appointing president, or other prominent politician of the president's party. Another nine had important political connections because of their political activism before their appointments to the bench. But almost all had reputations as prominent attorneys or jurists. Unlike their colleagues in the nineteenth century, these judges were "homegrown." All but two were born in Ohio, and most came from families who had lived and worked in Ohio for generations. All but five who had formal collegiate or legal educations attended either college or law school in Ohio, and sixteen received all their advanced education in Ohio. Despite what might appear to be provincialism, however, the judges of the twentieth and twenty-first centuries, like their earlier colleagues, see their role as upholding the U.S. Constitution and federal law rather than representing their region. Their job, as they see it, is to mediate, adjudicate, and provide a level playing field for those seeking to vindicate rights in the courts.[297]

# APPENDIX

## Judges of the Southern District of Ohio

*Their Backgrounds and Histories, a Summary*

| Name | Father's Profession[a] | Place of Birth | Preappointment Career | Appointing President | Political Affiliation | College Education/ Academic Background | Law School Education | Professional Public Service (e.g., Judge, Prosecutor, Defender) | Political, Partisan Activism | Age at Appointment | Tenure |
|---|---|---|---|---|---|---|---|---|---|---|---|
| Byrd, Charles W., 1803–1828 | Elite planter | plantation, VA | Appointed government position | Jefferson | Jeffersonian Republican | Tutored | No | Secretary, Northwest Territory | Delegate, Ohio constitutional convention | 33 | 25 years |
| Creighton, William, 1828–1829 | Unknown, probably elite | Western VA | Congressman | Adams | Jeffersonian Republican | Dickinson | No | U.S. attorney, Southern District of Ohio | Ohio secretary of state; U.S. congressman | 50 | 1 term 1828–29 recess |
| Campbell, John W., 1829–1833 | Poor farmer | Augusta Co., VA | Congressman | Jackson | Democrat | Tutored | No | County prosecutor | Ohio legislator; U.S. congressman | 47 | 4 years |
| Tappan, Benjamin, 1833–1834 | Minister; wealthy merchant | Northampton, MA | Ohio state senator; common pleas court judge | Jackson | Democrat | Common school | No | Common pleas judge | Elected judgeship; state senate; Jackson elector | 60 | 1 term Dec. 1833 recess |
| Leavitt, Humphrey H., 1834–1871 | Poor farmer, merchant | CT | Congressman | Jackson | Democrat | Private academy | No | County prosecutor | Congressman, Ohio legislator | 38 | 37 years |
| Swing, Philip B., 1871–1882 | Farmer | Southern OH | Private practice | Grant | Republican | None | No | County prosecutor | Town council; party leader | 51 | 11 years |
| White, William, 1883 | unknown | England | Chief judge, Ohio Supreme Court | Arthur | Republican | High school | No | County prosecutor; common pleas judge; Ohio Supreme Court judge | Elected judgeship | 61 | 0 |
| Sage, George R., 1883–1898 | Baptist minister | Erie, PA | Lucrative private practice | Arthur | Republican | Granville (Denison) | Cincinnati Law School | County prosecutor (briefly) | Related to influential politicians; active in party | 55 | 15 years |

[a] As indicator of social status at birth.

| Name/Term | Occupation | Origin | Prior Position | President | Party | College | Law School | Prior Legal/Judicial Experience | Political Background | Age | Tenure |
|---|---|---|---|---|---|---|---|---|---|---|---|
| Thompson, Albert C., 1898–1910 | Attorney | Brookville, PA | Congressman, private practice | McKinley | Republican | None | No | Probate judge; common pleas judge | Three-term congressman; elected judgeship; delegate Republican National Convention | 56 | 12 years |
| Sater, John E., 1907–1924 | Farmer | New Haven, OH | Lucrative private practice | T. Roosevelt | Republican | Marietta College | No | None | unknown | 53 | 17 years |
| Hollister, Howard C., 1910–1919 | Attorney | Cincinnati | Private practice | Taft | Republican | Yale | Cincinnati Law School | Assistant prosecutor; common pleas judge | Elected judgeship; involved in reform campaigns | 54 | 9 years |
| Peck, John Weld, 1919–1924 | Attorney/judge | Cincinnati | Private practice | Wilson | Democrat | Harvard | Cincinnati Law School | None | Ran for offices; campaigned for others; delegate Democratic National Convention; city council | 45 | 4 years |
| Hickenlooper, Smith 1923–1929 | Lieutenant governor of Ohio/business executive | Cincinnati | Superior court judge | Harding | Republican | University of Cincinnati | Harvard | County prosecutor; judge superior court | Elected judgeship | 43 | 6 years |
| Hough, Benson 1925–1935 | Successful farmer and stockman | Rural Delaware Co., OH | U.S. attorney | Harding | Republican | Ohio Wesleyan | Ohio State | City solicitor; Ohio Supreme Court judge; U.S. attorney | Elected judgeship | 49 | 10 years |
| Nevin, Robert R., 1929–1952 | Attorney, U.S. congressman | Dayton | Private practice | Coolidge | Republican | Ohio State | University of Cincinnati | County prosecutor | Delegate Republican National Convention; chair, county Republican Party | 51 | 24 years |
| Underwood, Mell, 1936–1967 | Farmer, businessman | Farm in Morgan Co., OH | Congressman | F. Roosevelt | Democrat | Ohio University | Ohio State | County prosecutor | County prosecutor; congressman | 45 | 31 years |

| Name | Father's Profession | Place of Birth | Preappointment Career | Appointing President | Political Affiliation | College Education/Academic Background | Law School Education | Professional Public Service (e.g., Judge, Prosecutor, Defender) | Political, Partisan Activism | Age at Appointment | Tenure |
|---|---|---|---|---|---|---|---|---|---|---|---|
| Druffel, John H., 1937–1967 | unknown | Cincinnati | Common pleas judge | F. Roosevelt | Democrat | Xavier | YMCA (night school) | Common pleas judge | City council; elected judgeship | 51 | 30 years |
| Cecil, Lester L., 1953–1959 | Hourly worker for traction company | Farm near Piqua, OH | Common pleas judge | Eisenhower | Republican | University of Michigan | University of Michigan | City prosecutor; municipal court judge; common pleas judge | Elected judgeship | 60 | 6 years |
| Weinman, Carl A., 1959–1979 | unknown | Steubenville | Private practice | Eisenhower | Republican | University of Michigan | University of Michigan | City solicitor; common pleas judge | Elected judgeship; member Ohio Republican State Committee | 56 | 20 years |
| Peck, John Weld, 1961–1966 | Attorney | Cincinnati | Private practice | Kennedy | Democrat | Miami University | University of Cincinnati | Common pleas judge; Ohio Supreme Court judge | Several appointed positions in state government; campaigned for others; county Democratic policy committee | 48 | 5 years |
| Hogan, Timothy S., 1966–1989 | Attorney/Ohio attorney general | Wellston, OH | Private practice | Johnson | Democrat | Xavier | University of Cincinnati | None | Ran for office; delegate Democratic Convention; active campaigner; member, Democratic policy committee | 57 | 23 years |
| Porter, David S., 1966–1989 | Teacher | Cincinnati | Common pleas judge | Johnson | Democrat | University of Cincinnati | University of Cincinnati | Common pleas judge | Elected judgeship | 57 | 23 years |
| Kinneary, Joseph P., 1966–2001 | Salesman | Cincinnati | U.S. attorney | Johnson | Democrat | Notre Dame | University of Cincinnati | Ohio assistant attorney general; U.S. attorney, Southern District of Ohio | Campaigned for others; delegate Democratic National Convention | 61 | 35 years |

| Name / Term | Prior Occupation | City | Prior Position | Appointing President | Party | Undergraduate | Law School | Prosecutorial/Judicial Experience | Political Activity | Age | Tenure |
|---|---|---|---|---|---|---|---|---|---|---|---|
| Rubin, Carl B., 1971–1995 | Tailor | Cincinnati | Private practice | Nixon | Republican | University of Cincinnati | University of Cincinnati | Briefly county prosecutor | Ran three Taft campaigns; active in party | 51 | 24 years |
| Duncan, Robert M., 1974–1985 | Factory worker | Urbana, OH | Judge, U.S. Court of Military Appeals | Nixon | Republican | Ohio State | Ohio State | City prosecutor; chief counsel Ohio attorney general; municipal judge; Ohio Supreme Court judge; judge U.S. Court of Military Appeals | Friend of William Saxbe (Ohio attorney general; U.S. attorney general; U.S. senator); some state government positions | 47 | 11 years |
| Holschuh, John D., 1980–present | Businessman; foreman, Works Progress Administration; millwright | Ironton, OH | Private practice | Carter | Democrat | Miami University Cincinnati | University of | None | None | 54 | Still on bench |
| Spiegel, S. Arthur, 1980–present | Municipal court judge | Cincinnati | Private practice | Carter | Democrat | University of Cincinnati | Harvard | None | Contributed money to some judicial campaigns | 60 | Still on bench |
| Rice, Walter H., 1980–present | Drug and tobacco jobber | Pittsburgh | Common pleas judge | Carter | Democrat | Northwestern | Columbia | County prosecutor; municipal court judge; common pleas judge | Elected judgeship; active campaigner | 43 | Still on bench |
| Weber, Herman J., 1985–present | Attorney | Lima, OH | Ohio court of appeals judge | Reagan | Republican | Otterbein College | Ohio State | Common pleas judge, Ohio Court of Appeals | City council/vice mayor; elected judgeship | 58 | Still on bench |
| Graham, James L., 1985–present | CPA | Columbus | Private practice | Reagan | Republican | Ohio State | Ohio State | None | Campaigned for judges; attorney for Republican Party | 47 | Still on bench |
| Smith, George C., 1987–present | Small businessman | Columbus | Common pleas judge | Reagan | Republican | Ohio State | Ohio State | City attorney; county judge; prosecutor; municipal court common pleas judge | City attorney; executive assistant to mayor; assistant Ohio attorney general | 52 | Still on bench |

| Name | Father's Profession | Place of Birth | Preappointment Career | Appointing President | Political Affiliation | College Education/ Academic Background | Law School Education | Professional Public Service (e.g., Judge, Prosecutor, Defender) | Political, Partisan Activism | Age at Appointment | Tenure |
|---|---|---|---|---|---|---|---|---|---|---|---|
| Beckwith, Sandra, 1992–present | Attorney | Norfolk, VA/Cincinnati[b] | Private practice | G. H. W. Bush | Republican | University of Cincinnati | University of Cincinnati | Common pleas judge; municipal court judge | County board of commissioners; elected judgeship | 49 | Still on bench |
| Dlott, Susan, 1995–present | Successful businessman | Dayton | Private practice | Clinton | Democrat | Northwestern | Boston University | Assistant U.S. attorney | Active on several political committees | 49 | Still on bench |
| Sargus, Jr. Edmund A., 1996–present | Attorney/Ohio state senator | St. Clairsville, OH | U.S. attorney, Southern District of Ohio | Clinton | Democrat | Brown | Case Western Reserve | Special council Ohio attorney; city law director; U.S. attorney Southern District of Ohio | City council; campaign for a senator; delegate Democratic National Convention; county Democratic Central Committee | 43 | Still on bench |
| Marbley, Algenon L., 1997–present | School-teacher | Nashville, N.C. | Private practice | Clinton | Democrat | University of North Carolina, Chapel Hill | North-western | Assistant regional attorney, HHS | None | 43 | Still on bench |
| Rose, Thomas M., 2002–present | Banker | Laurelville, OH | Common pleas judge | G. W. Bush | Republican | Ohio University | University of Cincinnati | County prosecutor; common pleas judge | Elected judgeship | 54 | Still on bench |
| Frost, Gregory L., 2003–present | Owner, oil and gas drilling firm | Newark, OH | Common pleas judge | G. W. Bush | Republican | Wittenburg | Ohio Northern | County prosecutor; municipal court judge; common pleas judge | Elected judgeships | 54 | Still on bench |

bJudge Beckwith is, in fact, a native Cincinnatian. She was born in Norfolk while her father was stationed there during World War II.

# NOTES

## INTRODUCTION

1. Judge Joseph P. Kinneary, 1999 interview, quoted in "Oldest Federal Judge Still Handling Cases to Retire," Associated Press State and Local Wire Service, July 27, 2001, and "Retired Federal Judge Joseph Kinneary Dead at 97," ibid., February 15, 2003, both in files of Rita Wallace, historian of the Sixth Circuit, Library of the Sixth Circuit and the District Court for the Southern District of Ohio, Cincinnati (hereafter Wallace Files).

2. John H. Metz, quoted in "Families Share Pain, Memories," *Cincinnati Enquirer,* June 18, 2000, B5.

3. Kinneary, quoted in Associated Press State and Local Wire Service, February 15, 2003.

4. Metz, quoted in *Cincinnati Enquirer,* June 18, 2000, B5.

5. Statistics from the Federal Judicial Center at www.fjc.gov/history/dc_bdy.html. Kevin L. Lyles argues that district judges increasingly play a policy-making role. Because only about 10 percent of all cases are appealed and because appellate courts are influenced by the initial fact finding of the district courts, district court judges are, more than ever, "gatekeepers," determining "what policy issues come into the federal court system and what policy effects or directives come out." Kevin L. Lyles, "Presidential Expectations and Judicial Performance Revisited: Law and Politics in the Federal District Courts, 1960–1992," *Presidential Studies Quarterly* 26 (Spring 1996): 447–48, 465–66. See also Wolf Heydebrand and Carroll Seron, *Rationalizing Justice: The Political Economy of Federal District Courts* (Albany: State University of New York, 1990), 20–22; James Williard Hurst, "The Functions of Courts in the United States, 1950–1980," *Law and Society Review* 14, nos. 3–4 (1980–1981): 402–70.

6. Robert A. Carp and Ronald Stidham, *The Federal Courts,* 3d ed. (Washington, DC: CQ Press, 1998), 23.

7. Judge James Graham, interview by author, July 15, 1999, Columbus.

8. Judge John W. Peck, speech at swearing-in ceremony in Cincinnati, October 13, 1961, Papers of John W. Peck, box 34, Cincinnati Historical Society, Cincinnati.

9. Judge Sandra Beckwith, interview by author, July 22, 1999, Cincinnati.

10. Judiciary Act of 1789, 1 Stat. 73.

11. Ibid.

12. Ibid. Criminal jurisdiction was limited to crimes committed in the district or on the high seas where the punishment did not exceed whipping, a $100 fine, or

six months in prison. Their common-law jurisdiction was limited to disputes valued at less than $100, and only where the United States was the plaintiff.

13. Ibid.; Judiciary Act of 1802, 2 Stat. 156.

14. Edwin C. Surrency, "Federal District Court Judges and the History of Their Courts," 40 *Federal Rules Decisions* (1966): 139, 144.

15. An Act to establish circuit courts of appeal . . . , 26 Stat. 826 (1891).

16. Judicial Code of 1911, 36 Stat. 1087 (1911). For a brief overview of the evolution of the federal court structure, see Edwin C. Surrency, *History of the Federal Courts* (New York: Oceana Publications, 1987), and Russell R. Wheeler and Cynthia Harrison, *Creating the Federal Judicial System*, 2d ed. (Washington, DC: Federal Judicial Center, 1994).

17. Heydebrand and Seron, *Rationalizing Justice*, 46, xvii–xviii.

18. Ibid., xvii. See also Steven Harmon Wilson, *The Rise of Judicial Management in the U.S. District Court, Southern District of Texas, 1955–2000* (Athens: University of Georgia Press, 2002), 3–6. See also chapter 6.

19. Clerk of the U.S. District Court for the Southern District of Ohio, annual report, 2000, clerk's office, Columbus, Ohio. (Hereafter referred to as Clerk's Annual Report.) See also Administrative Office of the U.S. Courts, annual report, 2000, available from www.uscourts.gov/judbus2000/contents.html. Before 2000, the Government Printing Office in Washington, DC, published these reports annually. (Hereafter referred to as AO Annual Report.)

20. John Weld Peck, "The Selection and Tenure of Judges," in *John Weld Peck: A Memorial*, ed. Jane Peck Alcorn (Cincinnati: n.p., 1938), 250.

21. See, e.g., Mary K. Bonsteel Tachau, *Federal Courts in the Early Republic: Kentucky, 1789–1816* (Princeton, NJ: Princeton University Press, 1978); Christian G. Fritz, *Federal Justice in California: The Court of Ogden Hoffman, 1851–1891* (Lincoln: University of Nebraska Press, 1991); Kermit L. Hall and Eric W. Rise, *From Local Courts to National Tribunals: The Federal District Courts of Florida, 1821–1990* (Brooklyn, NY: Carlson Publishing, 1991); Lawrence H. Larsen, *Federal Justice in Western Missouri: The Judges, the Cases, the Times* (Columbia: University of Missouri Press, 1994); Charles L. Zelden, *Justice Lies in the District: The United States District Court, Southern District of Texas, 1902–1960* (College Station: Texas A&M University Press, 1993); Tony Freyer and Timothy Dixon, *Democracy and Judicial Independence: A History of the Federal Courts of Alabama, 1820–1994* (Brooklyn, NY: Carlson Publishing, 1995); Jeffrey Brandon Morris, *Calmly to Poise the Scales of Justice: A History of the Courts of the District of Columbia Circuit* (Durham, NC: Carolina Academic Press, 2001); Richard Cahan, *A Court that Shaped America: Chicago's Federal District Court from Abe Lincoln to Abbie Hoffman* (Evanston, IL: Northwestern University Press, 2002); Peter Graham Fish, *Federal Justice in the Mid-Atlantic South: United States Courts from Maryland to the Carolinas, 1789–1835* (Washington, DC: Administrative Office of the U.S. Courts, 2002); Wilson, *Rise of Judicial Management*.

22. "Humphrey Howe Leavitt," *United States Law Magazine* 5 (1850–1852): 44.

23. Cited in Lisle W. Abrahamson, *The United States District Court for the District of Kentucky, 1789–1901* (Louisville: U.S. District Court for the Western District of Kentucky, 2001), 5.

24. Felix Frankfurter and James M. Landis, *The Business of the Supreme Court: A Study in the Federal Judicial System* (New York: Macmillan, 1928), 52n174.

1. William T. Utter, *The Frontier State, 1803–1825,* vol. 2, *The History of the State of Ohio,* ed. Carl Wittke (Columbus: Ohio State Archaeological and Historical Society, 1941–1944), 3.

2. Ibid., 3–13, 391–93; Donald J. Ratcliffe, *Party Spirit in a Frontier Republic: Democratic Politics in Ohio, 1793–1821* (Columbus: Ohio State University Press, 1998), 16–17, 122.

3. An Act to enable the people of the Eastern division of the territory northwest of the river Ohio to form a constitution and state government, 2 Stat. 173 (1802).

4. Ibid. For a brief history of this process, see Utter, *Frontier State,* 4–13.

5. An Act to provide for the due execution of the laws of the United States, within the state of Ohio, 2 Stat. 201 (1803).

6. Ibid. See also Judiciary Act of 1789, 1 Stat. 73. The U.S. attorney determines who is investigated, sued, and prosecuted in the district. Thus, he or she has broad discretion in determining what crimes are brought before the judges of the district courts.

7. An Act establishing Circuit Courts, and abridging the jurisdiction of the district courts in the districts of Kentucky, Tennessee, and Ohio, 2 Stat. 420 (1807). Initially, in the Judiciary Act of 1789, Congress had authorized three circuits encompassing the thirteen original district courts. See 1 Stat. 73 (1789). Congress changed this in 1802 to six circuits with one Supreme Court justice and one district court judge presiding over each circuit. See 2 Stat. 156 (1802). The 1807 law then added the Seventh Circuit for the three states west of the Appalachian Mountains. See, generally, Surrency, "Federal District Judges."

8. *Journal of the Executive Proceedings of the Senate of the United States,* 7th Cong., 2d sess., 447 (March 1, 1803).

9. Ibid., 5th Cong., 2d sess., 330 (December 20, 1797); Charles E. Rice, "Biographical Sketch," Charles E. Rice Collection, Ohio Historical Society, Columbus; Nelson W. Evans and E. B. Stivers, *A History of Adams County, Ohio: From Its Earliest Settlement to the Present Time* (West Union, OH: E. B. Stivers, 1900), 305, 526–32; Ratcliffe, *Party Spirit,* 39–40, 69; Carrington T. Marshall, ed., *A History of the Courts and Lawyers of Ohio* (New York: American Historical Society, 1934), 1:66–68; Andrew R. L. Cayton, "The Failure of Michael Baldwin: A Case Study in the Origins of Middle-Class Culture on the Trans-Appalachian Frontier," *Ohio History* 95 (Winter–Spring 1986): 36–37, 44. For more details on Byrd, his appointment, and his jurisprudence, see chapter 9.

10. *Senate Executive Journal,* 7th Cong., 2d sess., 447 (March 1, 1803).

11. Ratcliffe, *Party Spirit,* 114.

12. George A. Katzenberger, "Major David Ziegler," *Ohio State Archaeological and Historical Quarterly* 21 (April 1912): 127–74; Ratcliffe, *Party Spirit,* 114, 26–27, 78.

13. Ratcliffe, *Party Spirit,* 69, 108–9, 111, 114, 138; Evans and Stivers, *History of Adams County,* 508; Charles Theodore Greve, *Centennial History of Cincinnati and Representative Citizens* (Chicago: Biographical Publishing, 1904), 1:438–39; Cayton, "The Failure of Michael Baldwin," 35–36, 38–41, 43, 46. See Andrew R. L. Cayton, *The Frontier Republic: Ideology and Politics in the Ohio Country, 1780–1825* (Kent, OH: Kent State

University Press, 1986), 56–60, 68–70, 84–88, for a good discussion of the political ideology of Byrd and his colleagues and the growing tension between them and Baldwin.

14. Irwin S. Rhodes, "The History of the United States District Court for the Southern District of Ohio," *University of Cincinnati Law Review* 24 (Summer 1955): 340.

15. Order Books 1803–1938, vol. A, 2–18 (June term 1803), General Records, Western Division, Records of the U.S. District Court, Southern District of Ohio, RG 21, National Archives Branch Depository, Great Lakes Region, Chicago, IL (hereafter Order Books). Hereafter, all the records of the U.S. District Court, Southern District of Ohio, will be identified simply as RG 21.

16. See *Scioto Gazette,* March 19, 1803, and 1803–1818, passim; *Scioto Gazette and Fredonian Chronicle,* 1819–1821, passim; *Chillicothe Supporter,* 1810–1813 and 1818–1821, passim; *Cincinnati Western Spy,* 1803–1807, passim.

By contrast, state courts were the subject of much interest and hot political debates during this early period. Not only did newspapers occasionally print stories of trials in state court, but they followed with interest the controversy between the state judges and the legislature over the issue of the state courts' power to declare acts of the legislature unconstitutional. Within three years of statehood, the Ohio House of Representatives, dominated by an anticourt party, impeached two state judges (although the Senate failed to convict either) and enacted the "Sweeping Resolution" that ended the terms of all state judges in 1810 so they could be replaced with those more amenable to the views of the dominant legislative faction. William T. Utter, "Judicial Review in Early Ohio," *Mississippi Valley Historical Review* 14 (June 1927): 8–23. For a description of Ohio's judicial system, see Francis J. Amer, *The Development of the Judicial System in Ohio from 1787 to 1932* (Baltimore: Johns Hopkins Press, 1932).

17. Irwin Rhodes counted a total of sixty-one cases from 1803 to 1807. Rhodes, "History of the District Court," 340.

18. Order Books, passim.

19. See Order Books, vol. A, passim.

20. McCormick v. Sullivant, 23 U.S. 192 (1825); Order Books, vol. A (October term 1803; February term 1804; February term 1805). The summary of the court's activities above and below were compiled from Order Books and the Records (Journals), 1814–1842, General Records, W. Div., RG 21 (hereafter Records [Journals]). These are the only extant records in RG 21 for this period.

Before Congress divided the Ohio district court into two courts in 1855, Ohio had only one federal district court. The National Archives has filed all pre-1855 records with the records of what would become the Southern District of Ohio. Further, Congress divided the Southern District into an Eastern Division and a Western Division in 1880. The National Archives has filed all pre-1880 documents in the records of what would become the Western Division.

21. See, e.g., U.S. v. Burrell and U.S. v. Hammond, Order Books, vol. A, 101–2 (June term 1806).

22. See, e.g., two cases in ibid., 189–91 (September term 1816), in which the government filed bills of information for libel against defendants for selling dis-

tilled spiritous liquor without a license and the court found the defendants guilty; U.S. v. Totte, ibid., 226 (September term 1817).

23. An Act establishing Circuit Courts, and abridging the jurisdiction of the district courts in the districts of Kentucky, Tennessee, and Ohio, 2 Stat. 420 (1807).

24. Minor criminal cases were cases in which potential maximum punishments did not exceed thirty stripes, a fine of $100, or six months in jail.

25. District courts had exclusive jurisdiction over admiralty cases; seizures under federal laws of impost, navigation, or trade; and cases for penalties and forfeitures brought by the United States.

26. An Act altering the place of holding the circuit and district court in the district of Ohio, 3 Stat. 544 (1820). Congress also changed the dates of the courts' sessions. The circuit court convened on the first Monday of September and January, while the district court met on the second Mondays of those months.

27. Rhodes, "History of the District Court," 342.

28. See, generally, Order Books, vols. A, 1, and 2; Records (Journals), 1814–1842, vol. 1. The information on the Harrison case is in Records (Journals), 12:7–8 (July term 1831). The suit was brought in 1821; the bond had been executed in 1814. The case was delayed until the court disposed of the suit between the United States and Clarkson.

29. Under the Articles of Confederation, because there were no federal courts; the central government had to rely on state courts to enforce federal laws. See Articles of Confederation, art. XIII.

30. Irwin S. Rhodes calculated that the circuit court, from 1807 to 1820, handled a total of 267 cases, averaging about 20 a year. Rhodes, "History of the District Court," 341.

31. See *Scioto Gazette*, January 4, 1808, 2.

32. Ibid., January 11, 1808, 2–3.

33. Few slave owners filed their runaway slave cases in federal court because of the expense, the inconvenience, and the potential delay in getting a hearing. See Paul Finkelman, *An Imperfect Union: Slavery, Federalism, and Comity* (Chapel Hill: University of North Carolina Press, 1981), 236–39.

34. Order Books, vol. A, 229–31 (September term 1817).

35. Ibid., 231–32. See An Act to Regulate Black and Mulatto Persons, 2 Laws of Ohio 63, 65 (1803).

36. Order Books, vol. A, 231–32 (September term 1817). For provisions of the Fugitive Slave Act, see 1 Stat. 302 (1793). For a history of the passage of the Fugitive Slave Act, see Paul Finkelman, *Slavery and the Founders: Race and Liberty in the Age of Jackson*, 2d ed. (Armonk, NY: M. E. Sharpe, 2001), 81–104.

37. Order Books, vol. A, 231–32 (September term 1817). The Ayerses were early antislavery advocates, actively helping runaway slaves, hiding them in their barns, and even employing some as farm hands. Elsie Johnson Ayers, *The Hills of Highland* (Springfield, OH: H. K. Skinner and Son, 1971), 467. See also, generally, 458–74.

38. Order Books, vol. A, 451 (September term 1819); Ayers, *Hills of Highland*, 231–33, 451.

39. Don E. Fehrenbacher, *Slavery, Law, and Politics: The Dred Scott Case in Historical Perspective* (New York: Oxford University Press, 1981), 29.

40. Finkelman, *Imperfect Union*, 89–91, 237–43. See also ibid., 9 for an excellent discussion of the definition of "in transit."

41. See Fehrenbacher, *Slavery, Law, and Politics*, 29; Finkelman, *Imperfect Union*, 90–92.

42. Davis v. Casey, Order Books, 1:8–79 (September 12, 1820). Ohio did have strong laws against harboring fugitive slaves, and Governor Thomas Worthington, in 1817, insisted that Ohio enforce those laws as well as the federal Fugitive Slave Act of 1793. Leo Alilunas, "Fugitive Slave Cases in Ohio Prior to 1850," *Ohio State Archaeological and Historical Quarterly* 49 (April 1940): 164–66.

43. For the routine case load, see Journals (Order Books), 1807–1911 and Records (Journals), 1808–1868 in General Records, United States Circuit Court, Southern District of Ohio, W. Div., RG 21; Chancery Record Books, 1828–1911, Chancery Records, United States Circuit Court, Southern District of Ohio, W. Div., RG 21.

44. *Scioto Gazette*, October 23, 1806, 3.

45. Rice, "Biographical Sketch."

46. See, e.g., *Scioto Gazette*, October 24, 1805, 3; October 23, 1806, 3; October 30, 1806, 3; November 6, 1806, 2; November 13, 1806, 3; November 20, 1806, 2; November 27, 1806, 2; and December 26, 1806, 3. The paper continued to publish information on the conspiracy and the proceedings in the various federal courts against Burr and his fellow conspirators. See, e.g., ibid., January 8, 1807, 3; February 5, 1807, 2, 3; and February 12, 1807, 1–3.

47. *Scioto Gazette*, February 12, 1807, 3.

48. Indictment, Records relating to proposed trials of Aaron Burr and Harman Blennerhassett, August 1, 1805 to January 21, 1808, RG 21, microfilm T265. Indictments were returned in the January 1808 term. See also recognizance of Blennerhassett with a Mr. Smith and John Cummings as sureties and of Burr with Luther Martin and John Cummings as sureties, for their appearance before the Seventh Circuit Court at Chillicothe, dated October 20, 1807, and summons for various witnesses, ibid.; *Scioto Gazette*, October 1, 1807, 3; January 4, 1808, 2; January 11, 1808, 2; and September 6, 1808, 3; Edward Tiffin Papers, MIC 96, roll 1, Ohio Historical Society, Columbus; John Weld Peck, "The Federal Courts of Ohio," in Marshall, *History of the Courts and Lawyers of Ohio*, 3:707–8; Utter, *Frontier State*, 69–77. For information on Blennerhassett, see J. Fletcher Brennan, ed., *The Biographical Cyclopaedia and Portrait Gallery with an Historical Sketch of the State of Ohio* (Cincinnati: Western Biographical Publishing, 1883–1884), 1:46; *Dayton Daily News*, March 5, 1939, 9. Meigs, the grand jury foreman, later became chief justice of the Ohio Supreme Court, a U.S. senator from Ohio, and, in 1810, governor of Ohio. *Dayton Daily News*, March 5, 1939, 9; Peck, "Federal Courts of Ohio," 706. For information on Baldwin, see Evans and Stivers, *History of Adams County*, 509; Ratcliffe, *Party Spirit*, 111, 138.

These records were lost to the public for more than a hundred years until they were found in the courthouse basement. Then the records were reprinted in Ohio newspapers, educating citizens about one of the important roles the lower federal courts played in the nation's early history. The *Cincinnati Daily Times-Star*, July 4, 1927, 3, reprinted many of the documents including the indictment and some correspondence by Burr and President Thomas Jefferson. The *Dayton Daily News,* March 5, 1939, 9, published a story about the original documents along with Judge Robert Nevin's summary of the case.

49. Osborn v. Bank of U.S., 22 U.S. (9 Wheat.) 738 (1824).

50. A Lexis shepardizing search on December 9, 2003, gives an indication of the case's continued importance. The search yielded 1,625 citing decisions, 2,190 total citations, and over 500 references in law review articles.

51. See, e.g., Edward S. Kaplan, *The Bank of the United States and the American Economy* (Westport, CT: Greenwood Press, 1999), ix-x, 22–25, 29–33, 49–64, 97–139; James Roger Sharp, *American Politics in the Early Republic: The New Nation in Crisis* (New Haven, CT: Yale University Press, 1993), 38–41, 283–84.

52. Utter, *Frontier State,* 283. See also Ratcliffe, *Party Spirit,* 223–24.

53. Whereas the nation's population increased by one-third between 1810 and 1820, Ohio's population increased from 230,760 to 581,434, an increase of more than 150 percent.

54. Charles Clifford Huntington, *A History of Banking and Currency in Ohio before the Civil War* (Columbus: F. J. Heer Printing, 1915), 57–59. See also ibid., 41–42; Utter, *Frontier State,* 276–98.

55. Huntington, *History of Banking and Currency in Ohio,* 60–62.

56. Ibid., 62–71; Utter, *Frontier State,* 276, 290–98; Ratcliffe, *Party Spirit,* 224–25.

57. *Chillicothe Supporter,* September 2, 1818, 2; Huntington, *History of Banking and Currency in Ohio,* 86–87. For a history of Ohio's banking legislation, see Huntington, *History of Banking and Currency in Ohio,* 57–62, and Utter, *Frontier State,* 263–312.

58. Huntington, *History of Banking and Currency in Ohio,* 87.

59. Osborn v. Bank of U.S., 22 U.S. at 740; *Chillicothe Supporter,* January 17, 1819, 2–3 (see also September 6, 1818, 2 and September 16, 1818, 2); Huntington, *History of Banking and Currency in Ohio,* 86–89. Ohio was not the first state to come to these conclusions and recommend this solution. Maryland was the first state to place a tax on the activities of the bank's branches in its state. Kentucky followed suit. See Huntington, *History of Banking and Currency in Ohio,* 63–85.

60. Osborn v. Bank of U.S., 22 U.S. at 740.

61. McCulloch v. Maryland, 17 U.S. (4 Wheat.) 316 (1819).

62. Osborn v. Bank of U.S., 22 U.S. at 740–41; injunction, Case No. 1135, Osborn v. Bank of U.S., proceedings of U.S. Circuit Court, District of Ohio, Appellate Case Files of the United States Supreme Court, 1792–1831, RG M214, National Archives, reel 58.

63. Affidavit of Ralph Osborn, January 10, 1820, delivered to the Circuit Court of the United States for the Seventh Circuit and for the District of Ohio in Chillicothe before Hon. Thomas Todd and Charles W. Byrd on January 6, 1820, by Osborn's attorneys, Osborn v. Bank of U.S., RG M214, reel 58. James M'Dowell, the man the marshal authorized to serve Osborn, denied Osborn's claim. See Osborn v. Bank of U.S., 22 U.S. at 741.

64. Affidavits by William Creighton Jr., Abraham G. Claypoole, and John S. Harper detailing the events of September 17, 1819, Osborn v. Bank of U.S., RG M214, reel 58.

65. Osborn v. Bank of U.S., 22 U.S. at 741. See also proceedings of the Seventh Circuit, Osborn v. Bank of U.S., RG M214, reel 58.

66. See proceedings of the Seventh Circuit, Osborn v. Bank of U.S., RG M214, reel 58; Huntington, *History of Banking and Currency in Ohio*, 85–100; *Cincinnati Inquisitor and Advertiser*, September 28, 1819, 2 reprinting article in *Chillicothe Supporter*.

67. See, e.g., *Scioto Gazette*, February 10, 1820, 2, reprinting article from the *Steubenville Gazette* arguing that a federal court had no jurisdiction over this or any other such case and therefore that Harper and Orr were illegal detained; *Scioto Gazette and Fredonian Chronicle*, September 24, 1819, 4, and October 1, 1819, 2. See also Utter, *Frontier State*, 302–12; Ratcliffe, *Party Spirit*, 225–27.

68. These were resolutions written by Thomas Jefferson and James Madison in 1798 and passed by the legislatures of Kentucky and Virginia, attacking the constitutionality of the Sedition Act passed by Congress that year to curtail attacks on the Adams's administration and its foreign policy toward France. Jefferson and Madison argued that the federal government had no constitutional authority to enact sedition laws and that states could judge for themselves whether federal laws were constitutional.

69. *Cincinnati Inquisitor and Advertiser*, January 3, 1819, 2. See also ibid., January 3, 1821, for another committee report denouncing the federal court for exceeding its jurisdiction and reaffirming its belief in state sovereignty. See also *Cincinnati Advertiser*, October 12, 1819, 3, reporting a meeting of some Cincinnatians, urging caution in "array[ing] this state against the general government."

70. Osborn v. Bank of U.S., RG M214, roll 58, frame 147. See also Huntington, *History of Banking and Currency in Ohio*, 85–100; Brennan, *Biographical Cyclopaedia*, 52–53; Peck, "Federal Courts of Ohio," 727–30; Ethan A. Brown Papers and Charles Hammond Papers, Ohio Historical Society, Columbus.

71. Osborn v. Bank of U.S., 22 U.S. at 744 and 804; Peck, "Federal Courts of Ohio," 730. Hammond, a prominent Whig, editor of the *Cincinnati Gazette*, and a member of the Ohio General Assembly, had been the legislator who had proposed withdrawing the protection of Ohio's laws from the Bank of the United States. Ratcliffe, *Party Spirit*, 179–80. John Wright served as a representative from Ohio in the U.S. Congress in the 1820s and as a justice of the Ohio Supreme Court in the 1830s. See http://bioguide.congress.gov.

72. Osborn v. U.S., 22 U.S. at 804.

73. Ibid., 816–71.

74. Ibid., 871.

75. Evans and Stivers, *History of Adams County*, 509; Cayton, "Failure of Michael Baldwin," 46.

76. Byrd to Todd, January 29, 1812, Charles E. Rice Collection.

77. See Cayton, *Frontier Republic*, 76–80; Donald J. Ratcliffe, *The Politics of Long Division: The Birth of the Second Party System in Ohio, 1818–1828* (Columbus: Ohio State University Press, 2000), passim, but esp. 258, 299–335.

78. Utter, *Frontier State*, 63.

79. Ibid., 391–93.

80. Ratcliffe, *Politics of Long Division*, passim, but esp. 299, 305–35.

81. Ibid., 225.

82. Order Books, 2:170 (December term 1828). Presidents make recess appointments when Congress is not in session.

83. Quotation by Thomas C. Flournoy, an Adams Republican and Creighton supporter, cited in Ratcliffe, *Politics of Long Division,* 225. See also Bicentennial Committee of the Judicial Conference of the United States, *Judges of the United States,* 2d ed. (Washington, DC: Government Printing Office, 1983), 112. For detailed biographical information on Creighton, see chapter 9.

84. *Senate Executive Journal,* 20th Cong., 2d sess., 621 (December 11, 1828), 645 (February 16, 1829). See also *Cincinnati Advertiser,* February 18, 1829, 3.

85. Order Books, 2:170–73 (December 18–21, 1828).

86. *Senate Executive Journal,* 21st Cong., 1st sess., 6 (March 6, 1829), 7 (March 7, 1829). At the same time, Jackson nominated John McLean of Cincinnati to be an associate justice of the U.S. Supreme Court and the judge who would sit with Campbell as the court of the Seventh Circuit to replace Justice Todd, who had also died in 1828. McLean, too, was confirmed on March 7. McLean's slot was available because, at the same time that the Senate refused to vote on Creighton, they also refused to consider Adams's nomination of John Crittenden of Kentucky to the Supreme Court position. *Cincinnati Advertiser,* February 18, 1829, 3. For biographical information on McLean, see Marshall, *History of the Courts and Lawyers of Ohio,* 3:811–13.

87. Ratcliffe, *Politics of Long Division,* 124; John W. Campbell, *Biographical Sketches with Other Literary Remains of the Late John W. Campbell, Compiled by His Widow* (Columbus: Scott & Gallagher, 1838), 2–8. For more detailed biographical information on Campbell, see chapter 9.

88. Order Books, vol. 2, passim, and July term 1831; ibid., 12:1–6 and passim.

89. Because McLean missed only two sessions during the more than twenty years he sat with Judge Humphrey Leavitt, it is likely that Campbell and McLean sat jointly for the circuit court sessions. "Humphrey Howe Leavitt," 43.

90. Ewing v. Burnet, 8 F. Cas. 931 (C.C.D. Ohio 1835) (No. 4,591).

91. Frank G. Davis, "Lessee of Ewing v. Burnet," in *The Law in Southwestern Ohio,* ed. George P. Stimson (Cincinnati: Cincinnati Bar Association, 1972), 419.

92. See Lessee of Ewing v. Burnet, 36 U.S. (11 Pet.) 41 (1837); Ewing v. Burnet, 8 F. Cas. 931 (C.C.D. Ohio 1835) (No. 4,591). The circuit court, in charging the jury, explained that an adverse claimant need not actually occupy or cultivate the land to assert his claim, but need only show continued, public use. After hearing these instructions, the jury held for Burnet, the adverse claimant, finding that he had used or leased the land as a gravel pit continually from 1804. Justice Henry Baldwin, writing the Supreme Court's opinion affirming the lower court, emphasized that in determining adverse possession "so much depends on the nature and situation of the land [and] . . . the uses to which it can be applied," that the Court should not lay down any "precise rule." Continual use, appropriate for the land at issue, is sufficient. Lessee of Ewing v. Burnet, 36 U.S. at 53. Although McLean reported the circuit court charge to the jury, in his reports he published not only his rulings and orders but those of other judges as well.

93. Cincinnati v. Lessee of White, 31 U.S. (6 Pet.) 431, 433 (1832). In the original suit heard in the circuit court, White's lessee was the plaintiff. The parties were switched at the Supreme Court level, after the city lost the case in the lower court. Although the circuit court's proceedings are unpublished, the facts of the case are summarized in the Supreme Court's decision, which also reports Campbell's instructions to the jury fully.

94. Ibid. at 437–38. The Supreme Court's decision appears to have been unanimous. At least, no dissent was recorded or indicated. This case set a precedent upholding the validity of dedications of land for public use without written documentation; the government entity must only demonstrate that the owner had opened the land up to public use and that the government entity had never explicitly given the land back. See, e.g., Foster v. Bear Valley Irrigation Co., 65 F. 836 (C.C.S.D. Cal. 1895); Barney v. Baltimore, 2 F. Cas. 886 (C.C.D. Md. 1863) (No. 1,029); Sargeant v. State Bank of Indiana, 21 F. Cas. 491 (C.C.D. Ind. 1848) (No. 12,360). Although the Supreme Court's decision in *Charles River Bridge v. Warren Bridge*, 36 U.S. (11 Pet.) 420 (1837), adhering strictly to the provisions of the charter between the state of Massachusetts and the proprietors of the Charles River Bridge and refusing to imply anything beyond the letter of the contract, seemingly contradicted *Cincinnati v. Lessee of White,* the principle that the Court would favor public interests over private property rights remained consistent in both cases.

95. U.S. v. Gwynne, 26 F. Cas. 60, 61–62 (C.C.D. Ohio 1836) (No. 15,272). The Supreme Court case was *Wetmore v. U.S.* 35 U.S. (10 Pet.) 647.

96. Campbell, *Biographical Sketches,* 9.

CHAPTER 2

1. See Letters of Appointment and Recommendation during the Administration of Andrew Jackson in File of Letters of Appointment and Recommendations for Appointment to Federal Office (1791–1901), General Records of the Department of State, RG 59, National Archives Microfilm Publication M639. These records contain nominations or support letters for eight candidates. John Goodenow, Thomas Scott, and James Exum were prominent contenders. Others in the records who received nomination were N. P. Gains, W. W. Irvin, William Kennon, and Humphrey H. Leavitt, the man who eventually won confirmation.

2. Daniel Feller, "Benjamin Tappan: The Making of a Democrat," in *The Pursuit of Public Power: Political Culture in Ohio 1787–1861,* ed. Jeffrey P. Brown and Andrew R. L. Cayton (Kent, OH: Kent State University Press, 1994), 77.

3. Ibid., 71–78. For more detailed biographical information on Tappan, see chapter 9.

4. R. Mitchell to Jackson, October 2, 1833; petition from McConnelsville dated October 2, 1833, signed by thirteen citizens; John Thomson to Jackson, October 3, 1833; Micajah T. Williams to Jackson, October 3, 1833; letter of sundry citizens of Cadiz, October 11, 1833; and Humphrey Leavitt to Jackson, October 7, 1833, in Letters of Appointment and Recommendations during the Administration of Andrew Jackson, RG 59, M639, roll 24.

5. *Journal of the Executive Proceedings of the Senate of the United States,* 23d Cong., 1st sess., 344–45 (January 20, 1834), 402 (May 12, 1834), 412 (May 29, 1834); Feller, "Benjamin Tappan," 78–79; draft of article about Tappan in Benjamin Tappan Papers, Ohio Historical Society, Columbus. By the time Tappan's name came to a vote, Ruggles had been replaced by Democrat senator Thomas Morris, who voted to confirm.

6. Letters of Appointment and Recommendation during the Administration of Andrew Jackson, RG 59, M639.

7. Joseph Benson Foraker, *Notes of a Busy Life* (Cincinnati: Stewart & Kidd, 1916), 1:83, quoted in Irwin S. Rhodes, "The History of the United States District Court for the Southern District of Ohio," *University of Cincinnati Law Review* 24 (Summer 1955): 347n44.

8. "Humphrey Howe Leavitt," *United States Law Magazine* 5 (1850–1852): 37–44. For more detailed biographical information on Leavitt as well as fuller information on his political views, see chapter 9 and elsewhere in this chapter.

9. John Weld Peck, "The Federal Courts of Ohio," in *A History of the Courts and Lawyers of Ohio,* ed. Carrington T. Marshall (New York: American Historical Society, 1934), 3:709.

10. Ibid.; Brown and Cayton, *Pursuit of Public Power,* viii–x; Stephen E. Maizlish, *The Triumph of Sectionalism: The Transformation of Ohio Politics, 1844–1856* (Kent, OH: Kent State University Press, 1983), 1–6; Francis P. Weisenburger, *The Passing of the Frontier, 1825–1850,* vol. 3, *History of the State of Ohio,* ed. Carl Wittke (Columbus: Ohio State Archaeological and Historical Society, 1941–1944), 3–29.

11. Humphrey H. Leavitt, *Autobiography of the Hon. Humphrey Howe Leavitt Written for His Family* (New York: n.p., 1893), 64–66. Indeed, Leavitt had so much "leisure time," that he regularly delivered "public addresses on the subjects of education, temperance, agriculture, etc." Ibid., 66.

12. Judiciary Act of 1842, 5 Stat. 516, 517.

13. Fugitive Slave Act of 1793, 1 Stat. 302, 302–5; Fugitive Slave Act of 1850, 9 Stat. 462, 462–65.

14. An Act to Divide the State of Ohio into Two Judicial Districts, 10 Stat. 605 (1855). Although Leavitt was assigned to the southern district, the U.S. attorney and U.S. marshal for the District of Ohio were assigned to the northern district, requiring Leavitt to adjust to two new officers of the court who would be appointed by the president.

Before Congress divided the state into two districts, it experimented with one district sitting in two cities. In 1842, Congress mandated that the district court hold one session in Cincinnati and one session in Columbus each year. This obviously did not work well, and Congress ended the experiment in 1844. An Act to amend . . . "An act to change the time of holding the circuit and district courts in the district of Ohio," 5 Stat. 488, 488–89 (1842); An Act to repeal the act entitled "An act to amend . . . ," 5 Stat. 652 (1844). Congress also adjusted the circuit courts. In 1837, it established the eighth and ninth circuits and reconfigured the seventh to include Ohio, Indiana, Michigan, and Illinois. Kentucky and Tennessee along with Missouri composed the new Eighth Circuit. An Act to Establish the Eighth and Ninth Circuits, 5 Stat. 176 (1837).

15. Charles Theodore Greve, *Centennial History of Cincinnati and Representative Citizens* (Chicago: Biographical Publishing, 1904), 1:672; 10 Stat. 605 (1855). The court could also authorize additional sessions if its business required it.

16. *Ohio State Journal,* January 11, 1854, 2; February 17, 1854, 2.

17. Peck, "Federal Courts of Ohio," 710, quoting Leavitt's retirement speech of 1871. See also Leavitt, *Autobiography,* 73.

18. See Order Books, passim, General Records, Western Division, Records of the U.S. District Court, Southern District of Ohio, RG 21, National Archives Branch Depository, Great Lakes Region, Chicago, IL (hereafter Order Books); Records (Journals), 1814–1842, passim, General Records, Western Division, Records of the U.S. District Court, Southern District of Ohio, RG 21, National Archives Branch Depository, Great Lakes Region, Chicago, IL (hereafter Order Books). Hereafter, all the records of the U.S. District Court, Southern District of Ohio, will be identified simply as RG 21

19. Rhodes, "History of the District Court," 344–47.

20. See Civil Case Files (Old Series) 1847–1862, Civil Records, Circuit Court, W. Div., RG 21; Rhodes, "History of the District Court," 345; Peck, "Federal Courts of Ohio," 709–12. For violations of neutrality laws, see In re Charge to Grand Jury–Neutrality Laws, 30 F. Cas. 1018 (C.C.D. Ohio 1838) (No. 18,265); In re Charge to Grand Jury–Neutrality Laws, 30 F. Cas. 1021 (C.C.D. Ohio 1851) (No. 18,267); U.S. v. Lumsden, 26 F. Cas. 1013 (C.C.S.D. Ohio 1856) (No. 15,641).

21. Order Books, 2:235.

22. Civil (Law) Records, 1842–1918, vol. 2 (July term 1845 and November term 1849), Civil Records, W. Div., RG 21. There were regularly one to a dozen trespass cases each term during the antebellum period.

23. Mixed Case Files, 1856–1925, General Records, W. Div., RG 21, passim.

24. An act of Congress enacted in July 1838 required all steamboats engaged in interstate commerce to be licensed and to employ only licensed pilots. An Act to Provide for the Better Security of the Lives of Passengers on Board Vessels Propelled by Steam, 5 Stat. 304 (1838). In its November 1849 session, Leavitt promulgated rules to enforce a congressional law that extended the jurisdiction of district courts to certain cases on the lakes and navigable waters of the United States. Records (Journals), W. Div., 1:1–5; An Act making appropriations . . . , and for other Purposes, 9 Stat. 380, 382 (1849).

25. William J. Novak, *The People's Welfare: Law and Regulation in Nineteenth-Century America* (Chapel Hill: University of North Carolina Press, 1996), 131.

26. Greve, *Centennial History of Cincinnati,* 1:497–98, 540–44, 603–5.

27. Congress's regulation of river traffic was part of a broader movement to provide for a "well-regulated society." Both William Novak and Harry Scheiber document how state legislatures, and especially the Ohio legislature, promoted economic prosperity by regulating economic activities seen to be in the public interest as well as embarking on economic enterprises such as the construction of canals and the subsidization of railroads. Novak, *The People's Welfare,* x, 1–2; Scheiber, *Ohio Canal Era: A Case Study of Government and the Economy, 1820–1861* (Athens: Ohio University Press, 1969).

28. Leavitt, *Autobiography*, 73.

29. Although the four categories discussed below were the most common, Leavitt did occasionally hear a different type of case. One, for example, involved a "malicious assault" on the steamboat *Metropolis*. A jury found the ship's first engineer guilty of assaulting another crewmember. U.S. v. William Curley, Civil (Law) Records, W. Div., 2:188–89 (October term 1857) and Order Books, 3:173. While this case is archived in the law records, it might, indeed, be a criminal case: a grand jury indicted Curley for the assault, which, because it occurred on a steamboat engaged in interstate commerce, fell under federal jurisdiction.

30. See Order Books, vols. 2–3, passim. See, e.g., U.S. v. Sundry Goods, Order Books, 2:249 (July term 1835) and 2:291 (July term 1838); U.S. v. Schooner Hunter, ibid., 2:261 (December term 1835); U.S. v. The Water Witch, ibid., 2:271 (December term 1836); U.S. v. 128 Packages of Goods and 15 Blankets, ibid., 2:321–22 (December term 1839).

31. See U.S. v. The Steam Boat Warren, Order Books, 2:311 (July term 1839), 2:322–25 (December term 1839), and 2:336–40 (July term 1840); Campbell v. Pearce, Civil (Law) Records, 2:184 (June term 1857); Campbell v. Rogers, ibid., 2:184 (June term 1857) and 2:190–200 (October term 1857); U.S. v. Bougher, 24 F. Cas. 1205 (C.C.D. Ohio 1854) (No. 14,627). For the rules that the court followed in such proceedings, see Journals, 1849–1921, 1:1–5, General Records, W. Div., RG 21 (hereafter Journals, W. Div.). Leavitt proclaimed these rules at the court's November 1849 term after Congress extended the jurisdiction of the district courts to certain cases on the lakes and navigable waters of the United States.

32. U.S. v. The Steam Boat Warren, Order Books, 2:311 (July term 1839), 2:322–25 (December term 1839), and 2:336–400 (July term 1840). No records have been found that indicate what the *Warren* was worth, how much the government received from the sale, or whether Moore received any of the proceeds after his fine and costs were paid from the sale. But steamboats were certainly worth more than $500. The first steamboat built in Cincinnati, the *New Orleans,* was valued at $40,000 when it was launched in 1811. The *Jacob Strader,* built in 1853, cost $170,000. Benjamin F. Klein, ed., *The Ohio River: Handbook and Picture Album* (Cincinnati: Young and Klein, 1959), 165, 184.

33. See Davis v. Schooner Kewaumee and Garbit v. Schooner Chief Justice Marshall, Order Books, 2:293, 296 (July term 1838); Ball v. The Steam Boat Ambassador, Cassilly v. The Steamboat Ambassador, and sundry other unnamed suits against the *Ambassador,* Mixed Case Files, W. Div., Dis. Civ. boxes 13, 25, and 61; Decamp vs. The Steam Boat Kate French, Mixed Case Files, Dis. Civ. box 40; The Eolian, 8 F. Cas. 740 (C.C.S.D. Ohio 1860) (No. 4,504). A few cases provided Leavitt with the opportunity to assert federal supremacy over state laws. See, e.g., Dudley v. The Superior and Sexton v. The Troy, 7 F. Cas. 1160 (S.D. Ohio 1855) (No. 4,115) (deciding that workers and those repairing a ship in a port, all being local, cannot sue in admiralty, but have recourse only under state laws); The N. W. Thomas, 18 F. Cas. 502 (C.C.S.D. Ohio 1857) (No. 10,386) (affirming Leavitt's district court decision that, as between a purchaser enforcing an admiralty lien and a purchaser having a claim based on a state court order, the former has the better title).

34. Steamboat Nathan Holmes v. Owners of the Cuba, Mixed Case Files, W. Div., Dis. Civ. box 27; Delaware Mut. Safety Ins. Co. v. Davis, ibid., box 1. For examples of cases involving insurance policy claims, see Delaware Mutual Safety Insurance Co. v. Packages of Merchandise Shipped and Aetna Insurance Company v. Packages of Merchandise Shipped, Journals, W. Div., 1:25–45, March–April 1853. See also Scott v. The Dick Keyes, 21 F. Cas. 823 (S.D. Ohio 1857) (No. 12,528), aff'd, 7 F. Cas. 678 (C.C.S.D. Ohio 1863) (No. 3,898) (holding that a contract made by masters of two steamboats for the use of a barge on the Mississippi and Ohio rivers is cognizable in admiralty and affirming Leavitt's use of the laws of contract to decide the case). Additional information on this case is in Journals, W. Div., 1:58–59.

35. See, e.g., Thorpe v. The Steamboat Defender, Mixed Case Files, W. Div., Dis. Civ. boxes 35 and 36; Haywood v. Steam Boat Buckeye Belle and Mills v. The Steamer Nathaniel W. Holmes, ibid., box 27; Steam Boat Golden Gate v. Steam Boat Ohio and Steamboat Ambassador v. Keys, ibid., box 25; Lucas v. The Thomas Swann, 15 F. Cas. 1065 (D. Ohio 1854) (No. 8,588).

36. Ward v. The Ogdensburgh, 29 F. Cas. 199, 202 (D. Ohio 1853) (No. 17,158).

37. Ibid., 201.

38. Ibid., 203, 206; Ward v. Chamberlain, 29 F. Cas. 169 (C.C. Ohio 1855) (No. 17,151).

39. Ward v. Chamberlain, 29 F. Cas. at 175.

40. Ward v. Chamberlain, 62 U.S. 572 (1858).

41. McGinnis v. The Pontiac, 16 F. Cas. 112, 112–16 (D. Ohio 1852) (No. 8,801). For examples of other courts' application of Leavitt's new principle, see, e.g., The Connemara v. The Joseph Cooper Jr., 108 U.S. 352 (1883); The Western Star, 157 F. 489 (D. Wisc. 1907); Seven Coal Barges, 21 F. Cas. 1096 (C.C.D. Ind. 1870) (No. 12,677). See also the following treatises and legal authorities: "Place of Rendering Service," C.J.S. Salvage § 61 (2003); Martin J. Norris, "Crew Salving Own Vessel," The Law of Seamen (2002): § 9:27; Laura Hunter Dietz, "Master or Crew Salving Own Vessel," 68 Am. Jur. 2d Salvage § 48 (2003).

42. Genesee Chief v. Fitzhugh, 53 U.S. (12 How.) 443 (1852).

43. McGinnis v. The Pontiac, 16 F. Cas. at 116.

44. Note, "From Judicial Grant to Legislative Power: The Admiralty Clause in the Nineteenth Century," Harvard Law Review 67 (May 1954): 1214–37, esp. 1214–15 and 1225–26 (quote at 1226). One Ohioan attempted to persuade Congress to restore the tidewater limits doctrine. See Cincinnati Gazette, February 13, 1869, cited ibid., 1226 and note 89.

45. U.S. v. Bougher, 24 F. Cas. 1205 (C.C.D. Ohio 1854) (No. 14,627).

46. Ibid., 1206. Leavitt was interpreting the Steamboat Act of 1852 "to provide for the better security of the lives of passengers on board vessels propelled in whole or in part by steam" (Pamph. Laws, U.S., 32d Cong., 1st sess.). There were other occasions, outside of admiralty actions, where Leavitt again asserted federal authority over state courts. See Doe v. Johnston, 7 F. Cas. 803 (D. Ohio n.d.) (No. 3,958) (in an ejectment proceeding, asserting that because the federal court had authority based on diversity jurisdiction, there was no need to await the result of

proceedings in state court to determine proper title over the property in dispute); Hall v. Warren, 11 F. Cas. 275 (C.C.D. Ohio 1840) (No. 5,952) (asserting that the federal district court had broad authority in enforcing the country's revenue laws).

47. The N. W. Thomas, 18 F. Cas. 502 (C.C.S.D Ohio 1857) (No. 10,386).

48. Congress, on that date, enacted An act to establish a uniform system of Bankruptcy throughout the United States, 5 Stat. 440 (1841; repealed 1843). For a history of this law, its goals, and its political, economic, and legal implications, see David A. Skeel Jr., *Debt's Dominion: A History of Bankruptcy Law in America* (Princeton, NJ: Princeton University Press, 2001); Edward J. Balleisen, *Navigating Failure: Bankruptcy and Commercial Society in Antebellum America* (Chapel Hill: University of North Carolina Press, 2001).

49. Bankruptcy Decree Book, 1:49, Bankruptcy Records, W. Div., RG 21; Order Book, vol. 1, Bankruptcy Records, August 19, 1841, n.p.

50. Bankruptcy Decree Book, vol. 1, passim.

51. See, e.g., In re Hunter, 12 F. Cas. 950 (C.C. Ohio 1843) (No. 6,902); In re Book, 3 F. Cas. 867 (C.C. Ohio 1843) (No. 1,637); Collins v. Hood, 6 F. Cas. 129 (C.C. Ohio 1846) (No. 3,015). Leavitt rarely stopped bankruptcy proceedings, thereby siding, according to Balleisen, with the Whig judges who enforced the law, which favored voluntary bankruptcy, tending to see the law as giving debtors "a new lease on life." Balleisen, *Navigating Failure*, 114.

52. Leavitt, *Autobiography*, 65.

53. U.S. v. Hanks and U.S. v. Pickett, Order Books, vol. 3, n.p. (October 17–November 6, 1854).

54. See Order Books, vol. 3, passim.

55. Paul Finkelman, *An Imperfect Union: Slavery, Federalism, and Comity* (Chapel Hill: University of North Carolina Press, 1981), 155.

56. Ibid.; see also Greve, *Centennial History of Cincinnati*, 749.

57. Leo Alilunas, "Fugitive Slave Cases in Ohio Prior to 1850," *Ohio State Archaeological and Historical Quarterly* 49 (April 1940): 160.

58. Weisenburger, *Passing of the Frontier*, 50.

59. Marshall, *History of the Courts and Lawyers of Ohio*, 2:591; Simeon D. Fess, ed., *Ohio: A Four-Volume Reference Library on the History of a Great State* (Chicago: Lewis Publishing, 1937), 1:267; Finkelman, *Imperfect Union*, 156; Donald J. Ratcliffe, *Party Spirit in a Frontier Republic: Democratic Politics in Ohio, 1793–1821* (Columbus: Ohio State University Press, 1998), 86–87.

60. Eugene H. Roseboom, *The Civil War Era, 1850–1873*, vol. 4, *The History of the State of Ohio*, ed. Carl Wittke (Columbus: Ohio State Archaeological and Historical Society, 1941–1944), 111. Weisenburger, *Passing of the Frontier*, 350–51, 363–86, 456–57, 463–77; Charlotte Reeve Conover, *Dayton, Ohio: An Intimate History* (New York: Lewis Historical Publishing, 1902), 42–43; Utter, *Frontier State*, 328.

61. For Ohio's Black Laws, see An Act to Regulate Black and Mulatto Persons, 2 Laws of Ohio 63 (1803); An Act to amend . . . "An Act to Regulate Black and Mulatto Persons," 5 Laws of Ohio 53 (1807). For changing school laws, see Roseboom, *Civil War Era*, 193–94; David A. Gerber, *Black Ohio and the Color Line, 1860–1915* (Urbana: University of Illinois Press, 1976), 4–5, 72. But Paul Finkelman points out

that before the 1853 statute Ohio courts had held that some mulattos were not excluded by state statute from public schools. Moreover, some African American children attended private schools. Thus, in 1860 almost 40 percent of Ohio's black students attended school. Paul Finkelman, "Prelude to the Fourteenth Amendment: Black Legal Rights in the Antebellum North," *Rutgers Law Journal* 17 (Spring–Summer 1986): 474. For more details on Ohio laws, see Finkelman, "Prelude to the Fourteenth Amendment," 424–28; Alilunas, "Fugitive Slave Cases in Ohio," 160–67, 169–76.

62. Gerber, *Black Ohio*, 5–24; Andrew R. L. Cayton, *Ohio: The History of a People* (Columbus: Ohio State University Press, 2002), 110; Stanley W. Campbell, *The Slave Catchers: Enforcement of the Fugitive Slave Law, 1850–1860* (Chapel Hill: University of North Carolina Press, 1968), 90.

63. Cayton, *Ohio*, 26, 118–19; Maizlish, *Triumph of Sectionalism*, 7–8; Weisenburger, *Passing of the Frontier*, 3:40–42.

64. Maizlish, *Triumph of Sectionalism*, 7–8; Weisenburger, *Passing of the Frontier*, 40–42; Cayton, *Ohio*, 26, 109, 118–19; Greve, *Centennial History of Cincinnati*, 1:750–52; Henry A. Ford and Kate B. Ford, *History of Cincinnati, Ohio* (Cleveland: L. A. Williams, 1881), 102. Finkelman emphasizes that Ohio's black population grew continually, increasing from 9,568 in 1830 to 25,279 in 1850 and to 36,673 in 1860. He argues that this growth indicates that the laws restricting black migrants were not strictly enforced. Finkelman, "Prelude to the Fourteenth Amendment," 436–37. Although this is certainly true, the percentage of African Americans as a part of the total Ohio population increased from 1 percent to 1.6 percent between 1840 and 1860. Finkelman also emphasizes that Cincinnati by 1850 "ranked third among American cities in the number of free blacks owning property," indicating that, "despite the city's southern proximity and racist reputation, free blacks were relatively well accepted." Ibid., 436n127.

65. Fugitive Slave Act of 1793, 1 Stat. 302.

66. For Ohio's laws regarding the rendition of fugitive slaves, see the Act to Punish Kidnaping, 17 Laws of Ohio 56 (1819); Act Relating to Fugitives from Labor or Service from Other States, 37 Laws of Ohio 38 (1839). After the Supreme Court decision in *Prigg v. Pennsylvania*, 41 U.S. (16 Pet.) 539 (1842), declared that enforcement of the fugitive slave provision of the Constitution rested exclusively with the federal government, the Ohio legislature repealed its fugitive slave laws. An Act to repeal an Act entitled "An Act relating to Fugitives," 41 Laws of Ohio 13 (1843).

67. Alilunas, "Fugitive Slave Cases in Ohio," 167–69, 176–77.

68. Fess, *Ohio*, 1:268–69. See also Finkelman, "Prelude to the Fourteenth Amendment," 426.

69. Alilunas, "Fugitive Slave Cases in Ohio," 162–63; Marshall, *History of the Courts and Lawyers of Ohio*, 2:596; Fess, *Ohio*, 1:268–69, 4:74–77; Greve, *Centennial History of Cincinnati*, 1:593–94, 597–600; Weisenburger, *Passing of the Frontier*, 3:350–51, 363–86, 456–57, 463–77; Conover, *Dayton, Ohio*, 42–43; Ratcliffe, *Party Spirit*, 86–87; Utter, *Frontier State*, 2:328. Richard L. Aynes, "*Bradwell v. Illinois:* Chief Justice Chase's Dissent and the 'Sphere of Women's Work,'" *Louisiana Law Review* 59 (Winter 1999): 521–41; J. Fletcher Brennan, ed., *The Biographical Cyclopaedia and Portrait Gallery*

*with an Historical Sketch of the State of Ohio* (Cincinnati: Western Biographical Publishing, 1883–1884), 1:60. For a sample of Chase's arguments, see Jones v. Van Zandt, 13 F. Cas. 1047 (C.C.D. Ohio 1843) (No. 7,502), 46 U.S. 215 (1847), 13 F. Cas. 1054 (C.C.D. Ohio 1849) (No. 7,503), 13 F. Cas. 1056 (C.C.D. Ohio 1849) (No. 7,504), 13 F. Cas. 1057 (C.C.D. Ohio 1851) (No. 7,505); Driskill v. Parrish, 7 F. Cas. 1100 (C.C.D. Ohio 1845) (No. 4,089), 7 F. Cas. 1093 (C.C.D. Ohio 1847) (No. 4,087), 7 F. Cas. 1095 (C.C.D. Ohio 1849) (No. 4,088), 7 F. Cas. 1068 (C.C.D. Ohio 1851) (No. 4,075). For biographical information on Chase, see Marshall, *History of the Courts and Lawyers of Ohio,* 3:815–21.

70. Alilunas, "Fugitive Slave Cases in Ohio," 168; Fess, ed., *Ohio,* 1:271.

71. Campbell, *Slave Catchers,* 56–57.

72. Ford, *History of Cincinnati,* 87–92; Greve, *Centennial History of Cincinnati,* 1:597–600.

73. William C. Cochran, "The Western Reserve and the Fugitive Slave Law: A Prelude to the Civil War," *Collections of the Western Reserve Historical Society, Publication No. 101* (Cleveland: Western Reserve Historical Society, 1920), 110; Alilunas, "Fugitive Slave Cases in Ohio," 169–83.

74. Alilunas, "Fugitive Slave Cases in Ohio," 177–80, discussing State v. Hoppess, 1 Ohio Dec. Reprint 105 (1845), and Richardson v. Beebee, 10 Ohio Dec. Reprint 563 (1844). See also Finkelman, *Imperfect Union,* 167–71.

75. Don E. Fehrenbacher, *Slavery, Law, and Politics: The Dred Scott Case in Historical Perspective* (New York: Oxford University Press, 1981), 26–31. Finkelman, however, challenges this conclusion, citing an unreported 1817 case in which the Ohio chief justice "asserted that slaves brought into the state" voluntarily became free. Finkelman, "Prelude to the Fourteenth Amendment," 447–48. Although one case is significant, the general rule Fehrenbacher articulated prevailed during the first three decades of the nineteenth century.

76. Fehrenbacher, *Slavery, Law, and Politics,* 26–31.

77. Finkelman, *Imperfect Union,* 164–66.

78. Ibid., 238.

79. Jones v. Van Zandt, 13 F. Cas. 1040, 1045–46 (C.C.D. Ohio 1843) (No. 7,501), 13 F. Cas. 1047 (C.C.D. Ohio 1843) (No. 7,502), 46 U.S. (5 How.) 215 (1847). See also Alilunas, "Fugitive Slave Cases in Ohio," 180–82; Finkelman, *Imperfect Union,* 159, 245–47; John Niven, *Salmon P. Chase: A Biography* (New York: Oxford University Press, 1995), 76–83, 185. On the issue of the constitutionality of the 1793 Fugitive Slave Act, McLean and Leavitt "recorded a difference of opinion" so Chase could bring an appeal before the Supreme Court. While that case became "an important cause célèbre for the antislavery movement," the Supreme Court developed no new constitutional law, sustaining the Cincinnati jurors and McLean's charge to them. Finkelman, *Imperfect Union,* 246; Niven, *Salmon P. Chase,* 81. Even after the Supreme Court's decision, the case dragged on for another four years. Van Zandt died before the trial on the statutory damages, and the administrators of his estate resisted paying any of the damages. Eventually, the court held that the estate was liable for the damages incurred by the loss of the slave but not the statutory penalty, which could not be imposed on the estate but died with the person. Jones

v. Van Zandt, 13 F. Cas. 1054 (C.C.D. Ohio 1849) (No. 7,503), 13 F. Cas. 1057 (C.C.D. Ohio 1851) (No. 7,505).

80. William M. Wiecek, "Slavery and Abolition before the United States Supreme Court, 1820–1860," *Journal of American History* 65 (June 1978): 48. See also Robert M. Cover, *Justice Accused: Antislavery and the Judicial Process* (New Haven, CT: Yale University Press, 1975), 173.

81. Cover, *Justice Accused*, 119–22, 173–74.

82. Driskill v. Parrish, 7 F. Cas. 1100, 1104 (C.C.D. Ohio 1845) (No. 4,089), 7 F. Cas. 1095, 1100 (C.C.D. Ohio 1849) (No. 4,088). See also Alilunas, "Fugitive Slave Cases in Ohio," 182–83; Cochran, "Western Reserve and the Fugitive Slave Law," 110–12.

83. Fugitive Slave Act of 1850, 9 Stat. 462, 462–65.

84. Campbell, *Slave Catchers*, 56–57.

85. Ibid., 90.

86. *Maysville Eagle*, November 4, 1852, cited ibid., 57; Julius Yanuck, "The Garner Fugitive Slave Case," *Mississippi Valley Historical Review* 40 (June 1953): 50.

87. Campbell, *Slave Catchers*, 88–90. The legislature repealed the statute the following year.

88. Miller v. McQuerry, 17 F. Cas. 335, 340 (C.C.D. Ohio 1853) (No. 9,583); Roseboom, *Civil War Era*, 343; Cover, *Justice Accused*, 119–20, 122, 183; Greve, *Centennial History of Cincinnati*, 759–60. Carpenter, a "respected" member of the Cincinnati bar, resigned as commissioner a year after the McQuerry case, determined not to do that type of work again. Greve, *Centennial History of Cincinnati*, 760.

89. Weimer v. Sloane, 29 F. Cas. 599 (D. Ohio 1854) (No. 17,363); (Law) Records, 2:95ff and esp. 106–7.

90. See Yanuck, "Garner Fugitive Slave Case," 62n66; Maurice Joblin, *Cincinnati, Past and Present, or Its Industrial History* (Cincinnati: Elm Street Printing, 1872), 87; Leavitt, *Autobiography*, 77–78. Henry Howe cites Leavitt's charge to the jury in another case which he believed indicated that Leavitt opposed slavery but believed that federal law had to be enforced. Leavitt told the jury: "Christian charity was not the meaning or intent of the fugitive slave law, and it would not therefore answer as a defense for violating the law." Henry Howe, *Historical Collections of Ohio* (Cincinnati: C. J. Krehbiel, 1902), 1:979. Until the end of his career, Leavitt kept his political and ideological beliefs to himself. It was not until he wrote his autobiography, which some could argue was self-justifying, that he claims to have opposed slavery. But after his retirement from the bench, he actively supported international racial harmony. Fess, *Ohio*, 4:125. And one antebellum newspaper does, while criticizing one of his rulings, label him a Whig. "Federal Encroachments upon State Rights," *Ohio State Journal*, July 16, 1857, 2. Certainly his actions and decisions during the Civil War indicate that he had moved from being a Jacksonian Democrat to a Lincoln Republican.

91. Leavitt, *Autobiography*, 77–78.

92. Weimer v. Sloane, 29 F. Cas. at 603; Civil (Law) Records, 2:106–7.

93. Gibbons v. Sloane, 10 F. Cas. 294 (C.C. Ohio 1854) (No. 5,382). Although the record says "circuit court," the case was heard in district court. See Civil (Law) Records, 2:116.

94. Leavitt, *Autobiography*, 77–78.

95. J. W. Schuckers, *The Life and Public Services of Salmon Portland Chase* (New York: D. Appleton, 1874; reprint New York: Da Capo Press, 1970), 182.

96. Ex parte Robinson, 20 F. Cas. 969 (C.C.S.D. Ohio 1855) (No. 11,935).

97. Cover, *Justice Accused*, 183–85; Finkelman, *Imperfect Union*, 175–76; Greve, *Centennial History of Cincinnati*, 761.

98. Toni Morrison based her Pulitzer Prize–winning novel, *Beloved* (New York: Knopf, 1987), on this case.

99. Ex parte Robinson, 20 F. Cas. 965, 968–69 (C.C.S.D. Ohio 1856) (No. 11,934); *Daily Gazette*, February 1, 1856, cited in Yanuck, "Garner Fugitive Slave Case," 56. See also Yanuck, "Garner Fugitive Slave Case," 47–66; Greve, *Centennial History of Cincinnati*, 762–64; Campbell, *Slave Catchers*, 144–46.

100. Nevin, *Salmon P. Chase*, 184; Yanuck, "Garner Fugitive Slave Case," 62–66; Campbell, *Slave Catchers*, 146. To end the tragedy, the boat Garner and her fellow slaves were on as they headed to Arkansas had an accident; twenty-five passengers died, including another of Garner's children. Campbell, *Slave Catchers*, 146.

101. Ex parte Sifford, 22 F. Cas. 105 (S.D. Ohio 1857) (No. 12,848). For a detailed summary of the entire incident, see Campbell, *Slave Catchers*, 161–64; Benjamin F. Prince, "The Rescue Case of 1857," *Ohio State Archaeological and Historical Society* 16 (July 1907): 292–309.

102. Cited in Schuckers, *Life and Public Services of Chase*, 178–79.

103. Ex parte Sifford, 22 F. Cas. at 105, 111–12. Between 1857 and 1859, in addition to the Sifford case, Leavitt presided over at least six criminal cases in which the U.S. attorney indicted men for either harboring fugitives or obstructing U.S. process. Either some of these cases were weak or the federal law was not being vigorously enforced, because in three of them, the defendants did not appear, their recognizances were forfeited, and the government entered nolle prosequis. U.S. v. Cowan, U.S. v. Layton and Compton, and U.S. v. Taylor, Order Books, 3:172–77. In *U.S. v. Waits*, the jury, after a two-day trial, was unable to agree; the U.S. attorney then decided not to pursue the case further. Ibid., 173–74, 182. In 1859, however, a jury did convict Reuben Johnson of attempting to rescue a fugitive. He was sentenced to thirty days in the Hamilton County Jail and fined $5 plus court costs. U.S. v. Johnson, ibid., 225.

104. Leavitt, *Autobiography*, 79. For details on how other federal judges also upheld federal supremacy and lectured juries on their duty to enforce the 1850 Fugitive Slave Act, see Robert J. Kaczorowski, "Fidelity through History and to It: An Impossible Dream?" *Fordham Law Review* 65 (March 1997): 1663–93; Robert J. Kaczorowski, "The Tragic Irony of American Federalism: National Sovereignty versus State Sovereignty in Slavery and in Freedom," *University of Kansas Law Review* 45 (July 1997): 1015–45, esp. 1027–29.

105. Cited in Campbell, *Slave Catchers*, 108–9.

106. *Ohio State Journal*, July 14, 1857, 2, and July 21, 1857, 2. See also ibid., July 16, 1857, 2, and July 18, 1857, 2.

107. Ibid., July 21, 1857, 2, and July 31, 1857, 2. See also ibid., July 27, 1857, 2, August 10, 1857, 2, and August 13, 1857, 2.

108. Cited ibid., July 16, 1857, 2, and July 31, 1857, 2.

109. Greve, *Centennial History of Cincinnati,* 1:764.

110. Smith v. Swormstedt, 22 F. Cas. 663 (C.C. Ohio 1852) (No. 13,112).

111. Leavitt, *Autobiography,* 99.

112. Smith v. Swormstedt, 57 U.S. (16 How.) 288, 311–13 (1853).

113. See, e.g., Order Books, vol. 3, passim, but esp. September term 1858, September term 1859, and June and October terms 1860.

114. U.S. v. Lumsden, 26 F. Cas. 1013, 1014, 1016, 1019–20 (C.C.S.D. Ohio 1856) (No. 15,641); Peck, "Federal Courts of Ohio," 712; Rhodes, "History of the District Court," 346–47.

115. Leavitt, *Autobiography,* 76. For Leavitt's summary of the case, see ibid., 74–76.

116. U.S. v. Lumsden, 26 F. Cas. at 1013, 1014, 1016, 1019–20; Peck, "Federal Courts of Ohio," 712; Rhodes, "History of the District Court," 346–47. Judge McLean also had two occasions to deal similarly with filibuster activities against Cuba. See In re Charge to Grand Jury—Neutrality Laws, 30 F. Cas. 1018 (C.C. Ohio, 1838) (No. 18,265), and In re Charge to Grand Jury—Neutrality Laws, 30 F. Cas. 1021 (C.C. Ohio 1851) (No. 18,267).

117. See, e.g., Myers v. U.S., 17 F. Cas. 1120 (C.C.D. Ohio 1839) (No. 9,996); U.S. v. Pickett, 27 F. Cas. 528 (S.D. Ohio 1857) (No. 16,043); U.S. v. Hilliard, 26 F. Cas. 321 (C.C.D. Ohio 1843) (No. 15,368).

118. U.S. v. Smith, 27 F. Cas. 1139 (S.D. Ohio 1856) (No. 16,321); Civil (Law) Records, 2:174–76 (October term 1856).

119. U.S. v. Patterson, 27 F. Cas. 464 (C.C. Ohio 1842) (No. 16,009).

120. Sifford to Pugh, Cincinnati, June 18, 1857, in Records Relating to the Appointment of Federal Judges, Marshals, and Attorneys, Ohio (Southern) 1853–1901, box 526, General Records of the Department of Justice, RG 60, National Archives Branch Depository, College Park, MD. Pugh forwarded the complaint to the Attorney General Jeremiah Black.

121. Sifford to "Samuel," March 17, 1860, ibid., box 527.

122. Leavitt, *Autobiography,* 79. For a general history of Ohio during the Civil War, see, e.g., Roseboom, *Civil War Era;* E. O. Randall and Daniel J. Ryan, *History of Ohio,* vol. 4 (New York: Century History, 1912). For histories discussing dissent in Ohio, see Frank L. Klement, *The Copperheads in the Middle West* (Chicago: University of Chicago Press, 1960), and *The Copperheads of the North* (Shippensburg, PA: White Man Publishing, 1999); Jean H. Baker, *Affairs of Party: The Political Culture of Northern Democrats in the Mid-Nineteenth Century* (Ithaca, NY: Cornell University Press, 1981); Louis Leonard Tucker, "Cincinnati during the Civil War," *Publications of the Ohio Civil War Centennial Commission, No. 9* (Columbus: Ohio State University Press, 1962).

123. See Journals, W. Div., vol. 1, 1860–1865, passim; Mixed Case Files, W. Div., Dis. Civ., box 40; Order Books, vol. 3, 1861–1865, passim.

124. For all extant cases, see Journals, W. Div., vol. 1, 1860–1865, passim; Mixed Case Files, W. Div., passim; Order Books, vol. 3, passim.

125. U.S. v. 13 Colt's Navy Revolvers, Mixed Case Files, W. Div., Dis. Civ., box 40; Order Books, vol. 3, n.p. (June–July, 1861).

126. U.S. v. Six Boxes of Arms, 27 F. Cas. 1087, 1088–89 (S.D. Ohio 1861) (No. 16,295).

127. Confiscation Act, 12 Stat. 589 (1862).

128. Journals, W. Div., vol. 1, 1863–1865, passim. After the war, courts had to deal with litigation as heirs of the former rebels filed suit to get the confiscated real estate back. The Supreme Court affirmed that the rebel had only forfeited his life interest in his real property; after his death, the family was entitled to the real estate. Any purchaser of the condemned property only purchased a life estate; he had no right to title in fee simple. Jenkins v. Collard, 145 U.S. 546, 548, 559 (1892).

129. Leavitt, *Autobiography*, 85; Journals, W. Div., vol. 1, 1863–1865, passim.

130. U.S. v. One Hundred and Thirty Barrels of Whiskey, 27 F. Cas. 281, 282 (S.D. Ohio 1865) (No. 15,938).

131. Charge to Grand Jury–Treason, 30 F. Cas. 1036, 1036–38 (C.C.S.D. Ohio 1861) (No. 18,272). Other courts faced with similar charges copied Leavitt's words. See, e.g., U.S. v. Bolles, 209 F. 682 (W.D. Mo. 1913).

132. U.S. v. Chenoweth, Order Books, vol. 3, July 27, 1861.

133. No records could be found which recorded any further proceedings and there were no reports in the *Cincinnati Enquirer* about any trial.

134. Ex parte Vallandigham, 28 F. Cas. 874, 888 (C.C.S.D. Ohio 1863) (No. 16,816).

135. Michael Kent Curtis, *Free Speech, "The People's Darling Privilege": Struggles for Freedom of Expression in American History* (Durham, NC: Duke University Press, 2000), 301.

136. Ex parte Vallandigham, 28 F. Cas. at 874.

137. *The Trial of Hon. Clement L. Vallandigham, by a Military Commission: And the Proceedings under His Application for a Writ of Habeas Corpus in the Circuit Court of the United States for the Southern District of Ohio* (Cincinnati: Rickey and Carroll, 1863). For information on Vallandigham and details on his arrest, see Klement, *Copperheads in the Middle West;* Frank L. Klement, *The Limits of Dissent: Clement L. Vallandigham and the Civil War* (Lexington: University Press of Kentucky, 1970); Klement, *Copperheads of the North;* Jean H. Baker, "A Loyal Opposition: Northern Democrats in the Thirty-seventh Congress," *Civil War History* 25 (June, 1979): 139–55; Baker, *Affairs of Party.*

138. President Lincoln nominated Swayne as an associate justice of the U.S. Supreme Court January 21, 1862; the Senate confirmed his appointment three days later. Swayne replaced Justice McLean, who had passed away, thus also becoming the new circuit court justice for Ohio. Swayne, like McLean, was from southern Ohio. He had served as U.S. attorney for the District of Ohio in the late 1820s and the 1830s. For biographical information on Swayne, see Marshall, *History of the Courts and Lawyers of Ohio,* 3:813–15.

139. Ex parte Vallandigham, 28 F. Cas. at 874–919. Flamen Ball, a prominent antebellum Cincinnati attorney and active Republican, had been Salmon Chase's law partner during Chase's abolitionist years. Niven, *Salmon P. Chase,* n.p.

140. *Cincinnati Weekly Gazette,* May 20, 1863, 1; Leavitt, *Autobiography,* 88.

141. Ex parte Vallandigham, 28 F. Cas. at 923, 920; Leavitt, *Autobiography,* 83–84.

142. Ex parte Vallandigham, 28 F. Cas. at 921–22.

143. Ibid., 924. To bolster his arguments, Leavitt cited the recent statutes enacted by the Ohio legislature "in which the validity and legality of arrests in this state under military authority are distinctly sanctioned." He asserted that these laws were "a clear indication of the opinion of that body that the rights and liberties of the people are not put in jeopardy by the exercise of the power in question."

144. Ibid., 923–24. Pugh appealed Leavitt's decision to the U.S. Supreme Court. In February 1864 the Supreme Court, affirming Leavitt's ruling, declared that civilian courts had no authority to hear appeals from or review the decisions of military commissions. Ex parte Vallandigham, 68 U.S. 243 (1864).

145. Leavitt, *Autobiography*, 83.

146. Curtis, *Free Speech*, 319–21. See also *Cincinnati Enquirer*, May 17, 1863, 2, and September 22, 1863, 2. Leavitt also received numerous letters of praise from "loyal northerners." Leavitt, *Autobiography*, 82–83. For additional details on the Vallandigham case, press reaction to the judicial decisions, and the broader issue of the Lincoln administration's record on civil liberties during the war, see Mark E. Neely Jr., *The Fate of Liberty: Abraham Lincoln and Civil Liberties* (New York: Oxford University Press, 1991), 65–68, 161, 174–75, 196–97.

147. *Cincinnati Enquirer*, March 18, 1873, 4.

148. U.S. v. Cathcart, 25 F. Cas. 344, 344–50 (C.C.S.D. Ohio 1864) (No. 14,756).

149. U.S. v. Hughes, 26 F. Cas. 420, 420–21 (S.D. Ohio 1864) (No. 15,418). See also James H. Thompson, "Treason Trial in Ohio," in *A History of Adams County, Ohio: From Its Earliest Settlement to the Present Time*, ed. Nelson W. Evans and E. B. Stivers (West Union, OH: E. B. Stivers, 1900), 394–99. Thompson was Hughes's attorney.

150. File of A. C. Sands in Records Relating to the Appointment of Federal Judges, Marshals, and Attorneys, 1853–1901, box 527. By "loose," the Department of Justice meant that all those involved, including Leavitt, failed to follow strict accounting procedures. It, however, never accused Leavitt of any malfeasance in office.

151. Leavitt did have to deal with a few cases left over from the war, charging people with violating wartime trading regulations. See U.S. v. Moore, 26 F. Cas. 1300 (S.D. Ohio 1866) (No. 15,081); U.S. v. The Henry C. Homeyer, 26 F. Cas. 278 (S.D. Ohio 1868) (No. 15,353).

152. See William M. Wiecek, "The Reconstruction of Federal Judicial Power, 1863–1875," *American Journal of Legal History* 13 (October 1969): 333–59. Wiecek argued that "in no comparable period of our nation's history have the federal courts . . . enjoyed as great an expansion of their jurisdiction." Ibid., 333. See also Stanley I. Kutler, *Judicial Power and Reconstruction Politics* (Chicago: University of Chicago Press, 1968).

153. Wiecek, "Reconstruction of Federal Judicial Power," 341–42. See also Kutler, *Judicial Power and Reconstruction Politics*, 143–44, 154. See also chapter 3 for additional information on the Judiciary Act of 1875 and the impact of removal provisions.

154. An Act to fix the number of Judges of the Supreme Court of the U.S., and to Change certain Judicial Circuits, 14 Stat. 209 (1866). During the Civil War, Congress had placed Ohio and Indiana in the Seventh Circuit. Michigan, Illinois,

and Wisconsin composed the Eighth Circuit, and Kentucky, Tennessee, Louisiana, Arkansas, and Texas composed the Sixth.

155. Judiciary Act of 1869, 16 Stat. 44 (1869). For the final transformation of the district courts into the sole federal trial courts, see chapters 3 and 4.

156. Leavitt, *Autobiography,* 100. See also ibid., 91.

157. Table 2.1 and all the information on cases heard is derived from the following sources: Journals, W. Div., vols. 1 and 2; Court Docket Books, 1863–1872, vol. 2, General Records, W. Div., RG 21 (hereafter Court Docket Books, W. Div.).

158. U.S. v. Canter, 25 F. Cas. 281 (C.C.S.D. Ohio 1870) (No. 14,719).

159. Ibid. at 281.

160. Cayton, *Ohio,* 139; Roseboom, *Civil War Era,* 457, 464; Felice A. Bonadio, *North of Reconstruction: Ohio Politics, 1865–1870* (New York: New York University Press, 1970), 80, 92–106; Edgar Toppin, "Negro Emancipation in Historic Retrospect: Ohio; The Negro Suffrage Issue in Postbellum Ohio Politics," *Journal of Human Relations* 11 (Winter 1963): 232–46; William Gillette, *The Right to Vote: Politics and the Passage of the Fifteenth Amendment* (Baltimore: Johns Hopkins Press, 1969), 33, 139–44, 160–61. The Ohio legislature had ratified the Fourteenth Amendment in January of 1867, but the next year, with the Democrats in control, the General Assembly rescinded that ratification. Secretary of State Seward, however, never recognized this attempt to withdraw Ohio's approval and counted Ohio among the required three-fourths of the states needed for ratification. Thus, Ohio's status in ratification remained in limbo. A group of law students at the University of Cincinnati College of Law brought this to the attention of Ohio state legislators in 2003, and after some fanfare, Ohio, in September 2003, again ratified the Fourteenth Amendment, clearing up any ambiguity that might have remained. Roseboom, *Civil War Era,* 464; Roy Wood and Barry M. Horstman, "Ohio to Correct 'Crazy History,'" *Cincinnati Post,* September 10, 2003.

161. Cayton, *Ohio,* 200, 272; Gerber, *Black Ohio,* 199–208.

162. U.S. v. Canter, 25 F. Cas. at 281–82.

163. Ibid. at 282. What is surprising is that, according to both the Lexis Shepard service and Westlaw's Keycite, this case has never been cited by any other court. Indeed, only two law review articles mention the case, and they only in passing. See Michael G. Collins, "'Economic Rights,' Implied Constitutional Actions, and the Scope of Section 1983," *Georgetown Law Journal* 77 (April 1989): 1557–58; Michael J. Klarman, "The Plessy Era," *Supreme Court Review* (1998): 367.

164. Journals, W. Div., 2:284 (November 26, 1869).

165. See, e.g., Civil (Law) Records, W. Div., vol. 3. Most likely, most jury trials resulted in verdicts for the defendant because guilty defendants just didn't show up. See also Journals, W. Div., vols. 1 and 2; Court Docket Books, W. Div., vol. 2.

166. See, e.g., Civil (Law) Records, W. Div., vols. 3–4. Before the Civil War, most debt cases were against post office and other government officials who did not turn over money they had collected or against sureties and others against whom the government had claims after winning judgments in court.

167. See, e.g., U.S. v. Eight Hundred Caddies of Tobacco, 25 F. Cas. 989 (S.D. Ohio 1869) (No. 15,036); U.S. v. 78 Cases of Books, 27 F. Cas. 1030 (S.D. Ohio

1869) (No. 16,258), 27 F. Cas. 1033 (S.D. Ohio 1869) (No. 16,258a), 27 F. Cas. 1035 (S.D. Ohio 1869) (No. 16,258b); U.S. v. 78 Cases of Books, Journals, W. Div., 2:199, 205, 232, 235–38, 258, 274, 276, 385.

168. U.S. v. Turner, 28 F. Cas. 230, 232 (C.C.S.D. Ohio 1870) (No. 16,547).

169. Ibid. at 231.

170. U.S. v. Chaffee, 25 F. Cas. 380, 381–82 (S.D. Ohio 1867) (No. 14,772).

171. For a brief history of this short-lived act, see Skeel, *Debt's Dominion*. See also Balleisen, *Navigating Failure*, 133.

172. Order Book, vol. 1, Bankruptcy Records, W. Div., RG 21.

173. See, generally, Bankruptcy Journals, 1867–1898, vol. C, Bankruptcy Records, W. Div., RG 21.

174. See., e.g., Perry v. Langley, 19 F. Cas. 280 (S.D. Ohio 1868) (No. 11,006), *rev'd,* Langley v. Perry, 14 F. Cas. 1113 (C.C.S.D. Ohio 1869) (No. 8,067); Ahl v. Thorner, 1 F. Cas. 220 (S.D. Ohio 1869) (No. 103); Haughey v. Albin, 11 F. Cas. 837 (S.D. Ohio 1869) (No. 6,222); In re Webb, 29 F. Cas. 493 (S.D. Ohio 1869) (No. 17,313).

175. In re Manly, 16 F. Cas. 628, 629 (S.D. Ohio 1869) (No. 9,031).

176. Ex parte Ross, 20 F. Cas. 1228, 1228–31 (S.D. Ohio 1869) (No. 12,069).

177. The Cheeseman v. Two Ferryboats, 5 F. Cas. 528 (S.D. Ohio 1870) (No. 2,633).

178. Genesee Chief v. Fitzhugh, 53 U.S. (12 How.) 433 (1852).

179. The Cheeseman v. Two Ferryboats, 5 F. Cas. at 529–32. The court further held that the ferryboats were in danger, that the *Cheeseman* did perform the work of salvors, and that the libelants were due $1,200 for their services. Ibid., 532–33.

180. Roback v. Taylor, 20 F. Cas. 852, 853–54 (C.C.S.D. Ohio 1866) (No. 11,877).

181. Records Relating to the Appointment of Federal Judges, Marshals, and Attorneys, 1853–1901, box 529.

182. A. Hopeland to U.S. Grant, March 3, 1869, ibid., box 528. Hopeland urged Grant to appoint new district attorneys for the Southern District of Ohio and for districts in Indiana and Illinois where he found similar problems. He compared the abysmal record in southern Ohio with the efficiency of the district attorneys in St. Louis and Louisville. There is no indication from the records if the charges were correct, but there is also no indication why there should have been such delays or lack of prosecutions. Certainly the court's docket was not crowded.

183. *Senate Executive Journal,* 42d Cong., 1st sess., 46–47 (March 30, 1871). Leavitt was able to retire because of a provision in the Judiciary Act of 1869 that allowed judges with at least ten years of service who had reached the age of seventy to retire with full pay for the remainder of their lives. See § 5 of the Judicial Act of 1869, 16 Stat. 44.

184. *Cincinnati Enquirer,* March 20, 1873, 8. See also ibid., March 18, 1873, 1.

## CHAPTER 3

1. Eugene H. Roseboom, *The Civil War Era, 1850–1873,* vol. 4, *The History of the State of Ohio,* ed. Carl Wittke (Columbus: Ohio State Archaeological and Historical Soci-

ety, 1941–1944), 4–24, 111–16; J. Fletcher Brennan, ed., *The Biographical Cyclopaedia and Portrait Gallery with an Historical Sketch of the State of Ohio* (Cincinnati: Western Biographical Publishing, 1883–1884), 1:71–72; Phillip R. Shriver and Clarence E. Wunderlin Jr., eds., *The Documentary Heritage of Ohio* (Athens: Ohio University Press, 2000), 263; Philip D. Jordan, *Ohio Comes of Age 1873–1900,* vol. 5, *The History of the State of Ohio,* ed. Carl Wittke (Columbus: Ohio State Archaeological and Historical Society, 1941–1944), 4–13, 225–29.

2. Jordan, *Ohio Comes of Age,* 6, 13, 195–97, 309; Shriver and Wunderlin, *Documentary Heritage of Ohio,* 264–65; Andrew R. L. Cayton, *Ohio: The History of a People* (Columbus: Ohio State University Press, 2002), 226–31.

3. Jordan, *Ohio Comes of Age,* 5, 243, 308.

4. *Journal of the Executive Proceedings of the Senate of the United States,* 42d Cong., 1st sess., 46–47 (March 30, 1871); *Cincinnati Enquirer,* March 31, 1871, 2.

5. Bicentennial Committee of the Judicial Conference of the United States, *Judges of the United States,* 2d ed. (Washington, DC: Government Printing Office, 1983), 477–78; Carrington T. Marshall, ed., *A History of the Courts and Lawyers of Ohio* (New York: American Historical Society, 1934), 3:712; Bicentennial Committee of the Judicial Conference of the United States, *History of the Sixth Circuit* (Washington, DC: Bicentennial Committee of the Judicial Conference of the United States, 1976), 195. For more detailed information on Swing and his appointment to the bench, see chapter 9.

6. See William C. Howard to Attorney General B. H. Brewster, November 4, 1882, Records Relating to the Appointment of Federal Judges, Marshals, and Attorneys, Ohio (Southern) 1853–1901, box 530, General Records of the Department of Justice, RG 60, National Archives Branch Depository, College Park, MD; *Senate Executive Journal,* 48th Cong., 1st sess., 63, 65 (December 18, 1883), 111–12 (January 7, 1884); Senate Judiciary Committee, minutes, 48th Cong., 1st sess., 146 (January 7, 1884), Records of the U.S. Senate, RG 46, National Archives, Washington, DC.

7. "In Memoriam George Read Sage 1828–1898," *Pamphlets* (Cincinnati: Press of Curtis and Jennings 1899), 7:5. For more detailed information on Sage and his appointment to the bench, see chapter 9.

8. Circuit Courts of Appeal Act, 26 Stat. 826 (1891). See chapter 4 for a discussion of the 1911 statute abolishing the old circuit courts.

9. The Supreme Court's docket fell dramatically—from 623 cases in 1890 to 379 in 1891 and 275 in 1892. See http://air.fjc.gov/history.

10. Indeed, it seems that sometimes not even the clerk of the court could keep the two courts straight. In the late 1880s through the 1890s, in the order books for the district court, the clerk entered orders issued by the circuit court, including those issued by Circuit Court Judge William Howard Taft, alongside orders issued by Judge Sage sitting as a district court judge. See Order Books, vol. 4, passim. And although the circuit court heard all the patent and copyright litigation, it was District Court Judge Sage who was prominently known for his expertise in this area.

11. Russell R. Wheeler and Cynthia Harrison, *Creating the Federal Judicial System,* 2d ed. (Washington, DC: Federal Judicial Center, 1994), 16.

12. An Act to provide for circuit and district courts . . . at Columbus, 21 Stat. 63 (1880). The new counties were Union, Delaware, Morrow, Knox, Coshocton, Harrison, and Jefferson. The Eastern Division included Union, Delaware, Morrow, Knox, Coshocton, Harrison, Jefferson, Madison, Fayette, Franklin, Pickaway, Ross, Pike, Gallia, Jackson, Meigs, Vinton, Athens, Hocking, Fairfield, Licking, Perry, Muskingum, Morgan, Washington, Noble, Monroe, Belmont, and Guernsey counties. The Western Division included Adams, Brown, Butler, Champaign, Clark, Clermont, Clinton, Darke, Greene, Hamilton, Highland, Lawrence, Mercer, Miami, Montgomery, Preble, Scioto, Shelby, and Warren counties.

13. Irwin S. Rhodes, "The History of the United States District Court for the Southern District of Ohio," *University of Cincinnati Law Review* 24 (Summer 1955): 347–48.

14. Judiciary Act of 1875, 18 Stat. 470. Initially, only circuit courts had federal question jurisdiction. Specifically, the statute gave them concurrent jurisdiction with state courts "in all suits of a civil nature at common law or in equity" in which the sum at issue was $500 or more, "arising under the Constitution or laws of the United States, or treaties made . . . under their authority, or in which the United States are plaintiffs or petitioners."

15. See William M. Wiecek, "The Reconstruction of Federal Judicial Power, 1863–1875," *American Journal of Legal History* 13 (October 1969): 356–59; Tony A. Freyer, "The Federal Courts, Localism, and the National Economy," *Business History Review* 53 (Autumn 1979): 343–63.

16. Edward A. Purcell Jr., *Litigation and Inequality: Federal Diversity Jurisdiction in Industrial America, 1870–1958* (New York: Oxford University Press, 1992), 8.

17. Swift v. Tyson, 41 U.S. 1 (1842).

18. See Edward A. Purcell Jr., *Brandeis and the Progressive Era: Erie, the Judicial Power, and the Politics of the Federal Courts in Twentieth-Century America* (New Haven, CT: Yale University Press, 2000), 76.

19. Purcell, *Litigation and Inequality,* passim.

20. In 1888, Congress raised the jurisdictional minimum from $500 to $2,000. 25 Stat. 433. In 1911, Congress raised it again, to $3,000. 36 Stat. 1087, 1091.

21. Freyer, "The Federal Courts, Localism, and the National Economy," 359n48.

22. Andrews Ex'rs v. Garrett, cited in Merch. & Mfrs. Nat. Bank v. Wheeler, 17 F. Cas. 40 (C.C.S.D.N.Y. 1875) (No. 9,439), in Hoadley v. San Francisco, 12 F. Cas. 250 (C.C.D. Cal. 1875) (No. 6,544), and in Crane v. Reeder, 6 F. Cas. 758 (C.C.E.D. Michigan n.d.) (No. 3,356).

23. Stapleton v. Reynolds, 22 F. Cas. 1080 (S.D. Ohio 1876) (No. 13,303).

24. Wills v. Baltimore & Ohio R.R. Co., 65 F. 532 (C.C.S.D. Ohio 1895).

25. State ex rel. City of Columbus v. Columbus & Xenia Ry. Co., 48 F. 626 (C.C.S.D. Ohio 1891) (denying the railroad's writ to remove because it had not raised the federal question of its right to an existing street crossing in state court first); Rike v. Floyd, 42 F. 247 (C.C.S.D. Ohio 1890) (holding that the printing company had not shown the local prejudice complained of would prevent an impartial hearing by the state court as required by the removal statute). In 1903, Judge Thompson continued where Judge Sage left off, refusing to allow a railroad to re-

move a tort case initiated by an injured worker from state court, holding that diversity was achieved only by improper joinder. Axline v. Toledo, Walhonding Valley & Ohio R.R. Co., 138 F. 169 (C.C.S.D. Ohio 1903).

26. Wheeler and Harrison, *Creating the Federal Judicial System,* 16.

27. See table 3.1. "Terminated" is the term used by the U.S. attorney general and later by the Federal Judicial Center to indicate the number of cases disposed of by the courts in any of a variety of ways, including dismissal for lack of prosecution, pretrial settlement, plea bargaining in criminal cases, or a verdict after a trial.

28. See, generally, Daniel R. Ernst, "Law and American Political Development, 1877–1938," *Reviews in American History* 26 (March 1998): 205–19; Gerald Berk, *Alternative Tracks: The Constitution of American Industrial Order, 1865–1917* (Baltimore: Johns Hopkins University Press, 1994); Albro Martin, "Railroads and the Equity Receivership: An Essay on Institutional Change," *Journal of Economic History* 34 (September 1974): 685–709. Although Martin argues that "the adaptation of old equity-law receivership to the new problems of the industrial age" was almost inevitable, Berk believes there were alternatives which federal judges rejected, believing that the national railroad systems "needed protection." Therefore, Berk concludes, federal judges "systematically reallocated extant rights within the corporation from creditors (bondholders) to incumbent managers," ensuring "bigness and . . . the separation of ownership from managerial control" as well as "disempower[ing] creditors, thereby enabling incumbent managers to reduce debt . . . on reorganized railroads on average by one-third." Martin, "Railroads and the Equity Receivership," 686; Berk, *Alternative Tracks,* 47. Whereas the judges of the Southern District of Ohio heard no major receivership cases, the Sixth Circuit Court of Appeals affirmed St. Louis District Judge Samuel Treat's decision to allow management to reorganize at the expense of bondholders, explaining that the maintenance of an integrated railroad was essential to the country's prosperity. "If others choose to break up the line and deprive people of railroad facilities," he declared, "the consequence is not with this court." Cited in Martin, "Railroads and the Equity Receivership," 699. This doctrine was controlling authority for the Southern District of Ohio.

29. See Bankruptcy Journals, vols. C, D, and E, passim. These journals indicate that few businesses that filed for bankruptcy were placed in receivership. In general, the court ordered the company dissolved, the assets sold, and the proceeds distributed. These records show no railroad filing for bankruptcy during this period. In the equity records, there are no opinions that provide any data on receiverships, but it is clear that there were a number of them, including a few railroad receiverships. Perhaps the reason why there are no extended opinions in equity cases was because of pressures to move the docket along. Circuit and then Supreme Court Justice Horace Lurton explained in a letter to Judge Howard Hollister, after Hollister's appointment to the district court: "Do not acquire the habit of taking equity cases out for consideration after the argument. Four times out of five your judgment when you have heard a case well argued will be sound. . . . Do not bother about writing opinion; make short memorandums showing what you hold." Lurton to Hollister, March 12, 1910, Mixter Family Papers, box 2, folder 2, Cincinnati Historical Society, Cincinnati.

30. See table 3.1 and Civil Docket Book, 1853–1874, vol. 2 in General Records and Civil (Law) Dockets, vol. 3, in Law Records, W. Div., RG 21.

31. Journals, 1880–1925, 1:1–2, General Records, E. Div., RG 21 (hereafter referred to as Journals, E. Div.). See also 21 Stat. 63 (1880). The court met in Columbus on the first Tuesday of June and December and in Cincinnati in April and October.

32. Journals, E. Div., vol. 1. See also Law Records Books, Law Records, E. Div., RG 21. The types of cases heard in both divisions were the same.

33. The summary of the typical docket was compiled not only from the specific cases listed in the text, but more especially from the extant records in RG 21 as well as records still housed in the courthouse in Columbus while this author was doing research. See Journals, W. Div., vols. 3–6; Court Docket Book, W. Div., vol. 2; Order Books, vol. 4; Civil (Law) Dockets, Law Records, W. Div., RG 21, vol. 3; Civil (Law) Records, W. Div., vols. 5–7; Law Record Books, E. Div., vols. 1–2; Journals, E. Div., vol. 1; Columbus, Criminal Docket 1880–1897, unnumbered volume, federal courthouse, Columbus (hereafter referred to as Columbus Courthouse Criminal Docket). While this author was conducting research, several files were still stored at the courthouses in Columbus, Cincinnati, and Dayton. Most have since been sent to the National Archives Branch Depository, Great Lakes Region in Chicago, and incorporated into RG 21. Hereafter, those files will be identified as "Columbus Courthouse," "Cincinnati Courthouse," or "Dayton Courthouse" and then the name of the record, as the criminal docket cited above illustrates.

34. For examples of typical bankruptcy cases, see Pence v. Cochran, 6 F. 269 (S.D. Ohio 1881) (dealing with the issue of priority of liens of judgment); In re Henderson, 9 F. 196 (S.D. Ohio 1881) (defining "a proceeding in involuntary bankruptcy" and the procedures under such a proceeding).

35. See, e.g., U.S. v. 164 8/100 Proof Gallons Distilled Spirits, 82 F. 204 (S.D. Ohio 1897); U.S. v. Strauss, 55 F. 388 (S.D. Ohio 1893).

36. Beginning in 1888, the vast majority of orders recorded in the Order Book were decrees pro confesso. See Order Books, vol. 4, 1888–1895, passim.

37. U.S. v. Thornburg and U.S. v. Wise, 6 F. 41 (S.D. Ohio 1881), aff'd, U.S. v. Thornburg and U.S. v. Wise, 7 F. 190 (C.C.S.D. Ohio 1881). Neither side argued that freight rather than passenger boats could be used. Although several other district court judges adopted Swing's proshipper interpretation, others took the government's view, thus allowing the government to regulate the shippers more freely. See Note, "From Judicial Grant to Legislative Power: The Admiralty Clause in the Nineteenth Century," *Harvard Law Review* 67 (May 1954): 1231–33.

38. Longstreet v. Steam-Boat R. R. Springer, 4 F. 671 (S.D. Ohio 1880).

39. The Guiding Star, 9 F. 521 (S.D. Ohio 1881). See also The Thomas Sherlock, 22 F. 253 (S.D. Ohio 1884) (in which Judge Sage reiterates the priority of maritime over other claims when a boat is sold because debts cannot be paid).

40. The Charles Morgan, 5 F. Cas. 511 (S.D. Ohio 1878) (No. 2,618). For examples of citations by other district courts, see Hollyday v. The David Reeves, 12 F. Cas. 386 (D. Md. 1879) (No. 6,625); Homes v. Oregon & C. Ry. Co., 5 F. 75 (D.

Or. 1880). This case is exceptional in the fact that it went to trial. Litigants settled the vast majority of collision cases out of court.

41. Kineon v. The New Mary Houston, 69 F. 362 (S. D. Ohio 1895).

42. The Memphis & Cincinnati Packet Co. v. Hancock, Case No. 1742, Journals, W. Div., 6:318–19 (August 3, 1894).

43. I.C.C. v. Cincinnati, N.O. & T.P. Ry. Co., 64 F. 981 (C.C.S.D. Ohio 1894), 76 F. 183 (C.C.S.D. Ohio 1896), *certified question answered,* 167 U.S. 479 (1897), and *aff'd,* 104 F. 1005 (6th Cir. 1900). Quote at 76 F. at 183.

44. I.C.C. v. Bellaire, Zanesville & Columbus Ry., 77 F. 942 (C.C.S.D. Ohio 1897). See also The Gretna Green, 20 F. 901 (S.D. Ohio 1883) (Sage declaring that barges operating solely within the state of Kentucky are not subject to federal navigation laws even when operating on the Ohio River). Sage chose to interpret the Supreme Court's 1871 ruling in *The Daniel Ball* that a steamship operating solely within the state of Michigan still had to get a federal license because it was carrying goods on navigable waters of the United States and was thus an "instrument of interstate commerce" as inapplicable. See Note, "From Judicial Grant to Legislative Power," 1232–33.

45. In re Worthen, 58 F. 467 (C.C.S.D. Ohio 1891). Another important case dealing with the conflict between state and federal law involved the Adams Express Company and other telephone, telegraph, and express companies. Heard before the Circuit Court for the Southern District of Ohio with decisions rendered by Circuit Judge William Howard Taft and affirmed by the Supreme Court, federal courts upheld an Ohio tax placed on these companies, ruling that the statute was not an unconstitutional interference with interstate commerce nor did it deny the companies the equal protection of the laws. Moreover, Taft held that, in deciding whether a state statute violated the state's constitution, the decision of the supreme court of that state would be accepted as conclusive by federal courts. See Adams Express Co. v. Poe, 61 F. 470 (C.C.S.D. Ohio 1894), *reh'g granted, opinion set aside,* Adams Express Co. v. Poe and Western Union Tel. Co. v. Poe, 64 F. 9 (C.C.S.D. Ohio 1894), *aff'd,* Sanford v. Poe, 69 F. 549 (6th Cir. 1895), *aff'd,* Adams Express Co. v. Ohio State Auditor, 165 U.S. 194 (1897), *reh'g denied,* Adams Express Co. v. Ohio State Auditor, 165 U.S. 185 (1897).

46. For a general history of Ohio's union efforts, see Raymond Boryczka and Lorin Lee Cary, *No Strength without Union: An Illustrated History of Ohio Workers, 1803–1980* (Columbus: Ohio Historical Society, 1982); Shriver and Wunderlin, *Documentary Heritage of Ohio,* 287–90; Cayton, *Ohio,* 184–89; Charles Theodore Greve, *Centennial History of Cincinnati and Representative Citizens* (Chicago: Biographical Publishing, 1904), 1:998–1006.

47. See Thomas v. Cincinnati, N.O. & T.P. Ry. Co., 62 F. 803 (S.D. Ohio 1894), which was one of the earliest federal decisions upholding this right, and Michael H. Leroy and John H. Johnson IV, "Death by Lethal Injunction: National Emergency Strikes Under the Taft-Hartley Act and the Moribund Right to Strike," *Arizona Law Review* 43 (Spring 2001): 75.

48. Letter from C. B. Smirall, dated January 7, 1899, read at a memorial service held for Judge Sage by the Cincinnati Bar Association, "In Memoriam George Read Sage," 31.

49. Casey v. Cincinnati Typographical Union No. 3, 45 F. 135 (C.C.S.D. Ohio 1891).

50. Haggai Hurvitz, "American Labor Law and the Doctrine of Entrepreneurial Property Rights: Boycotts, Courts, and the Juridical Reorientation of 1886–1895," *Industrial Relations Law Journal* 8 (September 1986): 337.

51. Casey v. Cincinnati Typographical Union No. 3, 45 F. at 135; "In Memoriam George Read Sage," 48.

52. Casey v. Cincinnati Typographical Union No. 3, 45 F. at 143-44.

53. Consol. Steel & Wire Co. v. Murray, 80 F. 811, 829 (C.C.N.D. Ohio 1897), italics added, Sage sitting by designation in the Northern District. Between *Casey* and *Consolidated*, the Supreme Court decided *In re Debs*, 158 U.S. 564 (1895). Therefore, Sage cited *Debs* in *Consolidated* as authority for the federal court's right to exercise equity jurisdiction to end any obstructions impeding interstate commerce. In *Casey*, however, Sage merely cited a string of British and American cases to support his assertion that he had general equity jurisdiction. Casey v. Cincinnati Typographical Union No. 3, 45 F. at 144.

54. William E. Forbath, *Law and the Shaping of the American Labor Movement* (Cambridge, MA: Harvard University Press, 1991), 59–97; Leroy and Johnson, "Death by Lethal Injunction," 75–79; Hurvitz, "American Labor Law and the Doctrine of Entrepreneurial Property Rights," 307–52; Gary Minda, "The Law and Metaphor of Boycott, *Buffalo Law Review* 41 (Fall 1993): 872–73; William E. Forbath "The Shaping of the American Labor Movement," *Harvard Law Review* 102 (April 1989): 1172–74.

55. Forbath, *Law and the Shaping of the American Labor Movement*, 61. See also Purcell, *Brandeis and the Progressive Constitution*, 70.

56. Shriver and Wunderlin, *Documentary Heritage of Ohio*, 264–65, 270–72; Joseph William Singer, "No Right to Exclude: Public Accommodations and Private Property," *Northwestern University Law Review* 90 (Summer 1996): 1374. The General Assembly enacted the state law after the U.S. Supreme Court declared the Civil Rights Act of 1875 unconstitutional. The Civil Rights Cases, 109 U.S. 3 (1883).

57. George W. Hays, *Reminiscences of Hon. George W. Hays from 1890 to 1929*, compiled by Angry A. Smith and Lucia B. Keys (Cincinnati: Wm. P. Houston Printing, n.d.), 18–20.

58. Gray v. Cincinnati S. Ry. Co., 11 F. 683, 684–85 (C.C.S.D. Ohio 1882).

59. Civil Rights Act of 1875, 18 Stat. 335 (1875). The U.S. Supreme Court declared the statute unconstitutional in the *Civil Rights Cases*, 109 U.S. 3 (1883).

60. John Hope Franklin, "The Enforcement of the Civil Rights Act of 1875," *Prologue* 6 (Winter 1974): 226–28, 231–35. See also William Gillette, *Retreat from Reconstruction* (Baton Rouge: Louisiana State University Press, 1979), 277; Stephen J. Riegel, "The Persistent Career of Jim Crow: Lower Federal Courts and the 'Separate but Equal' Doctrine, 1865–1896," *American Journal of Legal History* 28 (January 1984): 20–21.

61. See Michael W. McConnell, "Originalism and the Desegregation Decisions," *Virginia Law Review* 81 (May 1995): 1061, 1073. Other historians argue that Congress's intent was unclear; some Republican congressmen believed the statute

only barred exclusion. Michael J. Klarman, "The Plessy Era," *Supreme Court Review* (1998): 303, 327; Michael J. Klarman, "Brown, Originalism, and Constitutional Theory: A Response to Professor McConnell," *Virginia Law Review* 81 (October 1995): 1881, 1884–1914; Earl M. Maltz, "Originalism and the Desegregation Decisions— A Response to Professor McConnell," *Constitutional Commentary* 13 (1996): 223.

62. There were only four reported federal cases before *Gray* that enforced equal accommodations, and only one, *U.S. v. Newcomer*, explicitly held the Civil Rights Act to be constitutional. Charge to Grand Jury–Civil Rights Act, 30 F. Cas. 999 (C.C.W.D.N.C. 1875) (No. 18,258); U.S. v. Newcomer, 27 F. Cas. 127 (E.D. Pa. 1876) (No. 15,868); U.S. v. Dodge, 25 F. Cas. 882 (D.C. Tex. 1877) (No. 14,976); Brown v. Memphis & Charleston R.R. Co., 5 F. 499 (C.C.W.D. Tenn. 1880). Franklin cites two unreported 1875 cases in which federal district court judges upheld the statute's constitutionality: Judge R. R. Nelson of Minnesota and Judge Alexander Rives of Virginia. Franklin, "Enforcement of the Civil Rights Act," 231. Three cases after the U.S. Supreme Court declared the Civil Rights Act unconstitutional still upheld the common law principles and affirmed a separate but equal doctrine for public conveyances. Logwood v. Memphis & Charleston R.R., 23 F. 318 (C.C.W.D. Tenn. 1885); Murphy v. W. & Atl. R.R., 23 F. 637 (C.C.E.D. Tenn. 1885); Houck v. S. Pac. Ry. Co., 38 F. 226 (C.C.W.D. Tex. 1888). In 1873, the Supreme Court in *Washington A. G. Railroad Co. v. Brown* construed a congressional statute providing that "no person shall be excluded . . . on account of color" to mean that facilities could not be segregated. Justice Davis, writing for the Court, relied on the legislative history of the statute, which applied to railroads operating in Washington, DC, to conclude that Congress intended their words to bar segregation. 84 U.S. 445, 447, 452–53 (1873).

63. Charge to Grand Jury–Civil Rights Act, 30 F. Cas. 1005 (C.C.W.D. Tenn. 1875) (No. 18,260); Cully v. Baltimore & Ohio R.R. Co., 6 F. Cas. 946 (D. Md. 1876) (No. 3,466); Smoot v. Kentucky Cent. Ry., 13 F. 337 (C.C.D. Ky. 1882); U.S. v. Washington, 20 F. 630 (C.C.W.D. Tex. 1883). See also Riegel, "Persistent Career of Jim Crow," 33.

64. Gray v. Cincinnati S. Ry. Co., 11 F. at 686–87. Swing cited *Day v. Owen*, 5 Mich. 520 (Supreme Ct. of Mich. 1858), as precedent but he could have also cited an 1859 Hamilton County, Ohio, common pleas court decision, *State v. Kimber*, which held that no public conveyance could deny a person his or her right to public transportation based on race; the common law allowed only reasonable discriminations, and discrimination based on race was not reasonable. 3 Ohio Dec. Reprint, 197. In the same year in which Swing decided *Gray*, Circuit Court Judge John Baxter, in *U.S. v. Buntin*, held that, although the state could establish schools segregated by race, those schools for African American children must be reasonably accessible and must afford "substantially" equal education to that afforded to white children. The jury, however, decided that requiring African American children to travel five miles to their designated school placed them at no material disadvantage with respect to their white neighbors, thereby upholding the segregation of the schools in a township in Clermont County, Ohio. 10 F. 730 (C.C.S.D. Ohio 1882). Ohio state courts had earlier held that segregated schools did not violate the

equal protection clause of the Fourteenth Amendment. Garnes v. McCann, 21 Ohio State 198 (1871). See also Klarman, "Plessy Era," 303; J. Morgan Kousser, *Dead End: The Development of Nineteenth-Century Litigation on Racial Discrimination in Schools* (Oxford: Clarendon Press, 1986).

65. Patricia Hagler Minter, "The Failure of Freedom: Class, Gender, and the Evolution of Segregated Transit Law in the Nineteenth-Century South," *Chicago-Kent Law Review* 70 (1995): 993–96.

66. Singer, "No Right to Exclude," 1377–78. See also Franklin, "Enforcement of the Civil Rights Act," 232. Riegel, however, contends that the separate but equal doctrine still promoted the underlying assumptions of racism. Railroads did have integrated cars. African Americans and whites sat together in the smoking cars; African Americans were excluded only from the "ladies" car, showing that federal judges, in applying the separate but equal doctrine, were "balancing the conflicting considerations of racial caste and economic class." Riegel, "Persistent Career of Jim Crow," 27.

67. Hallam v. Post Publ'g Co., 55 F. 456 (C.C.S.D. Ohio 1893).

68. Hallam v. Post Publ'g Co., 59 F. 530 (6th Cir. 1893). See also Donald L. Magnetti, "'In the End, Truth Will Out' . . . Or Will It? 'Merchant of Venice,' Act II, Scene 2," *Missouri Law Review* 52 (Winter 1987): 299–362 and esp. 302–3.

69. Criminal Dockets 1888–1931, Criminal Records, W. Div., RG 21, vol. 1 (hereafter Criminal Dockets, W. Div.); Columbus Courthouse Crim. Docket, unnumbered volume (1880–1897).

70. See Journals, W. Div., vol. 6; Columbus Courthouse Crim. Docket, unnumbered volume (1880–1897); U.S. v. White, 28 F. Cas. 546 (S.D. Ohio 1877) (No. 16,674).

71. Criminal Docket, W. Div., vol. 1. There is no indication as to why the government chose not to prosecute so many who had been indicted by the grand jury. This pattern does, however, continue. It could be that the accused could not be found, although there is no indication in the records that that was the case.

72. "In Memoriam George Read Sage," 5–6, 12; "Committee of the Bar . . . appointed to prepare a memorial of the life . . . of the late George R. Sage," Journals, E. Div., 1:438–41.

73. U.S. v. Britton, 17 F. 731, 732–34 (S.D. Ohio 1883).

74. Journals, W. Div., vol. 4. The breakdown, by nationality, in 1880, was 159 Germans, 19 from England, 10 from France, 7 from Switzerland, 6 from Ireland, 4 each from Russia, Hungary, Italy, and Scotland, 3 each from Holland and Austria, and 1 each from Belgium, Hindostan, Syria, Italy, and Canada. After these large numbers, the records indicate much smaller numbers being naturalized regularly.

CHAPTER 4

1. See, e.g., Sean Cashman, *America in the Age of Titans: The Progressive Era and World War I* (New York: New York University Press, 1988); John Chambers, *The Tyranny of Change: America in the Progressive Era, 1900–1917* (New York: St. Martin's Press, 1980); Steven J. Diner, *A Very Different Age: Americans of the Progressive Era* (New York: Hill and

Wang, 1998); Richard Hofstadter, *The Age of Reform from Bryan to F.D.R.* (New York: Random House, 1955); Gabriel Kolko, *The Triumph of Conservatism: A Re-interpretation of American History, 1900–1916* (Chicago: Quadrangle Books, 1967); Arthur S. Link, *Woodrow Wilson and the Progressive Era, 1910–1917* (New York: Harper, 1954); Arthur Mann, *The Progressive Era* (New York: Holt, Rinehart and Winston, 1963); Sidney M. Milkis and Jerome M. Mileur, eds., *Progressivism and the New Democracy* (Amherst: University of Massachusetts Press, 1999); Robert H. Wiebe, *The Search for Order, 1877–1920* (New York: Hill and Wang, 1967). For a good summary of the historiography of the progressive era, see Judith Sealander, *Grand Plans: Business Progressivism and Social Change in Ohio's Miami Valley, 1890–1929* (Lexington: University Press of Kentucky, 1988).

2. E. O. Randall, ed., *Ohio Centennial Anniversary Celebration at Chillicothe, May 20–21, 1903, under the Auspices of the Ohio State Archaeological and Historical Society* (Columbus: Ohio State Archaeological and Historical Society, 1903), 53.

3. John M. Weed, "Business—as Usual," in *Ohio in the Twentieth Century, 1900–1938*, comp. Harlow Lindley, vol. 6, *The History of the State of Ohio*, ed. Carl Wittke (Columbus: Ohio State Archaeological and Historical Society, 1941–1944), 159–60.

4. Phillip R. Shriver and Clarence E. Wunderlin Jr., eds., *The Documentary Heritage of Ohio* (Athens: Ohio University Press, 2000), 300; Sealander, *Grand Plans*, 7 and passim; Francis R. Aumann, "Ohio Government in the Twentieth Century: From Nash to White," in Lindley, *Ohio in the Twentieth Century*, 17.

5. Unidentified newspaper clipping, [1910], Mixter Family Papers, box 2, folder 3, Cincinnati Historical Society, Cincinnati.

6. Shriver and Wunderlin, *Documentary Heritage of Ohio*, 300; Aumann, "Ohio Government in the Twentieth Century," 17–54; Hoyt Landon Warner, *Progressivism in Ohio, 1897–1917* (Columbus: Ohio State University Press, 1964), vii–viii, 94–95, 483–87; Charles Hogan, "Timothy S. Hogan, Ohio's Crusading Attorney General" (master's thesis, Xavier University, 1972).

7. Edward A. Purcell Jr., *Brandeis and the Progressive Era: Erie, the Judicial Power, and the Politics of the Federal Courts in Twentieth-Century America* (New Haven, CT: Yale University Press, 2000), 20.

8. An Act to provide the appointment of an additional district judge in and for the southern district of Ohio, 34 Stat. Pt. 1 928 (1907); *Journal of the Executive Proceedings of the Senate of the United States*, 60th Cong., 1st sess., 34, 103 (December 3, 1907). Because federal judges are appointed for life (that is, for "good behavior"), a temporary judgeship is created by permitting an appointment with a proviso that, when a vacancy occurs because of a judge's resignation or death, there will be no replacement. Although the statute did not specify where the new judge would sit, it was understood that one judge would sit in Columbus and the other would hold court in Cincinnati. E. L. Taylor to Theodore Roosevelt, March 4, 1907, Records Relating to the Appointment of Federal Judges, Marshals, and Attorneys, 1901–1933, box 691, Ohio (Southern), General Records of the Department of Justice, RG 60, National Archives Branch Depository, College Park, MD. Presidents appoint judges to the district; the judges themselves determine at which congressionally authorized seat each judge will sit. They make their determination based on the overall needs of the court. And the judges cooperate, some sitting at multiple sites to

help clear dockets. As Horace Lurton, Supreme Court justice and former judge of the Sixth Circuit Court of Appeals, explained to the newly appointed Judge Hollister, in 1909: "Agree upon some mode of co-operation with Judge Sater." Noting that the Cincinnati docket was much larger than that in Columbus, Lurton advised that Sater "has plenty of time to do much work at Cincinnati and will be willing to do so if you divide the responsibility in some definite way with him." Lurton to Hollister, March 12, 1910, Mixter Family Papers, box 2, folder 2.

9. An Act providing for the appointment of an additional district judge, 36 Stat. 202 (1910).

10. An Act to provide for sittings of the U.S. Circuit and District Courts . . . , at the City of Dayton, 34 Stat. 1294 (1907). The statute provided that the judges of the Southern District of Ohio should hold two terms of both the circuit and district courts (there were still two trial courts) in Dayton each year, to convene on the first Monday in May and November. Grand and petit juries could be drawn from citizens residing anywhere in the district. Moreover, cases arising from anywhere in the district could be heard in Dayton—or in Cincinnati or Columbus. Either judge could sit in Dayton.

11. An Act to amend . . . "An Act to codify . . . the laws relating to the judiciary," 38 Stat. 1187 (1915). The Western Division comprised eighteen counties: Adams, Brown, Butler, Champaign, Clark, Clermont, Clinton, Darke, Greene, Hamilton, Highland, Lawrence, Miami, Montgomery, Preble, Scioto, Shelby, and Warren. There were thirty counties in the Eastern Division: Athens, Belmont, Coshocton, Delaware, Fairfield, Fayette, Franklin, Gallia, Guernsey, Harrison, Hocking, Jackson, Jefferson, Knox, Licking, Logan, Madison, Meigs, Monroe, Morgan, Morrow, Muskingum, Noble, Perry, Pickaway, Pike, Ross, Union, Vinton, and Washington. The Western Division sessions would meet in Cincinnati on the first Tuesday of February, April, and October. The Eastern Division would convene in Columbus on the first Tuesday in June and December and in Steubenville on the first Tuesday of March and September. Dayton sessions would be held on the first Mondays in May and November. Grand and petit jurors drawn in Columbus could be directed to serve in Steubenville "if in the opinion of the court the public convenience so requires." Civil suits arising in the eastern division and crimes committed in the eastern division could be tried either in Columbus or Steubenville "as the court may direct." Thus, while Dayton had its own docket and heard cases arising from anywhere in the district, Steubenville was an alternative seat for the Eastern Division only.

12. Judicial Code of 1911, 36 Stat. 1087. The statute also created a single code encompassing all statutes related to the judiciary and revised and unified existing laws. Congress enacted unification after long debates over the 1910 report of a commission it had appointed in 1899. The main areas of contention were the injunctive power of the courts over labor disputes (some congressmen wanted to restrict this power but that effort failed) and diversity jurisdiction. Those who wanted to limit the number of cases based on diversity of citizenship which could be filed in federal court prevailed; the minimum jurisdictional amount was raised to $3,000 by this statute.

13. *Senate Executive Journal,* 55th Cong., 3d sess., Pt. I, 1059, 1071 (December 13, 1898), 1098 (December 19, 1898), 1102 (December 20, 1898); Journals, W. Div., 7:240; Records Relating to the Appointment of Federal Judges, Marshals, and Attorneys, 1897–1901, box 542, RG 60; Charles Theodore Greve, *Centennial History of Cincinnati and Representative Citizens* (Chicago: Biographical Publishing, 1904), 2:109–10. For more information on Thompson and his appointment to the bench, see chapter 9.

14. George Irving Reed, ed., *Bench and Bar of Ohio: A Compendium of History and Biography* (Chicago: Century Publishing & Engraving, 1897), 1:305; John Weld Peck, "The Federal Courts of Ohio," in *A History of the Courts and Lawyers of Ohio,* ed. Carrington T. Marshall (New York: American Historical Society, 1934), 713.

15. "Obituary," *Ohio Law Reporter* 7 (January 31, 1910): 581–82.

16. "Sater dies," *Ohio State Journal,* July 19, 1937, A1, A5; *Who Is Who in and from Ohio* (Cincinnati: Queen City Publishing, 1912), 2:1083–84. For additional biographical information on Sater, as well as details about his nomination and the struggle over his confirmation, see chapter 9.

17. E. L. Taylor to Theodore Roosevelt, March 4, 1907, Records Relating to the Appointment of Federal Judges, Marshals, and Attorneys, 1901–1933, box 691.

18. Records Relating to the Appointment of Federal Judges, Marshals, and Attorneys, 1901–1933, box 691 and bound book of endorsements for John E. Sater, which includes a biography and comments by the Honorable H. J. Booth of Columbus. Organized labor, however, must not have been happy with many of his sweeping injunctions, discussed later in this chapter.

19. *Senate Executive Journal,* 61st Cong., 2d sess., 229–30 (February 24, 1910), 251 (March 7, 1910); Senate Judiciary Committee, minutes, 60th–62nd Congress (March 7, 1910); Senate Judiciary Committee, docket, 60th–61st Congress (February 25, 1910, and March 7, 1910), Records of the U.S. Senate, RG 46, National Archives, Washington, DC; Records Relating to the Appointment of Federal Judges, Marshals and Attorneys, 1901–1933, boxes 688, 690, and 692; Horace Lurton to Hollister, March 12, 1910, Mixter Family Papers, box 2, folder 2. Technically, Hollister was appointed to the permanent position created by Congress on February 24, 1910; Sater then completed Thompson's term. *Senate Executive Journal,* 61st Cong., 2d sess., 229–30 (February 24, 1910).

20. "Long Career on the Bench Is at End," *Cincinnati Enquirer,* September 25, 1919, 20; Howard Hollister, "William H. Taft at the Bar and Bench," *Green Bag* 20 (July 1908): 337–45.

21. "Tribute Paid by Foreign Born," *Cincinnati Enquirer,* September 27, 1919, 8. It is not known what Hollister did that won him this admiration.

22. "Long Career on the Bench Is at End," *Cincinnati Enquirer,* September 25, 1919, 20. For complete biographical information on Hollister, see chapter 9.

23. See Journals, E. Div., vols. 1–3; Civil (Law) Records, 1842–1918, vol. 6–7; Columbus Courthouse Crim. Journal, Book 1 (1901–1907); Columbus Courthouse Crim. Docket, 1882–1900.

24. "Obituary," *Ohio Law Reporter* 7 (January 31, 1910): 581.

25. See Bankruptcy Journal, vol. 1. For a history of this statute, see David A.

Skeel Jr., *Debt's Dominion: A History of Bankruptcy Law in America* (Princeton, NJ: Princeton University Press, 2001).

26. See, generally, Bankruptcy Docket Books, Bankruptcy Records, W. Div., RG 21, vol. 1 (1892–1900). See also Hicks v. Knost, 94 F. 625 (S.D. Ohio 1899), *question certified to the Supreme Court,* 104 F. 1005 (6th Cir. 1900), 178 U.S. 541 (1900); In re Welch, 100 F. 65 (S.D. Ohio 1899); Falter v. Reinhard, 104 F. 292 (S.D. Ohio 1900), *aff'd,* In re McGill, 106 F. 57 (6th Cir. 1901); In re Flick, 105 F. 503 (S.D. Ohio 1900); Stearns v. Flick, 103 F. 919 (S.D. Ohio 1900); In re Troth, 104 F. 291 (S.D. Ohio 1900); Strobel & Wilken Co. v. Knost, 99 F. 409 (S.D. Ohio 1900); In re John Morrow & Co., 134 F. 686 (S.D. Ohio 1901); In re Olman, 134 F. 681 (S.D. Ohio 1902); In re Bogen, 134 F. 1019 (S.D. Ohio 1904); and In re Karns, 148 F. 143 (S.D. Ohio 1905).

27. U.S. v. Geddes, 180 F. 480 (S.D. Ohio 1903), *aff'd,* 131 F. 452 (6th Cir. 1904).

28. I.C.C. v. Cincinnati, Hamilton, & Dayton Ry. Co., 146 F. 559 (C.C.S.D. Ohio 1905), *aff'd,* 206 U.S. 142 (1907). Congress had been debating the Hepburn Act for months when Thompson rendered his decision. That act explicitly stated that courts were not to review ICC findings de novo, but it did not become law until 1906. The Supreme Court, in *Illinois Central Railroad Co. v. I.C.C.,* 206 U.S. 441 (1907), agreed that it would not look at ICC findings anew.

29. U.S. v. Horman, 118 F. 780 (S.D. Ohio 1901), *aff'd,* 116 F. 350 (6th Cir. 1902), *cert. denied,* 187 U.S. 641 (1902). For a description of the law and its legislative history as well as a discussion of the broad and strict views and the significance of *U.S. v. Horman,* see Michael C. Bennett, "Borre v. United States: An Improper Interpretation of Property Rights," *De Paul Law Review* 42 (Summer 1993): 1499–1556, but esp. 1499–1510 (quotes at 1504); Courtney Chetty Genco, "What Happened to *Durland?* Mail Fraud, RICO, and Justifiable Reliance," *Notre Dame Law Review* 68 (1992): 333–98, esp. 359–62; Ellen S. Podgor, "Tax Fraud–Mail Fraud: Synonymous, Cumulative or Diverse?" *University of Cincinnati Law Review* 57 (1989): 903–33, esp. 905–6.

30. U.S. v. Horman, 118 F. at 782.

31. Barnes v. Berry, 156 F. 72 (C.C.S.D. Ohio 1907), 157 F. 883 (C.C.S.D. Ohio 1908), *aff'd,* 169 F. 225 (6th Cir. 1909). Irwin Rhodes, in his early history of the court, said that the decision "encountered some criticism as being favorable to corporate interests." Irwin S. Rhodes, "The History of the United States District Court for the Southern District of Ohio," *University of Cincinnati Law Review* 24 (Summer 1955): 350. Such criticism seems unwarranted, especially when one compares this ruling with injunctions the court issued in the following decades. The interpretation of the case by the author of this book is shared by E. H. Schopler, "Collective Bargaining Agreement as Restricting Right to Strike or Picket," *American Law Reports* 2 (1948): 1278, §§ 3(a), 3(e), and 6.

32. *Ohio Law Bulletin* 52 (April 22, 1907): 211. Kelley was the "featured case" of this edition of this weekly legal publication.

33. Kelly v. Herman, 155 F. 887 (C.C.S.D. Ohio 1906). No sources could be found that discuss Kelly's subsequent career.

34. Analysis of statistics and dockets is based on extant records in RG 21 and material at the courthouses in Cincinnati, Columbus, and Dayton. See Civil (Law) Dockets, W. Div., vols. 4–6; Criminal Dockets, W. Div., vols. 2–3; Columbus Courthouse Crim. Docket, vol. 2. See also U.S. attorney general, *Annual Reports of the Attorney General,* 1913–1919.

35. See, e.g., Law Record Books, E. Div. 1880–1913, vol. 2; U.S. v. Cincinnati, Hamilton & Dayton Ry. Co., Case No. 1993 (1910) (as an example of the Safety Appliance Act); U.S. v. 165 Pails, Buckets, and Kegs of Fish, Case No. 1998 (1910) and U.S. v. 50 cases of Champagne, Case No. 2021 (1911) (as examples of seizures under the Food and Drug acts), and U.S. v. Dayton & Union R.R. Co., Case No. 2006 (1910) (as an example of a violation of the twenty-four-hour law), all in Mixed Case Files, General Records, W. Div., RG 21 (hereafter cited as Case Files, W. Div.).

36. See, e.g., Dresser Mfg. Co. v. Dayton Pipe Coupling Co., Case No. 2204 (1912), Case Files, W. Div.; Wayman v. Louis Lipp Co., 222 F. 679 (S.D. Ohio 1912); Meccano, Ltd. v. Wagner, 234 F. 912 (S.D. Ohio 1916), *case reopened by* Wagner v. Meccano, Ltd., 235 F. 890 (6th Cir. 1916), *aff'd in part, rev'd in part,* 246 F. 603 (6th Cir. 1917).

37. See tables 4.1 and 4.4. For examples of cases and how they were dispatched see, e.g., U.S. v. McCalmont, Case No. 680 (1908) (indicted for sending obscene material through the mails); U.S. v. Baltimore & Ohio S.W. R.R. Co., Case No. 768 (1910) (indicted for violating the Quarantine Act for transporting sheep that had a potential contagious disease); U.S. v. Jacob Portney, Della Bennett, Emma Harris, Bessie Green and W. I. Overstreet, Case Nos. 795, 797, 798, and 800 (1911) (indicted for violating the White Slave Traffic Act); U.S. v. Adams Express, Case No. 863 (1912) (indicted for violating the Interstate Commerce Act by charging more than the posted rates); U.S. v. Galbreath and Davis, Case No. 950 (1913) (indicted for bank fraud); and U.S. v. Katz (indicted for violating the Reed Amendment regulating the transportation of liquor), Criminal Case Files, 1888–1965, Criminal Records, W. Div., RG 21.

38. *Cincinnati Enquirer,* April 18, 1913, 7. The Mann Act was "a splendid example" of the "politicalization of morality" typical of some progressive legislation. David Langum, *Crossing over the Line: Legislating Morality and the Mann Act* (Chicago: University of Chicago Press, 1994), 258–59. Langum provides a good history of the Mann Act, the public hysteria over "white slavery," and its links in some people's minds with immigration.

39. See, generally, Michael Les Benedict, *The Blessings of Liberty* (Lexington, MA: D. C. Heath, 1996), 247–66.

40. Ohio River & W. Ry. Co. v. Dittey, 203 F. 537, 548–49 (S.D. Ohio 1913); Equity Journal, Equity Records, E. Div., RG 21, 1:16–17. Because the panel realized the importance of its decision, it immediately certified it for appeal to the Supreme Court. In 1914, the Supreme Court affirmed the lower court's holding in this and its companion case, *Marietta, Columbus, & Cleveland Railroad Co. v. Creamer,* 232 U.S. 576 (1914). See also *Ohio State Journal,* July 19, 1937, A5, and *Columbus Evening Dispatch,* July 19, 1937, A6 on the significance of this decision. Three-judge panels,

authorized by the Judicial Code of 1911, heard cases where the constitutionality of a statute was called into question.

41. Hebe Co. v. Calvert, 246 F. 711, 716–717, 719–21 (S.D. Ohio 1917). See also Equity Journal, E. Div., 2: 323. The Supreme Court, in *Hebe Co. v. Shaw,* 248 U.S. 297 (1919), upheld the district court's decision.

42. Geiger-Jones Co. v. Turner, Coultrap v. Turner, and Rose v. Hall, 230 F.233 (S.D. Ohio 1916), *rev'd,* 242 U.S. 539 (1917) (upholding the statute as a legitimate police power).

43. Louisville & Nashville R.R. Co. v. Hughes, 201 F. 727, 751 (S.D. Ohio 1912). See also Case No. 6817, Equity Journal, Equity Records, W. Div., RG 21, vol. 1. Another three-judge panel, in *Air-Way Electric Appliance Corp. v. Archer,* upheld, as constitutional, an Ohio state franchise fee imposed on foreign corporations doing business in Ohio. 279 F. 878 (S.D. Ohio 1922), 3 F.2d 669 (S.D. Ohio 1922). In that case, however, the Supreme Court reversed the lower court, finding that the fee violated the equal protection clause of the Fourteenth Amendment and put an undue burden on interstate commerce. 266 U.S. 71 (1924).

44. U.S. v. Frank, 189 F. 195, 201 (S.D. Ohio 1911); Case No. 747, Criminal Case Files, W. Div.

45. U.S. v. Ferger, 256 F. 388 (S.D. Ohio 1918), *rev'd,* 250 U.S. 199 (1919) and 250 U.S. 207 (1919).

46. For a discussion of removal as a litigation strategy and its handling by Gilded Age judges, see chapter 3.

47. Green v. Chesapeake and Ohio Ry. Co., Case No. 2059, Case Files, W. Div. See also Barnes v. Pullman Co., Case No. 2104, ibid., Hollister concluding that the Pullman Company could be served a summons in Ohio, but that once the state common pleas court had jurisdiction, the defendant had the authority to remove the case. But cf. *State of Ohio ex rel. Erkenbrecher v. Cox,* 257 F. 334 (S.D. Ohio 1919), in which Hollister held that the district court had no jurisdiction in a suit by an Ohio taxpayer to enjoin the governor from sending to the state legislature for ratification the proposed Eighteenth Amendment inaugurating prohibition.

48. See LaBelle Box Co. v. McFarland, Equity Journal, E. Div., 1:41; Phillips Sheet & Tin Plate Co. v. Amal. Ass'n of Iron, Steel & Tin Workers, 208 F. 335 (S.D. Ohio 1913), and Equity Journal, E. Div., 1:129; Niles-Bement-Pond Co. v. Iron Moulders' Union Local No. 68, Equity Journal, W. Div., 2:176.

49. Michael H. Leroy and John H. Johnson IV, "Death by Lethal Injunction: National Emergency Strikes under the Taft-Hartley Act and the Moribund Right to Strike," *Arizona Law Review* 43 (Spring 2001): 64, 80. See also William E. Forbath "The Shaping of the American Labor Movement," *Harvard Law Review* 102 (April 1989): 1109–1256, esp. 1182.

50. See George B. Cotkin, "Strikebreakers, Evictions, and Violence: Industrial Conflict in the Hocking Valley, 1884–1885," *Ohio History* 87 (Spring 1978): 140–50.

51. Niles-Bement-Pond Co. v. Iron Moulders' Union Local No. 68, 246 F. 851, 855–56, 859–60 (S.D. Ohio 1917). The U.S. attorney also indicted one of the union members, William West, for perjury for denying, at the hearing before

Sater issued the injunction, that he had spoken in a threatening manner to a Mr. Wise about joining the union. After his conviction, West filed a motion for a new trial, which Judge Hollister denied, the denial being affirmed by the Sixth Circuit Court of Appeals. U.S. v. West, Case No. 1200, Criminal Case Files, W. Div. (October term 1917). West was sentenced to three years in the penitentiary. Case No. 1200, Criminal Dockets, W. Div. The government continued to prosecute West well into the 1930s. Having won a judgment against him for $1,500 plus court costs, the government filed suit to sell his property. U.S. v. West, Case No. 4004 (1930), Law Case Files, 1925–1938, Law Records, W. Div., RG 21.

52. Iron Moulders' Union Local. No. 68 v. Niles-Bement-Pond Co., 258 F. 408 (6th Cir. 1918), aff'd, 254 U.S. 77 (1920).

53. U.S. v. Long Chong, Case No. 1942, Case Files, W. Div. Congress enacted the nation's first Chinese exclusion law in 1882 and then amended it in 1888. This prosecution was under the 1888 statute.

54. U.S. v. Lee Shew, Case No. 2444, Case Files, W. Div., opinion delivered November 1914, italics added. The defendant appealed. Sater finally reheard the case and agreed with Hollister. The government deported Shew in 1919.

55. See Cancellation (November 11, 1909), U.S. v. Arnold Battaglini, Case No. 1982, Case Files, W. Div. In *Augusto Siniscalchi v. Thomas,* the court ordered Siniscalchi deported as undesirable, finding that he was under indictment for murder in Italy. Case No. 2033 (1911), ibid.

56. *Cincinnati Times-Star,* March 16, 1910, clipping in Mixter Family Papers, box 2, folder 3. For Hays's initial appointment, see chapter 3. Sater, on the other hand, claimed to have no right to reappoint Hays. Hays held his federal post for twenty-eight years.

57. Ford Motor Co. v. Union Motor Sales Co., 225 F. 373, 382 (S.D. Ohio 1914), aff'd, 244 F. 156 (6th Cir. 1917). See also Case No. 2147, Case Files, W. Div.

58. Dayton attorney and historian David Greer argues that the reason attorney Robert M. Nevin (later a district judge for the Southern District of Ohio) pushed for passage of the statute that provided for the sitting of the court in Dayton was to hold this trial in Dayton where, it was presumed, a friendly jury composed of those who lived in a community whose prosperity depended on NCR's success would acquit the NCR officers. The federal judges, however, refused to convene in Dayton because there was no federal courtroom. The Sixth Circuit Court of Appeals agreed, and the trial was held in Cincinnati. The result, Greer argues, was the construction of the federal courthouse in Dayton. David Greer, *Sluff of History's Boot Soles: An Anecdotal History of Dayton's Bench and Bar* (Wilmington, OH: Orange Frazer Press, 1996), 145. See also Bruce W. Ronald and Virginia Ronald, *Dayton: The Gem City* (Tulsa, OK: Continental Heritage Press, 1981), for a detailed description of NCR, its policies and practices, and the case.

59. *Cincinnati Enquirer,* November 21, 1912, cited in Greer, *Sluff of History,* 143.

60. U.S. v. Patterson, indictment, Case No. 862, Criminal Case Files, W. Div. For background information on Patterson and NCR, see Greer, *Sluff of History,* 141–42, 145–46.

61. Greer, *Sluff of History,* 142–43.

62. U.S. v. Patterson, Hollister overruling defense motion to move the trial to Dayton, November 19, 1912, Case No. 862, Criminal Case Files, W. Div. The jury, drawn from a broad cross-section of southern Ohio residents, included three farmers, one from West Union, one from Woodstock, and one from Campbellstown; a contractor from Hamilton; a Mechanicsburg hardware dealer; a Port William blacksmith; a canner from Mt. Washington; and four Cincinnatians—a secretary for a stationery company, the president of a lithographing company, the president of another company, and one whose occupation is unknown; and one whose origins are not known. *Cincinnati Enquirer*, November 21, 1912, 16.

63. U.S. v. Patterson, 205 F. 292, 300 (S.D. Ohio 1913).

64. Greer, *Sluff of History*, 143; U.S. v. Patterson, jury verdict, Case No. 862, Criminal Case Files, W. Div.; Case No. 862, Criminal Dockets, W. Div., vol. 2.

65. Wickersham to Hollister, February 19, 1913, Mixter Family Papers, box 2, folder 4.

66. U.S. v. Patterson, Case No. 862, Criminal Dockets, W. Div., vol. 2.

67. Newspaper clipping, n.d., Mixter Family Papers, box 2, folder 6.

68. Greer, *Sluff of History*, 143.

69. Wickersham to Hollister, February 19, 1913, ibid., box 2, folder 4.

70. E. E. Clark, M.D., Danville, IL, to Hollister, March 14, 1913, Emil Wetten, Chicago attorney, to Hollister, February 21, 1913, Curtis Manor of Dublin, OH, to Hollister, n.d., and anonymous correspondent to Hollister, n.d., ibid.

71. Greer, *Sluff of History*, 144; Editorial, *New York World*, February 18, 1913, 8. See also the *Piqua Leader-Dispatch*, February 20, 1913; the *Western Christian Advocate*, February 26, 1913; the *Literary Digest*, March 1, 1913, 444; clipping from the *Cincinnati Post*, n.d.; clippings from about a dozen other unidentified newspapers; all in Mixter Family Papers, box 2, folder 6. The *Literary Digest*'s list of other dailies that praised Hollister's sentences and the jury's verdict included the *St. Louis Republic*, the *Boston Advertiser*, the *Charleston News and Courier*, and the *New York Times*. *Literary Digest*, March 1, 1913, 444.

72. Greer, *Sluff of History*, 145.

73. Orton to Hollister, Chicago, April 2, 1913, Mixter Family Papers, box 2, folder 4; Greer, *Sluff of History*, 143–45.

74. U.S. v. Patterson, Case No. 862, Criminal Case Files, W. Div. and Criminal Dockets, W. Div., vol. 2; Patterson v. U.S., 222 F. 599 (6th Cir. 1915), *cert. denied*, 238 U.S. 635 (1915); Case No. 5802, Equity Journal, W. Div, 1:593. See also U.S. attorney general, *Annual Report*, 1913, 12; 1914, 18–19; 1915, 18; 1916, 24–25. The court retained jurisdiction and on at least two occasions took action against NCR and its officers to enforce the consent decree. See U.S. v. Nat'l Cash Register Co., Cincinnati Courthouse Civil Journal, 4:19; U.S. v. Wiffen, Case No. 3022, Criminal Case Files, W. Div. As of 1952, the decree was still in effect. See Cincinnati Courthouse Civil Journal., 4:19. See also Greer, *Sluff of History*, 143–45.

75. U.S. v. Van Tress, Hiatt, Gorsuch, and Williams, Case Nos. 1208, 1314, and 1463, Criminal Case Files, W. Div. Hollister seemed to be swayed by the audacity of the crime, the plight of the victims, and perhaps community pressure to condemn the fraud, but the court of appeals demanded clear evidence to prove, beyond a reasonable doubt, all the elements of a conspiracy. This, they held, had not

been done. For the publicity the case received, see *Cincinnati Enquirer*, September 25, 1919, 20.

76. U.S. v. Bathgate, Case Nos. 1136–1141, Criminal Case Files, W. Div.; Criminal Dockets, W. Div., vol. 3; Journals, W. Div., 12:354–55 (February term 1918). The government appealed to the Supreme Court, but the results are not known. It is also not known if local officials ever pursued the case.

77. U.S. attorney general, *Annual Report*, 1918, 14–20, 42–45. For an overview of the fate of civil liberties during the war, see Paul L. Murphy, *World War I and the Origin of Civil Liberties in the United States* (New York: W. W. Norton, 1979).

78. Ronald, *Dayton: The Gem City*, 111.

79. Murphy, *World War I*, 143.

80. Ibid., 166. For overviews of attitudes and activities in southern Ohio during the war, see H. Clyde Hubbart, "Ohio in the First World War, 1917–1918" in Lindley, *Ohio in the Twentieth Century*, 388–404; Shriver and Wunderlin, *The Documentary Heritage of Ohio*, 303–32, 348–49; Murphy, *World War I*, 143, 164–65; Cayton, *Ohio*, 235. For details on the Bigelow kidnapping and reactions in Ohio, see Herbert Shapiro, "The Herbert Bigelow Case: A Test of Free Speech in Wartime," *Ohio History* 81 (Spring 1972): 108–21.

81. *Cincinnati Enquirer*, September 25, 1919, 20.

82. Case Files on Detained Enemy Aliens 1917–1919, Criminal Records 1888–1965, RG 21, three boxes containing 145 files.

83. U.S. attorney general, *Annual Report*, 1918, 56–57.

84. See table 4.5 and Criminal Dockets, vol. 3; Journals, W. Div., 12:393–422, 446–97. Quotation from U.S. v. Weiss, Journals, W. Div., 12: 393.

85. U.S. v. Casey, F. 362, 364–66 (S.D. Ohio 1918).

86. U.S. v. Stickrath, 242 F. 151 (S.D. Ohio 1917). See also U.S. attorney general, *Annual Report*, 1918, 56–57, praising the decision. After a trial, the defendant was found guilty; his sentence does not appear in the records.

87. U.S. v. Bago, Case No. 1232, Criminal Case Files, W. Div.

88. U.S. v. Bisdorf, Case No. 1233, ibid.

89. U.S. v. Benner, Case No. 1172, ibid.

90. U.S. v. DeBolt, 253 F. 78 (S.D. Ohio 1918); Case No. 1105, Criminal Misc. Case Files, Criminal Records, E. Div., RG 21.

91. U.S. attorney general, *Annual Report*, 1918, 56.

92. U.S. v. Hammerschmidt, Case No. 1192, Criminal Case Files, W. Div. This file contains a copy of the flyers the Socialist Party printed and distributed, parts of which are quoted above. Hammerschmidt v. U.S., 287 F. 817 (6th Cir. 1923), overturned in Hammerschmidt v. U.S., 262 U.S. 736 (1923).

## CHAPTER 5

1. See, e.g., William E. Leuchtenburg, *The Perils of Prosperity, 1914–1932* (Chicago: University of Chicago Press, 1958); Barry Karl, *The Uneasy State: The United States from 1915 to 1945* (Chicago: University of Chicago Press, 1983); Morton Keller, *Regulating a New Society: Public Policy and Social Change in America, 1900–1933* (Cambridge, MA: Harvard University Press, 1994); Michael Parrish, *Anxious Decades: America in Prosperity*

and *Depression, 1920–1941* (New York: W. W. Norton, 1992); David S. Clark, "Adjudication to Administration: A Statistical Analysis of Federal District Courts in the Twentieth Century," *Southern California Law Review* 55 (November 1981): 110–17.

2. *Journal of the Executive Proceedings of the Senate of the United States*, 66th Cong., 1st sess., 474 (October 30, 1919), 478 (November 3, 1919), 484 (November 5,1919); Senate Judiciary Committee, minutes, 66th Congress (November 3, 1919); Senate Judiciary Committee, executive docket, RG 46, 66th Congress (November 13, 1919); Applications & Endorsements, 1901–1933, Ohio, Southern, Judges, boxes 688–692, Department of Justice, Records of Appointment Clerk, RG 60 National Archives Branch Depository, College Park, MD (hereafter referred to as Applications & Endorsements). Peck presented his commission and took the oath of office on November 19, 1919.

3. Obituary of John Weld Peck, Papers of John W. Peck, box 36, Cincinnati Historical Society, Cincinnati; clipping from *Cincinnati Times-Star*, August 10, 1937, n.p., ibid.; clipping from *Cincinnati Court Index*, March 20, 1939, ibid., box 34; speech at the Cincinnati Club, 1935, ibid. For more detailed biographical information on Peck, see chapter 9. Peck continued to hold these views after returning to private practice. He criticized Franklin Roosevelt and the New Deal and praised federal courts for having the courage to strike down the New Deal's regulatory statutes as unconstitutional. Speech at the Cincinnati Club, 1935, Papers of John W. Peck, box 34.

4. *Cincinnati Post*, April 3, 1923, A1.

5. *Senate Executive Journal*, 67th Cong., 4th sess., 347 (February 28, 1923), 363 (March 1, 1923), 397 (March 2, 1923), 402–3 (March 3, 1923).

6. "Judge Scion of Old Family," *Cincinnati Enquirer*, December 23, 1933, A10.

7. "Jurist Collapses," *Cincinnati Enquirer*, December 23, 1933, A1, A10; Bicentennial Committee of the Judicial Conference of the United States, *History of the Sixth Circuit* (Washington, DC: Bicentennial Committee of the Judicial Conference of the United States, 1976), 143–44. For additional biographical information on Hickenlooper, see chapter 9.

8. *Senate Executive Journal*, 68th Cong., 2d sess., 329 (January 31, 1925), 352 (February 7, 1925), 358 (February 9, 1925); Bicentennial Committee, *History of the Sixth Circuit*, 146–47. For more detailed biographical information on Hough, see chapter 9.

9. Ralph H. Beaton, "Tribute to Hough," January 8, 1936, in Wallace Files.

10. "Memorial to Hough," *Columbus Journal*, January 29, 1935, 7.

11. See, e.g., Hyde v. U.S., Case No. 4345, Law Case Files, W. Div. (a World War I veteran from Dayton trying to collect under his War Risk Insurance Policy); Irving Berlin, Inc. v. John Ramsey DBA Maple Lake Inn, Case No. 975, Columbus Courthouse Equity Journal (Berlin charging copyright infringement when the inn did not pay him royalties when entertainers there performed his music); Lektophone Corp. v. Crosley Radio Corp., 46 F.2d 126 (S.D. Ohio 1928) (Hickenlooper determining whether the product at issue was different enough from prior art to be patentable); Columbus Plate & Window Glass Co. v Miller, 38 F.2d 509 (S.D. Ohio 1930) (Hough interpreting a portion of the Internal Revenue Code).

See also, generally, Law Case Files, W. Div.; Columbus Courthouse Equity Journals; Columbus Courthouse Criminal Dockets.

12. Columbus Gas & Fuel Co. v. City of Columbus, 17 F.2d 630 (S.D. Ohio 1927), and Case No. 362, Columbus Courthouse Equity Journal, May, 1925, *appeal dismissed*, 55 F.2d 56 (6th Cir. 1931); *Columbus Evening Dispatch*, November 20, 1935, A6; *Columbus Citizen*, November 20, 1935, A2. See also Van Wert Gas Light Co. v. PUCO, Case No. 274, Columbus Courthouse Equity Journal, August 14, 1925 (a three-judge panel declaring that rates established by the PUCO were confiscatory and therefore void); Cincinnati N. R.R. Co. v. PUCO, Case No. 163, January 26, 1921, Equity Journal, E. Div., 2:530 (Sater enjoining the PUCO from requiring twenty railroads from charging rates in conflict with rates established by the ICC); Washington Gas & Elec. Co. v. City of Washington Court House, Case No. 162, February 10, 1921, ibid. (Sater enjoining the city from forcing the company to charge rates in an amount less than they are "legally entitled to charge"); Cleveland Refining Co. v. State Dir. of Commerce, Case No. 186, February 9, 1922, ibid., 2:646 (a three-judge panel enjoining the state from collecting a fee and forcing inspection of oil and other fluids); Union Gas & Electric Co. and the Cincinnati Gas & Elec. Co. v. City of Cincinnati, Case No. 153, December 13, 1919, Equity Journal, W. Div., vol. 2 (Peck declaring a city ordinance fixing the rates these companies could charge an unconstitutional impairment of the obligation of contract because the city had issued the companies franchises fixing rates for five years); Connor v. Bd. of Comm'rs of Logan County, 12 F.2d 789 (S.D. Ohio 1926) (Hough declaring that for the commissioners to establish a sewerage district without first holding hearings was a violation of the Fourteenth Amendment's due process and equal protection clauses); Commercial Nat'l Bank of Columbus v. Franklin County, 45 F.2d 213 (S.D. Ohio 1930), *rev'd*, 59 F.2d 479 (6th Cir. 1932) (Hough finding a tax on the stock of national banks to be discriminatory, the Sixth Circuit disagreeing); Western Union Tel. Co. v. Tax Comm'n of Ohio, 21 F.2d 355 (S.D. Ohio 1927) (divided three-judge panel enjoining state officials from proceeding with an assessment preparatory to instituting a tax).

13. Red Ball Transit Co. v. PUCO, Case. No. 382, Columbus Courthouse Equity Journal, December 12, 1925. The case was decided by a three-judge panel composed of Hough along with Sixth Circuit Judge Maurice H. Donahue and David C. Westenhaver, district judge for the Northern District of Ohio.

14. Ex parte Willman, 277 F. 819 (S.D. Ohio 1921); Case No. 3082, Case Files, W. Div.

15. U.S. v. Newton Tea & Spice Co., 275 F. 394 (S.D. Ohio 1920). See also U.S. v. 17 Bottles . . . of an Article of Drugs, 55 F.2d 264, 268 (D. Maryland 1932), describing the change Congress made as a result of Peck's ruling.

16. Consol. Coal & Coke Co. v. Beale, 282 F. 934, 734–36 (S.D. Ohio 1922).

17. See chapter 4.

18. Wheeling Steel & Iron Co. v. Gemas, Case No. 207, Equity Journal, E. Div., vol. 2, February–April 1922. Sater also issued a similar injunction against the United Mine Workers in Harmon Creek Coal Co. v. Hall, Case No. 214, ibid., vol. 3, May 22, 1922.

19. Clarkson Coal Mining Co. v. UMW, Case No. 537, Columbus Courthouse Equity Journal, January 4, 1928–October 7, 1929; Clarkson Coal Mining Co. v. UMW, 23 F.2d 208, 210 (S.D. Ohio 1927). By the time the case was over, all of the mining companies had been added as intervenors. In 1931, Judge Nevin, in *P. H. Davis Tailoring Co. v. Amalgamated Clothing Workers of America,* issued an essentially identical restraining order. That strike had gotten quite violent: rocks thrown through the window of one home narrowly missed striking a three-month-old infant. Case No. 726, Equity Journal, W. Div., vol. 3, April 3, 1931.

20. John Lyter, Clerk of Courts, Southern District of Ohio, interview by author, September 7, 2001, Westerville, OH; Judge James Graham, interview by author, July 15, 1999, Columbus.

21. Clarkson Coal Mining Co. v. UMW, Case No. 537, Columbus Courthouse Equity Journal, January 4, 1928–October 7, 1929; Clarkson Coal Mining Co. v. UMW, 23 F.2d at 210. Hough exercised equitable powers based on his conclusions that the mine owners had a right to seek a remedy in federal court and that they had no adequate remedy at law.

22. Phillip R. Shriver and Clarence E. Wunderlin Jr., eds., *The Documentary Heritage of Ohio* (Athens: Ohio University Press, 2000), 356–57; U.S. Department of Justice, *Bicentennial Report of the Northern District of Ohio 1789–1989* (Cleveland: U.S. Department of Justice, 1990), 35–36; Norman H. Clark, *Deliver Us from Evil: An Interpretation of American Prohibition* (New York: W. W. Norton, 1976), 93–102.

23. American Law Institute, *A Study of the Business of the Federal Courts* (Philadelphia: American Law Institute), pt. 2, 37.

24. Civil (Law) Dockets, W. Div., vol. 13.

25. For a study of plea bargaining, see John F. Badgett, "Plea Bargaining and Prohibition in the Federal Courts, 1908–1934," *Law and Society Review* 24 (April 1990): 413–50. Badgett argues that federal judges engaged in what he labels implicit plea bargaining, whereby they intensified sentence discounting rather than altering the plea. They did so to maintain their more elite image, developing a practice different from that of state courts, which they saw as engaging in "corrupt" explicit plea-bargaining practices.

26. Criminal Dockets, vol. 4. Calculations done by author.

27. Columbus Courthouse Crim. Docket, vol. 4.

28. U.S. v. Remus, 283 F. 685 (S.D. Ohio 1922); Case Nos. 3551, 3501–3505, 2142–2144, Criminal Case Files, W. Div.; Remus v. U.S., 291 F. 501, 506 (6th Cir. 1923).

29. Remus v. U.S., 291 F. at 506.

30. Edward Behr, *Prohibition: Thirteen Years That Changed America* (New York: Arcade Publishing, 1996), 92–95.

31. Ibid., 95–99; John Kobler, *Ardent Spirits: The Rise and Fall of Prohibition* (New York: G. P. Putnam's Sons, 1973), 315.

32. Behr, *Prohibition,* 100–3, 121–26; Kobler, *Ardent Spirits,* 319.

33. U.S. v. Remus, Case No. 2144, Criminal Case Files, W. Div. The nuisance charge was one standard device the government used to prosecute violations of the liquor laws.

34. U.S. v. Remus, 283 F. 685 (S.D. Ohio 1922), *aff'd in part, rev'd in part*, U.S. v. Remus, 260 U.S. 477 (1923); Case Nos. 3551, 3501–3505, 2141–2144, Criminal Case Files, W. Div.; Case Nos. 2141–2144, Criminal Dockets, vol. 5; Remus v. U.S., 291 F.501, 506 (6th Cir. 1923), *cert. denied*, Remus v. U.S., 263 U.S. 717 (1924); Remus v. U.S., 291 F. 513 (6th Cir. 1923); U.S. v. Remus, 12 F. 239 (6th Cir. 1926), *cert. denied*, Remus v. U.S., 271 U.S. 689 (1926).

35. Remus's departure to the Atlanta penitentiary "was one of the highlights of the social season" in Cincinnati. A "sizeable crowd" watched as Remus, "in pearl-gray suit, spats, and diamond tiepin," boarded the train with his wife at his side. "Accompanied by federal marshals (whom he treated like honored guests)," Remus and the other sentenced men boarded the luxury railroad car Remus had hitched to the regular Atlanta train. While the others ate lavishly prepared gourmet meals, Remus "spent most of the journey reading Dante's *Divine Comedy*." Behr, *Prohibition*, 127; Kobler, *Ardent Spirits*, 319. Remus's life turned from bad to worse. Just before his release from prison, Remus received a copy of a divorce petition from his wife. This is when Remus discovered that she had used the power of attorney he had given her to rob him of his fortune and then had taken Franklin Dodge, the special agent who had led the raid on the Death Valley Farm, as a lover. Enraged, the morning of the divorce hearing, Remus waited patiently for his wife to leave her hotel and then, "shouting obscenities," seized and shot her. After a spectacular trial in which Remus conducted most of the defense himself, the jury found him not guilty by reason of insanity. After spending six months in the Lima State Hospital for the criminally insane, Remus won his freedom, satisfying a judicial panel that he had fully recovered from his insanity. He died peacefully at age seventy-nine in Cincinnati. Kobler, *Ardent Spirits*, 320.

36. U.S. v. Borkowski, 268 F. 408 (S.D. Ohio 1920).

37. On December 15, 2003, a Keycite search on Westlaw resulted in more than 100 citations to this case by other courts; shepardizing via Lexis resulted in 105 citing decisions.

38. U.S. v. Rykowski, U.S. v. Kozman, and U.S. v. Keydoszius, 267 F. 866, 870–871 (S.D. Ohio 1920). Sater's decision was widely cited by courts across the country to establish standards for issuing proper search warrants. On December 15, 2003, a Keycite search on Westlaw resulted in sixty-six citations to this case by other courts in the 1920s; shepardizing via Lexis resulted in sixty-eight citing decisions. Despite the defendants' victory on the search issue, Sater refused to return their stills. They were, he declared, "contraband," which could be used again to break the law. As such they were not to be returned. By contrast, Peck in *U.S. v. Slusser* held that all illegally seized property had to be returned. 270 F.818 (S.D. Ohio 1921).

39. U.S. v. Slusser, 270 F. at 818. This case, too, was widely cited. On December 15, 2003, a Keycite search on Westlaw resulted in 102 citations to this case by other courts; shepardizing via Lexis resulted in 112 citing decisions.

40. John Marshall, assistant attorney general, to Hough, June 6, 1929, Applications & Endorsements, box 690. The results of the investigation are unknown. Congress authorized the position of U.S. commissioner to relieve some of the

judges' work load. See chapter 2. Congress abolished this position when it created magistrate judges in 1968. See chapter 6.

41. *National Cyclopedia of American Biography* (Clifton, NJ: J. T. White, 1893), 33:83. See also "Jurist Collapses," *Cincinnati Enquirer,* December 23, 1933, A10.

42. *Columbus Citizen,* November 20, 1935, A2. See also *Columbus Evening Dispatch,* November 20, 1935, A1.

43. Magee v. Chicago Nat'l League Ball Club, Case No. 2859, June 9, 1920, Case Files, W. Div.

44. Ex parte Daugherty, 299 F. 620, 635, 638 (S.D. Ohio 1924); Case No. 3389, Case Files, W. Div. For information on Mally Daugherty, see Charles B. Galbreath, *History of Ohio* (Chicago: American Historical Society, 1925), 5:199.

45. McGrain v. Daugherty, 273 U.S. 135 (1927).

46. Scripps v. Scripps, 40 F.2d 176, 180–81 (6th Cir. 1930). See also *Cincinnati Enquirer,* December 23, 1933, A1, A10.

47. See, e.g., Melvyn Dubofsky and Stephen Burwood, eds., *The American Economy During the Great Depression* (New York: Garland, 1990); Ronald Edsforth, *The New Deal: America's Response to the Great Depression* (Malden, MA: Blackwell, 2000); Robert Higgs, *Crisis and Leviathan: Critical Episodes in the Growth of American Government* (New York: Oxford University Press, 1987); Leuchtenburg, *Perils of Prosperity;* Robert S. McElvaine, *The Great Depression* (New York: Times Books, 1984); Parrish, *Anxious Decades;* Arthur M. Schlesinger Jr., *The Age of Roosevelt* (Boston: Houghton Mifflin, 1957).

48. Andrew R. L. Cayton, *Ohio: The History of a People* (Columbus: Ohio State University Press, 2002), 314.

49. Ibid.; Shriver and Wunderlin, *Documentary Heritage of Ohio,* 369.

50. *Senate Executive Journal,* 74th Cong., 2d sess., 132 (January 27, 1936), 158 (February 3, 1936), 170 (February 4, 1936); Senate Judiciary Committee, executive documents, 74th Cong., Doc. 94; Senate, Records, Papers re Nominations, File 74B-A3 (11), RG 46, National Archives, Washington, DC; Columbus Courthouse Journal, 1935–1938 (June term 1935).

51. Bicentennial Committee, *History of the Sixth Circuit,* 201; "In Memoriam: The Honorable Mell G. Underwood," unpublished memorial read at the Sixth Circuit Judicial Conference, May 24–27, 1972, Wallace Files; Judges Kinneary, Cecil, and Peck, "Memorial for Judge Underwood," September 28, 1972, Papers of John W. Peck. For more detailed biographical information on Underwood, see chapter 9.

52. *Senate Executive Journal,* 70th Cong., 2d sess., 324 (January 21, 1929); Senate Judiciary Committee, minutes, January 14 and January 21, 1929.

53. "In Memoriam Honorable Robert R. Nevin," unpublished manuscript presented at the Fourteenth Judicial Conference, Sixth Circuit meeting in Ann Arbor, MI, April 17–18, 1953, in Wallace Files. For more detailed biographical information on Nevin, see chapter 9.

54. *Senate Executive Journal,* 75th Cong., 1st sess., 3 (November 16, 1937), 87 (December 7, 1937), 89 (December, 9, 1937); Senate, Records, papers re nominations, File 75B-A4(4), RG 46. Senate Judiciary Committee, executive documents, 75th Cong., doc. 76.

55. Bicentennial Committee, *History of the Sixth Circuit,* 130–31; C. W. Taylor, ed., *Bench and Bar of Ohio, 1939–1940* (San Francisco: C. W. Taylor Jr., 1939), 187. See also Bicentennial Committee of the Judicial Conference of the United States, *Judges of the United States,* 2d ed. (Washington, DC: Government Printing Office, 1983), 138; Harry A. Abrams, speech at the presentation of Judge Druffel's portrait on June 18, 1965, at Cincinnati federal courthouse, Wallace Files; *Cincinnati Enquirer,* May 17, 1967, 14. For more detailed biographical information on Druffel, see chapter 9.

56. See undated clipping from *Dayton Journal Herald,* Scrapbook of Judge Lester Cecil, in the possession of his son Tom Cecil, Dayton, OH.

57. Rhodes, "History of the District Court," 348; Graham interview.

58. U.S. attorney general, *Annual Reports of the Attorney General,* 1935 and 1938; American Law Institute, *Study of the Business of the Federal Courts,* pt. 1, passim but esp. at 12; Columbus Courthouse Journal, 1935–1939; Dayton Courthouse Criminal Docket Book, vol. 3 (1931–1938) (showing, for example, that, of the ninety-four criminal cases heard in 1935, defendants pleaded guilty in seventy-two; only two defendants went to trial, one being found guilty and the other pleading guilty in the middle of the trial. The rest of the cases were either dropped or continued). Of course, a few of these criminal cases involved the government's efforts to enforce New Deal statutes. See, e.g., U.S. v. John Cannata, Case No. 6756, Criminal Miscellaneous Case File, E. Div., box 1 (the defendant being charged with criminal contempt for failing to pay minimum wages mandated by the Fair Labor Standards Act).

59. U.S. v. Gilbert, 29 F. Supp. 507 (S.D. Ohio 1939), 31 F. Supp. 195 (S.D. Ohio 1939); Bicentennial Committee, *History of the Sixth Circuit,* 176.

60. U.S. v. Fouts, Moran, Foster, and Summers, Case No. 2182, Dayton Courthouse Criminal Docket Book, 1946.

61. Figures from U.S. attorney general, *Annual Report,* 1935; calculations by author. Westlaw and Lexis searches by judge's name show them hearing dozens of bankruptcy cases a year.

62. In re Cole, 13 F. Supp. 283 (S.D. Ohio 1936).

63. Louisville Joint Stock Land Bank v. Radford, 295 U.S. 555 (1935).

64. In re Cole, 13 F. Supp. at 285–86.

65. Ibid., 284.

66. Ibid., 285. Italics added.

67. Ibid., 285–86. See also Hartford Accident & Indem. Co. v. Flanagan, 28 F. Supp. 415 (1939) (Nevin holding that the Bankruptcy Act will be liberally construed so as not to discharge in bankruptcy a liability which would not exist but for the fraudulent conduct of the bankrupt).

68. For Nevin's cases, see, e.g., Ceramic Process Co. v. Cincinnati Advertising Prods. Co. and Solar Labs. v. Cincinnati Adver. Prods. Co., 28 F. Supp. 794 (S.D. Ohio 1939) (holding that to invalidate a patent, proof of prior use or anticipation must be clear and convincing, that the commercial success of a patented invention may be considered as an element in determining its validity, and that once determined to be valid, the patent owner has the prerogative to fix the terms and

conditions under which licensees may operate); Petersime Incubator Co. v. Bundy Incubator Co., 43 F. Supp. 446 (S.D. Ohio 1942) (holding that a second court could reexamine the validity of a patent if that second court finds something that is clearly and substantially new and that diversity is not required for parties to file patent infringement cases in federal court), aff'd, 135 F.2d 580 (6th Cir. 1943); Mueller v. Campbell, 68 F. Supp. 464, 467 (S.D. Ohio 1945) (holding that "an essential requirement for the validity of a patent" is that "the subject matter display 'invention,'" and "'ingenuity'" more than "the work of a mechanic skilled in the art"), aff'd in part, modified in part, Campbell v. Mueller, 159 F.2d 803 (6th Cir. 1947). Judge Druffel's cases include Stowe-Woodward, Inc. v. Cincinnati Rubber Mfg. Co., 25 F. Supp. 56 (S.D. Ohio 1938); United Shoe Mach. Corp. v. Williams Mfg. Co., 29 F. Supp 1015 (S.D. Ohio 1939); and Hazeltine Corp. v. Crosley Corp., 39 F. Supp. 755 (S.D. Ohio 1941).

69. Zimmerman v. Village of London, 38 F. Supp. 582, 584 (S.D. Ohio 1941); Case No. 321, Columbus Courthouse Civil Docket, vol. 2.

70. See, e.g., Hartford Accident & Indem. Co. v. Flanagan, 28 F. Supp. 415 (S.D. Ohio 1939); Van Wormer v. Champion Paper & Fibre Co., 28 F. Supp. 813 (S.D. Ohio 1939); Wagner Mfg. Co. v. Cutler-Hammer, Inc., 10 F.R.D. 458, 480 (S.D. Ohio 1950).

71. AO annual report, 1941, 27, 62, 76.

72. See Clark, "Adjudication to Administration," 121–22.

73. Walker v. Chapman, 17 F. Supp. 308 (S.D. Ohio 1936). See also West Coast Hotel v. Parrish, 300 U.S. 379 (1937).

74. Adkins v. Children's Hosp., 261 U.S. 525 (1923).

75. Walker v. Chapman, 17 F. Supp. at 310–11.

76. Feldman v. Cincinnati, 20 F. Supp. 531, 541 (S.D. Ohio 1937); Case No. 1005, Misc. Equity Case Files, Equity Records, W. Div., RG 21; Equity Docket, Equity Records, W. Div., vol. 8, RG 21. But in Coblentz v. Sparks, 35 F. Supp. 605 (S.D. Ohio 1940), the court did invalidate a special assessment imposed by the Montgomery County Board of Commissioners as a violation of the Fourteenth Amendment because the court believed the commissioners had clearly abused their power.

77. United Fuel Gas Co. v. PUCO, 46 F. Supp. 309 (S.D. Ohio 1941), aff'd, 317 U.S. 456 (1943)

78. Ohio v. U.S. and U.S. v. Wheeling & L. Erie Ry. Co., 6 F. Supp. 386 (S.D. Ohio 1934), aff'd, 292 U.S. 498 (1934).

79. Ohio v. U.S. Civil Serv. Comm'n, 65 F. Supp. 776 (S.D. Ohio 1946).

80. In re Cole, 13 F. Supp. 283, 285–86 (S.D. Ohio 1936).

81. Case Nos. 931–961, 999, 1002, Equity Docket, 7:2 and Misc. Equity Case Files, W. Div.

82. U.S. v. Butler, 297 U.S. 1 (1936).

83. Lohrey v. Conner, Case Nos. 931–961, 999, 1002, Equity Docket, 7:2 and Misc. Equity Case Files, W. Div.

84. Cayton, Ohio, 324–25.

85. Ohio Custom Garment Co. v. Lind, 13 F. Supp. 533 (S.D. Ohio 1936).

86. Dayton Power & Light Co. v. Mathewson, Case No. 920, Equity Docket, vol. 7 and Misc. Equity Case Files, W. Div.

87. Ohio Custom Garment Co. v. Lockert, Case No. 954, ibid.

88. Surprisingly, the District Court for the Southern District of Ohio had no labor cases under the National Labor Relations Act, although the judges did hear other types of challenges to that act. For other cases in which the district court upheld New Deal legislation, see Bastian v. U.S., 118 F.2d 777 (6th Cir. 1941); Hatfield Campbell Creek Coal Co. v. Conner, Case No. 966, Equity Docket, 7:3; Cincinnati Soap Co. v. U.S., Case No. 5049, Law Case Files, W. Div.

89. U.S. v. Krechting, 26 F. Supp. 266 (S.D. Ohio 1939).

90. Wickard v. Filburn, 317 U.S. 111 (1942).

91. U.S. v. Krechting, 26 F. Supp. at 266, 268–69. See also Case Nos. 1041–1058, Equity Docket 1912–1938 and Miscellaneous Equity Case Files, W. Div.

92. U.S. v. Lopez, 514 U.S. 549, 560 (1995). Wickard came into prominence after the enactment of the Civil Rights Act of 1964, the Supreme Court using Wickard's "cumulative effect" doctrine to uphold that law and expand its scope. During the New Deal it "attracted relatively little contemporary attention," perhaps because the nation was more focused on World War II. Samuel S. Wilson, "National Power," at history.circ6.dcn.

93. Filburn v. Helke, 43 F. Supp. 1017, 1019 (S.D. Ohio 1942). Judge Allen, in her dissent, in addition to upholding the penalty, argued that the entire statute was constitutional. Her opinion developed many of the arguments the Supreme Court would use later in its decision. Allen maintained that "where it is claimed that the local activity sought to be regulated does not directly affect commerce, decision should not be made by examination of the effect of isolated individual activity, but must include due regard to the total effect of the attempted regulation." Ibid., 1021–22.

94. Wickard v. Filburn, 317 U.S. at 128–29.

95. AO annual report, 1945, 21–24 and tables C1 and D3; AO annual report, 1941, 23, 48.

96. See Columbus Courthouse Civil Docket, vols. 2–3; Judge Robert R. Nevin, "Historic Cases Involving Conflicts between the Civil Courts and Military Authorities in Time of War," Sixth Circuit Judicial Conference, Cincinnati, May 9, 1942, Wallace Files. There were probably condemnations in Cincinnati also, but there are no extant records to verify that.

97. Nevin, "Historic Cases," 1–3.

98. AO annual report, 1945, 24, 62 and tables C1 and D3.

99. See, e.g., Columbus Courthouse Civil Docket, vol. 4.

100. U.S. v. Lichter, 68 F. Supp. 19 (1946), aff'd, Lichter v. U.S., 106 F.2d 329 (6th Cir. 1947) and 334 U.S. 742 (1948).

101. Porter v. Montaldo's, 71 F. Supp. 372, 375 (S.D. Ohio 1946). See also Bowles v. Gotterdam, 72 F. Supp. 1022 (S.D. Ohio 1947) (denying the government's attempt to get treble damages based on the defendant's alleged overcharging of rent because the defendant admitted his liability, although he never returned the excess rent he charged) and Bowles v. Rugg, 57 F. Supp. 116 (S.D. Ohio 1944)

(allowing the administratrix of an estate to proceed with a sale of farm equipment in state court without interference from the OPA).

102. AO annual report, 1941, 23, 48, 95.

103. Ibid., 1945, 65.

104. Figures compiled by the author from extant Dayton and Columbus criminal dockets, housed at their respective courthouses. No criminal docket books for Cincinnati were found for these years, so the figures assume that the numbers would be about the same as those for Columbus.

105. Extant records showed only one case of sabotage, the defendant being indicted in July 1945, tried by a jury in a trial that lasted three days, and sentenced to prison. U.S. v. Neff, Case No. 2042, Dayton Courthouse Criminal Docket, 1945.

106. Dayton Courthouse Criminal Docket, 1942 and 1943; Columbus Courthouse Criminal Docket, 1942 and 1943. See also Curia v. Pillsbury, 54 F. Supp. 196 (S.D. Ohio 1944) (Underwood upholding the army's right to place someone in military prison who claimed to be a consciousness objector but whose request for that classification had been denied and then who had undergone all his examinations but refused to take the oath of allegiance; Underwood held that he did not have to take the oath to be considered in the military). World War II law, however, provided for more exemptions, at least for pacifists. Thus, fewer "deserving" men were tried.

107. In re Berue, 54 F. Supp. 252 (S.D. Ohio 1944). See also Nevin, "Historic Cases," where, in analyzing some Civil War cases, he emphasized the distinction between military authority over civilians and martial law. There is nothing in the record to indicate what the "incident" was about, what Berue was specifically convicted of, or what the term of his sentence was.

108. See Whirls v. Trailmobile Co., 64 F. Supp. 713 (S.D. Ohio, 1945), *aff'd*, 154 F.2d 866 (6th Cir. 1946), *rev'd*, 331 U.S. 40 (1947) (holding to the strict letter of the statute that seniority is preserved only for a year after the veteran returns). See also Riggle v. Cincinnati Union Terminal, 71 F. Supp. 456 (1947) (Druffel concluding that plaintiff was entitled to full seniority despite his withdrawal from the United Mine Workers).

109. See Trischler v. Universal Potteries, Inc., 78 F. Supp. 609 (S.D. Ohio 1947) (Underwood holding that, as long as a returning veteran moved to the head of the list in a craft training program, the employer did not have to make room for him when all the positions were currently full).

110. Brown v. Watt Car & Wheel Co., 91 F. Supp. 570 (S.D. Ohio 1949), *aff'd*, 182 F.2d 570 (6th Cir. 1950). See also Bhd. of Ry. and S.S. Clerks v. Ry. Express Agency, Inc., 137 F. Supp. 653 (S.D. Ohio 1955) (Druffel holding that a dishonorably discharged veteran is not entitled to the privileges of being rehired upon return from the armed forces), *aff'd*, 238 F.2d 181 (6th Cir. 1956).

111. AO annual reports, 1950 and 1954.

112. Ibid.; Cincinnati Courthouse Criminal Journal, vol. 7; Columbus Courthouse Criminal Docket, vols. 12–16; Dayton Courthouse Criminal Docket, 1950–1960. Most of the income tax evasion cases were prosecutions of people who simply tried to avoid paying their taxes; however, some challenged the application

of the law to them. In *Doogan v. U.S.*, Judge Druffel, for example, had to decide whether pension payments the taxpayer received after he retired from the Cincinnati Fire Department because of a physical disability incurred in the line of duty were subject to taxation as income or were compensation for his injuries; Druffel, siding with the taxpayer, decided the latter was the case. 154 F. Supp. 703 (S.D. Ohio 1957).

113. Cincinnati Courthouse Civil Journal, vol. 4; Columbus Courthouse Civil Docket, vols. 12–13, 19–21; Dayton Courthouse Civil Docket, 1956–1959. See, especially, as an example of an unusual patent case, Int'l Indus. & Devs., Inc. v. Farbach Chem. Co., 145 F. Supp. 34 (S.D. Ohio 1956) (Druffel finding that plaintiff had filed a patent infringement suit in bad faith, awarding treble damages to the defendant), and, for bargaining agreements, Hamilton Foundry & Mach. Co. v. Int'l Molders & Foundry Workers Union of N. Am., 95 F. Supp. 35 (S.D. Ohio 1951), *aff'd*, 193 F.2d 209 (6th Cir. 1951) (Druffel holding the agreement invalid because the evidence showed that both parties intended that neither would be bound until the agreement was signed and the local union had never signed the agreement); Smith v. Baltimore & Ohio R.R. Co., 114 F. Supp. 869 (S.D. Ohio 1956), *aff'd*, 325 F.2d 576 (6th Cir. 1963) (Druffel voiding part of a union agreement with the railroad as violating the Railway Labor Act because it destroyed the employment and seniority rights of conductors belonging to a different union).

114. *Congressional Record*, 83d Cong., 1st sess., 1 (April 1, 1953); "Judge Cecil's Nomination Approved by Senate Group," *Dayton Daily News*, April 20, 1953, n.p., clipping in Cecil Scrapbook.

115. "Cecil Appears Sure of U.S. Judge Post," *Daily News*, February 23, 1953, clipping in Cecil Scrapbook; "Judge Lester L. Cecil," *West Milton Record*, May 6, 1953, 1, clipping in Cecil Scrapbook; attorney David Greer's nomination of Judge Cecil for the Walk of Fame, 2002, Cecil Scrapbook; attorney Tom Cecil, interview by author, June 6, 2002, Dayton, OH; note from Judge Cecil to his son Tom, August 4, 1960, Cecil Scrapbook. For more detailed biographical information on Cecil, see chapter 9.

116. U.S. v. Universal Milk Bottle Serv., Inc., 85 F. Supp. 622, 627 (S.D. Ohio 1949).

117. U.S. v. Holophane Co., 119 F. Supp. 114, 119 (S.D. Ohio 1954); Case No. 2659, Columbus Courthouse Civil Docket, vol. 12. See also Joseph P. Griffin, "United States Antitrust Laws and Transnational Business Transactions: An Introduction," *International Lawyer* 21 (Spring 1987): 307–41. According to his clerk at the time, John Lyter, it was Underwood's two clerks who convinced him, after "endless hours" of debate, to issue this broad ruling. Underwood, a "strict constructionist" and "very conservative," initially maintained that jurisdiction extended only to the three-mile limit. John D. Holschuh, a future district court judge and then Underwood's other clerk, together with Lyter, argued that the court's jurisdiction was much broader and that, in the final analysis, the court was not exercising jurisdiction outside the United States; it was only making the company act properly within the United States, even though it affected business in Europe. Lyter interview.

118. U.S. v. Hupman, Case No. 2707, Dayton Courthouse Criminal Docket, vol. 7; U.S. v. Hupman, 127 F. Supp. 432 (S.D. Ohio 1953). See also "Perjury: Circumstantial Evidence is Sufficient for False-Swearing Conviction of Union Officer Filing Non-Communist Affidavit," *Harvard Law Review* 70 (December 1956): 383–85; Harry A. Abrams, speech at the presentation of Judge Druffel's portrait.

119. Hupman v. U.S., 219 F.2d 243, 249 (6th Cir. 1955).

120. Brown v. Bd. of Educ., 347 U.S. 483 (1954).

121. *Hillsboro News-Herald,* October 7, 1954, editorial section, 3.

122. Transcript of docket entries, Clemons v. Bd. of Educ. of Hillsboro, Ohio, Case No. 3440, Civil Case Files, W. Div., RG 21.

123. Complaint, transcript of docket entries, transcript of September 29, 1954, hearing, various notices of motions and motions for entry of orders, order by Druffel, final order and injunction, and all other legal filings associated with the case, Clemons v. Bd. of Educ., Case No. 3440, Civil Case Files, Civil Records, W. Div., RG 21. All of Druffel's rulings and orders are unpublished.

124. *Hillsboro News-Herald,* October 7, 1954, editorial section, 3. For a good history of the events surrounding the case, see also ibid., December 16, 1954, 1; January 5, 1955, 6; February 3, 1955, 1; February 10, 1955, 1; January 12, 1956, 1; January 19, 1956, 4; January 26, 1956, editorial section, 1; February 2, 1956, 1–2; February 16, 1956, 1, and editorial section, 1; February 23, 1956, 1; April 5, 1956, 1, 5; April 12, 1956, 1–2 and editorial section, 2, 7; April 19, 1956, 1–2, editorial section, 2.

125. Order, October 1, 1954, Clemons v. Bd. of Educ., Case No. 3440, Civil Case Files, W. Div.; *Hillsboro News-Herald,* January 6, 1955, 6.

126. Order, December 10, 1954, Clemons v. Bd. of Educ., Case No. 12,380, 6th Circuit, in files of Clemons v. Bd. of Educ., Case No. 3440, Civil Case Files, W. Div.

127. Opinion, January 28, 1955, Clemons v. Bd. of Educ., Case No. 3440, Civil Case Files, W. Div.; *Hillsboro News-Herald,* February 3, 1955, 1.

128. Clemons v. Bd. of Educ. of Hillsboro, Ohio, 228 F.2d 853, 856, 858 (6th Cir. 1956), *cert. denied,* 350 U.S. 1006 (1956). The three-judge circuit court disagreed on whether Druffel had, indeed, abused his discretion and disagreed on whether there should be immediate integration of the schools. One, if not two, of the judges were willing to give Druffel more discretion in deciding when integration would occur. Some other lower courts agreed with Druffel's view. See "Development in the Law—Injunction II. The Changing Limits of Injunctive Relief," *Harvard Law Review* 78 (March 1965): 1007–8.

129. *Hillsboro News-Herald,* January 12, 1956, 1.

130. Order, April 11, 1956, Clemons v. Bd. of Educ., Case No. 3440, Civil Case Files, W. Div.

131. *Hillsboro News-Herald,* April 19, 1956, editorial section, 2.

### CHAPTER 6

1. For an overview of how the court's functions have changed over time, see James Williard Hurst, "The Functions of Courts in the United States, 1950–1980," *Law and Society Review* 14, nos. 3–4 (1980–1981): 402–70.

2. Andrew R. L. Cayton, *Ohio: The History of a People* (Columbus: Ohio State University Press, 2002), 368–71, quote at 368.

3. *Dayton Daily News,* June 22, 2002, clipping in files of Rita Wallace, historian of the Sixth Circuit, Library of the Sixth Circuit and the District Court for the Southern District of Ohio, Cincinnati (hereafter Wallace Files).

4. Ben Kaufman, "U.S. Judges in Middle of Social Security 'Mess,'" *Cincinnati Enquirer,* December 28, 1985, C1.

5. 75 Stat. 80 (1961) authorized a temporary fourth judge, made permanent in An Act to provide for the appointment of additional circuit and district judges, 80 Stat. 75 (1966); An act to provide for the appointment of additional district judges, 84 Stat. 294 (1970); An Act to provide for the appointment of additional district and circuit judges, 92 Stat. 1629 (1978); An Act to amend Title 28 of the U.S. Code, 98 Stat. 347 (1984); 104 Stat. 5089, Title II (1990).

6. For Weinman's appointment, see *Journal of the Executive Proceedings of the Senate of the United States,* 68th Cong., 1st sess., 643 (July 28,1959), 706 (September 1, 1959), 707 (September, 2, 1959). For biographical information on Weinman, see "Memorial Proceedings for the Honorable Carl A. Weinman," 473 F. Supp. 1–19 (S.D. Ohio 1979). For additional information on Weinman, see chapter 9.

7. For Peck's appointment, see *Senate Executive Journal,* 87th Cong., 2d sess., 6 (January 15, 1962), 513–14 (April 11, 1962); file on Peck's district court nomination, Papers of John W. Peck, box 54, Cincinnati Historical Society, Cincinnati; letters from Senator Stephen Young to Peck, November 30, 1965, and from Peck to Young, December 28, 1979, ibid., box 61. For biographical information, see Bicentennial Committee of the Judicial Conference of the United States, *History of the Sixth Circuit* (Washington, DC: Bicentennial Committee of the Judicial Conference of the United States, 1976), 178–79; "Presentation of Portrait of the Honorable John W. Peck to the U. S. District Court for the Southern District of Ohio," May 16, 1972, Wallace Files; clippings from *Cincinnati Enquirer,* October 13, 1991, December 5, 1971, and September 8, 1993, from *Cleveland Plain Dealer,* September 9, 1993, and from *Cincinnati Post,* September 8, 1993, in Wallace Files; statement of John W. Peck, Judge, Supreme Court of Ohio, before the Ohio Legislative Service Commission's Study Committee on Capital Punishment, July 5, 1960, Papers of John W. Peck, box 45; "Four Year Report," remarks to the Cincinnati Bar Association, December 1, 1965, Miscellaneous Speeches, ibid; *Cincinnati Enquirer,* October 2, 1962, clipping ibid., box 70.

8. *Senate Executive Journal,* 89th Cong., 2d sess., 989 (September 30, 1966), 1061, 1063–64 (October 20, 1966); Bicentennial Committee, *History of the Sixth Circuit,* 145; clippings from *Cincinnati Post,* January 31, 1989, *Cincinnati Enquirer,* January 31, 1989, and February 1, 1989, in Wallace Files; Judge Peck's remarks at Hogan's Memorial Service, February 24, 1989, and Judges Rubin, Kinneary, Weber, Peck, Spiegel and William McD. Kite, "In Memory of Timothy S. Hogan," Papers of John W. Peck, box 57; "Memorial Resolution for Timothy Sylvester Hogan," *1989 Annual Report Presented to the Sixth Circuit Judicial Congress,* May 10–12, 1989, 42–43. For additional information on Hogan, see chapter 9.

9. 80 Stat. 75 (1966).

10. *Senate Executive Journal,* 89th Cong., 2d sess., 989 (September 30, 1966), 1061, 1063–64 (October 20, 1966); Sarah Livermore, executive ed., *The American Bench: Judges of the Nation,* 3d ed. (Sacramento, CA: Forster-Long, 1985), 1868; Bicentennial Committee of the Judicial Conference of the United States, *Judges of the United States,* 2d ed. (Washington, DC: Government Printing Office, 1983), 398; Bicentennial Committee, *History of the Sixth Circuit,* 182; Memorial Resolution for David Stewart Porter, *1989 Annual Report Presented to the Sixth Circuit Judicial Congress, May 10–12, 1989,* 41. Quote from Allen Howard, "Old Buddies to Honor David Porter," *Cincinnati Enquirer,* December 3, 1982, Wallace Files. For more information on Porter, see chapter 9.

11. *Senate Executive Journal,* 89th Cong., 2d sess., 664 (June 28, 1966), 705–8 (July 21, 1966); *Almanac of the Federal Judiciary* (New York: Aspen Law and Business, 1999), 1:75–76; Ruth A. Kennedy, ed., *The American Bench: Judges of the Nation,* 10th ed. (Sacramento, CA: Forster-Long, 1999), 1889; *Justices and Judges of the United States Courts* (Washington, DC: Administrative Office of the U.S. Courts, 1999), 301; Bicentennial Committee, *History of the Sixth Circuit,* 154–55; Martha Colaner, "Judge Joseph P. Kinneary," pamphlet by the University of Cincinnati College of Law provided to the author by Judge Kinneary; *Associated Press State and Local Wire,* July 27, 2001, Wallace Files. For additional information on Kinneary, see chapter 9.

12. 84 Stat. 294 (1970).

13. *Senate Executive Journal,* 92d Cong., 1st sess., 185 (April 29, 1971), 263 (May 19, 1971), 264–65 (May 20, 1971); Marie T. Finn, ed., *The American Bench: Judges of the Nation,* 8th ed. (Sacramento, CA: Forster-Long, 1995), 1917; Bicentennial Committee, *Judges of the United States,* 430; Bicentennial Committee, *History of the Sixth Circuit,* 186; Judges Holschuh, Weber, and Dlott, "Memorial Resolution for Carl B. Rubin," *1996 Annual Report and Roster of Judges, Sixth Circuit Judicial Conference, July 7–10, 1996;* Robert Reisch and Gregory J. Mazares, "The Legacy of Judge Carl B. Rubin," *Law Technology Product News* (June 1996): 29, in Wallace Files. Quote from Thomas R. Schuck, "Dedication: Honorable Carl B. Rubin," *University of Cincinnati Law Review* 64 (Spring 1996): 800–802. For additional information on Rubin, see chapter 9.

14. *Senate Executive Journal,* 93d Cong., 2d sess., 309 (May 1, 1974), 399 (June 12, 1974), 400–401 (June 13, 1974); Bicentennial Committee, *History of the Sixth Circuit,* 129–30; "Robert M. Duncan," available from air.fjc.gov; Judge Robert M. Duncan, interview by author, May 25, 2001, Columbus. For additional information on Duncan, see chapter 9.

15. 92 Stat. 1629 (1978); 98 Stat. 347 (1984).

16. *Senate Executive Journal,* 96th Cong., 2d sess., 210 (March 28, 1980), 238–39 (April 15, 1980), 320 (May 20, 1980), 326 (May 21, 1980).

17. Holschuh résumé provided to author by Judge Holschuh; Judge John D. Holschuh, interview by author, July 12, 1999, and July 30, 1999, Columbus; *Almanac of the Federal Judiciary* (1999), 1:77. For additional information on Holschuh, see chapter 9.

18. *Almanac of the Federal Judiciary* (New York: Aspen Law and Business, 2002), 1:69–70; John D. Holschuh, Robert L. Black Jr., Nathaniel R. Jones, James B. Helmer Jr., et al., "Dedication: Honorable S. Arthur Spiegel," *University of Cincinnati*

*Law Review* 64 (Fall 1995): 1–10; Judge S. Arthur Spiegel, interview by author, July 29, 1999, Cincinnati. For additional information on Spiegel, see chapter 9.

19. Judge Walter H. Rice, interview by author, June 14, 1999, Dayton; David Greer, *Sluff of History's Boot Soles: An Anecdotal History of Dayton's Bench and Bar* (Wilmington, OH: Orange Frazer Press, 1996), 454–58. For additional information on Rice, see chapter 9.

20. *Senate Executive Journal,* 99th Cong., 2d sess., 504 (August 15, 1986), 586 (September 19, 1986), 606 (September 26, 1986); ibid., 100th Cong., 1st sess., 485 (July 1, 1987), 690 (November 5, 1987), 695 (November 6, 1987).

21. Kennedy, *American Bench* (10th ed.), 1967–68; *Almanac of the Federal Judiciary* (2002), 1:78–79; Judge Herman J. Weber, interview by author, July 23, 1999, Cincinnati. For additional information on Weber, see chapter 9.

22. Mary Lee Bliss, ed., *The American Bench: Judges of the Nation,* 12th ed. (Sacramento, CA: Forster-Long, 2001), 2012; *Almanac of the Federal Judiciary* (2002), 1:73–74; clipping from *Columbus Dispatch,* November 18, 1986, files of the Clerk of Court, Columbus, Ohio (hereafter referred to as Columbus Clerk Files); Judge James Graham, interview by author, July 15, 1999, Columbus. For additional information on Graham, see chapter 9.

23. *Almanac of the Federal Judiciary* (2002), 1:76–78; Mary Lee Bliss, ed., *The American Bench: Judges of the Nation,* 13th ed. (Sacramento, CA: Forster-Long, 2002), 2062; Mark R. Abel, "Judge Smith Takes Senior Status," *BARbriefs,* February 2002, 13–14; Judge George C. Smith, interview by author, July 26, 1999, Columbus. For additional information on Smith, see chapter 9.

24. *Senate Executive Journal,* 102d Cong., 1st sess., 499 (July 26, 1991). The Senate confirmed the nomination on February 6, 1992. Ibid., 102d Cong., 2d sess., 86–87.

25. *Almanac of the Federal Judiciary* (2002), 1:70–72; Judge Sandra Beckwith, interview by author, July 22, 1999, Cincinnati; unpublished biographical questionnaire, Wallace Files. For additional information on Beckwith, see chapter 9.

26. *Senate Executive Journal,* 104th Cong., 1st sess., 557 (August 10, 1995), 705–6 (October 26, 1995), 839, 842, 846 (December 22, 1995); ibid., 104th Cong., 2d sess., 271 (May 9, 1996), 469 (July 22, 1996); ibid., 105th Cong., 1st sess., 354 (July 3, 1997), 527 (October 9, 1997), 548 (October 23, 1997), 559 (October 27, 1997).

27. *Almanac of the Federal Judiciary* (2002), 1:72–73; résumé provided to the author by Judge Dlott. For additional information on Judge Dlott, see chapter 9.

28. *Almanac of the Federal Judiciary* (2002), 1:75–76; Judge Edmund A. Sargus, interview by author, July 15, 1999, Columbus. For additional information on Judge Sargus, see chapter 9.

29. *Almanac of the Federal Judiciary* (2002), 1:74–75; Judge Algenon L. Marbley, interview by author, July 30, 1999, Columbus. For additional information on Judge Marbley, see chapter 9.

30. "New Federal Judge to Ease Rice's Load," *Dayton Daily News,* June 20, 2002, and "Senate Confirms Rose Unanimously," ibid., May 10, 2002, clippings in Wallace Files; Bliss, *American Bench* (12th ed.), 1982; résumé of Judge Frost furnished to the author by Judge Rice, August 13, 2003.

31. For information on judicial appointees from Franklin Roosevelt to the present, see Robert A. Carp and Ronald Stidham, *The Federal Courts,* 4th ed. (Washington, DC: CQ Press, 2001), 71–71; Sheldon Goldman, *Picking Federal Judges: Lower Court Selection from Roosevelt through Reagan* (New Haven, CT: Yale University Press, 1997), 348–50 and passim; Donald Dale Jackson, *Judges* (New York: Atheneum, 1974), 252–53.

32. The information used to compile profiles of district court appointees for the District Court for the Southern District of Ohio is found in the footnotes for the individual judges in this chapter and in chapter 9. For statistics on judges nationwide, see note 31, *supra.*

33. 153 Stat. 1223 (1939); 60 Stat. 902 (1948); 70 Stat. 497 (1957); 81 Stat. 664 (1967); Ben Kaufman, "U.S. Judges in Middle of Social Security 'Mess,'" *Cincinnati Enquirer,* December 28, 1985, C1.

34. 82 Stat. 1107 (1968).

35. Rice interview; Magistrate Judge Michael Merz, interview by author, May 22, 2001, Dayton; Magistrate Judge Mark Abel, interview by author, June 4, 2001, Columbus. See chapter 9 for details on the appointment process each of the district court judges experienced.

36. Rice interview.

37. Merz interview.

38. Federal Magistrate Act of 1979, 93 Stat. 643. See also 92 Stat. 2729 (1976) and Judicial Improvements Act of 1990, 104 Stat. 5089.

39. For an overview of the development of magistrates and their role in district courts, see, e.g., Peter G. McCabe, "The Federal Magistrate Act of 1979," *Harvard Journal on Legislation* 16 (1979): 343–401; Joseph F. Spaniol Jr., "The Federal Magistrates Act: History and Development," *Arizona State Law Journal* 4 (1974): 565–78; Carroll Seron, "The Professional Project of Parajudges: The Case of U.S. Magistrates," *Law and Society Review* 22 (July 1988): 557–74; Judith Resnik, "'Uncle Sam Modernizes His Justice': Inventing the Federal District Courts of the Twentieth Century for the District of Columbia and the Nation," *Georgetown Law Journal* 90 (March 2002): 607; Georgene M. Vairo, "Federal Magistrates," *National Law Journal,* July 14, 2003, 16.

40. AO report; Merz interview.

41. Abel interview; Duncan interview; Graham interview; Holschuh interview; Marbley interview; Merz interview; Rice interview; Weber interview; Judge Susan Dlott, interview by author, July 28, 1999, Cincinnati; Judge Joseph P. Kinneary interview by author, June 25, 1999, Columbus.

42. Bankruptcy Act of 1978, 92 Stat. 2657; amended after a 1982 Supreme Court decision by 98 Stat. 333 (1983).

43. In addition to reaching age sixty-five, to retire at full pay, the judges' age and years of service must total at least eighty years. Thus for example, one can retire at sixty-seven if one has been a federal judge for thirteen years. Act of February 10, 1954, 68 Stat. 12. Congress created senior status in 1919, allowing retired judges to continue serving on a part-time basis. Act of February 25, 1919, 40 Stat. 1156. See also "U.S. Judges in Middle of Social Security 'Mess,'" *Cincinnati Enquirer,* December 28, 1985, C1.

44. Beckwith interview; Smith interview. See also Graham and Holschuh interviews. In 1984, in the Sentencing Reform Act, Congress established a commission

to establish new guidelines that federal judges had to follow when sentencing those convicted of federal crimes. 98 Stat. 1987 (1984). The commission promulgated the guidelines in 1987. For a good history of the legislation and challenges to it, see Ilene H. Nagel, "Structuring Sentencing Discretion: The New Federal Sentencing Guidelines," *Journal of Criminal Law and Criminology* 80 (Winter 1990): 883–943. For a study of the views of district judges nationwide, which demonstrates their similarity to those in the Southern District of Ohio, see Molly Treadway Johnson and Scott A. Gilbert, *The U.S. Sentencing Guidelines: Results of the Federal Judicial Center's 1996 Survey* (Washington, DC: Federal Judicial Center, 1997).

45. Holschuh et al., "Dedication: Honorable S. Arthur Spiegel," 6–7.

46. Peck, "Four Year Report."

47. Holschuh interview.

48. Conclusions based on interviews by the author with district judges Beckwith, Dlott, Graham, Holschuh, Kinneary, Rice, Sargus, Smith, Spiegel, and Weber and with magistrate judges Abel and Merz; Magistrate Judge Timothy S. Hogan, interview by author, July 12, 2001, Cincinnati; former Magistrate Judge Robert Steinberg, interview by author, June 1, 2001, Cincinnati.

49. See chapter 8.

50. Greer, *Sluff of History,* 457, and chapter 7.

51. See chapter 7.

52. Thompson v. Midwest Found. Indep. Physicians Ass'n, 117 F.R.D. 108 (S.D. Ohio 1987); 124 F.R.D. 154 (S.D. Ohio 1988).

53. Enter. Energy Corp. v. Columbia Gas Transmission Co., 137 F.R.D. 240 (S.D. Ohio 1991).

54. Spiegel interview.

55. In his 1985 year-end report on the judiciary, Chief Justice Warren Burger praised Lambros and Spiegel for the innovation. *New York Times,* September 16, 1987, 10.

56. Holschuh et al., "Dedication: Honorable S. Arthur Spiegel," 6–7.

57. Ben Kaufman, "Summary Jury Trial Is Ordered" *Cincinnati Enquirer,* November 29, 1986, C1.

58. Ben Kaufman, "GE Defense-Fraud Suit Settled in Principle," *Cincinnati Enquirer,* February 23, 1989, C2. See also Ben Kaufman, "Top Officials Ordered to Attend Fernald Trial," ibid., April 29, 1989, C2; Holschuh et al., "Dedication: Honorable S. Arthur Spiegel," 6–7.

59. Holschuh et al., "Dedication: Honorable S. Arthur Spiegel," 4; Hudson v. Cincinnati Metro. Housing Auth., Case No. 92-CV-279 (S.D. Ohio 1994).

60. Georgene Kaleina, "Speeding up Justice Arbitration to Shorten Backlog of Federal Cases," *Cincinnati Enquirer,* April 18, 1984, D1.

61. Clerk's annual report, 1991, 5; ibid., 1992, 5.

62. Memo from Judge Rice to "Counsel" with attachment explaining the new process, October 31, 2001, Columbus Clerk of Court Files.

63. Some argue that such changes have transformed district court judges from adjudicators to administrators. See David S. Clark, "Adjudication to Administration," 110–17. Many district court judges in the Southern District of Ohio, based

on this author's interviews with them, would agree. Judges like Rubin who preached a jurisprudence of restraint most especially opposed judicial supervision. In ending court supervision of a desegregation consent decree involving the Cincinnati Fire Division, for example, Rubin declared: "Intervention and supervision by the federal courts should be limited to situations where there are constitutional violations and that supervision should cease as soon as such violations are corrected." Ben Kaufman, "Court Ends Supervision in Race Suit" *Cincinnati Enquirer,* January 10, 1989, A7.

64. See, e.g., NCR Corp. v. Gartner Group, Inc., 1997 WL 1774881 (S.D. Ohio 1997); Moriarty v. Gen. Tire & Rubber Co., 289 F. Supp. 381 (S.D. Ohio 1967).

65. See, e.g., Reynolds v. Int'l Amateur Athletic Fed'n, 841 F. Supp. 1444 (S.D. Ohio 1992) (Kinneary holding that the court had personal jurisdiction over an international athletic association); Moriarty v. Gen. Tire & Rubber Co., 289 F. Supp. 381 (S.D. Ohio 1967) (Porter holding that the court had personal jurisdiction over a Greek plastic hose manufacturer charged with violating the Sherman Antitrust Act).

66. See, e.g., Moriarty v. General Tire & Rubber Co., 289 F. Supp. 381 (S.D. Ohio 1967) (Porter holding that the federal court had pendent jurisdiction to hear the state claims as well as the federal claims). See also chapter 8, for the several Eleventh Amendment cases questioning the federal court's subject matter jurisdiction to hear suits filed against the state of Ohio, agencies and institutions created by the state, or state officials.

67. Moriarty v. General Tire & Rubber Co., 289 F. Supp. at 390. The Third Circuit Court of Appeals applied this test in *Max Daetwyler Corp. v. Meyer,* 762 F.2d 290 (3d Cir. 1985). Several district courts, including the District of Connecticut and the Northern District of Ohio, also adopted this nationwide theory. Cryomedics, Inc. v. Spembly, Ltd., 397 F. Supp. 287 (D. Conn. 1975); Graham Eng'g Corp. v. Kemp Prods. Ltd., 418 F. Supp. 915 (N.D. Ohio 1976). The Ninth Circuit, the District Court for the Eastern District of Pennsylvania, and probably the majority of other federal courts, however, refused to adopt this expansive theory. Wells Fargo & Co. v. Wells Fargo Express Co., 556 F.2d 406 (9th Cir. 1977); Superior Coal Co. v. Ruhrkohle, A.G., 83 F.R.D. 414 (E.D. Penn. 1979).

68. Dlott interview. See also Wexell v. Komar Indus., Inc., 1993 WL 650862 (S.D. Ohio 1993), *reconsideration denied,* 1993 WL 650863 (S.D. Ohio 1993), *aff'd,* 18 F.3d 916 (Fed. Cir. 1994) (Beckwith, in a patent dispute case, dismissing the case after plaintiffs repeatedly violated the court's discovery orders and disregarded discovery deadlines, thereby making undue "demands upon the time and budget of this Court") 1993 WL 650863 at *3.

69. Rice interview. Fed. R. Civ. P. 56 established summary judgment. For a discussion of the changing and conflicting attitudes on summary judgment, see Charles Alan Wright et al., *Federal Practice and Procedure* (St. Paul, MN: West Publishing, 1998), 3d ed., § 2727, which is the leading treatise on federal procedure, and Arthur R. Miller, "The Pretrial Rush to Judgment: Are the 'Litigation Explosion,' 'Liability Crisis,' and Efficiency Clichés Eroding Our Day in Court and Jury Trial Commitments," *New York University Law Review* 78 (June 2003): 982–1134. See also

Theresa M. Beiner, "The Misuses of Summary Judgment in Hostile Environment Cases," *Wake Forest Law Review* 34 (Spring 1999): 71–134; Gregory A. Gordillo, "Summary Judgment and Problems in Applying the Celotex Trilogy Standard," *Cleveland State Law Review* 42 (1994): 263–99; Paul W. Mollica, "Federal Summary Judgment at High Tide," *Marquette Law Review* 84 (Fall 2000): 141–226.

70. The Supreme Court established the standards for summary judgment, liberalizing the prerequisites and encouraging judges to grant more of these motions, in a trilogy of cases: Anderson v. Liberty Lobby, Inc., 477 U.S. 242 (1986); Celotex Corp. v. Catrett, 477 U.S. 317 (1986); Matsushita Elec. Indus. Co., Ltd. v. Zenith Radio Corp., 475 U.S. 574 (1986).

71. Street v. J. C. Bradford & Co., 886 F.2d 1472 (6th Cir. 1989). This language is now "boilerplate" for rulings on motions for summary judgment. See Mega Linx, Inc. v. U.S., 1998 WL 723145, *2 (S.D. Ohio 1998).

72. Spires v. Ohio State Univ., 2001 WL 506511, *2 (S.D. Ohio 2001).

73. See, e.g., interviews of district judges Beckwith, Dlott, Duncan, Graham, Holschuh, Marbley, Rice, Sargus, Smith, and Weber and with magistrate judges Hogan, Steinberg, and Merz.

74. AO annual report, 1960. The Administrative Office estimated that judges spent approximately 50 percent of their time in chambers, researching, writing opinions, drafting findings of fact and conclusions of law in nonjury cases, drawing up charges in jury cases, holding pretrial conferences, and preparing for trial. All the statistics in this section, unless otherwise noted, were compiled from the AO reports and the annual reports of the Clerk of the District Court for the Southern District of Ohio.

75. Peck to Young, November 23, 1965, Papers of John W. Peck, box 61.

76. AO annual report, 1980, 128. See table 6.2.

77. AO annual report, 1990, 6–8. See table 6.2.

78. See table 6.3.

79. Memo, Porter to Judges Kinneary, Hogan, Rubin, and Duncan, April 4, 1979, Columbus Clerk of Court files.

80. See chapter 8.

81. See, e.g., Klopp v. U.S., 148 F.2d 659 (6th Cir. 1945); Imboden v. U.S., 194 F.2d 508 (6th Cir. 1952).

82. See AO annual report, 1972, 135. See also "U.S. Jury Indicts Two Who Refused Induction," *Cincinnati Enquirer,* April 7, 1966; "3 Years in Prison Given to Draft Evader," ibid., November 22, 1966; "Draft Objector Gets 3-Year Term," ibid., December 8, 1966; "Ex-Wyoming Man Begins Term on Draft Conviction," ibid., December 31, 1966; "Loveland Draft Dodger Jailed," ibid., January 6, 1967; "College Student Indicted by Jury," ibid., March 25, 1967; "Won't Go in Army, Goes in Jail," ibid., March 31, 1967; "Five Men Indicted on Draft Evasion Charges," ibid., July 25, 1968; "10 Area Men Charged as Draft Violators," ibid., January 23, 1970.

83. Merz interview. In fifteen cases listed in the criminal docket for Columbus in 1966 and 1967, all defendants received suspended sentences requiring work, generally in a hospital, for between two to five years; two, however, served three to four months in jail before the judge suspended the remainder of their sentences on

the condition that they do the required work. Columbus Courthouse Criminal Docket, vol. 19. One sees the same pattern in vol. 20 for the years 1968–1969. The Cincinnati criminal docket lists sixteen cases for 1965 through 1967. Two defendants received presidential pardons, having never been found to be sentenced; three were found not guilty at trial. The rest either were found guilty, generally by a jury, or pleaded guilty and were sentenced from two to three years. In Cincinnati, however, nothing in the record indicates that these sentences were suspended. Cincinnati Courthouse Criminal Docket, vol. Y. In 1970, of the nine defendants indicted in Cincinnati for failing to report for the draft or for alternative duty, or for other violations of the Selective Service procedures, four had their cases dismissed, two were not found and eventually received presidential pardon in January of 1977, and two received probation and alternative civilian work. Only one served a jail term—two years. Cincinnati Courthouse Criminal Docket, 1970–1973, vol. AA. Whether those in the 1960s had their sentences suspended cannot be determined from available records. Cincinnati judges did seem to be a little harsher in sentencings in these cases then did Kinneary or Weinman. The articles in the *Cincinnati Enquirer* cited in note 82, *supra,* indicate that many men convicted in Cincinnati did serve three-year prison terms.

84. U.S. v. Green, Columbus Courthouse Criminal Docket, vol. 20.

85. Irons, after graduating from Harvard Law School, taught at several major universities and wrote books on New Deal lawyers and the Japanese internment. Peck, in answering Irons's charges, claimed that he helped Irons's career by inspiring him to go to law school. Peck to Irons, undated [1985] and April 12, 1974, Papers of John W. Peck, box 57.

86. Irons to Peck, May 29, 1985; memo to Peck from Ray Clark, May 29, 1974; copy of presentence report; Peck to Irons, undated [1985] and April 12, 1974, ibid.

87. AO annual report, 1975, 94, 225.

88. Ibid.

89. See, generally, Columbus Courthouse Civil Docket, 1975, esp. case numbers 75–3 through 75–57; Dayton Courthouse Civil Docket, 1980; Lemasters v. Weisberger, 397 F. Supp. 274 (S.D. Ohio, 1975); New v. Harris, 505 F. Supp. 721 (S.D. Ohio 1980). The court in Columbus heard most of these cases, although Dayton and Cincinnati each had a few.

90. Begley v. Weinberger, 400 F. Supp. 901 (S.D. Ohio 1975), *aff'd,* Begley v. Matthews, 544 F.2d 1345 (6th Cir. 1976); *cert. denied,* Begley v. Califano, 430 U.S. 985 (1977).

91. See, e.g., Auflick v. Weinberger, Case No. 75–57, Columbus Courthouse Civil Docket, 1975, the Sixth Circuit Court of Appeals holding up an appeal until its decision in the *Begley* case. After *Begley, Auflick* was also remanded to HEW for further review in light of the *Begley* doctrine.

92. Letter from Judge Edmund A. Sargus to the author, September 8, 2003.

### CHAPTER 7

1. Marilyn Dillon, "Spiegel Nominated to Court," *Cincinnati Enquirer,* November 15, 1979, A1.

2. Phillip R. Shriver and Clarence E. Wunderlin Jr., eds., *The Documentary Heritage of Ohio* (Athens: Ohio University Press, 2000), 388.

3. See chapter 5.

4. See, e.g., Michael W. Combs, "Federal Judiciary and Northern School Desegregation: Law, Politics, and Judicial Management," *Publius* 16 (Spring 1986): 33–52; Paul Gewirtz, "Choice in the Transition: School Desegregation and the Corrective Ideal," *Columbia Law Review* 86 (May 1986): 728–799, quote 732–33; Randolph D. Moss, "Participation and Department of Justice School Desegregation Consent Decrees," *Yale Law Journal* 95 (July 1986): 1811–35 and note 50.

5. Deal v. Cincinnati Bd. of Educ., Case No. 5483, Cincinnati Courthouse Civil Docket, vol. 37.

6. *Cincinnati Enquirer,* December 22, 1969, clipping in Papers of John W. Peck, box 70, Cincinnati Historical Society, Cincinnati.

7. Deal v. Cincinnati Bd. of Educ., 244 F. Supp. 572, 582 (S.D. Ohio 1965).

8. Ibid., 576–77.

9. Ibid., 576–77, 579, 582.

10. Ibid., 582, *aff'd and remanded,* 369 F.2d 55 (6th Cir. 1966), *cert. denied,* 389 U.S. 847 (1967), *appeal after remand,* 419 F.2d 1387 (6th Cir. 1969), *cert. denied,* 402 U.S. 962 (1971); Case No. 5483, Cincinnati Courthouse Civil Docket, vol. 37. In 1969, the Sixth Circuit Court of Appeals affirmed but remanded the case "for further findings on the issues of claimed discrimination in specific schools." Deal, 369 F.2d 55. By then, Peck was serving on the Sixth Circuit Court of Appeals, so Judge Hogan heard the case. Hogan affirmed Peck, and the Court of Appeals again affirmed. See also Lewis M. Steel, attorney for the plaintiffs, to Peck, July 8, 1968, and Peck to Norris Muldrow and others, attorneys for the City of Cincinnati, December 6, 1966, in Papers of John W. Peck, box 77; *Cincinnati Enquirer,* December 22, 1969, and *Cincinnati Post,* July 28, 1965, clippings ibid., box 70. Some have speculated that the plaintiffs' attorneys did not do effective discovery in this case; indeed, this was the first case fully litigated in the North that plaintiffs lost.

11. Bronson v. Bd. of Educ., City of Cincinnati, 510 F. Supp 1251 (S.D. Ohio 1980).

12. Barbara Zigli, "Countywide Pattern Seen in School Segregation Suit," *Cincinnati Enquirer,* August 10, 1979, B2.

13. Bronson v. Bd. of Educ., City of Cincinnati, 512 F.2d 718 (6th Cir. 1975), 525 F.2d 344 (6th Cir. 1975). See also Barbara Zigli, "NAACP Outlines Specifics in Local School Suit," *Cincinnati Enquirer,* August 10, 1979, B1; "Judge Disallows Older Evidence in School Suit," ibid., October 30, 1979, D3.

14. Bronson v. Bd. of Educ., 510 F. Supp 1251 and 535 F. Supp. 846 (S.D. Ohio 1982), *rev'd,* 687 F.2d 836 (6th Cir. 1982). On remand, the city moved for summary judgment, which Rice denied. Bronson v. Bd. of Educ., 573 F. Supp 759 (S.D. Ohio 1983). Rice also allowed plaintiffs to file an amended complaint. Bronson v. Bd. of Educ., 573 F. Supp at 767 (S.D. Ohio 1983). Rice believed that his arguments in support of his decision that the prior action did not have a collateral estoppel effect was "the best piece of work to ever come out of this office." Judge Walter H. Rice, interview by author, June 14, 1999, Dayton.

15. Bronson v. Bd. of Educ., 578 F. Supp. 1091 (S.D. Ohio 1984). See also Clifford P. Hooker, "Whither the Metropolitan Remedy: Bronson v. Board of Education of the City School District of the City of Cincinnati," *West's Education Law Reporter* 17 (1984): 731–42.

16. Bronson v. Bd. of Educ., 604 F. Supp. 68 (S.D. Ohio 1984).

17. Ibid., 82.

18. Rice interview. See also Lisa Hooker, "Desegregation Ruling Puts School's Plans in Motion," *Cincinnati Enquirer,* June 23, 1984, D3; Allen Howard, "Judge OKs Plan for Schools," ibid., A1; Ben L. Kaufman, "Judge Hears Final Arguments in School Suit," ibid., June 7, 1986, C1; Kaufman, "City Schools Win 12-Year-Old Suit," ibid., July 3, 1986; Kaufman, "Decree Gives Local Schools $2.9 million," ibid., February 18, 1987, C1.

19. Rice interview.

20. David Greer, *Sluff of History's Boot Soles: An Anecdotal History of Dayton's Bench and Bar* (Wilmington, OH: Orange Frazer Press, 1996), 456–57.

21. Bronson v. Bd. of Educ., 1991 WL 1101072 at *14 (S.D. Ohio 1991). In 1994, a new settlement was reached whereby complaints go to the superintendent. If they are not satisfactorily resolved, the district court has the right of review. Rice interview. In 1999, the case went back to Judge Rice because of low achievement on standardized tests in predominantly African American schools. "Desegregation Case Goes Back to Judge," *Cincinnati Post,* June 8, 1999.

22. Penick v. Columbus Bd. of Educ., Case No. C-2–73–0248, Documents 1, 19, and 22 in case files at Columbus courthouse and 429 F. Supp. 229 (S.D. Ohio 1977). See also Robert L. Pegues Jr., "A Documentary Research of the Role of the School Superintendent in School Federal Desegregation Court Trials: Four Major Large Ohio Cities, 1964–1984" (Ph.D. diss., Kent State University, 1989).

23. Order by court filed July 29, 1977, document 168, Columbus case files for Penick v. Columbus Bd. of Educ.; opinion and order by the court, filed March 8, 1977, document 154, ibid. and published as 429 F. Supp. 229 (S.D. Ohio 1977). Duncan was not the only federal judge who bemoaned the fact that courts had to be involved or that others should be addressing this issue. See Combs, "Federal Judiciary and Northern School Desegregation," 39–44. See chapter 9 for biographical information on Duncan.

24. Penick v. Columbus Bd. of Educ., 429 F. Supp. 229, *aff'd,* 583 F.2d 787 (6th Cir. 1978), *aff'd,* 443 U.S. 449 (1979). Duncan also held that the state board and the state superintendent were liable. Penick v. Columbus Bd. of Educ., 519 F. Supp 925 (S.D. Ohio 1981), *aff'd,* 663 F.2d 24 (6th Cir. 1981).

25. Andrew R. L. Cayton, *Ohio: The History of a People* (Columbus: Ohio State University Press, 2002), 382. But Cayton also argues that the peaceful integration of Columbus was largely due to political and demographic factors. Further, he maintains that in the long run Columbus failed to face the racial and educational problems that lingered, creating new problems and a decline in the quality of the Columbus schools. Ibid. In general, the hopes for integrating schools have not been realized throughout the nation. See Peter H. Irons, *Jim Crow's Children: The Broken Promise of the Brown Decision* (New York: Viking, 2002).

26. Judge Robert M. Duncan, interview by author, May 25, 2001, Columbus. In 2001, twenty-six black parents and students in Columbus filed a new suit against the Columbus Board of Education, nine Columbus suburban school boards, and others, alleging that they discriminated against African Americans, maintaining a segregated system and thereby restricting their educational opportunities. Judge Sargus granted the defendants' motions to dismiss, although he invited the plaintiffs to file an amended complaint on one count. Moss v. Columbus Bd. of Educ., 2001 WL 1681117 (S.D. Ohio 2001).

27. Brinkman v. Gilligan and Brinkman v. Dayton Bd. of Educ., 503 F.2d 684, 685–86 (S.D. Ohio 1974); Paul R. Dimond, *Beyond Busing: Inside the Challenge to Urban Segregation* (Ann Arbor: University of Michigan Press, 1985), 124, 126. For a more detailed history of desegregation in the Dayton schools, see Joseph Watras, *Politics, Race, and Schools: Racial Integration, 1954–1994* (New York: Garland Publishing, 1997), 181–206; Harriet Elaine Glosson Adair, "Trends in School Desegregation: An Historical Case of Desegregation in Dayton, Ohio, Denver, Colorado, Los Angeles, California, and Seattle, Washington, 1954–1985" (Ed.D. diss., Brigham Young University, 1986).

28. Brinkman v. Dayton Bd. of Educ., 503 F.2d at 685–86.

29. Dimond, *Beyond Busing*, 124–50.

30. Brinkman v. Gilligan, 503 F.2d. at 687, 700–701, 703; Greer, *Sluff of History*, 399. Upon remand, Rubin entered a decision again favoring the board majority's plan; again the Sixth Circuit Court of Appeals reversed his ruling and remanded the case back to him. Brinkman v. Gilligan, 518 F.2d 853 (6th Cir. 1975).

31. Brinkman v. Gilligan, 539 F.2d 1084 (6th Cir. 1976).

32. Dayton Bd. of Educ. v. Brinkman, 433 U.S. 406 (1977).

33. Brinkman v. Gilligan, 446 F. Supp. 1232 (S.D. Ohio 1977). See also Greer, *Sluff of History*, 399–400.

34. Brinkman v. Gilligan, 583 F.2d 243, 247 (6th Cir. 1978).

35. Dayton Bd. of Educ. v. Brinkman, 443 U.S. 526 (1979). In 1985, Rubin found that the state board and the state superintendent were jointly and severally liable for racial segregation existing in Dayton and had to share in the costs of remedying the constitutional violation. Brinkman v. Gilligan, 610 F. Supp. 1288 (S.D. Ohio 1985).

36. Goodwine v. Taft, 2002 WL 1284228 (S.D. Ohio 2002). Dayton was the last Ohio city to remain under court-ordered busing. In December of 2001, Rice appointed John Garland, the president of Central State University, to mediate between the parties to end cross-town busing. After the parties reached a settlement, Rice lifted the desegregation order, ending twenty-five years of busing. *Cincinnati Enquirer,* December 22, 2001, B2. The agreement stipulated that Dayton would spend $30 to $35 million over the next five years to improve academic achievement in the public schools. The NAACP agreed to the end of busing because integration was impossible with a school population that was 73 percent black. Improving academic achievement became a more pressing goal. *Cincinnati Enquirer,* December 12, 2000, April 13, 2002, and April 16, 2002, clippings in Wallace Files and 5 *Ohio Lawyer's Weekly* 304 (2002), in Wallace Files.

37. Stanley Chesley et al., "Presentation of the Portrait of and Memorial to Honorable Carl B. Rubin," October 20, 1995, en banc session of the United States District Court for the Southern District of Ohio, xvii, in Wallace Files.

38. *Dayton Journal Herald*, July 28, 1978, 10, clipping in Papers of John W. Peck, box 55; Greer, *Sluff of History*, 400–402; Chesley et al., "Presentation of the Portrait of and Memorial to Honorable Carl B. Rubin," xvii–xviii.

39. Combs, "Federal Judiciary and Northern School Desegregation," 33–52, quotes at 51–52.

40. 42 U.S.C. § 2000e.

41. Dozier v. Chupka, 395 F. Supp. 836, 859–60 (S.D. Ohio 1975).

42. For African Americans and the Columbus police, see Naynie v. Chupka, 1975 U.S. Dist. LEXIS 14328 (S.D. Ohio 1976), and Police Officers for Equal Rights v. City of Columbus, 644 F. Supp. 393 (S.D. Ohio 1985), 916 F.2d 1092 (6th Cir. 1990). For women and Columbus firefighters, see Brunet v. City of Columbus, 642 F. Supp. 1214 (S.D. Ohio 1986).

43. City of Richmond v. Croson, 488 U.S. 469 (1989).

44. Brunet v. Columbus, 1992 WL 540716 (S.D. Ohio 1992).

45. Judge James Graham, interview by author, July 15, 1999, Columbus. The Sixth Circuit Court of Appeals affirmed Graham in the essentials of his order, agreeing that the city's affirmative action plan discriminated against male applicants and that neither the city nor the female firefighters had proven that the plan was based on past discrimination. Brunet v. Columbus, 1 F.3d 390 (6th Cir. 1993).

46. Youngblood v. Dalzell, 1973 WL 170 (S.D. Ohio 1973), 1976 WL 709 (S.D. Ohio 1976), 625 F. Supp. 30 (S.D. Ohio 1985), *aff'd*, 804 F.2d 360 (6th Cir. 1986); *cert. denied*, 480 U.S. 935 (1987). Rubin did affirm the use of quotas in *Youngblood v. Dalzell*, 123 F.R.D. 564 (S.D. Ohio 1989).

47. Youngblood v. Dalzell, 704 F. Supp. 137 (S.D. Ohio 1989). Porter turned the case over to Rubin when his health began to fail. On the day Porter died, Rubin signed the order ending court supervision of the consent decree Porter had helped to craft. Ben L. Kaufman, "Court Ends Supervision in Race Suit," *Cincinnati Enquirer*, January 10, 1987, A7.

48. Kaufman, "Court Ends Supervision in Race Suit," *Cincinnati Enquirer*, January 10, 1987, A7.

49. Youngblood v. Dalzell, 704 F. Supp. 137 (S.D. Ohio 1989), *remanded by* 925 F.2d 954 (6th Cir. 1991), *on remand to* 777 F. Supp 1382, 1386 (S.D. Ohio 1991); Jansen v. City of Cincinnati, 904 F.2d 336 (6th Cir. 1990), 758 F. Supp. 451 (S.D. Ohio 1991); *order vacated*, 977 F.2d 238 (6th Cir. 1992), *cert. denied*, 508 U.S. 911; Tye v. City of Cincinnati, 794 F. Supp. 824 (S.D. Ohio 1992). Occasional signs of lingering wariness on the part of whites over the affirmative action programs initiated in these consent decrees can be seen in *Meyers v. City of Cincinnati*, 728 F. Supp. 477 (S.D. Ohio 1990), involving charges that the assistant fire chief was helping unqualified individuals obtain jobs. For blacks and females against the Cincinnati police, see U.S. v. City of Cincinnati, 1883 WL 508 (S.D. Ohio 1983), 1984 WL 1123 (S.D. Ohio 1984), 1984 WL 1124 (S.D. Ohio 1984), *aff'd in part, va-*

*cated in part, rev'd in part,* 771 F.2d 161 (6th Cir. 1985); Vogel v. City of Cincinnati, 1991 WL 334859 (S.D. Ohio 1991), *aff'd,* 959 F.2d 594 (6th Cir. 1992). Dayton, too, faced litigation, but not until the late 1980s. Most cases are unreported. Rice tried but failed to negotiate a consent degree and eventually dismissed a case filed by minorities and women against the Dayton police and fire departments because the plaintiffs, in a class action suit, did not have a proper plaintiff representing the class. Rice interview; Campbell v. City of Dayton, 1991 WL 1092501 (S.D. Ohio 1991). Judge Merz later dismissed a suit alleging discrimination in promotions based on gender. Smith v. City of Dayton, 1991 WL 1092497 (S.D. Ohio 1991), 830 F. Supp. 1066 (S.D. Ohio 1993), *aff'd,* 37 F.3d 1499 (6th Cir. 1994).

50. Firefighters Local No. 1784 v. Stotts, 467 U.S. 561 (1984). The Supreme Court, in deciding this case, reversed the decision of the three-judge panel of the Sixth Circuit Court of Appeals. Judge Duncan, sitting by designation from the District Court of the Southern District of Ohio, together with circuit court judges Damon J. Keith and Boyce F. Martin Jr. unanimously had upheld affirmative action over union seniority plans. Stotts v. Memphis Fire Dept., 679 F.2d 541 (6th Cir. 1982).

51. "Police Layoffs Must Follow Affirmative-Action Rules," *Cincinnati Enquirer,* April 13, 1984, C3; Allen Howard, "Rubin Willing to Reconsider Layoff Ruling," ibid., June 16, 1984, A1; "Seniority to Decide Firefighters' Layoffs," ibid., June 23, 1984, D2; Allen Howard, "Order Barring City Layoffs to be Dissolved by Judge," ibid., June 29, 1984, A1; Allen Howard, "Police Layoffs Ordered by Seniority," ibid., June 30, 1984, A1.

52. In 2000, in the Southern District of Ohio, for example, 652 civil rights cases were filed. The Supreme Court, in *McDonnell Douglas Corp. v. Green,* 411 U.S. 792 (1973), established clear procedures to handle such cases. These cases are now fact-specific. In general, the cases either settle out of court, go to jury trial, or, if the plaintiff cannot establish the prima facie case required by *McDonnell Douglas,* are dismissed on summary judgment. Plaintiffs successfully stopped several discriminatory employment practices based on "cultural sexual conditioning" and other stereotypes about women. See, e.g., Heath v. Westerville Bd. of Educ., 345 F. Supp. 501 (S. D. Ohio 1972); Hosey v. Williamson, Case No. C-2–97–1047 (S.D. Ohio 1998).

53. Senter v. General Motors Corp., 383 F. Supp. 222–25, 227–29 (S.D. Ohio 1974), *aff'd,* 532 F.2d 511 (6th Cir. 1976). It is interesting to note that Rubin never insisted that plaintiff's attorney follow Rule 23 of the Federal Rules of Civil Procedures to certify the suit as a class action; however, although the Sixth Circuit Court of Appeals criticized Rubin for failing to follow prescribed procedures, it upheld the decision, concluding that "no one was misled as to the class nature of the action" and that plaintiff satisfied all the requirements necessary to represent the class under federal rules. Senter v. General Motors Corp., 532 F.2d at 520–26. On many occasions, the court has also enforced the equal protection rights of women as well as of minorities. The judges have insisted that stereotypical treatment of women that attempts, for example, to restrict their choice of a child's name

or their access to collegiate sports, be eliminated. See, e.g., Brill v. Hedges, 738 F. Supp. 340 (S.D. Ohio 1991); Miami Univ. Wrestling Club v. Miami Univ., 195 F. Supp. 2d, 1010, 1015–16 (S.D. Ohio 2001), aff'd, 302 F.3d 608 (6th Cir. 2002). The attorney for the male athletes challenging the implementation of Title IX rules at Miami University argued that Beckwith "broke new legal ground when she said that Miami does not always have to apportion its sports budget according to the percentages of men and women on campus." *Cincinnati Enquirer,* January 31, 2001, clipping in Wallace Files.

54. EEOC v. United Association of Journeymen and Apprentices of the Plumbing and Pipefitting Indus. of the U.S. and Canada, Local Union No. 189, 311 F. Supp. 468 (S.D. Ohio 1970); Dobbins v. Local 212, Int'l Bhd. of Elec. Workers, AFL-CIO, 292 F. Supp. 413 (S.D. Ohio 1968), *supplemented by* 1969 WL 120 (S.D. Ohio 1969).

55. Ethridge v. Rhodes, 268 F. Supp. 83 (S.D. Ohio 1967).

56. See Associated Gen. Contractors of Ohio, Inc. v. Drabik, 1998 WL 812241 (S.D. Ohio 1998) and 50 F. Supp. 2d 741 (S.D. Ohio 1999), aff'd, 214 F.3d 730 (6th Cir. 2000), *cert. denied,* Johnson v. Associated Gen. Contractors of Ohio, Inc., 531 U.S. 1148 (2001); Associated Gen. Contractors of Am. v. City of Columbus, 936 F. Supp. 1363 (1996). In response, the state hired a consulting firm to do a study of past and current discrimination. Then, when the state fired the minority-owned business it hired to do the study, Judge Marbley enjoined them from taking that action, finding that they had themselves discriminated in that decision. D. J. Miller & Assocs., Inc. v. Ohio Dept. of Admin. Servs., 115 F. Supp. 2d 872 (S.D. Ohio 2000), and 4 O.L.W. 1068 (2000). Judge Rice also followed *Croson* in an unreported Dayton case. Rice interview.

57. See, e.g., *Clemons v. Runck,* 402 F. Supp. 863 (S.D. Ohio 1975), and *Newbern v. Lake Lorelei, Inc.,* 308 F. Supp. 407 (S.D. Ohio 1968), in which plaintiffs were successful and *Marr v. Rife,* 503 F.2d 735 (6th Cir. 1974), in which the court held that the plaintiffs had not provided sufficient evidence.

58. Laufman v. Oakley Bldg. & Loan Co., 408 F. Supp. 489, 494, 496, 500 (S.D. Ohio 1976); S. Arthur Spiegel, "David S. Porter Memorial," Papers of John W. Peck, box 58.

59. See, e.g., Kelly v. Romney, 316 F. Supp. 840 (S.D. Ohio 1970), and Coalition of Concerned Citizens Against I-670 v. Damian, 608 F. Supp. 110 (S.D. Ohio 1984).

60. Spiegel, "Porter Memorial."

61. Tyehimba v. Cincinnati, 2001 WL 1842470 (S.D. Ohio 2001); "The Biggest Case in Town Is in Her Court," *Cincinnati Enquirer,* February 17, 2002, A1; "Linking Cases Greased Deal's Final Resolution" ibid., April 4, 2002, A1; Magistrate Judge Michael Merz, interview by author, November 10, 2003, Dayton.

62. "Key Players in the Negotiations," *Cincinnati Enquirer,* April 4, 2002, A4; "Judge Wants to Confirm Progress in Negotiations" ibid., February 24, 2002, B1; "Mediation Marathon Drags On," ibid., April 3, 2002, A1; "The Biggest Case in Town Is in Her Court," ibid., February 17, 2002, A1; "Linking Cases Greased Deal's Final Resolution," ibid., April 4, 2002, A1; "Settlement Oversight," ibid.,

April 5, 2002, A4. Information on the rioting is in "Settlement," ibid., April 4, 2002, AI, A4.

63. "Cincinnati May Set a Precedent," ibid., April 4, 2002, A4; "Settlement," ibid., AI; "Vote: City Council Poised," ibid., April 5, 2002, A4; "Settlement Oversight," ibid.; "Adding Up the Costs of Police Settlement," ibid.; "Both Sides Wary of Profiling Settlement," ibid., June 7, 2002, AI; "Profiling Settlement Approved," ibid., August 6, 2002, AI, A6. Dlott's approval of the settlement was delayed two months after the June 6 fairness hearing because of squabbles over attorney fees. Optimism that the agreement would last faded within a year as Dlott and several of the parties disagree as to the settlement's continued viability. "Agreement's Yield: Contention," ibid., April 30, 2003, A12.

64. Greer, *Sluff of History*, 461–63.

65. Ibid., 462; Urseth v. City of Dayton, 680 F. Supp. 1084 (S.D. Ohio 1987), and 680 F. Supp. 1150 (S.D. Ohio 1987); Rice interview.

66. U.S. v. Clemmer, 748 F. Supp. 1249 (S.D. Ohio 1989); U.S. v. Clemmer, 918 F.2d 570 (6th Cir. 1990). For other examples of charges of police misconduct, see Belcher v. Stengel, 522 F.2d 438 (6th Cir. 1975), *cert. dismissed*, 429 U.S. 118 (1976); In the Matter of Disclosure of Grand Jury Transcripts, 309 F. Supp. 1050 (S.D. Ohio 1970); U.S. v. Smith and Moton, Case No. 11788, Cincinnati Criminal Dockets, vol. GG (1971).

67. See, e.g., Glover v. Williamsburg Local Sch. Dist. Bd. of Educ., 20 F. Supp. 2d 1160, (S.D. Ohio 1998).

68. Equality Found. of Greater Cincinnati, Inc. v. City of Cincinnati, 838 F. Supp. 1235, 1241–42 (S.D. Ohio 1993); *Cincinnati Enquirer,* January 17, 1995, C1. The Supreme Court, in June 2003, articulated a similar position ten years after Spiegel asserted this constitutional proposition. Lawrence v. Texas, 539 U.S. 558 (2003).

69. Equality Found. of Greater Cincinnati v. City of Cincinnati, 860 F. Supp. 417, 422 (S.D. Ohio 1994), 838 F. Supp. at 1241–42; *Cincinnati Enquirer,* January 17, 1995, C1. For an overview of the history of the amendment and the court decisions, see Sarah Sturmon and Sharon Moloney, "Anti-Gay Law Upheld by Court," *Cincinnati Post,* May 12, 1995; "Rights and Wrongs/Reversal of Anti-Issue 3 Ruling May Itself Be Reversed on Appeal," *Cincinnati Enquirer,* May 16, 1995; "Supreme Court May rule on City's Gay Ordinance," *Cincinnati Post,* August 10, 1995; "Top Court Tackles Gay Rights," ibid., October 10, 1996; Ben L. Kaufman, "Gay-Rights Backers Weigh Legal Options," *Cincinnati Enquirer,* October 15, 1997; Sharon Moloney, "Gay Rights Showdown Brewing," *Cincinnati Post,* October 14, 1998; "Court Lets Stand Law Denying Gay Protection," *Cincinnati Enquirer,* October 14, 1998, AI, A8: "Issue 3: Anti–Gay Rights Law Ruled Legal," ibid., May, 13, 1999; "Issue 3 Drew Activism out of Voters," ibid.; "Cincinnati Gay-Rights Debate," ibid., May 21, 1999. All clippings in Wallace Files.

70. Spiegel interview.

71. Equality Found. v. Cincinnati, 860 F. Supp. at 421.

72. Equality Found. v. Cincinnati, 54 F.3d 261, 265–66 (6th Cir. 1995).

73. Romer v. Evans, 517 U.S. 620 (1996).

74. Equality Found. v. Cincinnati, 518 U.S. 1001 (1996).

75. Equality Found. v. Cincinnati, 1998 WL 101701, *2 (6th Cir. 1998).

76. Equality Found. v. Cincinnati, 525 U.S. 943 (1998); Spiegel interview.

77. Socialist Labor Party v. Rhodes, 290 F. Supp. 983, 986 (S.D. Ohio 1968), quoting Wesberry v. Sanders, 376 U.S. 1 (1964).

78. Nolan v. Rhodes, 218 F. Supp. 953 (S.D. Ohio 1963), *rev'd,* 378 U.S. 556 (1964), *on remand,* 251 F. Supp. 584 (S.D. Ohio 1965), *aff'd,* 383 U.S. 104 (1966).

79. Mallory v. Eyrich, 717 F. Supp. 540 (S.D. Ohio 1989), *appeal dismissed,* 898 F.2d 154 (6th Cir. 1990) (challenging municipal judge elections); Clarke v. City of Cincinnati, 1993 WL 761489 (S.D. Ohio 1993), *aff'd,* 40 F.3d 807 (6th Cir. 1994) (challenging at-large representation for Cincinnati city council); Mallory v. Ohio, 38 F. Supp. 2d 525 (S.D. Ohio 1997), *aff'd,* 173 F.3d 377 (6th Cir. 1999), *cert. denied,* 528 U.S. 951 (1999) (challenging at-large elections for state judges). In 1997, a three-judge panel also heard a challenge to Ohio's congressional districting plan, arguing that it was the result of "bipartisan political gerrymandering." Judge Smith granted summary judgment to the defendants, finding that apportionment was an inherently political process. Miller v. Ohio, C2–94–1116 (S.D. Ohio 1996); the Supreme Court affirmed. See *Almanac of the Federal Judiciary* (New York: Aspen Law and Business, 2002), 1:77.

80. See Ohio Rev. Code §§ 3505.10, 3513.05–3513.191, 3517.01–04. For a summary of all the requirements, see Kinneary's dissent in Socialist Labor Party v. Rhodes, 290 F. Supp. 983, 998 (S.D. Ohio 1968).

81. George Wallace, former governor of Alabama and a staunch segregationist, broke with the Democratic Party and launched a bid for the presidency in 1967. But to wage a successful national campaign, the Wallace forces had to challenge ballot restrictions across the nation.

82. Socialist Labor Party v. Rhodes, 290 F. Supp. at 992–93 and passim; 393 U.S. 23 (1968).

83. Socialist Labor Party v. Rhodes, 318 F. Supp. 1262 (S.D. Ohio 1970), *appeal dismissed,* Socialist Labor Party v. Gilligan, 406 U.S. 583 (1972), *aff'd,* Sweetenham v. Gilligan, 409 U.S. 942 (1972).

84. Anderson v. Celebrezze, 499 F. Supp. 121 (S.D. Ohio 1980). In 1976, another three-judge court held the provision that barred a candidate from running in a primary because he had voted for another party four years previous was unconstitutional as applied to a candidate whose previous party no longer existed. Kay v. Brown, 424 F. Supp. 588 (S.D. Ohio 1976).

85. Brown v. Socialist Workers '74 Campaign Committee (Ohio), Case No. C-2-75-92, Papers of John W. Peck, box 31.

86. Brown v. Socialist Workers '74 Campaign Committee (Ohio), 459 U.S. 87 (1982). For a detailed analysis of the Supreme Court decision, see Steve Sloan, "*Brown v. Socialist Workers '74 Campaign Committee* and the Constitutionality of Campaign Disclosure Requirements as Applied to Minor Political Parties," *Journal of Law and Politics* 1 (1983): 195–210.

87. Socialist Labor Party v. Rhodes, 290 F. Supp. at 995.

88. Pestrak v. Ohio Elections Comm'n, 670 F. Supp. 1368, 1378 (S.D. Ohio 1987), 677 F. Supp. 534 (S.D. Ohio 1988), *aff'd in part, rev'd in part,* 926 F.2d 573

(1991); Walter v. Cincione, 2000 WL 1505945 at *4–5 (S.D. Ohio 2000). See also Chamber of Commerce of the U.S. v. Ohio Election Comm'n, 135 F. Supp. 2d 857 (S.D. Ohio 2001) (Judge Sargus staying action challenging Ohio election laws regarding advertisements and disclosure of contributors until the state courts decided a pending case); *Cincinnati Enquirer,* October 13, 2001, clipping in Wallace Files (reporting that Judge Dlott had issued a temporary restraining order preventing Cincinnati from enforcing its ordinance regulating the size of political signs and the times during which they may be displayed).

89. Judge James Graham, interview by author, July 15, 1999, Columbus.

90. ACLU of Cent. Ohio v. County of Delaware, 726 F. Supp. 184 (S.D. Ohio 1989).

91. See, e.g., Ronald A. Carp and C. K. Rowland, *Policymaking and Politics in the Federal District Courts* (Knoxville: University of Tennessee Press, 1983); Kevin L. Lyles, *The Gatekeepers: Federal District Courts in the Political Process* (Westport, CT: Praeger, 1997); Kevin L. Lyles, "Presidential Expectations and Judicial Performance Revisited: Law and Politics in the Federal District Courts, 1960–1992," *Presidential Studies Quarterly* 26 (Spring 1996): 447–48, 465–66; Wolf Heydebrand and Carroll Seron, *Rationalizing Justice: The Political Economy of Federal District Courts* (Albany: State University of New York, 1990), 20–22; James Williard Hurst, "The Functions of Courts in the United States, 1950–1980," *Law and Society Review* 14, nos. 3–4 (1980–1981): 402–70; Robert A. Carp and Ronald Stidham, *The Federal Courts,* 3d ed. (Washington, DC: CQ Press, 1998).

92. ACLU of Cent. Ohio v. County of Delaware, 726 F. Supp. 184 (S.D. Ohio 1989); County of Allegheny v. ACLU, 492 U.S. 573 (1989); Graham interview. See also Turnington v. Standard Register Co., 1997 WL 1806 (S.D. Ohio 1977), in which Judge Weinman did the same thing—postponed announcing a decision in a case until the Supreme Court ruled in a different, but related, case.

93. Congregation Lubavitch v. City of Cincinnati, 807 F. Supp. 1353 (S.D. Ohio 1992), *aff'd,* 997 F.2d 1160 (6th Cir. 1993); Knight Riders of the Ku Klux Klan v. City of Cincinnati, 863 F. Supp. 587 (S.D. Ohio 1994), *aff'd in part, vacated in part,* 72 F.3d 43 (6th Cir. 1995).

94. Ben L. Kaufman, "Menorah Opposition Outlined," *Cincinnati Enquirer,* December 11, 1990, B1. See also Ben L. Kaufman, "Menorah Dispute Is Taken to Court," ibid., December 8, 1990, C5; Ben L. Kaufman, "Judge Rules for Fountain Square Menorah," December 12, 1990, A1.

95. Pinette v. Capitol Square Review and Advisory Bd., 844 F. Supp. 1182, 1188 (S.D. Ohio 1993), *aff'd,* 30 F.3d 675 (6th Cir. 1994), *aff'd,* 515 U.S. 753 (1995). In the same case, Graham also held that the city could not deny the Klan a permit to hold a rally at Capitol Square on Martin Luther King Jr.'s birthday. Pinette v. Capitol Square Review and Advisory Bd., 874 F. Supp. 791 (S.D. Ohio 1994). For Graham's views on interpreting the First Amendment, see chapter 9.

96. The Supreme Court established this three-prong test for determining whether a governmental action violates the establishment clause of the First Amendment in *Lemon v. Kurtzman,* 403 U.S. 602 (1971). The challenged action must have a secular purpose; its primary effect must neither advance nor inhibit religion; and it must not excessively entangle government with religion.

97. Capitol Square Review and Advisory Bd. v. Pinette, 515 U.S. 753 (1995); Desmond H. Staple, "*Capitol Square Review and Advisory Board v. Pinette:* The Dismantling of the 'Endorsement Test,'" *Capitol University Law Review* 25 (1966): 487–516; Brant W. Bishop, "Protecting Private Religious Speech in the Public Forum: *Capitol Square Review and Advisory Board v. Pinette,*" *Harvard Journal of Law and Public Policy* 19 (Winter 1996): 602–11; Nina Kraut, "Speech: A Freedom in Search of One Rule," *Cooley Law Review* 12 (Hilary Term 1995): 177–96. The district court has also recently upheld the First Amendment rights of Jehovah's Witnesses to solicit door-to-door, free of burdensome city regulations. Watchtower Bible and Tract Soc. of New York, Inc. v. Village of Stratton, 61 F. Supp. 2d 734 (S.D. Ohio 1999), *aff'd*, 204 F.3d 553 (6th Cir. 2001), *rev'd*, 536 U.S. 150 (2002) (the Supreme Court declaring even broader First Amendment rights and fewer restrictions than the district court granted). The court, however, found that the state had sufficient reason to prohibit roving solicitation at the Ohio State Fair by religious groups, especially since they were permitted booths for solicitation. Int'l Soc'y for Krishna Consciousness, Inc. v. Evans, 440 F. Supp. 414 (S.D. Ohio 1977). On the other hand, Judge Kinneary held that an elementary school's decision to allow a student Bible club to meet at 6:30 PM on school grounds but not immediately after school did not violate the students' First Amendment rights; rather, to meet directly after school would violate the establishment clause because the teacher who was active in the club would be seen as merely continuing her teaching duties and thus endorsing one particular religion. Quappe v. Endry, 772 F. Supp. 1004 (S.D. Ohio 1991).

98. ACLU v. Capitol Square Review and Advisory Bd., 20 F. Supp. 2d 1176, 1180 (S.D. Ohio 1998), *aff'd*, 243 F.3d 289 (6th Cir. 2001). The Sixth Circuit was quite divided. The original three-judge panel held 2 to 1 against Graham. 210 F.3d 703 (6th Cir. 2000). Then the first en banc court vacated the opinion. 222 F.3d 268 (6th Cir. 2000).

99. Marsh v. Chambers, 463 U.S. 783 (1983).

100. ACLU v. Capitol Square Review and Advisory Bd., 20 F. Supp. 2d at 1180. Graham rejected the argument that the motto showed the state's preference to Christianity because the motto is from the New Testament, Matthew 19:26. Graham held that the displayed motto had no attribution to the New Testament and that the statement was merely "generically theistic." Ibid., 1178–79.

101. Ganulin v. U.S., 71 F. Supp. 2d 824 (S.D. Ohio 1999).

102. Cayton, *Ohio*, 390.

103. Contemporary Arts Ctr. v. Ney, 735 F. Supp. 743 (S.D. Ohio 1990); Amy Adler, "What's Left: Hate Speech, Pornography, and the Problem for Artistic Expression," *California Law Review* 84 (December 1996): 1499–1572 at 1535 and note 154; Ben L. Kaufman, "Various Shades of Meaning," *Cincinnati Enquirer,* April 8, 1990, A1; Ben L. Kaufman, "Judge to Police: Keep Hands off Exhibit," ibid., April 9, 1990, A1; Ben L. Kaufman, "Trial to Reach Verdict in Art vs. Obscenity," ibid., September 24, 1990, A1. For other obscenity cases heard in the District Court for the Southern District of Ohio, see Peto v. Cook, 339 F. Supp. 1300 (S.D. Ohio 1971) (a three-judge district court holding that to the extent Ohio laws prevent licensees from dealing in publications not declared obscene in an adver-

sary hearing they were unconstitutional), *vacated* 409 U.S. 1071 (1972), *on remand,* 364 F. Supp. 1 (S.D. Ohio 1973) (three-judge court upholding the statute to a certain extent, but ruling it in violation of the First Amendment to a certain extent and holding that the massive seizure of magazines without warrant violated the Fourth Amendment), *aff'd,* Guggenheim v. Peto, 415 U.S. 943 (1974); Old 74 Corp. v. Union Township Bd. of Trs., 166 F.3d 1214 (6th Cir. 1998) (Spiegel upholding the Supreme Court doctrine that nude dancing was constitutionally protected expression under the First Amendment); Currence v. City of Cincinnati, 2000 WL 1357918 (S.D. Ohio 2000), *aff'd,* 2002 WL 104778 (6th Cir. 2002); and Wolfe v. Village of Brice, 37 F. Supp. 2d 1021 (S.D. Ohio 1999) (while still acknowledging that nude dancing is protected expression, the court upheld ordinances regulating sexually oriented businesses as reasonable regulations). In general, when the district court judges hear obscenity cases, they examine the specific facts in light of standards established by the Supreme Court to determine whether the material is indeed obscene. See e.g., U.S. v. Carver, Case No. 4695, June 3, 1970, Dayton Courthouse Criminal Docket, vol. 1966–1968.

104. United Food & Commercial Workers Union, Local 1099 v. S.W. Ohio Reg'l Transit Auth., 163 F.3d 341 (6th Cir. 1998); *Cincinnati Enquirer,* November 1, 1997, September 29, 1998, and December 11, 1998, clippings in Wallace Files. Under the strict scrutiny test for determining whether there has been a denial of equal protection, the burden is on the government or the governmental agency to prove that it has a compelling interest to justify the restriction, that the restriction furthers some compelling governmental purpose, and that the restriction is narrowly tailored to achieve that compelling purpose.

105. "Judge Allows Metro to Reject Hyland Ads," *Cincinnati Post,* September 30, 1998; "Decision Due Today on Candidate's Bus Signs," *Cincinnati Enquirer,* September 29, 1998; "Hyland Loses Round in Bus Signs Fight," ibid., September 30, 1998; "Hyland Loses the Battle of Bus Ads," ibid., October 2, 1998, B1; "Decision Today on Bus Ads," *Cincinnati Post,* October 2, 1998, n.p. All clippings in Wallace Files. See also Kelly v. U.S. Postal Serv., 492 F. Supp. 121 (S.D. Ohio 1980) (upholding the right of a postal worker to wear political buttons as a legitimate expression of free speech).

106. Note from Ben L. Kaufman to the author, December 15, 2003.

107. See, e.g., Peoples Rights Org. v. City of Columbus, 925 F. Supp. 1254 (S.D. Ohio 1996), *aff'd,* 152 F.3d 522 (6th Cir. 1998).

108. See, e.g., Pembaur v. City of Cincinnati, 745 F. Supp. 446 (S.D. Ohio 1990).

109. Wade v. Bethesda Hosp., 356 F. Supp. 380 (S.D. Ohio 1973), 337 F. Supp. 671 (S.D. Ohio 1971).

110. E-mail from Magistrate Judge Abel to the author, January 26, 2004.

111. See, e.g., Planned Parenthood Affiliates of Ohio v. Rhodes, 477 F. Supp. 529 (S.D. Ohio 1979) (Kinneary granting a preliminary injunction preventing enforcement of Ohio statute placing limits on the use of public funds for medically necessary abortions); Roe v. Ferguson, 389 F. Supp. 387 (S.D. Ohio 1974) (Duncan holding that Ohio's statute prohibiting the use of Medicaid monies for elective

abortions conflicted with the mandatory provisions of the Social Security Act), *stay denied*, 389 F. Supp. 393 (S.D. Ohio 1974), *rev'd and remanded*, 515 F.2d 279 (6th Cir. 1975).

112. Doe v. Barron, 92 F. Supp. 2d 694 (S.D. Ohio 1999), and Roe v. Leis, 2001 WL 1842459 (S.D. Ohio 2001); "The Biggest Case in Town Is in Her Court," *Cincinnati Enquirer*, February 17, 2002, A1.

113. Planned Parenthood v. Casey, 505 U.S. 833 (1992).

114. Women's Med. Prof'l Corp. v. Voinovich, 911 F. Supp. 1051 (S.D. Ohio 1995), *aff'd*, 130 F.3d 187 (6th Cir. 1997), *cert. denied*, 523 U.S. 1036 (1998); Women's Med. Prof'l Corp. v. Taft, 162 F. Supp. 2d 929 (S.D. Ohio 2001).

115. Rice interview.

116. Frisby v. Schultz, 487 U.S. 474 (1988).

117. Vittitow v. City of Upper Arlington, 830 F. Supp. 1077, 1081–82 (S.D. Ohio 1993). Judge Smith, in an interview with the author, explained that what he was trying to do was provide the police, who were "in a real quandary," with a rule to help them keep the peace. But he admitted that he just "made up" the two-house rule. He noted, "That was the judicial activism in my career, and the court of appeals didn't buy it." Judge George C. Smith, interview by author, July 26, 1999, Columbus.

118. Vittitow v. City of Upper Arlington, 43 F.3d 1100 (6th Cir. 1995), *cert. denied*, 515 U.S. 1121 (1995).

119. Freedom of Access to Clinic Entrance Act, 108 Stat. 694 (1994).

120. U.S. v. Operation Rescue, 111 F. Supp. 2d 948 (S.D. Ohio 1999), 112 F. Supp. 2d 696 (S.D. Ohio 1999).

121. *Cincinnati Enquirer*, February 17, 2002, A1; April 14, 2002, B1; April 15, 2002, B1; April 17, 2002, A1; April 18, 2002, B1, B9; April 19, 2002, A1, A10.

## CHAPTER 8

1. Davison v. Dept. of Def., 560 F. Supp. 1019, 1023–25 (S.D. Ohio 1982). Ultimately, the air cargo facility was built. As of January 1, 2004, the RPA merged with the Columbus International Airport. The Columbus Regional Airport Authority now operates the facility that includes an airport, cargo buildings, industrial property, and an international transportation center. The Department of Defense still owns a portion of the land that houses the Ohio Air National Guard. For a sample of other cases arising under national environmental statutes in which Judges Rubin, Graham, and Weber ruled against the proenvironmentalist position, see Belville Mining Co., Inc. v. U.S., 763 F. Supp. 1411 (S.D. Ohio 1991), *rev'd in part and aff'd in part*, 999 F.2d 989 (6th Cir. 1993); Sierra Club v. Robertson, 845 F. Supp. 485 (S.D. Ohio 1994), *rev'd*, Sierra Club v. Thomas, 105 F.3d 248 (6th Cir. 1997), *vacated and remanded*, Ohio Forestry Ass'n, Inc. v. Sierra Club, 523 U.S. 726 (1998); U.S. v. M/G Transp. Servs., Inc., 173 F.3d 584 (6th Cir. 1999).

2. Carroll E. Dubuc and William D. Evans Jr., "Recent Developments under CERCLA: Toward a More Equitable Distribution of Liability," *Environmental Law Reporter* 17 (June 1987): 10197.

3. U.S. v. Chem-Dyne, 572 F. Supp. 802, 805–9 (S.D. Ohio 1983).

4. Dubuc and Evans, "Recent Developments," 10197. See also David L. Markell, "The Federal Superfund Program: Proposals for Strengthening the Federal/State Relationship," *William and Mary Journal of Environmental Law* 18 (Fall 1993): 14n34; Alfred R. Light, "The Importance of 'Being Taken': To Clarify and Confirm the Litigative Reconstruction of CERCLA's Text," *Boston College Environmental Affairs Law Review* 18 (Fall 1980): 5–6.

5. Robert M. Elkins and Ben L. Kaufman, "Fired Foreman's Suit Claims GE Cheating," *Cincinnati Enquirer,* November 4, 1984, C2; Ben L. Kaufman, "Lawsuits Settled by GE," ibid., February 24, 1989, B1.

6. Gravitt v. Gen. Elec. Co., 680 F. Supp. 1162 (S.D. Ohio 1988), *appeal dismissed,* 848 F.2d 190 (6th Cir. 1988), *cert. denied,* 488 U.S. 901 (1988); Ben L. Kaufman, "Judge Rules U.S. Mishandled Case," *Cincinnati Enquirer,* January 25, 1988, A8. See also Ben L. Kaufman, "Voucher Settlement Fair, Magistrate Says," *Cincinnati Enquirer,* August 25, 1987, A8.

7. U.S. v. Gen. Elec. Co., 808 F. Supp. 580 (S.D. Ohio 1992); Ben L. Kaufman, "Lawsuits Settled by GE," *Cincinnati Enquirer,* February 24, 1989, B1.

8. Kaufman, "Lawsuits Settled by GE."

9. Note from Ben Kaufman to the author, December 15, 2003. For a complete history of this case, see James B. Helmer Jr. and Robert Clark Neff Jr., "War Stories: A History of the Qui Tam Provisions of the False Claims Act, the 1986 Amendments to the False Claims Act, and Their Application in the *United States Ex Rel. Gravitt v. General Electric Co.* Litigation," *Ohio Northern University Law Review* 18 (1991): 35–75.

10. Ex parte Young, 209 U.S. 123 (1908). The Supreme Court continued to limit the states' Eleventh Amendment sovereign immunity throughout the twentieth century, ruling that Congress could abrogate the Eleventh Amendment in laws enacted pursuant to its powers under Section 5 of the Fourteenth Amendment or its enumerated Article I powers, as long as Congress abrogated the states' sovereign immunity in clear language. Fitzpatrick v. Bitzer, 427 U.S. 445 (1976); Atascadero State Hosp. v. Scanlon, 473 U.S. 234 (1985). See generally William E. Thro, "The Eleventh Amendment Revolution in the Lower Federal Courts," *Journal of College and University Law* 25 (Winter 1999): 501–25.

11. Tyus v. Ohio Dept. of Youth Servs., 606 F. Supp. 239 (S.D. Ohio 1985).

12. Martin v. Voinovich, 840 F. Supp. 1175, 1187 (S.D. Ohio 1993). More than nine thousand mentally retarded and handicapped persons had sued state officials under the Rehabilitation Act and ADA for discrimination in providing community housing based on the severity of the handicap. See also Weaver v. Univ. of Cincinnati, 758 F. Supp. 446 (S.D. Ohio 1991) (Rubin holding that, although the Eleventh Amendment barred suits in federal court against the university, plaintiffs could sue university officers to halt continuing violations of federal law).

13. Seminole Tribe of Florida v. Florida, 517 U.S. 44 (1996).

14. City of Boerne v. Flores, 521 U.S. 50 (1997).

15. Wilson-Jones v. Caviness, 99 F.3d 203 (6th Cir. 1996).

16. Quote from Judge Algenon L. Marbley, interview by author, July 30, 1999, Columbus. For cases, see Thorpe v. Ohio, 19 F. Supp. 2d 816, 821–22 (S.D. Ohio

1998); Williams v. Ohio Dept. of Mental Health, 960 F. Supp. 1276 (S.D. Ohio 1997); Pease v. Univ. of Cincinnati Med. Ctr., 6 F. Supp. 2d 706 (S.D. Ohio 1998); Hines v. Ohio State Univ., 3 F. Supp. 2d 859 (S.D. Ohio 1998); Meekison v. Voinovich, 17 F. Supp. 2d 725 (S.D. Ohio 1998). See also Judge Edmund A. Sargus, interview by author, July 15, 1999, Columbus.

17. Value Behavioral Health, Inc. v. Ohio Dept. of Mental Health, 966 F. Supp. 557 (S.D. Ohio 1997).

18. Maine v. Thiboutot, 448 U.S. 1 (1980).

19. Section 1983 incorporates the Civil Rights Act of 1871 into the U.S. Code. During the Reconstruction Era after the Civil War, Congress, concerned that southern state courts would not protect newly freed African Americans' rights proclaimed in the Constitution and federal laws, authorized, in the 1866 and 1871 Civil Rights Acts, district courts to hear suits for alleged violations of federal law as well as the Constitution. Collins, "'Economic Rights,' Implied Constitutional Actions, and the Scope of Section 1983," *Georgetown Law Journal* 77 (April 1989): 1493–94.

20. Value Behavioral Health, Inc. v. Ohio Dept. of Mental Health, 966 F. Supp. at 563–65, 575–76. Initially, plaintiff argued he could sue the state because Ohio had violated a federal law passed pursuant to Congress's power under the spending clause of Article I of the Constitution; he argued that the state of Ohio, by accepting federal Medicare money, agreed to be bound by the conditions Congress placed on the state Medicaid programs; however, the second amended complaint focused on subject matter jurisdiction via § 1983 of the U.S. Code.

21. The court of appeals never reviewed the merits of Sargus's opinion. Rather, it vacated his order after the successful bidder merged with the unsuccessful one. The new company then petitioned the Sixth Circuit Court of Appeals to dismiss the appeal and vacate the judgment. Sargus interview.

22. Nihiser v. Ohio E.P.A., 979 F. Supp. 1168, 1176 (S.D. Ohio 1997), *aff'd in part, rev'd in part,* 269 F.3d 626 (6th Cir. 2001), *cert. denied,* 536 U.S. 922 (2002). William E. Thro examines the split in the Southern District of Ohio as well as in other lower federal courts in "The Eleventh Amendment Revolution in the Lower Federal Courts," 501–25 and esp. notes 32, 33, 109, and 110. See also S. Elizabeth Wilborn Malloy, "Whose Federalism?" *Indiana Law Review* 32 (1998): 45–69.

23. Thomson v. Ohio State Univ. Hosp., 5 F. Supp. 2d 574, 577–580 (S.D. Ohio 1998), *aff'd,* 238 F.3d 424 (6th Cir. 2000).

24. Katzenbach v. Morgan, 384 U.S. 641 (1966).

25. Thomson v. Ohio State Univ. Hosp., 5 F. Supp. 2d at 577–80. See also Sims v. Univ. of Cincinnati, 1999 WL 221107 (S.D. Ohio 1999) (Weber, citing Graham's *Thomson* decision, dismissing for lack of subject matter jurisdiction another suit alleging that the university violated FMLA).

26. Keaton v. Ohio, 2002 WL 1580567 (S.D. Ohio 2002); Gerhardt v. Lazaroff, 2002 WL 2008165 at *23 (S.D. Ohio 2002). The exceptions are when Congress clearly abrogates states' immunity in statutes enforcing substantive Fourteenth Amendment guarantees pursuant to its Section 5 authority and when the state implicitly waives its immunity by accepting federal funds conditioned on their agreement to comply with the provisions of the statute involved.

27. Matteson v. Ohio State Univ., 2000 WL 1456988 (S.D. Ohio 2000). See also Keaton v. Ohio, 2002 WL 1580567 (S.D. Ohio 2002).

28. Weaver v. Ohio State Univ., 1997 WL 1159680 (S.D. Ohio 1997).

29. Martin v. Taft, 2002 WL 31101079 (S.D. Ohio 2002). Plaintiffs sought an injunction to force Ohio to provide additional community-based services for them and others similarly situated in compliance with requirements of the ADA and the Rehabilitation Act. Claiming that it agreed that community-based facilities were desirable, Ohio argued it lacked the financial resources to proceed as quickly as federal statutes required.

30. In re Beverly Hills Fire Litig., 639 F. Supp. 915 (E.D. Ky. 1986). A fire occurred at the Beverly Hills Supper Club in Southgate, Kentucky, a suburb about ten miles south of Cincinnati and part of the greater Cincinnati metropolitan area. Judge Rubin sat by designation in the U.S. District Court for the Eastern District of Kentucky.

31. Karen A. Gedulig, "Casey at the Bat: Judicial Treatment of Mass Tort Litigation," *Hofstra Law Review* 28 (Fall 2000): 309–42 and esp. 309–10.

32. In re Beverly Hills Fire Litig., 639 F. Supp. at 917.

33. Stanley Chesley, "Presentation of the Portrait of and Memorial to Hon. Carl B. Rubin," October 20, 1995, en banc Session of the United States District Court for the Southern District of Ohio, xiii, in Wallace Files. The *Cincinnati Post* wrote that Rubin was one of the first judges in the country to "recognize the significance of mass tort action." *Cincinnati Post*, August 3, 1995, 1A. See also "Limited Funds Behind Ruling on Fire Suits," *Cincinnati Enquirer*, December 21, 1977, A1; Bob Fogarty, "Court Calls Fire Suits One Action," ibid.

34. Fed. R. Civ. P. 23(b)(1)(B) provides that class action is appropriate when individuals, if suing separately, might exhaust available money before all cases were heard. Specifically, it says that "an action may be maintained as a class action" if "the prosecution of separate actions by . . . individual members of the class would create a risk of . . . adjudications with respect of individual members of the class which would as a practical matter be dispositive of the interests of the other members not parties to the adjudications or substantially impair or impede their ability to protect their interest."

35. In re Beverly Hills Fire Litig., 695 F.2d 207, 212, 216–17 (6th Cir. 1982), *cert. denied*, 461 U.S. 929 (1983). Plaintiff attorneys now generally oppose bifurcated trials. Although the practice helps focus the jury on one issue at a time, it also removes from the jury, during the first stage, the emotional part of the case—the injuries to the plaintiff—which are heard during the liability phase, if the trial reaches that point. Plaintiff attorneys believe that if the jurors do not hear about injuries, they are "likely to think the case is not a very significant one." Moreover, it leads to a disjointed trial. See, e.g., "Selling the Jury in a Bifurcated Trial," *National Law Journal*, August 19, 2002, B7; Jonathan Harr, *A Civil Action* (New York: Random House, 1995).

36. The $2.9 million original settlement came from the insurance policies held by the Schilling family, who owned the Beverly Hills Supper Club. A judge from the eastern Kentucky district court presided at the second trial. In re Beverly Hills

Fire Litig., 695 F.2d. at 210–12. See also http://www.enquirer.com/beverlyhills /litigation.html.

37. In re Ohio River Disaster Litig., 579 F. Supp. 1273 (S.D. Ohio, 1984), *rev'd*, 862 F.2d 1237, 1242 (6th Cir. 1988), *cert. denied*, 493 U.S. 812 (1989).

38. In re Ohio River Disaster Litig., 862 F.2d at 1241–42, 579 F. Supp. at 1274, 1276. The District Court for the Southern District of Ohio has been hearing admiralty cases since the court's early years. Such litigation continues through the present. In general, the litigation involves two categories of cases: collisions on the Ohio River and litigation under the Jones Act wherein "injured seamen seek to recover damages for injuries sustained in the course of their service aboard tow boats" or other service. Gordon C. Greene, "Ohio River Law: The Practice of Admiralty on Dry Land," in *The Law in Southwestern Ohio*, ed. George P. Stimson, comp. Frank G. Davis (Cincinnati: Cincinnati Bar Association, 1972), 133–34.

39. In re Ohio River Disaster Litig., 862 F.2d at 1238–44, 579 F. Supp. at 1277, 1279–84.

40. Public Law 90–296, announced in press release by the Supreme Court, Papers of John W. Peck, box 55. For another example of a different type of multidistrict case, see In re Air Crash Disaster, Dayton, Ohio, 350 F. Supp. 757 (S.D. Ohio 1972).

41. In re Richardson-Merrell Inc. [Bendectin Products Liability Litigation], 533 F. Supp. 489 (Judicial Panel on Multi-district Litigation 1982); Ben L. Kaufman, "800 Hope Bendectin Trial Will Bring Restitution," *Cincinnati Enquirer*, January 27, 1985, C1.

42. Ben L. Kaufman, "Parents Protest Exclusion," *Cincinnati Enquirer*, February 26, 1985, B2. All the other cases involved individual plaintiffs proceeding in separate trials. Of the thirty trials, plaintiffs won eight, Merrell won nineteen, two resulted in hung juries, and one ended in a mistrial. Rubin's 818 cases was one of the nineteen class actions that Merrell won. See Joseph Sanders, "From Science to Evidence: The Testimony on Causation in the Bendectin Cases," *Stanford Law Review* 46 (November 1993): 4–6. One of the suits not part of the multidistrict litigation, this one heard in the U.S. District Court for the Southern District of California, resulted in one of the most significant changes in the admissibility of expert testimony in recent times. In *Daubert v. Merrell Dow Pharmaceuticals*, the Supreme Court, vacating and remanding the decision of the district court in southern California, articulated what is now known as the *Daubert* test: that scientific testimony and evidence, to be admissible, not only must be relevant but also must be reliable. Daubert v. Merrell Dow Pharm., 509 U.S. 599 (1993). Before *Daubert*, U.S. courts used the so-called *Frye* test, which required that scientific testimony be generally acceptable in the particular field before it could be offered as proof of causation. In light of the difficulty of establishing that a particular scientific theory had achieved "general acceptance," the test eliminated many claims.

43. Anne Brataas, "6 Jurors Chosen to Try Maker of Morning-Sickness Pill," *Cincinnati Enquirer*, June 12, 1984, C2.

44. Anne Brataas, "Bendectin Cases Now Class Action," ibid., June 19, 1984, B1.

45. Ben L. Kaufman, "Bendectin Retrial Requested," ibid., August 3, 1985, D4.

46. In re Richardson-Merrell, Inc. Bendectin Prods., 624 F. Supp. 1212, 1269 (S.D. Ohio 1985); In re Bendectin Litig., Hoffman v. Merrell Dow Pharm., 857 F.2d 290, 293–94 (6th Cir. 1988); Sanders, "From Science to Evidence," 29–30, 39, 53–54; "Jury Concludes Bendectin Caused No Defects," *Cincinnati Enquirer*, March 13, 1985, A1. Since Merrell Dow's victory in Rubin's consolidated case, Merrell has refused to settle any of the other cases out of court. Also, it is probable that the small number of claims against Merrell Dow was due to the lack of success plaintiffs had in this and several other cases. See Sanders, "From Science to Evidence," notes 9 and 10. Of course, plaintiffs appealed, but the Sixth Circuit Court of Appeals upheld all of Rubin's rulings, and the U.S. Supreme Court refused to review that decision. "Plaintiffs Lose Appeal of Bendectin Verdict," *Cincinnati Enquirer*, August 31, 1988, D1; "Supreme Court Refusal Signals Victory for Merrell Dow," ibid., January 10, 1989, A8.

Judge Rubin used scientific expert witness testimony in another way in the sixty-five asbestos bodily injury cases he heard in 1986. Again, his innovative mind came up with a solution to a perpetual problem in tort litigation—the battle of the experts. Normally, the plaintiff calls several experts who testify one way; the defense then counters with its many experts who testify to the exact opposite. In the asbestos litigation, Rubin appointed court experts to examine all reports, x-rays, and other pertinent material. These court-appointed experts found that almost two-thirds of the plaintiffs did not have an asbestos-related condition. In the sixteen cases in which the court-appointed experts testified, the juries returned eleven defense verdicts and five plaintiff verdicts. See Carl B. Rubin and Laura Ringenbach, "The Use of Court Experts in Asbestos Litigation," *Federal Rules Decisions* 137 (October 1991): 37–40; Ben L. Kaufman, "Expert Panels Established in Asbestos Cases," *Cincinnati Enquirer*, January 9, 1987, C2.

Another multidistrict litigation case Rubin presided over, *In re Chubb Corporation Drought Insurance Litigation*, involved eight civil suits against Chubb Insurance Corporation for refusing to sell insurance to farmers when it was clear that a drought was imminent. That case resulted in a monetary settlement to the farmers to cover the amount they would have received had they been insured. See 1988 U.S. Dist. LEXIS 17026 (Judicial Panel on Multi-district Litigation 1988); Ben L. Kaufman, "Attorneys Compete for Chubb Case," *Cincinnati Enquirer*, August 10, 1988, B2; Ben L. Kaufman, "Judge Merges Suits against Chubb Group," ibid., August 11, 1988, C4; Ben L. Kaufman, "Arbitrator Chosen," ibid., November 17, 1988, D3; Ben L. Kaufman, "Chubb Insurance, Broker Will Pay Drought Claims," ibid., December 16, 1989, C2.

47. See Mark G. Kobasuk, "Hon. Sandra S. Beckwith Judge, Southern District of Ohio," *Federal Lawyer* 47 (July 2000): 16–18.

48. In re Cincinnati Radiation, 874 F. Supp. 796, 800, 803, 809–11, 820 (S.D. Ohio 1995).

49. In re Cincinnati Radiation, 1997 WL 1433832 (S.D. Ohio 1997); "Citing *Amchem Products*, Ohio Judge Denies Certification of Class of Cancer Patients," *Andrews*

*Mass Tort Litigation Reporter* (October 1977): 25365; "Southern District of Ohio Won't Amend Order Approving University of Cincinnati Experiment Class Settlement," *Andrews Toxic Chemicals Litigation Reporter* 1998 (January 12, 1998): 25494.

50. Judge Sandra Beckwith, interview by author, July 22, 1999, Cincinnati.

51. In re Cincinnati Radiation Litig., 1999 WL 321882 (S.D. Ohio 1999); "Ohio Judge Gives Final OK to $3.5 Million Radiation Exposure Class Settlement," *Andrews Toxic Chemicals Litigation Reporter* 17 (June 7, 1999): 10. Beckwith approved the settlement after a fairness hearing at which none of the class objected. "3.5 Million Class Settlement Approved in Ohio Radiation Exposure Litigation," *Andrews Toxic Chemicals Litigation Reporter* 16 (April 19, 1999): 11; "$5.4M Pact Ends Lawsuit over Radiation," *Cincinnati Post,* May 5, 1999, clipping in Wallace Files. Twelve families opted out of the settlement, arranging their own deal valued at approximately $1.8 million. See "Ohio Judge Gives Final OK to $3.5 Million," *Andrews Toxic Chemicals Litigation Reporter* 17 (June 7, 1999): 10.

52. "$5.4M Pact Ends Lawsuit over Radiation," *Cincinnati Post,* May 5, 1999, clipping in Wallace Files.

53. Ibid.

54. Kobasuk, "Hon. Sandra S. Beckwith," 18.

55. "Families Share Pain, Memories," *Cincinnati Enquirer,* June 18, 2000, B1, B5. One of the plaintiffs noted that Beckwith "displayed 'courage, moxie and guts' in her handling of the case."

A second class action case involved the harvesting of corneas from plaintiffs' decedents without plaintiffs' consent by the county coroner of Hamilton County. Brotherton v. Cleveland, 733 F. Supp. 56 (S.D. Ohio 1989), *rev'd,* 923 F.2d 477 (6th Cir. 1991), *on remand,* 908 F. Supp. 502 (S.D. Ohio 1995), *aff'd in part, rev'd in part, and remanded,* 173 F.3d 552 (6th Cir. 1999), *on remand,* 141 F. Supp. 2d 894 (S.D. Ohio 2001). Here, too, the case was settled before trial. An even more recent case was filed in 2001. A class of two hundred plaintiffs, families of deceased persons taken to the Hamilton County morgue, filed suit against a photographer and the then assistant coroner for intentional infliction of emotional distress and for violating the deceased persons' property and privacy rights by taking photographs of corpses without the permission of the families. *Cincinnati Enquirer,* November 8, 2001, n.p., clipping in Wallace Files.

56. S. Arthur Spiegel, "Settling Class Actions," *University of Cincinnati Law Review* 62 (April 1994): 1565–79. For other cases settled by Spiegel after summary jury trials, see Crawford v. Nat'l Lead Co., No. C-1–85–0149 (S.D. Ohio, 1989), cited in *Almanac of the Federal Judiciary* (New York: Aspen Law and Business, 2002), 1:83; Cincinnati Gas & Elec. Co. v. Gen. Elec. Co., 659 F. Supp. 49 (S.D. Ohio 1986), and 117 F.R.D. 597 (S.D. Ohio 1987).

57. In re Fernald Litig., 1986 WL 81382 (S.D. Ohio 1986) and 1989 WL 267039 (S.D. Ohio 1989); Day v. NLO, 811 F. Supp. 1271 (S.D. Ohio 1992), 147 F.R.D. 148 (S.D. Ohio 1993), *rev'd,* 5 F.3d 154 (6th Cir. 1993), 814 F. Supp. 646 (S.D. Ohio 1993), 851 F. Supp. 869 (S.D. Ohio 1994), 864 F. Supp. 40 (S.D. Ohio 1994).

58. Ben L. Kaufman, "DOE Motion at a Glance," *Cincinnati Enquirer,* October 7, 1988, E2; Ben L. Kaufman, "Luken Calls Hearing on Plant's Hazards," ibid., October 8, 1988, C1.

59. Judge S. Arthur Spiegel, interview by author, July 29, 1999, Cincinnati.

60. See chapter 6 for a description of a summary jury trial.

61. In re Fernald Litig., 1989 WL 267039 (S.D. Ohio 1989); Lawrence G. Cetrulo, "Summary Jury Trial," *Toxic Torts: A Complete Personal Injury Guide* (St. Paul, MN: West Group, 1993), § 17:9; Stanley M. Chesley, Louise M. Roselle, and Paul M. DeMarco, "The Plaintiff's Perspective: The Need for Class Certification in Radiation Cases," *Gonzaga Law Review* 30 (1994–1995): 587–88.

62. Day v. NLO, 147 F.R.D. 148 (S.D. Ohio 1993; 5 F.3d 154 (6th Cir. 1993); 851 F. Supp. 869 (S.D. Ohio 1994); 864 F. Supp. 40 (S.D. Ohio 1994); Chesley, Roselle, and DeMarco, "Plaintiff's Perspective," 588–90.

63. Spiegel interview. The DOE, in Spiegel's words, "tried to welch" on the deal. He then ordered the secretary of energy to come to Cincinnati. When the secretary refused, Spiegel cited him for contempt. Although Spiegel later backed down, he did succeed in forcing the DOE to pay its obligation. The cases became even more complicated as cleanup proceeded. In 1997, after an employee of Fluor Daniel Fernald filed a federal whistleblower suit against his company for cheating taxpayers out of more than $92 million in the cleanup of Fernald, the company settled for $8.4 million, making it the largest award in history for a whistleblower case litigated by private attorneys rather than the Department of Justice. *Cincinnati Enquirer,* June 20, 1997, A1, A4.

64. Ben L. Kaufman, "DOE Sends Portion of Debt for Fernald," *Cincinnati Enquirer,* March 16, 1990, D3.

Spiegel presided over two other major products liability cases. *Bowling v. Pfizer* involved heart valves that sometimes failed. The parties worked out the settlement themselves, without the need for a summary jury trial. The unique feature of the *Bowling* settlement is that it allows future claimants, that is, those whose heart valves had not fractured, to opt out later. It also provided compensation for those with the heart valves as well as money for the funding of research and development to produce better heart valves and better techniques to detect fractures in existing heart valves. Bowling v. Pfizer, 143 F.R.D. 141, 147–50 (S.D. Ohio 1992). *In re Telectronics,* a class action suit with a worldwide class of pacemaker recipients, involved defective pacemaker lead retention wires. The case consisted of 450 individual cases filed in courts across the country, all transferred, under multidistrict litigation, to the Southern District of Ohio. After Spiegel held a four-day summary jury trial, the summary jury found the defendant liable in negligence, strict liability, and several other theories the plaintiffs had advanced. The parties then, with Spiegel's help, worked out a settlement. Initially, the settlement did not have an opt-out clause, that is, all class members had to agree to the settlement. The Sixth Circuit Court of Appeals held that was unfair, and the parties negotiated a new settlement with the opt-out feature. In re Telectronics, 164 F.R.D. 222 (S.D. Ohio 1995); 186 F.R.D. 459 (S.D. Ohio 1999), *rev'd,* 221 F.3d 870 (6th Cir. 2000); 137 F. Supp. 2d 985 (S.D. Ohio 2001).

65. Since the 1960s, these cases tend to be companies suing unions for breach of no-strike clauses. See, e.g., Stillpass Transit Co. v. Ohio Conference of Teamsters and Local Union 103, Case No. 5772, Cincinnati Courthouse Civil Docket, vol. 38; Riverton Coal Co. v. UMW, Case No. 5805, ibid. Another large category is suits against unions for engaging in secondary boycotts in violation of the National Labor Relations Act. See NLRB v. Local Union No. 98 of the Sheet Metal Workers' Int'l Ass'n, 291 F. Supp. 638 (S.D. Ohio 1968); NLRB v. United Steelworkers of Am., 1973 WL 1163 (S.D. Ohio 1973).

66. There is no pattern to patent, trademark, and copyright disputes. Most are fact-specific cases requiring the judges to determine whether the patent, trademark, or copyright was valid, and, if so, whether the other party infringed on it. Protection of patents, trademarks, and copyrights is important for the economic health of the nation and for the prevention of unfair competition. See, e.g., Dow Chem. Co. v. Monsanto Co., 256 F. Supp. 315 (S.D. Ohio 1966), 315 F. Supp. 416 (S.D. Ohio 1970), Case No. 5916, Cincinnati Courthouse Civil Docket Book, vol. 38; G.M. Corp. v. Toyota Motor Co., Case No. 76–28, Dayton Courthouse Civil Docket, 1976; Wurzburger Hofbrau Aktiengesellschaft v. Shoenling Brewing Co., 331 F. Supp. 497 (S.D. Ohio 1971); Frisch's Restaurants Inc. v. Elby's Big Boy of Steubenville, Inc., 514 F. Supp. 704 (S.D. Ohio 1981); Coal Processing Equip., Inc. v. Campbell, 578 F. Supp. 445 (S.D. Ohio 1981); Wendy's Int'l v. Big Bite, Inc., 576 F. Supp. 816 (S.D. Ohio 1983); Dragani v. Eastman Kodak Co., 576 F. Supp. 755 (S.D. Ohio 1983).

67. One of the major bankruptcy cases of the 1980s was Baldwin-United Corporation. Litigation went on for at least eight years, with charges of securities fraud complicating the bankruptcy proceedings. In re Baldwin-United Corp. Litig., 581 F. Supp. 739 (Judicial Panel on Multi-district Litigation, 1984); Stoller v. Baldwin-United Corp., 1984 WL 2454 (S.D. Ohio 1984), 956 F.2d 1164 (6th Cir. 1992).

68. For an example of a federal securities fraud case, see *Ayers v. Sutliffe,* a pyramid-scheme case involving the refinancing of several nursing homes, in which, to try the case, Rubin fully automated his courtroom. After a seventeen-day trial, the jury ruled for the plaintiffs against defendants that included prominent law and accounting firms. Ayers v. Sutliffe, 1992 WL 207235 (S.D. Ohio 1992). For an adjudication of insider trading brought by the Securities and Exchange Commission, see SEC v. Brethen, 1992 WL 420867 (S.D. Ohio 1992).

69. There are far fewer cases in the twenty-first century involving disputes with the ICC than there were before World War II. Once both sides (the regulator and the regulated) get used to the rules and the procedures, litigation generally declines, no matter what the area of regulation. During the post-1960s era, one case stands out, *Cincinnati, New Orleans & Texas Pacific Railway Co. v. U.S.,* in which several railroads sought injunctive relief from an ICC order reducing rates for multiple-car grain shipments. A three-judge district court agreed with the railroads, declaring the ICC's order null and void. Cincinnati, New Orleans & Texas Pac. Ry. Co. v. U.S., 220 F. Supp. 46 (S.D. Ohio 1963), 229 F. Supp. 572 (S.D. Ohio 1964), *vacated and remanded,* 379 U.S. 642 (1965).

70. U.S. v. E. W. Scripps Co., 1971 WL 513 (S.D. Ohio 1971), Case No. 5656, Cincinnati Courthouse Civil Docket, vol. 37.

71. U.S. v. Mead Corp., 1970 WL 490 (S.D. Ohio 1970), 1986 WL 955 (S.D. Ohio 1986).

72. U.S. v. Gen. Elec. Co., 869 F. Supp. 1285 (S.D. Ohio 1994); *Almanac of the Federal Judiciary* (2002), 1:77.

73. Elder-Beerman Stores, Inc. v. Federated Dept. Stores, Case No. 3316, Dayton Courthouse Civil Docket, 1966; 459 F.2d 138 (6th Cir. 1972); David Greer, *Sluff of History's Boot Soles: An Anecdotal History of Dayton's Bench and Bar* (Wilmington, OH: Orange Frazer Press, 1996), 382–85, quotes at 385.

74. See In re Elder-Beerman Stores Corp., 1997 WL 1774880 (S.D. Ohio 1997), and 1997 WL 1774875 (S.D. Ohio 1997).

75. Lexis, one of the major legal database corporations, was at the time part of Mead Data Central, but has since been sold. Magistrate Judge Michael Merz, interview by author, November 10, 2003, Dayton.

76. Wayne Buckhout, "Government Seeks to Bar Occidental Vote," *Cincinnati Enquirer*, December 7, 1986, B6.

77. Greer, *Sluff of History*, 412–17.

78. Mobil Corp. v. Marathon Oil Co., 1981 WL 1713 (S.D. Ohio 1981).

79. Allen Howard, "Jury OKs Marathon's Merger Deal," *Cincinnati Enquirer*, June 23, 1983, D2.

80. Judge James Graham, interview by author, July 15, 1999, Columbus. Graham, complimenting Judge Kinneary, who presided over the trial, noted that Kinneary "worked us to death."

81. Allen Howard, "Armstrong Defends Marathon-U.S. Steel Deal in Trial," *Cincinnati Enquirer*, June 14, 1983, C3.

82. Luxottica Group S.P.A. v. United States Shoe Corp., 919 F. Supp. 1085 (1995). Judge Graham, however, refused to declare the Ohio statute unconstitutional, contending that the issue was not yet ripe. In *United Dominion Industries, Ltd. v. Commercial Intertech Corporation*, Graham refused to enjoin the hostile tender takeover target from using the Control Share Acquisition Act, finding that it did not impermissibly conflict with the Williams Act in this particular case. United Dominion Indus., Ltd. v. Commercial Intertech Corp., 943 F. Supp. 857 (S.D. Ohio 1996). See also Thomas E. Geyer, "The Vitality of the Ohio Laws Designed to Encourage Negotiated Takeovers," *University of Dayton Law Review* 23 (Spring 1998): 515–58 and esp. 523–40.

A particularly bitter hostile takeover of DuBois Chemicals, Inc., by "industrial giant" W. R. Grace & Company resulted in a suit for unlawful appropriation of trade secrets and customer information, unlawful inducement of Grace's recently acquired employees to breach their contracts to work for a new competitor company, and breach of a noncompete covenant. W. R. Grace & Co. v. Hargadine, 392 F.2d 9, 20–21 (6th Cir. 1968), Case Nos. 5723, 5516, and 5517, Cincinnati Courthouse Civil Docket, vols. 37–38.

83. Wheeling-Pittsburgh Steel Corp. v. Mitsui & Co., 35 F. Supp. 2d 597 (S.D. Ohio 1999), aff'd, 221 F.3d 924 (S.D. Ohio 2000); Sargus interview and letter to the author, September 8, 2003.

84. Anton v. Ford Motor Co., 400 F. Supp. 1270 (S.D. Ohio 1975).

85. Ibid., 1271, 1273, 1275, 1281, and note 11. See also Judge Robert M. Duncan, interview by author, May 25, 2001, Columbus. Duncan rejected the approach taken by Judge Weinman in the only other Ohio automobile products liability case, *Shumard v. General Motors Corp.*, in which Weinman concluded that an automobile manufacturer has no duty to design fireproof cars or to prevent second collision injuries. Shumard v. Gen. Motors Corp., 270 F. Supp. 311 (S.D. Ohio 1967). Duncan argued that *Shumard* was decided before more recent cases fleshed out all the arguments and therefore should not be followed because that court did not have the "benefit of many court decisions and commentaries" Duncan had before he rendered his decision. Anton v. Ford Motor Co., 400 F. Supp. at 1280–81.

86. Cincinnati Gas & Elec. Co. v. Gen. Elec. Co., 656 F. Supp. 49 (S.D. Ohio 1986), 117 F.R.D. 597 (S.D. Ohio 1987); *Almanac of the Federal Judiciary* (New York: Aspen Law and Business, 1999), 1:76–77. See also *Cincinnati Enquirer*, June 5, 1987, D1, February 22, 1989, A4.

87. Ben L. Kaufman, "Owners Filed New Lawsuit over Zimmer," *Cincinnati Enquirer*, February 18, 1986, D1. See also chapter 6 for a discussion of the summary jury trial and the reaction of Jack Welch, CEO of General Electric. In hearings before the Public Utitlities Commission of Ohio, state officials were very careful to ensure that consumers would not carry the entire financial burden for the failed Zimmer plant; stockholders of the utilities bore much of the cost, along with stockholders at General Electric after the settlement of that suit.

88. CompuServe, Inc. v. Cyber Promotions, Inc., 962 F. Supp. 1015 (S.D. Ohio 1997). A Westlaw Keycite search found seventeen cases and more than two hundred articles citing this case.

89. See, e.g., U.S. v. Charbonneau, 979 F. Supp. 1177 (S.D. Ohio 1997); U.S. v. Elmore, 177 F. Supp. 2d 773; U.S. v. Mathis, 1997 WL 683648 (S.D. Ohio 1997).

90. See, e.g., U.S. v. Neufeld, 949 F. Supp. 555 (S.D. Ohio 1996), *aff'd,* 149 F.3d 1185 (6th Cir. 1998), *cert. denied,* 525 U.S. 1020 (1998); Tucker v. Prelesnik, 1999 WL 374105 (6th Cir. 1999).

91. Kutschbach v. Davies, 885 F. Supp. 1079 (S.D. Ohio 1995); Putnam v. Davies, 169 F.R.D. 89 (S.D. Ohio 1996); Beckwith interview.

92. Rose v. Giamatti, 721 F. Supp. 924 (S.D. Ohio 1989) and 721 F. Supp. 906 (S.D. Ohio 1989); Bernie Karsko, "Judge in Pete Rose Case Known for His Thoroughness," *Columbus Dispatch*, July 6, 1989, clipping in Columbus Clerk of Courts Files; Ben L. Kaufman, "Rose, Giamatti to Square Off in Court," *Cincinnati Enquirer*, June 20, 1989, A1. Rose originally filed his lawsuit in Hamilton County Court of Common Pleas, but Giamatti, seeking a more neutral arena, filed a notice of removal, which automatically removed the case to federal court. After Holschuh was assigned the case, he made the important ruling that the federal court had jurisdiction based on the diversity of the parties. He noted that this involved "some thorny legal issues, and I spent a lot of time" researching the question. He then worked hard to get the parties to settle, which they finally did. Judge John D. Holschuh, interview by author, July 12, 1999, and July 30, 1999, Columbus; Ben

L. Kaufman, "Rose Case Moves to Columbus Federal Court," *Cincinnati Enquirer,* July 4, 1989, A1; Ben L. Kaufman, "Next Inning for Rose Case," ibid., July 5, 1989, A1. Although Rose agreed to the settlement with Giamatti, he continued to claim he never bet on baseball until he published his autobiography in 2004, when he finally admitted that he had placed bets not only on baseball but also on the Cincinnati Reds while he managed the club.

Judge Rubin should have heard the case, but before Giamatti filed his notice of removal, Rubin had questioned Giamatti's objectivity, criticizing his investigation of Rose and accusing the commissioner of "engaging in a vendetta against Rose." After pressure from the press and some in the legal community, Rubin recused himself from hearing the Rose case against Giamatti. Ben L. Kaufman, "Judge Defends His Position," *Cincinnati Enquirer,* April 27, 1989, A1; Ben L. Kaufman, "Rubin Drops Peters Case," ibid., April 28, 1989, A1.

93. Spiegel interview; Ben L. Kaufman, "Rose to Plead Guilty in Tax Case," *Cincinnati Enquirer,* April 20, 1990, A1; Ben L. Kaufman, "Sentence Options: Probation to Jail," ibid., April 21, 1990, A1. Andrew R. L. Cayton, *Ohio: The History of a People* (Columbus: Ohio State University Press, 2002), 393–97. Cayton describes how many Cincinnatians continued to "admire" and "worship" Rose as a hero who epitomized someone who through hard work and perseverance rose to one of the best in his field.

94. U.S. v. Russell, Case No. CR-2–95–044, Columbus Courthouse, criminal case file. See also Judge George C. Smith, interview by author, July 26, 1999, Columbus. Smith was inundated with handwritten letters, mostly from mothers and grandmothers of many of the defendants, pleading with him to go easy on the defendants at sentencing time, saying that they were good boys caught in a web of circumstances or that they had been law-abiding citizens for years after they participated in the drug conspiracy and should not be punished for actions that occurred years before. U.S. v. Russell, Case No. CR-2–95–044, Columbus Courthouse, criminal case file.

95. Smith interview.

96. "Editorial," *Columbus Dispatch,* April 6, 1995, A10. The presumption against bail applies in cases involving the use of firearms, crimes of violence, or drug offenses involving a potential maximum sentence of ten years or more. Sargus letter.

97. U.S. v. Sutton, 605 F.2d 260 (6th Cir. 1979), *reheard en banc,* 642 F.2d 1001 (6th Cir. 1980), 700 F.2d 1078 (6th Cir. 1983).

98. Ohio Constitution, article I, § 10.

99. U.S. ex rel Shott v. Tehan, 382 U.S. 406, 416–19 (1966). See also U.S. ex rel. Shott v. Tehan, 337 F.2d 990 (6th Cir. 1964); Bicentennial Committee of the Judicial Conference of the United States, *History of the Sixth Circuit* (Washington, DC: Bicentennial Committee of the Judicial Conference of the United States, 1976), 89.

100. A Westlaw Keycite search shows more than twelve hundred citations for the 1970s alone. During that same period, law reviews published fifteen case notes on the case.

101. Granting the writ essentially overturned Sheppard's conviction; he would be released unless he were convicted in a new trial.

102. Sheppard v. Maxwell, 231 F. Supp. 37 (S.D. Ohio 1964).

103. "Memorial Proceedings for the Honorable Carl A. Weinman," 473 F. Supp. 1; Bicentennial Committee, *History of the Sixth Circuit*, 204–5; "Memorial Resolutions: The Honorable Carl A. Weinman," *Report of the Proceedings of the Judicial Conference of the United States, March 7–9, 1979* (Washington, DC: Government Printing Office, 1979), 46–47; Memorial Service, April 20, 1979, Papers of John W. Peck, box 28; Greer, *Sluff of History*, 311.

104. Sheppard v. Maxwell, 231 F. Supp. 37 (S.D. Ohio 1964), *rev'd*, 346 F.2d 707 (6th Cir. 1965), *rev'd*, 384 U.S. 333 (1966). See also Sheryl A. Bjork, "Indirect Gag Orders and the Doctrine of Prior Restraint," *University of Miami Law Review* 44 (September 1989): 175–76. After the Supreme Court's decision, Sheppard was retried in state court and acquitted.

105. Beckwith interview. See also Dlott, Holschuh, Marbley, Rice, and Spiegel interviews.

106. Beckwith, Dlott, Duncan, Graham, Kinneary, Rice, and Spiegel interviews. Indeed, the position of U.S. attorney has greatly increased in importance since its inception in the Judiciary Act of 1789. For example, in 1985, the U.S. attorney for the Southern District of Ohio supervised more than two dozen lawyers and about fifty employees in Cincinnati, Dayton, and Columbus. More important, he or she determines the type of crimes investigated and prosecuted in the district, having "wide discretion in deciding who will be investigated, sued and prosecuted." Ben L. Kaufman, "U.S. Attorney Barnes Resigns," *Cincinnati Enquirer*, June 28, 1985, C1.

107. Merz 2003 interview.

108. U.S. v. Rodriguez, 882 F.2d 1059, 1061–62, 1065–68 (6th Cir. 1989), *cert. denied*, 493 U.S. 1084 (1990). Quote from Ben L. Kaufman, "Federal Guidelines Just That," *Cincinnati Enquirer*, August 20, 1989, B8.

109. U.S. v. Joan, 883 F.2d 491 (6th Cir. 1989).

110. Weinberger v. U.S., 71 F. Supp. 2d 803 (S.D. Ohio 1999), *aff'd in part, rev'd in part*, 268 F.3d 346 (6th Cir. 2001), *cert. denied*, 535 U.S. 967 (2002).

111. U.S. v. Moored, 992 F.2d 139 (6th Cir. 1993).

112. Wilford Berry on February 19, 1999, J. D. Scott on June 14, 2001, John Byrd on February 19, 2002, Alton Coleman on April 26, 2002, and Robert Buell on September 25, 2002. See sources, notes 113–16, *infra*, for Berry and Byrd. For Jay D. Scott, see "Jay D. Scott" at http://www.ohiodeathrow.com; for Coleman, see "Ohio Executes Alton Coleman," at http://www.nbc4columbus.com; for Buell, see "Ohio Death Penalty News," at http://www.ohiodeathrow.com.

113. Franklin v. Francis, 997 F. Supp. 916 (S.D. Ohio 1998), *vacated*, 144 F.3d 429 (6th Cir. 1998), *cert. denied*, 525 U.S. 985 (1998); Marbley interview.

114. Franklin v. Francis, 36 F. Supp. 2d 1008 (S. D. Ohio 1999), *aff'd*, 168 F.3d 261 (6th Cir. 1999), *cert. denied*, 525 U.S. 1132 (1999). See also *Cincinnati Enquirer*, February 14, 1999, A1, A14, February 18, 1999, A1, A11; February 19, 1999, A1, A4; February 20, 1999, A4; November 30, 1999, B5, B9; *Cincinnati Post*, February 18, 1999, 4A; *Kentucky Enquirer*, February 20, 1999, A1; "Case of Wilford Berry," at http://www.agitator.com; *Columbus Dispatch*, February 19, 1999, at http://www.dispatch.com.

115. In re Byrd, 21 F.3d 427 (6th Cir. 1994), *aff'd*, 510 U.S. 1185 (1994); *Columbus Dispatch*, March 29, 1994, n.p., clipping in Columbus Clerk of Courts Files.

116. Byrd v. Collins, 209 F.3d 486 (6th Cir. 2000), 269 F.3d 544 (6th Cir. 2001), *amended by* 269 F.3d 561 (6th Cir. 2001), *remanded*, 269 F.3d 585 (6th Cir. 2001); In re Byrd, 2001 WL 1512986 (S.D. Ohio 2001), 277 F.3d 804 (6th Cir. 2002); Byrd v. Bagley, 37 Fed. Appx. 94 (6th Cir. 2002). Tensions among several judges of the Sixth Circuit became apparent as disputes arose over these many appeals. See, e.g., In re Byrd, 270 F.3d 984 (6th Cir. 2001) (Judge Suhrheinrich complaining that he was not informed of some hearings on motions). For the execution, see "Byrd Executed at Lucasville," http://www.ccadp.org.

For other death penalty appeals, see Strickland v. Marshall, 632 F. Supp. 590 (S.D. Ohio 1986); Smith v. Anderson, 104 F. Supp. 2d 773 (S.D. Ohio 2000); Henderson v. Collins, 262 F.3d 615 (6th Cir. 2001); Tucker v. Warden, 175 F. Supp. 2d 999 (S.D. Ohio 2001); Fautenberry v. Mitchell, 2001 WL 1763438 (S.D. Ohio 2001); Jamison v. Collins, 100 F. Supp. 2d 647 (S.D. Ohio 2000), *aff'd*, 291 F.3d 380 (6th Cir. 2002); Sowell v. Anderson, 2001 WL 1681142 (S.D. Ohio 2001); Nabinger v. Hurley, 2002 WL 1584285 (S.D. Ohio 2002); Godfrey v. Beightler, 2002 WL 485015 (S.D. Ohio 2002); Loza v. Mitchell, 2002 WL 1580620 (S.D. Ohio 2002); Ashworth v. Bagley, 2002 WL 485006 (S.D. Ohio 2002).

117. Carl Rubin, "Section 1983: A Limited Access Highway," *University of Cincinnati Law Review* 52 (1983): 977, 979; e-mail from Magistrate Judge Abel to the author, December 16, 2003. For arguments that the federal courts should be able to exercise greater oversight of state criminal court proceedings, see Edward Lazarus, *Closed Chambers: The First Eyewitness Account of the Epic Struggles inside the Supreme Court* (New York: Random House, 1988), 503, 509–10; Eric M. Freedman, *Habeas Corpus: Rethinking the Great Writ of Liberty* (New York: New York University Press, 2001), 147–53.

118. See Rubin to John Lyter, clerk, District Court for the Southern District of Ohio, July 22, 1980, Columbus Clerk of Court Files; memo from Lyter and unsigned response to Rubin's memo to judges in the Southern District of Ohio, [1981], ibid.; Rubin, "Section 1983," 977.

119. Rice interview.

120. Memo from Porter to Kinneary, Hogan, Rubin, and Duncan, April 4, 1979, Columbus Clerk of Court Files; memo from Lyter to Porter, n.d., ibid.; memo from Rubin to Miriam Librach, October 2, 1984, ibid.; memo from Rubin to Robert Pellicoro, chief, Clerk's Division, Administrative Office of the U.S. Courts, n.d., ibid.

121. Rubin, "Section 1983," 978, 985.

122. Ibid. For a sample of cases, see, e.g., Hasenmeier-McCarthy v. Rose, 986 F. Supp. 464 (S.D. Ohio 1998); Kelly v. Wehrum, 956 F. Supp. 1369 (S.D. Ohio 1997), *aff'd*, 182 F.3d 917 (6th Cir. 1999); Clerk v. Bradley, 880 F.2d 414 (6th Cir. 1989).

123. Pollock v. Marshall, 656 F. Supp. 957 (S.D. Ohio 1987).

124. Aqeel v. Seiter, 781 F. Supp. 517 (S.D. Ohio 1991); Blanken v. Ohio Dept. of Rehab. and Corr., 944 F. Supp. 1359 (S.D. Ohio 1996). See also Davie v.

Wingard, 958 F. Supp. 1244 (S.D. Ohio 1997); Rashaad v. Seiter, 690 F. Supp. 598 (S.D. Ohio 1987). In 2002, Judge Sargus upheld the Religious Land Use and Institutionalized Persons Act, which permitted the interest in safety and security to outweigh any inmate's claim to religious accommodation, as a legitimate exercise of Congress's spending power. Gerhardt v. Lazaroff, 2002 WL 2008165 (S.D. Ohio 2002).

125. Chapman v. Rhodes, 434 F. Supp. 1007 (S.D. Ohio 1977), *aff'd*, 624 F.2d 1099 (6th Cir. 1980), *rev'd*, 452 U.S. 337 (1981). See also Tom Brinkmoeller and David Beasley, "Most Inmates Have Mental Disorders, Doctors Maintain," *Cincinnati Enquirer*, May 25, 1977, C2; Tom Brinkmoeller, "Two Different Worlds but Cell or Courtroom Still Means One Thing to Prisoner—Confinement," ibid., May 27, 1977, D1; Tom Brinkmoeller, "Prisoners' Suit Long, Detailed, Rather Boring," ibid., May 31, 1977, D4; Tom Brinkmoeller, "Judge Hogan Breaks Spell in Prison Crowding Trial," ibid., June 19, 1977; Tom Brinkmoeller, "Court Ruling Bans Doubling up Cells at Ohio's Lucasville Prison," ibid., June 30, 1977, B2; Tom Brinkmoeller, "The Lucasville Precedent," ibid., July 24, 1977, B1.

126. Charles Durfey, "County Jail 'Unfit for Humans' Lawsuit Charges," *Cincinnati Enquirer*, November 1, 1977, A7; "County Ordered to Deliver Plan for Jail Space," ibid., December 20, 1980, B2; David Wells, "Judge Prepared to Order Jail's Construction," ibid., January 21, 1982, D5; Ben L. Kaufman, "County, Legal Aid Agree to Settlement on Conditions at Jail," ibid., September 13, 1985, C1; Ben L. Kaufman, "Jail Crowding Eases, but Tight Controls Sought," ibid., July 24, 1986, D4; Ben L. Kaufman, "Action Pushed on Jail," March 5, 1987, A1; Ben L. Kaufman, "Leis Accused of Reneging on Jail Limits," ibid., June 8, 1988, F1; Ben L. Kaufman, "Legal Aid Asks Court to Fine County for Jail Conditions," ibid., September 12, 1990, D1.

127. "Dayton Jail to Close over Complaints about Conditions," ibid., September 1, 2002, B4; Rice interview.

128. Stewart v. Rhodes, 473 F. Supp. 1185 (S.D. Ohio 1979), *aff'd*, 785 F.2d 310 (6th Cir. 1986).

129. White v. Morris, 811 F. Supp. 341 (S.D. Ohio 1992).

130. White v. Morris, 832 F. Supp. 1129 (S.D. Ohio 1993).

131. In re Southern Ohio Corr. Facility, 173 F.R.D. 205 (S.D. Ohio 1997), *aff'd in part, rev'd in part, and remanded*, 2001 WL 1667267 (6th Cir. 2001). See also "Lucasville Update," *Cincinnati Post*, June 11, 1996, n.p.; "Lucasville Prisoners Win $4.1 million," ibid., January 22, 1997, n.p.; "Inmates' Hearings Closed to Public," *Cincinnati Enquirer*, June 7, 1996, n.p.; "Prison Summary 'Trial' Put on Hold," ibid., June 11, 1996, n.p.; "Court Rules Inmates' Suit Can Be Kept from the Public," ibid., August 2, 1996, n.p.; "*Enquirer* Appeals Judge's Ban on Press at Civil Trial," ibid., August 14, 1996, all clippings in Wallace Files; "Lawyers' Fees Upset Lucasville Inmate," *Cincinnati Enquirer*, February 15, 1997, B10; "Hearing to Decide Payment in Lucasville Riot Claims," ibid., April 15, 1997, B4; "Lucasville Settlement OK'd," ibid., April 16, 1997, B1; "Judge Fears Inmates Are Getting Ripped Off," ibid., September 20, 1997, A1, A4.

132. Beckwith interview.

CHAPTER 9

1. Edwin C. Surrency, "Federal District Court Judges and the History of Their Courts," 40 *Federal Rules Decisions* (1966): 139.

2. "Sketches of the Establishment of the Federal Courts by States [jurisdiction] and Their Judges," 212 *Federal Rules Decisions* (April 2003): 611.

3. Republican Party of Minnesota v. White, 536 U.S. 765, 777–78 (2002).

4. See introduction, note 21, *supra*.

5. Kermit L. Hall, "Social Backgrounds and Judicial Recruitment: A Nineteenth-Century Perspective on the Lower Federal Judiciary," *Western Political Quarterly* 29 (June 1976): 243.

6. See generally Michael J. Gerhardt, *The Federal Appointments Process: A Constitutional and Historical Analysis* (Durham, NC: Duke University Press, 2000), 100–31.

7. See ibid., 100, 119–20; Sheldon Goldman, *Picking Federal Judges: Lower Court Selection from Roosevelt through Reagan* (New Haven, CT: Yale University Press, 1977), 173–74, 236–63, 283–345; Ronald Stidham and Robert A. Carp, "Regionalism in the Federal District Courts," *Publius* 18 (Fall 1988): 113–15; Kevin L. Lyles, "Presidential Expectations and Judicial Performance Revisited: Law and Politics in the Federal District Courts, 1960–1992," *Presidential Studies Quarterly* 26 (Spring 1996): 458–63.

8. Kermit L. Hall, "The Children of the Cabins: The Lower Federal Judiciary, Modernization, and the Political Culture, 1789–1899" *Northwestern University Law Review* 75 (1980): 424, 429–31, 464–65. See also Kermit L. Hall, *The Politics of Justice: Lower Federal Judicial Selection and the Second Party System, 1829–1861* (Lincoln: University of Nebraska Press, 1979); Hall, "Social Backgrounds and Judicial Recruitment."

9. Surrency, "Federal District Court Judges and the History of Their Courts," 150; Gerhardt, *Federal Appointments Process*, 50–58.

10. Surrency, "Federal District Court Judges and the History of Their Courts," 150.

11. Gerhardt, *Federal Appointments Process*, 123.

12. Ibid., 64–65, 118, 146–47; Kevin L. Lyles, *The Gatekeepers: Federal District Courts in the Political Process* (Westport, CT: Praeger, 1997), 44–45. Whereas Gerhardt asserts that this tradition of submitting more than one name has continued with presidents since Carter, the experience of judges appointed by William Clinton and both George Bushes to the District Court for the Southern District of Ohio has been that the senators have presented the president with one clear choice. Letter from Judge Edmund Sargus to the author, September 8, 2003; Ben L. Kaufman, "Beckwith Is the Favorite," *Cincinnati Enquirer*, April 2, 1991, A1.

13. Gerhardt, *Federal Appointments Process*, 123. See also biographies of Judges Creighton, Tappan, Sater, and Sargus in this chapter.

14. Lyle, *Gatekeepers*, 45.

15. Hall, "Children of the Cabins," 429, 462.

16. Robert A. Carp and C. K. Rowland, *Policymaking and Politics in the Federal District Courts* (Knoxville: University of Tennessee Press, 1983), i, 42–43, 165.

17. Stidham and Carp, "Regionalism in the Federal District Courts," 114.

18. Carp and Rowland, *Policymaking and Politics in the Federal District Courts*, i, 42–43, 165.

19. *Journal of the Executive Proceedings of the Senate of the United States,* 7th Cong., 2d sess., 447 (March 1, 1803).

20. Thomas Worthington to James Madison, November 17, 1802; Edward Tiffin to James Madison, December 5, 1802; Byrd to Madison, February 12, 1807, in File of Letters of Appointments and Recommendations for Appointment to Federal Office (1791–1901), General Records of the Department of State, RG 59, National Archives, microfilm publication M418; Donald J. Ratcliffe, *Party Spirit in a Frontier Republic: Democratic Politics in Ohio, 1793–1821* (Columbus: Ohio State University Press, 1998), 114. Another leading candidate, Samuel Huntington, sought the help of Jefferson's postmaster general, Gideon Granger, to get the appointment to the court. Jeffrey P. Brown, "The Political Culture of Early Ohio," in *The Pursuit of Public Power: Political Culture in Ohio 1787–1861,* ed. Jeffrey P. Brown and Andrew R. L. Cayton (Kent, OH: Kent State University Press, 1994), 3.

21. See Hall, "Children of the Cabins," esp. 433–35.

22. For Adams's appointment and Senate confirmation of Byrd as secretary of the Northwest Territory, see *Senate Executive Journal,* 5th Cong., 2d sess., 330 (December 20, 1797), 331 (December 31, 1797). For biographical information, see Charles E. Rice, "Biographical Sketch," Charles E. Rice Collection, Ohio Historical Society, Columbus; Rush R. Sloane, "Organization and Admission of Ohio into the Union and the Great Seal of the State," in *Ohio Centennial Anniversary Celebration at Chillicothe, May 20–21, 1903, under the Auspices of the Ohio State Archaeological and Historical Society,* ed. E. O. Randall (Columbus: Ohio State Archaeological and Historical Society, 1903), 104–5; Irwin S. Rhodes, "The History of the United States District Court for the Southern District of Ohio," *University of Cincinnati Law Review* 24 (Summer 1955): 340; Charles B. Galbreath, *History of Ohio* (Chicago: American Historical Society, 1925), 3:275; Nelson W. Evans and E. B. Stivers, *A History of Adams County, Ohio: From Its Earliest Settlement to the Present Time* (West Union, OH: E. B. Stivers, 1900), 305, 526–32; Ratcliffe, *Party Spirit,* 39–40, 69; Bicentennial Committee of the Judicial Conference of the United States, *Judges of the United States,* 2d ed. (Washington, DC: Government Printing Office, 1983), 71–72. For information on Massie, see Andrew R. L. Cayton, "The Failure of Michael Baldwin: A Case Study in the Origins of Middle-Class Culture on the Trans-Appalachian Frontier," *Ohio History* 95 (Winter–Spring 1986): 36.

23. Byrd to Arthur St. Clair, December 30, 1802, published in *Scioto Gazette,* January 15, 1803, 2. See also ibid., 3; Carrington T. Marshall, ed., *A History of the Courts and Lawyers of Ohio* (New York: American Historical Society, 1934), 1:65, 3:707–8.

24. Rice, "Biographical Sketch."

25. "Sketch, Charles Willing Byrd," *Weekly Law Bulletin* 24 (1882–1894): 417.

26. Rice, "Biographical Sketch"; Bicentennial Committee of the Judicial Conference of the United States, *History of the Sixth Circuit* (Washington, DC: Bicentennial Committee of the Judicial Conference of the United States, 1976), 118–19; Evans and Stivers, *History of Adams County,* 526–32.

27. Ratcliffe, *Party Spirit,* 69.

28. The Era of Good Feelings was that time, following the War of 1812, when, supposedly, there were no political parties. All Americans considered themselves

Jeffersonian Republican-Democrats; however, there were always factions within this broad category. That factionalism became clear during the maneuvers in the House of Representatives in 1824, when the House voted for president. See, e.g., Donald B. Cole, *The Presidency of Andrew Jackson* (Lawrence: University Press of Kansas, 1993); Donald B. Cole, *Martin Van Buren and the American Political System* (Princeton, NJ: Princeton University Press, 1984); Lawrence E. Kohl, *The Politics of Individualism: Parties and the American Character in the Jackson Era* (New York: Oxford University Press, 1989); Paul Nagel, *John Quincy Adams: A Public Life, A Private Life* (New York: Knopf, 1997); Arthur M. Schlesinger Jr., *The Age of Jackson* (New York: Book Find Club, 1945); Joel H. Silbey, *The Partisan Imperative: The Dynamics of American Politics before the Civil War* (New York: Oxford University Press, 1985). For a discussion of the second party system and judicial appointments, see Hall, *Politics of Justice.*

29. Donald J. Ratcliffe, *The Politics of Long Division: The Birth of the Second Party System in Ohio, 1818–1828* (Columbus: Ohio State University Press, 2000), 225.

30. Order Books, 2:170 (December term 1828). Presidents make interim or what are often called recess appointments when Congress is not in session.

31. John Weld Peck, "The Federal Courts of Ohio," in Marshall, *History of the Courts and Lawyers of Ohio,* 3:709; *Dictionary of American Biography* (New York: Charles Scribner's Sons, 1928–1936), 2:536–37; Bicentennial Committee, *Judges of the United States,* 112; Nelson W. Evans, *A History of Scioto County, Ohio, together with a Pioneer Record of Southern Ohio* (Portsmouth, OH: Nelson W. Evans, 1903), 167–68; Bicentennial Committee, *History of the Sixth Circuit,* 125; Randall, *Ohio Centennial Anniversary,* 9; *Who Was Who in America: Historical Volume, 1607–1896,* rev. ed. (Chicago: Marquis Who's Who, 1967), 196; Ratcliffe, *Party Spirit,* 77–78. Creighton continued in politics after the Senate refused to confirm his appointment to the court. Reelected to Congress in 1830, he served until 1833, when he returned to his hometown, Chillicothe, and private practice. Creighton died at home on October 8, 1851. The Creightons had four children.

32. Ratcliffe, *Politics of Long Division,* 225.

33. *Senate Executive Journal,* 20th Cong., 2d sess., 621 (December 11, 1828).

34. Ibid., 645 (February 16, 1829). The Senate voted 22 to 19 in support of the committee's recommendation. Both Ohio senators, Jacob Burnet and Benjamin Ruggles, voted with the committee and against Creighton.

35. *Cincinnati Advertiser,* February 18, 1829, 3.

36. *Senate Executive Journals,* 20th Cong., 2d sess. (1828–29) and 21st Cong., 1st sess. (1829), passim. For the appointment practices of the Jackson administration, see Goldman, *Picking Federal Judges,* 7; Gerhardt, *Federal Appointments Process,* 50–52.

37. Andrew R. L. Cayton, *The Frontier Republic: Ideology and Politics in the Ohio Country, 1780–1825* (Kent, OH: Kent State University Press, 1986), 119, 139.

38. Order Books, December 18–21, 1828, 2:170–73.

39. *Senate Executive Journal,* 21st Cong., 1st sess., 6 (March 6, 1829), 7 (March 7, 1829).

40. John W. Campbell, *Biographical Sketches with Other Literary Remains of the Late John W. Campbell, Compiled by His Widow* (Columbus: Scott & Gallagher, 1838), 2–8; Peck, "Federal Courts of Ohio," 709; J. Fletcher Brennan, ed., *The Biographical Cyclopaedia and Portrait Gallery with an Historical Sketch of the State of Ohio* (Cincinnati: Western Biographical

Publishing, 1883–1884), 2:446–48; Bicentennial Committee, *Judges of the United States*, 77; Evans and Stivers, *History of Adams County*, 301–2; Ratcliffe, *Politics of Long Division*, 124, 173, 227, 307; Ratcliffe, *Party Spirit*, 148.

41. Goldman, *Picking Federal Judges*, 7.

42. Ratcliffe, *Politics of Long Division*, 173; Evans and Stivers, *History of Adams County*, 301; Hall, *Politics of Justice*, 5–6.

43. Thomas Gillespie to an unidentified correspondent, February 18, 1829, Letters of Appointment and Recommendation during the Administration of Andrew Jackson 1829–1837, M639, roll 4.

44. Daniel Feller, "Benjamin Tappan: The Making of a Democrat," in Brown and Cayton, *Pursuit of Public Power*, 77; Hall, *Politics of Justice*, 5–6.

45. Russell to Jackson, March 3, 1829, February 23, 1829, Letters of Appointment and Recommendation, Administration of Jackson, M639, roll 4.

46. Russell to Jackson, February 23, 1829, ibid.

47. Campbell, *Biographical Sketches*, 8.

48. Brennan, *Biographical Cyclopaedia*, 2:448.

49. William Russell to Jackson, March 3, 1829, Letters of Appointment and Recommendation, Administration of Jackson, M639, roll 4; Campbell, *Biographical Sketches*, 8, 13, and passim. See also Hall, *Politics of Justice*, 6.

50. Campbell, *Biographical Sketches*, 9; Peck, "Federal Courts of Ohio," 709; Brennan, *Biographical Cyclopaedia*, 2:447.

51. See Letters of Appointment and Recommendation, Administration of Jackson, M639. These records contain nominations or support letters for the eight candidates. John Goodenow, Thomas Scott, and James Exum were also prominent contenders. Others in the records who received support were N. P. Gains, W. W. Irvin, and William Kennon. For Jackson's position on judicial appointments, see Hall, *Politics of Justice*, 9–10, 24–25.

52. Hall, *Politics of Justice*, 9–10, 24–25; Feller, "Benjamin Tappan," 77.

53. Feller, "Benjamin Tappan," 69–82; Ratcliffe, *Party Spirit*, 28, 90; Donald J. Ratcliffe, "The Autobiography of Benjamin Tappan," *Ohio History* 85 (Spring 1976): 109–57; *Dictionary of American Biography*, 9: 300–301; E. O. Randall and Daniel J. Ryan, *History of Ohio*, vol. 4 (New York: Century History, 1912), 117; Randall, *Ohio Centennial Anniversary*, 361; Henry Howe, *Historical Collections of Ohio* (Cincinnati: C. J. Krehbiel, 1902), 1:978; Bicentennial Committee, *Judges of the United States*, 481; E. A. Holt, "Party Politics in Ohio, 1840–1850," pts. 1–3, *Ohio Archaeological and Historical Quarterly* 37 (July 1928): 439–591; 38 (January 1929): 47–182; 38 (April 1929): 260–402; Bicentennial Committee, *History of the Sixth Circuit*, 195.

54. See R. Mitchell to Jackson, October 2, 1833; petition from McConnelsville dated October 2, 1833, signed by thirteen citizens; John Thomson to Jackson, October 3, 1833; Micajah T. Williams to Jackson, October 3, 1833; letter of sundry citizens of Cadiz, October 11, 1833; Humphrey Leavitt (himself a candidate) to Jackson, October 7, 1833; all in Letters of Appointments and Recommendations, Administration of Jackson, M639, roll 24.

55. Quotes from Feller, "Benjamin Tappan," 78. See also *Senate Executive Journal*, 23d Cong., 1st sess., 344–45 (January 20, 1834), 402 (May 12, 1834), 412 (May

29, 1834); draft of article about Tappan in Benjamin Tappan Papers, Ohio Historical Society, Columbus; Peck, "Federal Courts of Ohio," 709. By the time Tappan's name came to a vote, Ruggles had been replaced by Democrat senator Thomas Morris, who voted to confirm.

Seeing himself as a political martyr, Tappan swore to get his vengeance, which he did, winning election to the U.S. Senate from Ohio in 1838. He served in the Senate until 1845. He then left the Democratic Party to become a Free-Soiler. Moses M. Granger claims that the Senate rejected Tappan because a majority of senators were "temporarily hostile to President Jackson." Moses M. Granger, *The Judiciary of Ohio, 1803–1903* (Columbus: Ohio State Archaeological and Historical Society, 1903), 31. Although Leavitt denied it, many thought that he or his supporters had pushed for Tappan's defeat. Indeed, Ruggles was Leavitt's early mentor. Humphrey H. Leavitt, *Autobiography of the Hon. Humphrey Howe Leavitt Written for His Family* (New York: n.p., 1893), 60–61.

56. Leavitt, *Autobiography*, 59–60; Letters of Appointment and Recommendation, Administration of Jackson, M639, rolls 14 and 24. On September 28, 1833, early in his campaign for the judgeship, Leavitt had written to Vice President Van Buren, asking him to speak to Jackson on his behalf, correctly fearing that his recent reelection to Congress would be an impediment to his appointment to the federal bench. Letters of Appointment and Recommendation, Administration of Jackson, M639, roll 14.

57. *Senate Executive Journal*, 23d Cong., 1st sess., 435–36 (June 18, 1834).

58. Hall, *Politics of Justice*, 25.

59. Hall, "Children of the Cabins," 465.

60. Leavitt, *Autobiography*, 62–70.

61. Ibid., 1–17, 26–52, 69–70; "Humphrey Howe Leavitt," *United States Law Magazine* 5 (1850–1852): 37–44; S. B. Nelson, ed., *History of Cincinnati and Hamilton County* (Cincinnati: S. B. Nelson, 1894), 545–46; Howe, *Historical Collections of Ohio*, 1:978–79; Bicentennial Committee, *Judges of the United States*, 289; Maurice Joblin, *Cincinnati, Past and Present, or Its Industrial History* (Cincinnati: Elm Street Printing, 1872), 84–88; Bicentennial Committee, *History of the Sixth Circuit*, 158–59.

62. Leavitt, *Autobiography*, 44.

63. Ibid., 52. Later in life, Leavitt expressed some doubts about his earlier views on the bank.

64. Ibid., 77–78.

65. Simeon D. Fess, ed., *Ohio: A Four-Volume Reference Library on the History of a Great State* (Chicago: Lewis Publishing, 1937), 4:125.

66. Leavitt, *Autobiography*, 61–64.

67. Ibid., 64–65, 72; "Humphrey Howe Leavitt," 43–44.

68. Speech by Mr. Stanberry on the occasion of Leavitt's retirement dinner sponsored by the Cincinnati bar on March 30, 1871, *Cincinnati Commercial*, March 31, 1871, 7, and *Cincinnati Enquirer*, March 31, 1871, 3.

69. Leavitt, *Autobiography*, 88–89.

70. Speech by Leavitt on the occasion of his retirement dinner, *Cincinnati Commercial*, March 31, 1871, 7, and *Cincinnati Enquirer*, March 31, 1871, 3.

71. Leavitt, *Autobiography,* 90–91.

72. Ibid., 93–94, 115–16; Fess, *Ohio,* 4:125.

73. For salary information see Register of Officers and Agents . . . in the Service of the United States [in] . . . 1875 (Washington, DC: Government Printing Office, 1876).

74. Records Relating to the Appointment of Federal Judges, Marshals, and Attorneys, Ohio (Southern) 1853–1901, box 528, General Records of the Department of Justice, RG 60, National Archives Branch Depository, College Park, MD. See also *Cincinnati Enquirer,* March 31, 1871, 2.

75. Ibid.

76. Ibid., box 529.

77. *Senate Executive Journal,* 42d Cong., 1st sess., 46–47 (March 30, 1871).

78. Journals, W. Div. 2:471 (April 6, 1871).

79. William C. Howard to B. H. Brewster, attorney general, November 4, 1882, Records Relating to the Appointment of Federal Judges, Marshals, and Attorneys, 1853–1901, box 530.

80. Bicentennial Committee, *Judges of the United States,* 477–78; Marshall, *History of Courts and Lawyers of Ohio,* 3:712; Bicentennial Committee, *History of the Sixth Circuit,* 195.

81. W. C. Howard to the U.S. Marshal for the district, March 6, 1882, Records Relating to the Appointment of Federal Judges, Marshals, and Attorneys, 1853–1901, box 530.

82. *Senate Executive Journal,* 47th Cong., 2d sess., 640 (February 10, 1883).

83. *Cincinnati Enquirer,* November 2, 1882, 4.

84. Records Relating to the Appointment of Federal Judges, Marshals, and Attorneys, 1853–1901, boxes 530–31.

85. Ibid.

86. Ibid., box 530.

87. McLean to Grant, December 14, 1882, ibid. For information on Halstead, see Eugene H. Roseboom, *The Civil War Era, 1850–1873,* vol. 4, *The History of the State of Ohio,* ed. Carl Wittke (Columbus: Ohio State Archaeological and Historical Society, 1941–1944), 201.

88. Cowen to Butterworth, January 2, 1883, Records Relating to the Appointment of Federal Judges, Marshals and Attorneys, 1853–1901, box 530.

89. Hickenlooper to Butterworth, December 29, 1882, ibid.

90. *Senate Executive Journal,* 47th Cong., 2d sess., 642 (February 10, 1883), 653 (February 19, 1883); Senate Judiciary Committee, minutes, 47th Cong. (February 19, 1883), 132.

91. Granger, *Judiciary of Ohio,* 26. See also "In Memoriam Honorable William White," 38 Ohio State v–viii (1883); Marshall, *History of Courts and Lawyers of Ohio,* 1:251, 3:712; Randall and Ryan, *History of Ohio,* 151–54; White married Rachel Stout, who traced her lineage back to the early settlers of Springfield, Ohio. The Whites had three children.

92. Granger, *Judiciary of Ohio,* 26.

93. *Senate Executive Journal,* 48th Cong., 1st sess., 63, 65 (December 18, 1883), 111–12 (January 7, 1884); Senate Judiciary Committee, minutes, 48th Cong. (January 7, 1884), 146.

94. Peck, "Federal Courts of Ohio," 712; Bicentennial Committee, *History of the Sixth Circuit*, 186–87; Charles Theodore Greve, *Centennial History of Cincinnati and Representative Citizens* (Chicago: Biographical Publishing, 1904), 1:969; Marshall, *History of Courts and Lawyers in Ohio*, 3:712–13; Bicentennial Committee, *Judges of the United States*, 432; "Committee of the Bar . . . appointed to prepare a memorial of . . . the late George R. Sage," February 24, 1899, Journals, E. Div., 1: 438–39.

95. Records Relating to the Appointment of Federal Judges, Marshals, and Attorneys, 1853–1901, boxes 527, 540, and 542. Sage's resignation letter to President McKinley was dated August 24, 1898, and McKinley's letter of acceptance dated August 26.

96. Journals, E. Div., 1:438–41, dated February 24, 1899; Rhodes, "History of the District Court," 348–49.

97. Journals, W. Div., 7:240; Records Relating to the Appointment of Federal Judges, Marshals, and Attorneys, 1853–1901, box 542; *Senate Executive Journal*, 55th Cong., 3d sess., 1059, 1071 (December 13, 1898), 1098 (December 19, 1898), 1102 (December 20, 1898).

98. Bicentennial Committee, *History of the Sixth Circuit*, 198–99; Greve, *Centennial History of Cincinnati*, 1:969, 2:107–110; Peck, "Federal Courts of Ohio," 713; George Irving Reed, ed., *Bench and Bar of Ohio: A Compendium of History and Biography* (Chicago: Century Publishing & Engraving, 1897), 1:304–5; Brennan, *Biographical Cyclopaedia*, 5:1132; Evans, *History of Scioto County*, 47, 55, 143, 152, 159, 161, 195–97; Evans and Stivers, *History of Adams County*, 324–26; Bicentennial Committee, *Judges of the United States*, 484–85.

99. Reed, *Bench and Bar of Ohio*, 1:305; Peck, "Federal Courts of Ohio," 713.

100. "Obituary. Judge Thompson," *Ohio Law Reporter* 7 (January 31, 1910), 581–82.

101. Reed, *Bench and Bar of Ohio*, 434; Harold Chase et al., comps., *Biographical Dictionary of the Federal Judiciary* (Detroit: Gale, 1976), 245; Bicentennial Committee, *History of the Sixth Circuit*, 187–88; Peck, "The Federal Courts of Ohio, 713; *Who Is Who in and from Ohio*, 2:1083–1084; John William Leonard, *Who's Who in Jurisprudence: A Biographical Dictionary of Contemporary Lawyers and Jurists* (Brooklyn, NY: John W. Leonard, 1925), 1247; Henry A. Ford and Kate B. Ford, *History of Hamilton County, Ohio* (Cleveland: L. A. Williams, 1881), 288; Bicentennial Committee, *Judges of the United States*, 435; "The New Federal Judge: Hon. John E. Sater," *Ohio Law Bulletin* 52 (April 15, 1907): 197. Biographers differ on Sater's private life. A few say he was married twice, once to Elizabeth Jones Sater and then later, in 1889, to Mary Lyon Sater. Others just mention Mary as his wife. Most agree that he had three children.

102. E. L. Taylor to Roosevelt, March 4, 1907, Records Relating to the Appointment of Federal Judges, Marshals, and Attorneys, 1901–1933, box 691. See also Records Relating to the Appointment of Federal Judges, Marshals, and Attorneys, 1901–1933, box 691 for bound book of endorsements for John E. Sater and especially the Honorable H. J. Booth's biography and comments on Sater.

103. Leonard, *Who's Who in Jurisprudence*, 1247.

104. E. L. Taylor to Roosevelt, March 4, 1907, and bound volume of endorsements and Booth's biography of Sater, Records Relating to the Appointment of Federal Judges, Marshals, and Attorneys, box 691.

105. Records Relating to the Appointment of Federal Judges, Marshals, and Attorneys, box 691, and especially letters from Taylor and Booth, as well as a letter from Thomas J. Duncan to the new president, William Howard Taft, March 1, 1909.

106. *Senate Executive Journal,* 60th Cong., 1st sess., 34, 103 (December 3, 1907), 60th Cong., 2d sess., 31, 83 (December 8, 1908), 243 (March 1, 1909); Senate Judiciary Committee, minutes, 60th Cong., December 19, 1907; Senate Judiciary Committee, docket, 60th Cong., December 3, 1907, December 4, 1907.

107. Fess, *Ohio,* 5:4–5; *Ohio State Journal,* July 19, 1937, A1, A5.

108. Records Relating to the Appointment of Federal Judges, Marshals, and Attorneys, 1901–1933, boxes 688–92; Goldman, *Picking Federal Judges,* 9.

109. Records Relating to the Appointment of Federal Judges, Marshals, and Attorneys, 1901–1933, boxes 688–92.

110. Ibid., boxes 688, 689.

111. Editor and manager of the *Locomotive Firemen and Engineer's Magazine* to William Loeb Jr., secretary to the president, ibid., box 688.

112. *Senate Executive Journal,* 60th Cong., 2d sess., 31, 83 (December 8, 1908), 243 (March 1, 1909); Senate Judiciary Committee, minutes, 60th Cong., December 14, 1908, March 1, 1909; Senate Judiciary Committee, docket, 60th Cong., December 14, 1908, December 10, 1908, March 1, 1909.

113. *Ohio State Journal,* July 19, 1937, A1, A5.

114. *Columbus Evening Dispatch,* July 19, 1937, A6.

115. Fess, *Ohio,* 5:5.

116. *Biographical Dictionary of the Federal Judiciary,* 245; Bicentennial Committee, *History of the Sixth Circuit,* 187–88; *Ohio State Journal,* July 19, 1937, A1, A5; *Columbus Evening Dispatch,* July 19, 1937, A1, A6; Fess, *Ohio,* 5:5–6.

117. *Cincinnati Enquirer,* January 27, 1910, 2; Records Relating to the Appointment of Federal Judges, Marshals, and Attorneys, 1901–1933, box 691. Before Thompson's death, it was assumed that the president would need to reappoint Sater whenever Congress made the second judgeship a permanent position.

118. Pogue to Taft, February 17, 1910, and Pogue to Clarence D. Clark, chairman of the Senate Judiciary Committee, February 17, 1910, Records Relating to the Appointment of Federal Judges, Marshals, and Attorneys, 1901–1933, box 688.

119. *Senate Executive Journal,* 61st Cong., 2d sess., 229–30 (February 24, 1910), 251 (March 7, 1910).

120. *Cincinnati Enquirer,* September 25, 1919, 20.

121. Gerhardt, *Federal Appointments Process,* 100. See also Goldman, *Picking Federal Judges,* 9.

122. Taft to Hollister, February 27, 1910; Taft to Bellamy Storer, February 27, 1910; Taft to Clark, February 28, 1910; all in Mixter Family Papers, folder 1, box 2, Cincinnati Historical Society, Cincinnati; unidentified newspaper clipping, February 23, 1910, February 24, 1910, ibid., box 2, folder 3; clippings from *Marietta Register-Leader,* February 25, 1910, *Akron Times,* February 26, 1910, *Cincinnati Enquirer,* February 26, 1910, ibid. The *Cincinnati Post* reported that the price for the Cox organization eventually going along with Hollister's nomination was the "absolute re-

pudiation by President Taft of Wade Ellis, Chairman of the Republican State executive committee." Clipping from *Cincinnati Post,* March 7, 1910, ibid.

123. Records Relating to the Appointment of Federal Judges, Marshals, and Attorneys, 1901–1933, boxes 688, 690, and 692; Clark to Hollister, March 12, 1910; Henry M. Hoyt to Hollister, March 9, 1910; Horace Lurton to Hollister, March 12, 1910; all in Mixter Family Papers, folder 2, box 2. Hollister was the near-unanimous choice of the bench, bar, and community leaders; his file contained hundreds of letters from the bench, the bar, and the community supporting his appointment. Only two other men had more than one or two letters of support. Edgar Belden had ten letters and George R. Young of Dayton presented a thick file with support from attorneys mainly in Dayton as well as the bars of Montgomery and Preble counties and from some area business people. Records Relating to the Appointment of Federal Judges, Marshals, and Attorneys, 1901–1933, boxes 688, 690, and 692.

124. Records Relating to the Appointment of Federal Judges, Marshals, and Attorneys, 1901–1933, box 690.

125. Clark to Taft, March 3, 1910, Mixter Family Papers, box 2, folder 2.

126. *Senate Executive Journal,* 61st Cong., 2d sess., 229–30 (February 24, 1910), 251 (March 7, 1910); Senate Judiciary Committee, minutes, 61st Cong., March 7, 1910; Senate Judiciary Committee, docket, 61st Cong., February 25, 1910, March 7, 1910; *Cincinnati Enquirer,* September 25, 1919, 20.

127. Peck, "Federal Courts of Ohio," 713.

128. Bicentennial Committee, *History of the Sixth Circuit,* 145–46; George Mortimer Roe, *Cincinnati: The Queen City of the West* (Cincinnati: C. T. Krehbiel, 1895), 305–6; *Who Is Who in and from Ohio,* 1060; William W. Morris, *The Bench and Bar of Cincinnati* (Cincinnati: New Court House Publishing, 1921), 91; Reed, *Bench and Bar of Ohio,* 2:350; Greve, *Centennial History of Cincinnati and Representative Citizens,* 2:931–32; *Cincinnati Enquirer,* September 25, 1919, 20 and September 27, 1919, 8.

129. *Senate Executive Journal,* 66th Cong., 1st sess., 474 (October 30, 1919), 478 (November 3, 1919), 484 (November 5, 1919); Senate Judiciary Committee, minutes, 66th Cong., November 3, 1919; Senate Judiciary Committee, executive docket, 66th Cong., November 13, 1919; Applications & Endorsements, 1901–1933, Ohio, Southern, Judges, boxes 691, Department of Justice, Records of Appointment Clerk, RG 60 National Archives Branch Depository, College Park, MD. Peck presented his commission and took the oath of office on November 19, 1919.

130. Pomerene to the attorney general, November 1, 1919, and subcommittee minutes, November 13, 1919, Senate Judiciary Committee, executive docket, 66th Cong., Doc. No. 52; A. Mitchell Palmer to Wilson, October 18, 1919, Smith W. Bennett to Palmer, October 11, 1919, James M. Cox to Palmer, October 14, 1919, and Alfred G. Allen to Palmer, October 7, 1919, Applications and Endorsements, 1901–1933, box 691; file on H. L. Ferneding, ibid., box 688; miscellaneous letters for other candidates, ibid., boxes 688, 691, and 692.

131. *Cincinnati Enquirer,* August 11, 1937, A1, A2; obituary of John Weld Peck, Papers of John W. Peck, box 36; clipping from *Cincinnati Times-Star,* August 10, 1937, ibid.; clipping from *Cincinnati Court Index,* March 20, 1939, ibid., box 34; Biographical

Sketch in Applications and Endorsements, 1901–1933, box 691; Taylor, *Bench and Bar of Ohio*, 391; Morris, *Bench and Bar of Cincinnati*, 40; Bicentennial Committee, *Judges of the United States*, 385–86; Leonard, *Who's Who in Jurisprudence*, 1124; Bicentennial Committee, *History of the Sixth Circuit*, 179–80. Peck's first wife died in 1931. Two years later he married Alma Helm Peck, who died in 1937.

132. *Cincinnati Enquirer*, August 11, 1937, A2, A4.

133. Clipping from *Cincinnati Times-Star*, August 10, 1837, in Papers of John W. Peck, box 36; obituary, ibid.

134. Speech to the Cincinnati Club, November 12, 1935, ibid., box 34.

135. Applications and Endorsements, 1901–1933, box 691.

136. *Cincinnati Post*, April 3, 1923, A1; Applications and Endorsements, 1901–1933, boxes 688, 691.

137. *Senate Executive Journal*, 67th Cong., 4th sess., 347 (February 28, 1923), 363 (March 1, 1923), 397 (March 2, 1923), 402–3 (March 3, 1923); Senate Judiciary Committee, minutes, 67th Cong., February 28, 1923, March 3, 1923; Senate Judiciary Committee, executive docket, 67th Cong., Doc. Nos. 34 and 44; Applications and Endorsements, 1901–1933, Box 690.

138. "Jurist Collapses," *Cincinnati Enquirer*, December 23, 1933, A10; Bicentennial Committee, *History of the Sixth Circuit*, 143–44; Leonard, *Who's Who in Jurisprudence*, 690; Bicentennial Committee, *Judges of the United States*, 219–20; Morris, *The Bench and Bar of Cincinnati*, 38; Services in Memory of Judge Hickenlooper held in Cincinnati November 7, 1934 in the United States Circuit Court of Appeals, Wallace files; Rhodes, "History of the District Court," 352–53.

139. Services in Memory of Judge Hickenlooper held in Cincinnati November 7, 1934, in the United States Circuit Court of Appeals, Wallace files.

140. "Jurist Collapses," *Cincinnati Enquirer*, December 23, 1933, A10.

141. Bicentennial Committee, *History of the Sixth Circuit*, 146–47; Peck, "Federal Courts of Ohio," 714; *Biographical Dictionary of the Federal Judiciary*, 129–30; Bicentennial Committee, *Judges of the United States*, 232; letter of resignation from the Ohio National Guard in VFM 2696 Frank B. Willis file, Ohio Historical Society, Columbus; *Who Is Who in and from Ohio*, 2:1060; Galbreath, *History of Ohio*, 3:12–13; "Benson Hough Dies: Heart Attack Is Fatal to Federal Judge, 60," *Cincinnati Enquirer*, November 20, 1935, A1; Ralph H. Beaton, "Benson W. Hough: An Appreciation," unpublished manuscript dated January 18, 1936, Columbus, Ohio, in Wallace files. Hough continued his interest in baseball. A classmate of Branch Rickey, general manager of the St. Louis Cardinals, he regularly attended World Series games.

142. *Senate Executive Journal*, 68th Cong., 2d sess., 329 (January 31, 1925), 352 (February 7, 1925), 358 (February 9, 1925); Senate, Records, Papers re nominations, 68th Cong., File 68B-A3(6); Senate Judiciary Committee, minutes, 1923–1925, February 7, 1925; Senate Judiciary Committee, executive docket, 68th Cong., February 2, 3, and 9, 1925.

143. Thompson to Coolidge, December 2, 1924, Applications and Endorsements, 1901–1933, box 688.

144. Senate, Records, Papers re nominations, 68th Cong., File 68B-A3(6).

145. Applications and Endorsements, 1901–1933, boxes 688–90.

146. Ibid., box 688.

147. Lyle to Stone, January 3, 1925, ibid.

148. Affidavit of G. C. Weitzel, February 25, 1925, ibid., box 689.

149. Ibid., box 691. Many others writing about the appointment supported Hough if they had to choose between him and Foster. Harding faced the dilemma of being unable to accede to senatorial courtesy, because the state's two Republican senators vigorously opposed one another's choice. When Harding finally settled on Hough, Senator Fess wrote to Stone that he had been humiliated before the people of Ohio and that Foster had been smeared. He sought the records so he could clear Foster's name—and his. Fess to Stone, February 3, 1925, ibid., box 689.

150. Tribute by Ralph H. Beaton, January 8, 1936, Wallace files.

151. *Columbus Citizen*, November 20, 1935, A2.

152. Tribute by Beaton, Wallace Files.

153. "Judge Hough's Death Mourned," *Columbus Evening Dispatch*, November 20, 1935, A1; "Editorial," ibid.

154. Judges Nevin, Weygandt, and Edward Matthias, "Memorial to Judge Hough," *Columbus Courthouse Journal* (January 27, 1936), 1–9.

155. "Editorial," *Columbus Evening Dispatch*, November 20, 1935, A1.

156. Judges Nevin, Weygandt, and Edward Matthias, "Memorial to Judge Hough," *Columbus Courthouse Journal*, January 27, 1936, 7–8.

157. *Columbus Citizen*, November 20, 1935, A1–A2.

158. "Editorial," *Columbus Evening Dispatch*, A1. See also ibid., A1–A4, A6 for additional information on Hough.

159. *Senate Executive Journal*, 70th Cong., 2d sess., 324 (January 21, 1929); Senate Judiciary Committee, minutes, 1927–1929, January 14, 21, 1929. There are no records in the appointment files indicating any competition for this position. Applications and Endorsements, 1901–1933, passim.

160. "In Memoriam Honorable Robert R. Nevin," Wallace Files; *Who Was Who in America*, 3:635; Leonard, *Who's Who in Jurisprudence*, 1074; Peck, "Federal Courts of Ohio," 714; Taylor, *Bench and Bar of Ohio*, 164; Bicentennial Committee, *Judges of the United States*, 367; Bicentennial Committee, *History of the Sixth Circuit*, 175; Daniel W. Iddings, "The Bench and Bar of Dayton and Montgomery County, Ohio," in *Dayton and Montgomery County: Resources and People*, ed. Charlotte Reeve Conover (New York: Lewis Historical Publishing, 1932), 2:782; "Biographies," ibid., 3:31–32; "Judge Nevin Dies at 77," *Dayton Journal Herald*, January 1, 1953, 1; "Judge Nevin Marked Career with Wit, Dignity and Work," *Dayton Journal Herald* (January 1953), n.p., clipping in Cecil Scrapbook; "Federal Judge Robert R. Nevin Expires, *Cincinnati Enquirer*, January 1, 1953, A1; *Columbus Citizen*, January 1, 1953, A1. While Colonel Nevin, Judge Nevin's father, had pushed through the bill that provided for court sessions in Dayton in the National Cash Register case (chapter 4), the court refused to hold the trial in Dayton because, in part, Dayton had no adequate facilities. Indeed, federal judges consistently refused to hear cases in Dayton until adequate facilities were built. Iddings, "Bench and Bar of Dayton and Montgomery County," 782.

161. "'Not Retiring' from Bench, Nevin Says," *Dayton Journal Herald* [1952–53], n.p., Cecil Scrapbook; *Cincinnati Enquirer*, January 1, 1953, A1.

162. "Judge Nevin Dies at 77," *Dayton Journal Herald*, January 1, 1953, p. 1; "Judge Nevin Marked Career with Wit, Dignity and Work," *Dayton Journal Herald* [January, 1953], n.p., Cecil Scrapbook; *Cincinnati Enquirer*, January 1, 1953, A1; Columbus Citizen, January 1, 1953, A1.

163. "In Memoriam Honorable Robert R. Nevin"; "Judge Nevin Dies at 77," *Dayton Journal Herald*, January 1, 1953, 1; "Judge Nevin Marked Career with Wit," *Dayton Journal Herald*, n.p., Cecil Scrapbook; Robert Snell, Clerk of Court, interview by author, Dayton, Ohio, July 9, 2001.

164. David Greer, *Sluff of History's Boot Soles: An Anecdotal History of Dayton's Bench and Bar* (Wilmington, OH: Orange Frazer Press, 1996), 219.

165. "Judge Nevin Dies at 77," *Dayton Journal Herald*, January 1, 1953, 1.

166. Telegram to Senate Judiciary Committee chairman, January 30, 1936, Senate, Records, Papers re Nominations, File 74B-A3 (11). The examination to which Mrs. Hoffman referred is one required of attorneys to practice in federal court. There are, however, no requirements to be a federal judge other than nomination by the president and confirmation by the Senate.

167. *Senate Executive Journal*, 74th Cong., 2d sess., 132 (January 27, 1936), 158 (February 3, 1936), 170 (February 4, 1936); Senate Judiciary Committee, executive documents, 74th Cong., Doc. No. 94; *Columbus Courthouse Journal*, April 1, 1935–September 2, 1938, June term 1936.

168. Goldman, *Picking Federal Judges*, 17–25, 39; attorney Tom Cecil, interview by author, June 6, 2002, Dayton, OH.

169. Lyter interview; Bicentennial Committee, *History of the Sixth Circuit*, 201.

170. Galbreath, *History of Ohio*, 5:461; Bicentennial Committee, *Judges of the United States*, 503; Taylor, *Bench and Bar of Ohio, 1939–1940*, 328–29; Columbus Courthouse Journal, April 1, 1935–September 2, 1938, June term 1936; Bicentennial Committee, *History of the Sixth Circuit*, 201; "In Memoriam The Honorable Mell G. Underwood," Wallace Files; *Who Was Who in America*, 5.

171. Columbus Courthouse Journal, June term 1936, June 2, 1936.

172. "In Memoriam the Honorable Mell G. Underwood," Wallace Files.

173. Ibid.; attorney Tom Cecil, interview by author, June 6, 2002, Dayton, OH; Judge John D. Holschuh, interview by author, July 12, 1999, and July 30, 1999, Columbus; Lyter interview.

174. Donald Dale Jackson, *Judges* (New York: Atheneum, 1974), 275.

175. *Senate Executive Journal*, 75th Cong., 1st sess., 3 (November 16, 1937), 87 (December 7, 1937), 89 (December 9, 1937); Senate, Records, Papers re Nominations, File 75B-A4(4); Senate Judiciary Committee, executive documents, 75th Cong., Doc. No. 76.

176. Bicentennial Committee, *History of the Sixth Circuit*, 130–31; Taylor, *Bench and Bar of Ohio*, 187; Bicentennial Committee, *Judges of the United States*, 138; speech by Harry A. Abrams at the presentation of Judge Druffel's portrait on June 18, 1965, Wallace Files; *Cincinnati Enquirer,* May 17, 1967, 14.

177. Clippings from *Cincinnati Post & Times-Star*, December 29, 1964, and June 18, 1965, Papers of John W. Peck, box 70; Judges Weinman, Kinneary, Hogan, Porter

and others, Memorial to Honorable John H. Druffel at his Memorial Service, November, 1967, ibid., box 77.

178. *Congressional Record*, 83d Cong., 1st sess., 1 (April 1, 1953); *Dayton Daily News*, April 20, 1953, n.p., clipping in Cecil Scrapbook.

179. Cecil interview.

180. "Judge Nevin Successor Seen after Jan. 20," *Dayton Journal Herald* [December, 1952], "Federal Judgeship Vacancy Causes Big Stir in Political Circles Here," *Dayton Daily News*, January, 11, 1953, "Senate to Get Cecil's Name Next Week," *Dayton Journal Herald*, March 28, 1953, all clippings in Cecil Scrapbook; Greer, *Sluff of History*, 220; Cecil interview. As Eisenhower's first judicial appointment, Cecil was called to the White House to meet the president. "Eisenhower Chats With Daytonian," *Dayton Journal Herald*, March 30, 1953, clipping in Cecil Scrapbook.

181. "GOP Tussle Seen over Judgeship," *Dayton Daily News* [n.d., c. January 1953], clipping in Cecil Scrapbook. See also "Dayton Attorney Reported Likely Nevin Successor," *Dayton Journal Herald* [n.d.], and "Bar Pondering Cecil to Take Nevin's Place," *Dayton Journal Herald*, January 6, 1953, clipping ibid.

182. "GOP to Select Candidate for Nevin's Post," *Dayton Journal Herald*, January 10, 1953, "Federal Judgeship Vacancy Causes Big Stir in Political Circles Here," *Dayton Daily News*, January 11, 1953, "Take It Over," *Dayton Journal Herald*, January 14, 1953, "County GOP Is Suffering Political Indigestion" and "Bar to Decide on Giving Nod for Nevin Job," *Dayton Journal Herald*, January 17, 1953, "County GOP Squabble Seen over Judgeship," *Dayton Daily News*, January 18, 1953, "Replacement for Nevin Studied," *Dayton Journal Herald*, January 20, 1953, "Scrap May Cost Dayton Judgeship," *Dayton Daily News*, January 20, 1953, "Cecil 1st Pick of Dayton Bar," *Dayton Journal Herald*, January 23, 1953, "Cecil Backed by GOP For U.S. Bench," *Dayton Journal Herald*, January 24, 1953, "GOP Backs Judge Cecil," *Dayton Daily News*, January 25, 1953, "Lawyer Seen in Race for Judgeship," *Dayton Journal Herald*, January 26, 1953; "Opposition Is Growing to Cecil Appointment," *Dayton Journal Herald*, January 28, 1953, "Young Seeks Cecil Backing," *Dayton Journal Herald*, January 31, 1953, all clippings in Cecil Scrapbook. Some objected to the political battles, arguing that the best person should be selected. See letters to the editor of the *Dayton Journal Herald*, January 23, 1953. See also "Only One Measure," editorial in *Dayton Daily News*, January 11, 1953, "GOP Party Harmony Fractured," *Dayton Daily News*, February 1, 1953, "Darke County Man Indorsed for Judgeship," *Dayton Journal Herald*, February 4, 1953, "Bricker Expects Delay on Judge," ibid., February 12, 1953, "Judge Post to Greenville Man?" *Dayton Daily News*, February 15, 1953, "Cecil Indorsed by Mrs. Brown for Judgeship," *Dayton Journal Herald*, February 21, 1953, "Mrs. Brown Backs Cecil for U.S. Post," *Dayton Daily News*, February 21, 1953, "Taft, Bricker Support Cecil," *Dayton Journal Herald*, February 23, 1953, 1, "Sen. Taft's '11th-Hour' Phone Call Swayed Mrs. Brown on Choice," *Dayton Daily News*, February 25, 1953, "Minor Cataclysm in GOP Ranks," ibid., March 1, 1953, all clippings in Cecil Scrapbook.

183. *Congressional Record*, 83d Cong., 1st Sess., 1 (April 1, 1953); "Taft, Bricker Support Cecil," *Journal Herald*, February 23, 1953, 1, clipping in Cecil Scrapbook.

184. "Presentation of Portrait of the Honorable Lester L. Cecil," October 10, 1984, 801 F.2d lxxxv–xciii (S.D. Ohio 1986), quote at lxxxvii.

185. Bicentennial Committee, *Judges of the United States*, 84; George C. Edwards, "United States Circuit Judge Lester L. Cecil, 1893–1982," *Toledo Law Review* 14 (Spring 1983): 738–39; Taylor, *Bench and Bar of Ohio*, 49; Bicentennial Committee, *History of the Sixth Circuit*, 120; attorney David Greer's nomination of Judge Cecil for the Walk of Fame, 2002, document in the possession of Thomas Cecil; Cecil interview; Greer, *Sluff of History*, 309; *Cincinnati Enquirer*, June 30, 1977, E-16; "Taft, Bricker Support Cecil," *Dayton Journal Herald*, February 23, 1953, "Cecil Appears Sure of U.S. Judge Post," *Dayton Daily News*, February 23, 1953, "Judge Lester L. Cecil," *West Milton Record*, May 6, 1953, 1, clippings in Cecil Scrapbook.

186. "Cecil Appears Sure of U.S. Judge Position," *Dayton Daily News*, February 23, 1953, clipping in Cecil Scrapbook.

187. "Presentation of Portrait of the Honorable Lester L. Cecil," 801 F.2d at xci.

188. Note from Judge Cecil to his son Tom, August 4, 1960, document in possession of Thomas Cecil.

189. David Greer's nomination of Judge Cecil for the Walk of Fame, 2002, document in the possession of Thomas Cecil. See also "Cecil Appears Sure of U.S. Judge Post," *Dayton Daily News*, February 23, 1953, clipping in Cecil Scrapbook.

190. Bicentennial Committee, *History of the Sixth Circuit*, 120–21; *Senate Executive Journal*, 68th Cong., 1st sess., 643 (July 28, 1959).

191. *Senate Executive Journals*, 68th Cong., 1st sess., 643 (July 28, 1959), 706 (September 1, 1959), 707 (September 2, 1959).

192. "Memorial Proceedings for the Honorable Carl A. Weinman," 473 F. Supp. 1–9 (S.D. Ohio 1979); Bicentennial Committee, *Judges of the United States*, 523; Taylor, *Bench and Bar of Ohio*, 19; "Memorial Service," April 20, 1979, Papers of John W. Peck, box 20. After Weinman's first wife died in 1969, the judge married Frances Elaine Glerum. Bicentennial Committee, *History of the Sixth Circuit*, 204–205.

193. Judge Kinneary said that Bailey "was the most impressive person" he had seen in the courtroom. Judge Joseph P. Kinneary interview by author, June 25, 1999, Columbus.

194. *Dayton Journal Herald*, February 6, 1979, 1.

195. Ibid.

196. Ibid.; "Memorial Service," April 20, 1979, Papers of John W. Peck, box 28; "Memorial Proceedings for the Honorable Carl A. Weinman," 473 F. Supp. at 8–10.

197. "Memorial Proceedings for the Honorable Carl A. Weinman," 473 F. Supp. at 9.

198. Greer, *Sluff of History*, 310–11; article by Joe Fenley, *Dayton Daily News*, February 6, 1979, clipping in Papers of John W. Peck, box 28.

199. Article by Joe Fenley, *Dayton Daily News*, February 6, 1979, clipping in Papers of John W. Peck, box 28.

200. Ibid. See also *Dayton Journal Herald*, February 6, 1979, 1; "Memorial Service"; Greer, *Sluff of History*, 310–11; "Memorial Resolutions: The Honorable Carl A. Weinman," 46–47; Bicentennial Committee, *History of the Sixth Circuit*, 204.

201. *Senate Executive Journal,* 87th Cong., 2d sess., 6 (January 15, 1962), 513–14 (April 11, 1962); file on Peck's district court nomination, box 54, and letters from Young to Peck and Peck to Young, Papers of John W. Peck, box 61; "Naming of Peck as Successor to Druffel Expected Soon," *Cincinnati Post and Times-Star,* August 21, 1961, ibid. At his swearing in ceremony, Peck thanked those who supported him, saying "it would be ostrich-like to pretend that judicial appointments are made without consideration of political factors." He was selected over Timothy Hogan, who would be appointed judge in 1966. Speech by Peck, October 13, 1961, Cincinnati, Papers of John W. Peck, box 34.

202. Bicentennial Committee, *History of the Sixth Circuit,* 178–79; Cincinnati Chapter of the Federal Bar Association, "Presentation of Portrait of the Honorable John W. Peck to the U.S. District Court for the Southern District of Ohio," May 16, 1972, Papers of John W. Peck, box 58.

203. Bicentennial Committee, *Judges of the United States,* 385; Bicentennial Committee, *History of the Sixth Circuit,* 178–79; "Presentation of Portrait of the Honorable John W. Peck," Papers of John W. Peck, box 58; "New U.S. Judge Likes People Better Than Books," *Cincinnati Post & Times-Star,* September 27, 1961, 14; Libby Lackman, "Appeals Court Judge Has Unique Past," *Cincinnati Enquirer,* December 5, 1971; Ben L. Kaufman, "30 Years and Counting: Federal Judge Presides over Changes Good and Bad," *Cincinnati Enquirer,* October 13, 1991; Lori McClung, "Judge Peck Dies," *Cincinnati Post,* September 8, 1993; Smita Madan Paul and Kristen Delguzzi, "John Peck, 80: A Lifetime of Jurisprudence," *Cincinnati Enquirer,* September 8, 1993; "6th Circuit Judge Dies at Age 80," *Cleveland Plain Dealer,* September 9, 1993; various newspaper clippings in Papers of John W. Peck, boxes 34 and 36.

204. Unidentified newspaper clipping in Papers of John W. Peck, box 36.

205. Peck to John A. Wiethe, October, 1961, ibid., box 35.

206. Speech by Peck, October 13, 1961, ibid., box 34.

207. "New U.S. Judge Likes People Better Than Books," *Cincinnati Post & Times-Star,* September 27, 1961, 14; Speech by Peck, "Upstairs, Out of Sight," Cleveland Bar Association, Cleveland, Ohio, November 14, 1966, Papers of John W. Peck, box 78. See also Peck to Stephen Young, July 7, 1961, ibid., box 54.

208. Speech, "Upstairs, Out of Sight," Papers of John W. Peck, box 78.

209. *Cincinnati Enquirer,* September 8, 1993, and *Cleveland Plain Dealer,* September 9, 1993.

210. Statement of John W. Peck, Judge, Supreme Court of Ohio, before the Ohio Legislative Service Commission's Study Committee on Capital Punishment, July 5, 1960, Papers of John W. Peck, box 34. Although he would have liked to see the death penalty abolished in Ohio, as a practical, political compromise, he proposed to the committee that it change the system from one in which the penalty for first-degree murder is death unless the jury recommends mercy to one in which the automatic penalty was imprisonment for life unless the jury recommended the death penalty. This, he felt, would "virtually abolish electrocution in Ohio." Ibid.

211. John W. Peck, address in Cheviot, Memorial Day, May 30, 1951, ibid., box 36; John W. Peck, "Law Protects Freedom," address at Xavier University, June 19, 1959, ibid.; John W. Peck, talk on brotherhood, Dayton, February 14, 1960, ibid.

See also letter from Peck to Judge A. Leon Higginbotham Jr., March 13, 1992, praising Higginbotham's open letter to the then newly appointed Supreme Court Justice Clarence Thomas urging Thomas not to forget the history of the struggle for racial justice and to remember that he was replacing Justice Thurgood Marshall and should honor that jurist's memory by continuing his work. Ibid., box 57. (For Higginbotham's letter, see "An Open Letter to Justice Clarence Thomas from a Federal Colleague," *University of Pennsylvania Law Review* (January 1992): 1005–28.) But while Peck urged equal justice, he also believed that part of the struggle for freedom entailed fighting its enemies. We must, he said, continue to struggle to remain "free of Communistic domination." Address in Cheviot, ibid., box 36.

212. *Senate Executive Journal*, 89th Cong., 2d sess., 989 (September 30, 1966), 1061, 1063–64 (October 20, 1966). 80 Stat 75 (1966) created the new judgeship.

213. William A. Geoghegan to Ernest Friesen, assistant deputy attorney general, September 1, 1965, director of the FBI to acting attorney general, October 18, 1966, NARA screened material; *Cincinnati Enquirer*, September 16, 1966, 4; *Court Index of Hamilton County*, September 15, 1966, 1; Peck to Attorney General Ramsey Clark, September 19, 1966, and Clark to Peck, October 21, 1966, Papers of John W. Peck, box 34.

214. Robert R. Lavercombe, chairman, Judicial Selection Committee, to the committee, August 11, 1965, Geoghegan to Friesen, September 1, 1965, NARA screened material.

215. Goldman, *Picking Federal Judges*, 173; "Judge Shortage Hits Federal Court," *Cincinnati Enquirer*, September 16, 1966, 4.

216. Robert Elkins, "U.S. Judge Timothy Hogan," *Cincinnati Enquirer*, January 31, 1969, A10.

217. Judge Peck quoting Rubin in Peck's remarks at Hogan's Memorial Service, February 24, 1989, Papers of John W. Peck, box 57.

218. Elkins, "U.S. Judge Timothy Hogan," *Cincinnati Enquirer*, January 31, 1989, A10.

219. Ibid.; Judge Peck's remarks at Hogan's Memorial Service, Papers of John W. Peck, box 57; "Memorial Resolution for Timothy Sylvester Hogan," 42–43. For additional sources providing biographical material on Hogan, see Sarah Livermore, executive ed., *The American Bench: Judges of the Nation*, 3d ed. (Sacramento, CA: Forster-Long, 1985), 1835; Bicentennial Committee, *Judges of the United States*, 225; Bicentennial Committee, *History of the Sixth Circuit*, 145; "Judge Timothy S. Hogan: Funeral Service Today for U.S. District Court Jurist," *Cincinnati Enquirer*, February 1, 1989, clipping in Wallace Files.

220. "Memorial Resolution for Timothy Sylvester Hogan," 42–43.

221. Judges Rubin, Kinneary, Weber, Peck, Spiegel, and William McD. Kite, "In Memory of Timothy S. Hogan," Papers of John W. Peck, box 57.

222. "Judge Timothy Hogan Dead at 79," *Cincinnati Post*, January 31, 1989, 1B.

223. Elkin, "U.S. Judge Timothy Hogan," *Cincinnati Enquirer*, January 31, 1989, A10.

224. Judges Rubin, Kinneary, Weber, Peck, Spiegel, and William McD. Kite, "In Memory of Timothy S. Hogan," Papers of John W. Peck, box 57.

225. Judge Peck's remarks at Hogan's Memorial Service, Papers of John W. Peck, box 57.

226. Unidentified newspaper clipping, ibid.

227. Ben L. Kaufman, obituary article, *Cincinnati Enquirer,* January 7, 1989, ibid., box 58.

228. The fact that Hogan and Porter were appointed, confirmed, commissioned, and took office the same day and were also born the same day created a problem when it came time to decide who would assume the job of chief judge for the district. The chief judge is the active judge who has not reached the age of seventy with the most seniority based on the judges' commission date. When the commission bears the same date, precedence is determined by who is the older, but because both had received their commissions on the same day and had the same birthday, Judge Kinneary, who was just completing his term as chief judge, suggested a compromise; each would take a two-year term, with whoever was born first going first. Since Hogan was born eight hours before Porter, Hogan became chief judge first, on September 18, 1975. After he served for two years, Porter took over. The two judges took senior status in September 1979. Both died in January 1989, Porter on January 5 and Hogan on January 30. Untitled typewritten note probably by Judge Peck in Papers of John W. Peck, box 57; "Judge Timothy Hogan Dead at 79," *Cincinnati Post,* January 31, 1999, 1B; Judge Joseph P. Kinneary, interview by author, September 7, 2001, Columbus, Ohio.

229. Livermore, *American Bench,* 3d ed., 1868; W. Stuart Dornette and Robert R. Cross, *Federal Judiciary Almanac* (New York: John Wiley and Sons, 1984–1987), 748; *Bench Press,* December 1980, Wallace Files; Bicentennial Committee, *Judges of the United States,* 398; Bicentennial Committee, *History of the Sixth Circuit,* 182; "Memorial Resolution for David Stewart Porter," 41; Ben L. Kaufman, obituary article, *Cincinnati Enquirer,* January 7, 1989, Papers of John W. Peck, box 58.

230. "Memorial Resolution for David Stewart Porter," 41; Allen Howard, "Old Buddies to Honor David Porter's Senior Status," *Cincinnati Enquirer,* December 3, 1982, Papers of John W. Peck, box 58; Spiegel, "David S. Porter Memorial," ibid.; Ben L. Kaufman, "Obituaries: Judge David S. Porter," *Cincinnati Enquirer,* January 7, 1989, C3.

231. Ben L. Kaufman, "Obituaries: Judge David S. Porter," *Cincinnati Enquirer,* January 7, 1989, C3.

232. *Senate Executive Journal,* 89th Cong., 2d sess., 664 (June 28, 1966), 705–8 (July 21, 1966).

233. *Almanac of the Federal Judiciary,* 1999, 1:75–76; Ruth A. Kennedy, ed., *The American Bench: Judges of the Nation,* 10th ed. (Sacramento, CA: Forster-Long, 1999), 1889; Bicentennial Committee, *Judges of the United States,* 274; *Justices and Judges of the United States Courts* (Washington, DC: Administrative Office of the U.S. Courts, 1999), 301; Bicentennial Committee, *History of the Sixth Circuit,* 154–55; *Cincinnati Enquirer,* February 17, 2003, available at http://www.enquirer.com; *Columbus Dispatch,* February 15, 2003, A1–A2; "Hard Work, Impartiality, Respect," *Daily Reporter,* November 27, 1995, 11; "Bench Mark," *Columbus Dispatch,* March 16, 1986, in Columbus Clerk of Courts Files; Kinneary interviews 1999 and 2001.

234. Office memorandum, William A. Geoghegan, assistant deputy attorney general, to Robert Kennedy, attorney general, April 6, 1961; John A. Wiethe, chairman of the Hamilton County Democratic Party, to Byron White, deputy attorney general, June 7, 1961; William Geoghegan to Byron White, June 30, 1961; unidentified clipping, NARA files screened. It is evident from this correspondence that the posts of U.S. attorney and his assistants were viewed as political positions, with political considerations ranking as high as legal qualifications in the decision-making process. Kinneary's nomination for U.S. attorney was not without opposition. Some in power, including Judge Underwood and Governor DiSalle, opposed Kinneary, pushing the appointment of another Columbus attorney, General Loren G. Windom, who had been first assistant U.S. attorney in the Southern District of Ohio during the Truman administration. But Senator Young and many other powerful Democrats refused to yield; they insisted on Kinneary. Kinneary then proceeded to reorganize that office, staying in Cincinnati rather than moving to Columbus and appointing assistants to head each of the main divisions—criminal and civil. At that point, his appointments of assistants also got embroiled in patronage, many insisting that one or the other of the candidates deserved the post more because of his service to the party. But at all times the debate also centered on who was the most qualified for the position. Therefore competence, as well as politics, were key considerations.

By the 1980s, partisanship played a lesser role in the selection of U.S. attorney, at least for the Southern District of Ohio. According to Christopher K. Barnes, U.S. attorney for the Southern District of Ohio from 1981 to 1985, the previous two U.S. attorneys for the Southern District of Ohio, William Milligan and James Cissell, worked to minimize politics. Ben L. Kaufman, "U.S. Attorney Resigns, Will Return to Private Law," *Cincinnati Enquirer*, June 28, 1985, C1.

235. Peck to Young, February 24, 1966, Papers of John W. Peck, box 61. This was not only Peck's way of praising Kinneary's abilities, but also his not-so-subtle way of criticizing Underwood's record as a judge.

236. "A Commemoration of the Presentation to the United States District Court for the Southern District of Ohio of a Portrait of the Honorable Joseph P. Kinneary," July 22, 1986, Wallace Files.

237. Kinneary 1999 interview; Robert Ruth, "Legendary Federal Judge had a Flair for the Dramatic," *Columbus Dispatch*, February 15, 2003, A1.

238. "Bench Mark," *Columbus Dispatch*, March 16, 1986, in Columbus Clerk of Courts Files.

239. Other judges have also dealt firmly with jurors or potential jurors who failed to do their duty. In 1985, after only twenty-three of the thirty potential jurors who had been sent notices appeared for jury duty, a "furious" Judge Rubin sent U.S. marshals "out to corral prospective jurors who were AWOL." He fined the three who were found $25 each. Ben L. Kaufman, "Judge Fines Potential Jurors Who Didn't Appear in Court," *Cincinnati Enquirer*, September 24, 1985, C2. In 1990, the judges of the Southern District of Ohio, after a meeting in Dayton, voted to "enforce, with appropriate action," jury summonses. Those who did not appear for jury service when called were subject to a maximum $100 fine and three days in

jail. *Columbus Dispatch,* March 18, 1990, Columbus Clerk of Courts Files. That same year, Graham fined no-show jurors $50 each and lectured them for shirking their responsibilities as U.S. citizens. Two years later, Holschuh also fined no-shows $50 and chastised them, maintaining that "jury service is one of the most important responsibilities of citizenship." The next year, Beckwith fined nine more potential jurors $50 each, although she, like her predecessors, suspended the fines placed against some of the jurors when they agreed to accept further jury duty. Clippings from *Columbus Dispatch,* March 15, 1990, March 28, 1990, July 16, 1992, July 8, 1993, all in Columbus Clerk of Courts Files.

240. Martha Colaner, "Judge Joseph P. Kinneary"; "Bench Mark," *Columbus Dispatch,* March 16, 1986; Robert Ruth, "Legendary Federal Judge Had a Flair for the Dramatic," *Columbus Dispatch,* February 15, 2003, A1; Associated Press State and Local Wire, July 27, 2001, Wallace Files; *Daily Legal News & Cleveland Recorder,* November 9, 1995, 1; "LaFatch Judge Just Like a Drill Sergeant," *Akron Beacon Journal,* March 28, 1974, C1; Charley Gillespie article in *Cincinnati Post,* September 29, 1999, clipping in Wallace Files; "A Commemoration of the Presentation to the United States District Court Southern District of Ohio of a Portrait of the Honorable Joseph P. Kinneary," July 22, 1986, ibid.

241. "Bench Mark," *Columbus Dispatch,* March 16, 1986, December 9, 1986, clippings in Columbus Clerk of Courts Files; *Cincinnati Enquirer,* February 17, 2003; *Columbus Dispatch,* February 15, 2003, A1–A2.

242. *Senate Executive Journal,* 92d Cong., 1st sess., 185 (April 29, 1971), 263 (May 19, 1971), 264–65 (May 20, 1971). 84 Stat. 294 (1970) authorized the position.

243. "Presentation of the Portrait of and Memorial to Honorable Carl B. Rubin, 1920–1995," 948 F. Supp. at lxvii.

244. Marie T. Finn, ed., *The American Bench: Judges of the Nation,* 8th ed. (Sacramento, CA: Forster-Long, 1995), 1917; Bicentennial Committee, *Judges of the United States,* 430; Bicentennial Committee, *History of the Sixth Circuit,* 186; *Cincinnati Post,* August 3, 1995, 1A; Ben L. Kaufman, "Judge Carl Rubin, 1920–1995: 24 Years as 'Tough but Fair' Jurist," *Cincinnati Enquirer,* August 3, 1995, A1, A7; "Presentation of the Portrait of and Memorial to Honorable Carl B. Rubin, 1920–1995," 948 F. Supp. at lxiii.

245. John D. Holschuh, Herman Weber, and Susan Dlott, "Memorial Resolution for Carl B. Rubin."

246. Rubin to Peck, undated, and Peck to Rubin, March 15, 1990, Papers of John W. Peck, box 58.

247. *Cincinnati Post,* August 3, 1995, 1A, quoting Larry Kane, Rubin's former law partner.

248. Ibid.

249. See Congregation Lubavitch v. Cincinnati, 807 F. Supp. 1353 (S.D. Ohio 1992); Knight Riders of the Ku Klux Klan v. Cincinnati, 847 F. Supp. 85 (S.D. Ohio 1993); 863 F. Supp. 587 (S.D. Ohio 1994).

250. Thomas R. Schuck, "Dedication: Honorable Carl B. Rubin," 800–802.

251. Mallory v. Eyrich, 666 F. Supp. 1060, 1062–63 (S.D. Ohio 1988).

252. Youngblood v. Dalzell, 777 F. Supp. 1382, 1386 (S.D. Ohio 1991).

253. Ben L. Kaufman, "Expert Panels Established in Asbestos Cases," *Cincinnati Enquirer*, January 9, 1987, C2.

254. *Cincinnati Post*, August 3, 1995, A1; Holschuh et al., "Memorial Resolution for Carl B. Rubin"; *Law Technology Product News*, June 1996, 29; Douglas Frantz, "High-Tech Ohio Courtroom Provides Glimpse of Future," *New York Times*, August 19, 1994, A16; Stanley M. Chesley to John Peck, writing a recommendation for Judge Rubin for the 1990 Edward J. Devitt Distinguished Service to Justice Award, September 27, 1990, all in Papers of John W. Peck, box 65; Ben L. Kaufman, "24 Years as 'Tough but Fair' Jurist," *Cincinnati Enquirer*, August 3, 1995, A1, A7.

255. Holschuh et al., "Memorial Resolution for Carl B. Rubin."

256. *Cincinnati Enquirer*, August 7, 1995, A1, A5; Ben L. Kaufman, "Rubin Vows Slowdown over Denial of Pay Raise," *Cincinnati Enquirer*, February 10, 1989, Papers of John W. Peck, box 65; former Magistrate Judge Robert Steinberg, interview by author, June 1, 2001, Cincinnati.

257. Goldman, *Picking Federal Judges*, 200–202, 209.

258. *Senate Executive Journal*, 93d Cong., 2d sess., 309 (May 1, 1974), 399 (June 12, 1974), 400–401 (June 13, 1974); Judge Robert M. Duncan, interview by author, May 25, 2001, Columbus.

259. Bicentennial Committee, *History of the Sixth Circuit*, 129–30; air.fjc.gov; Duncan interview.

260. Duncan interview.

261. *Senate Executive Journal*, 96th Cong., 2d sess., 210 (March 28, 1980), 238–39 (April 15, 1980), 320 (May 20, 1980), 326 (May 21, 1980).

262. Lyles, "Presidential Expectations and Judicial Performance Revisited," 458–59; Gerhardt, *Federal Appointments Process*, 119–20; Goldman, *Picking Federal Judges*, 236–63.

263. Holschuh interview; Judge S. Arthur Spiegel, interview by author, July 29, 1999, Cincinnati; Judge Walter H. Rice, interview by author, June 14, 1999, Dayton; Marilyn Dillon, "Spiegel Nominated to Court," *Cincinnati Enquirer*, November 15, 1979, A1.

264. Résumé provided to author by Judge Holschuh; Holschuh interview; *Almanac of the Federal Judiciary* (1999), 1:75; "Counselor online," Winter 2001, website of the University of Cincinnati School of Law, 6.

265. Résumé provided to author; Holschuh interview; *Almanac of the Federal Judiciary* (1999), 1:75.

266. Marilyn Dillon, "Spiegel Nominated to Court," *Cincinnati Enquirer*, November 15, 1979, A1; Spiegel interview.

267. *Almanac of the Federal Judiciary* (1999), 1:76–77; Holschuh et al., "Dedication: Honorable S. Arthur Spiegel," 1–10; Spiegel interview; S. Arthur Spiegel, "Affirmative Action in Cincinnati," *Cincinnati Historical Society Bulletin* 37 (Summer 1979): 79–88. Ben Kaufman, the *Cincinnati Enquirer*'s longtime reporter of the district court, labeled Spiegel "the most liberal of the three full-time U.S. District Court judges in Cincinnati" as of 1995. Clipping, *Cincinnati Enquirer*, n.d., n.p., Columbus Clerk of Courts Files.

268. Rice interview; *Almanac of the Federal Judiciary* (2002), 1:69–70; Greer, *Sluff of History*, 454–58; *Dayton Daily News*, n.d., [June 22, 2002] n.p., clipping in Wallace Files.

269. *Almanac of the Federal Judiciary* (2002), 1: 8–79; Kennedy, *American Bench*, 10th ed. 1967–68; Judge Herman J. Weber, interview by author, July 23, 1999, Cincinnati.

270. Lyles, "Presidential Expectations and Judicial Performance," 463; Gerhardt, *Federal Appointments Process*, 120.

271. Weber interview.

272. *Almanac of the Federal Judiciary* (2002), 1:78–79; Weber interview.

273. Kinneary interview; *Columbus Dispatch*, November 18, 1986, Columbus Clerk of Court Files.

274. Judge James Graham, interview by author, July 15, 1999, Columbus.

275. Ben L. Kaufman, "U.S. Judges in Middle of Social Security 'Mess,'" *Cincinnati Enquirer*, December 28, 1985, C1.

276. Paul D. Kamenar, "The Role of the American Bar Association in the Judicial Selection Process," in *Judicial Selection: Merit, Ideology, and Politics*, ed. Henry J. Abraham (Washington, DC: National Legal Center for the Public Interest, 1990), 96. The ABA Standing Committee on the Federal Judiciary, composed of fifteen members "hand-picked" by the ABA's president, has investigated, evaluated, and rated judicial nominees "at the behest of the Department of Justice" since 1952. Although it claims that it never considers politics or ideology when rating candidates, Kamenar believes that the Graham example proves otherwise. Ibid., 93–94.

277. *Senate Executive Journal*, 99th Cong., 2d sess., 504 (August 15, 1986), 586 (September 19, 1986), 606 (September 26, 1986).

278. *Almanac of the Federal Judiciary* (2002), 1:73–74; Mark R. Abel, "Graham Marks Fifteen Years on the Bench," *BARbriefs*, October 2001, 14; *Columbus Dispatch*, November 18, 1986, n.p., and November 23, 1986, 2C, Columbus Clerk of Courts Files; Mary Lee Bliss, ed., *The American Bench: Judges of the Nation*, 12th ed. (Sacramento, CA: Forster-Long, 2001), 2012.

279. *Senate Executive Journal*, 100th Cong., 1st sess., 485 (July 1, 1987); Kinneary interview. Indeed, Smith was first considered for Duncan's replacement along with Graham. *Columbus Dispatch*, July 17, 1986, 8C.

280. Judge George C. Smith, interview by author, July 26, 1999, Columbus; *Columbus Dispatch*, December 9, 1986, n.p., Columbus Clerk of Courts Files; *Senate Executive Journal*, 100th Cong., 1st sess., 690 (November 5, 1987), 695 (November 6, 1987).

281. *Almanac of the Federal Judiciary*, 1:76–78; Mark R. Abel, "Judge Smith Takes Senior Status," *BARbriefs*, February, 2002, 13–14; "Here's One Federal Judge Who Will Miss Campaigning," *Daily Reporter*, November 27, 1987, 1; Smith interview.

282. *Senate Executive Journal*, 102d Cong., 1st sess., 499 (July 26, 1991), 102d Cong., 2d sess., 86–87 (February 6, 1992). It took the Senate Judiciary Committee over six months to report on Beckwith's nomination because the committee was distracted by the contentious confirmation hearing of Clarence Thomas to the U.S. Supreme Court. There is no indication that there were any problems or controversies surrounding Beckwith's appointment. Once the Senate Judiciary Committee

recommended her confirmation on February 6, the Senate unanimously confirmed her en bloc with many others the same day.

283. Ben L. Kaufman, "Beckwith Is the Favorite," *Cincinnati Enquirer*, April 2, 1991, A1. See also Judge Sandra Beckwith, interview by author, July 22, 1999, Cincinnati.

284. Beckwith interview.

285. *Almanac of the Federal Judiciary* (2002), 1:70–72; Mark G. Kobasuk, "Hon. Sandra S. Beckwith Judge, Southern District of Ohio," *Federal Lawyer* 47 (July 2000): 16–22; Beckwith interview; unpublished biographical questionnaire, Wallace Files.

286. *Journal of the Executive Proceedings of the Senate of the United States,* 104th Cong., 1st sess., 557 (August 10, 1995), 705–706 (October 26, 1995), 842, 846 (December 22, 1995); *Columbus Dispatch* [August 1995], 5B, Columbus Clerk of Court Files.

287. *Columbus Dispatch* [August 1995], 5B, Columbus Clerk of Court Files.

288. *Almanac of the Federal Judiciary* (2002), 1:72–73; résumé provided to the author by Judge Dlott; Judge Susan Dlott, interview by author, July 28, 1999, Cincinnati.

289. "The Biggest Case in Town Is in Her Court," *Cincinnati Enquirer*, February 17, 2002, A1, A16.

290. Dlott interview.

291. *Senate Executive Journal,* 104th Cong., 1st sess., 839 (December 22, 1995), 104th Cong., 2d Sess., 271 (May 9, 1996), 469 (July 22, 1996); Judge Edmund A. Sargus, interview by author, July 15, 1999, Columbus; "Judge Rubin Dies, Leaves Second Vacancy," *Columbus Dispatch* [August 1995], 5B in Columbus Clerk of Courts Files; Howard Wilkinson, "Rubin Successor South," *Cincinnati Enquirer*, August 4, 1995, n.p., Wallace Files.

292. *Almanac of the Federal Judiciary* (2002), 1:75–76; Sargus interview; letter from Sargus to the author, September 8, 2003; "Judge Conducts Pretrials Using 'Hands-On' Approach," *Ohio Lawyer's Weekly*, April 30, 2001, 1, 26; Nature's Dairy v. Glickman, 173 F.3d 429, (6th Cir. 1999) (Sargus, writing for the court and sitting on the Sixth Circuit Court of Appeals by designation, arguing that courts must pay "appropriate respect" to the "power of Congress to regulate commerce among the states").

293. *Senate Executive Journal,* 105th Cong., 1st sess., 354 (July 31, 1997), 527 (October 9, 1997), 548 (October 23, 1997), 559 (October 27, 1997); Judge Algenon L. Marbley, interview by author, July 30, 1999, Columbus.

294. *Almanac of the Federal Judiciary* (2002), 1:74–75; Marbley interview; résumé provided to the author by Judge Marbley.

295. "New Federal Judge to Ease Rice's Load," *Dayton Daily News,* June 20, 2002; "Senate Confirms Rose Unanimously," ibid., May 10, 2002, clippings in Wallace Files; Bliss, ed., *American Bench,* 13th ed., 1982; air.fjc.gov;

296. Résumé provided to author, August 13, 2003; http://www.ohsd.uscourts .gov/jfrost.htm; http://www.law.yale .edu/outside/scr/library/nom/detail.asp?rec_num=21.

297. See appendix for a tabular summary of the judges' backgrounds.

# SELECTED BIBLIOGRAPHY

## JUDICIAL RECORDS

The bulk of the material upon which this history is based are the records of the court itself, primarily the decisions of the judges of the court. Some of these decisions, especially in modern times, have been published in the various federal reporters. Much of the record of the court, however, is available only in manuscript form, either in case files or various journals. Those collections are listed below.

Cincinnati federal courthouse, Criminal and Civil Journals and Dockets of the Southern District of Ohio, Western Division meeting in Cincinnati, not yet shipped to the National Archives Branch Depository, Great Lakes Region, Chicago, IL.

Columbus federal courthouse, Criminal and Civil Journals and Dockets and Equity Journals of the Southern District of Ohio, Eastern Division meeting in Columbus, not yet shipped to the National Archives Branch Depository, Great Lakes Region, Chicago, IL.

Dayton federal courthouse, Criminal and Civil Docket Books of the Southern District of Ohio, Western Division meeting in Dayton, not yet shipped to the National Archives Branch Depository, Great Lakes Region, Chicago, IL.

National Archives Branch Depository, Great Lakes Region, Chicago, IL. Records of the U.S. District Court, Southern District of Ohio. RG 21.

———. Records of the U.S. Circuit Court, Southern District of Ohio. RG 21.

National Archives Microfilm Collection, Records Relating to Proposed Trials of Aaron Burr and Harman Blennerhassett. RG 21, microfilm T265.

———. Proceedings of the U.S. Circuit Court, District of Ohio, Appellate Case Files of the United States Supreme Court, 1792–1831. RG M214, reel 58.

## OTHER GOVERNMENT RECORDS

Administrative Office of the United States Courts. Annual Reports. Washington, DC: Government Printing Office.

Clerk of the U.S. District Court for the Southern District of Ohio. Annual Reports. Unpublished. Columbus: Office of the Clerk of the U.S. District Court for the Southern District of Ohio.

National Archives Branch Depository, College Park, MD. Records Relating to the Appointment of Federal Judges, Marshals, and Attorneys, Ohio (Southern). General Records of the Department of Justice. RG 60.

———. Applications and Endorsements, Ohio, Southern Judges. Department of Justice Records of Appointment Clerk. RG 60.

National Archives Main Branch, Washington, DC. Senate Judiciary Committee, docket. Records of the United States Senate. RG 46.

———. Senate Judiciary Committee, executive docket. Records of the United States Senate. RG 46.

———. Senate Judiciary Committee, executive documents. Records of the United States Senate. RG 46.

———. Senate Judiciary Committee, files. Records of the United States Senate. RG 46.

———. Senate Judiciary Committee, minutes. Records of the United States Senate. RG 46.

National Archives Microfilm Collection. Letters of Appointment and Recommendation during the Administration of Andrew Jackson, General Records of the Department of State. RG 59, Microfilm Publication M639.

U.S. Attorney General. *Annual Reports of the Attorney General of the United States.*

U.S. Congress. Senate. *Journal of the Executive Proceedings.*

## MANUSCRIPT COLLECTIONS

Ethan A. Brown Papers, Ohio Historical Society, Columbus (OHS)

Scrapbook of Judge Lester Cecil, in the possession of his son Tom Cecil, Dayton, Ohio

Charles Hammond Papers, OHS

Mixter Family Papers, Cincinnati Historical Society (CHS)

Papers of John W. Peck, CHS

Charles E. Rice Collection, OHS

Benjamin Tappan Papers, OHS

Edward Tiffin Papers, OHS

Frank B. Willis File, OHS

## INTERVIEWS

*All interviews were conducted by the author.*

Abel, Mark. Columbus, June 4, 2001.

Beckwith, Sandra. Cincinnati, July 22, 1999.

Cecil, Thomas. Dayton, June 6, 2002.

Dlott, Susan. Cincinnati, July 28, 1999.

Duncan, Robert M. Columbus, May 25, 2001.

Graham, James. Columbus, July 15, 1999.

Hogan, Timothy S. Cincinnati, July 12, 2001.

Holschuh, John D. Columbus, July 12, 1999, and July 30, 1999.

Kinneary, Joseph P. Columbus, June 25, 1999, and September 7, 2001.

Lyter, John. Westerville, OH, September 7, 2001.
Marbley, Algenon L. Columbus, July 30, 1999.
Merz, Michael. Dayton, May 22, 2001, and November 10, 2003.
Rice, Walter H. Dayton, June 14, 1999, and October 23, 2001.
Sargus, Edmund A., Jr. Columbus, July 15, 1999.
Smith, George C. Columbus, July 26, 1999.
Spiegel, S. Arthur. Cincinnati, July 29, 1999.
Steinberg, Robert. Cincinnati, June 1, 2001.
Weber, Herman J. Cincinnati, July 23, 1999.

NEWSPAPERS

*Chillicothe Scioto Gazette*
*Chillicothe Scioto Gazette and Fredonia Chronicle*
*Chillicothe Supporter*
*Cincinnati Advertiser*
*Cincinnati Commercial*
*Cincinnati Enquirer*
*Cincinnati Gazette*
*Cincinnati Inquisitor and Advertiser*
*Cincinnati Post*
*Cincinnati Times-Star*
*Cincinnati Western Spy*
*Columbus Citizen*
*Columbus Evening Dispatch*
*Columbus Journal*
*Dayton Daily News*
*Dayton Journal Herald*
*Hillsboro News-Herald*
*Ohio State Journal (Columbus)*

SECONDARY SOURCES

Abel, Mark R. "Graham Marks Fifteen Years on the Bench." *BARbriefs* (October 2001): 14.
———. "Judge Smith Takes Senior Status." *BARbriefs* (February 2002): 13–14.
Abrahamson, Lisle W. *The United States District Court for the District of Kentucky, 1789–1901.* Louisville: United States District Court for the Western District of Kentucky, 2001.
Adair, Harriet Elaine Glosson. "Trends in School Desegregation: An Historic Case of Desegregation in Dayton, Ohio, Denver, Colorado, Los Angeles, California and Seattle, Washington, 1954–1985." Ed.D. diss., Brigham Young University, 1986.
Adler, Amy. "What's Left: Hate Speech, Pornography, and the Problem of Artistic Expression." *California Law Review* 84 (December 1996): 1499–1572.
Alilunas, Leo. "Fugitive Slave Cases in Ohio Prior to 1850." *Ohio State Archaeological and Historical Quarterly* 49 (April 1940): 160–84.

*Almanac of the Federal Judiciary.* New York: Aspen Law and Business, 1999.

———. New York: Aspen Law and Business, 2002.

Amer, Francis J. *The Development of the Judicial System in Ohio from 1787 to 1932.* Baltimore: Johns Hopkins Press, 1932.

American Law Institute. *A Study of the Business of the Federal Courts.* Philadelphia: American Law Institute, 1934.

Aumann, Francis R. "Ohio Government in the Twentieth Century: From Nash to White." In *Ohio in the Twentieth Century,* comp. Harlow Lindley. Vol. 6. of *History of the State of Ohio,* ed. Carl Wittke. Columbus: Ohio State Archaeological and Historical Society, 1942.

Ayers, Elsie Johnson. *The Hills of Highland.* Springfield, OH: H. K. Skinner and Son, 1971.

Aynes, Richard L. "*Bradwell v. Illinois:* Chief Justice Chase's Dissent and the 'Sphere of Women's Work,'" *Louisiana Law Review* 59 (Winter 1999): 521–41.

Badgett, John F. "Plea Bargaining and Prohibition in the Federal Courts, 1908–1934." *Law and Society Review* 24 (April 1990): 413–50.

Baker, Jean H. *Affairs of Party: The Political Culture of Northern Democrats in the Mid-Nineteenth Century.* Ithaca, NY: Cornell University Press, 1981.

———. "A Loyal Opposition: Northern Democrats in the Thirty-seventh Congress." *Civil War History* 25 (June 1979): 139–55.

Balleisen, Edward J. *Navigating Failure: Bankruptcy and Commercial Society in Antebellum America.* Chapel Hill: University of North Carolina Press, 2001.

Beiner, Theresa M. "The Misuses of Summary Judgment in Hostile Environment Cases." *Wake Forest Law Review* 34 (Spring 1999): 71–134.

Benedict, Michael Les. *The Blessings of Liberty.* Lexington, MA: D. C. Heath, 1996.

Bennett, Michael C. "*Borre v. United States:* An Improper Interpretation of Property Rights." *DePaul Law Review* 42 (Summer 1993): 1499–1556.

Berk, Gerald. *Alternative Tracks: The Constitution of American Industrial Order, 1865–1917.* Baltimore: Johns Hopkins University Press, 1994.

Bicentennial Committee of the Judicial Conference of the United States. *History of the Sixth Circuit: A Bicentennial Project.* Washington, DC: Bicentennial Committee of the Judicial Conference of the United States, 1977.

———. *Judges of the United States.* 2d. ed. Washington, DC: Government Printing Office, 1983.

Bishop, Brant W. "Protecting Private Religious Speech in the Public Forum: *Capitol Square Review and Advisory Board v. Pinette.*" *Harvard Journal of Law and Public Policy* 19 (Winter 1996): 602–11.

Bjork, Sheryl A. "Indirect Gag Orders and the Doctrine of Prior Restraint." *University of Miami Law Review* 44 (September 1989): 165–95.

Bliss, Mary Lee, ed. *The American Bench: Judges of the Nation.* 12th ed. Sacramento, CA: Forster-Long, 2001.

———, ed. *The American Bench: Judges of the Nation.* 13th ed. Sacramento, CA: Forster-Long, 2002.

Bonadio, Felice A. *North of Reconstruction: Ohio Politics, 1865–1870.* New York: New York University Press, 1970.

Boryczka, Raymond, and Lorin Lee Cary. *No Strength without Union: An Illustrated History of Ohio Workers, 1803–1980.* Columbus: Ohio Historical Society, 1982.

Brennan, J. Fletcher, ed. *The Biographical Cyclopaedia and Portrait Gallery with an Historical Sketch of the State of Ohio.* Cincinnati: Western Biographical Publishing, 1883–84.

Brown, Jeffery, and Andrew R. L. Cayton, eds. *The Pursuit of Power: Political Culture in Ohio, 1787–1861.* Kent, OH: Kent State University Press, 1994.

Cahan, Richard. *A Court that Shaped America: Chicago's Federal District Court from Abe Lincoln to Abbie Hoffman.* Evanston, IL: Northwestern University Press, 2002.

Campbell, John W. *Biographical Sketches with Other Literary Remains of the Late John W. Campbell, Compiled by his Widow.* Columbus: Scott and Gallagher, 1838.

Campbell, Stanley W. *The Slave Catchers: Enforcement of the Fugitive Slave Law, 1850–1860.* Chapel Hill: University of North Carolina Press, 1968.

Carp, Robert A., and C. K. Rowland. *Policymaking and Politics in the Federal District Courts.* Knoxville: University of Tennessee Press, 1983.

Carp, Robert A., and Ronald Stidham. *The Federal Courts.* 3d ed. Washington, DC: CQ Press, 1998.

Cashman, Sean. *America in the Age of Titans: The Progressive Era and World War I.* New York: New York University Press, 1988.

Cayton, Andrew R. L. "The Failure of Michael Baldwin: A Case Study in the Origins of Middle-Class Culture on the Trans-Appalachian Frontier." *Ohio History* 95 (Winter–Spring 1986): 34–48.

———. *The Frontier Republic: Ideology and Politics in the Ohio Country, 1780–1825.* Kent, OH: Kent State University Press, 1986.

———. *Ohio: The History of a People.* Columbus: Ohio State University Press, 2002.

Cetrulo, Lawrence G. "Summary Jury Trial." *Toxic Torts: A Complete Personal Injury Guide.* St. Paul, MN: West Group, 1993, § 17:9.

Chambers, John. *The Tyranny of Change: America in the Progressive Era, 1900–1917.* New York: St. Martin's Press, 1980.

Chase, Harold, ed. and comp. *Biographical Dictionary of the Federal Judiciary.* Detroit: Gale Research, 1976.

Chesley, Stanley M., Louis M. Roselle, and Paul M. DeMarco. "The Plaintiff's Perspective: The Need for Class Certification in Radiation Cases." *Gonzaga Law Review* 30 (1994–1995): 573–98.

Clark, David S. "Adjudication to Administration: A Statistical Analysis of Federal District Courts in the Twentieth Century." *Southern California Law Review* 55 (November 1981): 65–152.

Clark, Norman H. *Deliver Us from Evil: An Interpretation of American Prohibition.* New York: W. W. Norton, 1976.

Cochran, William C. "The Western Reserve and the Fugitive Slave Law: A Prelude to the Civil War." *Collections of the Western Reserve Historical Society.* Publication No. 101. Cleveland: Western Reserve Historical Society, 1920.

Colaner, Martha. "Judge Joseph P. Kinneary." Cincinnati: University of Cincinnati College of Law, n.d.

Cole, Donald B. *Martin Van Buren and the American Political System.* Princeton, NJ: Princeton University Press, 1984.

———. *The Presidency of Andrew Jackson.* Lawrence: University Press of Kansas, 1993.

Collins, Michael G. "'Economic Rights,' Implied Constitutional Actions, and the Scope of Section 1983." *Georgetown Law Journal* 77 (April 1989): 1493–1566.

Combs, Michael W. "Federal Judiciary and Northern School Desegregation: Law, Politics, and Judicial Management." *Publius* 16 (Spring 1986): 33–52.

Conover, Charlotte Reeve, ed. *Dayton and Montgomery County: Resources and People.* New York: Lewis Historical Publishing, 1932.

———. *Dayton, Ohio: An Intimate History.* New York: Lewis Historical Publishing, 1902.

Cotkin, George B. "Strikebreakers, Evictions and Violence: Industrial Conflict in the Hocking Valley, 1884–1885." *Ohio History* (Spring 1978): 140–150.

Cover, Robert M. *Justice Accused: Antislavery and the Judicial Process.* New Haven, CT: Yale University Press, 1975.

Curtis, Michael Kent. *Free Speech, "The People's Darling Privilege": Struggles for Freedom of Expression in American History.* Durham, NC: Duke University Press, 2000.

"Development in the Law: Injunction II. The Changing Limits of Injunctive Relief." *Harvard Law Review* 78 (March 1965): 997–1021.

*Dictionary of American Biography.* New York: Charles Scribner's Sons, 1928–1936.

Dietz, Laura Hunter. "Master or Crew Salving Own Vessel," 68 Am. Jur. 2d. *Salvage,* 2003, § 48.

Dimond, Paul R. *Beyond Busing: Inside the Challenge to Urban Segregation.* Ann Arbor: University of Michigan Press, 1987.

Diner, Steven J. *A Very Different Age: Americans of the Progressive Era.* New York: Hill and Wang, 1998.

Dornette, W. Stuart, and Robert R. Cross. *Federal Judiciary Almanac.* New York: John Wiley and Sons, 1984–1987.

Dubofsky, Melvyn, and Stephen Burwood, eds. *The American Economy during the Great Depression.* New York: Garland, 1990.

Dubuc, Carroll E., and William D. Evans, Jr. "Recent Developments under CERCLA: Toward a More Equitable Distribution of Liability." *Environmental Law Reporter* 17 (June 1987): 10197.

Edsforth, Ronald. *The New Deal: America's Response to the Great Depression.* Malden, MA: Blackwell, 2000.

Edwards, George C. "United States Circuit Judge Lester L. Cecil, 1893–1982." *Toledo Law Review* 14 (Spring 1983): 738–39.

Ernst, Daniel R. "Law and American Political Development, 1877–1938." *Reviews in American History* 26 (March 1998): 205–19.

Evans, Nelson W. *A History of Scioto County, Ohio, Together with a Pioneer Record of Southern Ohio.* Portsmouth, OH: Nelson W. Evans, 1903.

Evans, Nelson W., and E. B. Stivers. *A History of Adams County, Ohio: From Its Earliest Settlement to the Present Time.* West Union, OH: E. B. Stivers, 1900.

Fehrenbacher, Don E. *Slavery, Law, and Politics: The Dred Scott Case in Historical Perspective.* New York: Oxford University Press, 1981.

Fess, Simeon D., ed. *Ohio: A Four-Volume Reference Library on the History of a Great State.* Chicago: Lewis Publishing, 1937.

Finkelman, Paul. *An Imperfect Union: Slavery, Federalism, and Comity.* Chapel Hill: University of North Carolina Press, 1981.

———. "Prelude to the Fourteenth Amendment: Black Legal Rights in the Antebellum North." *Rutgers Law Journal* 17 (Spring–Summer 1986): 415–82.

———. *Slavery and the Founders: Race and Liberty in the Age of Jackson.* 2d ed. Armonk, NY: M. E. Sharpe, 2001.

Finn, Marie T., ed. *The American Bench: Judges of the Nation.* 8th ed. Sacramento, CA: Forster-Long, 1995.

Fish, Peter Graham. *Federal Justice in the Mid-Atlantic South: United States Courts from Maryland to the Carolinas, 1789–1835.* Washington, DC: Administrative Office of the United States Courts, 2002.

Forbath, William E. *Law and the Shaping of the American Labor Movement.* Cambridge, MA: Harvard University Press, 1991.

———. "The Shaping of the American Labor Movement." *Harvard Law Review* 102 (April 1989): 1109–1256.

Ford, Henry A., and Kate B. Ford. *History of Cincinnati, Ohio.* Cleveland: L. A. Williams, 1881.

———. *History of Hamilton County, Ohio.* Cleveland: L. A. Williams, 1881.

Frankfurter, Felix, and James M. Landis. *The Business of the Supreme Court: A Study in the Federal Judicial System.* New York: Macmillan, 1928.

Franklin, John Hope. "The Enforcement of the Civil Rights Act of 1875." *Prologue* 6 (Winter 1974): 225–35.

Freedman, Eric M. *Habeas Corpus: Rethinking the Great Writ of Liberty.* New York: New York University Press, 2001.

Freyer, Tony A. "The Federal Courts, Localism, and the National Economy, 1865–1900." *Business History Review* 53 (Autumn 1979): 343–63.

Freyer, Tony A., and Timothy Dixon. *Democracy and Judicial Independence: A History of the Federal Courts of Alabama, 1820–1994.* Brooklyn, NY: Carlson Publishing, 1995.

Fritz, Christian G. *Federal Justice in California: The Court of Ogden Hoffman, 1851–1891.* Lincoln: University of Nebraska Press, 1991.

"From Judicial Grant to Legislative Power: The Admiralty Clause in the Nineteenth Century." *Harvard Law Review* 67 (May 1954): 1214–37.

Galbreath, Charles B. *History of Ohio.* Chicago: American Historical Society, 1925.

Gedulig, Karen A. "Casey at the Bat: Judicial Treatment of Mass Tort Litigation." *Hofstra Law Review* 28 (Fall 2000): 309–42.

Genco, Courtney Chetty. "What Happened to *Durland?* Mail Fraud, RICO, and Justifiable Reliance." *Notre Dame Law Review* 68 (1992): 333–98.

Gerber, David A. *Black Ohio and the Color Line, 1860–1915.* Urbana: University of Illinois Press, 1976.

Gerhardt, Michael J. *The Federal Appointment Process: A Constitutional and Historical Analysis.* Durham, NC: Duke University Press, 2000.

Gewirtz, Paul. "Choice in the Transition: School Desegregation and the Corrective Ideal." *Columbia Law Review* 86 (May 1986): 728–98.

Geyer, Thomas E. "The Vitality of the Ohio Laws Designed to Encourage Negotiated Takeovers." *University of Dayton Law Review* 23 (Spring 1998): 515–58.

Gillette, William. *Retreat from Reconstruction*. Baton Rouge: Louisiana State University
Press, 1979.

———. *The Right to Vote: Politics and the Passage of the Fifteenth Amendment*. Baltimore: Johns
Hopkins Press, 1969.

Goldman, Sheldon. *Picking Federal Judges: Lower Court Selection from Roosevelt through Reagan*.
New Haven, CT: Yale University Press, 1977.

Gordillo, Gregory A. "Summary Judgment and Problems of Applying the Celotex
Trilogy Standard." *Cleveland State Law Review* 42 (1994): 263–99.

Granger, Moses M. *The Judiciary of Ohio, 1803–1903*. Columbus: Ohio State Archaeological and Historical Society, 1903.

Greer, David. *Sluff of History's Boot Soles: An Anecdotal History of Dayton's Bench and Bar*. Wilmington, OH: Orange Frazer Press, 1996.

Greve, Charles Theodore. *Centennial History of Cincinnati and Representative Citizens*. Chicago:
Biographical Publishing, 1904.

Griffin, Joseph P. "United States Antitrust Laws and Transnational Business Transactions: An Introduction." *International Lawyer* 21 (Spring 1987): 307–41.

Hall, Kermit L. "The Children of the Cabins: The Lower Federal Judiciary, Modernization, and the Political Culture, 1789–1899." *Northwestern University Law Review* 75 (1980): 423–71.

———. *The Politics of Justice: Lower Federal Judicial Selection and the Second Party System, 1829–61*.
Lincoln: University of Nebraska Press, 1979.

———. "Social Backgrounds and Judicial Recruitment: A Nineteenth-Century Perspective on the Lower Federal Judiciary." *Western Political Quarterly* 29 (June 1976):
243–57.

Hall, Kermit L., and Eric W. Rise. *From Local Courts to National Tribunals: The Federal District Courts of Florida, 1821–1990*. Brooklyn, NY: Carlson Publishing, 1991.

Heydebrand, Wolf, and Carroll Seron. *Rationalizing Justice: The Political Economy of the Federal District Courts*. Albany: State University of New York Press, 1990.

Higgs, Robert. *Crisis and Leviathan: Critical Episodes in the Growth of American Government*. New
York: Oxford University Press, 1987.

Hofstadter, Richard. *The Age of Reform from Bryan to F.D.R.* New York: Random House,
1955.

Hogan, Charles. "Timothy S. Hogan, Ohio's Crusading Attorney General." Master's thesis, Xavier University, 1972.

Holschuh, John D., Robert L. Black, Jr., Nathaniel R. Jones, James B. Helmer, et.
al. "Dedication: Honorable S. Arthur Spiegel." *University of Cincinnati Law Review* 64
(Fall 1995): 1–10.

Holt, Edgar Allan. "Party Politics in Ohio, 1840–1850." Pts. 1, 2, and 3. *Ohio Archaeological and Historical Quarterly* 37 (July 1928): 439–591; 38 (January 1929):
47–182; 38 (April 1929): 260–402.

Hooker, Clifford P. "Whither the Metropolitan Remedy: *Bronson v. Board of Education
of the City School District of the City of Cincinnati*." *West's Education Law Reporter* 17 (1984):
731–42.

Howe, Henry. *Historical Collections of Ohio.* Cincinnati: C. J. Krehbiel, 1902.

Hubbart, H. Clyde. "Ohio in the First World War, 1917–1918." In *Ohio in the Twentieth Century,* comp. Harlow Lindley. Vol. 6 of *History of the State of Ohio,* ed. Carl Wittke. Columbus: Ohio State Archaeological and Historical Society, 1942.

"Humphrey Howe Leavitt." *United States Law Magazine* 5 (1850–52): 44.

Huntington, Charles Clifford. *A History of Banking and Currency in Ohio before the Civil War.* Columbus: F. J. Heer Printing, 1915.

Hurst, James Williard. "The Functions of Courts in the United States, 1950–1980." *Law and Society Review* 14 (1980–81): 401–70.

Hurvitz, Haggai. "American Labor Law and the Doctrine of Entrepreneurial Property Rights: Boycotts, Courts, and the Juridical Reorientation of 1886–1895." *Industrial Relations Law Journal* 8 (September 1986): 307–61.

"In Memoriam, George R. Sage, 1828–1898." *Pamphlets.* Cincinnati: Press of Curtis and Jennings, 1899.

Irons, Peter H. *Jim Crow's Children: The Broken Promise of the Brown Decision.* New York: Viking Press, 2002.

Joblin, Maurice. *Cincinnati, Past and Present, or Its Industrial History.* Cincinnati: Elm Street Printing, 1872.

Johnson, Molly Treadway, and Scott A. Gilbert. *The U.S. Sentencing Guidelines: Results of the Federal Judicial Center's 1996 Survey.* Washington, DC: Federal Judicial Center, 1997.

Jordan, Philip D. *Ohio Comes of Age, 1873–1900.* Vol. 5 of *History of the State of Ohio,* ed. Carl Wittke. Columbus: Ohio State Archaeological and Historical Society, 1943.

*Justices and Judges of the United States Courts.* Washington, DC: Administrative Office of the United States Courts, 1999.

Kaczorowski, Robert J. "Fidelity through History and to It: An Impossible Dream?" *Fordham Law Review* 65 (March 1997): 1663–93.

———. "The Tragic Irony of American Federalism: National Sovereignty versus State Sovereignty in Slavery and in Freedom." *University of Kansas Law Review* 45 (July 1997): 1015–45.

Kaplan, Edward S. *The Bank of the United States and the American Economy.* Westport, CT: Greenwood Press, 1999.

Karl, Barry. *The Uneasy State: The United States from 1915 to 1945.* Chicago: University of Chicago Press, 1983.

Katzenberger, George A. "Major David Ziegler." *Ohio State Archaeological and Historical Quarterly* 21 (April 1912): 127–74.

Keller, Morton. *Regulating a New Society: Public Policy and Social Change in America, 1900–1933.* Cambridge, MA: Harvard University Press, 1994.

Kennedy, Ruth A., ed. *The American Bench: Judges of the Nation.* 10th ed. Sacramento, CA: Forster-Long, 1999.

Klarman, Michael J. "Brown, Originalism, and Constitutional Theory: A Response to Professor McConnell." *Virginia Law Review* 81 (October 1995): 1881–1936.

———. "The Plessy Era." *Supreme Court Review* (1998): 303–411.

Klein, Benjamin F., ed. *The Ohio River: Handbook and Picture Album.* Cincinnati: Young and Klein, 1959.

Klement, Frank L. *The Copperheads in the Middle West*. Chicago: University of Chicago Press, 1960.

———. *The Copperheads of the North*. Shippensburg, PA: White Man Publishing, 1999.

———. *The Limits of Dissent: Clement L. Vallandigham and the Civil War*. Lexington: University Press of Kentucky, 1970.

Kobasuk, Mark G. "Hon. Sandra S. Beckwith, Judge, Southern District of Ohio." *Federal Lawyer* 47 ( July 2000): 16–18.

Kohl, Lawrence E. *The Politics of Individualism: Parties and the American Character in the Jackson Era*. New York: Oxford University Press, 1989.

Kolko, Gabriel. *The Triumph of Conservatism: A Re-interpretation of American History, 1900–1916*. Chicago: Quadrangle Books, 1967.

Kousser, J. Morgan. *Dead End: The Development of Nineteenth-Century Litigation on Racial Discrimination in Schools*. Oxford: Clarendon Press, 1986.

Kraut, Nina. "Speech: A Freedom in Search of One Rule." *Cooley Law Review* 12 (Hilary Term 1995): 177–96.

Kutler, Stanley I. *Judicial Power and Reconstruction Politics*. Chicago: University of Chicago Press, 1968.

Langum, David. *Crossing over the Line: Legislating Morality and the Mann Act*. Chicago: University of Chicago Press, 1994.

Larsen, Lawrence H. *Federal Justice in Western Missouri: The Judges, the Cases, the Times*. Columbia: University of Missouri Press, 1994.

Lazarus, Edward. *Closed Chambers: The First Eyewitness Account of the Epic Struggles inside the Supreme Court*. New York: Random House, 1988.

Leavitt, Humphrey H. *Autobiography of the Hon. Humphrey Howe Leavitt Written for His Family*. New York: n.p., 1893.

Leonard, John William. *Who's Who in Jurisprudence: A Biographical Dictionary of Contemporary Lawyers and Jurists*. Brooklyn, NY: John W. Leonard, 1925.

Leroy, Michael H., and John H. Johnson IV. "Death by Lethal Injunction: National Emergency Strikes under the Taft-Hartley Act and the Moribund Right to Strike." *Arizona Law Review* 43 (Spring 2001): 63–134.

Leuchtenburg, William. *The Perils of Prosperity*. Chicago: University of Chicago Press, 1958.

Light, Alfred R. "The Importance of 'Being Taken': To Clarify and Confirm The Litigative Reconstruction of CERCLA's Text." *Boston College Environmental Affairs Law Review* 18 (Fall 1980): 1–52.

Lindley, Harlow, comp. *Ohio in the Twentieth Century*. Vol. 6 of *History of the State of Ohio*, ed. Carl Wittke. Columbus: Ohio State Archaeological and Historical Society, 1942.

Link, Arthur S. *Woodrow Wilson and the Progressive Era, 1910–1917*. New York: Harper, 1954.

Livermore, Sarah, ed. *The American Bench: Judges of the Nation*. 3d ed. Sacramento, CA: Forster-Long, 1985.

Lyles, Kevin L. *The Gatekeepers: Federal District Courts in the Political Process*. Westport, CT: Praeger, 1997.

———. "Presidential Expectations and Judicial Performance Revisited: Law and Politics in the Federal District Courts, 1960–1992." *Presidential Studies Quarterly* 26 (Spring 1996): 447–72.

Magnetti, Donald L. "'In the End, Truth Will Out' . . . Or Will It? 'Merchant of Venice,' Act II, Scene 2." *Missouri Law Review* 52 (Winter 1987): 299–362.

Maizlish, Stephen E. *The Triumph of Sectionalism: The Transformation of Ohio Politics, 1844–1856.* Kent, OH: Kent State University Press, 1983.

Malloy, S. Elizabeth Wilborn. "Whose Federalism?" *Indiana Law Review* 32 (1998): 45–69.

Maltz, Earl M. "Originalism and the Desegregation Decisions: A Response to Professor McConnell." *Constitutional Commentary* 13 (1996): 223–30.

Mann, Arthur. *The Progressive Era.* New York: Holt, Rinehart and Winston, 1963.

Markell, David L. "The Federal Superfund Program: Proposals for Strengthening the Federal/State Relationship." *William and Mary Journal of Environmental Law* 18 (Fall 1993): 1–82.

Marshall, Carrington T., ed. *A History of the Courts and Lawyers of Ohio.* 4 vols. New York: American Historical Society, 1934.

Martin, Albro. "Railroads and the Equity Receivership: An Essay on Institutional Change." *Journal of Economic History* 34 (September 1974): 685–709.

McCabe, Peter G. "The Federal Magistrate Act of 1979." *Harvard Journal on Legislation* 16 (1979): 343–401.

McConnell, Michael W. "Originalism and the Desegregation Decisions." *Virginia Law Review* 81 (May 1995): 947–1140.

McElvaine, Robert S. *The Great Depression.* New York: Times Books, 1984.

Milkis, Sidney M., and Jerome M. Mileur, eds. *Progressivism and the New Democracy.* Amherst: University of Massachusetts Press, 1999.

Miller, Arthur R. "The Pretrial Rush to Judgment: Are the 'Litigation Explosion,' 'Liability Crisis,' and Efficiency Clichés Eroding Our Day in Court and Jury Trial Commitments." *New York University Law Review* 78 (June 2003): 982–1134.

Minda, Gary. "The Law and Metaphor of Boycott." *Buffalo Law Review* 41 (Fall 1993): 807–937.

Minter, Patricia Hagler. "The Failure of Freedom: Class, Gender, and the Evolution of Segregated Transit Law in the Nineteenth-Century South." *Chicago-Kent Law Review* 70 (1995): 993–1009.

Mollica, Paul W. "Federal Summary Judgment at High Tide." *Marquette Law Review* 84 (Fall 2000): 141–226.

Morris, Jeffrey Brandon. *Calmly to Poise the Scales of Justice: A History of the Courts of the District of Columbia Circuit.* Durham, NC: Carolina Academic Press, 2001.

Morris, William W. *The Bench and Bar of Cincinnati.* Cincinnati: New Court House Publishing, 1921.

Moss, Randolph D. "Participation and Department of Justice School Desegregation Consent Decrees." *Yale Law Journal* 95 (July 1986): 1811–35.

Murphy, Paul L. *World War I and the Origin of Civil Liberties in the United States.* New York: W. W. Norton, 1979.

Nagel, Ilene H. "Structuring Sentencing Discretion: The New Federal Sentencing Guidelines." *Journal of Criminal Law and Criminology* 80 (Winter 1990): 883–943.

Nagel, Paul. *John Quincy Adams: A Public Life, A Private Life.* New York: Knopf, 1997.

*National Cyclopedia of American Biography.* Clifton, NJ: J. T. White, 1893.

Neely, Mark E., Jr. *The Fate of Liberty: Abraham Lincoln and Civil Liberties.* New York: Oxford University Press, 1991.

Nelson, S. B., ed. *History of Cincinnati and Hamilton County.* Cincinnati: S. B. Nelson, 1894.

Niven, John. *Salmon P. Chase: A Biography.* New York: Oxford University Press, 1994.

Norris, Martin J. "Crew Salving Own Vessel." *The Law of Seamen* (2002): § 9:27.

Novak, William J. *The People's Welfare: Law and Regulation in Nineteenth-Century America.* Chapel Hill: University of North Carolina Press, 1996.

Parrish, Michael. *Anxious Decades: America in Prosperity and Depression, 1920–1941.* New York: W. W. Norton, 1992.

Peck, John Weld. "The Federal Courts of Ohio." In *A History of the Courts and Lawyers of Ohio,* ed. Carrington T. Marshall. New York: American Historical Society, 1934.

———. "The Selection and Tenure of Judges," in *John Weld Peck: A Memorial,* ed. Jane Peck Alcorn. Cincinnati: n.p. 1938.

Pegues, Robert L., Jr. "A Documentary Research of the Role of the School Superintendent in School Federal Desegregation Court Trials: Four Major Large Ohio Cities, 1964–1984." Ph.D. diss., Kent State University, 1989.

"Perjury: Circumstantial Evidence is Sufficient for False-Swearing Conviction of Union Officer Filing Non-Communist Affidavit." *Harvard Law Review* 70 (December 1956): 383–85.

Podgor, Ellen S. "Tax Fraud—Mail Fraud: Synonymous, Cumulative or Diverse?" *University of Cincinnati Law Review* 57 (1989): 903–33.

Prince, Benjamin F. "The Rescue Case of 1857." *Ohio State Archaeological and Historical Society* 16 (July 1907): 292–309.

Purcell, Edward A., Jr. *Brandeis and the Progressive Era: Erie, the Judicial Power, and the Politics of the Federal Courts in Twentieth-Century America.* New Haven, CT: Yale University Press, 2000.

———. *Litigation and Inequality: Federal Diversity Jurisdiction in Industrial America, 1870–1958.* New York: Oxford University Press, 1992.

Randall, E. O., ed. *Ohio Centennial Anniversary Celebration at Chillicothe, May 20–21, 1903, under the Auspices of the Ohio State Archaeological and Historical Society.* Columbus: Ohio State Archaeological and Historical Society, 1903.

Randall, E. O., and Daniel J. Ryan. *History of Ohio.* New York: Century History, 1912.

Ratcliffe, Donald J. "The Autobiography of Benjamin Tappan." *Ohio History* 85 (Spring 1976): 109–57.

———. *The Politics of Long Division: The Birth of the Second Party System in Ohio, 1818–1828.* Columbus: Ohio State University Press, 2000.

———, ed. *Party Spirit in a Frontier Republic: Democratic Politics in Ohio, 1793–1821.* Columbus: Ohio State University Press, 1998.

Reed, George Irving, ed. *Bench and Bar of Ohio: A Compendium of History and Biography.* Chicago: Century Publishing and Engraving, 1897.

*Register of Officers and Agents . . . in the Service of the United States [in] . . . 1875.* Washington, DC: Government Printing Office, 1876.

Reisch, Robert, and Gregory J. Mazares. "The Legacy of Judge Carl B. Rubin." *Law and Technology Product News* (June 1996): 29.

Resnik, Judith. "'Uncle Sam Modernizes His Justice': Inventing the Federal District Courts of the Twentieth Century for the District of Columbia and the Nation." *Georgetown Law Journal* 90 (March 2002): 607–84.

Rhodes, Irwin S. "The History of the United States District Court for the Southern District of Ohio." *University of Cincinnati Law Review* 24 (Summer 1995): 338–54.

Riegel, Stephen J. "The Persistent Career of Jim Crow: Lower Federal Courts and the 'Separate but Equal' Doctrine, 1865–1896." *American Journal of Legal History* 28 (January 1984): 17–40.

Roe, George Mortimer. *Cincinnati: The Queen City of the West.* Cincinnati: C. T. Krehbiel, 1895.

Ronald, Bruce W., and Virginia Ronald. *Dayton: The Gem City.* Tulsa, OK: Continental Heritage Press, 1981.

Roseboom, Eugene H. *The Civil War Era, 1850–1873.* Vol. 4 of *History of the State of Ohio,* ed. Carl Wittke. Columbus: Ohio State Archaeological and Historical Society, 1944.

Rubin, Carl. "Section 1983: A Limited Access Highway." *University of Cincinnati Law Review* 52 (1983): 977–85.

Sanders, Joseph. "From Science to Evidence: The Testimony on Causation in the Bendectin Cases." *Stanford Law Review* 46 (November 1993): 1–85.

Scheiber, Harry N. *Ohio Canal Era: A Case Study of Government and the Economy, 1820–1861.* Athens: Ohio University Press, 1969.

Schlesinger, Arthur M., Jr. *The Age of Jackson.* New York: Book Find Club, 1945.

———. *The Age of Roosevelt.* Boston: Houghton Mifflin, 1957.

Schopler, E. H. "Collective Bargaining Agreement as Restricting Right to Strike or Picket." *American Law Reports 2d.* (1948): 1278 §§ 3(a), 3(e), and 6.

Schuck, Thomas R. "Dedication: Honorable Carl B. Rubin." *University of Cincinnati Law Review* 64 (Spring 1996): 800–802.

Schuckers, J. W. *The Life and Public Services of Salmon Portland Chase.* New York: D. Appleton, 1874; reprint New York: Da Capo Press, 1970.

Sealander, Judith. *Grand Plans: Business Progressivism and Social Change in Ohio's Miami Valley, 1890–1929.* Lexington: University Press of Kentucky, 1988.

Seron, Carroll. "The Professional Project of Parajudges: The Case of U.S. Magistrates." *Law and Society Review* 22 (July 1988): 557–74.

Shapiro, Herbert. "The Herbert Bigelow Case: A Test of Free Speech in Wartime." *Ohio History* 81 (Spring 1972): 108–21.

Sharp, James Roger. *American Politics in the Early Republic: The New Nation in Crises.* New Haven, CT: Yale University Press, 1993.

Shriver, Philip R., and Charles E. Wunderlin Jr., eds. *The Documentary Heritage of Ohio.* Athens: Ohio University Press, 2000.

Silbey, Joel H. *The Partisan Imperative: The Dynamics of American Politics before the Civil War.* New York: Oxford University Press, 1985.

Singer, Joseph William. "No Right to Exclude: Public Accommodations and Private Property." *Northwestern University Law Review* 90 (Summer 1996): 1283–1495.

Skeel, David A., Jr. *Debt's Dominion: A History of Bankruptcy Law in America*. Princeton, NJ: Princeton University Press, 2001.

"Sketches of the Establishment of the Federal Courts by States [Jurisdiction] and their Judges." 212 *F.R.D.* (April 2003): 611–19, 750–54.

Sloan, Steve. *"Brown v. Socialist Workers '74 Campaign Committee* and the Constitutionality of Campaign Disclosure Requirements as Applied to Minor Political Parties." *Journal of Law and Politics* 1 (1983): 195–210.

Smith, Angry A., and Lucia B. Keys, comps. *Reminiscences of Hon. George W. Hays from 1890 to 1929*. Cincinnati: William P. Houston Printing, n.d.

Spaniol, Joseph F., Jr. "The Federal Magistrates Act: History and Development." *Arizona State Law Journal* 4 (1974): 565–78.

Spiegel, S. Arthur. "Affirmative Action in Cincinnati." *Cincinnati Historical Society Bulletin* 37 (Summer 1979): 79–88.

———. "Settling Class Actions." *University of Cincinnati Law Review* 62 (April 1994): 1565–79.

Staple, Desmond H. *"Capitol Square Review and Advisory Board v. Pinnette:* The Dismantling of the 'Endorsement Test.'" *Capitol University Law Review* 25 (1996): 487–516.

Stidham, Ronald, and Robert A. Carp. "Exploring Regionalism in the Federal District Courts." *Publius* 18 (Fall 1988): 113–25.

Stimson, George P., ed. *The Law of Southwestern Ohio*. Cincinnati: Cincinnati Bar Association, 1972.

Surrency, Edwin C. "Federal District Judges and the History of Their Courts." 40 F.R.D. 139–52 (1966).

———. *History of the Federal Courts*. New York: Oceana Publications, 1987.

Tachau, Mary K. Bonsteel. *Federal Courts in the Early Republic: Kentucky, 1789–1816*. Princeton, NJ: Princeton University Press, 1978.

Taylor, C. W., ed. *Bench and Bar of Ohio, 1939–1940*. San Francisco: C. W. Taylor Jr., 1939.

Thompson, James H. "Treason Trial in Ohio" In *A History of Adams County, Ohio: From Its Earliest Settlement to the Present Time*, ed. Nelson W. Evans and E. B. Stivers. West Union, OH: E. B. Stivers, 1900.

Thro, William E. "The Eleventh Amendment Revolution in the Lower Federal Courts." *Journal of College and University Law* 25 (Winter 1999): 501–25.

Toppin, Edgar. "Negro Emancipation in Historic Retrospect: Ohio, the Negro Suffrage Issue in Post-bellum Ohio Politics," *Journal of Human Relations* 11 (Winter 1963): 232–46.

*The Trial of Hon. Clement L. Vallandigham, by a Military Commission: And the Proceedings under His Application for a Writ of Habeas Corpus in the Circuit Court of the United States for the Southern District of Ohio*. Cincinnati: Rickey and Carroll, 1863.

Tucker, Louis Leonard. "Cincinnati during the Civil War." *Publications of the Ohio Civil War Centennial Commission*. No. 9. Columbus: Ohio State University Press, 1962.

United States. Department of Justice. *Bicentennial Report of the Northern District of Ohio 1789–1989*. Cleveland: U.S. Department of Justice, 1990.

Utter, William T. *The Frontier State, 1803–1825*. Vol. 2 of *History of the State of Ohio*, ed. Carl Wittke. Columbus: Ohio State Archaeological and Historical Society, 1942.

——. "Judicial Review in Early Ohio." *Mississippi Valley Historical Review* 14 (June 1927): 8–23.

Warner, Hoyt Landon. *Progressivism in Ohio 1897–1917.* Columbus: Ohio State University Press, 1964.

Watras, Joseph. *Politics, Race, and Schools: Racial Integration 1954–1994.* New York: Garland Publishing, 1997.

Weed, John M. "Business—As Usual." In *Ohio in the Twentieth Century,* comp. Harlow Lindley. Vol. 6 of *History of the State of Ohio,* ed. Carl Wittke. Columbus: Ohio State Archaeological and Historical Society, 1942.

Weisenburger, Francis P. *The Passing of the Frontier, 1825–1850.* Vol. 3 of *History of the State of Ohio,* ed. Carl Wittke. Columbus: Ohio State Archaeological and Historical Society, 1941.

Wheeler, Russell R., and Cynthia Harrison. *Creating the Federal Judicial System.* 2d ed. Washington, DC: Federal Judicial Center, 1994.

*Who Is Who in and from Ohio.* Cincinnati: Queen City Publishing, 1912.

*Who Was Who in America: Historical Volume, 1607–1896.* Rev. ed. Chicago: Marquis Who's Who, 1967.

Wiebe, Robert H. *The Search for Order, 1877–1920.* New York: Hill and Wang, 1967.

Wiecek, William M. "The Reconstruction of Federal Judicial Power, 1863–1875." *American Journal of Legal History* 13 (October 1969): 333–59.

——. "Slavery and Abolition before the United States Supreme Court, 1820–1860." *Journal of American History* 65 (June 1978): 34–59.

Wilson, Steven Harmon. *The Rise of Judicial Management in the U.S. District Court, Southern District of Texas, 1955–2000.* Athens: University of Georgia Press, 2002.

Wright, Charles Alan, et al. *Federal Practice and Procedure.* 3d ed. § 2727. St. Paul, MN: West Publishing, 1998.

Yanuck, Julius. "The Garner Fugitive Slave Case." *Mississippi Valley Historical Review* 40 (June 1953): 47–66.

Zelden, Charles L. *Justice Lies in the District: The United States District Court, Southern District of Texas, 1902–1960.* College Station: Texas A & M University Press, 1993.

# INDEX

The letter *t* following a page number denotes a table or chart. Endnotes are indicated by the letter *n* following the page number followed by the note number on that page.

Hoover, Herbert, 118, 212
*Horman, U.S. v.*, 82
hostile takeover attempts, 197–99
Hough, Benson, 105, 108, 110, 116, 118,
    125, 237–39
House of Representatives (Ohio), 18
Housing and Urban Development, De-
    partment of, U.S. (HUD), 170
housing discrimination, 159, 169–70
Hughes, Charles Evans, 117
*Hughes, U.S. v.*, 54
Human Services, Department of, Ohio,
    186
Hupman, E. Melvin, 133
*Hupman, U.S. v.*, 133–34
Hyde, Udney, 44–45

*Iams v. KalKan*, 150
*I.C.C. v. Bellaire, Zanesville & Columbus Railway Co.*,
    71
*I.C.C. v. Cincinnati, Hamilton & Dayton Railway Co.*,
    81–82
Illinois, 3
immigration restriction, 104
Independent Republican Party (Ohio), 63,
    80
Indiana, 3
*In re* cases. *See name of party or res.*
International Printing Pressmen and As-
    sistants' Union, 82
Interstate Commerce Act, 71
Interstate Commerce Commission (ICC),
    71, 81–82, 90, 125, 360n69
Ireland, 48
*Iron Moulders' Union Local No. 68, Niles-Bement-
    Pond Co. v.*, 91–92
Irons, Peter, 155
Issue 3, 172–73

Jackson, Andrew, 21, 22, 25, 215–16, 218,
    219–20, 222
Jacksonians, 25, 32
    judicial appointments and, 21, 216–17,
    218
    jurisprudence, 23, 32–33, 60–61, 219
Jefferson, Thomas, 8, 9, 16, 17, 20, 21,
    214
Jefferson County, 110
Jeffersonian Democrats, 105
Jeffersonian Republicans, 21, 35, 212,
    276t
Jehovah's Witnesses, 123–24
*J. N. Green v. Chesapeake & Ohio Railway Co.*, 90

John Shillito Company, 67
Johnson, Andrew, 60
Johnson, John H., IV, 91
Johnson, Lyndon B., 139, 157, 211, 252
Jolliffee, John, 40–41
Jones, Nathaniel R., 164–65
*Jones v. Van Zandt*, 38–39
judges
    backgrounds and experience, 142,
        273–74, 276t–80t
    case loads, 153t
    recruitment and appointment, 211–13,
        273–74
    salaries, 8, 20, 213, 222, 223
    *See also specific judges*
judgeships, 79, 119, 138, 139, 140,
    232–33, 251
judicial activism, 176, 258, 264, 265,
    268–69, 270, 281n5, 292
Judicial Code (1911), 79
judicial review, 123
Judiciary Act, 2–4, 29
juries, 384–85n239
Jurisdiction and Removal Act, 55, 66–67
Justice, Department of, U.S. (DOJ), 54,
    98, 132–34, 168, 170–71, 184–85,
    198
    role in judicial appointments, 211, 265

*KalKan, Iams v.*, 150
*Katzenbach v. Morgan*, 188
Keifer, J. Warren, 225–26
Kelly, Michael, 83
*Kelly v. Herrman*, 83
Kelso, Fred, 101, 103
Kennedy, John F., 138
Kentucky, 8, 35, 43
Kentucky Resolves, 19
*Kineon v. The New Mary Houston*, 70
King, Norah McCann, 143
Kinneary, Joseph P., 139, 143, 155, 167,
    174, 178–79, 198, 254–57
*Knight Riders of the Ku Klux Klan v. City of Cincinnati*,
    176
*Krechting, U.S. v.*, 126
Krupansky, Robert B., 173
Ku Klux Klan, 176–77

labor-management litigation, 104, 109–10
labor unions, judicial appointments and,
    231–32, 238
Lambros, Thomas, 148
land condemnations, 128–29

Morehead, Charles S., 43
Morgan, John, 54
*Morgan, Katzenbach v.,* 188
*Moselle* (steamboat), 29–30
motions, pretrial, 149–50
Motley, Constance Baker, 134
motor vehicle standards, 109
motto, Ohio, 177
*Mount Vernon Banner,* 46
Muller, Mike, 119
Muskingum County Children's Services
  Board, 179

narcotics peddlers, 116
National Archives and Records Adminis-
  tration, Great Lakes Region, 5
National Association for the Advancement
  of Colored People (NAACP), 159,
  161, 164
National Cash Register Corporation
  (NCR), 62, 80, 93–97
National Environmental Policy Act
  (NEPA), 183–84
National Labor Relations Act, 91, 126
National Labor Relations Board, 126
National Lead Company (NL), 194–96
National Lead of Ohio (NLO), 195–96
National League, 83
National Prohibition Act, 111–13
national uniform common law, 66–67
nativity scene, Delaware County, 176
Natural Gas Act,, 125
naturalization, 47, 76, 84t, 106t, 107t,
  108t, 248
Nevin, Robert R. (Jake), 119, 123–29, 132,
  239–41, 319n8, 327–28n68
New Deal, 118–28
*New Mary Houston, Kineon v.,* 70
*New York Herald,* 46
*New York Times,* 198
*New York World,* 96
*Niles-Bement-Pond Co. v. Iron Moulders' Union
  Local No. 68,* 91–92
Niles Tool Company, 91
Ninth Amendment, 3–4, 138, 158,
  179–81, 194
Nixon, Richard M., 139, 140
*NLO, Day v.,* 194–96
Northwest Territory, 7, 9
Nuremberg Code, 194

Oberlin College, 37
Occidental Petroleum, 197–98

Office of Price Administration (OPA),
  128, 129
*Ogdensburgh* (steamboat), 31
Ohio, 3, 5, 177
  economic development, 21, 26, 55,
    62–63, 78–79, 137
  election laws, 174, 175
  General Assembly, 16, 111
  immigration, 77–78
  national government and, 21
  National Guard, 105, 110
Ohio Anti-Slavery Society, 37
*Ohio Custom Garment Co. v. Locket,* 126
*Ohio Department of Mental Health, Value Behavioral
  v.,* 187
*Ohio Law Reporter,* 81
Ohio Public Utilities Commission, 108
Ohio River, 4, 7, 31, 35
*Ohio River & Western Railway Co. v. Dittey,* 88–89
Ohio River Disaster Litigation, 190–91
*Ohio State Journal,* 27, 46
*Ohio Tax Cases. See Ohio River & Western Railway
  Co. v. Dittey*
*Ohio v. U.S.,* 125
*Ohio v. U.S. Civil Service Commission,* 125
O'Neill, John H., 49
Organized Crime Control Act,, 203
Orton, Herbert E., 96
Osborn, Ralph, 18–19
*Osborn v. Bank of the United States,* 17–20

*Parrish, Driskill v.,* 39
*Parrish, West Coast Hotel v.,* 124
patent rights, 93, 95, 196
Patterson, John, 48
Patterson, John H. (NCR), 62, 93, 97
*Patterson, U.S. v.,* 93–97
Peck, John Weld (1919–1924), 5, 25,
  103–5, 109, 111–13, 115–16, 117,
  203, 234–36
Peck, John Weld (1961–1966), 138–39,
  147, 152, 155, 159–60, 203,
  249–51, 381n210
*Penick v. Columbus Board of Education,* 162–63
pension cases, 75
perjury standards, 133–35
Perry County, 128
*Philadelphia Record,* 96
Pickaway County, 128
picketers, 109–10
picketing, residential, 180
*Pinette v. Capitol Square Review and Advisory Board,*
  176–77